THE ATLAS OF NEW LIBRARIANSHIP

For information about special quantity discounts, please email special_sales@mitpress.mit.edu

This book was set in Adobe Garamond Pro and Helvetica Neue by the MIT Press. Printed and bound in Singapore.

Library of Congress Cataloging-in-Publication Data

Lankes, R. David.
  The atlas of new librarianship / R. David Lankes.
     p. cm.
  Includes bibliographical references.
  ISBN 978-0-262-01509-7 (alk. paper)
  1. Library science—Philosophy. 2. Library science—Forecasting. 3. Libraries and community. 4. Libraries and society. I. Title.
  Z665.L36 2011
  020.1—dc22
                    2010022788

10 9 8 7 6 5 4 3 2

THE ATLAS OF NEW LIBRARIANSHIP

R. David Lankes

The MIT Press
Cambridge, Massachusetts
London, England

Association of College & Research Libraries
A Division of the American Library Association

This book is dedicated to Joanne Silverstein, who, from the time we were doctoral students together, has always been my intellectual traveling companion.

CONTENTS

PREFACE *xi*

ACKNOWLEDGMENTS *xiii*

AN INTRODUCTION TO THE ATLAS *1*

NAVIGATING THE FUTURE *2*

THE FOUNDATIONS OF THE ATLAS *2*

FINDING A CENTER IN THE DYNAMIC *3*

A NOTE ON RHETORIC *3*

THE ATLAS *5*

A NOTE ON VISUALIZATION *6*

HOW TO NAVIGATE THE ATLAS *6*

READERS OF THE ATLAS *11*

LIMITATIONS OF THE ATLAS *11*

THREADS *13*

MISSION *15*

THE MISSION OF LIBRARIANS IS TO IMPROVE SOCIETY THROUGH FACILITATING KNOWLEDGE CREATION IN THEIR COMMUNITIES *15*

IMPORTANCE OF WORLDVIEW *15*

LONGITUDE EXAMPLE *16*

IMPORTANCE OF THEORY AND DEEP CONCEPTS *18*

　Libraries and Theory *22*

CONVERSATION THEORY *23*

　Credibility *24*

OTHER INFORMATIVE CONCEPTS AND THEORIES *24*

　Dialectic Theories *25*

　Sense-Making *25*

　Motivation Theories *26*

　Motivation *26*

　Learning Theory *27*

　Constructivism *27*

　Postmodernism *27*

CREATING A NEW SOCIAL COMPACT *28*

　Evolution of the Social Compact *29*

THREAD CONCLUSION *29*

KNOWLEDGE CREATION *31*

THE MISSION OF LIBRARIANS IS TO IMPROVE SOCIETY THROUGH FACILITATING KNOWLEDGE CREATION IN THEIR COMMUNITIES *31*

KNOWLEDGE IS CREATED THROUGH CONVERSATION *31*

CONVERSATION THEORY *31*

　Conversants *32*

　Service Is Not Invisibility *33*

　Language *33*

　Evolution of Systems *35*

SYSTEM VIEW *36*

USER-BASED DESIGN *37*

USER SYSTEMS *38*

　Social Network Sites *39*

AGREEMENTS *39*

　Artifacts *41*

　Source Amnesia *42*

　Invest in Tools of Creation over Collection of Artifacts *42*

　Death of Documents *44*

　Memory *48*

　Entailment Mesh *49*

　Annotations *49*

Limitations of Tagging   51

Cataloging Relationships   53

SCAPES   53

REFERENCE EXTRACT   60

LIBRARIES ARE IN THE KNOWLEDGE BUSINESS, THEREFORE THE CONVERSATION BUSINESS   63

FACILITATING   65

THE MISSION OF LIBRARIANS IS TO IMPROVE SOCIETY THROUGH FACILITATING KNOWLEDGE CREATION IN THEIR COMMUNITIES   65

TRUE FACILITATION MEANS SHARED OWNERSHIP   65

Members Not Patrons or Users   66

MEANS OF FACILITATION   66

ACCESS   67

Publisher of Community   67

Shared Shelves with the Community   68

Meeting Spaces   69

KNOWLEDGE   72

Library Instruction   72

Need for an Expanded Definition of Literacy   73

Gaming   75

Social Literacy   76

ENVIRONMENT   77

MOTIVATION   78

Intrinsic   79

Extrinsic   79

THREAD CONCLUSION   80

COMMUNITIES   83

THE MISSION OF LIBRARIANS IS TO IMPROVE SOCIETY THROUGH FACILITATING KNOWLEDGE CREATION IN THEIR COMMUNITIES   83

PRESSURE FOR PARTICIPATION   84

Boundary Issues   85

DIGITAL ENVIRONMENTS   86

Internet Model Example   86

Infrastructure Providers   86

TCP/IP   86

Application Builders   87

Open Source   87

Information Services   88

Web 2.0   89

User   90

CREDIBILITY   90

From Authority to Reliability   91

Authoritative versus Authoritarian   91

Putting It All Together: The Participatory Digital Library   92

PHYSICAL ENVIRONMENTS   93

Topical Centers with Curriculum   93

HYBRID ENVIRONMENTS   94

DIFFERENT COMMUNITIES LIBRARIANS SERVE   95

PUBLIC   96

Free Library of Philadelphia   97

Entrepreneurium   98

Writing Center   99

Music Center   100

ACADEMIC   101

Issues of Institutional Repositories   103

Scholarly Communications   104

GOVERNMENT   105

Department of Justice   105

ASSESSMENT   106

Mapping Conversations   107

SPECIAL   111

SCHOOL   112

Growing Importance of Two-Way Infrastructure   112

ARCHIVES   113

GO TO THE CONVERSATION   114

Embedded Librarians   114

TRULY DISTRIBUTED DIGITAL LIBRARY   114

THREAD CONCLUSION   115

IMPROVE SOCIETY   117

THE MISSION OF LIBRARIANS IS TO IMPROVE SOCIETY THROUGH FACILITATING KNOWLEDGE CREATION IN THEIR COMMUNITIES   117

IMPORTANCE OF ACTION AND ACTIVISM   117

SERVICE   118

Service Is Not Invisibility   119

CORE VALUES   119

Learning   120

Openness   121

Intellectual Freedom and Safety   122

Intellectually Honest Not Unbiased   122

Ethics   124

SOCIAL JUSTICE ISSUES   *124*

POLICY   *125*

　　Democracy and Openness Overshadowed by Technology   *126*

INNOVATION   *127*

　　Innovation versus Entrepreneurship   *128*

CREATING AN AGENDA   *129*

　　Risks of Data   *131*

LEADERSHIP   *132*

　　Obligation of Leadership   *134*

THREAD CONCLUSION   *135*

LIBRARIANS   *137*

THE MISSION OF LIBRARIANS IS TO IMPROVE SOCIETY THROUGH FACILITATING KNOWLEDGE CREATION IN THEIR COMMUNITIES   *137*

CORE SKILLS   *137*

TRANSITION OF TRADITIONAL SKILLS   *137*

INFORMATION ORGANIZATION   *137*

　　Cataloging Relationships   *139*

　　Evolution of Integrated Library Systems   *144*

INFORMATION SEEKING   *153*

PUBLIC SERVICE   *154*

　　Reference   *154*

COLLECTION DEVELOPMENT   *157*

　　Community as Collection   *159*

　　Issues of Institutional Repositories   *159*

ADMINISTRATION   *160*

　　Warehousing Functions   *161*

　　Shelving   *166*

　　Circulation   *166*

IMPORTANCE OF TECHNICAL SKILLS   *167*

AMBIGUITY IS ESSENTIAL FOR PROFESSIONAL WORK   *168*

ABILITY TO WORK IN INTERDISCIPLINARY TEAMS   *170*

　　Relation to Other Domains   *170*

　　Information Science   *171*

　　Getting Past the L v I Debate   *171*

　　Communications   *172*

　　Computer Science   *174*

　　Humanities   *176*

　　Education   *176*

　　Paraprofessionals   *177*

LIS EDUCATION   *177*

　　Shift in Innovation from Academy to Ubiquity   *178*

　　Co-Learning   *179*

INCREASE FRICTION IN THE PROCESS   *179*

　　Every Course Has Symposia and Practica   *179*

CURRICULUM OF COMMUNICATION AND CHANGE OVER TRADITIONAL IDEAS OF LEADERSHIP   *180*

　　Recognize a School as a Participatory Network   *181*

　　From School to School of Thought   *181*

　　Avoiding the Florentine Dilemma   *182*

NEED TO EXPAND THE EDUCATIONAL LADDER   *183*

　　Bachelor of Information and Instructional Design   *183*

　　Need for an Executive Doctorate   *184*

　　Institute for Advanced Librarianship Idea   *184*

　　Vital Roles of Mentors   *185*

OBLIGATION OF LEADERSHIP AND THREAD CONCLUSION   *185*

THREADS POSTSCRIPT   *186*

PRACTITIONERS   *186*

LIBRARY AND INFORMATION SCIENCE SCHOLARS   *186*

STUDENTS   *186*

MEMBERS   *187*

THE WHOLE COMMUNITY OF LIBRARIANSHIP   *187*

WEB CITATIONS   *189*

AGREEMENT SUPPLEMENTS   *193*

ABILITY TO WORK IN INTERDISCIPLINARY TEAMS   *195*

ACADEMIC   *197*

ACCESS   *199*

ADMINISTRATION   *199*

AGREEMENTS   *200*

AMBIGUITY IS ESSENTIAL FOR PROFESSIONAL WORK   *201*

ANNOTATIONS   *202*

APPLICATION BUILDERS   *204*

ARCHIVES *205*

ARTIFACTS *206*

ASSESSMENT *207*

AUTHORITATIVE VERSUS AUTHORITARIAN *209*

AVOIDING THE FLORENTINE DILEMMA *210*

BACHELOR OF INFORMATION AND INSTRUCTIONAL DESIGN *210*

BOUNDARY ISSUES *211*

CATALOGING RELATIONSHIPS *212*

CIRCULATION *213*

CO-LEARNING *213*

COLLECTION DEVELOPMENT *214*

COMMUNICATIONS *214*

COMMUNITY AS COLLECTION *215*

COMPUTER SCIENCE *215*

CONSTRUCTIVISM *216*

CONVERSANTS *219*

CONVERSATION THEORY *220*

CORE SKILLS *224*

CORE VALUES *225*

CREATING A NEW SOCIAL COMPACT *227*

CREATING AN AGENDA *229*

CREDIBILITY *230*

CURRICULUM OF COMMUNICATION AND CHANGE OVER TRADITIONAL IDEAS OF LEADERSHIP *231*

DEATH OF DOCUMENTS *232*

DEMOCRACY AND OPENNESS OVERSHADOWED BY TECHNOLOGY *234*

DEPARTMENT OF JUSTICE *236*

DIALECTIC THEORIES *246*

DIFFERENT COMMUNITIES LIBRARIANS SERVE *249*

DIGITAL ENVIRONMENTS *250*

EDUCATION *250*

EMBEDDED LIBRARIANS *251*

ENTAILMENT MESH *252*

ENTREPRENEURIUM *252*

ENVIRONMENT *257*

ETHICS *258*

EVERY COURSE HAS SYMPOSIA AND PRACTICA *261*

EVOLUTION OF INTEGRATED LIBRARY SYSTEMS *261*

EVOLUTION OF SYSTEMS *262*

EVOLUTION OF THE SOCIAL COMPACT *264*

EXTRINSIC *266*

FREE LIBRARY OF PHILADELPHIA *266*

FROM AUTHORITY TO RELIABILITY *267*

FROM SCHOOL TO SCHOOL OF THOUGHT *267*

GAMING *268*

GETTING PAST THE L V I DEBATE *270*

GO TO THE CONVERSATION *270*

GOVERNMENT *271*

GROWING IMPORTANCE OF TWO-WAY INFRASTRUCTURE   *274*

HUMANITIES   *274*

HYBRID ENVIRONMENTS   *275*

IMPORTANCE OF A WORLDVIEW   *276*

IMPORTANCE OF ACTION AND ACTIVISM   *278*

IMPORTANCE OF TECHNICAL SKILLS   *280*

IMPORTANCE OF THEORY AND DEEP CONCEPTS   *281*

INCREASE FRICTION IN THE PROCESS   *283*

INFORMATION ORGANIZATION   *283*

INFORMATION SCIENCE   *284*

INFORMATION SEEKING   *284*

INFORMATION SERVICES   *285*

INFRASTRUCTURE PROVIDERS   *285*

INNOVATION   *286*

INNOVATION VERSUS ENTREPRENEURSHIP   *287*

INSTITUTE FOR ADVANCED LIBRARIANSHIP IDEA   *287*

INTELLECTUAL FREEDOM AND SAFETY   *295*

INTELLECTUALLY HONEST NOT UNBIASED   *297*

INTERNET MODEL EXAMPLE   *297*

INTRINSIC   *299*

INVEST IN TOOLS OF CREATION OVER COLLECTION OF ARTIFACTS   *300*

ISSUES OF INSTITUTIONAL REPOSITORIES   *300*

KNOWLEDGE   *303*

KNOWLEDGE IS CREATED THROUGH CONVERSATION   *304*

L_0 *305*

L_1 *305*

LANGUAGE   *306*

LEADERSHIP   *309*

LEARNING   *311*

LEARNING THEORY   *311*

LIBRARIES ARE IN THE KNOWLEDGE BUSINESS, THEREFORE THE CONVERSATION BUSINESS   *317*

LIBRARY INSTRUCTION   *318*

LIMITATIONS OF TAGGING   *319*

LIS EDUCATION   *320*

LONGITUDE EXAMPLE   *321*

MAPPING CONVERSATIONS   *322*

MASSIVE SCALE   *322*

MEANS OF FACILITATION   *329*

MEETING SPACES   *331*

MEMBERS NOT PATRONS OR USERS   *333*

MEMORY   *333*

MOTIVATION   *334*

MOTIVATION THEORIES   *336*

MUSIC CENTER   *336*

NEED FOR AN EXECUTIVE DOCTORATE   *337*

NEED FOR AN EXPANDED DEFINITION OF LITERACY   *337*

NEED TO EXPAND THE EDUCATIONAL LADDER   *338*

OBLIGATION OF LEADERSHIP *339*

OPEN SOURCE *339*

OPENNESS *340*

PARAPROFESSIONALS *340*

PHYSICAL ENVIRONMENTS *341*

POLICY *342*

POSTMODERNISM *344*

PRESSURE FOR PARTICIPATION *346*

PUBLIC *347*

PUBLIC SERVICE *349*

PUBLISHER OF COMMUNITY *349*

RECOGNIZE A SCHOOL AS A PARTICIPATORY NETWORK *350*

REFERENCE *350*

REFERENCE EXTRACT *351*

RELATION TO OTHER DOMAINS *351*

RISKS OF DATA *352*

SCAPES *352*

SCHOLARLY COMMUNICATIONS *366*

SCHOOL *368*

SCHOOL INFORMATION MANAGEMENT SYSTEMS *371*

SELECTIVE DISSEMINATION OF INFORMATION *371*

SENSE-MAKING *372*

SERVICE *378*

SERVICE IS NOT INVISIBILITY *379*

SHARED SHELVES WITH THE COMMUNITY *379*

SHELVING *380*

SHIFT IN INNOVATION FROM ACADEMY TO UBIQUITY *381*

SOCIAL JUSTICE ISSUES *382*

SOCIAL LITERACY *386*

SOCIAL NETWORK SITES *388*

SOURCE AMNESIA *392*

SPECIAL *394*

SYSTEM VIEW *397*

TCP-IP *397*

THE MISSION OF LIBRARIANS IS TO IMPROVE SOCIETY THROUGH FACILITATING KNOWLEDGE CREATION IN THEIR COMMUNITIES *398*

TOPICAL CENTERS WITH CURRICULUM *399*

TRANSITION OF TRADITIONAL SKILLS *399*

TRUE FACILITATION MEANS SHARED OWNERSHIP *400*

TRULY DISTRIBUTED DIGITAL LIBRARY *401*

USER *401*

USER SYSTEMS *402*

USER-BASED DESIGN *403*

VITAL ROLES OF MENTORS *404*

WAREHOUSING FUNCTIONS *404*

WEB 2.0 *405*

WRITING CENTER *405*

ATLAS POSTSCRIPT *407*

PREFACE

I've always had a hard time figuring out the purpose of a preface. If it's important stuff, why isn't it just chapter 1? Well, here's where I ended up on the topic and why you are now reading a preface. It is not about the content itself; it is more about the author's intent and frame of mind. Ironically, it is written last and, although a bit self-indulgent, gives me a chance to reflect on the whole process.

The first thing I'd like to make clear before you read this is that I do not claim that everything in here has sprung like Athena from my head. There are some old ideas in here. In some cases, they are brilliant and radical ideas that have either become lost or so widely adopted that we have forgotten they were once radical.

There are also some current ideas culled from dedicated practitioners from around the globe. It may not seem like a large chunk of text is an interactive process (it is not—as I hammer on over and over again—it is an artifact), but the thinking behind the Atlas was very interactive. From the initial forums set up to comment on the first drafts of a white paper in 2006, to the hours of sometimes heated debate in an office, an airport, a conference center, or over good food in good cities, the Atlas may be my words, but it is the thoughts and experiences of hundreds.

This leads me to a personal note. The writing of the Atlas and the years of work that it took to develop these ideas have renewed my faith in librarianship. It is easy, in the daily grind, to see the worst of our profession. Often I am invited in to help fix outdated practices and ideas. It seems like conferences are just as much an opportunity to bemoan what is not happening as to learn about what is possible. What I have come to understand is that the complaints about the recalcitrant old school librarians that don't "get it" have, in fact, increased because there are more folks who do "get it" to complain.

It's like that scene in the West Wing when a liberal staffer is complaining about the National Rifle Association (NRA) and a conservative Republican points out that if everyone who wanted to ban assault rifles simply joined the NRA, they could vote the organization out of existence. In other words, if people like me would simply stop yelling about the laggards and look around the room at everyone else who is complaining, we might realize that there are fewer and fewer folks left to complain about.

One last note; a plea really. This book is all about conversations. The Atlas is my latest contribution to that conversation, and it is really an invitation for you to join in. What do you agree with? What do you disagree with? What is offensive or supportive? What did I miss? What should I know? What do we need to change? Let's talk.

ACKNOWLEDGMENTS

I was in a meeting with Lewis Hyde, author of *The Gift*, where he talked about different narratives on intellectual property. One narrative, often used by large media companies, is that creativity and the creation of intellectual property are acts of individual genius: that an author or artist sits back, gets inspired, and makes something. The other narrative is that creativity and creation are an act of a community: that while you may paint something unique, you were able to do so from a lifetime's inspiration and input from those around you. I very much subscribe to the latter of these narratives.

The Atlas may be my work, but that is only useful in assigning blame. The good stuff in here comes from the brilliance of the library community. I have done my best to package their ideas and represent them together as they make sense to me. What I got wrong is my fault. What is right is most likely from them.

CONTRIBUTORS

This Atlas is the result of a large number of smart and generous people. They contributed everything from writing of Agreement Supplements, to editing, to providing feedback on the drafts. Where possible I have noted their contributions in the text, but I wanted to begin by thanking them here.

ATLAS RESEARCH TEAM

This is the crew that did the heavy lifting on the Atlas manuscript through editing, reviewing, arguing, and generally getting it done.

Todd Marshall, Angela Usha Ramnarine-Rieks, Heather Margaret Highfield, Jessica R. O'Toole, Nicole Dittrich, and Xiaoou Cheng. Special thanks to Julie Strong for her help.

AGREEMENT RESEARCHERS

One of the advantages of being in an innovative school like Syracuse University's iSchool is that every so often I get to make classes up. So I did. The students did a fantastic job of slogging through rough drafts of the threads and doing a lot of really amazing work on the agreements and discussion questions.

Jocelyn Clark, Amy Edick, Elizabeth Gall, Nancy Lara-Grimaldi, Michael Luther, Kelly Menzel, Andrea Phelps, Jennifer Recht, Sarah Schmidt, and William Zayac.

PARTICIPATORY NETWORKS WHITE PAPER

The work in this Atlas really began with the formation of participatory librarianship. That happened because Rick Weingarten and Carrie Lowe of the American Library Association's Office for Information and Technology Policy (OITP) commissioned a white paper on social networking in libraries. Much of the foundational work on these concepts came from long hours of conversation between my co-authors, Joanne Silverstein and Scott Nicholson.

From the white paper on, OITP has been a great support in the work. I thank them and all the folks at ALA's Washington Office: Emily Sheketoff, Rick Weingarten, Carrie McGuire, and Alan Inouye.

STARTER KIT SITES

Most of the examples and experiments throughout the Atlas come from a wide variety of library and information settings. The following folks were gracious enough to open their doors for me and share their insights.

Blane Dessy and the librarians of the Department of Justice Law Libraries.

Linda Johnson and Sandra Horrocks of the Free Library of Philadelphia Foundation, and Elliot Shelkrot, Joe McPeak, Kyle Smith, and all of the great librarians (past and present) of the Free Library.

Jeff Penka, Susan McGlamery, Paula Rumbaugh, and Tam Dalrymple of OCLC's QuestionPoint service.

Robert Johnston and the librarians of LeMoyne College.

Elizabeth Stephens of the Glendale Library.

PARTICIPATORY LIBRARIANSHIP RESEARCH GROUP

After the white paper was out, a group of talented faculty and doctoral and master's students worked with me to further refine the ideas now in this Atlas: Todd Marshall, Angela Usha Ramnarine-Rieks, Joanne Silverstein, Jaime Snyder, Keisuke Inoue, David Pimentel, Gabrielle Gosselin, Agnes Imecs, and Sarah Webb.

Special thanks to Meg Backus for her ideas on innovation.

MIT PRESS

Marguerite Avery, Senior Acquisitions Editor, for giving the book a chance.

ACRL

Kathryn Deiss, for insisting that I had to publish with ACRL, and Mary Ellen Davis, who told me I was allowed to piss off anyone I needed to.

THE ILEADU TEAM, THE STATE LIBRARY OF ILLINOIS, AND IMLS

Thanks to Anne Craig, Gwen Harrison, and all the folks involved with the ILEADU Project for giving me a chance to try out some of these ideas.

THE JOHN D. AND CATHERINE T. MACARTHUR FOUNDATION

Thanks to Kathy Im and Elspeth Revere for supporting a study on the future of libraries and the development of the Reference Extract Idea. It is a rare treat to find funders who are great collaborators and ask the best questions. Also thanks to Connie Yowell for support on my credibility work.

Reference Extract is very much a product of brilliant collaborators like Jeff Penka, Mike Eisenberg, Eric Miller, and Uche Ogbuji.

IDEAS AND REACTIONS

I do practice what I preach. Most of my learning happens in conversations over lunch, coffee, and in hallways. What I love about the field of librarianship is that you are never at a loss for interesting company. I am going to miss a lot of people in making this list, but I wanted to give a shout out to some of the folks who had patience with me droning on about new librarianship.

Scott Nicholson, Joanne Silverstein, Meg Backus for the brilliant concepts on innovation versus entrepreneurship, Joe Janes, Eli Neiburger, Jill Hurst-Wahl, Mary Ghikas, George Needham, Chuck McClure, Michael Eisenberg, Joe Ryan, Megan Oakleaf, Blythe Bennett (who cemented the name for the Atlas), and Buffy Hamilton.

An apology to those I forgot.

GENERAL ACKNOWLEDGMENTS

Thanks to my family, who had to see a lot of my back while I was typing in my office. Riley, I marvel every day at the man you are becoming. Andrew, you are the epitome of infectious joy. Anna Maria, my wife and love of my life, you make me a better man and the world a better place.

Thanks to all of the audiences of my presentations. Your questions, comments, and challenges honed these ideas. What's more, they demonstrated that the best days of librarianship are ahead of us.

Thanks to the University of North Carolina, Greensboro, for the time to write this book.

Thanks to the Free Library of Fayetteville for the place to write. I can't tell you the number of tough fixes I worked through on the Stickley furniture.

To Ray von Dran, who taught me true mentorship. He gave me my first real job, his trust, and faith. His time on Earth was too short, but his impact was great.

To my dad, who taught me that everything is retail. Whether you're selling ink or ideas, you still have to sell. I miss him every day.

To my mom, who has every one of my books and may well be the only one to have read them all (including me).

To Michael Eisenberg, my one-time advisor, but always mentor and friend.

To Chuck McClure, who has shown me that staying on the top of your game throughout your career is possible.

To Joan Laskowski, my real boss.

To Lisa Pawlewicz for all her hard work in helping me play with technology.

To Marie Radford, who covered for my Atlas obsession on that other book.

Thanks to the creators of Galcon who gave me the perfect activity to think things through (well technically, take a break from thinking things through). And damn you Plants vs. Zombies for that lost week!

LIBRARIANS WHO HAVE AND CONTINUE TO INSPIRE ME

Abby Kasowitz-Scheer, Blythe Bennett, Joann Wasik, Pauline Shostack, Holly Sammons, Rivkah Sass, Sari Feldman, Stewart Bodner, Stephen Bell, Stephen Francoeur, Donna Dinberg (who is no doubt whipping Heaven's reference desk into shape as we speak), Franceen Gaudet, Joe Janes, Nicolette Sosulski (a one-woman reference SWAT team), Jenny Levine, Karen Schneider, Joan Stahl, John Collins, Linda Arret, Nancy Morgan, Melanie Gardner, Joe Thompson, Buff Hirko, Caleb Tucker-Raymond, Nancy Huling, Jane Janis, Joyce Ray, Bob Martin, Tasha Cooper, Mary Chute, Keith Stubbs (although you may not have the degree, you have the brain, heart, and soul of a librarian), Joe Ryan (the first and second), Linda Smith, Pauline Nicholas, Kathleen Kerns, Meg Backus, Mary Fran Floreck, Kate McCaffrey, and Lorri Mon.

INTRODUCTION TO THE ATLAS

atlas |ˈat-ləs|

noun

1 (pl. **atlases**) a book of maps or charts *: I looked in the atlas to find a map of Italy | a road atlas.*

• a book of illustrations or diagrams on any subject *: Atlas of Surgical Operations.*

This atlas is written for you. It seeks to bolster the defiant who stand bravely before the crushing weight of the status quo and seeks to give hope to those silenced by the chorus of the mediocre and resistant to change. It seeks to show the way forward for librarians in a time of great challenge, change, and opportunity. It is also a statement that you are not alone, you are not crazy, you are right: It is not about cataloging, or books, or buildings, or committees—it is about learning, knowledge, and social action.

But being right is irrelevant if it is not followed by real action and change. As I said at the 2002 Virtual Reference Desk conference, we must be brave and bold in addition to being right. We must be brave and stand up to the inertia of colleagues unwilling to change and an antiquated stereotype of librarians within our communities. We must be bold, in that this is no time for small ideas or limited action. A committee on innovation and a few brown bag talks about change are not going to help the world.

The work in the Atlas is founded on the simple precept that the very definition of our field, its perception, and its ultimate effect are in the hands of librarians—our hands. Thousands of years of tradition serve as inspiration for our future, not as a set of shackles binding us.

As Israel Zangwill, the English writer, once wrote[1]:

> The Past: Our cradle, not our prison; there is danger as well as appeal in its glamour. The past is for inspiration, not imitation, for continuation, not repetition.

The ultimate goal of this book is to enumerate and express the inexpressible: that stripped of your collections and policies and organizations, you still stand noble. Your nobility comes from a mission no less than the preservation and improvement of society. Our nobility is not found in collections, or walls, or organizational structures, or even in our history—it is found in our action. The nobility of librarianship is earned every day by the dedicated action of thousands of individuals around the globe. That nobility is found in inspiring someone to read, in helping someone find a job, in connecting an abused wife to social services to save her life, and in a Philadelphia café at the central library staffed by dedicated personnel in transition from homelessness to work.

The nobility of librarianship is found in schools where library media specialists prepare our future in the children they teach. It is in the government librarian who preserves freedom in the halls of political power. The nobility of librarians can be seen in the corporate offices, hospitals, law firms, departments of transportation, and colleges throughout the world. Although it has been cloaked in an air of service and hidden away behind quaint and romantic stereotypes, it is time for that nobility to shine and to be brought into clear focus for our communities.

NAVIGATING THE FUTURE

There is a theme that pervades this atlas. It is navigation. This is not merely a convenient metaphor or simple literary conceit. Rather, it emerges from the dynamic nature of the topic. Librarians are on a journey that started literally millennia ago and continues to this day. It is a journey that will continue for centuries to come—so long as we don't lose our way. In any journey, there are milestones—key moments that allow us to stop and review our course. As the web explodes, the world economy stumbles, the newspaper industry implodes, the media landscape fragments, and societies around the world face social unrest, librarians have not only an opportunity but an obligation to find their center and the means to continue a centuries-long mission to use knowledge to better understand the past, make a better today, and invent an ideal future.

1. http://www.quotationspage.com/quote/4482.html

These are lofty goals, and it would be pure hubris to claim that the Atlas could accomplish all of this. Indeed, as is discussed at length, no artifact, however compelling, can accomplish anything. It is only people who make change. The highest hope I can have for this Atlas is to inspire positive change and to move forward a conversation on the role of librarians that has all too often become mired in an obsession with things, processes, and defining boundaries.

The Atlas is also an attempt to answer the most frequent and important question asked at all of those conferences where the preachers, prophets, and demagogues of librarianship speak: "Now what?" The work to recast librarianship to date has focused on core concepts and generating examples. It has lacked a set of marching orders and some key tools in reinvention. The Atlas seeks to be a tool. It is intended to be a textbook, conversation guide, platform for social networking, and inspirational sermon.

THE FOUNDATIONS OF THE ATLAS

The Atlas is the result of more than 100,000 miles of travel to 29 locations on three continents; input from hundreds of librarians and professors from 14 accredited library programs, 25 formal presentations to more than 50 conferences, and 14 publications. The foundational data for this book come from large organizations and small; national, public, academic, school, and special libraries; associations with local, regional, national, and international reach; doctoral and master's students; librarians, lawyers, historians, programmers, venture capitalists, and teachers. The whole point of all of this effort was to discover and develop a new approach to librarianship from the ground up. This means good theory, good practice, and real examples.

The result of all this work was a concept called "participatory librarianship," and it serves as the basis for the "new librarianship" detailed in this work. Simply put, new librarianship recasts librarianship and library practice using the fundamental concept that knowledge is created through conversation. Librarians are in the knowledge business; therefore, librarians are in the conversation business. New librarians approach their work as facilitators of conversation. Be it in practice, policies, programs, and/or tools, librarians seek to enrich, capture, store, and disseminate the conversations of their communities.

However, although you will read a great deal about participation, you will not see many specific references to "participatory librarianship." This is intentional. Modifiers and titles are useful in gaining attention, but the ultimate success of any idea is the loss of a modifier.

"Virtual reference" becomes simply "reference" when the ideas put forth are widely incorporated throughout practice. "Digital libraries" are quickly becoming simply "libraries" as they become integrated into the larger organizations and collections of a library. So too must participatory librarianship, if it is to be successful, become part of the overall concept of librarianship.

The central concepts of participatory librarianship have not changed—that conversation and knowledge are core to all that librarians do. This central principle has been explored, expanded, and detailed over the years. It will continue to be refined after the initial release of the Atlas as well. The Atlas is incomplete, in the same way the field of librarianship is incomplete. New times, new ideas, and new needs within the community create a dynamic world for librarians. Librarians and their work must be equally dynamic.

FINDING A CENTER IN THE DYNAMIC

The Atlas is about reaffirming the roots of librarianship not in buildings and collections, but in knowledge, community, and advancing the human condition (not human documents). The approach outlined in the Atlas does not discount books, buildings, or ivy, but it does put these tools in their proper perspective… as tools. Remember, we are the future of libraries, not buildings, although they may stand for centuries still. We—you and I—are the future of libraries. Ivy may grow on the columns, coffee may well be served, and books may be shelved. But they shall be done so by our decision in response to the needs of our communities.

Some have attributed the dynamic nature of the librarian's world to technology. The web, social networking, blogging, and so forth, they will say, have totally changed the world, and librarians must abandon old ways of thinking and embrace the new world of openness, participation, and so on. I would say that technology has indeed brought about revolutionary change and indeed requires librarians to adopt (and, I would argue, create) new tools. However, seeing technology as the sole driver for change is short-sighted in the extreme.

Here is the truth: The world is changing radically—just like it always has. It does no good to ignore that librarians and society as a whole have faced times of massive change in the past. Can anyone really argue that the scale of change offered by today's digital ubiquity (in the so-called developed world) is of greater magnitude than the advent of movable type? Is the Internet a seismic shift of greater magnitude than, say, the advent of universal public education? Is to-day's youth culture any more radical than the counterculture of the fabled 1960s—or the beatnik generation? Which is having a greater effect on society: the World Wide Web or the fact that over the past century life expectancy for U.S. citizens has gone from 47 to 77?[2] Which is a greater challenge to credibility: the fact that I just cited Wikipedia or the fact that three candidates in the 2008 presidential race "indicat[ed] they did not subscribe to Charles Darwin's theory of evolution?"[3]

What is amazing is that, through all of these changes and even greater ones over the centuries (the Renaissance, the Enlightenment, indoor plumbing), the concept of the library has survived. To be more precise, the concept of libraries has been able to evolve to meet a changing world. This is an important difference because those who may be comforted that libraries survive should not be lulled into believing either that it has done so by being a fixed point in a world of change or that it has done so without wrenching and fierce debate as to its mission. Just as physicians, universities, and farmers have existed for millennia, they have done so by adapting.

Let me be clear: The world we live in *IS* changing. It is not your imagination. The world of information is moving faster, new technologies are making it to market in less time, new markets are emerging as you are reading this, and, yes, the world we lived in just 5 years ago is now gone. You cannot ignore the change, and you cannot ignore the victories of the past in accommodating the change.

The Atlas before you is an attempt to follow Israel Zangwill's advice and look to the history of the field for the core and constant while looking to even deeper theory of how people know to help shape the future.

A NOTE ON RHETORIC

The Atlas is a combination of topical map, scholarly theory, practical example, persuasive argument, textbook, and inspirational sermon. The rhetoric seeks to match. There are plenty of sections of the Atlas that do dwell on the scholarly and theoretical. They are not in here to make me sound smart; they are in here because the deeper our understanding, the better our decisions and the better our practice. I shall not, however, shy away from the personal by masking it behind

2. http://en.wikipedia.org/wiki/Life_expectancy
3. http://www.cnn.com/2007/POLITICS/06/05/debate.evolution/index.html.

the third-person passive voice. When I talk of passionate topics, I do so with passionate rhetoric.

Some may fault me for the use of inspirational and even over-the-top rhetoric. I feel this field is in need of some inspiration. All too often we seem to reserve passionate and inspiring rhetoric for our political speeches and action movies. Why? Why divorce the everyday struggles of a noble profession like librarians from soaring words? Are we not worthy of it? Why are the struggles of librarians less deserving of a sermon and some inspiration than the politician running for office or the football team seeking the next victory? It is time that those who seek to unlock the imagination and power of our society, the librarians, get a few supportive and overheated words themselves.

What can be more inspiring than knowledge and those who seek it out? Some in academia feel that knowledge is a cold thing, a dispassionate examination of facts and limitations. Yet knowledge is anything but cold and dispassionate. Scholarship is a passionate quest approached with dispassionate tools. The questions that push the quest forward come from deeply personal parts of us. We seek the truth from a faith that it exists, that it is discoverable, and that finding it will make things better.

Any attempt by librarians to wrap ourselves in the rhetoric and attitudes of some mythic, detached scholar misses the point of understanding. Look at the examples of the greatest minds that have moved the world—scholars who talk of epiphanies. The quest of truth is often described not as a methodical description of facts but of discovery. After all, Einstein unlocked the secrets of the atom and then was a tireless advocate for containing nuclear weapons. The top law schools don't just teach the law; they go into court to defend civil liberties. MIT doesn't simply teach mathematics, it builds software. Example after example shows that discovery of knowledge carries an equal obligation to fight ignorance and act. Scholarship is activism, truth is teaching, and librarianship is radical change. One must be both right and righteous. The rhetoric of the Atlas can be nothing less.

THE ATLAS

The Atlas is a topical map represented by a series of agreements in relation to one another organized into a series of threads. While many terms are discussed in detail throughout the Atlas, it is useful to at least provide a basic definition before we proceed:

• *Agreement*   An understanding about the field of librarianship that may include a skill area, a relevant theory, a practice, or an example. One might be tempted to think of these as facts that lack context—for example, the fact that Mt. Everest is 29,029 feet high. That fact is useful but not nearly as important as when teamed with the fact that your plane can only climb to 29,000 feet. Agreements are more like persuasive arguments that are related to each other. This teaming of agreements is context, and within the Atlas this is achieved through relationships.

• *Relationships*   True knowledge lies not in facts but in the relationships among them. Relationships provide context to agreements and sit between them. These are aggregated together for explanatory purposes into threads.

• *Threads*   Threads are intended to tell the story of key concepts in the Atlas. For example, one thread focuses on the conceptual foundations of the Atlas, whereas another focuses on the skills and values that librarians need. Taken together, the threads, relationships, and agreements are visually represented in the Map.

• *Map*   The Map is the visual representation that acts as an index to the entire Atlas. It is a snapshot that allows the reader to explore and navigate through an emerging, grounded understanding of the field of librarianship. It is the centerpiece of the Atlas.

• *Atlas*   The Atlas is the sum total of this work. It is the visual Map, as well as the detailed discussions of agreements and threads.

There is one other term used throughout the Atlas that must be clarified: "member." While this is fully explored within the agreement

"Members Not Patrons or Users," it is worth explaining its use here. What do you call the people whom librarians serve? In the aggregate, I'll call them community, realizing that the community might be the faculty, staff, and students of a university; taxpayers in a city; or employees in a commercial firm. Individually I refer to them as members—as opposed to patrons, customers, or users. I picked up this term from Joan Frye Williams, the librarian and information technology consultant who solved the naming problem by doing something amazing—she asked folks in the library what they wanted to be called.

I like the term because it implies belonging, shared ownership, and shared responsibility. It is, frankly, a bit awkward to talk about membership in a work dedicated to an individual, the librarian (after all, can someone be a member of a librarian?), but I am willing to deal with the awkwardness to reinforce the idea of member as stakeholder. After all, a user connotes a consumer who takes without giving, and a customer implies a lopsided relationship where service is bought and paid for. Patron is fine but derives from the concept of patronage, which has always struck me as a bit paternalistic. So I use member. They are members of a community, a library, or a conversation (and often all three at the same time).

A NOTE ON VISUALIZATION

The shape of the Map—that is, how it is actually displayed—is arbitrary. The current "picture" in the Atlas was chosen as a compact design that is easy to navigate and aesthetically pleasing. The true map of agreements and relationships can be displayed in a nearly infinite number of ways. Indeed, the beginning of each thread and agreement changes the position of agreements to maximize clarity and space. For example, in the overall Map, the "Mission" thread has the shape seen in figure 1.

While in the discussion of this thread, it is represented more compactly as figure 2.

The relationships and agreements are the same; simply the position is different.

The Atlas as a whole can also be displayed in various ways. For example, it can be seen as a hyperbolic tree in figure 3.

This format is actually better for exploration and direct interaction but more difficult for static viewing and understanding the whole.

The Map could also be displayed simply as a sort of textual outline, say for a Wiki interface in figure 4. Although this format is efficient for navigating the agreements, it all but obscures the relation-

ships between them, implying only a rigid hierarchy. After all, the Map is actually a mesh not a hierarchy.

One could imagine three-dimensional views of the Map or simple aesthetic changes in the colors. The point is not the actual picture but rather the agreements and relationships contained within it.

HOW TO NAVIGATE THE ATLAS

The Atlas is divided into three major components: "The Map," "Threads," and "Agreement Supplements." If the Atlas is seen as a course, the Map is the syllabus, the Threads are the lectures, and the Agreement Supplements contain the accompanying readings and discussion materials. The Map shows agreement titles and their relations to one another. The bulk of information about these agreements and their relationships is explained under Threads. Agreements are expanded in entries within the Agreement Supplements.

It is suggested that the first time through the Atlas, you read the Threads in a linear way and then refer to the Agreement Supplements as needed to find more information on a given area or idea. As you become more familiar with the overall concepts of the Atlas, the Agreement Supplements become more useful in application. To help you explore concepts throughout the Threads, some headers will have a "*" next to them with an accompanying bolded footnote indicating that additional information beyond index data can be found in the Agreement Supplements.

The Map is read in a top-to-bottom manner. That means that the relationships expressed are phrased as coming from the top node to the bottom node. For example, take a look at figure 5.

This relationship is read as " 'Creating a new social compact' results in the 'Evolution of that social compact.' " However, this is just the phrasing. The relationship in reading bottom to top is the same but would be phrased differently: " 'Evolution of the social compact' results from 'Creating a new social compact.' " The relationship is still "resulting," but the phrasing is slightly different. Ultimately, the choice of top to bottom, a sort of deductive presentation, is chosen to make explaining the whole Atlas easier.

The size differences between agreements represent their relative importance. As you can see, the emphasis in the preceding relationship is on the creation of a new social compact. The evolution of the compact is important but not as fully explored in the Atlas, or at least not as fully emphasized.

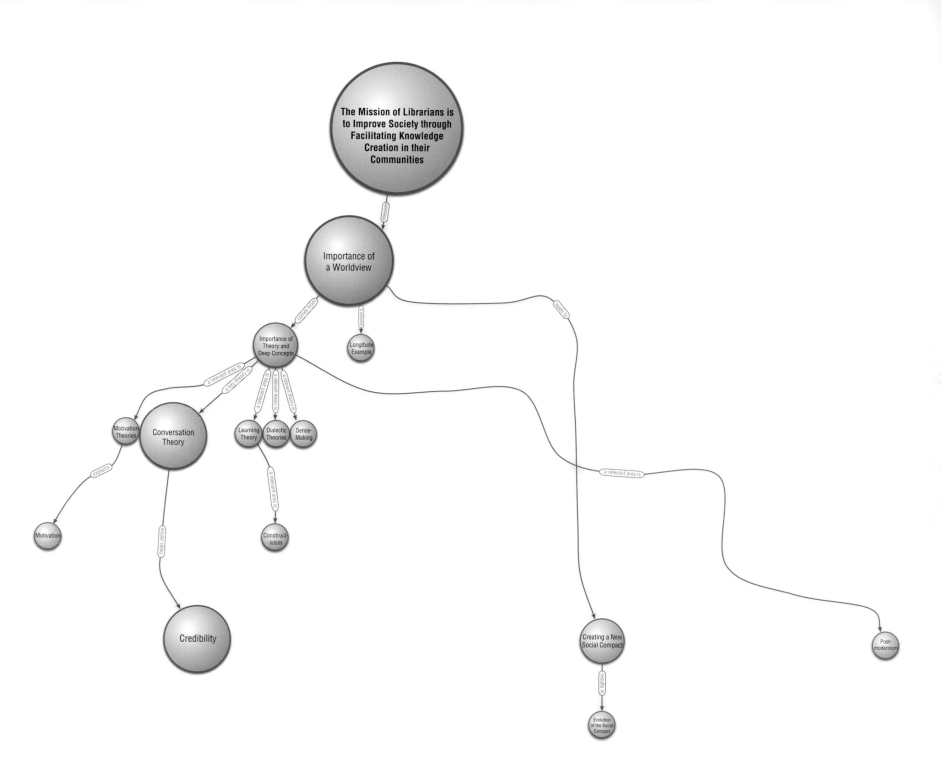

Figure 1

Figure 2

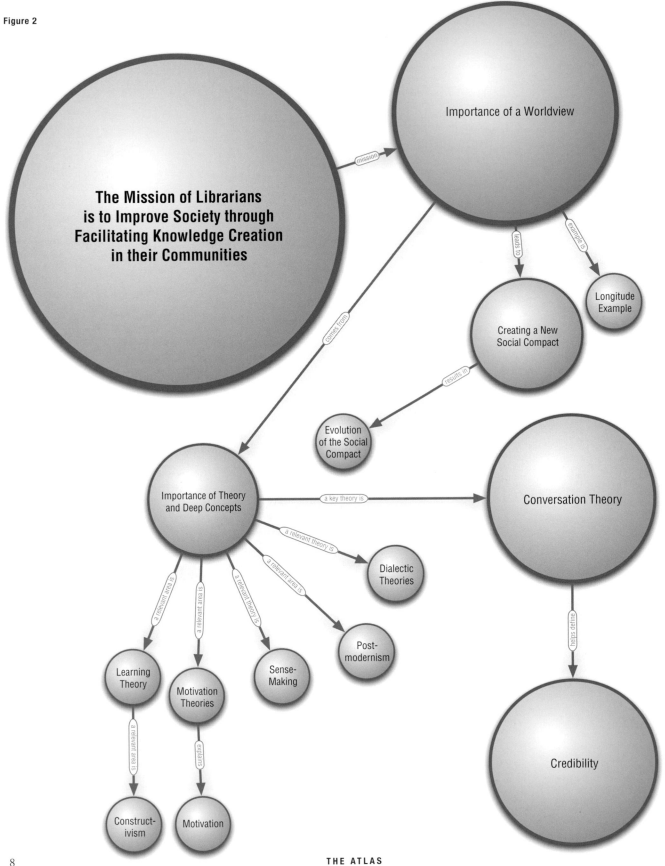

Figure 3

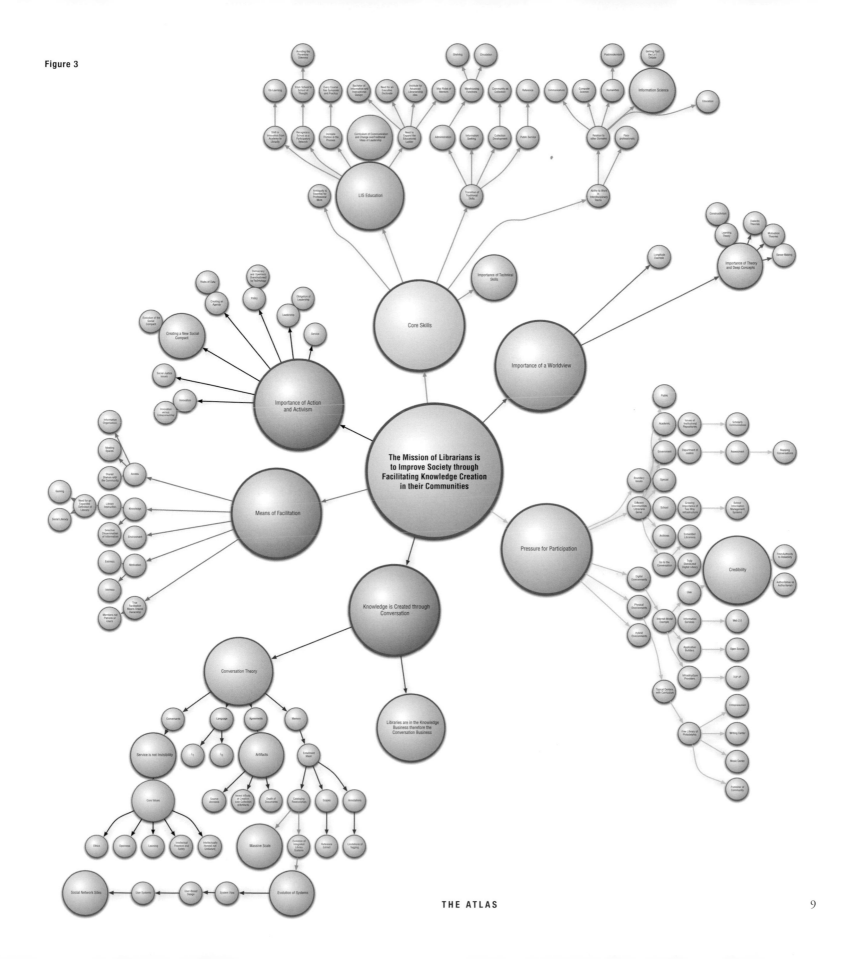

The Mission of Librarians is to Improve Society through Facilitating Knowledge Creation in their Communities

- ## Knowledge is Created through Conversation
  - ### Libraries are in the Knowledge Business therefore the Conversation Business
- ## Pressure for Participation
  - Boundary Issues
  - Different Communities Librarians Serve
    - Public
      - Free Library of Philadelphia
        - Entrepreneurium
          - Innovation versus Entrepreneurship
        - Writing Center
        - Music Center
        - Publisher of Community
    - Academic
    - Government
      - Department of Justice
        - Assessment
          - Mapping Conversations
    - Special
    - School
      - Growing Importance of Two Way Infrastructure
        - School Information Management Systems
    - Archives
    - Go to the Conversation
      - Embedded Librarians
      - Truly Distributed Digital Library
  - Digital Environments
    - Internet Model Example
      - User
        - ### Credibility
          - From Authority to Reliability
          - Authoritative vs Authoritarian
      - Information Services
        - Web 2.0
      - Application Builders
        - Open Source

Figure 5

Figure 4

READERS OF THE ATLAS

This Atlas, although not an encyclopedia, tries to capture the whole of librarianship. As such, it is not an easy one sitting read. It also covers a lot of different topics that may have variable interest for different audiences.

The primary audience for the Atlas is practitioners; librarians in the field. Practitioners are the implied antecedent to pronouns like "you." It is vital that current librarians act as thoughtful or reflective practitioners who seek to understand the why of service and not simply the how and what. Although a practitioner may want to jump right to the more applied parts of the Atlas (namely, the "Communities" and "Librarians" threads), they shouldn't. All of the examples and specifics are derived from the mission, a deep understanding of knowledge, and the means of facilitation covered in the first three threads.

Another audience for the Atlas is Library and Information Science (LIS) scholars. Although the rhetoric of the threads is definitely and deliberately not "scholarly" in tone, the ideas are being put forth to the scholarly community for consideration and validation. There are plenty of studies implied here and assertions in need of testing. There is an overall challenge throughout the Atlas for scholars: Can we think bigger? Each agreement may well be a dissertation waiting to be written, but aren't we as scholars also obliged to try and integrate our own valuable and detailed work into a larger whole? I think so. The Atlas is my attempt at this goal.

The last purposeful audience I have written for is the corps of LIS students. You are our future. Although we all have a role to play, you, as a student, right now, have a unique position that will never come again. You are new to the field. Even if you have worked in or around a library, you are now breaking through our dense crust of language and acronyms (which I apologize have not entirely disappeared in this work) to see what it is we do and why. Why is being new to something so special? As Michael Brooks observes in his book *13 Things That Don't Make Sense: The Most Baffling Scientific Mysteries of Our Time*[1]:

> Kuhn observed that his paradigm shift model means that major discoveries are only made by people who are either very young or very new to that particular scientific discipline.

That's you. Don't waste your precious gift of a fresh perspective by reading these words or listening to the voices of your faculty and assuming we are right. We are preparing you to be librarians not clones.

---

1. Brooks, M. (2008). *13 things that don't make sense: The most baffling scientific mysteries of our time*. New York: Doubleday.

I also hope that members and communities beyond librarians find value in the Atlas. I think there is a lot of food for thought for board members, college presidents, principals, and elected officials who oversee libraries in these pages. However, I hope that is true for members of the general public as well. Within these pages is a call to engage our communities—you—in a new social compact. This social compact spells out the true value of the library and librarians, what is expected from them, and by them. You—as a parent, as a job seeker, as a reader, as a web surfer, as a gamer, as a child, as a student, as a business man—have a voice in the future of libraries. I hope this Atlas helps you find that voice.

LIMITATIONS OF THE ATLAS

The Atlas is formative. Although it contains examples, it doesn't go into the specifics of all skills mentioned. Rather, it lays out a broad framework and a direction. This is important because I don't intend to necessarily negate current understandings and work. However, in many places, it does call for reexamination of functions and assumptions. There is value in taking such a high-level perspective: It gives us all a chance to step back and reflect. Much of current practice has been encased in decades (centuries) of practice and evolution. This history, although certainly representing the aggregate efforts of best thoughts in the profession, can also serve as baggage weighing down needed reform. Any standard, policy, or practice results not only from true insight but also compromise, and it reflects the limitations of attitudes and technology of the time. So although we don't want to throw the baby out with the bathwater, it is good to every so often ask whether the baby is clean enough.

Another limitation of the Atlas is that it reflects a decidedly North American perspective. This is obvious, for example, in the discussion of LIS education because bachelor's-level librarianship degrees exist in many countries already. Although efforts were made to learn from and think about the librarian experience in other countries, the truth is that most of my time and energy have been spent around libraries in the United States and Canada. I certainly hope the Atlas can serve as a springboard for further conversations globally (preferably starting with in-person dialogs about librarianship in the South of France).

There are, no doubt, other limiting perspectives in this work, and it is your responsibility to point them out and my responsibility to listen and work with you to correct or at least account for them.

An important thing to remember as you read through the Threads is this: to question something is not to seek weakness but rather to seek fitness. If an idea is good or an approach is valid, it should not only stand up to scrutiny, but it should welcome it. A major reason for the Atlas is to get the library community to ask hard questions so that we are fully ready for hard scrutiny from our members and beyond.

OK, let's get started.

THREADS

As detailed throughout this Atlas, knowledge is not simply a set of accumulated facts but rather a web of personal truths and their relationship to one another (the context). As such, this Atlas is not simply a list of definitions about librarianship but a set of agreements with relationships, with many agreements contextualizing any single agreement. Threads are a construct—a way of explaining the arrangement and logic that sit around the agreements. Threads are context and a means of understanding the full set of agreements and relationships.

The Threads of the Atlas are organized around the six major concepts in the mission of librarians, seen highlighted here:

The **mission** *of* **librarians** *is to* **improve society** *through* **facilitating knowledge creation** *in their* **communities.**

Rather than take each Thread in order, I present them in a building sequence. I first establish the case for a new mission and definition of librarianship in the "Mission" Thread, and I then lay the foundations of this new mission in the way knowledge is created. Upon this foundation, I lay the means of facilitating knowledge creation—the proposed role for librarians—and examine the concept of communities in today's increasingly interconnected world. Finally, I show the importance of action and activism, and I discuss the particular skills, values, and preparation of new librarians.

In general, the Threads form a sort of funnel, starting with broad concepts (the conceptual foundations of new librarianship) and then moving to more narrowly conceived examples and aspects. Each thread builds on the previous. So that an example in the "Communities" Thread is an expression of how people create knowledge outlined in the "Knowledge" Thread, which helps reinforce a worldview first put forth in the "Mission" Thread.

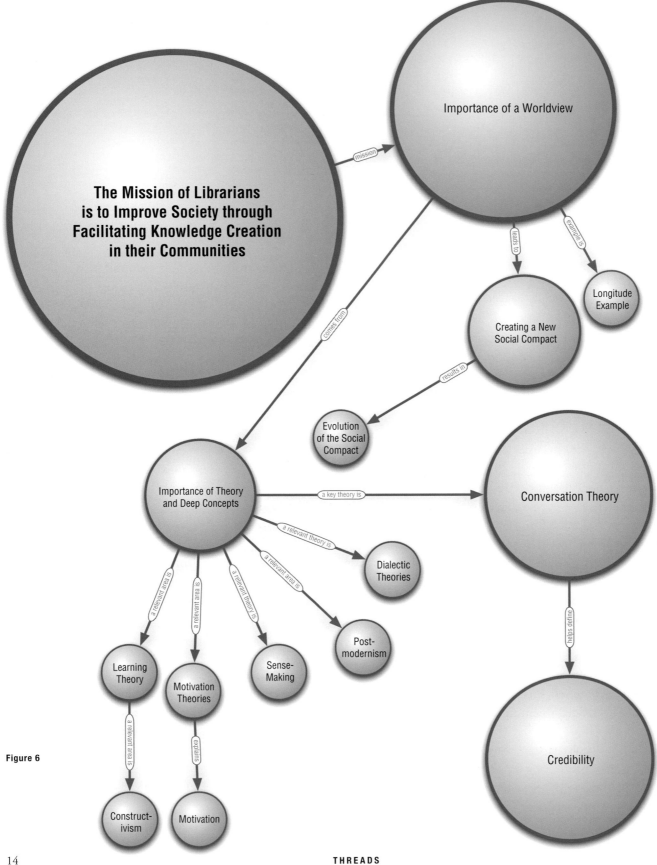

The Mission of Librarians is to Improve Society through Facilitating Knowledge Creation in their Communities

Importance of a Worldview

Longitude Example

Creating a New Social Compact

Evolution of the Social Compact

Importance of Theory and Deep Concepts

Conversation Theory

Dialectic Theories

Post-modernism

Sense-Making

Learning Theory

Motivation Theories

Credibility

Construct-ivism

Motivation

Figure 6

MISSION

The library is not a shrine for the worship of books. It is not a temple where literary incense must be burned or where one's devotion to the bound book is expressed in ritual. A library, to modify the famous metaphor of Socrates, should be the delivery room for the birth of ideas.
—Norman Cousins

THE MISSION OF LIBRARIANS IS TO IMPROVE SOCIETY THROUGH FACILITATING KNOWLEDGE CREATION IN THEIR COMMUNITIES

The mission of librarians is to improve society through facilitating knowledge creation in their communities. There are some important things to note about this mission statement. First, it is not the mission of a library or an organization; it is the mission of a librarian. It focuses the field on information professionals, but it also makes the responsibility personal to an individual. It doesn't matter whether a librarian works in a library or hospital, a law firm, a search engine company, or out of his or her own home; the mission still stands.

Although other threads in the Atlas unpack some of the key phrases in the mission statement, one must first answer the most basic question: Why bother having a field-wide mission statement anyway?

A mission, vision, or goal provides a yardstick by which to gauge efforts and judge options. When librarians are faced with decisions, as they increasingly are in times of tight budgets, they must have some means of making the decision. Should a public librarian spend precious resources on popular materials? Databases? Longer hours? Without a common and deeply held mission, these decisions come down to personal or political choice often based on unquestioned assumptions.

For example, I was on the board of a public library. The board had made a goal before I joined of constantly increasing the materials budget by 10%. When hard times hit, the goal remained, and so come budget time, the initial proposal to the board was to increase the collection budget and lay off staff. After a quick discussion about how having books that could not be found, shelved, or even circulated didn't make much sense, it was decided to cut the materials budget and retain the staff.

This might seem like an easy choice to the librarians reading this (even a victory), but that is not the point. Why was the initial proposal put forth in the first place? The answer comes down to the world-view that the mission of the library is situated within it. If you see the library's primary value being the maintenance of a collection—that is, the mission of a library is the collection and provision of materials—then it makes a lot of sense to increase the materials budget. In contrast, if you see the main asset of a library as the professional or, even better, the potential positive effect librarians can have on a community, then it makes no sense at all.

IMPORTANCE OF WORLDVIEW*

In many ways, this entire Atlas is intended to make clear a worldview of librarianship not founded on materials, but outcomes and learning. Once again, this may seem like an easy or even obvious approach. However, look at the budgets that most libraries spend on materials and the activities surrounding them. Between buying, licensing, cataloging, shelving, housing, and circulating things, what is left? If you have a hard time answering that question beyond "reference," you are not alone. The worldview of librarians has become so fixated on artifacts (books, CDs, etc.) that they have a hard time separating out their goals from the tools they use to achieve them. Allow me to illustrate with a story.

A foundation was working with a large urban library to design a physical space for youth to explore new modes of learning. The library had identified an underutilized storage space and turned it over to researchers funded by the foundation. The researchers went about designing the space to be open, collaborative, and infused with technology. All seemed to be going well until architectural plans for the new space came in and the librarians asked, "Where are we going to put the books?" The researchers were dumbfounded. The library didn't need the space for collections, and the researchers felt that a lot of shelving would deaden the space they envisioned. In a state of confusion, they asked me what was going on.

My short answer was that the foundation researchers had run smack into a materials-centered librarian worldview. In essence, the librarians were trying to identify their own contributions and value in the new space. Without collections, they felt they had no value. Ironically, the researchers saw great value in the librarians as moderators and facilitators. Youth were going to be entering new spaces and would need help and guidance. In fact, one of the reasons the foun-

*See Agreement Supplement for an annotated bibliography of worldviews in librarianship.

dation had originally approached the library was because of the great perceived value of librarians in a network of learning that included schools, museums, and homes.

Ask yourself, how artifact-centric is your worldview? Assume for a moment "they" are right…you know, them: The ones who say that the Internet/Mass Digitization/Search Engines/Wikipedia/Document Right Management/whatever is going to put libraries out of business. Assume that the stacks are bare, the coffee bars are empty, and the ivy is left to run riot over the columns. Is there still a library? If that strikes you as an odd question, let me ask you another one. Is the future of the library a question of stacks, coffee bars, or ivy?

I have long contended that a room full of books is simply a closet but that an empty room with a librarian in it is a library. Will that librarian build a collection of artifacts over time to help in his or her mission of facilitating knowledge? Probably. If that empty room has an Internet connection, there is a good chance that the room will soon also serve out a web page full of links. Over time, the room may fill with magazines, computers, or (hopefully) whiteboards and meeting spaces. However, these things come from the librarians doing their jobs; they are not the job itself.

Librarianship is not the only profession currently dealing with a worldview that has too closely co-mingled a mission with the tools of the trade. Take the current media obsession with the death of newspapers. Around the nation, newspapers are folding or facing tremendous financial difficulties. Many have said this signals the death of journalism. However, reporters at local, national, and cable television news outlets might disagree. What is dying is a medium of delivery and a business model for print. Journalism—and its methods of credibility, ethics, and even overarching mission of telling truth—is still very needed and alive.

What we must develop, and what this Atlas puts forth as a first effort, is a new worldview of librarianship that transcends tools, and even former missions like information organization (a means to an end), and maintaining recorded knowledge (an oxymoron that is discussed later). It is vital to do so not simply to survive the current times but to open up a world of possibilities.

LONGITUDE EXAMPLE

It might seem a bit grand to think that something as abstract as a worldview can "open up a world of possibilities," but that is precisely what happened in eighteenth-century England. At the time, commerce and the wealth of nations was very much centered on a nation's sea fleet and its ability to navigate the world. Since ancient times, seagoing vessels have plied the waters of Europe and the Mediterranean for trading purposes. Since ancient times, this type of navigation was based on the concepts of latitude and landmarks.

Latitude is the measure of one's relative position north and south on the Earth. In modern times, it is defined by how far you are from the equator. Early sailors determined their latitude by the use of landmarks. Seeing a certain cliff wall or a certain lighthouse on the shore would determine their location along the coast. Later sailors could use the stars and star charts to determine their north and south location.

However, sailors had to stay close to the shore because they had no way of determining how far east or west they were (a measure we now call longitude). If a crew lost sight of land, they would have no way of determining their true location and might as well have fallen off the edge of a flat Earth. Even when it was widely known that the Earth was round (long before Columbus sailed the ocean blue starting as far back as Aristotle), making use of that information was difficult and treacherous. Massive fleets and treasure were lost trying to go beyond the sight of land.

Huge amounts of money were spent trying to figure out a method of determining longitude by the position of the moon and stars. Proposals were even put forth to build a system of cannons across the ocean that would fire at precise times each day to set up shipping lanes. Finally, in an early version of crowdsourcing, governments put up huge rewards for the person who could figure out a method of determining longitude accurately and effectively.[1]

The winner, it turns out, was a man named John Harrison who invented an extremely accurate clock. With an accurate clock, you can determine what time it is at some fixed point of longitude (today we use a line that goes right through Greenwich, England), say noon. You can then determine noon at your current location (when the sun is at its highest point). By using the difference in the two times and a little math, you can accurately determine your location east/west.

Using these two concepts, longitude and latitude, you can now chart the globe. You no doubt have seen a map like the one in figure 7. The lines on the map, latitude running from top to bottom and longitude left to right, don't actually exist in nature. They are a purely human construct. Yet with this construct—quite literally a

1. Sobel, D. (1995). *Longitude: The true story of a lone genius who solved the greatest scientific problem of his time*. New York: Walker.

Physical Map of the World, June 2009

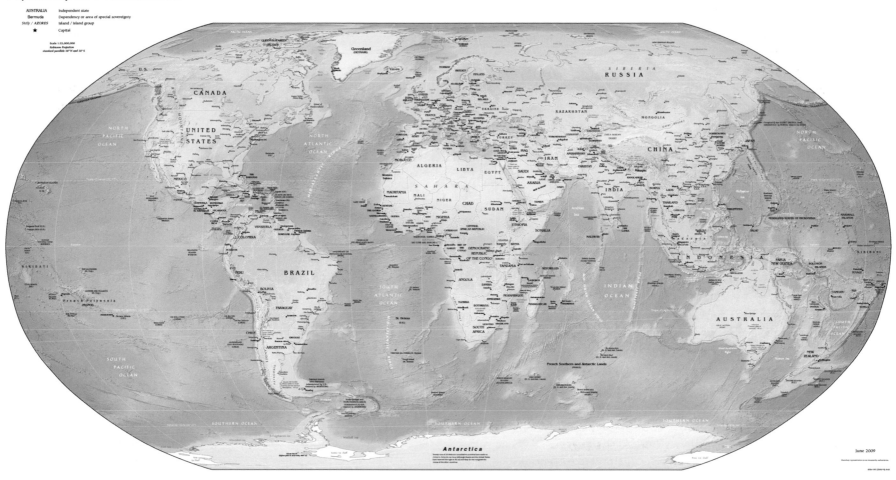

Figure 7

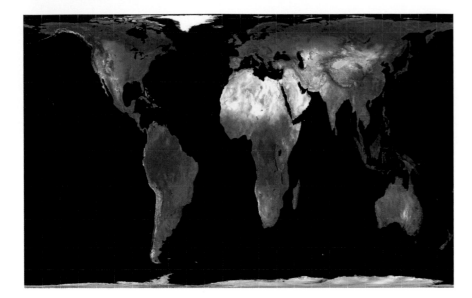

Figure 8

worldview—one can understand not only where you are but where everything else is and how to get there. It is such a powerful worldview that it is still used today, although the stars and moon have been replaced by satellites and Harrison's clock replaced by digital clocks in our global positioning system (GPS) units.

It should be noted that even this map represents a view of the world that is far from universal. After all, this is a flat map of a sphere. In fact, throughout the twentieth century, many cartographers advocated for the use of the "Gall-Peters Projection" (as seen in figure 8) that some felt better represented the distribution of land on the globe.

This is a different view than the maps based on the "Mercator Projection" most of us grew up with, where Greenland and Africa appear to be about the same size even though Africa is 14 times larger. Some maps in Australia actually put South at the top of the map (who says North has to be "up"). The bottom line is this: How we envision the world influences our navigation through it and the decisions we make.

Throughout this Atlas, I attempt to articulate a worldview so that we cannot only determine where we are but what our options are and where we can go next. Further, this worldview must be independent of any given set of tools and/or technologies because we know they change rapidly. The worldview must be based on theory and deep concepts. Allow me to illustrate the point with a joke.

IMPORTANCE OF THEORY AND DEEP CONCEPTS*

So Albert Einstein goes to a party. The host is keen to show off the world-famous physicist to his mostly blue-collar friends, so he escorts Einstein around, introducing him.

The first guest asks Einstein, "So what is it you do, Albert?"

Einstein replies, "I seek to understand time."

"Wow," says the guest, "We're in the same business. I sell watches."

The host introduces him to the second guest, who asks, "So Albert, what is it you do?"

Einstein, trying to impress, replies, "I seek to understand how all the planets and stars in heaven move about the universe."

"Wow," says the second guest, "We're in the same line of work. I build telescopes."

A third guest asks Einstein, "What is it you do?"

Einstein replies, "I have discovered how light, magnetism, and electricity are connected."

"Wow," says the third guest, "We're in the same business. I repair TVs!"

The host takes a now depressed and exasperated Einstein to meet a fourth guest.

"What is it you do, Albert?" asks the fourth guest.

Now completely deflated, Einstein says, "Nothing. I don't sell anything. I don't build anything. I can't even repair anything. I'm useless."

"Wow," says the fourth guest, "I'm a tenured professor too!"

Few would actually see a watch salesman, a telescope builder, and a TV repairman as in the same business as Einstein, but the joke illustrates an important point: Functional definitions of professions in general, and of librarianship in particular, do not work. That is, if you seek to define the worldview of librarians by the functions they do, you will run into all sorts of problems—problems we have all seen played out at conferences and on blog posts.

Let us recast the joke. This time it is a librarian being introduced around instead of Albert Einstein (feel free to put a snide comment here).

"What do you do?" asks the first guest.

"I help people find information," says the librarian.

"Wow," says the guest, "We're in the same business. I work at Google [or Bing, or Yahoo]."

*See Agreement Supplement for an annotated bibliography on theory in libraries.

To the second guest, the librarian answers, "I provide access to books, CDs, and all types of materials."

"Wow," says the second guest, "We're in the same business. I work at Amazon."

To the third guest, the librarian replies, "I answer people's questions when they ask."

"Wow," says the third guest, "We're in the same business. I work at the Sears Helpdesk."

I'll let you fill in the punch line (although I think it should either involve a belly dancer or a politician). The point remains the same. If you define the whole of librarianship as a set of tasks or functions, you end up with a lot of confusion and understandable concern about the future. This, by the way, I see as the major shortcoming of ALA's "Core Competencies of Librarianship."[2] It is a document that lists functions with no explicit declaration of worldview (although it is clearly based on one that is strongly artifact-centric).

The keen reader is quick to point out that, although the worldview behind the functions may be different, the average users of these functions may not be able to tell the difference. If there is no functional difference, then why does worldview matter (or at least a worldview that seeks to go beyond following the landmarks of the search engines and such)?

The short answer is time. As is obvious to anyone in librarianship, the world is changing. It is dynamic. It is changing not just in the technology it produces and uses but also in other more profound ways. I've already mentioned that over the past century, life expectancy for U.S. citizens has gone from 47 to 77 years.[3] Profound changes in technology, demographics, connectivity, and more mean that functions are also changing, and it is the ability to change in the direction of current and *future* service that will spell success or disaster (or an uncomfortable stasis). That ability to change and anticipate is a product of a worldview.

Let me walk you through three examples to show you what I mean. The first is silly and is only presented to make the point obvious. Imagine I gave you a task: pick an animal to run a land race and win. You might pick a cheetah, the world's fastest animal. You could also pick a dog (let's say a greyhound). Functionally, both could run a race. However, given that the task is to win, the cheetah might seem the obvious choice. What is missing, and what becomes obvious over

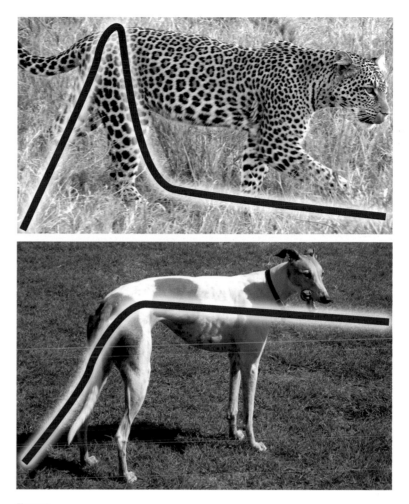

Figure 9

2. http://www.ala.org/ala/educationcareers/careers/corecomp/corecompetences/final-corecompstat09.pdf
3. http://en.wikipedia.org/wiki/Life_expectancy

time, is that the real variable you need to consider is mentioned nowhere in the task…the length of the race.

You see, while the cheetah is very fast, it is not very fast for very long. Its explosive speed is short-lived and helps it hunt. After a quick burst of speed, most of the cat's energy is used up, and it requires a very long nap to restore its energy. Dogs, on the other hand, while not as fast, can maintain their top speed for a long time. So if the race is a 100-yard dash, the cheetah would win. If it is a marathon, the dog is the best bet (see figure 9).

You may think this is cheating, holding out a key aspect of the task. Yet that is exactly what happens in the real world. As the param-eters of the environment change, an important aspect of a task, organization, or worldview may not become apparent at any given moment. It is only over time that one approach wins out over the other. Let me move off the simple example of a race to one in the real world.

Take Wikipedia and Encarta in 2004. Both were online encyclopedias. Both had freely available content. Both had a wide range of topics. Yet something interesting happened over the next two years. As the graph in figure 10 shows, Wikipedia exploded while Encarta imploded.

In retrospect, we can say the fact that users could add their own content made the big difference, and that a "2.0" approach was the

Figure 10

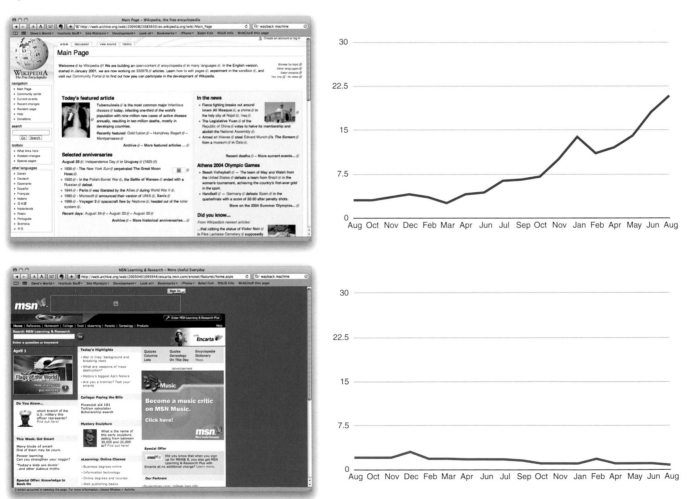

obvious winner. However, put yourself back in 2004. Microsoft funded Encarta. Encarta had a huge number of existing users through its CD-ROM products (particularly in the K–12 domain) and was professionally edited and designed. Wikipedia had no advertising budget, no expert editors, and no real organizational backing. What Wikipedia did have was a different worldview—that of radical openness. Over time, as the web changed, that worldview proved more successful (Encarta eventually closed shop). Simply saying that Encarta and Wikipedia were functionally similar misses the whole point.

Take, as another example, MySpace and GeoCities. Functionally they provided the same basic function: a personal space on the web.

Both were situated as social in nature. But as time moved forward, the more restricted nature of GeoCities and its limited ability for customization changed their adoption as shown in figure 11.

We could continue with examples that range from web search (with Alta Vista looking at the web as a set of documents and Google seeing it as a set of connections) to nondigital examples, such as how Dewey's classification system took off while other systems, such as Ranganathan's faceted classification, did not. However, the point is clear: Over time, functional views don't and can't capture the dynamic nature of the world. What's more, they tend to lead to stagnation and an inability to adapt.

Figure 11

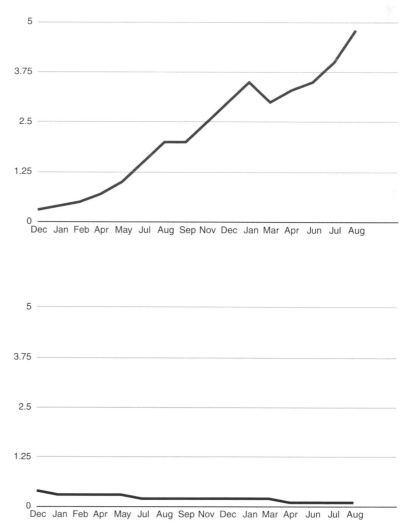

If, on the other hand, we build a worldview on theory and deep conceptual foundations (such as latitude and longitude), we should be able to build a more robust mission statement, allow functions to change as the environment changes, and still retain a core identity as librarians. So when the public library in Gilbert, Arizona, drops Dewey, we don't have to ask, "Is it still a library?" Although the tools have changed, the core mission of knowledge creation and societal improvement remains. Their identities as librarians are not predicated on whether they catalog but by how they see the world (worldview) and determine whether they should or shouldn't catalog (a function). The reasoning behind the decision is much more important over time than the decision itself.

The worldview of new librarianship put forth in this Atlas is founded on a theory of how people learn called Conversation Theory. It is also informed by other key theories and concepts such as Motivation Theory, Sense-Making, and Postmodernism. All of these combined approaches call out for a new social compact among librarians and those they seek to serve.

Libraries and Theory

Before we proceed into the theories and conceptual frameworks that lie at the base of new librarianship, it is worth exploring a bit on why theories on learning and conversation are being used over library-specific theories.

There are two answers: Library science as currently constituted is not rich in strong theory, and what theory there is revolves around functional approaches. The field of library science as seen in journals and books is overwhelmingly about empirical explorations and system building. So there are ample data on how members feel about a given function (surveys on catalog usage, behavioral studies on web-based information seeking, content analysis of digital reference questions) but little attempt to answer why the results turn out the way they do. There are, of course, some exceptions. McGrath,[4] for example, has tried to determine a grand theory of library science. However, on the whole, few have put forth library-specific theories, and what is there is more like theories of cataloging, reference, and so on.

Some have taken this lack of theoretical work to claim that library science is an atheoretical field. However, this notion is not true. Take a run through the reference literature. You have Brenda Dervin's development of neutral questioning[5] to Marie Radford's work on reference encountering.[6] However, here the use of theory is not about the library per say but about the action that is taken in a library (namely, asking and answering questions).

When you think about it, this makes sense. Theories and science are all about explaining and exploring natural or organic things. Social scientists use theories and methods to explore how humans make their way through the world. Theories from the natural sciences study how the physical world reacts. Even in areas where the study is explicitly about organizations, such as economics, management, or systems theory, the emphasis is on general behaviors, not tied to a specific type of organization.

Science always looks for the general. Having a theory of libraries is like having a theory about General Motors or the grand unified theory of McDonald's. Because libraries are artificial creations of people (societies, communities), one must look to the underlying drivers that lead to the act of creation.

In other words, to learn about why organizations are shaped the way they are, we try to understand what drives people to organize. Likewise, to improve libraries, we don't look to theories of buildings but to theories that drive the goals that librarians seek to accomplish.

For decades, those have been presumed to be theories of information. From Shannon and Weaver's Theory of Information[7] to the more specific information-seeking world, to the human–computer interaction world that seeks to understand how people interact with information systems. To be sure, these theories have been of great utility and shall continue to be useful. However, in terms of setting a worldview and grounding a mission, they fall short. After all, how does a library mission of "informing" help us determine what to do next? "Keep informing" is not a satisfying answer.

Setting aside the inability of the library and information science field to develop a universally satisfying definition of information (Is it in our heads or what is transmitted? What is the difference between data and information and knowledge anyway? What is the unit of

4. McGrath, W. E. (2002a, Winter). Explanation and prediction: building a unified theory of librarianship, concept and review. *Library Trends*. Available: http://www.findarticles.com/p/articles/mi_m1387/is_3_50/ai_88582619
5. Dervin, B., & Dewdney, P. (1986). Neutral questioning: A new approach to the reference interview. *Reference Quarterly, 25*(4), 506–513.
6. Radford, M. L. (1999). *The reference encounter: Interpersonal communication in the academic library* (ACRL publications in librarianship, no. 52). Chicago: Association of College and Research Libraries.
7. Shannon, Claude E., & Weaver, Warren. (1949). *The mathematical theory of communication*. Champaign, IL: University of Illinois Press.

analysis for information?), the fact is that we have yet to encounter any organization, society, or individual who doesn't use information. How can something so universal help guide libraries?

Let's take just a quick example. Cognitive studies show us that people can processes about seven (plus or minus two) pieces of information at a time.[8] That is, if I give you a phone number, you can probably remember it, but if I give you a credit card number, you have to write it down. OK, so this may be useful in a reference interview (how many sources to cite) or a catalog interface (number of results to show), but does it help you determine why you do reference or cataloging?

For this reason, I go to learning and knowledge. Here we have a rich array of conceptual tools on which to draw. It also fits squarely into the mission of libraries over their history (after all, libraries do not collect resources just to fill space). It has wide applicability over the types of organizations libraries serve, and it is about the individuals (both the individuals who are learning, as well as the individuals who are facilitating that learning).

To be sure, not everyone agrees with this choice. There are some who even question the need for theory at all. When living in such a data-rich world, why not just let the data tell you where to go next or how to act?[9] When Google wants to make any changes, including itty bitty cosmetic changes to its home page, it creates a new version of the site and randomly feeds it out to a few hundred thousand users.[10] It then has plenty of data to determine whether the change was beneficial. However, such an approach would never have invented Google in the first place. It takes insight and a mission to even know what data are important.

So let us now proceed into theory; theory that looks past any institution and into human nature itself.

CONVERSATION THEORY*

Conversation Theory[11] serves as the conceptual foundation of the worldview set forth in this Atlas. As such the theory is covered in greater detail elsewhere (see the "Knowledge Creation" Thread or the "Conversation Theory" Agreement Supplement). What is essential to understand in terms of mission and worldview is that Conversation Theory focuses on learning and knowledge. This is a departure from a current focus on information, access, and artifacts. More precisely, in the lens of conversation, artifacts and access are only useful in that they are used to (or results of) build knowledge through active learning.

The fundamental shift is from things to human knowledge. It changes the focus of the work of librarians from artifacts and the products of learning (like books, web pages, and DVDs) to the learning process. Rather than being concerned with some externalized concept such as information (or, worse, "recorded knowledge"), it places the focus of librarianship squarely on behavior and the effects of services on the individual. In essence, the value of a book, or librarian for that matter, is evaluated against the need of the library member's ability to learn. Even the need for a library to collect artifacts (materials) is determined by the learning needs of the member or the aggregated needs of the community. So a library where people are learning and building their knowledge may have no books, no computers, no DVDs, and no building. What it will have is a librarian facilitating the process. This may seem odd, if not outright wrong. Allow me to present you two scenarios of a library with no books: the first historical, and the second proposed.

Many people trace the history of libraries back to the Library of Alexandria in ancient Egypt. Most talk about its enormous collection of scrolls and documents from around the known world. One of my favorite aspects of the library was that any ship entering into Alexandria, a major trading port, would have all of its documents confiscated. The library would then copy the documents and return the copies to the ship.

What many people don't recall in this history was that the library was not actually one big building. It was more of a campus. The documents were stored in several buildings, including a structure dedicated to the Muses called the Museion—the origin of the term "museum." The campus was a dormitory and working space for scholars. Scholars and thinkers were paid to take up residence in Alexandria, and the buildings were designed with colonnades to maximize their interaction. If these scholars had some great thought or wrote down some new insight, the artifact was then retained. The library was much more a precursor to today's university systems or even to economic incubators.[12] The library existed for the scholars' interactions, and the librarian of Alexandria was seen not as a caretaker but an advisor to the rulers of the city-state.

8. Miller, G. A. (1956). The magical number seven, plus or minus two: Some limits on our capacity for processing information. *Psychological Review*, *63*(2), 81–97.
9. http://www.wired.com/science/discoveries/magazine/16-07/pb_theory
10. http://gizmodo.com/5181402/googles-design-problem-all-data-no-vision
*See Agreement Supplement for an overview of conversation theory and more links to the literature.
11. Pask, G. (1976). *Conversation theory: Applications in education and epistemology.* New York: Elsevier.
12. For more on the library as a think tank, see Casson, L. (2001). *Libraries in the ancient world.* New Haven, CT: Yale University Press. 32–39.

Just a quick note on worldview before I move on to the next example. Many have heard of the Library of Alexandria, but few have heard about the campus and the use of the library beyond the collection. History is often a narrative that reinforces worldviews rather than challenging them. In this case, the worldview is that libraries are storehouses for materials.

Now let us think about a modern library that would not carry books. You might expect a discussion of digital libraries or web spaces, but in truth these can be seen as store houses of artifacts where the artifacts are web pages and digital files. What we want is a library of behaviors and learning.

Let us first set up a few concepts. There are plenty of things that cannot be well taught through text or even video; they must be learned by doing. There are also people who learn much better through hands-on experience. So what if we wanted to set up a library of manufacturing? We want to build a space that facilitates knowledge of building things. Our first instinct might be to go and collect materials on how-tos, industry reports, and the like. While in reality we might well do this, let's stick to the task: a library without traditional information artifacts.

Why not fill the space with manufacturing equipment? What's more, we need to fill the space with experts who can teach folks how to use this equipment. Members of our manufacturing library might come into the space with their own building projects, work with experts to learn the equipment, and build. We might have apprenticeship programs where members get certified. We might even have spaces filled with Legos, building blocks, and Tinker Toys for kids to learn the basics of structure and construction.

Why is this a library and not a trade school or vocational academy? The answer is because it is brought together and managed by a librarian. Not just in title but in what the librarian brings to the space. The role of the librarian in this space will not seem so different from what you might do today. The librarian must know the community and its needs. He or she might conduct surveys or have focus groups to identify the most useful manufacturing equipment. The librarian must also build a collection. Rather than this being a collection of documents, it would be a collection of expertise and processes. The librarian would organize programs, answer reference questions, and even complete an inventory of projects through some form of cataloging. The manufacturing library is a library not because of these functions, however, but because a librarian brought his or her worldview of knowledge and learning to a community (including his or her values, which we review in the "Improve Society" Thread).

Conversation Theory shapes our mission. It focuses us on learning and, as I detail elsewhere, shapes the means of facilitation into a unique profession. Our worldview and our mission must accommodate learning theories and focus on individual learning and responsibilities. Conversation Theory also provides insight into one of the greatest assets a librarian has: credibility.

Credibility

The prime value of librarians is not their skill set or their credentials. These things will change. The enduring value of librarians on which everything flows is their credibility. Building and holding the trust of the community is the scaffolding on which all facilitation is built. The reason that credibility is discussed in conjunction with Conversation Theory is that the predominant means of determining credibility of a source is shifting. In an increasingly networked world, credibility determinations have shifted from a basis of authority—the abdication of personal credibility judgments to another source (the authority)—to one of reliability—polling a number of sources for commonalities.

The effect of this on the mission of librarians is at least two fold: Librarians must understand that they are only one source among many for a community, and librarians must be at least aware of the views of many sources on topics. This is not new by any means. One could argue that this is exactly how librarians have become seen as honest and credible agents. Not by seeking to be the authority on a source but rather by openly and transparently guiding members through multiple sources seeking consistency. This would indicate that as librarians move forward, they must be willing to move beyond any one class of resources (such as artifacts over experts).

OTHER INFORMATIVE CONCEPTS AND THEORIES

Before we proceed, it is worth a quick revisit to theory. Don't worry; this is not a textbook on theory and theory development. It is just important to understand what I mean by theory and how several theories can relate to a new librarianship. It is also important that as a librarian, you understand and appreciate theory—it is a fundamental difference between a job position and a profession. If you are uncomfortable with theory or you question its importance to practice, you are not alone—it is an unfortunate side effect of the field and LIS education's myopic focus on process and functions. Part of being a librarian in the new librarianship worldview is to be aware of theory and, therefore, be a reflective practitioner.

The term "theory" has a lot of possible meanings depending on your background and the situation. Some use theory to mean "educated guess." On the other end of the spectrum is the use of theory by physicists to describe a strong and well-vetted explanation of a given set of evidence. Certainly, Gordon Pask, the originator of Conversation Theory, would say that Conversation Theory is not a guess but rather a thorough and tested explanation of how people learn.

In the social sciences, there is even an informal distinction between "big T" Theory and "little t" theory, where Theories spelled with a big "T" are broad in their applicability and more basic in nature (think the Theory of Evolution, Complexity Theory, the Theory of Relativity). Little "t" theories, in contrast, are specific. LIS is rife with these examples, from theories of information retrieval to theories of virtual reference. I would consider Conversation Theory a big "T" Theory because it seeks to understand broadly and fundamentally how people learn—that is, how they learn in libraries, schools, their homes, anywhere.

The reason for giving you a primer in theories is that often theories can be combined or at least used together. For example, in the Atlas, Conversation Theory really serves as the basic theory informing worldview and indeed most aspects of what new librarianship is. Yet it is broad and a bit dated. Many of the concepts that Pask labored to explain are now more commonly held and better understood. These more recent refinements don't refute, but rather add to, Pask's work.

For example, in his book on Conversation Theory,[13] Pask devoted nearly a whole chapter to the idea that it is impossible to separate out the conditions of an experiment from the results of the experiment. So, for example, when you ask a student to come into a laboratory and perform some test, the fact that the student is in a laboratory (instead of, say, his own room) will have an impact on the results of the test. The ideas of researcher bias, limitations of controlled experiments, and the fact that context can affect performance are now well understood and accounted for. If Pask were writing today, he would have just cited this or even assumed the reader understood that.

Conversation Theory defines the basic theoretical underpinnings of the Atlas but is also informed by numerous other approaches. An informing theory is one where I gain insight from it but don't worry about how the outcome of my work refines (or redefines) that theory. For example, you do mathematics every day by being informed by number theory, but you don't spend too much time trying to discover how to change the basics of addition.

There are a host of these theories and concepts that inform new librarianship. The following sections outline key bodies of work to consider. These sections are not much more than glorified pointers here. There are more details in the associated agreements.

Dialectic Theories*

Conversation Theory belongs to a larger class of complementary theoretical constructs called dialectic theories. These theories, while emphasizing different facets such as human cognition, learning, concept acquisition, sociology, or interpersonal communications, all address the acquisition of knowledge through iterative messages—roughly conversation.

Many of these theories and their applied methods compliment the more holistic Conversation Theory and help bring Pask's concepts up to date, filling in aspects of conversation beyond Pask's more system-oriented thinking. Theories such as Speech Act Theory and methodologies such as discourse analysis have been important in advancing and refining the worldview of new librarianship presented in the Atlas.

Sense-Making*

Sense-making is a set of concepts and methods for determining how individuals understand the ideas and tasks they encounter and how they communicate those ideas and tasks. As Marshall[14] wrote:

> Dervin's Sense-Making focuses on the individual as he or she moves through time and space. As this happens, gaps are encountered where the individual must "make sense" of the situation to move, physically or cognitively, across the gap. The key components in this process are the situation, gap, and uses. The situation is the context of the user, the gap is that which prevents movement, and the use is the application of the sense which is constructed. (Dervin, 1999[15])

*See Agreement Supplement for a much deeper discussion of these theories.
*See Agreement Supplement for a greatly expanded discussion of Sense-Making.

14. Marshall, T. (2009). *Participatory networks in a nonprofit organization: An interpretive case study*. Unpublished doctoral dissertation proposal, Syracuse University, Syracuse, NY.
15. Dervin, B. (1999, May). *Sense-making's theory of dialog: A brief introduction*. Paper presented at a nondivisional workshop held at the meeting of the International Communication Association, San Francisco, CA.

13. Pask, G. (1976). *Conversation theory: Applications in education and epistemology*. New York: Elsevier.

It is an approach that seeks to focus on individuals and their cognitive processes. It is closely aligned to Sensemaking (look, Ma, no dash), in which Weick seeks to understand how organizations understand their environment.[16]

These approaches to how people and organizations move through an uncertain world help enrich our worldview and mission. Dervin,[17] Dewdney, and Nilan's[18] work, for example, provides numerous methods for determining how library members perceive problems. Many of Dervin's ideas already lie at the heart of the reference interview with concepts such as neutral questioning.[19]

Motivation Theories

As with dialectic theories, the Motivation Theories agreement represents a number of conceptual approaches to the question of what leads a person to action. These theories include Attribution Theory,[20] Expectancy Theory,[21] Goal-Setting Theory,[22] and Self-Determination Theory.[23] In essence, what cognitive processes and/or reward systems are in play when a person decides to learn, adopt, or act on something? There is a great deal of work around the concept of motivation in the field of education, where the driving question is, "What engages learners?" or, more broadly, "What drives someone to learn?"

Some theories of motivation focus on fulfilling fundamental needs. Abraham Maslow proposed a "hierarchy of needs,"[24] in which human needs are arranged in a sort of pyramid where basic physiological needs (need for food, warmth, etc.) must be satisfied before safety needs (the need to feel protected), before social needs (the need for friendship), before esteem needs (the need to feel good about oneself), and before self-actualization (the need to learn and grow). One must satisfy the basic needs before preparing for greater motivations.

This set of theories is tremendously helpful in the areas of outreach and public service by librarians. How can we expect the homeless to learn new skills or find new occupations if their basic needs for food and shelter are not met? Ideas of motivation are also useful when talking about how to facilitate knowledge.

For the purposes of the Atlas, motivations are seen as a combination of extrinsic rewards (where the reward for accomplishment comes from another person or outside source), intrinsic rewards (where the reward for accomplishment comes from within the individual), and a series of other factors such as perceived ability or competency (the likelihood of success).

*Motivation**

Let me pause here for a moment to show how understanding theory directly affects practice. Even those who already see the library as a learning place, or part of a larger network of learning, tend to assume a particular kind of motivation: intrinsic. That is, much of how libraries are set up now assumes that the people who use them do so voluntarily. Even when presenting library service as essential, it is often couched in terms of the motivation for use coming from outside of the library. So the student using an academic library to work on a paper is impelled to do so from a professor. A child attending story hour either does so of his or her own volition or is impelled to do so by a parent or guardian.

There is a danger to this view. It implies that library use is driven solely by external forces, and it also implies that the library is somehow passive (it is unable to compel use on its own). One clear departure from this approach can be seen in the rise of teaching information literacy skills in primary and secondary education. Here school library media specialists have their own goals, curricula, and place in the school. They become an extrinsic motivational force to move students along a path. This sets up a different relationship not only with library members (in this case students) but also with other school personnel.

* See Agreement Supplement for more on motivation.

16. Weick, K (1995). *Sensemaking in organizations*. Thousand Oaks, CA: Sage.
17. http://communication.sbs.ohio-state.edu/sense-making/default.html is a great starting place for learning more on sense-making.
18. For example, see Dalrymple, P. W. (2001). A quarter century of user-centered study: The impact of Zweizig and Dervin on LIS research. *Library & Information Science Research*, *23*(2), 155–165. Retrieved on September 13, 2009, from Library, Information Science & Technology Abstracts with Full Text. <http://search.ebscohost.com/login.aspx?direct=true&db=lih&AN=ISTA3700451&site=ehost-live>; Dewdney, P., & Ross, C. (1986). Effective question asking in library instruction. *Reference Quarterly*, *25*(4), 451–454; and Nilan, M. S., Newby, G. B., Paik, W., & Lopatin, K. (1989). User-oriented interfaces for computer systems: A user defined online help system for desktop publishing. *Proceedings of the ASIS Annual Meeting*, *26*, 104–110.
19. Dervin, B., & Dewdney, P. (1986). Neutral questioning: A new approach to the reference interview. *Reference Quarterly*, *25*(4), 506–513.
20. Roesch, S. C., & Amirkham, J. H. (1997). Boundary conditions for self-serving attributions: Another look at the sports pages. *Journal of Applied Social Psychology*, *27*, 245–261.
21. Vroom, V. H. (1964). *Work and motivation*. New York: Wiley.
22. Tetlock, P. E., & Kim, J. (1987). Accountability and judgment in a personality prediction task. *Journal of Personality and Social Psychology: Attitudes and Social Cognition*, *52*, 700–709.
23. Deci, E. L., & Ryan, R. M. (1985). *Intrinsic motivation and self-determination in human behavior*. New York: Plenum Press.
24. Maslow, A. H. (1943). A theory of human motivation. *Psychological Review*, *50*(4), 370–396.

In terms of developing a mission for new librarians, it is crucial that librarians have a better understanding of motivation. By having a better understanding of why members use the service (and why non-members don't), librarians can begin to, with some fidelity and craft, compel use where it makes sense and be much more proactive in the knowledge life of their members. We revisit this idea in the "Facilitating" Thread.

*Learning Theory**

Learning theories constitute a broad range of conceptual frameworks devoted to the hows and whys of learning. This includes things such as Motivation Theory and Conversation Theory. It also involves cognitive and behavioral theories. Perhaps the most notable thing about learning theories in relation to librarianship is their startling absence from librarian preparation outside of some school media programs.

How can you as a librarian hope to design effective services and systems to help people learn if you don't have a basic understanding of the process and variables involved (e.g., learning styles and modalities for the catalog)? What learning theory adds to librarianship and our worldview is an understanding that simply providing access to a concept is insufficient to learn that concept. One theory that speaks more to worldview and the conceptual underpinnings of new librarianship is constructivism.

*Constructivism**

One of the distinguishing characteristics of learning theories from many other bodies of theory has to do with the underlying philosophies that shape these concepts. Beyond the neurological and basic cognitive studies, there is a great deal of debate in education in terms of the role of the learner and that of the teacher. For example, structural approaches believe that, particularly for novice learners, guiding a student through a topic is the most effective means of learning. Such approaches range from university lectures to so-called "drill-and-kill" pedagogies that emphasize memorization and the role of the teacher.

An alternative approach is constructivism.[25] Here the emphasis is on active learning, where students learn by doing, and the ultimate meaning they derive from learning is individual. At the heart of a constructivist approach is the belief that someone can create conditions for learning, but it is impossible to impose knowledge or learning on someone. This approach is evident throughout the Atlas.

Note, for example, the wording of the mission: "facilitate knowledge creation." It is not about transferring knowledge or teaching a community. Rather, the role of the librarian is as facilitator, and the knowledge created of concern is resident within the learner at the end of the facilitation process. It is also the reason that librarians are not referred to as teachers. Teaching is a profession with its own norms and boundaries, and a teacher is someone who can make learning happen.[26] Librarians don't make learning happen; rather they both create the conditions for learning and fulfill the need for learning on the part of the member. Constructivism and motivation are very much about a member-centric view. The effect of librarians is seen in the member. The power is ultimately resident in the member.

This, by the way, in no way contradicts the idea that librarians must be active and strong partners in a conversation. After all, although a customer ultimately gets to decide whether he or she likes the food in a restaurant, the cook still has to make the dish.

*Postmodernism**

Talking about postmodernism[27] is somewhat akin to tap dancing in a minefield. Because the entire movement is one based on interpretation and criticism, postmodernist debates are often debates about the character of the one who is doing the interpreting. I had one student who groaned when I mentioned it because she had fled an English program for librarianship to avoid heated postmodernist debates.

Postmodernism is brought up in this context as a way of emphasizing individual action and interpretation in the work of librarianship. In essence, the collections that librarians currently work with are artifacts that prompt conversations that lead to knowledge. The collections by themselves are not knowledge. When someone reads a book, he or she is engaged in a conversation—not with the author but with him or herself about how to interpret and use the ideas generated in reading. This is why books, CDs, and web pages are referred to

*See Agreement Supplements for a deeper discussion of learning theories.
*See Agreements Supplement for a much more thorough discussion of constructivism, include links to the relevant literature.
25. Delia, J. G., O'Keefe, B. J., & O'Keefe, D. J. (1982). The constructivist approach to communication. In F. E. X. Dance (Ed.), *Human communication theory* (pp. 147–191). New York: Harper & Row.
26. To be fair, there are many teachers and education scholars who don't believe that teachers can make anything happen if the learner does not want to engage.
*See Agreement Supplement for more on postmodernism.
27. http://plato.stanford.edu/entries/postmodernism/

throughout the Atlas as artifacts as opposed to "recorded knowledge." You can't record knowledge; it is an inherently human thing. All you can do is promote and hope to shape conversations.

CREATING A NEW SOCIAL COMPACT*

So where are we? We started talking about missions, grounded the statement in a worldview, and just tripped quickly through a load of theories. Are we done yet? Not quite. Although I have attempted to show you the importance of having a mission, and how the particular mission of improving society through facilitating knowledge creation in our communities is grounded in deep concepts and worldviews, this is still only half of what we need to succeed. Just as knowledge comes from a conversation between at least two parties, a mission to improve society is only effective if it is mutually agreed on by two parties: the party doing the improving and the party being improved or, more accurately, the two parties that must work together to improve.

As an example, I work in Syracuse, New York. The city has the same problems that trouble most urban centers: violence, poverty, racial tensions, and so on. For years the University would send researchers and students into the city to "help" the community. I put help in quotes because, after a while, city residents made it clear that certain departments of the University were no longer welcome. While the University felt it was bringing needed assistance to the community as part of a mission, the community felt like it was always being told how it was broken. Community residents became tired and angry with being an experiment to a distant university community on the hill. This feeling is hardly unique to Syracuse. The "town and gown" divide exists all over the United States.

My point is that having a mission is important, but if it is not supported by the larger community served, it is useless. There must be a social compact between the community and the librarians. This is ultimately the most important conversation that librarians can have with the community and not just when budgets are on the line. In many ways, this Atlas is in response to a current social compact that is fraying, with librarians seeking to either reify the old or push the new, and a community that is all too often unaware of the debate.

These social compacts can happen gradually, such as the growing expectation among many geographic communities that public libraries serve as Internet hubs. They can also happen rapidly, such as in

*See Agreement Supplement for readings on social compacts and higher education.

service use agreements in social networks like Facebook. In all cases, they never happen unnoticed. Whether brought on by crisis—such as the unfolding reformation of the regulatory apparatus in the financial markets brought on by the worldwide economic downturn—or by opportunity—such as the expectation of technological advances and planned obsolesce in the technology sector—there is debate and agreement between stakeholders in the compact.

It is one thing to say that librarians are now central and that their role is in learning not collections or books. It is quite another to have academies, municipalities, schools, corporations, and governments agree. In some cases, it is simply bringing stakeholders up to speed with a new situation and reality. In some cases, it is a true clash of value systems.

I would argue that the ideas presented within this Atlas, although not ubiquitous, are present in many forms throughout librarianship now. Some vary in form or extent—there will certainly be disagreements over parts of the whole picture—but there is a growing understanding that libraries have gone from quiet buildings with loud rooms to loud buildings with quiet rooms. Libraries have gone from a place to gather knowledge to a place to create and transmit knowledge. They have long ago gone beyond books—first to other media, but now to ideas, experts, and services with no resource element. Yet librarians all too often have strived to do so quietly or in a way that has avoided potentially rancorous debate between other librarians and the community served.

Yet look at what has happened when librarians were not quiet and passive in their ideals. Look at issues of free speech, access, and member privacy.[28] Here librarians were far from quiet and got into fights. Rather than damaging the community, I would argue that, in these areas, we have earned respect.

I was presenting some of these ideas at a conference some years ago. During the questions, someone asked that if librarians are aggressive in their new mission, wouldn't they be inviting increased scrutiny, particularly by policymakers? My response was simple: If you want the illumination of the spotlight, you must be prepared for the heat.

If we expect support from our communities in the form of taxes, budget lines, or endowments, we must not shy away from negotiat-

28. A few places to start looking include ALA's Office for Intellectual Freedom [http://www.ala.org/ala/aboutala/offices/oif/index.cfm], the *New York Times* [http://www.nytimes.com/2003/09/28/magazine/WLN104134.html], and the WIRED article, "Don't Mess With Librarians Is Just Fun" [http://www.wired.com/politics/security/news/2004/09/64945].

ing the terms on which we are supported. If we allow the funding to continue based on old perceptions of quiet book repositories, we will soon find that funding going away. People will say that they don't need book warehouses and cut us. Then it will be too late for us to show what we have really been up to: knowledge and empowerment.

To establish a new social compact, we must do so loudly, with transparency, and we must actively shape the conversation. We don't market innovation or find our future in surveys. We dream, plan, and execute in an open way.

Evolution of the Social Compact*

It is clear from the preceding discussion that social compacts evolve. They often begin simply and grow more complex over time. Understandings, like standing contracts, are amended and refined. What begins as a simple agreement evolves into standards, policies, and cooperatives. Sometimes the origins of the original intent are lost. In the cases where social compacts become either irrelevant (the ethical code of the scrivener) or so burdened with specificity that they become inflexible, it is time to start fresh.

In effect, the current compact on libraries (as opposed to librarians) has been encased in a growing crust of praxis, policies, standards, cooperatives, curricula, and risk aversion that has frozen the profession when it is so desperately in need of agility. This is a moment, a moment of our choosing and creation, to scour the old compact for original intent, best practices, and effective services and to mix these with opportunities, current realities, and visions of a new ideal future to forge a new social compact. A compact that builds on the work of people like Andrew Carnegie, who said[29]:

> There is not such a cradle of democracy upon the earth as the Free Public Library, this republic of letters, where neither rank, office, nor wealth receives the slightest consideration.

Where 100 years ago Andrew Carnegie built libraries to further democracy, we must now build librarians to further a knowledge-based society.

THREAD CONCLUSION

The greatest asset any library has is a librarian. Librarians go well beyond a collection of skills and tasks. They are on a mission to improve society through facilitating knowledge creation in their communities. Of course a mission statement is just words. It must be grounded in an overarching worldview and deep conceptual foundations. Only through these can the field of librarianship evolve to meet new challenges.

At the heart of the mission are knowledge and innovation (as is explored in other Threads). A librarian must understand that knowledge is not some artifact or item, but rather a uniquely human resource arrived at through active conversation. In other Threads, the mission is further refined, but the themes of innovation and knowledge remain constants.

It is this mission and associated worldview that truly define librarians. It is also our mission and worldview that we must actively bring to our communities to forge a new social compact where libraries are rewarded and held accountable not for the items we maintain but for the real improvements we facilitate.

---

*See Agreement Supplement for a deeper discussion of evolving social compacts.
29. http://www.quotegarden.com/libraries.html.

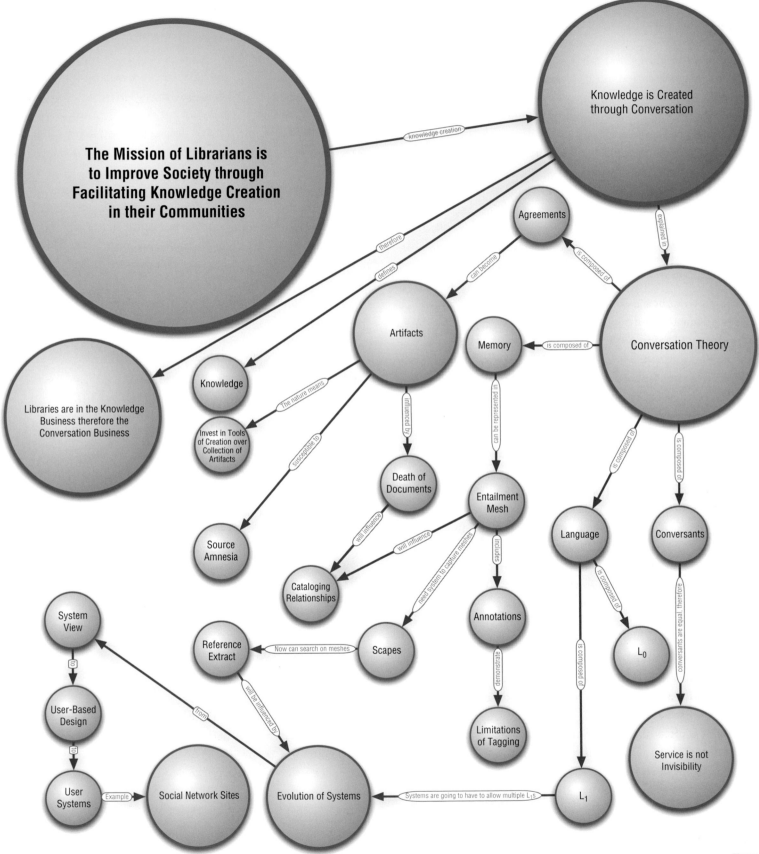

The Mission of Librarians is to Improve Society through Facilitating Knowledge Creation in their Communities

Knowledge is Created through Conversation

knowledge creation

therefore

defines

Libraries are in the Knowledge Business therefore the Conversation Business

Knowledge

The nature means

Invest in Tools of Creation over Collection of Artifacts

susceptible to

Source Amnesia

Agreements

can become

is composed of

Artifacts

Memory

is composed of

Conversation Theory

explained in

influenced by

can be represented in

is composed of

is composed of

Death of Documents

Entailment Mesh

Language

Conversants

will influence

will influence

includes

Cataloging Relationships

Annotations

is composed of

L₀

conversants are equal, therefore

need system to capture meshes

System View

to

User-Based Design

to

Reference Extract

Now can search on meshes

Scapes

demonstrate

is composed of

Service is not Invisibility

User Systems

Example

from

will be influenced by

Social Network Sites

Evolution of Systems

Systems are going to have to allow multiple L₁S

Limitations of Tagging

L₁

Figure 12

30

KNOWLEDGE CREATION

> The time was when a library was very much like a museum, and a librarian was a mouser in musty books.... The time is when a library is a school, and the librarian is the highest sense a teacher.
> —Melvil Dewey

THE MISSION OF LIBRARIANS IS TO IMPROVE SOCIETY THROUGH FACILITATING KNOWLEDGE CREATION IN THEIR COMMUNITIES

With our mission in hand, we can now begin to ground it in theory and deep concepts that will allow it to span any set of technologies or peculiarities of a single setting. So let us start with the most fundamental of questions for a knowledge-based organization: What is knowledge? How can it be created? These are the central questions we must answer to form a new librarianship. But before diving into the details of defining and denoting the underpinnings of knowledge, I must address something that knowledge is not—cold and impersonal.

There is a perception among many that knowledge is somehow a dispassionate accumulation of facts. We see the lofty professor or tireless scientist who slaves away in a laboratory, unaffected by the outside world, seeking knowledge. We have images of quiet and reverent spaces associated with knowledge—a perception that has guided many a library design over the past century.

But knowledge is not cold. Knowledge is heat, passion, and light. To *know* is to seek truth—a noble quest. In his book *The Age of Wonder: How the Romantic Generation Discovered the Beauty and Terror of Science,*[1] Richard Holmes talks of an era in the eighteenth and nineteenth centuries when science became a rich combination of personal quest and romantic ideal. It was an era when the Enlightenment collided with personal achievement to create the myth of the lone genius seeking truth at almost any cost. In some sense, we have lost some of that romanticism.

Today we try to see science as objective and clinical. Knowledge becomes something abstract. Yet science is a passionate quest pursued with dispassionate tools. Any good scientist conducts his or her experiments with a concern for validity, reliability, and the ability to reproduce results. But what led that scientist to the experiment in the first place? It is often obsession or an insatiable curiosity—a need to know. So it is with science, so it is with religion, or governance, and so it should be for librarianship.

We talk of great thinkers, and we use words such as "eureka" or "epiphanies," denoting an almost spiritual revelation of understanding. This is knowledge. Ultimately, it is the belief that forces us to act—it is what we do and why we do it. It is the understanding that forces us to not only see the world, but to see it differently, and to change it for the better.

This Thread delves into the theory of knowledge and the specifics of that theory. As such, it presents knowledge as a seemingly clinical object. There is value in that because, by doing so, librarians can understand not only how to shape their service to meet member needs but also shape the future of our own profession. In this respect, you may think this is the boring and dry Thread. But never forget—just like the formula for gunpowder can look static on the page, its effects are explosive. By grounding libraries in knowledge, we gain an inheritance not of quiet bookishness but of explosive power to shape how people see the world.

KNOWLEDGE IS CREATED THROUGH CONVERSATION

Gordon Pask wanted to teach machines to think. As a cyberneticist, he was centrally interested in making interactive machines and, ultimately, creating artificial intelligence. Mind you, this was in the 1960s, and the quest for interactive machines was much more about hardware than programming at the time.

So Pask was looking for something to model his machines on. He decided to start with how people learn. After all, why not use natural intelligence until artificial intelligence catches up? This began a long, thorough examination of learning behavior. The conclusion he came to can be summed up in a seemingly simple concept: Knowledge is created through conversation.

These conversations might be with a teacher, friend, or, most often, with ourselves. These "back and forths" allow the conversants to try out ideas, come to agreements, and eventually change what we know. The specifics require delving into Conversation Theory.

CONVERSATION THEORY*

Conversation Theory details the iterative process by which we know things. It is worth noting that I use "knowledge" throughout this Atlas as a noun. It is a convention that is hard for me to break. However, Pask only uses the verb "know" or gerund "knowing." He would say

---

1. Holmes, R. (2008). *The age of wonder: How the romantic generation discovered the beauty and terror of science.* New York: Pantheon Books.

*See Agreement Supplement for an overview of Conversation Theory and more links to the literature.

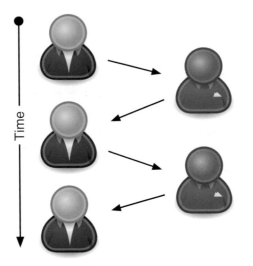

Figure 13

that how we know something is determined in conversation. Knowing is dynamic and changing. Although I use "knowledge," the same must be understood—knowledge is what we do and why we do it, not something that can be boxed up, transferred, or archived. It is also in constant flux as we encounter new situations and new interactions.

So how do we come to know things? What is dynamic? Knowledge is a set of agreements in relation to one another through a memory that is derived from language exchange between conversants. See—perfectly clear.

OK, a bit dense and in need of unpacking. Let's look at knowledge as a process. Two people (or organizations, societies, or even parts of oneself) engage in a back-and-forth dialog over time. It might look like figure 13.

What they are exchanging is language. It may be spoken language or nonverbal. With each interaction, both parties are trying to come to an agreement about something (the time of day, the weather, the politics). Also, there is persistence to this conversation over time—that is, the conversants remember what they just said. Piece of cake, right? It seems practically intuitive. Except, of course, in its application. What do I mean that someone can converse with themselves? How does this lead to anything like knowledge and not just idle chit-chat? What if the agreement they come up with is just plain wrong? For this, let's dive into the elements of Conversation Theory at much greater depth: conversants, language, agreements, and memory.

In scholarly language, "conversants" are cognizing agents that seek agreement. A cognizing agent is something that can be interactive: take input and create a reasoned response. Why not just say a person? Well, that's where things get a bit complicated. Certainly, people can be agents, but so can groups. Take, for example, a library negotiating with a vendor for a software product. The organizations (library and vendor) are acting as conversants. The reasoned response may well come from an aggregation of a number of people, but at this level of analysis the organizations are the conversants. The agreement they seek may be a price, specifications, or some other contractual stipulation. We can keep this aggregating up and have consortia converse, states, or nations. In the humanities, whole cultures and societies can converse.

If we are comfortable aggregating up, then we can also divide down. For example, if you just read that last statement and asked, "What does he mean by that?" I ask you: Who were you talking to? The idea of an internal dialog is nothing new. Instructional librarians are familiar with concepts such as critical thinking or meta-cognition. In the arts, there is the concept of "apperception"—the act of perceiving oneself perceiving (as in "I cannot believe how choked up I'm getting at the ending of this book").

We have many of these internal dialogs. In fact, much of librarianship is based on a particular kind of internal dialog: reading. When you are reading this, another book, or a web page, you are learning (hopefully[2]). Conversation Theory then says you must be engaged in a conversation. Many of us like to think we are in a dialog with the author. Pardon the bluntness of this statement, but it is important—that is wrong. While you are reading this, I am not sitting alone somewhere on the other end of a conversation. When you wonder just what Hamlet's beef is, Bill Shakespeare is not thinking about your question. He is dead. Sorry.

So if reading is not a conversation with the author, then whom? Yourself. You are constantly engaged in an attempt to relate what you are reading to what you already know. This is a conversation with yourself. As the author, I am doing my best to guide your internal conversation, but ultimately it is up to you and… well, you, to figure

---

2. I won't spend too much time on this, but reading a book for pleasure is still a learning experience. You can learn about the art of writing, foreign places, or new ideas. You learn what you like and what you don't. A good piece of fiction can teach us a lot about ourselves.

it out. That's why two different people reading this can come to different conclusions: Lankes is crazy or Lankes got it right. This would be a good time to mention postmodernism. There, I mentioned it.

The bottom line is that conversants can be within us or external to us. It is a scalable concept. It can be scaled up to organizations and communities (such as having a conversation with your community about a new social compact) or scaled down to aspects of ourselves.

Service Is Not Invisibility

Before we jump to other aspects of Conversation Theory, it is worth a quick pause here to talk about one important implication of conversants. It takes at least two conversants to make a conversation. Each conversant plays a part and has a voice that guides the conversation. This means that in, say, a reference interview, the librarian is not invisible or somehow neutral. He or she plays an active role in that conversation. The library, in a debate about how a community defines good and bad information, needs to be part of that conversation to have a voice.

Put simply: to be of service in building knowledge means to be part of a conversation. To be part of a conversation means to have a voice and be active in shaping that conversation. To be active is not to be invisible. This concept will be discussed in more depth in the "Service Is Not Invisibility" agreement and in the "Improve Society" Thread. For now, let us continue our discussion of Conversation Theory's components.

*Language**

Language is a truly incredible thing. In written form, it only takes 26 characters to express all the ideas, emotions, history, and dreams of the English-speaking world. With our voices, we can conjure, inspire, lament, confound, and confront. But language goes beyond syntax and vocabulary. With our bodies, even with our fingers, we can express joy, hatred, and longing.

There are entire fields of study and the arts devoted to language. From linguistics and natural language processing, to poetry and rhetoric, brilliant minds are dedicated to exploring the symbols and signs we use to convey meaning. The following examination of language does not attempt to take in all its complexities. Rather, it presents an operational view targeted to language and learning. As Karl Popper said, "Science may be described as the art of systematic oversimplification."[3] Let the oversimplification begin.

Conversation Theory lays out two distinct levels of language used in learning: L_0 and L_1. Pask uses these two levels to classify language used to negotiate a conversation (L_0) and those that actually further a conversation (L_1). For the Atlas, I expand these different levels of language usage to represent different levels of understanding of a domain under investigation. Understanding these different levels is also key to understanding both the successes and failures of library systems. It also points a direction to where library systems (digital and nondigital) need to go. Last, using these two levels of language, we can begin to understand the power of social networking sites on the web.

And you thought language was going to be boring.

L_0

Think back to the worst computer training you have ever received. My guess is it went something like this: "Click here, now click here, now click here." If you ever asked why you were clicking or what you were clicking, you were most likely ignored. Yet this sort of directional and function-based training is a fantastic representation of L_0 in action. You also have to admit that there have been times when all you wanted was to know what button to click, and you really didn't care why.

L_0 language is used by conversants with low preexisting knowledge of a domain. They are almost always directional: How do I do this? Where do I go? What is the next step? You may already be picking up the parallels between L_0 and functional understandings of things like librarianship. When you are new to a domain, it is simply easier to find your way around than to try and figure out the underlying reasons for the course; worse yet, you find there is no underlying reason.

As you learn more and more about a domain, you move up to L_1 language use. However, there are plenty of places where we retain L_0 and it satisfies our needs. What's amazing is the proliferation of interfaces that work quite well in the L_0 level. Figure 14 is one of the most widely used and successful.

Think about it: What do you put in that box? A few words and hit return. How many users of Google have any idea what happens after they hit return? Yet for most users, it works just fine. That's because Google assumes an L_0 interaction and uses algorithms and assumptions to guess at the details that will satisfy the user's query. These are

See Agreement Supplement for a further discussion of language and L_0 and L_1.

3. Brooks, M. (2008). *13 things that don't make sense: The most baffling scientific mysteries of our time*. New York: Doubleday.

simple assumptions, such as "the most-referenced web pages have the greatest chance of meeting a user's need." However, we have all been in situations where these assumptions are wrong.

Take, for example, a search on the term "apple." The first couple hundred pages are results for Apple, Inc. and their computers and iPods. Not a fruit in sight. The assumption is that, with no further information given, you would want the information that is most prevalent on the web. There are more geeks than gardeners on the web, apparently. By the way, if you are looking for apples to eat, use "apples" or "apple fruit."

Now, keeping this in mind, think about the current trend of libraries to replace multiple complicated library-resource interfaces with a simple "Google-like" search box. Now ask yourself an L_0 question. If a member types in a simple directional query, what are you going to use—what assumptions are you going to make—to fill in the member's query and get him or her to the right information? Popularity? Importance? There are many reasons that a single search box is problematic for existing library resources (see the agreements on "Cataloging Relationships" and "Evolution of Integrated Library Systems"), but our ability to respond to L_0 language by being able to infer what the member really means is a big one.

L_1

Now take a look at the Google interface again. If you've been a librarian long enough, it actually might seem vaguely familiar. It is really just the web equivalent of a command line interface, like the old version of Dialog. If you know the underlying query language, then instead of typing in "apples" you could type in "+apples + 'new york' state fruit 'gala' -computers" and gotten only results about the Gala variety of apples in New York State (the best-tasting apples in my humble opinion).

What is going on here? The interface doesn't force an L_0 conversation; it simply accommodates it. As you gain greater understanding of the interaction you are having, your language changes. You can begin to have a much deeper and richer dialog that occurs with specialized vocabulary and syntax.

Part of what defines a profession is the use of specialized vocabulary. To us, "MLS" means Masters of Library Science instead of Major League Soccer. Librarians understand that a catalog is for looking up holdings, not shopping for sweaters. None of us is born speaking Boolean or Dewey. We learn it. When we started learning, we were

using directional L_0 language (What is a 400? What is an "and" vs. an "or"?). As we gained basic concepts, we could leave the "hows" and "whats" and move to the "whens" and "whys." Like, why did Dewey put "cookery" under business and industry?

This separation of the levels of language also explains one of those recurrent research results that drives librarians crazy: evaluation of catalog interface effectiveness. When you look at how well people do when they are looking something up in catalogs, members come out doing very poorly, and librarians come out doing very well.

However, when you look at this in terms of L_0 and L_1, it makes sense. Like Google, our catalogs allow for both levels of language, but unlike Google, they only really work with L_1. Librarians are loath to give up catalogs, not because of tradition or resistance to change (OK, a bit of that), but because they find them so useful. Here we run into a recurrent theme of the Atlas—that success can actually stifle innovation like our earlier example with encyclopedias.

I just gave a bunch of technological examples of language use, but there are plenty of times we encounter this in nondigital settings. The reference interview often begins with a negotiation of language. Each party in the negotiation is attempting to identify whether this will be an L_0 exchange because at least one of the conversants does not have strong domain knowledge, or L_1, because the conversants involved do have high preexisting knowledge. Note that in this negotiation, it is often the librarian who forces the conversation down to L_0 in terms of the topic (because the member knows more about the topic) and the member who forces down to L_0 in terms of process (because the librarian knows more about searching).

Figure 14

One of the core aspects of librarianship over the past 100 years has been the use of specialized, or L_1, language. Classifications, taxonomies, specialized subject thesauri, and even authority files (where we turn names, people, and places into specialized language) are prime examples of the L_1 versus L_0 split. There is also no question about the effectiveness of specialized language—when it is used by those who have an L_1 understanding of the specialized terms.

So what to do about mismatches? Well, you really only have three options: build systems that assume L_0 and serve the least common denominator, bring the members up to L_1, or radically rethink how we build systems. The first option is tough because it may work well for the generalists, but it will then underserve all of the experts (including librarians). The second option of trying to bring members up to L_1 is actually the dominant approach in libraries today—how many classes do we offer in searching for information? Much of the current focus on instructional librarians and information literacy is all about bringing members up to speed with the L_1 language they find in library systems.

There is actually a good model of bringing the user from L_0 to L_1, and that is videogames. Time was that games of any complexity came with a pretty hefty manual. The manual would include basic game controls (press the "A" button to shoot or "B" to jump), plus, for narrative games, the back-story ("You are a soldier in Earth's last battalion…"). You don't find too many of those manuals these days. Increasingly, games have integrated the manual into the game itself.

Take, for example, Halo.[4] The game opens with an Earth ship being pursued and attacked by the Covenant, a vague coalition of hostile enemy forces. The introductory movie (a cut scene) ends with the captain's order to wake up the Master Chief (the character you play). The next thing you know, you are waking up first person in a "cryotube." The technicians then check and calibrate your battle suit's systems. How do they do this? By asking you to perform basic actions ("OK, chief, let's make sure your targeting sensors work—look up!") and explaining any new systems you have installed. It is part of the flow of the game, but it is a tutorial. It also introduces the specialized vocabulary of the game.

However, while we are getting smarter about using gaming concepts in training folks in specialized languages, there are some real limitations. The gaming approach assumes the person being trained is highly motivated; it also assumes the person learning has sufficient time to learn. It also assumes there is only one L_1 that is relevant. In essence, it ignores the fact that a person may well already have an L_1 understanding of a useful domain.

For these reasons, in general systems like library systems, I advocate for the last option—a radical new approach. It is an approach currently evolving on the web and in libraries around the world. In this approach, where you do not choose between L_0 or L_1, you recognize that there is a whole host of L_1 systems of language that can all co-exist. It is the language use modeled in Flickr and Facebook. However, the implications go well beyond sharing photos and updating friends. It is nothing less than the evolution of system design. So bear with me as we take a slight but significant detour from my explanation of Conversation Theory to the evolution of systems.

And you thought language was going to be boring!

Evolution of Systems*

Normally when folks are talking about systems, they are talking about software or hardware systems. In essence, they are talking about technology. Yet systems are really just organized processes and resources with a goal. They might be software to read web pages or find documents or libraries with buildings to serve a public. It is, to say the least, a broad concept.

That is not, however, to say that systems are a nebulous concept. There have been some smart folks who have spent a lot of time thinking about systems, how they work, and how to make them efficient. For example, a gentleman named Karl Ludwig von Bertalanffy, a Viennese professor of biology, developed something called General Systems Theory[5] that he and others felt could describe any system—from an ecosystem to a computer program. His work was so influential that you've probably run into it at some point. If you've ever spent any time thinking about inputs, processes, or outputs, thank Bertalanffy (posthumously). It is in fact indirectly thanks to Bertalanffy that Gordon Pask developed Conversation Theory.

Pask was a cyberneticist. The whole cybernetics movement[6] was founded on the belief that General Systems Theory missed something. There needed to be a loop from the output of a system to its input, a feedback loop. This loop allowed a system to be interactive and self-correcting.

4. http://en.wikipedia.org/wiki/Halo_(series)
*See Agreement Supplement for citations and links to additional information on systems and General Systems Theory.
5. Bertalanffy, L. V. (1969). *General system theory; Foundations, development, applications.* New York: G. Braziller.
6. Here are a few starting points or learning more about cybernetics: IEEE's Systems, Man, and Cybernetics Society (http://www.ieeesmc.org/) and Derek J. Smith's Basic of Cybernetics (http://www.smithsrisca.demon.co.uk/cybernetics.html).

However, when these concepts were applied to building information-retrieval systems, what was considered part of the system and what was input to the system became conceptualized in a specific way. That way is best characterized by how you answer the following question: Is the member part of your library system?

Ever wonder why only drug dealers and computer scientists talk of users? Because early models of information systems put the person asking questions outside the bounds of the system. The modern equivalent is the use of the term "customer" or "client." It is a model in which one sets up a system that is used by an actor outside of the system. "Patron" and "member," in contrast, imply that the beneficiaries of library services are part of the service and help to shape it. Remember that the word "patron" comes from "patronage"—to give support. This will loop back to the use of language soon in how the system deals with different language levels (after all, if you are part of a system, the system had better be able to handle your language).

This division between whether one is a user or a member represents an evolution of thinking in information systems. The beginning point of that evolution is the system view.

SYSTEM VIEW

Read the early information-retrieval literature from the 1970s, and even into the 1980s, and you will run across a comparatively simple view of the world (see figure 15). There is a user, an interface, a collection of documents, and an algorithm, as well as a process to sort through the documents. The system under examination—the part that was under the control of the developer—did not include the user.[7]

This is a digital system, but many folks did and still do see a library this way, as in figure 16. In this model, the user is a consumer of the service and exists outside of it. He or she does not directly affect the workings of the system.

This paradigm, known as the "system view," predominated early information-retrieval approaches. It was remarkably effective as well. Concepts that emerged from this model focus almost exclusively on algorithms and document analysis and include probabilistic retrieval and vector-based retrieval.[8] They also strongly influenced cataloging efforts.

It also goes a long way toward explaining why librarians can rock the catalog while members (or users, in this view) flounder. Librarians, you see, are in the box—part of the system. The user? Outside.

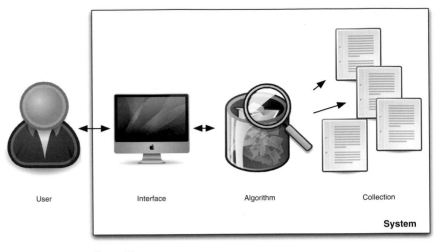

User   Interface   Algorithm   Collection

System

Figure 15

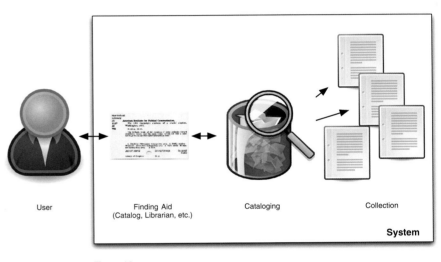

User   Finding Aid (Catalog, Librarian, etc.)   Cataloging   Collection

System

Figure 16

7. I am using "user" and not "member" to emphasize how the concept of systems evolve.
8. Manning, C. D., Raghavan, P., & Schutze, H. (2008). *Introduction to information retrieval*. New York: Cambridge University Press.

Librarians have an L_1 understanding of how the collection is organized and how the algorithms work. In fact, much of that algorithm and organization is based on the librarian.

Think for a moment of the books around you. They may be in your office or in your home. Can you find the one you need? Probably without too much trouble. How are they organized? If they are by Dewey, you must know you are the exception. Mine are by pile, sometimes by room (fiction in the bedroom—tech books in the den). Now, invite me into your home or office and see how well I do in finding a book. You are part of the system, I am not.

It is at this point that our recurrent theme—that success can actually stifle innovation—pops up again. You see, those damned users kept getting in the way. It was one thing when computer time was expensive and so every user had to be highly trained to use the system. It was quite another when systems starting showing up on people's desktops. As the type of users of systems became more diverse and less specially trained, they failed more often. More than that, as users became more self-sufficient and had a wider array of systems to choose from, system designers were finally forced to confront the user head on. They could no longer simply design systems from the standpoint of experts and documents; they had to design the system for the user.

USER-BASED DESIGN*

Robert Taylor was a great man. In 1968, he wrote my favorite article ever on Question Negotiation.[9] Here he really nailed the fact that a person had a hard time formulating questions. After all, how do you explain something you don't know? However, many librarians familiar with Taylor's work in reference may not know of his work in information systems. He came up with something called the Value-Added Model of Information Systems.[10]

The heart of this model is simple—if a system does not make a user's life better, no matter how good the algorithm or collection of information, it is useless (I am overstating this a bit—but just a bit). He laid out a whole array of factors that a system had to account for, such as saving a user time or making it easier for the user to sort through the results of a search. This might seem like "no duh" stuff, but there are still catalog systems that rank their results by the order in which the MARC records were entered.

The point of all this? Not only did the user matter, but if you didn't design the whole system from the user's perspective, you were lost. This work was later refined and augmented into a whole host of research methods and theories, like Sense-making, that I talked about in the "Mission" Thread.

The basic premise of user-based design is simple. You first seek to understand the problem the user is trying to solve (write a paper, surf the web, cure cancer). You then build a system that meets those needs. Usability, Human Computer Interaction, Web Design, and Information Architecture are all examples of putting the user front and center in the design process.

I am proud to say that the School of Information Studies at Syracuse University, where I completed my doctorate, was a strong player in establishing and espousing the user-based perspective. No doctoral student was able to escape the snowy North until he or she could recite the value-added model from memory. You can imagine, then, just how well Andrew Dillon, the dean of the iSchool at the University of Texas, was received a few years ago when he got up before the faculty and announced that the user-based approach was meaningless. You can also imagine just how shocked I was to find myself agreeing with him.

Dillon's point was not that users don't matter or even that when designing systems we shouldn't start with the user; it was just that the practice of designing systems had twisted the concept.

Think of it this way. Let's say you work for a library and have been given the task of redesigning the library's website. Now, you have some opinions on what would make a better site. In fact, you have some pretty strong opinions about how the website should be designed. Still, you have been told that user-based design is the way to go, so you start talking to users. Which ones? Ah, there's the rub. If you ask enough users, you are sure to find some folks who agree with your ideas. In fact, there is a good chance that, even with the best of intentions, you will pick out users and user comments that just happen to agree with you. Worse still, even if you are conscientious, there is a good chance you'll discover something profoundly disturbing: Users have no idea what they want.

Study after study shows that users are great at telling you what they like and what exists, but they are lousy at telling you what they need. Ask a bunch of users about your current site, and they are filled with opinions. Ask them what they want in its place, and you'll hear

*See Agreement Supplement for links to more on user-based design.
9. Taylor, R. (1968). Question negotiation and information seeking in libraries. *College & Research Libraries, 29*, 178–194.
10. Taylor, R. (1986). *The value-added process in information systems*. Norwood, NJ: Ablex.

a lot of references to existing sites (many having nothing to do with libraries).

The last rub is where we loop back to language (and you thought I forgot). When you design a general-purpose system that serves a diverse user population (such as a library, database, catalog, or operating system), you find out that it is not as simple as some folks using L_1 because they are expert users and others using L_0 because they are novices. What you find out is that every user uses L_1, but not all users use the same L_1s.

Take, for example, the writer and the artist. Both have a robust and rich concept of the creator of a work. Both understand that works have histories, authenticity, and influences. Yet for the artist, the creator of a work is, well, an artist. For the writer, it is a writer. Artists talk of periods (like Picasso's Blue Period), while writers talk about a writer's influence. Add to this the museum curator who talks of provenance, and you begin to see the problem. It is not that one group of users is simple and one is complex, one expert and one amateur. All of these groups are using high-level language, just not the same one.

The user-based paradigm traded one problem for another. Where the system view forced only one L_1, defined by who was within the bounds of the system, and who was outside, the user-based folks brought in the Tower of Babel for systems that spanned user groups. Systems that spanned user groups had to suddenly deal with multiple L_1 groups.

So where are we to go from here? Well, that's where the whole "radically rethink how we build systems" option comes back into play. Mind you, a good librarian is familiar with all of these approaches because there are still plenty of places where the systems approach and the user approach still work (in environments of trained system operators and where the user population is relatively homogenous). What we want to now explore is the next step in the chain of centering the user in the system—to truly transform from users to members. I call this next stage User Systems.

USER SYSTEMS

I ask you to recall the graphs showing the relative market shares of Wikipedia versus Encarta and MySpace versus GeoCities from the "Mission" Thread. At that point, I said, "In retrospect, we can say the fact that users could add their own content made the big difference, and that a '2.0' approach was the obvious winner." But what is the "2.0 approach?" I would argue that it is not about blogs and wikis or tagging or mashups. In fact, I would argue that it is not even about 2.0. The thing that made these systems win over time is something that will be with us in Web 2.0, 3.0, 4.0, and so on. That concept is about where the user, or now member, fits in the system and, consequently, how that system handles the member's language.

A lot of this member inclusion into systems is covered in the "Communities" Thread, so for now I limit my focus to the use of language in "User Systems." This is a term I coin to talk about an emerging approach to not building systems with a user focus, but for members building the systems themselves. We might just as easily call them participatory systems, conversational systems, or member systems. I use "User Systems" to show continuity with previous approaches.

In a systems approach, the language in use was that of a select L_1 community. In essence, the system was optimized around a language familiar (or learned) by experts. However, novice users, or users with expertise represented by a different L_1, were out of luck. In user-based design, the system was optimized around a generic user (or, more often than not, an expert selected user group). This was better for the selected user population but equally frustrating to members outside of the selected user groups. If you want to see this in action, take a casual Mac user and put him or her in front of Windows or vice a versa. Concepts such as the "Dock" and the "Start Menu" are far from universal human constants.

However, instead of basing the system on any one user group, User Systems provide a lot of limited functions that can be easily combined by members with little existing structure. Members essentially build the system around themselves, combining little applets of functionality (posting text, adding tags to photos, giving someone's blog posts a thumbs up) together to form a grander whole. The end result is a system that is tuned toward that member's understandings and using the member's language. Of course each little applet requires learning or expanding some language, but the additional language acquisition is minimal and at the member's discretion.

I want to emphasize that this approach is of limited utility, where a member community has a relatively homogenous L_1 or where an application requires great complexity by its very nature. (Mathematica, a highly complex mathematical modeling program, is easy to use to do complex mathematics; unfortunately, you have to understand complex mathematics to begin with.) However, for librarians who work across members or in a general setting, the User Systems approach is preferred.

Think for a moment about the library catalog. Is it more like Mathematica or the iPhone? The answer is currently that it acts more like Mathematica with its use of controlled vocabularies, MARC displays, and fielded searching. But members need something much more like the iPhone, and I don't just mean something trendy and pretty.

Think about the iPhone. It is a complex piece of technology. In its glass and metal, it holds a Unix-based operating system, three different radios (GPS, WiFi, and 3G), a multitouch capacitive display, and more. To write an application for the iPhone requires knowledge of Objective C, a compiled programming language. Yet it is built for the generalist audience. It is in many ways easier to use than basic phones with a numeric keypad and camera. Why? Well, one cannot discount good design, but it also comes down to the App store. The App store built into the phone allows individuals to make the iPhone uniquely theirs. They want their iPhone to play games? They add an app. They want it to do accounting? Add an app.

Adding apps may seem like a standard consumer behavior, but they are building an information and telecommunications system around themselves. This model has been so successful in such a short time that all other phone makers and carriers are scurrying to catch up (plus eBook producers and printer companies).

Think about the library catalog now. The member wants to search for books? Add an app. Search databases too? Add an app. Map the books they find to a Google Map? Add an app. Keep track of articles, websites, and their own documents not on the library system? Add an app. Next-generation catalogers have it wrong. We don't add next-generation functionality to the catalog; we let the members do it. We may create the apps, but the member needs to add them. ILS vendors need to evolve to the same model, where they become more about marketplaces of apps than creators and bundlers of them. Of course, I think we should scrap the catalog completely and start again, but we'll get there later. For now, let's take a look at how User Systems are already finding their way into the work of librarians.

*Social Network Sites**

It has been interesting to watch the quick adoption of social networking sites in the library domain. I believe it has more to do with the often-unconscious recognition of User Systems than an attempt to be trendy. After all, there are plenty of other technology trends that have not found such fertile ground in libraries, including Geographic Information Systems (GIS) and the Green movement (I didn't say no ground, but certainly, not adoption at the scale and pace of social networking).

Sites like Flickr do little more than allow a person to upload images to the web. However, members can add tags if they want, or geolocation information, and they can build much more functional systems around their uploaded photos. Facebook is just a wall and friends, and yet one can add quizzes, videos, web links, and profile information and truly create one's own space on the web in a comfortable language. Both Flickr and Facebook then allow you to create peer communities that often have a corresponding L_1. Even sites like Amazon, through their lists functions, allow communities and members to create paths through resources in their own terms and discourse.

The theme of participation and the lessons librarians can learn from (and ultimately teach back to) social networking come up often in the Atlas. The role that language plays in such systems is only part of the picture—these sites ultimately allow for the member to create a learning space on the web. However, language is a vital part. You see, language is not just a simple act of applying a label to a thing or concept. Instead, language shapes and is shaped by deep cognitive processes that ultimately shape the world around us.

The old line that Eskimos have 52 names for snow does not mean they had more time to assign terms to snow, it means they saw snow differently than someone who lives in the tropics. Librarians must build systems that understand that language is not labels but rather individuality and understanding. Renaming the catalog will not work—one must change how librarians use and understand language. This ultimately means changing the tools of librarianship.

AGREEMENTS*

Let us return to Conversation Theory with a simple question: Why do conversants bother to exchange language of any sort back and forth? Pask's answer is to reach an agreement. These conversants might seek an agreement on the time of day, the solution to a nuclear crisis, the solution to a reference question, or even within an individual that a sound came from an object he or she saw fall to the floor.

*See Agreement Supplement for more on social networking.
*See Agreement Supplement for some additional example of agreements.

Agreements, and their relationships to one another, form the basis of what we know. How we prejudge a situation comes from our past experience. That experience is composed of agreements (It is January in Syracuse, it will probably be cold). But they are not simply static, flat facts; they are also agreements on processes of change (Let me check the temperature on my thermometer to see whether it is cold outside anyway).

It would be tempting to call agreements facts. We agree that two added to two is four, or we agree that my name is David. But the word "fact" is limiting, and it brings with it a huge set of baggage. Our politics come from our agreements, and our religious beliefs are encoded as a set of agreements we call faith. Anything we learn, including what things we consider good and bad, are agreements.

Agreements and their relationships are also flexible—they can be added to, taken away, or changed from individual experience (conversations with ourselves) or conversations with others. The way you see librarianship is a set of agreements you came to throughout your life. Your interaction with your school librarian, your experience as an undergraduate, your professional education, and the colleagues with whom you interact as part of your professional life have shaped your worldview by bringing you to a set of agreements about the profession ("There is a future for librarianship," "We are doomed," "The folks in public service don't get it," etc.).

What I attempt to do now is bring about an internal conversation (your reading this) and hopefully many external conversations (with your colleagues and community) to create a new set of agreements about the profession. To do that, I may use facts (empirical evidence) that show the rise of social networking sites. I may use logical argument (theoretical evidence), such as walking you through Conversation Theory. I may use my background and reputation (experiential evidence), such as talking about the libraries I have worked with. Failing these, I may use more crude persuasive techniques to inspire you to my way of thinking. All of these approaches include language I use to bring about agreements. In person or in an interactive environment, I might use these in a conversation between you and me. In writing, I can only be an artifact that you use to come to your own conclusions.

It should be noted that one of the most important types of agreements is an agreement not to agree. As you read this Atlas, there are no doubt things I write that make sense to you and reinforce an existing agreement. There are things I write that may create new agreements—things you had not thought about before but now you agree with.

There are also no doubt things I write about that you reject. If this were an interactive discussion, we would simply have to say, "Well, I guess we aren't going to solve that problem, so we will simply agree not to agree and move on." If the point is central to a conversation, that might end it. If not, you may simply proceed on to another topic.

Here is where I am forced to bring up the weird concept that if you find yourself disagreeing with a point I write about, you are in a twisted way disagreeing with yourself. You are disagreeing with that part of you that took an affirmative position on a statement that is read. You may not put up too much of a fight with yourself, or you may find yourself "churning" on an issue over a few days. While you and I may personally disagree on something, you can't tell that (come to that agreement) from just reading this.

OK, let me prove it to you with an example. Let's say I wrote the following line:

Librarians must not listen only to their communities.

The point of this sentence is that librarians, as equal conversants within a community, are allowed to disagree and push the community.

However, let's say the editor changed the wording by mistake (not my editor, of course, he or she is perfect in every respect) to:

Librarians must not listen to their communities.

OK, so along you come as the reader and don't (hopefully) agree with the second sentence. I wouldn't either. We would both disagree with the voice within ourselves that is reading those words.

Now, let me say that this can be taken to a ridiculous extreme. I am NOT forgiving authors who write purposefully hateful, malicious, or incorrect things. There is a responsibility that I have as an author. However, my role is ultimately one of facilitating, not dictating, a conversation. Just as we cannot excuse the author who spreads hate, we cannot condemn the author whose words are deliberately misused. After all, God would have a lot to answer for if he were ultimately to blame for idiots with holy texts in one hand and hate in their hearts (feel free to substitute Darwin or Marx for God).

My obvious point here is that agreements can be encoded into artifacts, but that artifacts do not contain the agreement—or, more broadly, knowledge.

Artifacts *

OK, I've alluded to it a few times already, but let me get this off my chest. I hate the phrase "recorded knowledge." I loathe it. To me the phrase "recorded knowledge" makes as much sense as the phrase "intelligent rock." Why? Well, let me show you…with a rock (see figure 17).

OK, not just any rock, but a rock outside of Taliesin West, Frank Lloyd Wright's camp in Arizona. Now I look at it and I see a rock, but a geologist might see a particular kind of rock. He or she could determine the type of rock, how it was formed, where it came from, and even how old it is. An archeologist might note the ideograms scratched into the surface and understand the significance of this rock to a Native American culture.

My point is that the knowledge of composition, type, age, or cultural significance is not in the rock. It is brought to the rock from the geologist or archeologist. In fact, when I see this rock, I think about my trip to Scottsdale with my wife.

Well, what's true for the rock is true for books. There is no such thing as "recorded knowledge" because knowledge is resident in humans not in inanimate objects. It is dynamic—it can't be static (recording something is making it static and inflexible).

This is why I use the term "artifact." Artifacts like books, CDs, web pages, DVDs, and so on are not knowledge but rather things that result from a knowledge activity (at least that's how I use the term in the Atlas). For example, this Atlas is an artifact. The conversations that went into the writing of this manuscript, the conversations that come as a result, your agreements and knowledge, all of these things are ethereal. They exist in your head. Until we get to the day when we can map memories and thoughts and transfer them directly from neu-

ral pathway to neural pathway, we are stuck with iterations in conversation and representing knowledge as a pale ember called an artifact.

Bob Taylor said this much more elegantly in 1968 when he first discussed Question Negotiation[11] in the reference process. He talked about representations of an information need. He said people have four levels of forming their questions. The first is the "visceral need," where a member knows he or she has a question but can't really express it. Then there is the "conscious need," the "within-brain description of the need." The first time a librarian may hear a person's need, it is a "formalized need" (the best way a member can express his or her need or question). Finally, there is the "compromised need," which can actually be acted on by a system. The point is that, by the time anything ends up expressed or recorded, it has been encoded, translated, and ultimately compromised. Taylor used this notion to stress the need for an interview. I use it to make the clear demarcation between knowledge, or what's in a person's head, and artifact, what can be represented.

It may seem like a pretty commonsense notion to some, but it clearly is not universal. For example, I feel it important now to state that I am not anti-book or anti-artifact. They are amazingly useful tools and are indeed amazingly effective in helping transfer knowledge. However, to be precise, I should say books and artifacts are amazingly effective at the re-creation of knowledge from conversant to conversant. Remember, there was a time when most knowledge was transferred in actual face-to-face conversations in a strong oral tradition.

So why bring up artifacts in relation to agreements? Because often, but not always—in fact, most likely in the minority of cases—agreements have some relation to an artifact and/or a conversant that was instrumental in the development of an agreement. For example, when I talk about artifacts, I cite Taylor's work, where I really started to think about the difference between what is in our head and what we share. For this agreement, I have an artifact I relate to it. Note, the relation is mine, and, as is standard practice in academia, I make it explicit through citation. I don't, however, imply through the citation that Bob Taylor would see the connection.

Figure 17

*See Agreement Supplement for an annotated bibliography on the concept of artifacts and recorded knowledge.
11. Taylor, R. (1968). Question negotiation and information seeking in libraries. *College & Research Libraries, 29,* 178–194.

I say academia because there have been a lot of studies that show that the whole idea of citing sources and making explicit links between agreements and artifacts is not really a natural process—as we see in our next agreement.

Source Amnesia*

Here is how *not* to stop a rumor: tell people that the rumor is not true. I know it sounds counterintuitive, but brains have a hard time keeping track of pesky little details, such as the word "not."[12] According to Sam Wang and Sandra Aamodt, the brain re-creates and then re-stores the information we recall. In the process, it often loses track of the context from which it came. It also tends to remember things it writes down often. So even though you are refuting something, you are also often repeating the falsehood, thus strengthening your recall of it.

What's more, your brain quickly loses track of where you got a given idea. So you may well know that clouds are made of water vapor, but can you tell me where you learned that? Probably not (unless the situation was particularly memorable).

Here I have an embarrassing admission to make. It happens to me. I was giving a presentation in which I gave an example of how knowledge can be connected in things such as history. I said look at how James Burke associates the North winning the U.S. Civil War with the advent of the modern computer. I then filled in how the North was supposed to lose the Civil War because they had fewer troops, and common military wisdom was that more troops equals victory. The North changed the equation because they had greater manufacturing and could bring more artillery to bear. This logic continued up until World War II. The problem was that, to shoot artillery, you need to do some heavy calculations that couldn't be done in the field, so human mathematicians called computers made firing tables up. In World War II, they couldn't keep up, so the computer was invented and so on.

It was a good presentation. I got very excited. I was happy. I then got an email from an audience member who said it was great except all my stuff on the Civil War was dead wrong. The North had plenty of soldiers, and the South had plenty of cannons. I decided to review my source, James Burke's *The Day the Universe Changed* (an awesome book), and it wasn't there. I looked over his other books—nope. I

even watched the original TV series he produced (even better than the book)—no Civil War. I put up a rather timid statement on my blog and begged forgiveness. I still shiver.

Not only had I gotten the facts wrong, I had misattributed them to James Burke's book. It made sense to me. I was 100% sure it was there. It wasn't. I now triple check all my references.

The point of this little digression and confession is not to talk about how your memory works (that's coming) but to emphasize the secondary role that artifacts play in what we know—not unimportant, just secondary. I acted (spoke) based on a set of agreements I attributed to an artifact, not what was in the artifact. Also, artifacts are only one class of tools that librarians can use in their mission of knowledge creation. In fact, increasingly, librarians have become overreliant on a set of artifacts referred to as "Document Like Objects."

Invest in Tools of Creation over Collection of Artifacts

An interesting thing happened on the way to the video store…it went away. Time was that getting a video you could watch at home, at a time of your choosing, was difficult. Enter the video player, Beta and VHS, later just VHS, later DVD. Now a machine allowed you to watch what you wanted, when you wanted. But it was expensive to buy all of that media, not to mention that there were few things you could be certain you would want for the long haul. So the solution? Create an agent, in this case a commercial agent, that would centralize the buying and storing of videos and rent them out on demand with a usage fee. Pay for only what you wanted for the time you used it. This became the local video store on the corner; that became Blockbuster.

Then a couple of things happened. The first and most obvious was the development and wide-scale deployment of the DVD format. DVDs were not only smaller but cheaper to produce and more durable. Suddenly it was not only easier to view movies, it was much cheaper to produce video content for distribution. Can you imagine a 50-box set of the Brady Bunch on Betamax? But now, for pennies a disk and an entire season on one small disk—why not?

Enter the Internet phase 1 (I explain that in a second) and a little company called Netflix. Netflix not only was more willing to warehouse a much larger selection of DVDs, but it figured out that with a DVD's light weight and durability, it became practical to ship them right to your door. Blockbuster tried to keep up, but it is on the ropes as more and more folks realize that all the benefits of watching the video you want when you want it can be had at home.

---

*See Agreement Supplement for much more on source amnesia.

12. http://www.nytimes.com/2008/06/29/opinion/29iht-edwang.1.14069662.html

Now you might think there is an obvious next chapter here about DVDs going away in favor of digital delivery, but that's still playing out, and Netflix has already more or less said that the future is in digital downloads anyway and is well on its way to making that a reality.

No, the next step in this story is actually something called the Paradox of Choice, as proposed by Barry Schwartz, a psychologist at Swarthmore College. You see, Netflix's problem has little to do with business models and distribution and much more to do with too much of a good thing. Netflix has too many videos to choose from (more than 100,000 according to its website[13]). It is such a problem that it has a running competition to improve the recommender engines with a top prize of a million dollars.[14]

Why offer a prize? Because, Schwartz says, with too much choice, people become paralyzed and get less satisfied with the choices they do make. As you have more to choose from, you begin to defer the decision, not wanting to take the time to investigate the possibilities. When you do make a choice, you realize that (1) there were plenty of opportunities to choose something better, and (2) the person to blame for not having potentially made a better choice is you. Schwartz even goes so far as to suggest that the rise in depression and suicide in the industrialized world is in no small part a result of this paradox.

Netflix is hardly alone. iTunes, the largest music download site, has more than 10 million songs[15] available. But if you think those numbers are big, how about WorldCat, which holds records for 1.4 billion items? However, go take a look at iTunes or Amazon. Note that they don't brag about how many items they have on their front pages. Instead they are desperately trying to create systems that minimize choice (while improving the accuracy of the choices they do provide). That is, except for Worldcat (take a look at figure 18).

Doesn't that screen just say, "Go ahead, find what you're looking for in 1.4 billion items, I dare you."

My point here is that being in the aggregation of artifacts business (books, DVDs, music) is a losing game for two reasons: You can never get it all, and if you did, your members would actually be less satisfied and more frustrated. Why do you think search engines stopped playing the "My index of web pages is bigger than yours" game years ago? Now it is all about fewer better results, not more and more.

Where does this leave us as librarians? Right back at our mission. Librarianship is not about artifacts, it is about knowledge and facilitating knowledge creation. So what should we be spending our precious resources on? Knowledge creation tools, not the results of knowledge creation.

Figure 18

Does that mean books in some communities where the members are looking for inspiration and examples? Sure. Does it mean keyboards and podcasting stations in some? Yup. What about computers for public use? Yup, if that is what the community needs to create knowledge.

This agreement is not about saying that any one tool is better than another. It is about saying they are tools, and tools fit a purpose. As a librarian, you must be open to all tools that aid members in their knowledge creation process; you should not start with what you have and market it to fit. It is in the member's success and the increased knowledge of our communities that we must define success, not in the amount of stuff we collect. If your community needs a workshop, build a workshop, not a collection of books about building workshops. You have limits to your budget, and you need to invest that money in the tools that yield the maximum results. How do you determine that? By having a conversation with the community where you identify the most pressing knowledge-creation needs.

Stop thinking in terms of resources. Stop thinking in terms of recorded knowledge. Stop thinking in terms of collections or artifacts, or traditions, or circulation! Think only of knowledge in the community. That is your collection!

Of course, if you do think in terms of artifacts, you are going to have a hard time because they are transforming before your very eyes.

13. http://netflix.mediaroom.com/index.php?s=43&item=307
14. http://www.netflixprize.com/
15. http://www.apple.com/itunes/features/#purchasing

*Death of Documents**

It seemed like an innocuous question. The question was, "Do you like your Kindle?" and it was asked by an audience member at the Program for Cooperative Cataloging's annual meeting at the American Library Association (ALA). My answer was, yes, I loved it. I could read and take notes, and if I finished a book, I could, wherever I was, go online and get another book.

Of course, I said, I am really intrigued by what the Kindle could become.[16] With its ubiquitous network connection, not only could I take notes, but I could bring them up with cited passages online and send them to colleagues and friends. Imagine, I said, if I could do this in real time. In fact, right now I can look up a word as I am reading, but imagine that I am struggling with a passage beyond a simple definition. I could bring in a colleague in real time to work through my confusion.

Imagine reading this Atlas on a future e-book reader. I keep saying that you are having a conversation with yourself, but what if you could in fact be having conversations with the author, friends, or co-workers as you are reading? Imagine a device that was more of a social access mechanism through text than a display reader.

Now, ask yourself, in that environment, is an e-book really a book at all? By turning printed text into 1s and 0s, are we in fact making a much more profound change? Is an e-journal that allows real time per paragraph commenting and annotating the same thing as a printed journal on a screen?

The answer is no. When we transform books, journals, and traditional documents into a digital sphere, we use the terms "book" and "journal" as metaphors. They are book-like or journal-like. It took centuries for the book as we know it to evolve. Introduction of things such as titles, tables of contents, page numbers, glossaries, indexes, and such emerged as people discovered new technical and use possibilities for the newly mass-produced bound book. Where once the goal of the printer was to mimic the illuminated manuscripts as closely as possible, now we have a whole new beast with its own conventions. In fact, almost any book you read today (as in 99.999%) is in fact an electronic document that has been bound to paper. Even if authors

hand write (or draws) out texts, they are transcribed and laid out as digital items. We maintain the physical form for convenience and to perpetuate a business model centered on items with hard boundaries among other reasons.

Why, for example, do I ever have to finish writing this Atlas? I could release it as I am writing it and continually add to, edit, and prune it. I could open it up for you to do the same. Is it still a book? Why wait for editions when I could use Wiki-style edit histories? Don't get me wrong, there are plenty of reasons to finish the book and make editions (citations, version control, etc.), but they are now choices, not rules dictated by the medium.

I go through this whole exercise to point out that the whole world of "document like objects" that has for so long dominated the work of librarians is vanishing. What is a Facebook profile? What does a MARC record look like for Google? Do we really want to apply the Library of Congress subject headings to every blog post? Where are the hard boundaries for a web page—the end of the HTML? The page plus its links?

To be sure, these are hard questions, and I am far from the first to highlight them. I do so for two reasons: to stress that librarians need to be the ones confronting these problems, and to show that we need to do so with a different approach. We cannot sit back and wait for things to settle out.

I propose that, rather than spend so much time on containers, we spend a lot more time on the use of containers (and even more time of those using the containers, but that should be obvious). For example, why is so much of cataloging intent on the front of a book—titles, ISBNs, copyrights, publishers, and so on—when the really cool stuff is often in the back or the footnotes? It is there where an author connects his or her ideas to the broader universe. But, you say, what about fiction or items that have no footnotes? Then we need to see what connections our members make.

Let me use an example of how thinking in documents can be problematic. The chart in figure 19 shows the entire web page presented on *Harry Potter and the Sorcerer's Stone* in a few library catalogs and Amazon.com.

OCPL is the Onondaga County Public Library, and the last column is Amazon. In case you are wondering what is taking up all that space, figure 20 is a breakdown of the Amazon column.

Note that if you combine "Sales Information" with "Bibliographic Data" in the Amazon column, you have about the same amount of information displayed as those pages from library catalogs.

**See Agreement Supplement for conversation starters and related resources on how to define and think about documents.

16. As I submit this manuscript, Apple has just announced the iPad with the iBook software. A month before, the Consumer Electronics Show was dominated by a whole raft of new e-book readers. My point is, Kindle, iPad, Sony e-Book, whatever the brand, the future has more to do with conversations than the brand of the display.

OCLC Open WorldCat

OCPL

National Library of Australia

Library of Congress

Amazon

Figure 19

Identity and Branding

Sales Information

Sales Recommendations

"Quality" Reviews

Bibliographic Data

Recommendations Based on Purchase and Tags

"Open" Reviews

Pathfinders

Discussion Tools

Marketing Info and Tools

Figure 20

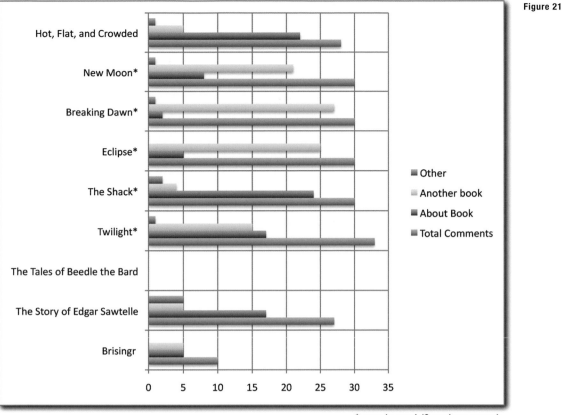

Figure 21

* sample used (first three pages)

Now, what does this have to do with the death of documents? After all, this is all about documents in the most traditional sense. The answer is that the length of that page has many advantages but shows a fundamental flaw of logic. If you actually read the "open reviews," you find out that a lot of them are not about the book at all. They may start at the book, but you get comments such as:

> The novel opens with Harry living under the cupboard with his abusive aunt and uncle. He has had a mean, depressed life, and though an active boy, the sheer amount of trauma he must have endured would scar any child. But the door opens out of this lifestyle. I've read an interesting theory (obviously not true), that a much different writer than Rowling would have ended Book 7 with Harry having imagined all this fantasy world, where he was so prominent and famous, to help escape the neglect and abuse from the Dursleys.[17]

Now is this comment about the book, the series, or an uncited reference to another literary critic? If you read through these comments, you'll find a lot of them are talking about the series as a whole or comparing the plot of Book 1 to Book 6, and so on. *Harry Potter* is not alone. I did a quick analysis of the comments on Amazon's top sellers for a given week and made figure 21.

There is a lot of talk going on about multiple documents here, but because Amazon is fixated on documents (after all, that's what it is selling), they all get forced into one document-like object. People don't think like that, and so the page balloons and, in doing so, loses value.

We are increasingly being confronted by resources that don't fit neatly into document metaphors or rigid boundaries. Efforts such as FRBR[18] are not helping either. Apply FRBR to a search engine, an ongoing listserv discussion, MySpace, or…well, you get my point. We take this up again when talking about cataloging relationships, but

17. http://www.amazon.com/Harry-Potter-Sorcerers-Stone-Anniversary/dp/054506967X/ref=sr_1_4?ie=UTF8&s=books&qid=1250868783&sr=8-4
18. http://www.ifla.org/en/publications/functional-requirements-for-bibliographic-records

the point here is that the dominance of documents, no, the tyranny of documents, is actually holding librarians back. How we define a document should not be by bindings or title pages but by a member-defined "atom" of a resource they find helpful. Will the transition to this approach be easy? No way. Is it necessary? Absolutely.

Memory

Getting back to Conversation Theory, we have conversants exchanging language to seek agreements. There is one more vital ingredient to making this all work: memory. We have already touched a bit on the nature of memory, but now let us dive in deeper and see in what unexpected ways it might take us.

First, why memory? If knowledge is dynamic and always changing, does that mean there is nothing durable in how we see the world? Of course not. The role of memory is to keep track of previous agreements (as best it can) and make them available in new situations. In essence, in a conversation, you need to be able to recall previous agreements from that conversation and previous ones.

It seems simple enough, but there are some major implications in how that memory appears to work. The primary feature is that memory is relational. We remember things not as discreet buckets of information but as a sort of oddly tangled web of ideas and their contexts. Let me give you two examples to show this to you. The first is a word game, and the second is a joke.

Let's start with the word game. I'm going to give you a word, and you think about what that word means. Here's you first word: "run."

OK, did you think of run as in the verb to move quickly by foot? How about run, as in to operate, like run a business? How about run as a noun, like a run in stockings? They all fit right. Of course we all know this problem as librarians because we all have had to disambiguate words in questions and classifications. Yet if you search a library catalog for "run," you are as likely to get running as a sport as you are to get items on running a business.

OK, another word: "bank."

Did you think of the financial institutions? The sides of a river? Or perhaps to put aside for later use, like banking favors? Others?

One more: "OMG."

I'm going to go ahead and assume you didn't think of the Object Management Group or the OMG company that manufactures roofing materials. I'm almost certain you thought "OH MY GOD!" from texting or instant messaging.

What's going on here? Why do run and bank make sense in so many varied ways? Why can I, not knowing you, guess what you were thinking about with OMG? What's going on is that in your mind you have a plethora of agreements as to what words such as "bank" and run" mean and many relationships between those agreements and others. When asked you to pick one, you do so, but without much context your brain just grabs one at hand. For example, when I have done this in the past, I use "formula" as a chemical combination, a mathematical equation, or something to give babies so they don't starve. It gets easy to pick out the audience members who are recent parents or grandparents. However, with something like OMG, there are few agreements with few relationships. Your brain has few to pick from.

By the way, these ideas can be coupled to create whole new concepts, such as, "A run on the bank?! OMG!"

Now the joke:
A woman goes into her local green grocer and asks for a pound of broccoli.

"I'm sorry," says the grocer, "we don't have any broccoli, but I have some nice spinach."

"That's great," says the woman, "I'll take a pound of broccoli."

"I'm sorry ma'am, but we are out of broccoli, perhaps some cauliflower?"

"Wonderful," says the woman, "I'll take a pound of broccoli."

"Lady," says the grocer, "We have no broccoli, but we do have peas."

"OK," says the lady, "I'll have a pound of broccoli."

Exasperated, the grocer asks, "Pardon me ma'am, but can you spell, for example, cat, as in catastrophic?"

"Of course C-A-T."

"How about dog, as in dogmatic?"

"D-O-G."

"Great, how about stink, as in broccoli?"

"Hey, there's no stink in broccoli!"

"That's what I'm trying to tell you, lady, there's no stinkin' broccoli!"

OK, so maybe not the best joke in the world, but it actually tells you a lot about how your brain remembers things. Note the structure of the joke: There is a pattern established, actually two: lady asks for broccoli, grocer makes alternative suggestion, lady ignores him; and man asks for spelling with suggestion, woman replies. Then, what makes it a joke: The pattern is broken with an unexpected, but still meaningful, twist. Go back and look at the Einstein joke in my discussion of "Importance of Theory and Deep Concepts." Same thing—pattern with an unexpected but still meaningful twist. Your brain is set to look for patterns. Once it establishes one, the break of the pattern is a surprise and that the surprise makes sense makes humor (at least one type).

This also, by the way, explains why it is so hard to remember a good joke. In a piece in the *New York Times*,[19] Natalie Angier explains how the brain looks for patterns to store. By adding a punch line—breaking the pattern—the brain has a hard time remembering the joke, at least the punch line.

As we have seen before when talking about source amnesia or Amazon's open comments, the way in which we think is relational. We often remember something because the situation in which it occurred was meaningful, such as when I asked you where you learned that clouds were made up of water vapor. There is a chance you actually did remember if, say, it was in your favorite science class or you learned about it on a special trip to a museum.

It doesn't just happen with "facts" and ideas. Smells, for example, have one of the most direct connections to the brain. They are amazingly powerful ways of triggering memories. Smelling a fresh baked pie might take you back to your youth. There are entire industries that bank on using smells to evoke memories, such as candle stores. Maybe we should make all our textbooks scratch and sniff (what do you think the smell of worldview is?).

Allow me for a moment to revisit the question of source amnesia. The fact that the brain re-creates information as it remembers it, and the fact that that information can be re-created incorrectly, plus the fact that a lot of information doesn't fit into nice patterns, points out an important role for librarians in terms of memory. The peculiarities of human memory point out a strong need for librarians to reliably remember things. This leads into the important areas of archives and preservation. Librarians preserve artifacts to enhance conversations through a reliable and accurate memory.

Now before you yell "AHA! It's all about the artifacts after all," let me say two things: I never said artifacts were unimportant, simply secondary, and artifacts without context are not really memory. You may have an ancient volume that tells you how folks lived in first-century China, but if it is written in a language that cannot be translated, did you really preserve the memory or the object? Preservation, digitization, and archives are an important function of librarianship in that

they are our focus on memory, and our focus on memory is there to enrich current conversations, not to collect artifacts.

Entailment Mesh

Pask represented the relationship of agreements as an "entailment mesh." It is simply a graphical way to display agreements and their contexts. The Map at the beginning of this Atlas is an entailment mesh (although technically Pask would call it an entailment structure because it has been pruned and refined). It is an external representation, in that Pask does not pretend this is how things are actually stored in your head. It is more like Taylor's Compromised Need, in that it has been encoded and transformed to be shared.

One benefit of making this kind of representation is that it makes it easier for learners to both grasp the whole of a concept and burrow into the details. In essence, by seeing the domain of librarianship laid out, you can more quickly come up to speed on how I see the field than with all of this darned writing. You can then use this overall concept to fit the writing together. I didn't make an Atlas just because I think maps make pretty pictures.

Annotations*

This concept of entailment mesh also changes the way we look at annotations. An annotation is a seemingly simple concept of adding a note or some comment or context to an item. The problem is, when actually trying to implement this idea, things get suddenly more complex. In the metadata world, there is a concept called an ordered object. An object of the first order is the primary item. It serves as the parent for all lower ordered items. So in FRBR, the work is a first-order object, whereas all the expressions would be lower or second-order objects. It seems pretty straightforward. All this ordering helps determine what you describe (assign metadata to) and at what depth.

The problem comes in that life is not quite so accommodating. Take, for example, all those comments on the *Harry Potter* book we looked at before. The first-order object is the book. The comments—annotations—are second-order objects. Simple. Except that in my use, it is actually the comments that serve as the item under primary

19. http://www.nytimes.com/2009/03/17/science/17angi.html?_r=1&sq=&st=cse&%2334;=&scp=1&%2334;In%20One%20Ear%20and%20Out%20the%20Other=&pagewanted=print

*See Agreement Supplement for discussion questions and pointers to resources on annotations.

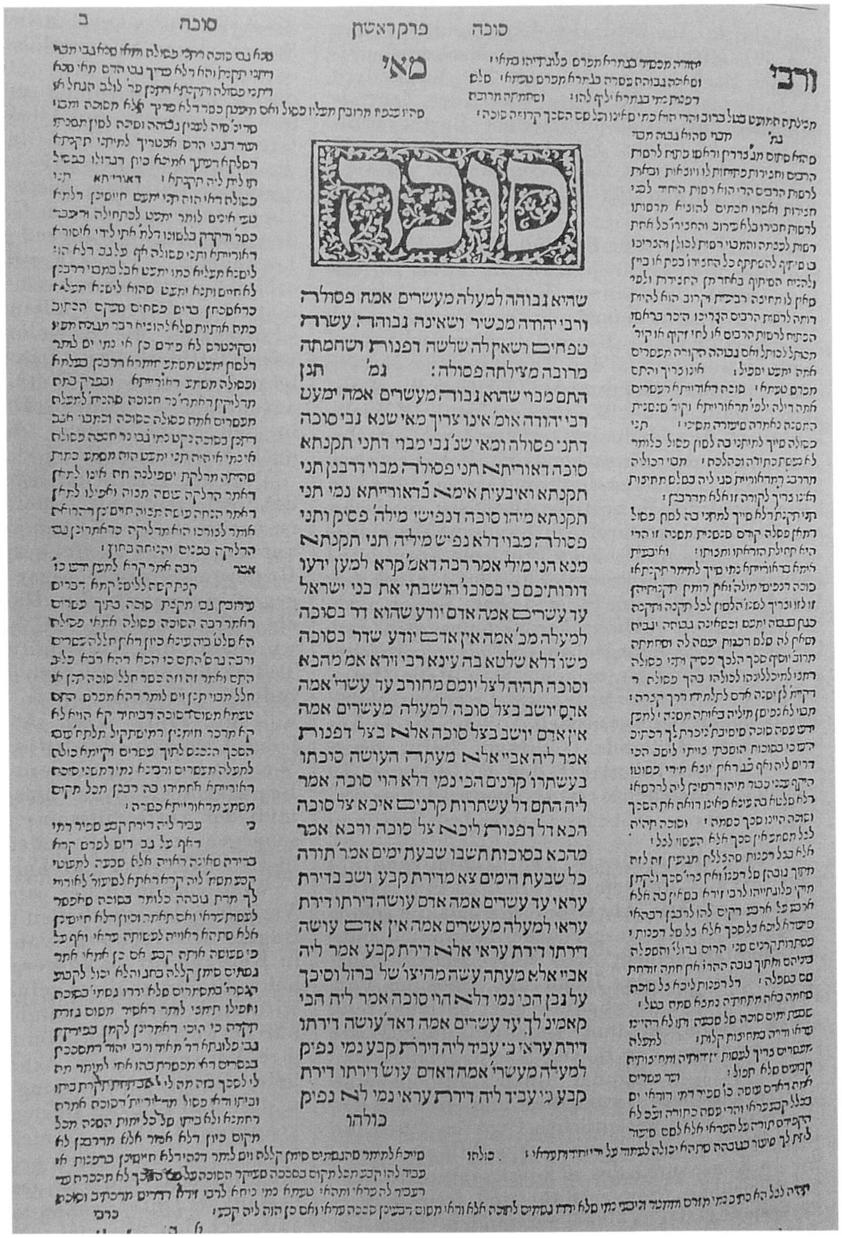
ב סוכה פרק ראשון סוכה

מאי

ורבי

סוכה

שהיא גבוהה למעלה מעשרים אמה פסולה ורבי יהודה מכשיר ושאינה גבוהה עשרה טפחים ושאין לה שלשה דפנות ושחמתה מרובה מצילתה פסולה:

Figure 22

consideration—a first-order object. Also, although Amazon relates the comments to the book, it also relates it to the person who wrote them (the more quality comments you write, the greater your visibility in the system). So which is the first-order object? The person or the book?

My absolute favorite example of this dilemma is the Babylonian Talmud. Here, religious scholars look at a specific Jewish text and comment (or debate) about how it is to be interpreted. Take a look at the page from the Talmud in figure 22.

See that ornate boxed writing in the top middle of the page? That's the topic. All the other columns snaking out in a spiral are the writings of rabbis commenting on and interpreting the topic. This page is quite literally a representation of an ongoing conversation (I never claimed I invented the concept). So, which is the annotation and which is the content? Before you say it is obvious, ask yourself: Why would you look at the Talmud and not just the original text alone? The whole purpose of the Talmud is the annotation—that is, its unique content.

The use of conversation has the potential to break through all of this first- and second-order business. Everything is first order, but everything is also sequenced and connected. Rather than thinking hierarchically, one must think of meshes and ontologies. First order, second order, and so forth are dictated by the conversation they are referenced within, not from the artifacts themselves.

Another point to make in relation to annotation is that systems are having us annotate the wrong things. We need to be able to annotate the linkage between agreements (concepts, artifacts, etc.). The real meat of understanding, or knowledge, is in relationships. Yes, I can annotate a given paragraph in an article, but I also need to be able to annotate a link between that paragraph and a paragraph in an entirely different context.

Think about hyperlinks on the web. At one point (and probably still), the number one piece of anchor text for a link on the web (i.e., the words you click on to make the link happen) were "click here." It tells you nothing about why you might want to click. It may, of course, be embedded in the text surrounding "click here," but often a search engine won't see it or know it is related. It is the difference between a list of readings and an annotated bibliography. The connections between things on a list, between two web pages, or between two ideas are vitally important. Annotation tools need to explicitly allow for annotations on links and relationships, not just artifacts. This becomes clear when talking about annotation through tagging.

One might imagine I would be a big fan of tagging because it allows people to put their own spin on content and add context. However, I see tagging as having severe limitations, especially at the individual level.

Now, I have to pause here because I nearly got into a Twitter fight with Tim Spalding of LibraryThing over this. And you just haven't lived until you felt the adrenaline rush of a tense back and forth 140 characters at a time. Tagging can mean a lot of things to a lot of folks, so let me be clear. I think the idea of member-created vocabularies (better known as folksonomies) have a lot of virtue. After all, this is really an expression of L_1 for a member or community. What I am really talking about here is keyword tagging.

The problem should be pretty apparent after the discussion of memory. Words as labels tend not to work unless they are specialized words with few agreements and relationships. Otherwise, the grouping of words often lacks sufficient connective tissue to truly capture the context they are meant to convey.

Take a random object from your surroundings. Assign it three tags not using a proper noun. Hand the list to someone outside of that room and ask him or her to come up with what you were describing. Hide the list from yourself for 6 months and see whether you can tell what you were describing. We can see the problem with a quick sampling of images brought back by Google Images using the tag "brother," as in figure 23. The full set of results includes Brother sewing machines, the movie *Undercover Brother*, monks, and even Orwell's Big Brother.

This is not to say that tagging has no uses. It turns out that when you aggregate tags in a group of people, it has great utility. This makes sense because the group that uses the utility probably has a large overlapping L_1 vocabulary. Also, the group is sloppy enough to fill in the cracks where someone might miss a tag. Look, for example, at the first page of image results from Flickr searching for the tag "brother" in figure 24.

However, tagging is far from a panacea. It requires careful consideration before implementing such a system, and it needs to be based on the knowledge of the community's needs and, of course, how knowledge works. It also needs to take into consideration that tags are often more useful when describing a relationship between two objects.

Figure 23

Figure 24

"Brother"

"Brother"

"Brother"

"Brother"

Figure 25

"Brother"

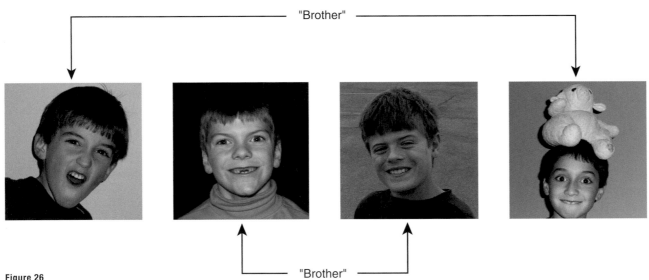

Figure 26

"Brother"

Take the Amazon example again. People's comments were really a form of annotation (they can tag items, too). Yet we often see that they are attempting to annotate not a single artifact but a series of them.

Take a look at the pictures in figure 25 with their tags.

Now take a look at what you get if you annotate between artifacts in figure 26.

There are plenty of articles and discussions on tagging, so I do not belabor the point here. What I want you to walk away with is that the gold of tags, and indeed knowledge, is relationships—not single isolated artifacts or facts. When we put tagging into library systems, we would do well to remember this.

Cataloging Relationships

Although cataloging relationships is discussed in greater detail in the "Librarians" Thread, it is worth noting that the underlying conceptual foundation for focusing on the space between items, as opposed to items themselves, comes directly from the way memory works.

SCAPES*

Scapes is a conceptual digital reference software system that embodies concepts of Conversation Theory. It seeks to recast the digital reference process from the foundations of conversation, rather than the tradition of the reference desk. In essence, Scapes is an entailment mesh maker. It allows an individual or group of folks to come around a common tool to build an entailment mesh of the concept, agreement, or domain under consideration.

Think of it this way: Rather than having someone walk up to a reference desk or the virtual equivalent of finding a library's reference form and having them enter their information, we give our members a big table from which to work. On this table, they begin to pile artifacts—perhaps notes they have made on index cards or books they think are relevant. As they put more information on the table, they begin to build piles. One pile is of books that take stance A, another is B. They can connect the piles with string and note what the relationship is (e.g., "Pile A disagrees with B"). As they are working, they can invite friends in to help or experts with whom to consult. When they have a question, they can invite the librarians over.

*See Agreement Supplement for Questions and Answers on possible Scapes development.

Figure 27

Here is where things get a little more interesting. Now the librarian not only has the question the member is asking, but the librarian can see the table of what they have already looked at and even how they are conceptualizing their worldview on the topic. No more asking if they have searched Google, or looked at book X, because there it is.

By making the table digital, we can add a sort of recommender system. Put down three books and their relationships, and the "digital table," or Scape, suggests a fourth ("80% of folks who used this book also used this one"). Not only that, but now the member can pull in not just books and materials but also other scapes. Now they get whole agreement sets they can include, and by doing so they build a web of agreements and perspectives that span the community.

The following figures show my first guess at what an interface to create a "Scape" looks like. Let's start with the opening screen in figure 27.

The interface is deliberately sparse, just like the empty table from the previous scenario. This sparse interface and limited tools allow the member to organize their materials in their own fashion, not confined by some preexisting organizational scheme (remember our discussion of User Systems). The three tools in the top right are simply "add objects," "talk to a person," and "search." The functions of these buttons become obvious soon.

In this set of screens, a man named John was driving home from work one day listening to the radio and heard the song "Rich Girl" by Gwen Stefani. John thought he had heard a song like that before, but he couldn't remember where. Arriving home, he went to his library online and started a Scape on the subject. The first thing John did was perform a simple search on "rich girl" (figure 28).

Figure 28

It is a basic search, so it brings up a lot of results. John finds the song at the bottom of the list and drags it into the Scape. A simple click on the song would play it and show standard bibliographic data, such as that stored in catalogs. With a click, he can make a standing link between the song and the album it came from (figure 29).

This doesn't really tell John what he is interested in—it is a remake—so he brings in a friend to help think about this. John uses the second button in the upper right of the screen, and he adds a chat session with his friend, Jeff. John asks Jeff whether he knows where to find the lyrics to the song. Jeff does a search (using the same tools available to John—as seen in figure 30) and finds that someone has already created a public Scape on the lyrics to this song.

Jeff drags the existing object into John's workspace. Because this is not a simple text file but another Scape, meaning a complete workspace with relationships and context, John gets not only the lyrics but the links someone has made between parts of the lyrics and additional information. In this case, this added scape includes four threads based on the lyrics (as seen in the lower right portion of figure 31).

Following one of the threads, "I'd get me four Harajuku girls to (uh huh)," John can find out that the Harajuku Girls are Gwen Stafani's backup dancers and even a link to Wikipedia to see that they took their name from a fashionable subway stop in Tokyo.

Still, as interesting as this is, it is not helping John on his quest to find the origin of this song. John goes back to his "talk to a person" button and brings in a librarian (figure 32). John then asks the librarian, "Hi...do you know if this song is a remake?" to which the librarian replies, "Actually it is a remake of a song from *Fiddler on the Roof.*"

The librarian then uses the "add objects" button to bring up a window (visible and available to all and seen in figure 33) and adds links to the original *Fiddler on the Roof* song, "If I Were a Rich Man," and links that song to information on the musical soundtrack.

Happy with the results, all sign off. Because this Scape may be useful to others, John leaves it public so that others may see it (and include it), and John allows all the original participants to edit the Scape whenever they want.

In fact, later that night, as Jeff is driving home, he hears another Gwen Stefani song, "Start It Up," which contains elements from *The Sound of Music*. He logs back into the Scape, and he adds that information as well (as seen in figure 34). John will be alerted to the change through RSS and can always keep this document live or lock it down.

So looking at the final result, what was built? In terms from conversation theory, it is an entailment mesh or a representation of

Figure 29

Figure 30

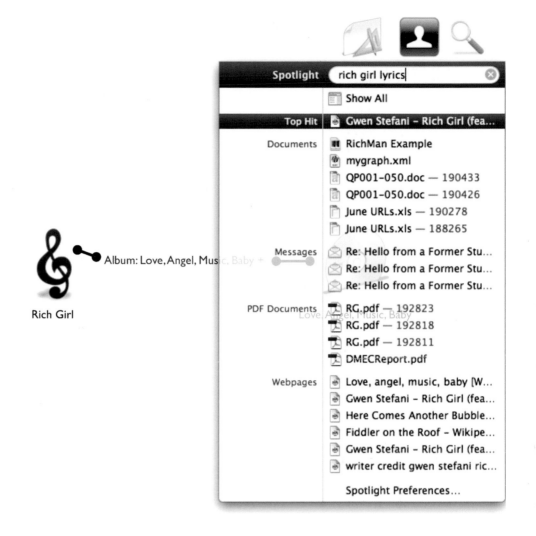

Rich Girl

Album: Love, Angel, Music, Baby +

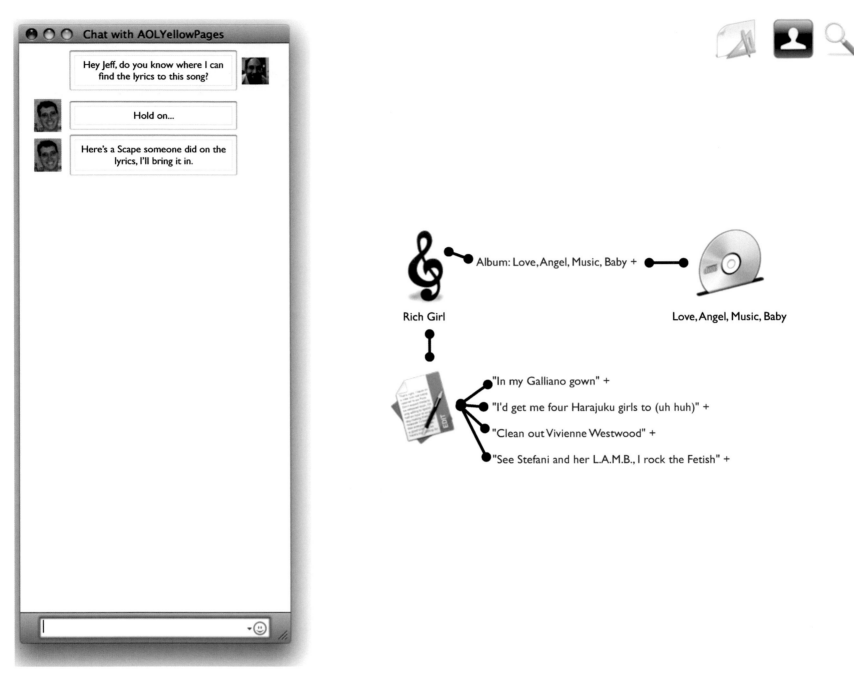

Figure 31

http://en.wikipedia.org/wiki/Harajuku_Girls

Figure 32

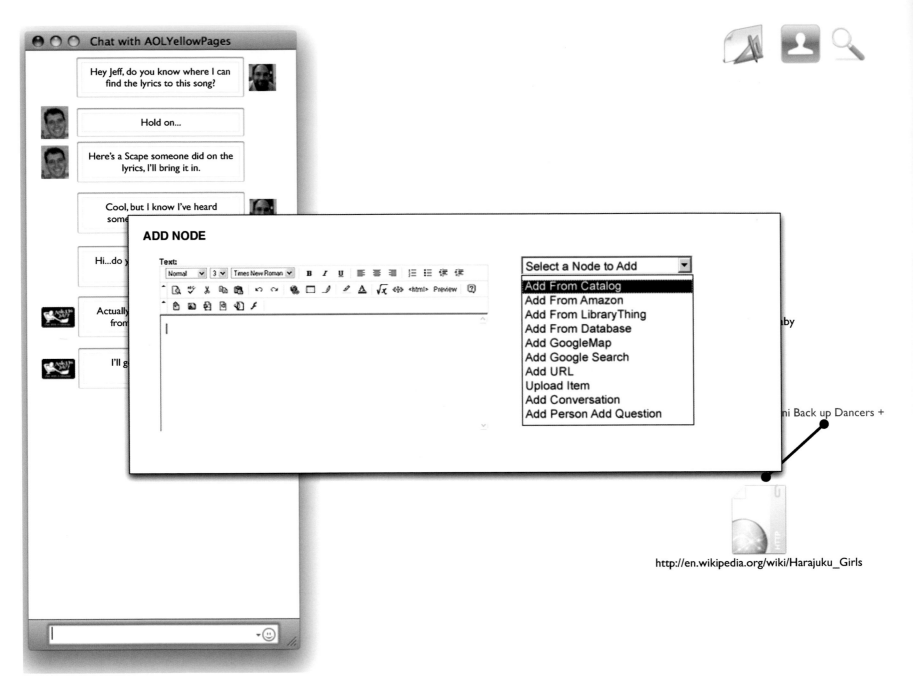

Figure 33

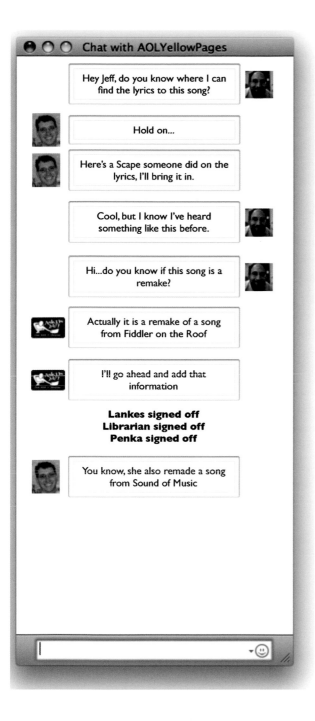

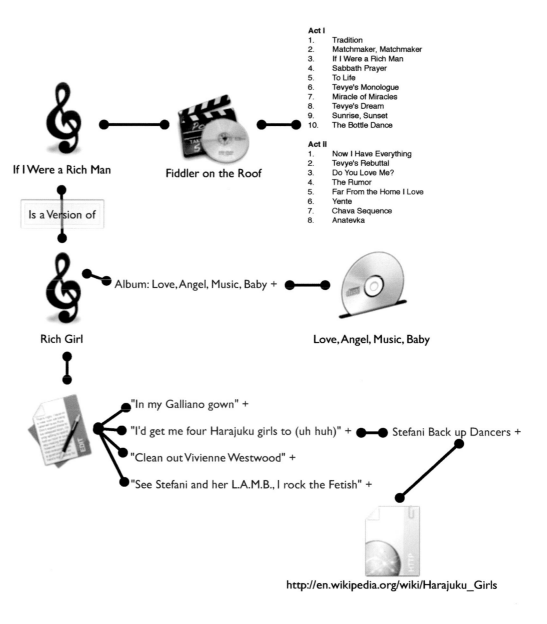

knowledge. It was built through conversation and contains agreements in the form of established links. It is participatory and all about learning. What's more, it looks nothing like existing library software. Not because we set out to make it look different, but because it was built from a grounded conceptual framework, not as an incremental evolution of existing systems. It was built around how people learn, not around how librarians built catalogs or did reference at a desk for the past century.

This is not altogether unlike a Wiki environment. After all, people can collaborate and link things. But in wikis, you are stuck with blobs of text where the underlying system can do little to augment your work. By making the entailment mesh explicit, the system can perform all sorts of functions, such as finding other people who may share common relationships or finding a path through agreements that lead to unexpected outcomes.

Imagine using a Scape as a community tool where the library facilitates a community-wide discussion on youth violence. Community organizations, the police force, local government, and individuals could gather around a virtual table and begin laying out the problem as they see it. One group might put up crime statistics. Another group might link those statistics to a map showing where the crimes took place. Another individual might then add economic data, believing there is a strong link between economic opportunity and violence. Still another person might link to an article that refutes that view, and so on.

At the end of the day, you may not end up with a picture that everyone agrees with, but rather a map of where the conversation and knowledge of the situation stands. That would be a great starting point for the conversation, and it would still be available three years hence when the discussion reemerges, or it could be linked into a town planning discussion, and so on.

Todd Marshall says that a Scape is the recognition that, just as we have spreadsheets to manage numbers and word processors to handle words, we need a knowledge processor to handle the results of our learning. Further, it is the library that should build the system because it is core to their mission. The catalogs we provide now? They only provide the raw materials for a knowledge process; we need to support the process.

I have said, a bit unkindly, that librarians serve their communities with a shovel in one hand and a catcher's mitt in the other. When someone is starting his or her knowledge discovery process, we are happy to search databases, catalogs, and the web and present the member with a ton of potential resources. We then step back and wait for knowledge to be developed and put into artifact form (a published article, a book, a song, a plan). That's when we pull out the catcher's mitt to capture the artifact and shelve it. It is time for librarians to be there at every step of the knowledge-creation process. Just as with the community example, they need to be there helping the community formulate their agreements, helping them discuss it, helping them document it, and then helping them implement it.

REFERENCE EXTRACT

So what else can librarians do with all these entailment meshes? How does a Scape suggest possibly related resources? One idea I developed, working with Mike Eisenberg at the University of Washington, Jeff Penka at Online Computer Library Center, and the MacArthur Foundation—with a lot of input from scholars, librarians, and technologists—is called Reference Extract: a credibility engine. It is envisioned as a system that takes the resources that librarians see as credible, plus the contexts in which they find them credible, and use them to help members find credible information on the Internet.

However, in terms of finishing off this thread, think of Reference Extract as a topology engine. That is a fancy way of saying it searches not for specific items but for a network of things. Google, and most general-purpose search engines these days, use topology engines to do their work. They not only find a web page that uses the words you are looking for, but they also take into account how those documents relate to other pages. Page Rank, which drives Google results, can be simplified to the right words in the most-linked-to (or popular) page as seen in figure 35.

However, the Page Rank process, being automated, is open to some weaknesses. Aside from an overall bias toward shopping and technology sites (a search for "apple," as we've seen, yields many sites about Apple computers and few on fruit), it is also open to manipulation. Advertisers quickly learned ways of creating many false sites that drove up the ranking of their clients and created an entire industry around Search Engine Optimization (SEO). So-called "Google Bombing" was a process where certain words would lead to unwanted results. (In 2003, a search on "miserable failure" would point to the George W. Bush's White House page because a group of bloggers agreed to use those keywords to point to the White House. Within days, this same technique was used to point to various Democratic figures until Google manually adjusted the search results.) What this

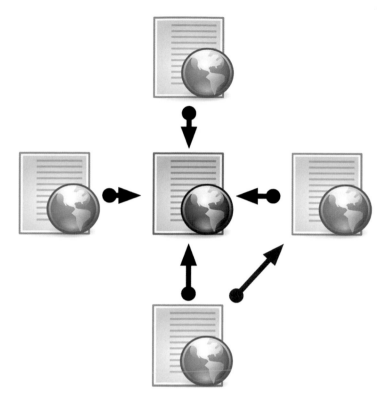

Figure 35

coming in and built-in mechanisms for diversity (reference at academic libraries, government, public, school, etc.). What's more, we can link this system right into a Scape (or a catalog) to suggest new connections and resources.

We can also connect it into digital reference systems such as QuestionPoint to help suggest good resources as part of the reference process. Even better, if the reference librarian doesn't find a good resource in Reference Extract while answering a question, he or she adds a new one, improving Reference Extract. It becomes a feedback loop: The more the system is used, the better it gets, and the use is tied into existing processes not as some new burden or task.

Now I love reference librarians, but they are never, ever going to be as fast as web crawlers in terms of adding new resources to Reference Extract. To some degree, this is good. We only want the good stuff, not everything. But with all this rich linkages/context/topology, Reference Extract can start to infer what might be credible. A page not directly cited but from the same site? Maybe credible. A page pointed to by a credible resource? Probably credible. One can image giving members a choice: fewer more dependable resources or more resources with less assurance?

But let's keep going here. After all, up to this point, I've only talked about librarians connections being used in Reference Extract.

shows is that ranking results by naturally occurring links or referrals is effective. However, completely automating this process can lead to noncredible results.

Reference Extract seeks to add another dimension to search—credibility. Reference Extract takes the success of the page rank approach and uses it to highlight credible (not just popular) sites. It does this by using the judgments of a highly credible population, librarians, to determine which sites are searched and the order of the search results.

In essence, linkages between web pages by anyone are replaced by citations to web pages by highly trained librarians in their daily work of answering the questions of scholars, policymakers, and the general population. Instead of page rank, I refer to this as "reference weighting," as shown in figure 36.

There are a lot of advantages to this approach (and some real drawbacks we get to in a second). First, some preliminary research shows that members perceive the information they get from librarians as highly credible. Second, by linking this into ongoing reference activities in libraries, we have a built-in way to keep new information

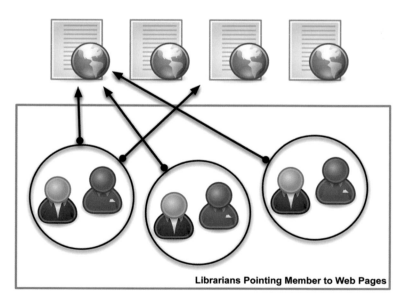

Librarians Pointing Member to Web Pages

Figure 36

But what about all of those Scapes out there by our members? Why not bring them in too? Well, this actually makes a lot of sense, but it must be tied to some mechanism of choosing which Scapes you want. The current idea is from people you trust. So give me resources from librarians and my friends. Or librarians, and professors, and my friends. Eventually you end up with a set of credibility communities that you built and can draw on.

All of this topology information, by the way, is why all those simple single search boxes that librarians are putting on web pages are doomed to fail, at least when compared to Google, Bing, Yahoo!, and the open search engines. You see, the search engines looks at the entire web as one big map: This page leads to that page, which leads to that page, and so on. The stores of metadata that the library's unified search box spans have much less topology to work with, and we currently make use of much less still. The items in our databases are not linked to the items in our catalog; we are just doing multiple searches and fusing them…somehow (see figure 37).

That's not to say that there aren't plenty of interesting topologies we could use today. Circulation data could be useful, for example—linking circulated items borrowed together. In academic situations, we could use inclusion of readings in syllabi. In law libraries, inclusion of items in common briefs, and so on. Ultimately, I would argue that we need systems such as Scapes as a primary interface for our members to gather their explicit relationships and then systems such as Reference Extract to make use of those connections.

I leave you with the main point: When you change your thinking from artifacts and items to conversations and knowledge, new possibilities open up—new systems for us to develop (not simply adopt or copy), new services to offer, and a whole new relationship with our members.

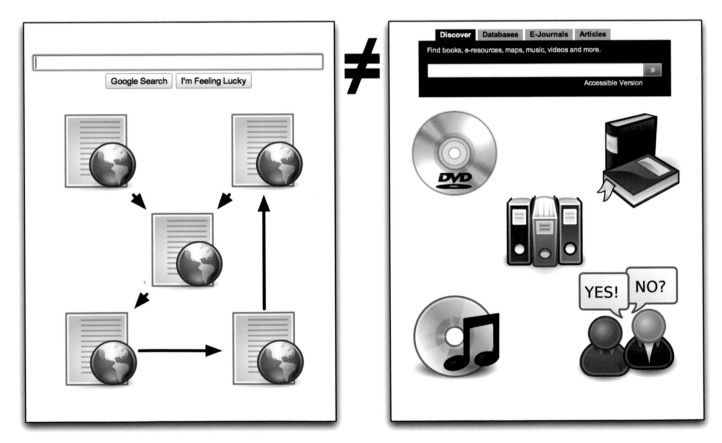

Figure 37

LIBRARIES ARE IN THE KNOWLEDGE BUSINESS, THEREFORE THE CONVERSATION BUSINESS

This of course brings us back to the beginning: our mission. Librarians are not caretakers of artifacts. Librarians are not finders of things. Librarians are much more profoundly useful and powerful. Librarians are in the knowledge business. They—you—facilitate the creation of knowledge, and by doing so you improve society. Rather than building book museums, we—you and I—must build edifices of bricks and code to promote knowledge. Where once Carnegie built temples to books, we shall build workshops of the mind.

Of course, now with the foundations of Conversation Theory under our belts, we know that being in the knowledge business, we are in the conversation business. We engage in conversations, we help shape them, we support them, and we even capture the results of them to enrich our communities, serve as a vital memory, and ultimately be a powerful partner for the creation of a joint ideal future.

Now that we know what knowledge is, it is time to get to the brass tacks of how to facilitate its creation.

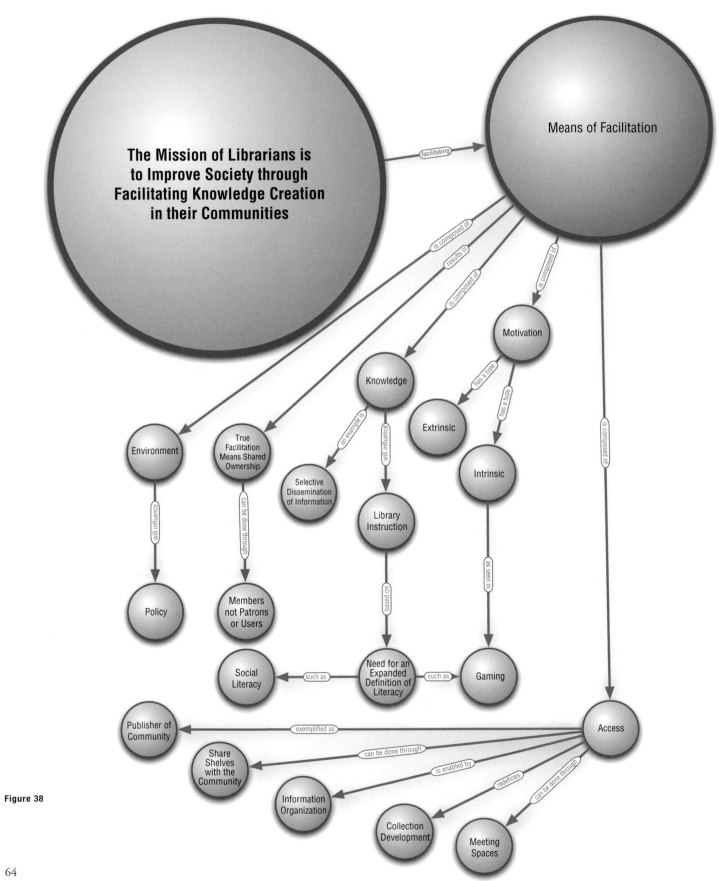

Figure 38

FACILITATING

> The librarian must be the librarian militant before he can be the librarian triumphant.
> —Melvil Dewey

THE MISSION OF LIBRARIANS IS TO IMPROVE SOCIETY THROUGH FACILITATING KNOWLEDGE CREATION IN THEIR COMMUNITIES

As always, our Thread begins with the mission of librarians: to improve society through facilitating knowledge creation in their communities. But what do I mean by "facilitate knowledge creation"? We know from the previous Thread that it has something to do with conversations, but I need to be much more specific. Where the "Mission" Thread was broad and the "Knowledge" Thread was conceptually specific, this Thread begins to transform the concept and mission into the applied. At least as applied as possible because the ultimate specifics and shapes of services will be unique and negotiated with your community.

This Thread revolves around four means of facilitation: access, knowledge, environment, and motivation. At this point, think of it as getting people to the conversation, making sure they know what is being discussed, making sure they feel safe to be part of the conversation, and finding the right encouragement for them to engage in the conversation.

Before we begin with the specifics, I need to make clear one guiding principle that winds throughout facilitation, and indeed the entire Atlas: True facilitation means shared ownership.

TRUE FACILITATION MEANS SHARED OWNERSHIP

I could have saved this agreement for the big soaring rhetoric at the end of the Thread, but it is too important to wait. This Atlas is all about you, the librarian. However, your ultimate measure of success comes not from you, or from me, but from the success of your members. You are in good company. Just as doctors must be evaluated by the success of their patients and lawyers their clients, the nature of our profession is ultimately one of service. This means members and librarians are true partners, both with a stake in the outcome of a knowledge endeavor.

Just as we share in the successes, responsibilities, and failures of our members, we must cede some of our own responsibilities to the members as well. As in a conversation, when you must stop and listen, thus sharing control of the conversation, so too must we allow our services to listen, that is, be influenced by our members. Doing so not only flows from our concepts, it builds trust and ultimately builds the relationship necessary for a new compact with our communities. Allow me to demonstrate this with an example already in practice today.

I mentioned a project in the "Mission" Thread where a group of researchers worked with a large urban library to create a digital learning space. In the course of those conversations, a researcher called the public library a "public space." I corrected her. The public library, I said, is a civic space. What is the distinction? A public space is not truly owned. It is an open space. Things in the public domain, for example, are free to use and reproduce. A civic space, on the other hand, is a regulated space on behalf of the public. That means it is beholden to a whole raft of policy and law. A group can gather in a public space. They have to have permission to do so in a civic space, and that permission must be given in an equitable and nondiscriminatory way.

Why do I bring this up? It is an existing example of a partnership between member and librarian. Members give the public library money and space, but they also insist on some conditions (law and policy). It is a jointly owned enterprise.

What is obvious and regulated in the civic sphere is also true in other contexts such as academia, where, in most cases, faculty governance puts conditions on the operation of the library and librarians (from tenure to budgets). In schools, teachers and the administration team with school library media specialists to shape the media center. In law firms, law libraries are accountable to partners, and so on. What you must also understand is that this joint ownership process must extend to all the services.

This is not about the whole 2.0 language of radical trust, where an organization must be open to online communities for a sort of greater good. "Radical trust" implies first that such a co-owned relationship is radical: It is not. Co-ownership is about the nature of knowledge. As we see throughout all Threads in the Atlas, people construct their knowledge, and they need to shape the systems by which they do so. The second false implication of radical trust is that we, librarians, own something and are letting the members participate. Once again, in the knowledge game, if members do not participate, they are not learning. It is they who are allowing us to participate in their learning. To paraphrase Anne Lipow,[1] it is we who are remote from members, not the other way around. They trust us to help them.

1. http://techinlibraries.com/kresh.pdf

Eli Neiburger is an amazingly talented and smart man. He is a true innovator in the library space. Part of what makes him so good is how well he listens to his community. He told me about a great idea that one of his members had. This member asked: Why couldn't the member use the material-sharing tools the library has to also share member-owned materials? Just like the catalog lists books on the shelves of the different branches that are available to borrow, why can't it also list the personal items people are willing to share? It actually harkens back to the origin of public libraries in North America.

If, as a librarian, you see the library and collected resources as something outside of the community, this is an odd and possibly troubling idea. If, on the other hand, you see the library as a part of the community, then it makes perfect sense. Is the library, to put this in a political context, an institution *of* the people or *for* the people?

Your answer to that question ultimately defines how you see facilitation. If you are for the people, you are a tool and separate. To facilitate is to act on a population. You have users and customers, not members. If, in contrast, you feel as I do that the library is of the people, then to facilitate is to engage and help the community because you are helping yourself. You have members. If you see yourself as a tool for the people, you have a job. If you see yourself as a member of the community, you have a vocation—a calling—a mission.

I had a former student in a hushed tone once say she saw her role as a librarian akin to being a parish minister. She needed to get out among the community to see how their minds and spirits needed tending. I actually think this is a wonderful analogy. Of course some librarians might be horrified by this analogy. What a great place to start a conversation.

MEANS OF FACILITATION*

So how do librarians facilitate knowledge creation? They do so through access (building a bridge between conversants), knowledge (the requisite domain understanding necessary to converse), environment (providing a platform where a member can feel safe to participate), and motivation (understanding, supporting, and, in some cases, imparting a desire to participate).

Marcia Mardis, Todd Marshall, and others have thought a lot about this and actually defined these as a set of new digital divides.[2] The fist divide is access. The original digital divide debate centered on the urban poor being left behind (primarily in an economic opportunity sense) because they could not afford computers or online access fees. This was one of the main impetuses for the e-rate funds in the United States.[3]

Marshall and Mardis would argue that this is only the first such divide. The second is a knowledge divide. It is great that urban schools now have computers to explore the online world and engage the global community in conversation. However, if the students don't know how to work these computers, they can get little use from them. In essence, hardware is not enough. They need the knowledge of how to use the computers and get online.

Marcia Mardis then posits a third divide. So now that students are online and know how to get to a conversation, can they? Filters may prevent access from vital conversations. The third divide is then the environment (primarily seen in use policies) in which the students work. I was one author in a book about credibility as it relates to digital media, youth, and learning.[4] At least three of us came to the conclusion independently: that primary and secondary schools as they currently operate are terrible places to teach students about the credibility of online information.[5]

The logic goes something like this. To teach about credibility, you need negative as well as positive examples. Communities are loath to allow noncredible information into schools (do you want to be the one at the school board who asks for more crap in the classroom?). In fact, there is national policy that insists on filtering "bad" sites on the Internet to prevent students from accessing them. Therefore, you are limited in teaching students about online credibility because you can't show the negative examples.

It gets worse. Because we have created such a rarified online experience in schools, students have a hard time dealing with the rough-and-tumble Internet they experience. So when students have access

*See Agreement Supplement for a quick overview to the means of facilitation and citations to additional thoughts on facilitation in general.

2. http://conversants.syr.edu/journal/?p=28 and Mardis, M. A., Hoffman, E. S., & Marshall, T. E. (2008). A new framework for understanding educational digital library use: Re-examining digital divides in US schools. *International Journal on Digital Libraries, 9*(1), 19–27.

3. http://www.fcc.gov/learnnet/

4. Metzger, M. J., & Flanagin, A. J. (2008). *Digital media, youth, and credibility. The John D. and Catherine T. Macarthur Foundation series on digital media and learning.* Cambridge, MA: MIT Press.

5. See Frances Jacobson Harris' chapter in particular: http://www.mitpressjournals. org/doi/abs/10.1162/dmal.9780262562324.155

to trained teachers and guides who can turn any negative online experience into a teachable moment, we prevent such experiences. Yet when they are alone online, we do nothing. Please note that I am not universally opposed to filters. I just think we use them as blunt instruments with little thought for the consequences.

The fourth divide that Todd Marshall points out is in terms of motivation. Members can have access to the online world, knowledge of how to use the tools, and permission to enter into the conversations. However, if they are unwilling to participate, the other three levels don't matter. This can best be summed up with the phrase, "You can lead a horse to water, but you can't make it drink." A librarian must understand what motivates participation.

Let's now break down these means of facilitation in greater detail. We start with one that for centuries has been seen as central to librarians and their core activities and values: access.

ACCESS

Access is getting a person to a conversation or some artifact of a conversation. As I have said, books, videos, journal articles, and so on aren't conversations, but they come from conversations. Although librarians have been focused on access to artifacts, digital networks allow librarians and their members to get closer and closer to the actual point of knowledge creation, the conversation itself. Now, you cannot only provide an article, but you can also get a member in touch directly with the article's author.

This new reality of access is easily seen in the sciences where open access publishing and online conversations have supplanted published journal articles as the primary means of sharing knowledge.[6] In many science disciplines, published articles have become archives of new knowledge and post-facto forums of official review. If one truly wants access to the physics conversation, for example, the best "resource" to point people to is online, real time, and ongoing. This trend seems to be expanding into other disciplines. Although open access publishing models have been adopted to various degrees, the concept of open access alone has put real pressure on faculty to post their pre-print versions of papers online and for associations and traditional journal publishers to increasingly provide low barrier access to articles.

Much of library education, and indeed library science as a whole, is focused on access. Cataloging, metadata, information retrieval, and

6. See, for example, http://arxiv.org

search engines are examples of access. Librarians have created an array of tools, such as subject classification, to make access to information and materials efficient and effective. To be precise, however, much of library science has been focused on providing access to artifacts. Access to actual conversations and knowledge has been a much more recent development, and still it is not well integrated into common library practice.

There is another aspect of access often overlooked by librarians—namely, that access for members is a two-way street. Not only do members need help to get to other people's conversations, they need help in providing access to their own knowledge and artifacts. This is a key part of new librarianship. The Ann Arbor case of sharing members' materials is one example, and Scapes is another. We need to stop thinking of librarianship as accumulating materials provided by other parties (publishers, websites, etc.) and then giving members access to our accumulation. We really need to stop thinking about access just in terms of materials!

Several libraries have implemented the idea of "checking out" librarians and other experts from the community. A member can have an hour with a librarian, firefighter, lawyer, accountant, and so on. One of the early ideas in the digital reference world was using librarians as an access point for an academic faculty. As member questions come in, librarians would build a system to route them to faculty and then store the answers and make them available. Faculty would benefit because librarians could weed out the repeated questions and only take the faculty's time with unique and relevant questions. This is access.

I foresee the day in the near future when librarians spend the majority of their time working with community members and community organizations making their content accessible: where acquisition is a matter of production, not purchasing. The future of libraries (and librarians) is in becoming publishers of the community.

Publisher of Community

So while Eli was telling me about the member sharing idea, he also talked about having "production librarians." Aside from some limited duties producing media projects for the library, they spend their time working as freelance production assistants with community members. The artifacts they produce are then made available through the library.

Once again, this is not, by itself, a radical new concept in librarianship. Historians ran most academic libraries a century ago because they were using the materials as part of their scholarship. What is new is the ability of the library to not only feed knowledge production but to self-produce and disseminate it as well.

This is not a call for every library to get into the publishing business. Why trade one set of crises for another? Rather, think in terms of being an access provider to the community. This means not only giving the community access to extra-community resources, as we primarily do now, but giving others access to the community—community-produced artifacts, members' expertise, community conversations, and so on. Instead of helping a member find a blog, host one for them.

Everything within the community, you ask? That depends on the community. Elsewhere in the Atlas (in the "Communities" Thread), I describe some topical centers developed as part of a planning process at the Free Library of Philadelphia: one in music, one in business, and one in writing. Both the music and writing centers had strong community publishing aspects. For the writers it was a print-on-demand service for member works, and for musicians it was a growing repository of community-created and performed music.

The remarkable thing is that the publishing standards for both differed radically. The writers wanted no filters or selection processes. If a member wrote it, it was in. The musicians, in contrast, only wanted to include scores and works that had been performed. A curator appointed by the community would be selecting what things were performed.

The point is that the community determined norms and review processes. In essence, they determined what would be published and how they wanted themselves presented both within and outside of the community.

This determination of publishing can push down to individual members. Can you share my digital reference questions? Can you share my circulation data? Can you share my Scape, story, song, profile? Members can decide.

It has always struck me as ironic that librarians are so concerned about privacy that we remove options from our members. In essence, we are making the same mistake with member privacy as policymakers made with credibility in the schools. In our zeal to protect members, we have taken away the best privacy classroom imaginable, leaving members to make their mistakes in commercial systems after they sign away all their rights. Part of being a community publisher and part of facilitating access is to promote a rich knowledge of privacy online and off.

I promised some specifics in this Thread, so let's get down to them. I'll tackle new perspectives on traditional access topics such as Information Organization and Collection Development in the "Librarian" Thread. For now, let me present two immediate access ideas that at first glance involve physical spaces.

Shared Shelves with the Community

I love the Free Library of Philadelphia. One of the reasons I love the Free Library, aside from the incredible people who work there, is that it was there I saw my first original Maxfield Parrish work. It is housed, along with the stuffed raven that is said to have inspired Edgar Allen Poe, in the Rare Book Department on the top floor of the Central Library. Also in that department on the top floor you will find the entire library of William McIntire Elkins. I don't mean just his book, I mean his entire physical library, including desk, carpet, and even simulations of the views out of his windows. The room and materials were a gift to the library. It makes the stories of donated National Geographic magazines seem quaint, doesn't it?

Librarians have a long tradition of taking donated works. Community libraries can begin with donated books, scholars leave their papers, artists bequeath paintings, and rich Philadelphians, apparently, sometimes donate parts of their houses. But these donated free materials are, as the saying goes, free like puppies. They require care and upkeep. Librarians routinely catalog the items, shelve them, and, in some cases, preserve and secure them.

But what if they didn't? What if, like Eli Neiburger's member-sharing tools, the materials were just collocated with other librarian-controlled resources? Why not just give a community group some space? Here historical society are 10 linear feet—do with them as you please. Here manga student group is your book case. Here Mrs. Hlywa's English class is your shelf. If you would like them to be findable in the catalog, it will cost you this much. If you are worried about them staying in order, I would suggest you have a member of your organization show up once or twice a day/week/month to take care of that.

Yes but, you say, if we give space to one group, we must give it to all who ask. Why? Policy. Who sets policy? People. If the policy doesn't allow it, the policy needs to be changed. If it is a university policy, then go to the university. If it is a city policy, go to the city.

But how will we know what belongs where when we find it on the table? Put a sticker on it. But what if it is stolen? That's the chance the partnering organization decided to take. Remember when I started this Thread and I talked about how true facilitation means shared ownership? The flip side is shared responsibility and risk.

Tim Spalding, who created LibraryThing, once talked about how people tag a lot more items on LibraryThing than on Amazon.com (13 million tags versus 1.3 million).[7] His conclusion from this was the following:

> Tagging works well when people tag "their" stuff, but it fails when they're asked to do it to "someone else's" stuff. You can't get your customers to organize your products, unless you give them a very good incentive. We all make our beds, but nobody volunteers to fluff pillows at the local Sheraton.

Don't worry, I'm not diving back into the whole "of the people or by the people" thing, but I want to make a much more tactical point here. The more we instill a sense of ownership in the physical spaces we maintain and the artifacts within them, the more the community will trust and use those spaces. Why stop at our physical spaces? What about offering up digital shared shelves as well?

At a federal agency, I met a man who had developed a history of that agency. He had done it for internal purposes, but he knew that many folks outside of government were interested in it. In fact, he received regular requests for it. He was worried about the integrity of the document, so with every request, he would print it out and send the artifact via the postal service. I suggested that the agency library might be able to help out. Sure enough, the library was able to create a secured PDF version of the document and put it online. They also agreed to print it out on demand as long as the author (or rather the author's department) would cover the postage. The document lived on the library's website, but the responsibility of maintaining the document also stayed with the author. The library website became, in a limited way, a true information commons.

But what if the document gets out of date? Or the author wants to pull it down, the server gets hacked, or the encryption on the document is broken? Yup, these risks exist. They are, however, shared by both parties.

At this point, if I were saying this in a presentation, I would most likely have a government librarian (perhaps federal or state) who will begin citing policies about public information and such. In fact, one of my favorite stories happened at a national library in the United States. For those of you outside of the United States, realize that we don't have just one national library, but rather we have a bunch in medicine, agriculture, education, and even transportation. For a while in the 1990s, it was all the rage to start a national library on some topic.

In any case, this national library received a notification that it had to take any access to the library's catalog off the web. Why? Because it allowed people to access nongovernmental information. Seriously. There was agency policy that said that no information produced outside the agency could be disseminated through the website. The catalog was doing just that because the catalog was providing access to the holdings of the national library, and it turns out the agency had not in fact authored all the books in the catalog. So there you go. There was a policy. The case was clearly closed.

Except it wasn't. The librarians went to bat. They talked with the agency lawyers, they sent memos, and they ultimately made a convincing case that the library was a special place, and the catalog was fundamentally different than a report or agency publication. And the agency agreed.

For every case I have cited of a policy that prevented action, I have a case of a librarian who changed the policy, found a loophole, or just did it anyway and got away with it. When you are of the people (OK, I lied, I am going there) and your services are of the people, the people support it. Shared shelving, both physical and virtual, is one way to ensure that the community knows that not only your operations are at stake, but their well-being is as well. Another way to remind them of their own self-interest is to hold a meeting—literally.

*Meeting Spaces**

In the U.S. federal government, there is something called "convening power." It means that a governmental body is authorized to bring people together—literally, the power to have meetings with folks outside of itself. Frankly, it sounds like one of the weaker governmental powers compared with things such as spying, arresting, and waging war, but it is an amazingly effective tool for getting things done (although it does make a poor recruiting poster: Join the government and you too can go to MEETINGS!). Bringing people together for conversations, particularly the right people, is how things get done (it is, after all, the way knowledge is created).

7. http://www.librarything.com/thingology/2007/02/when-tags-works-and-when-they-dont.php
*See Agreement Supplement for some ideas of types of meeting spaces and links to the literature.

If you are ever in Philadelphia, go visit Independence Hall. It was where:

George Washington was appointed commander in chief of the Continental Army in 1775 and the Declaration of Independence was adopted on July 4, 1776. In the same room the design of the American flag was agreed upon in 1777, the Articles of Confederation were adopted in 1781, and the U.S. Constitution was drafted in 1787.[8]

What struck me when I went was how small it was. It had no marble, no statues, no mall, or obelisks. It was a spartan room with simple tables. No more than 50 or so people could cram themselves into the space, a far cry from the palaces of Europe or the monuments of Rome. Yet in this small space something remarkable happened. A few of the right people came together and changed the world. Librarians must use this power of convening to improve their communities. They must provide access to the right members.

Sure enough, no library is built or redesigned today without some meeting space. Yet nowhere in the ALA Core Competencies is there a spot for meeting planning or space management. I know of no LIS curriculum that offers a party-planning elective. This, of course, is an example of an artifact-centric view. Why worry about how people meet when we need to manage stuff and manage people to manage stuff? Access is about getting to stuff, right? It's like we teach people how to buy the party favors and bake the cake, but we forget to invite anyone to celebrate.

Access to things is one sort of access, but it is insufficient. We need to provide access to members, and in the physical world that means giving them a place to meet.

I do not pretend to be an architect. I do not offer you diagrams and floor plans, but I share some of the elements of meeting spaces that seem to work. The first is flexibility. Walls need to be able to move, and tables need to be able to push together or disappear altogether. Seats need to be comfortable. Windows need to show the time of day but darken easily. Oh, and the room needs to be agnostic to time and space.

Huh?

In 1776, it was imperative for representatives of the colony to travel to Philadelphia. Today they would need to videoconference. They would need to come together, yes, but only for the final roll-up-their-sleeves-browbeat-Adams-into-submission-photo-op part of the

8. http://www.nps.gov/inde/independence-hall-1.htm

process. Today's librarian-provided meeting spaces need to be hybrid. Those who can attend in person should be able to connect to the Internet seamlessly and wirelessly. They should have ample tools to synthesize what they find with SMART Boards and wall-sized white boards. Those who can't get to the place need to video and/or audio conference in (plus see and interact with the white boards). Those who can't get there at the right time should be able to see what happened and leave their own thoughts.

Mind you, this is a rather generic picture, and the community will ultimately need to dictate the capabilities of that hybrid space (including seeing what the community can afford). A music librarian might want access to a performance space. An art librarian may want a studio space or a gallery space. The emphasis is on the hybrid nature of the place.

Now, here is the kicker: We need digital meeting rooms as well. Calling for cool and connected meeting spaces in libraries these days is like calling for indoor plumbing. So why is it that librarians, who are busy building great places to get together in real space, build websites that aren't?

Here's another quick story. My wife and several of her friends began a Moms Club. The idea was for them to organize play dates, field trips for the kids, and get-togethers for nights out, and to be a general support group of mothers with small children. The group quickly became a sort of barter economy, where high chairs and car seats found new homes or were loaned out for family vacations. Over time, the group went from 10 and 12 members to 50, and it is now about 500 members strong. It quickly grew beyond a phone tree and monthly organizing meetings. They needed a better way to communicate, and online made good sense. They looked around for a place to post messages, minutes, opportunities, and such.

Being the geek type that I am, I set them up a website. It got hacked. I set up another one. It got hacked. They needed something to rely on, and they finally turned to Yahoo! Groups. It served their needs, and life was good.

My question: Where was the library? Here was a local community group that was all about building and sharing knowledge on parenting. Its members needed a place to meet. They did use library meeting rooms for events, and many of the activities involved public library services. But when they went online, the library wasn't there. Why not? Why was it possible for the library to accommodate people in a building but not online?

The answer is that librarians keep looking at the online environment as a place to provide information, not as a place to facilitate

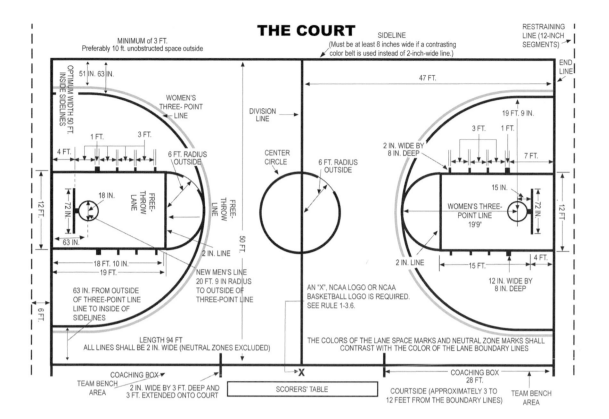

THE COURT   Figure 39

knowledge and conversation. We broadcast our catalogs and our physical presences, but when it actually comes to doing work and building a community, our services consist of asking one-on-one digital reference questions and putting things on hold (feel free to read that as a metaphor).

In academia, for example, professors and scholars are getting funded to do research. An increasing number of these efforts involve some form of online dissemination or community building (advisory panels, workshops, etc.). Scholars expert in their topical areas rarely are also masters of web building. What's more, as Helen Tibbo points out, they are even worse about archiving their online work.[9] Where are the librarians to facilitate access to their work both in process and after the fact? Things are getting better, with librarians now offering to host workgroup servers and faculty blogs, but these are not universal services, and little thought has been put into how these project-specific sites fit into the librarians' online reality.

Excuse me while I digress a moment on language use. Note that I keep talking about librarians' presence online. Libraries have web pages like Mickey Mouse has a Facebook profile–he didn't really do it. Librarians build web pages and need to take responsibility for that. If the library website sucks, it is the fault of the librarians not the bricks and mortar. Calling it "the library's website" is technically called "anthropomorphizing" (from the *Oxford English Dictionary*, "the attribution of human characteristics or behavior to a god, animal, or object"), and it is a grammatical no-no.

If the librarian's job is to facilitate knowledge creation through conversation, the tools that librarians build should do so as well. It is all nice and easy to talk about meeting spaces online and in real space, but as I already said, walls don't make a library. Neither does code. Conversations can be easy, tense, avoided, rancorous, or boring. To facilitate is to guide and ensure that no matter the mode, knowledge is gleaned. Access to the space, as we see, is vital but insufficient.

Let me end our discussion of access with an analogy. Barbara Quint once compared a library after hours to a coral reef without the fish.[10] Beautiful but formed not as sculpture or interesting shaped rocks all at once, but as a result of life and action. I, without Quint's eloquence, instead see it as a basketball court. Take a look at the basketball court diagramed in figure 39. It is a rectangle bisected in the

9. http://www.ibiblio.org/minds/
10. http://www.infotoday.com/searcher/jun06/voice.shtml

center with hoops on posts at either end. Under each hoop, or basket, is a painted rectangle (or trapezoid in some leagues). There is a semicircle that radiates onto the court from each end.

You can tell a lot just by looking at the court. From the shape of the free-throw line, you can tell whether you are in North America or Europe. The distance of the three-point line to the basket tells whether you are playing college ball or professional. You can tell where play begins (the center circle) and even where players will stand for free throws. The physical surface represents the rules of the game. Yet it is nothing. The surface and the lines do not play the game, they are paint. It is the players who make watching and playing the sport worthwhile. By knowing how to structure the court, you have no idea how the game will end up or even how it will be played (strategy). What's more, you don't even need the court to play the game. On asphalt parking lots and driveways around the United States, kids play just fine. Around the world, they play with literal baskets on hard-packed earth.

Build meeting spaces. Build physical ones with comfy couches and huge displays. Build virtual meeting spaces and host blogs. But remember that by doing so you have simply painted the lines on the court. For your members to play, they need coaches, referees, and even an audience. They also need to know the rules of the game, which leads to our next major area of facilitation.

KNOWLEDGE

If access to artifacts or conversations were sufficient for knowledge, then anyone with Internet access would be brilliant. In fact, some have argued that access can in fact provide on-demand or commoditized knowledge. Today there is a discussion of the end of memory and the end of theory because of the massive quantity of easy-to-access information.

David Weinberger, the author of *Everything Is* Miscellaneous,[11] talks about a meeting where the topic of the 1996 Telecommunications Act was being discussed.[12] One colleague not familiar with the law went online and read a Wikipedia article on the topic, increased their knowledge in real time, and therefore could better participate in the conversation. In fact, while I am literally going to skim over it here, this is much of the thinking behind Selective Dissemination of Information (SDI)—get people select packets of information and let them absorb it on demand. It may be true that a person can come up to speed quickly with a visit to Wikipedia, but it misses the fact that the increase in knowledge did not come from simply accessing the page. For example, the colleague had to know how to read and had to have a working knowledge of the English language. They had to know that Wikipedia exists. They probably had to have a basic concept of telecommunications and law. The point is, they were adding to their existing knowledge, which was the result of a huge number of previous conversations.

Librarians have understood this need to go beyond access for some time in the form of instructional librarians. From earlier concepts of bibliographic instruction,[13] instructional librarians have now engaged members to increase their basic information-seeking skills. Academic librarians are offering students tutoring services and creating spaces to collocate library and instructional assistance services. This concept of instruction is also evident in how reference librarians are prepared. Reference staff are taught to go beyond simply providing answers and provide instruction—to not merely provide information but teach the member how to search independently.

Library Instruction *

However, librarians are only now confronting the reality of instruction, and that is the need for better integration into the complete instructional environment of their members and the reality that true instruction requires evaluation. For example, if a professor simply stood before a room and talked on a topic for 30 minutes, does that necessarily mean that anyone learned? It is impossible to tell without evaluating the impact of the talk on the audience members. Whether it is a test, accomplishment of a task, or even some ethnographic study on changed behaviors, without evaluation it is impossible to determine whether learning truly occurred. It is this logic that underlies an increasing shift from outputs to outcome-based evaluation by accrediting agencies (there is more about this in the Assessment agreement).

The need for librarians to move beyond access grounds the need for instructional skills in all librarians regardless of title or function. Reference staff, technical staff, and administrators are all part of the instructional process and need to have a true sense of how to teach

11. Weinberger, D. (2008). *Everything is miscellaneous: The power of the new digital disorder*. New York: Holt Paperbacks.
12. http://www.kmworld.com/Articles/Column/David-Weinberger/The-commoditization-of-knowledge-40810.aspx
13. Please, please, please stop using this phrase, or worse BI.
*See Agreement Supplement for citations on library instruction.

and how to evaluate the effectiveness of that teaching. Although certainly some librarians will develop a deeper understanding and set of instruction skills, basic knowledge of learning is important to all librarians. It is also time to expand what we call information literacy.

I was taught information literacy by the best: Mike Eisenberg. He, with Bob Berkowitz, created the Big 6 Information Literacy skills system.[14] The name comes from the six primary steps someone should take in solving an information problem (not necessarily in order):

1. Task Definition, where you define the information problem and identify the information needed to solve it.
2. Information Seeking, where you use strategies to determine all possible relevant sources and then select the best sources to use.
3. Location and Access, where you locate sources (intellectual and physical) and find information within sources.
4. Use of Information, where you engage (e.g., read, hear, view, touch) information and extract relevant information.
5. Synthesis, where you organize information from multiple sources and present the information.
6. Evaluation, where you judge the product (effectiveness) and process (efficiency).

The other thing I learned from Mike was how to take a good idea and apply it everywhere you can. Mike and Bob have the Super 3, the Little 12, bookmarks, cards, videos, and workshops, and I'm sure if you asked they'd make Big 6 boxer shorts.

While I haven't sat down with Mike to see how the Big 6 and the new librarianship outlined within the Atlas match up, my guess (not surprisingly) is that there would be a pretty big overlap. After all, it is not a far stretch to talk about defining the knowledge needed, coming up with strategies to determine the necessary conversations, locate those conversations (including within yourself), engage conversants, synthesize (relate) the agreements that come from the conversation, and then evaluate how effective your new knowledge and the learning processes were.

Yet the Big 6 (and, to be equitable in my praise, Kuhlthau's work on information literacy[15] is also very good, although it has seven steps and no bookmarks) and much of information literacy show an unstated bias toward artifacts and the things from which we can extract information.

In information literacy courses, librarians emphasize artifacts: how to pick good ones, how to search for them, how to cite them,

and even a good dose of how to process them with technology tools. Don't get me wrong, these are still vital skills. However, we also need to teach about effective communication skills. Eisenberg has another legacy in which I am well versed. He helped create IST 444 or "4 x4" (four-by-four) as he called it. It is an undergraduate course taught at Syracuse University's iSchool, where he was a doctoral student and then faculty member.

The 4x4 class was developed because the faculty noted that students were getting good at system design and analysis but had real problems communicating the solutions they developed. In essence, they came up with a great recipe but couldn't teach people how to cook. The solution was a course in information presentation and design. Students would learn how to transform information technology solutions into effective presentations, online materials, and even technical manuals. The course is still one of the most requested courses at the school.

Librarians can impart all the instruction they want on how to search and evaluate sources, but if we don't also facilitate the knowledge of transforming all of that new knowledge into an effective conversation (online, in person, or otherwise), we have created a closed loop with limited benefit to the community in general. So information literacy must include the idea of conversational literacy. Indeed, concepts of new librarianship call for a host of expansions in all sorts of literacy.

Need for an Expanded Definition of Literacy

I hate the READ posters.[16] There, I've said it.

OK, I don't hate the posters (the one with Yoda is my favorite). It just drives me crazy that:

1. The most successful collective marketing effort of libraries is around a task that people can do regardless of whether a librarian or library is involved, and
2. We portray reading as something to fall in love with versus something that is an essential skill in today's society. It would be like mathematicians putting up pictures of Britney Spears talking about the seductive lure of long division.

14. http://www.big6.com/what-is-the-big6/
15. Kuhlthau, C. C. (2004). *Seeking meaning: A process approach to library and information services.* Westport, CT: Libraries Unlimited.
16. http://www.alastore.ala.org/searchresult.aspx?categoryid=158

What I would put in their place is Ask posters. This idea has made a few rounds on the dig_ref listserv,[17] and its time has come. We need some way to inspire people to learn and explore, and we need to show that librarians are valuable resources in that process.

If there are sacred cows in librarianship—and who are we kidding, we mint them regularly—none is more sacrosanct than literacy. Let's face it, reading is a good thing, but we have built a substantial mythology around it that is not altogether healthy. Why just read books? Why do people have to love reading? I read. Do I love to read? No. It just turns out it is the most efficient way to get to what I like: good stories, good thinking, and so on. I read because it gives me power! A funny word, power—I'd like to think on it for a moment.

In the health care debate occurring in the United States as I write this, there is an interesting bit of political theater going on. Across the country, town hall meetings with members of Congress are being disrupted by an organized protest campaign. A spokesman for the group responsible for at least some of this organizing, Freedom Works, was interviewed on my favorite NPR show, *On the Media*.[18]

In the interview, Freedom Works spokesman Adam Brandon said something interesting. He says the first thing anyone does that joins the very right-leaning organization is read Saul Alinsky's *Rules for Radicals*,[19] a handbook written by a far left radical during the unrest of the 1960s. It is a fascinating read.

Alinsky wrote the book out of "desperation, partly because it is what they [the youth, particularly the youth protesting the Vietnam War] do and will do that will give meaning to what I and the radicals of my generation have done with our lives." In essence, he was frustrated because of a leadership crisis. The radicals who fought so hard against McCarthyism had died, been imprisoned, or simply disappeared, and there was no one left to teach the art of protest to the next generation. "My fellow radicals who were supposed to pass on the torch of experience and insights to a new generation just were not there."[20]

What follows throughout the book are extreme and explicitly Machiavellian tactics for achieving change, some of which we return to in the "Improve Society" Thread. What I want to point out, however, is Alinsky's take on the word "power."

The question may legitimately be raised, why not use other words—words that mean the same but are peaceful, and do not result in such negative emotional reactions? There are a number of fundamental reasons for rejecting such substitution. First, by using combination of words such as "harnessing the energy" instead of the single word "power," we begin to dilute the meaning; and as we use purifying synonyms, we dissolve the bitterness, the anguish, the hate and love, the agony and the triumph attached to these words, leaving an aseptic imitation of life.[21]

I told you it was a fascinating read.

Power is not bad or evil. Alinsky would say the evil is when you don't have power. Without power you don't make decisions, things are decided for you. Librarians need to be powerful. They need to be able to shape agendas, lead the community, and empower members to do the same. We seek out power not as an end but as a means to make the world a better place. To serve, to truly serve, you need to be powerful so you can steward the community.

Why this trip through radicalism and political protest? Because it lies at the heart of how we are to interpret the role of literacy in librarianship. If we see the role of librarians as supplementing other educational processes (teaching reading in schools or literacy organizations, or supporting parents), then literacy is a somewhat limited concept. It is something done by public libraries and school libraries. After all, corporate, medical, and, for that matter, academic librarians just don't have as their main drivers basic skills in reading and writing.

However, if we look at literacy as empowerment, literally to gain power, then we have a different take on literacy altogether. Librarians, I would argue, need to view literacy as a means of acquiring power—more often than not, power for the powerless. I can already hear the chorus talk about the role of libraries in pleasure reading. Am I calling for a purely utilitarian agency that only contains textbooks and technology manuals? Far from it.

In the *Rules for Radicals*, Alinsky lays out characteristics of a good leader. The first three? Curiosity, irreverence, and imagination. Want a radical text? *Tom Sawyer*, *Harry Potter*, *Twilight*, *1984*, *Catcher in the Rye*, *The Fountainhead* (for me in high school, it was *My Name Is Asher Lev*). Even a Danielle Steele novel can tell us something about ourselves (what we like, what we hope for, the escapes we seek). Fiction is every bit as empowering and radical as any manifesto. I'm not saying that all reading is deliberately targeted toward "fighting the man." I

17. http://www.ub.uni-dortmund.de/listen/inetbib/msg04148.html
18. http://www.onthemedia.org/transcripts/2009/08/07/01
19. Alinsky, S. D. (1971). *Rules for radicals: A practical primer for realistic radicals*. New York: Random House.
20. Pages xiii–xiv.
21. Ibid, Alinksy.

am simply asking that you think of literacy not as a pleasant activity or even a socially agreed-on skill. Rather, I ask you to see literacy as a proactive act of power, a necessary skill in service not to some larger societal ideal, but for the power of the individual.

Once again, I don't claim this is my unique conception. Literacy efforts around the world are geared toward immigrants and the underclass. Banned book week is all about literacy as power. Do you want people to read so they will be too distracted to notice they have no power? Do you want people to read so that they obey the rules? Or do you want them to participate in democratic processes (including voting and peaceful protest) to ensure the rules are right? Do you want them to read to question the rules? Perhaps Yoda's glass eyes staring at me from the READ poster is something more than a nod to the pleasantries of reading. Perhaps in the puppet face of a wise old Jedi master is a gleam of the revolutionary.

Of course librarians, as with the rest of society, can't resist taking useful words and bending and expanding their meaning. Literacy has come to mean much more than reading and writing. With modifiers, literacy has come to mean ability or proficiency in something. So "information literacy" is not about reading information, it is about a proficiency in accessing and using information. The same is true for math literacy, economic literacy, technical literacy, and so on. Most of these areas concern themselves with some sense of mastery: To be literate in something means to be proficient. But what if we take a "power" perspective?

To be "literate in" means to be able to use something to gain power. Now librarians in all situations have literacy as their core skill. It is not just librarians in the public sphere or the schools that promote literacy. No, in our new librarianship, we facilitate literacy in members to empower. Reading, writing, processing information, and gaming (as we see) are not exclusively about passing the time or doing well in established tasks. No, literacy is about the power to excel and, when necessary, break the rules to improve society and the community.

With this expanded notion of literacy—librarians facilitating skills in the acquisition of power—let's look at just two examples beyond reading and writing. Although both of them look trendy and some have dismissed them as just about passing the time, they are, in fact, vital ways of understanding and acquiring power.

Gaming*

If you would like a clear example of where a type of literacy can be used to empower or placate, take a look at gaming. Scott Nicholson takes games very seriously. As a professor at Syracuse University's iSchool, he takes gaming in libraries very very seriously, and he has built his research agenda around it. As part of this work, he looked at the history of gaming in libraries. He found a very interesting article about how gaming was used in 1800s England for "moral betterment." Libraries built billiard halls, smoking parlors, and game rooms to lure members out of the pubs and into a more respectable establishment.[22] Here gaming was used not to grant power but to reify the power of the prevailing cultural norms. It is more than a bit ironic, then, that there is so much debate about gaming in libraries today.

So how can librarians use gaming to empower members and facilitate knowledge creation? Well, we have already discussed the use of gaming to build L_1 language use in the "Knowledge" Thread. With respect to language games—and here I am talking about videogames, board games, card games, puzzles, really a whole class of structured activities that depend strongly on internal motivation of the participants—have really shown an amazingly effective way to turn internal motivation (I want to play the game) into effective knowledge building (therefore I need to learn the rules) and storytelling (and I learn the rules by playing the game).

But gaming allows for a whole host of literacy instruction, from the basic forms of literacy where children must learn to read to really play Pokemon games, to complex information literacy activities. Take, for example, one of my favorite games of all time: Myst.[23] I wasn't alone in my love (and addiction) to Myst when it was released in the 1993. It was the best-selling game of all time until 2002.[24]

As you wander through rendered landscapes of an island with an odd assortment of buildings and statues, you have to piece together what is going on (classic Big 6-style task definition). In fact, throughout the game's different challenges and levels (well, worlds in Myst), you go through all the levels of information literacy activities from locating information sources, to putting them together (synthesis), to evaluating your process.

*See Agreement Supplement for more on gaming in libraries.
22. http://www.youtube.com/watch?v=Hdg0FdhKEJ4
23. http://en.wikipedia.org/wiki/Myst
24. http://www.gamespot.com/pc/strategy/simslivinlarge/news_2857556.html

When I first built the AskERIC Virtual Library, a website for the Department of Education's ERIC program, I always had images of slipping behind the virtual stacks in a Myst-like way. I can still imagine embedding games in the tools that librarians provide their members. Want to teach undergraduates about the physical library facilities? Host a murder[25] and have them go from floor to floor to solve it.

If that sounds odd, look at what Dan Brown and his publisher did with *The Da Vinci Code*.[26] The book was covered in puzzles, anagrams, and clues. Online you could start a game that involved going to other websites, making phone calls, and reading other books. Talk about effective viral marketing! Librarians can go beyond marketing their services by highlighting gaming, and they can use gaming to market their services. This, of course, would be using gaming literacy to empower librarians as much as their members.

What I have always found impressive is that the best librarians I know treat their work as gaming. I have some friends who are good reference librarians. I mean really good ones. We're talking the kind of folks "who chase you out of the building because they just found that one other article" kind of good. The kind of folks who pray to Saint Christopher, the patron saint of lost things, just in case it gives them that extra edge. To them, the search for information is a game.

I know catalogers who take the concept of literary warrant as a sort of game with language. There is a great presentation by Erin McKean, a lexicographer at the *Oxford English Dictionary*, who saw her job not as being a gatekeeper of words but as being a fisherman of language seeking out new words and their meaning,[27] language as a game.

The most amazing library directors I have met are gamers. Their playing fields are universities, municipal governments, and bureaucracies. Their pieces are services and budgets. Before they begin negotiating with unions, they devour collective bargaining agreements like rulebooks and see the union representatives as respected players, as both challengers and fellow gamers.

Gaming should not be a loss leader for librarians. Do not use gaming programs to get "the kids" into the library so you can trick them into reading. Your goal with literacy is empowerment, power to create knowledge. Gaming, when done right, will accomplish these goals on its own.

Of course, that is if you can find enough free computers and tables from people updating their Facebook profiles.

*Social Literacy**

So we all know that social networking sites on the Internet are a new milestone in the annals of human history—or they are built on fundamental human needs to be part of a group that is as old as the species itself. MySpace is a site about personal empowerment and self-expression—or the best place for trolling pedophiles. Twitter is a waste of time or, of course, the new public square. Facebook is for the young—or the middle-aged. Trendy, old school, revisionary, evolutionary, retrograde. It's enough to make a librarian long for the good old days of microfiche versus microfilm.

Brian Williams, the anchor of NBC's "Nightly News," once joked about using his iPod Touch in an elevator. A colleague excitedly told him that they now had an app where he could listen to live streaming audio, to which Williams replied, "So would that make it a radio?" The point being that just because something is new it is not necessarily original.

This Atlas is about deep concepts that span any specific technology, and so when I talk about social literacy, I must talk beyond Facebook, MySpace, or even digital applications. To be sure, these tools highlight issues, but they are persistent issues that span human social interactions. We have already touched on privacy and the fact that what you share on Facebook is a teachable moment with the concept of sharing, not sharing, and consequences. We have also tackled the need for communication skills.

Add to these "literacy" ideas of authenticity, credibility, and social good. I would sum these up as issues of identity. To be sure, identity is an internal issue. How we come to understand who we are and what we believe is an important part of being human. Librarians can facilitate this process, although they might want to leave good parts of this to spiritual leaders and psychologists. Identity is also about who we are externally or how we present ourselves to each other. Social literacy can be summed up as the power of identity in groups.

One of the problems that librarians have with facilitating this literacy of identity is the frighteningly simplistic ways that librarians have defined identity within a library. Within most library organizations, there are two identities: "librarian" and "not librarian." Who gets to add records to the catalog? Librarians. Who gets to change a

25. The game "Host a Murder" please…do not really murder anyone.
26. Brown, D. (2003). *The Da Vinci code: A novel*. New York: Doubleday.
27. http://www.ted.com/talks/lang/eng/erin_mckean_redefines_the_dictionary.html
**See Agreement Supplement for more on social literacy and a librarian's role in promoting it.*

record? Librarians. If an author runs across an error in the record for one of my books, can he or she change it? Nope, he or she is not a librarian.

This identity has even affected the relationship between librarians and other professionals and paraprofessionals. I can't tell you the number of talented folks I meet in libraries that, if hit by a bus, would stop major library operations dead and yet who are not afforded equal respect by librarians with a master's of library science (MLS). Can't there be a way to earn entrance into the club outside of a large student loan? Librarians must start to think of themselves as a meritocracy, where we take on the power to expand and collapse our social group; to include members and other people in order to extend our power—our power to do good, to affect technology, to further the needs of the community, to increase our ability to facilitate knowledge creation.

The process of doing this—of defining and expanding social groupings to further our aims—is social literacy. Just as you need to master it, so too you need to facilitate it in your members. Teach folks how to get on Facebook, limit access to their sensitive information online, and teach them how to communicate. Then teach them how to market themselves and how to organize others to form movements around their aims.

Whether you sit on the right or the left, conservative, liberal, progressive, fundamentalist, communist, or anarchist, you are in the power business. As librarians, you gather power to impart it in others, but you still must be adept at gathering power. As a librarian, you do so through social action, by working with others. This Atlas makes the argument that this is all done through conversation; and make no mistake about it, librarianship is a radical profession, and literacy is a radical topic.

ENVIRONMENT

So far we have talked about people getting to a conversation (or taking their conversation to people) and preparing them to participate in it as equals (access and knowledge). Now we need to ensure that they feel safe to participate, create, and learn. Safety here refers to both a sense of physical safety, often emphasized in public library settings, and intellectual and cultural safety.

Librarians use safety to facilitate knowledge in many contexts. When you moderate an Internet mailing list to prevent spamming and flaming, you are providing the subscribers with a sense of safety (I can open my inbox to this feed). When you design an effective user interface to a web application, you provide safety (I don't think I'm going to break this). Perhaps an area where you can serve a major need in your community is by moderating in-person meetings, ensuring safety from those seeking to dominate the conversation, or sidelining a conversant.

I was part of a review panel for a new untenured faculty member. During our discussions, the panel identified a need for the faculty member to participate more fully in meetings. "It seems like you come to meetings and then remain quiet," we said. "You have a lot to contribute, and we all benefit from you sharing your ideas." We then went into a discourse about how we are a faculty of one and need for all the members to share. It was pretty close to a "we're a big happy family, and no one is allowed to skip dinner-time discussion" theme.

The untenured faculty member's response floored us. "I would, but I don't feel welcome to do so. I tried this in my first year, and it was made clear that my opinion wasn't needed."

"How so?"

"There are folks who have been on this faculty for a long time, and every time I'd offer an opinion, I would get a long history lesson on the topic."

There it was. The thing we on the panel most valued, participation, was threatened by something else we equally valued, a durable and long-standing culture. In essence, we expected participation, but we had created a situation where this faculty member didn't feel safe sharing. Needless to say, it seemed as if the panel had failed the review, and a lot of healthy conversations about collegiality ensued.

Librarians should be able to facilitate meetings, ensuring equal participation and safety. Imagine the positive benefits of a reputation for running effective meetings among a faculty, business, or community. Imagine what you can learn about the knowledge needs of a community by being directly part of the knowledge-creation conversation.

Then there is that power thing that pops up again. One of the lessons I learned early when pursuing funding was to always volunteer to write the proposal. If you are in a meeting brainstorming a funding opportunity, volunteer to write up the proposal. While everyone sees you doing this activity as saving them time, it is guaranteeing that you are part of the proposal and get the last word on the resources that come out of it.

Librarians have long considered questions of intellectual safety as well. With concepts of intellectual freedom and privacy, one could argue that safety is a core value of any library. It would be simple to say that as a librarian you need to have policy skills and a deep understanding of privacy and intellectual property and leave it at that. However, the question of environment is more complicated. Allow me to revisit the areas of privacy and intellectual freedom.

Conversation theory tells us that memory, the ability to recall concepts and artifacts and their relationships, is vitally important. In essence, new learning is scaffold on previous learning. If the library is about facilitating knowledge, it must be about supporting a member's (student's, scholar's, employee's) memory. Yet can a member find out from the library the books he or she checked out previously? Can the member annotate journal articles in our online tools to highlight and revisit key points? Can the member see all the articles flagged in a previous search? To be sure there are some, and fortunately there is an increasing number of librarians who can say yes to these questions. However, many librarian-created policies and library software prevent such memory features because of a fear of retaining member data. In essence, the policy of many librarian-created environments works against the intended work of librarians and facilitating knowledge.

Then there is the additional unintended consequence to building an environment on a simplistic view of member privacy that I raised before. Rather than teaching members how to make effective privacy choices (understanding the consequences of giving out personal information) in the safe librarian-mediated environment, librarians tend to enforce a monolithic view of retaining no personal data, making any real conversation of privacy in the library meaningless. Rather than librarians choosing a single approach to privacy, it would be better for us to be equipped to have a privacy conversation with our communities and determine appropriate privacy policies based on the needs and understanding of that community.

Another more nuanced approach to policy can be seen in content filtering. A public library I visited did not filter their computers. Members could visit any site they wished. The local police learned that registered sex offenders were visiting this public library, as was their right. The police, as was their right, on a regular basis started visiting the library and standing behind members using the public access computers watching for banned Internet usage. The net effect was that they were watching all members in an obvious way, creating a chilling effect within the library. To get the police not to provide such an obvious and chilling presence, the librarians installed content filters (which could be turned off by librarians on member request). The effect was a greater sense of intellectual safety for the patrons because they didn't have authorities watching over their shoulders. The

public library example is hardly an endorsement of filtering. Rather, it demonstrates that true environmental facilitation requires a complex understanding of policy and principles.

Many examples could be given of good services that were shut down by lawyers and managers out of fear of breaching policy. If a librarian does not have a good grasp of policy and legal issues, service may suffer out of an "assume the answer is no" mentality. I'll spend a lot more time on this in the "Improve Society" Thread when we get to talk about policy in some depth.

One last thing I have to say before we leave our discussion of environment: A safe environment is necessary, but we should look at that as a sort of least common denominator. What we really want to build are compelling, challenging, and inspiring environments where members feel comfortable enough to risk and reach. To get to this place, we must mix environments and motivation. We'll talk about this in much greater depth in the different environments under the "Communities" Thread, but for now let's talk about motivation.

MOTIVATION

So the member is at the conversation, knows what is going on, and feels safe to participate. Mission accomplished, right? Well it may seem obvious, but if the member does not want to engage in the conversation or is not incented to do so, the conversation will not occur. Librarians often underplay the importance of motivation in conversations. Members often seek out the library and its resources of their own accord or are compelled to do so for assignments.

Efforts to market the library are a partial response to the question of motivation. Marketing campaigns seek to raise awareness of the library (note here that I am deliberately not using the term "librarians") and, if they are properly targeted, can motivate a person to use the library. However, all too often these approaches seek to bring people to the library, rather than to bring the library to the person or, even further, to bring the librarian to the people.

I have to take a second out of our motivation conversation to say that you have got to resent playing second fiddle to an integrated library system. I mean seriously, stop putting pictures of the building on the web page and start putting people on it. It's like promoting a Rolling Stones concert by printing sheet music on the poster. ("Oh look honey! A B flat!") OK, I'm better now. Where were we? Oh yes, how to use existing or intrinsic motivation to market librarians (note here that I am deliberately not using the term "libraries").

Intrinsic

Let's take as an example the question of faculty tenure in a university. A colleague preparing his tenure package called the library looking for help doing a citation analysis. Because publication and citation analysis form the bulk of tenure consideration at his university, he wanted to know how many times he had been cited and by whom. The librarian he talked with told him they would be glad to spend an hour to show him or his graduate assistant how to use Web of Science.

Now, think about that response and ask yourself what it is really saying. It is saying that the most important professional task in a professor's career warranted about an hour of time and, even worse, that the entire considerable bibliographic skill set of a professional librarian could be imparted to a graduate assistant in an hour.

What if, instead, knowing that faculty are highly motivated in terms of citation analysis and tenure librarians proactively reached out to faculty members coming up for tenure to interview them and work with them to do a citation analysis? This would recognize the intrinsic motivation of the faculty member (the need for tenure) and the crucial extrinsic motivation from the faculty member's department. There is no better opportunity to demonstrate the value of a librarian in a university. What's more, if the tenure decision is positive, the library has become a trusted resource that the faculty can start recommending to the students and colleagues. If the tenure decision is negative, the faculty member won't be around long enough to bad mouth the library service.

The equivalent to the tenure opportunity exists in other settings that librarians serve. One of my favorites comes from a law library. At this particular law firm, there are huge efforts around expert witnesses. These are scientists, authors, and other experts brought in to persuade a judge or jury to interpret a fact or concept a certain way.

In almost any case, lawyers spend a lot of their time either finding an expert witness to support their side of a case or learning about expert witnesses called against them. The idea is that if David Lankes is called to the stand against me, I need to know everything about him and everything he has ever written so I can find some way to disqualify his testimony. ("Ah, but Dr. Lankes, in 1992, you said Gopher was the greatest Internet technology, and now here you are touting something called the web? Clearly you will say anything to advance your diabolical agenda!")

So one day a lawyer pops his head into the librarian's office. "Can you help me?" asks the lawyer. "I've just spent an entire day and night trying to find something about this guy, and I have to get to court in two hours and I have nothing." A few minutes later, the librarian was printing off reams of articles from full-text databases and handing them to an appreciative lawyer.

I could stop the story here, but it gets *so* much better. The next week, the librarian begins offering weekly "Character Assassination 101" workshops. Every week to a full room of lawyers and paralegals, the librarian would walk through good sources for expert information. All the time the librarian would say, "So you can do this to search this database…or you could just have me do it." It was such a successful strategy that several lawyers started considering the librarians part of their litigating teams.

The point is that a librarian must understand motivation to build services that aren't simply useful to members but recognize and reward the members' reasons for using the service. Marketing is one approach in a broad way, but each conversation has its own motivation dynamic. We have already talked about how this works in gaming. But what if the member just isn't internally motivated to participate?

Extrinsic

In the "Mission" Thread, I ended my brief discussion of motivation with the following line:

> By having a better understanding of not only why members use the service (and why non-members don't), librarians can begin to, with some fidelity and craft, compel use where it makes sense, and be much more proactive in the knowledge life of our members.

It may sound extreme or even distasteful to talk about librarians compelling members to do something, but they already do. After all, in public libraries supported by taxes, people are compelled to pay for library use if the levy is approved. In primary and secondary education, students are compelled to use the library media center by teachers and administration (and state law in some cases). In higher education, many librarians work with faculty to put compulsory usage into syllabi. In all of these cases, the community, including community librarians, sees the benefits of library usage outweighing some freedoms on the part of the community.

Of course, "compel" is an odd word. As a verb it means to force or, in this context, provide extrinsic motivation. As an adjective, however, compelling is to make use irresistible (intrinsic motivation). While many librarians draw back from the idea of compelling use, they are all for making use of the library more compelling (isn't English a wonderful language?). From blogs to marketing to new outreach, librarians are working to make their services more and more compelling.

One final note on compelling before we leave motivation. Although it is possible to compel members to be present with a librarian, it is impossible to compel actual learning or use. Ultimately, if a member is unwilling to enter into a conversation, they will not do it. All sorts of incentives and disincentives can be put in place to encourage use (extrinsic motivations), but it is ultimately a decision on the part of a member. If this wasn't the case, no one would ever fail a course, and all four-year-olds would eat their vegetables.

THREAD CONCLUSION

So there you have it, four means of facilitation (access, knowledge, environment, and motivation) that boils down to: get them to a conversation knowing what they are doing and help them feel safe and compelled to participate. Why get to conversations? Because that is how we build knowledge. How are they compelled? Either of their own free will or through the use of external incentives and/or disincentives. We also have seen that, in all of this, there are issues of power. As the cliché goes, knowledge is power, yes. But also, the quest for knowledge requires power.

Reading, gaming, getting people's attention, driving people to the table, and mediating communications between members require a powerful facilitator, not a weak or subservient one. To be a librarian is to be powerful. The tactics of facilitation are ultimately about empowering you and your members. The power may be quiet, the way a kindergarten teacher can quiet a room of five-year-olds by simply raising a hand in the air. It may be loud, like Alinsky's protests or the shouting at town hall meetings. But in the hands of librarians, power is the ability to make our communities, and ultimately our society, a better place.

I end this thread with a story that to me best illustrates the power of the librarian. The Free Library of Philadelphia's Central Library had a problem with homelessness. Every morning before the library opened, the homeless of the central city would congregate in a park before the grand Beaux-Arts building. Once the doors of the library would open, the homeless would crowd in to use the bathrooms and find a place to rest. A board member of the library complained about the conditions of the bathrooms after attending the library's world-class lecture series.

Every day one man would go straight up the grand staircase to a large unabridged dictionary on the second floor and check to see whether the word "masturbation" was still in it and then proceed to discuss the finer points of the definition with the librarians.

The librarians of the central library had a choice to make. The homeless were powerless. Much of the advice the librarians received from various sources had to do with keeping out the homeless. Policy changes they could make, use of the law, and so on to "minimize" the problem. The librarians of the Free Library chose a different path.

The first thing they did was to hire homeless men and women to be bathroom attendants to keep the bathrooms clean. Social services began to provide meals in a park across from the front entrance. Then the library started a café. The café was a community-wide effort. Major funding came from Bank of America. The coffee and equipment were donated by Starbucks. The food came from a neighborhood bakery. The café was staffed, trained, and managed by formerly homeless men and women now in a program to transition to work.

That is the power of being a librarian. To look at people not as problems but as members in need—in need of services, support, and, yes, literacy. But ultimately in need of power. The power to support themselves and live dignified lives. The power to create and learn, not simply to survive. Did the Free Library of Philadelphia solve the homelessness problem in central Philly? No. Instead they decided not to stand by and ignore it. They did not "minimize the problem." They also leveraged the power of the members (homeless) to deal with the problem, which the librarians had previously been powerless to address. The members, even homeless ones, have potential power that will help the librarians.

The power of librarians is not just about an "A" student, a suburban family, a trial attorney, or a doctor. It is also about the failing student, the battered wife, the pro bono client, and the indigent patient. That is what makes librarians powerful AND noble.

Every librarian I have ever met has the story. It is that little narrative—a memory—that librarians keep close to their heart. It is the story that they tell to themselves after a boring meeting or the twentieth set of directions to the bathroom or the last toner cartridge replacement. Perhaps it is a story of a seven-year-old who shone from within as he or she retold the plot from a book he or she read on the librarian's recommendation. Perhaps it is the story of a job the librarian helped find for the laid-off father of five, the criminal who went to jail, or the patient cured. Whatever that story is, no matter how big or small, those stories that librarians tell me have one thing in common:

They are about people. There is always a conversation. There is always a point when the librarian and member shared a triumph and the world, even if just for a moment, or just in a miniscule way, became a better place. True and successful facilitation is when a librarian helps a member find his or her own story.

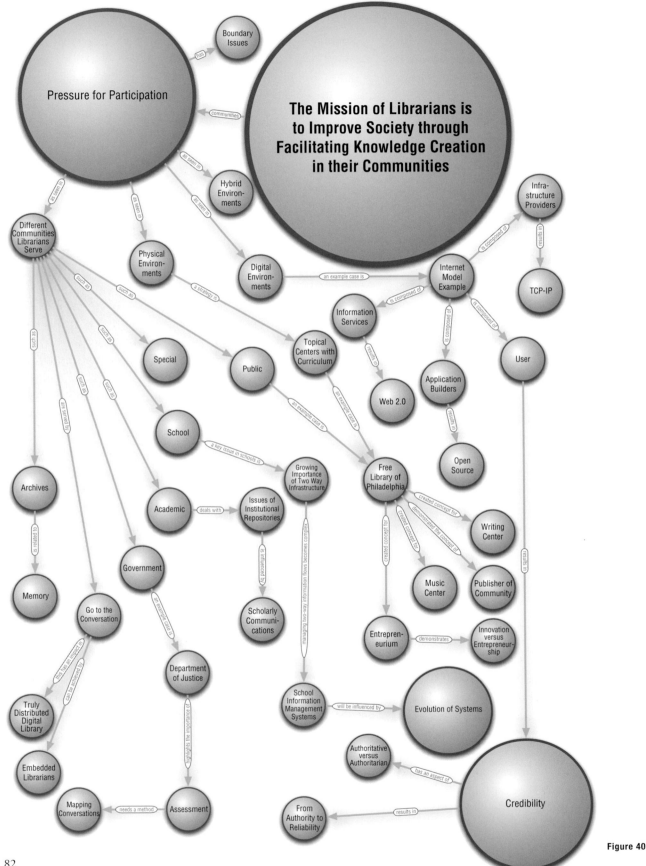

Boundary Issues

Pressure for Participation

has

communities

The Mission of Librarians is to Improve Society through Facilitating Knowledge Creation in their Communities

as seen in

Hybrid Environments

Infra-structure Providers

results in

as seen in

Different Communities Librarians Serve

as seen in

Physical Environments

Digital Environments

an example case is

Internet Model Example

is composed of

TCP-IP

such as

a strategy is

Information Services

is composed of

is composed of

User

such as

Special

Public

Topical Centers with Curriculum

results in

Application Builders

such as

is composed of

Web 2.0

results in

such as

School

a key issue in schools is

Growing Importance of Two Way Infrastructure

Free Library of Philadelphia

Open Source

such as

Archives

Academic

deals with

Issues of Institutional Repositories

created concept for

demonstrated the concept of

Writing Center

is related to

is influenced by

managing two-way information flows becomes complex

created concept for

created concept for

Memory

Go to the Conversation

Government

Scholarly Communications

Music Center

Publisher of Community

this has an impact in

Truly Distributed Digital Library

can be achieved by

an example case is

Department of Justice

Entrepren-eurium

demonstrates

Innovation versus Entrepreneur-ship

highlights the importance of

results in

Embedded Librarians

School Information Management Systems

will be influenced by

Evolution of Systems

Authoritative versus Authoritarian

has an aspect of

Mapping Conversations

needs a method

Assessment

From Authority to Reliability

results in

Credibility

Figure 40

COMMUNITIES

One of the things I learned in library school is that when people have an information need, they'll always ask people they know before they ask a librarian. The trick is making sure that librarians are some of the people they know.

—Jessamyn West

THE MISSION OF LIBRARIANS IS TO IMPROVE SOCIETY THROUGH FACILITATING KNOWLEDGE CREATION IN THEIR COMMUNITIES

We begin as we begin every thread, with the mission of the librarian. To this point, we have explored the need for a mission and its corresponding worldview. We have explored the nature of knowledge and its creation through conversation. We have also looked at means of facilitating knowledge creation through access, knowledge, environment, and motivation.

However, even with examples and stories, we have yet to see prescriptive advice and detailed service plans. You may be asking, "So what exactly should I be doing?" The very short answer is: Ask your community. Do your members need collections? Do they need digital libraries? Do they even need a building? Ask your community.

I realize for some of you, this may seem like a cop out. However, you should have seen it coming. After all, I did spend a good amount of time on co-ownership with the community and the importance of developing a social compact. But let's take an example: Should a public library offer story hours in the morning?

It may seem like a simple question, and many libraries do. However, to whom do these services cater? According to the Population Reference Bureau,[1] "Only 7 percent of all U.S. households consisted of married couples with children in which only the husband worked. Dual-income families with children made up more than two times as many households." So are these public libraries intentionally offering a service to an elite few who can afford to either stay home with their children or have a nanny who can take the kids to story hour?

Of course, there are plenty of potential reasons to offer story hours in the mornings: parents who can't afford child care and have to stay home with the kids, nontraditional child care such as cooperatives, and even the fact that in your community there is a healthy-sized number of families with a parent who stays home out of choice. My point is not to have all story hours in the evening but to make sure you know *why* you are offering them in the morning and that the decision was a mutual one with the community.

In the end, the primary tactic advocated throughout this Atlas is what Mike Eisenberg called the "Anti-Field of Dreams Model." Rather than build it and they will come, it is invite them in and then scramble like hell to meet the needs they bring. Of course, you need something to invite them into, but there are already plenty of libraries that exist; if you are the entire library (a one-librarian library), then you are the bait. You are the loss leader to find out what they need. Let me give you an example of the importance of seeking community input in determining library service.

I grew up in a suburb of Cincinnati, Ohio, called Glendale. Glendale is one of those towns that looks like a patch of trees next to its more developed neighbors in Google Maps. It has a population of 2,500; is on the National Historic Registry; and has a quaint village, grand old Victorian homes, a tiny train museum, and, as of two years ago, a library three days a week.

The library was started by a group of residents who thought that every community needs a library. They started with a book drive and a volunteer core. The donated books now line the shelves of a building that was once a library closed decades ago but more recently a community center.

It is not a well-trafficked library, however. Initial book club meetings have shrunk, and walk-in traffic is limited (a person or two a day). When you think about it, why does Glendale need a library consisting mostly of second-hand books the residents have already read? These are folks with broadband, ready access to Amazon, an easy drive to three existing public libraries, and well-stocked school libraries.

Instead of building a shared book resource, why not build a volunteer corps of "citizen librarians?" Send this corps into the community, laptop and 3G card in hand. Send librarians into the homes of those looking for new jobs. Send librarians into the apartments and houses to answer questions. Send the librarian corps into the community centers and schools armed with a single question: "What do you need to know?" Then look at what's being asked and what the community needs. Maybe a building. Maybe a collection. Maybe not.

Before you begin listing the "why nots" (the biggest one being that free books are easy to gather, librarians are not), just take it as a thought experiment. If the community group wanted a library as a status symbol, then a building makes sense. After all, the public library is often an aspirational institution. It is a place that represents what a community thinks are its best aspirations: learning and knowledge.

1. http://www.prb.org/Articles/2003/TraditionalFamiliesAccountforOnly7PercentofUSHouseholds.aspx

If, on the other hand, the group starting the library wanted to make a difference, then perhaps they should have looked to their borders where they are surrounded by poverty and a growing immigrant community. If they wanted a shared collection of used books, why did they call it a library? Because to many outside of the profession, libraries are about books. Unfortunately for us, too many of us inside the profession think this way as well.

My point is that what we do is a joint agreement with our communities. Why we do them, that's ours. That is what makes us a profession (this is the focus of the "Improve Society" Thread). This Thread is all about how librarians shape their services to a unique kind of pressure exerted by communities: the pressure of participation. It seeks to tackle the questions: Are there any generalized features of community that can inform new librarianship, and how do we define our communities anyway? We begin with this unique aspect of community—their desire to be active creators of knowledge and the force this need exerts on librarians.

PRESSURE FOR PARTICIPATION

Let me restate a foundation of new librarianship: Knowledge is created through conversation. Let this concept play out for a minute. A conversation involves at least two conversants. Conversations are defined as a participatory exchange. It takes at least two conversants, and both conversants have to participate. Otherwise you have a monologue, and that is only good for transmitting what you already know, not creating new knowledge. So to learn, a member has to participate.

Participation in a system, however minimal, exerts pressure on that system. It changes things. This concept is so fundamental that we see it in physics (the mere act of observation changes something), in biology (merely by being alive you use resources), the humanities (postmodernists see the act of reading as interpretation and meaning making), and beyond. Even the world's largest religions see participation in the community as essential to worship (through acts of charity, for example).

The concept of participation is so fundamental to the work of new librarians that much of the thinking and work captured in the Atlas was developed under the rubric of "participatory librarianship." You will still see vestiges of this language on the web and in the Agreements. It is with the creation of this Atlas that I drop the "participatory" modifier because these concepts are too central to be sidelined as a subgroup. In essence, there can't be both participatory and non-

participatory librarians. Even if you don't buy many of the arguments in the Atlas, even if you don't buy any of them, you are still actively affecting the lives of your members; you are participating in their lives and in your communities even if you are just taking taxes, tuition, or a salary from the community. By existing, you change the community. New librarianship simply seeks to make these changes conscious efforts for the betterment of the community.

The fundamental source of the pressure in librarianship is the members' desire, often unrecognized, to participate in learning. It follows from the necessity of member involvement that they want to shape the systems in which they learn. They may want to change digital system interfaces, the times given services are available (e.g., later library hours), or how information is organized. This pressure is not always consciously brought to bear and can be subtle (it can also be loud and disruptive). This relates back to Bob Taylor's concepts of unstated needs and an inability to articulate exactly what a member needs.[2] This calls for a process to find out what members need, which we talk about throughout this Thread.

So here are the first two contributors to the pressure of the community: Members need to be active in the learning processes and their accompanying desire to shape the systems they use. It should be noted that the inability of a member to accurately communicate how they want a system changed is another part of the pressure. Wanting something different, but not knowing what, is a real frustration, and ultimately helping a member figure this out is a service that librarians must provide.

The third origin of the pressure for participation comes from the social nature of members. As Clay Shirky says, "Human beings are social creatures—not occasionally or by accident but always."[3] We can see this social nature reflected in how we keep memories where we relate and create connections. As we learn, we build networks: networks of ideas, agreements, artifacts, and people. Note the use of the verbs here: relate, build, converse. They are action verbs. Building knowledge is an active process, it is not done through osmosis, and it cannot happen passively with someone making you learn or imparting knowledge. To know is to participate—to be active.

Our fourth form of pressure was previewed in the Netflix versus Blockbuster example. If you went to the video store and asked for a video and the store didn't have it, what would you do? If this store were one outlet of many, you could simply move to the next option (like folks who switched from Blockbuster to Netflix). However, if that were your only option, you might complain to the manager or lobby to get the video or simply complain that your title was not available. This is our fourth form of pressure: one based on the limitations of resources within a community. This pressure can range from simple irritation as a member waits for an item, to social action if a group of members feels some needed resource is being withheld or censored.

The fifth major contributor to the pressure comes in the nature of boundaries and how we use them to define communities.

Boundary Issues

The ideal boundaries for a community would be set by conversations, a porous perimeter with conversants coming and going. However, librarians are rarely faced with such organic communities (though these communities are growing rapidly due to increased access to peers over the Internet). Instead, boundaries are often set by more arbitrary and historic conglomerations of members such as those in a location or in institutional structures. Not that this is all bad. Certainly these boundaries represent a master or driving set of conversations ("How can I make a better living here?" "What is the best way to teach this topic?" How can we make more money?"). They also present a sense of stability in which services can evolve and anticipate.

However, conversations and knowledge are dynamic. They often push up against boundaries creating pressure. Why push up against boundaries? Because the whole concept of community, like knowledge, is dynamic. A member spans many communities, most of which they have only fuzzy awareness of in terms of the limits and size of the community. I am a professor, a father, a son, a resident of New York, a lover of science fiction, a casual gamer, and a member of ALA and the Association for Library and Information Science Education (ALISE). None of these roles define me, and yet all of them taken together provide a sense of context. Still, when I seek to build knowledge in one of my communities, I can't help but be informed by my other communities.

Not only that, but within the boundaries of any one of my communities, there are members who will amplify my approach and those who will cancel it out. There are even members of those communities who will actively try to stop some of my actions. In each of these communities, and often between them, I am engaged in conversations and monologues. Some of my interactions in one community raise my expectations for participation in others as well.

The point of all this is that our members and our communities (aggregations of members) need to participate. If you frustrate that desire, they will seek out participation elsewhere. Don't ever make the mistake of thinking that because community members don't respond to a blog asking for input they have no input to give. Instead, seek out where the communities are participating and see why and whether you can help.

This was all summed up for me by an excellent presentation by Laural Winter of Multnomah County Library System at the 2008 Oregon Virtual Reference Summit.[4] Her group had done focus groups to find out what teens wanted from the library's websites and were a bit shocked to hear that teens wanted librarians to blog. Now here is the important part and what in my mind makes Laural's work so outstanding: They didn't just stop there. A functional approach taken by many librarians would have simply been to put up a blog or several. Laural's group looked deeper and found a strong desire for conversation, specifically about books.

What the teens wanted was online readers' advisory services. Rather than getting simple lists of good books (a list of artifacts), they wanted to know who said these were good books and why. The teens wanted to get to know the librarians before they could decide the value of the recommendations.

If the library just had blogs put up by librarians, there is a good chance the teens might have found them. However, had these blogs been professional and anonymous in tone, the teens would most likely have ignored them. They would have gone elsewhere, to another one of their communities, and sought conversation there.

All too often, those on both sides of the "participatory debate" miss the true point of participatory technologies. On one side you get the doubters, those who see the "blog people" as superficial or the technologies as sinking standards to the lowest common denominator. These folks miss the fact that, unless librarians build participatory tools, they have no chance to engage their members in conversation and thus raise the bar for the whole community.

On the other side are the participatory utopians who see blogs, Wikis, and tagging as a sort of magic dust that can be sprinkled on existing systems to make them more attractive and valuable to members. They miss the fact that it is not the technology that creates pressure for participation but rather an underlying human need. In a real way, it is a selfish need to learn that drives folks to social networks (online and

2. Taylor, R. (1968). Question negotiation and information seeking in libraries. *College & Research Libraries, 29*, 178–194.
3. http://us.penguingroup.com/static/pages/specialinterests/currentaffairs/2009/herecomeseveryone.html
4. http://www.oregonlibraries.net/videos/remote_users-2008-summit

off). If a library does not address the underlying need for participation in learning, no open-radically-trusted-mashable-crowd-sourced web technology is enough to spark conversation. It has to help someone build knowledge.

Let's see how this pressure for participation from communities plays out in different settings. We start with a macro view of how it has affected digital environments.

DIGITAL ENVIRONMENTS

One of the things I do as a professor is review articles submitted for journal publication. Do me a personal favor and stop using the words "revolutionary," "unprecedented," or "paradigm" in your articles about participatory technologies. Really, to read some of these submissions, you'd think we'd jumped from fire to the blog in one swift movement. It is not that participatory technologies are not new or don't have substantial impact, but it would be wrong to assume that they are somehow aberrant, that they represent some unique and isolated new activity. In fact we have seen participation driving changes in the digital domain for a long time. To show you, I first need to give a quick model of the Internet.

Internet Model Example*

The Internet is a big thing by all measures. It has 1,668,870,408 users.[5] Google estimates there are more than a trillion unique uniform resources locators (URLs) on the web.[6] The Internet is used by men, women, and children in cars, on computers, and on mobile phones. We now even have pacemakers directly connected to the Net.[7] It can be a little overwhelming and hard to find long-term, large-scale trends in such a large network. To help, let me present the Internet as four interacting layers:

- Infrastructure: These people and technology provide basic connectivity services (from T1 lines to server farms).

- Application Builders: These individuals and organizations produce software to ship and decode information around the Internet (from the Apache web server, to Firefox, to the folks who wrote your e-mail software).

- Information Services: These services use the software created by application builders to distribute information and services over the Internet's infrastructure (from Google to the Library of Congress).

- Users: These people engage information services to solve a problem (from curious or bored individuals to students writing term papers).

It should be noted that these are, as with all people-based borders, porous boundaries (Google writes software as well as provides a service), but they provide a 30,000-foot way of looking at the effects of the pressure for participation on the digital networked environment.

Infrastructure Providers

The Internet was neither the first nor is it the only large-scale digital network available to a wide variety of users. Although there are a large number of examples to pick from (including the phone network on which the early Internet was built), I focus on the online networks of the 1980s and early 1990s. America Online (AOL), Prodigy, and CompuServe all provided means for people to get online and interact over a wide area. Their approach to infrastructure, however, was different than the Internet's. These proprietary networks built a proprietary infrastructure and access points (initially modem dial up points in key area codes). A subscriber who joined AOL or CompuServe didn't have any choice in how this infrastructure was developed or its characteristics. Although a subscriber could buy a faster modem, these companies did not need to provide matching speed on their end. Furthermore, these were just access points. If an organization wanted a much faster connection through broadband telecommunication lines, the companies did not have to accommodate these.

Although few folks think about the power of community in terms of T1 lines and dedicated fiber linkages, it is there. The pressure for participation acted on these proprietary companies, screaming for wide area networks that could be customized and shaped for the needs of the organization and individual. In fact, the pressure was so powerful it simply overran these proprietary services and put most of them out of business.

TCP/IP

You see, the Internet was and is a different kind of wide area network in terms of infrastructure. In fact, it is not really a single network at

---

*See Agreement Supplement for more on the Internet Model and how it relates to credibility.

5. http://www.internetworldstats.com/stats.htm
6. http://googleblog.blogspot.com/2008/07/we-knew-web-was-big.html
7. http://www.reuters.com/article/internetNews/idUSTRE5790AK20090810?feedType=RSS&feedName=internetNews&pageNumber=1&virtualBrandChannel=0&sp=true

all. The Internet is a cooperative of independent networks with their own infrastructures that agree to speak the same networking languages: the Transmission Control Protocol and the Internet Protocol, better known as TCP/IP. These two protocols take data from one device (a PC, a phone, a car, a pacemaker), break it up into chunks, and then forward those chunks from one point to another, again and again, until they reach the destination device designated by an address (an IP address).

However, what's interesting is that not every point along the way has to forward all the information. Plenty of networks will block certain types of data (e.g., chat data) or data from certain places (e.g., pornography sites). There is no grand wizard who enforces all data to all places. Compare this to the initial AOL infrastructure that literally controlled the network from end to end.

This simple protocol suite, TCP/IP, embedded into routers and network hardware, is what has made the Internet so big (and, some would also add, such a security nightmare). Each node along the chain, however, can participate in the network and shape it. If your organization wants faster connections, they can upgrade their own infrastructure. If you want a static IP address versus one that changes every time you connect, you can buy that (not from the Internet, but from your own network or Internet Service Provider).

Even the protocols and addressing are based on a cooperative governance structure where network representatives suggest changes. For example, when the Internet was running out of addresses to give out, these cooperative groups created an updated version of the IP protocol called IPv6. It allows the potential billions of new devices to get an address. CompuServe or Prodigy would simply come up with a new standard and implement it, whereas IPv6 was created more than 10 years ago and has yet to be widely implemented.

The point of this trip into telecommunications is that the Internet approach of participation has won. Not only have other networks gone away (e.g., CompuServe, Prodigy) or simply adopted this new infrastructure (AOL is now simply another network on the Internet from an infrastructure perspective), the phone system that the original Internet was based on is now being re-created to use the Internet as its infrastructure model.

Application Builders*

Take another look at AOL. It used to be that, once you connected to AOL, AOL provided you with your e-mail package and the software used to access AOL data. If you didn't like the e-mail package, you were out of luck. On the Internet, however, as long as your software can speak TCP/IP, it can come from any source, including writing your own. The next major software advance is as likely to come from a 16-year-old in Egypt as it is to come from Microsoft in Redmond, Washington.

Software on the Internet is not centrally controlled. If you create the next greatest web browser, you don't have to submit it to some central authority for approval or pass some kind of test. You simply create it and use it (or sell it or give it away). This means that folks have the ability to participate in how software is selected and, increasingly, how it is created.

Open Source

There are few places on the network where the pressure for participation is more obvious than the open source movement. Open source started as the simple idea that when I create an application I make available the source code. Others could download the source and make their own modifications. However, open source has come to be more of a philosophy. There is now formal open source licensing (GNU, Apache, MIT, Mozilla Public License, etc.), as well as regular debates about whether open source is the same thing as free and public domain or whether it is a business model.

This open source philosophy (or, more precisely, these philosophies) is evident when you look at the debates around electronic voting. On one side of the debate are proprietary solutions that feel that the way to keep the voting software secure is to follow rigorous development standards and hide the source code. Because hackers can't see the source code, they can't find exploitable bugs or loopholes. On the other side of the argument, the open source folks say that the best way to secure the process is to release the code widely and have everyone try and break it so you know where the bugs and loopholes are and can fix them. While the proprietary folks hold up examples such as military systems, the open source folks point to Linux and Apache as very secure.

What's remarkable about the pressure exerted in this debate is how it has radically changed the software production model (that you as a librarian have to deal with). For example, there is now a concept of perpetual beta. Time was that a company would produce a piece of

*See Agreement Supplement for a more specific definition of application builders.

software and hire professional testers to look for bugs and potential improvements. The coders would work with the developer version, then the professional testers would work with the alpha version (the sort of first draft), and then a second, larger set of testers would play with a beta version (closer to the final draft). These beta testers would be a mix of paid employees and close partners with the developer. Only after this beta period was software released to the public.

If this process sounds clunky or even inaccurate, it is because you live in an Internet environment where the pressure of participation has totally changed this process. Beta code has always been released early in the development process in the open source world. Because of the growing success of open source products, the proprietary software world now releases their beta software much earlier and much wider. In essence, organizations are crowd sourcing their beta tests.

Even more interesting is that beta now is not only a search for bugs but a search for audience. Google, for example, keeps a service in beta until it feels there is a sufficient user base to commit to its continued existence. Gmail, Google's e-mail system, was in beta for 5 years.

Open source and perpetual beta are the results of pressure for participation at the software level. As people experienced and then expected more options and more say into the software they used, software publishers changed their practices.

Information Services

Information services are people and organizations that have services to share. You may say that you have information to share as well, but in fact all you ever share is a service. Access to information is a service; the organization of resources is a service; the search, maintenance, and persistence of information is a service. It is impossible to separate out information from service. Let me demonstrate this through an example.

The National Science Foundation has funded digital library research since the early 1990s. At first they funded more basic research on technologies such as speech to text, video indexing, image retrieval, and large-scale computing. In the early part of this century, they began looking toward application. They wanted to show how digital libraries could make a direct impact on the teaching of science, technology, engineering, and mathematics (the so-called STEM discipline). They launched the National Science Digital Library (NSDL) program to build a national resource for STEM education.

The plan for the library shows a distinct artifact-centric view (in this case, the artifacts were primarily born digital web resources).

The NSDL was to consist of collections, services, and a core integration service to bring it all together (primarily through harvested metadata from collections). So the collections would make available three-dimensional models of chemicals, weather simulations, lesson plans, and so on. Services would busily write code for searching the collections, answering questions posed to scientists, and using information visualization for complex mathematics. The core integration group would then tie this all together to make it look like one seamless library.

A funny thing happened, however, when the core integration team went to tie everything together. Instead of pristine collections, they found websites. These sites had their own search engines, their own classification systems, and their own sets of services. More than that, the content was shaped not only to take advantage of these services but to depend on these services. The NSDL discovered that a digital library was not a set of collections with some services on top but rather a set of services with some associated content.

Access, you see, is a service (as I talked about in the "Facilitation" Thread). The way something is organized, displayed, and addressed is a service that varies by the community that puts up the content. It used to be said that content was king, but on the web it seems that context rules the castle.

Of course, you may say that this is a rookie mistake. Sure, how data are displayed on the web is a service, no big deal. Libraries have known for a long time that data can be disconnected from the display. A Machine-Readable Catalog (MARC) record is not tied to the catalog system displaying it. Data and service can be separated. This leads nicely into my next example that seems like an exception. Linked data services: the technologies and strategies behind the mashup craze.

The push these days is to let data be free. Not free in a monetary sense, necessarily (although that is certainly a pressure), but free of its interface. Through the use of Application Programming Interfaces (APIs, a way for two pieces of software to exchange requests and data) and RESTful interfaces (think of it as sending a really long URL and getting back a chunk of data), you can get at the raw data used by a website and create your own interface. You've either seen, heard about, or built these kinds of linked data services. A library embedding an interactive Google Map to its location on the library website would be one example.

There are plenty of other examples as well, including sending Amazon a title and getting back a book cover or sending OCLC's WorldCat an ISBN number and getting back bibliographic details. You can even set up a service that pulls down product information from Best Buy and use that description to search Google. You can send a request to a library catalog and get back a MARC record. You might think that these are examples of content without context. Nope.

The service providing the data sets the questions it can be asked and the data that are returned. You can't, for example, ask Google for black-and-white versions of their maps. There was the case of the iPhone app Delicious Library that used the Amazon API to display book covers of books you owned. One day, Amazon announced that it was no longer supporting that kind of data export. Delicious Library for iPhone was dead. It is an interesting cautionary tale in what can happen to organizations that depend on data they do not own, such as libraries and full-text databases.

Another example of how context and services shape content and data can be seen in the disastrous attempts to provide anonymized data. The idea here is that personal identity information can be stripped out of search logs and such, thus rendering them safe to share. Of course, tell that to AOL, which released a ton of anonymized search results only to find there was little difficulty in identifying folks within it. (Who knew people would search their own social security numbers?) As an article in Ars Technica[8] puts it:

> Such work by computer scientists over the last fifteen years has shown a serious flaw in the basic idea behind "personal information": almost all information can be "personal" when combined with enough other relevant bits of data.

Bottom line? Data can never be truly stripped of context.

But I digress. Where is the pressure for participation here? Well, the fact that Amazon, Best Buy, Google, and such even offer these mashup services is from a pressure on the part of Internet users to create their own interfaces and data combinations. However, the clearest example of the impact of the pressure for participation on information services is the whole Web 2.0 phenomenon.

Web 2.0

Let's get this out of the way right at the start. I am not a big fan of "Web 2.0" or "Library 2.0." I'm particularly not a fan of Library 2.0. You'd think that counting from the Library of Alexandria, to the monasteries of medieval Europe, to the overflowing libraries of Muslim Spain, to the grand libraries of the Renaissance, Enlightenment,

chained libraries of the oldest universities, subscription libraries, to the public libraries of the United States, we should be at least on Library 12.5 beta or something.

My main problem with Web 2.0 is that it is an unfocused buzzword that invites quick succession (go right now and do a web search on "Web 4.0" if you don't believe me). Also, as I am writing this, saying Web2.0 is like saying "Golly Gee!" and "Daddio" in some circles. However, although I'm not a fan of the nomenclature, there is something profoundly new and interesting happening on the web of today, something that has been bubbling up through our Internet layers and will shape the web well into versions 2, 3, 4, and 5. People want to participate.

No longer are members content to simply see the web as "brochure-ware," where they inactively absorb information. They have begun to expect something beyond web applications where they can do work online. Increasingly, our members want to shape the services they use. They have a need to make the systems match their learning styles, to remember for them, and to help them move from one conversation to the next.

Many look at social networking sites and see vanity or some vacuous need to be part of some group. Although we cannot discount the need for ego and the strong pull of the limelight, ultimately what drives the pressure to participate is an in-built, some might say selfish, need to learn and situate the environment. Members look to friends, experts, artifacts, organizations, media, and more to learn. The more that the systems they encounter help them do this *the way they want*, the more use the systems will get. I realize this may sound frighteningly obvious—members use systems that help them—but it seems to be often overlooked. Application builders in library-land keep piling on new social features, and librarians keep deploying them more out of a need to be current than to be useful.

It is like Stephen Abrahms says, members don't want to search for information; they want to find information.[9] Members don't want to tag, blog, or edit Wikis; they want to accomplish some goal. If that goal is learning, then librarians should thoughtfully deploy these functions. Deploying them just in case someone wants to use them is often ineffective, in that they can get in the way of members who don't want to use them.

8. http://arstechnica.com/tech-policy/news/2009/09/your-secrets-live-online-in-databases-of-ruin.ars
9. http://www.sirsidynix.com/Resources/Pdfs/Company/Abram/20091116_Darien.pdf

This also means when determining whether to deploy a given feature you must do careful analysis of what members are trying to accomplish. Even better, go re-read the section on building User Systems and let them do it themselves.

User

In fact, if you do go re-read the User Systems section, you realize that the lines between the User layer and the Information Services layer in this model are dissolving. Although not for every application, or for every member, the User layer as a distinct idea is still useful in our look at how the pressure for participation has shaped digital networks. For one thing, it highlights a growing paradox for our members: namely, the paradox of "information self-sufficiency."

The paradox, discussed in greater detail in the "Credibility" agreement, goes something like this. There is a push from information providers to have members become more self-sufficient online (buy their airplane tickets without an agent, track their own packages via the web, fill out their own government forms, etc.). This push is matched by a strong pull from members to become more self-sufficient as well (search out their own medical information, organize their own vacations, track repairs, etc.). This push/pull combination is referred to as disintermediation.

But there is an interesting disconnect that leads to our paradox. Members are becoming both more self-sufficient (they are obligated to seek out information and make decisions by their own desire or through limited options and incentives on the part of information providers) and more dependent on the information provided by information services. Think about it: You now have to book your own flight, but who provides the system that you use to do the booking? Now you can find the best prices of electronics online, but who provides the pricing information? In an open network environment, you have the ability to access much more information (really access services) and to do more yourself, but you are more reliant on those providing the tools and services to do so.

So as shown in our previous Delicious Library iPhone App example, as a user of the App, you can organize your own materials online. However, to do so, you are dependent not on the App's author, but on Amazon (without being aware of it), plus, of course, the phone service provider. This is the paradox that librarians must wade into neck-deep to grab the hands of those users who are drowning in a torrent of conflicting capabilities and dependencies and bring them

safely to the shore of knowledge. This turbulent confluence of dependencies and a librarian's role can be seen in the question of credibility.

CREDIBILITY

It was a grisly crime. Anne E. Harper, an honors student at Hollins College, was murdered in Boston while home visiting her parents for Thanksgiving in 1995. Her body, with an incriminating stab wound, was incinerated in a house fire set to cover the crime. Detective June Boyle (a detective later at the center of the DC Sniper case) was on the case.

Armed with a forensic report, Detective Boyle interviewed witnesses and family members. Her keen eye lighted on a bloodstain on the jeans of Matthew Harper, Anne's brother. In a scene out of a TV crime drama, Boyle laced together a case of evidence that led to Matthew's confession and the dramatic close of a murder case.

Except that it didn't happen that way. There was indeed a murder and fire, but no blood stain and no confession. Those "facts" were added by the *New York Times*' Jayson Blair.[10] Blair was the *Times* reporter fired after being discredited on a number of national stories where he made up facts and/or plagiarized from other sources.

Of course, the *New York Times* isn't the only one with these problems. Oprah Winfrey was so moved by Herman Rosenblat's memoir, *Angels at the Fence*, that she called it "the single greatest love story" she'd ever featured on her show.[11] Unfortunately, the story of how Rosenblat met his wife at the gates of the Buchenwald concentration camp in World War II turned out to be a lie. At least this time Oprah was able to cancel the show before the Rosenblat story went on the air, unlike the case with James Frey.[12] Frey told of a harrowing life of addictions and lost love. It would have been nice if it were in fact his life as he presented it to be.

Episodes of deceit and error assaulting the credibility of individuals and organizations could fill up an entire series of manuscripts. From politicians who go "hiking the Appalachian trail"[13] to televangelists selling exclusive membership to nonexistent properties,[14] the list is an outstanding case of schadenfreude[15]—the pleasure of watching others' misfortune. In some cases, these lapses of credibility have

10. http://www.nytimes.com/2003/03/03/us/making-sniper-suspect-talk-puts-detective-in-spotlight.html
11. http://abcnews.go.com/Entertainment/story?id=6543206&page=1
12. http://www.time.com/time/arts/article/0,8599,1897924,00.html
13. http://www.politico.com/news/stories/0609/24146.html
14. http://www.time.com/time/magazine/article/0,9171,956551,00.html
15. http://www.merriam-webster.com/dictionary/schadenfreude

ended careers, whereas in others they have resulted in heartfelt apologies and later triumph.

Perhaps as a society we are becoming more tolerant of occasional lapses of credibility. Perhaps not. What is for sure is that the way our members are determining credibility online is changing. In fact, in many ways, it is becoming much closer to the way librarians have been determining credibility for quite some time.

From Authority to Reliability

Let me first be clear about my definition of credibility. It is a personal determination of "believability" of information that lets an individual act. To feel that information is credible is to not only believe it but allow that information to change your behavior. To put this in terms of knowledge and Conversation Theory, which sits at the foundation of new librarianship, it is an affirmative agreement (as opposed to an agreement not to agree) on some concept used to shape your worldview. So an artifact cannot be credible; only someone's perception of that artifact can be credible.

Some find Fox News to be credible, whereas others do not. Fox News can try and influence folks in making that determination, but they cannot make it happen. Once again, we see a recurring theme of new librarianship: Credibility, like knowledge and learning, rests in the control of the member not us.

Now this is not to say that people make detailed credibility determinations of everything they encounter. It is impossible. There are plenty of times you have to simply trust the judgment of others either because the result of that judgment is not consequential, because you have determined the judgment to be consistently in line with yours, or because you simply have no choice. This deferred credibility is authority. You grant a person or an organization, or an artifact for that matter, authority to determine what should be agreed on.

The cases of Blair, Frey, and Rosenblat impugned the authority of the *New York Times* and Oprah. These cases forced people to reevaluate their previous decision to trust their credibility determinations. In some cases, such as Oprah and the *Times*, the reevaluation process by the majority of readers and viewers seems to have been reaffirmed. In the case of the televangelist and the politician, this has not been the case.

The alternative approach to authority is reliability. Reliability is a scientific term with great methodological meaning. In essence, reliability is a measurement of consistency, how often did the predicted event actually occur? If you add one apple to one apple, you always get two apples; it is a reliable result. If you pour vinegar onto baking soda, you will always get a release of carbon dioxide. However, if you had asked James Frey whether there was anything in his book that didn't happen, the answer changed over time.

Note that reliability over time can become authority. If a person or institution gives you consistently credible information time after time, you will simply trust his or her (or its) word. However, it only takes one unreliable incident to destroy authority.

Now some will say that authority is dead. But this is far from true. Reliability and authority models of credibility have always been around. It is just that in today's digital networked environment, the potential sources of information available to our members are so great and so varied that they can become their own experts in many more areas. In essence, with the large number and large variety of information sources on the web, members can build credibility determinations from the consistent repetition of key factors across these sources.

Now, think about yourself and your training as a librarian. Were you taught to simply look for a single source by some authority? I hope not. Librarians are (or should be) taught to look at multiple sources and multiple perspectives. We are reliability people. This is a crucial distinction because it means that librarians are a special kind of credible: They are authorities not authoritarians.

Authoritative versus Authoritarian

Way back in the "Mission" Thread, I said "one of the greatest assets a librarian has: his or her credibility." I remind you of this to once again draw your attention to the language; that the asset is of the librarian—his or her credibility—your credibility. It is your asset and your responsibility. This has always been the case, but it is even more so in these days of librarians being increasingly disconnected from artifacts and traditional institutional borders.

Think about a library. Perhaps it is one you work in, hope to work in, or simply visited. There are artifacts in the library that are full of inaccuracies. In fact, Worldcat.org tells me that James Frey's "memoir" is still in more than 2,800 libraries.[16] Hitler's *Mein Kampf*? 3, 866.[17] Don't even get me started on movies, musical scores, and the newspapers. You'd think folks would look at libraries not as places of knowledge but as central repositories of deceit (of course, there are certainly those who do mostly because we circulate the *Harry Potter* books).

16. http://www.worldcat.org/oclc/51223590&referer=brief_results
17. http://www.worldcat.org/oclc/178218&referer=brief_results

Yet they don't (by and large). Why? Because librarians don't claim to know "good" information from "bad" information. For those of you who disagree, perhaps I should say they *shouldn't* claim to know good information from bad information. For those of you who still don't agree, let me explain.

Librarians should be taught not what a good site is and what a bad site is but what is good for a given member (and, by extension, a community). Say a reporter walks up to you and asks for good Internet sites for a story he is doing on hate groups using the web to recruit youth. The Ku Klux Klan's (KKK's) website is a good resource for the reporter. Now, a 13-year-old comes in and asks for a good site for after-school activities. Is the KKK's site still a good site? Context matters.

What is good and what is bad, what is credible and what is untrustworthy, are the determinations of members and communities. This approach—the contextual approach of knowledge and conversation—is where reliably giving good information makes authorities. We gain trust by consistently giving members a variety of sources and perspectives. We facilitate the member to make a good choice. The alternative approach, to predetermine good and bad sources and conversations, is authoritarian.

We've already seen the difference in the examples in the Atlas to this point: in the case of the teens in Multnomah County who wanted to know the librarians before they determined the credibility of their reading selections; in the law librarian who gained credibility by helping lawyers with expert witnesses; in a library that built trust between public access users and law enforcement through filters; and in building a trust relationship with the community through shared shelves and meeting spaces. All of these examples turn on building credibility with members and communities through a conversation and repeated engagement, not status and uniform applications of good and bad.

In the end, credibility is your greatest asset, and you build it through conversation and openness not through dictates. What good is a collection of artifacts if I can't trust the collector? What good is a meeting space if I can't trust the host? What good is advice, or sources, or facilitation, or policy, or communication if there is not credibility? They are all dust. You earn this credibility every day with every question you answer pointing to multiple sources, by every book you catalog consistently, and by every set of services you create. No title or degree can grant you credibility. No building ensures your word, and no institution can guarantee your word and your professionalism. That's all you.

Putting It All Together: The Participatory Digital Library

Syracuse University offers a Certificate of Advanced Study in Digital Libraries. It is nationally ranked. Yet the students in the first course, an overview of the field, all have the same problem by the end of the course: explaining what a digital library is. This isn't a fault of the students or the instructors. It is an issue in the field. Take, for example, two definitions of digital libraries:

> Digital libraries are organizations that provide the resources, including the specialized staff, to select, structure, offer intellectual access to, interpret, distribute, preserve the integrity of, and ensure the persistence over time of collections of digital works so that they are readily and economically available for use by a defined community or set of communities.
> —Digital Libraries Federation[18]

and

> Digital library is a managed collection of information, with associated services, where information is stored in digital formats and accessible over a network.
> —Bill Arms[19]

Now normally I contrast these two definitions to show how one sees the digital library as an organization and one sees it as a distributed network utility. Yet look closely, and you'll see that they both share an artifact-centric view. The Digital Library Federation sees people, but they are there to "ensure the persistence over time of a collection of digital works." Digital stuff, in other words. Arms at least sees stuff plus services but ends the definition talking about digital formats (stuff).

What are the characteristics of a digital library in new librarianship? Well, we have just reviewed most of them, but let's put it together.

It is a facilitated collection of services (access, structure, search, etc.) that allows for member-supplied organization (aka Scapes, tags, annotations) and provides tools for content creation based on supplied conversation opportunities that match the norms of the community.

18. http://www.diglib.org/about/dldefinition.htm
19. Arms, W. Y. (2000). *Digital libraries. Digital libraries and electronic publishing.* Cambridge, MA: MIT Press.

The librarian also ensures that these services go where the conversation is, but we'll get into that in more depth later in the Thread.

Does a digital library look like a collection of stuff? Well, if that's what the community needs. Does it look like a big threaded discussion board? If that's what the community needs. Does it look like a static, one-way broadcast of existing documents? Never. In fact, increasingly digital libraries need to look more like physical libraries.

PHYSICAL ENVIRONMENTS

If you ever have the chance to see the Graduate Reading Room of the Suzzalo Library at the University of Washington, take it. Likewise the main reading room at the Library of Congress' Jefferson Building. They are spectacular spaces. High vaulted ceilings with classical wooden tables. They are the kind of places filmmakers go when they want to scream "library." Of course, scream might be the wrong word; more like shush. Physical places of all sorts say something.

Stuart Sutton, an associate professor at the University of Washington and a good friend, has one of those backgrounds that just make you feel like you've been wasting your time. He has been in the theater, a law librarian, library director, professor, and a program director. He is also a lawyer. Just about everything in this Atlas that I got right I learned from him. All the wrong stuff is mine. He told me a great story about law offices.

You go into a lawyer's office and sit in a little chair. The lawyer sits in a big chair. Arrayed prominently in the office, either the lawyer's personal office, or near the waiting area, will be volumes upon volumes of law books. They are there, like the big chair, to impress. There is an excellent chance they have never been opened.

The vaulted ceilings of the reading rooms are there to impress. They are aspirational edifices, the soaring ceilings and dark desks are really more a painting of knowledge, a sort of devotional sculpture to how a community wishes to be seen as glorious and knowledgeable.

You might get the impression from my discussion of the Glendale library that I am in some way against or indifferent to physical spaces. You would be wrong. I understand well both the functional and affective dimensions of architecture. When Carnegie built libraries a century ago, he built secular temples to knowledge. In Seattle, Salt Lake City, San Antonio, and Vancouver, new library buildings are a way of raising the visibility of the work of librarians and creating a tangible monument for the community.

There are many people smarter than me working on the design and utilization of physical spaces. Much can be learned in librarian-created online sites from the trends in today's physical libraries. Casual seating, coffee bars, and meeting rooms aren't just the latest trend; they recognize the value of social interaction and conversation. People may go to Starbucks for the coffee, but they stay for the conversation.

You may ask yourself, where is the agreement on the learning commons (or information commons)? After all, shouldn't I be excited about interdisciplinary spaces that fuse services, expertise, and technology? I am, actually, I just think that limiting these types of spaces to one area is wrong. I think that should describe the entire library.

The conceptual foundation of new librarianship adds a few requirements for physical spaces that will be familiar to the commons movement. Much of these are discussed in the review of the Free Library of Philadelphia, but one I wanted to highlight was the development of topical centers.

Topical Centers with Curriculum

One of the core concepts in cataloging is collocation: putting like things together. So the cooking books are together and the books on physics show up next to each other (either physically on shelves or logically in systems). Topical centers seek to extend this concept not only to artifacts (across media types) but also to the inclusion of services (and, in some cases, services without associated artifacts). The idea is not simply to put like things together, but rather to aid like conversations to progress from agreement to agreement by putting like conversations together (as opposed to like artifacts).

The progress from one agreement to another is not automatic. Although it is ultimately the choice of the member what he or she learns next, or how they explore a given domain of knowledge, in many cases, members are more than willing to follow experts or other guides. This is why credibility is so essential to librarians. Part of facilitation is guiding members from their current state of knowledge to a new state, agreement by agreement. They will be willing to follow if they trust us, or we can prove consistently trustworthy guides. So topical centers within a library are more than just collocation, they also have direction.

Take, for example, an entrepreneur with a new business idea. Let's call her Joanne. Joanne can go to the library and find an area of business resources. She can read about the industry she is targeting and find artifacts about marketing and law. However, without a business plan, the likelihood that Joanne will ever actually start the business is low. How does Joanne know this? There may well be a great book on putting together a business plan in the library, but how does she know to look for it?

Once Joanne figures out a business plan, she will need accounting advice, legal help, and even a place to work (we talk about this later as part of the Entrepreurium). She needs access to these experts as well, but in the right sequence. In essence, to truly build her knowledge and solve her information needs, Joanne needs a course in starting a business. This is the idea behind a topical center. It's like a pathfinder for conversations.

Where does the curriculum originate? Well, it depends on the nature of the community being served and the conversation. One can imagine that, in an academic setting, academic departments will provide the curriculum and the librarian will array library resources and services to meet the department's requirements. This is a cornerstone of school librarianship: curriculum mapping. Find out what is happening in the curriculum and tie services and resources to it. It improves usage and outcomes, and it makes assessment much easier (and better).

For the public library, the curriculum might come from a partnering academic institution or other community partner (e.g., local economic development agency for entrepreneurship). For business settings, it may be matching industry certifying guidelines or unit leaders.

Increasingly, however, the curriculum is being developed by communities. In Philadelphia, there was a discussion of teaming up the public library, the public television station, and a lifelong learning organization to use retired experts and professionals to develop courses that could be offered over the air as well as in the library. The best curriculum for emerging technologies is often on the Internet.

So which curriculum? If a topical center is a set of services brought together with a curriculum of some sort, what are the topics? I know it is a bit redundant to even type this, but they come from the community. What are the topics that your community sees as crucial not simply to support but to showcase and move forward?

Realize that these centers may and, in fact, should change over time. One can imagine sort of long-term centers handling large and durable concerns of the community (innovation, age group concerns) and a set of centers that have short, defined lives. Some of the innovative librarian-created programs I have seen have turned foyers into public laboratories and sandboxes. Like museums, librarians set up temporary exhibits to get the community to either focus on a given topic or explore new ideas.

An industry idea worth exploring is "hot desking." New projects and ideas are given a temporary space with desks, white boards, and computers. Teams are brought together to explore the idea and see where it goes. If it turns into something more durable, a more durable home is found. If the idea runs its course, the resources are made available for a new project. These teams can be librarians and a panoply of community members.

This raises one of the issues that almost every organization has to confront. The problem is not developing new initiatives but closing initiatives down. This notion is explored in greater depth in the Topical Centers with Curriculum agreement. This notion is also discussed in more detail later in the Thread. For now, let us turn to the true reality of physical and digital environments—they no longer exist in isolation.

HYBRID ENVIRONMENTS

On the video, you see a hand with a phone in it. The phone faces the ground and displays a live video feed of the road below. As the phone pans up, the video feed is overlaid with text boxes and arrows. As the phone pans to the left and right, the boxes move in unison synched to the objects entering and leaving the frame. As the video feed focuses on a building, the phone's owner hits a text box and up pops a window with more information on the building's architecture. In another video, a person uses his phone to overlay directions to the subway overtop the live video.

They are calling this "augmented reality," and by the time you read these words, it will either be commonplace, passé, or still obscure (my bet is on the first). Long the area of science fiction, the idea of a live heads-up display (in this case, a phones-up display, I suppose) overlaying information on what you see is becoming a reality. Rather than the pure digital realm of cyberspace, augmented reality is an example of a true hybrid environment: the seamless interaction of the digital with the virtual. What you need to realize is that in many places it is already here.

For example, millions of cars each day get stopped by red lights controlled by intelligent transportation management systems that seek to mediate crowded roadways. Through ATM machines, the digital world of finance is translated into paper money. While my office is real enough, the temperature is controlled by an environmental model running on a computer a mile away.

I had a dinner in Key West with a school superintendant from Pennsylvania who talked about having to install metal detectors in his schools. I asked whether the parents of his students had complained. Quite the opposite, he told me, the parents wanted more security. He then went on to outline how he could monitor his school even from several states away. When the students came to school, they brought their school IDs with them. The IDs had RFID chips in them. The chips allowed for automatic attendance and tracked where the students were throughout the day. He had also installed cameras in the halls that he could monitor remotely on his laptop, virtually walking the halls of the schools at any time of day.

The majority of librarians in the world today function in hybrid environments of one sort or another. From full-text CD-ROMs, to virtual branches, to digitized collections, librarians have embraced digital technology to either augment or replace physical services. But the convergence of the physical to the digital into a hybrid environment exists along a sort of continuum. At one end of the spectrum are librarians who have replaced the card catalog with the online catalog. At the other end of the spectrum is augmented reality, making it difficult to separate the physical from the digital.

In between, librarians must understand that physical spaces make excellent feeders to digital worlds. Lecture series can be podcast, meetings can be streamed, and works can be digitized. Likewise, digital environments can be brought into real spaces. Why not simulcast the symphony to library members? Webcasts can be played in classrooms as well as workstations. One of the coolest examples I have seen is at the Seattle Public Library, where the back of the information desk is a video wall with a real-time visualization of catalog searches and borrowing.

Yet in between is also a difficult place to be, as evidenced by librarian-created catalogs. Catalogs were created to maintain physical collections, and it shows. The attempts to truly intermingle digital and physical items have been problematic at best. MARC records for something as dynamic as a website don't work, and few find Dublin Core sufficient for books. Not to mention all of the nonartifact services librarians offer that can never be truly captured and integrated into catalogs. Even with FRBR, the idea of entering an event that needs to disappear from the catalog after it has occurred, while relating it to a recoding of the event (or ongoing discussion that emerges from the event) simply blows up many of the processes set up to capture "information packages." Yet that is what we need.

The point, of course, is not that we must have hybrid environments or augmented reality. As I set out in the "Mission" Thread, we must look deeper than the current trend or technology to what is durable. Then what is durable in the hybrid realm? What reality makes sense to augment? Much of this again depends on your community. In the so-called developed or industrialized world, certainly most information lives are already hybridized. From electronic bank records recording our real debit and credits, to the nearly inescapable digital tracks we leave as we move through the solid streets and buildings, librarians have a role.

Librarians, to this point, have attempted to make the library a sort of sanctuary from the growing surveillance society. Through our fights against the Patriot Act in the United States, to the regular elimination of borrowing records, we preserve intellectual freedom at our borders. However, these borders are increasingly irrelevant. For example, why care if librarians regularly destroy borrowing records when each keystroke a member makes is recorded by his or her Internet Service Provider? Protecting members at our borders is simply no longer enough. As we talk about in the "Improve Society" Thread, we must work with our communities to create appropriate member protections throughout the community.

DIFFERENT COMMUNITIES LIBRARIANS SERVE

One of the highlights of my career was working with an amazing team of talented librarians to put on seven Virtual Reference Desk conferences. At the end of every conference, I would moderate a group plenary to identify themes in the conference, brainstorm new initiatives, and generate ideas on how to improve the conference. One comment was guaranteed to come up: a call for more library-specific tracks (digital reference in academic libraries, serving public library members, etc.). We had specifically designed the conference not to make such distinctions, and I admit to at times being less than diplomatic in resisting such a fragmentation.

I was sharing my frustration with Donna Dinberg, an unsung hero in digital reference. She came up with the best answer. She said, "When they ask for these tracks, tell them that it is their job to take what they learn and apply it to their settings." She went on to eloquently talk about the reality of how each community would be different and how one could never have enough tracks to satisfy all communities (digital reference in Canadian rural libraries with two librarians). Then she talked about the professional responsibility of the attendees to participate. This, she said, is the difference between being part of a movement and simply attending continuing education. If you are in a movement, you digest, synthesize, enact, evaluate, and report. You're not an audience, you are a missionary.

I bring up the conferences as a prelude to discussing specific library types to remind you that the Atlas is not a recipe book. New librarianship is not a hammer in search of nails. Certainly, differences exist between public librarians and academic librarians, but we are all librarians, and our communities do not conform to some standard of "public-ness" or "academic-ness." Librarianship is a common root that must branch out in unique ways to cover our communities.

I was commissioned by the MacArthur Foundation to study the future of libraries. As part of this effort, I would call up librarians and library directors. I would call up a public library director and ask him or her what the future of the library was. "Well, I can't tell you about academic libraries because they're screwed, but the future of public libraries is as a community space focused on learning." I then would call up an academic library director, who would say, "Well, I can't tell you about public libraries because they're screwed, but the future of public libraries is as a community space focused on learning." I just wanted to make two calls and hold the handsets up to each other.

What is my take on the idea that there are fundamental differences between library types? Stop it! You tell me why the New York Public Library is more different from the Yale Library than from a single-room library in rural West Virginia. Well, you say, one has to support students. OK, two thirds of the current MLS class at Syracuse University is comprised of distance students. You're telling me they don't use their public libraries for class at all? How about the fact that many a public librarian will talk about how their children's books collections are greatly reduced once school starts because they are checked out by school librarians? Our communities are not as segmented as we would like to imagine, and neither should our librarians be.

So why break these distinctions out at all in the Atlas? Part of this is a nod to tradition but mostly as a bridge for a field that has already established boundaries. To emphasize the fact that public, academic, special, legal, and so on are contexts that librarians work in, I shift from using librarian to talking about libraries. Why? Because librarians are in a profession and are rooted in the common; libraries are contexts and are grounded in the specific.

You may be tempted to skip through the following section ("I'm a public librarian, so I can skip the academic discussion"), but don't do it. It is not written that way. For example, the agreement on assess-ment is connected to government libraries not because it only applies to government libraries, but because that is the context in which I started addressing the issue.

PUBLIC*

I have visited one-room/one-librarian libraries in the coastal towns of Maine. I have visited the glass and steel urban libraries of New York City. I have been in Swedish libraries that shared space with a symphony and community theaters. From Boston to London to Cincinnati to Beijing, I have seen the mosaic of institutions that share one powerful community idea: They are set up by the public to serve the public.

As I have said before, libraries are aspirational institutions: They are not purely utilitarian. They have become a sort of secular cathedral used to revitalize downtowns, impress a community, and demonstrate a community's commitment not to books but to learning and knowledge. In an age of utilitarian civic structures, the library has often remained a statement in glass, marble, and hard wood.

And why not? It is one of the few civic institutions that span the range of a geographic community. The library provides a connective tissue between young and old, rich and poor. The children of the white collar sit with the children of the blue to listen to story hour. The library is open to banker and beggar alike.

This gives librarians power: power to understand and help improve the community. The public library has become Ray Oldenburg's Third Place:

> Public places on neutral ground where people can gather and interact. In contrast to first places (home) and second places (work), third places allow people to put aside their concerns and simply enjoy the company and conversation around them.[20].

It is increasingly seen as a vital part of a web of learning that includes home, school, and work.

However, public does not mean "all things to all people." Just because you pay taxes doesn't mean you get to drive the fire truck around on the weekends. Public libraries must become masters of mediation, gathering consensus around the conversations of critical importance to the community and then targeting services to those conversations.

*See Agreement Supplement for more on Public Libraries and their communities.
20. http://www.pps.org/info/placemakingtools/placemakers/roldenburg

This work is often hindered by a sort of romantic ideal of libraries. I called it being loved to death.

"What do you think of libraries?" I ask.

"I love libraries," they say. "All the books and the comfortable retreat from the world."

"When's the last time you went to a library?"

"Oh, never."

This is a form of benign neglect. Although it may seem like a positive for the libraries ("At least they say they love us"), come tax time, love tends to fall to money. If you haven't yet, go read OCLC's *From Awareness to Funding*.[21] Go ahead, right now. I'll wait.

What you just read was that, although libraries enjoy widespread support and admiration, they can only count on 7.1% of voters to consistently support increased public funding, with another 32% being "persuadable." What you also read was that the willingness to support the library was not correlated to the frequency of use. Those who love us don't necessarily use us. The good news is that those who do frequently use the library are persuadable:

> Conversely, the Just for Fun segment of Probable Supporters reports by far the most frequent use of the library with more than three times the average. However, this segment is only somewhat more likely than average to definitely vote in favor of a library funding measure.[22]

The authors of the report and I come to different conclusions based on those data. They say:

> The most frequent library visitors are not the right target market for a library funding campaign. Library support is driven by voter attitudes and beliefs, not by awareness of library services or the frequency of library usage.[23]

I wholeheartedly agree that we need to focus on voter attitudes and beliefs in terms of funding. However, I also say the "Just for Fun" group is worthy of targeting. We should strive to turn them into co-owners so they are invested in the continued support of the library. What other industry can say that the most skeptical customers are its biggest users?

All of these factors were brought front and center when I started to work with the Free Library of Philadelphia and their campaign to expand their Central Library.

Free Library of Philadelphia

The Free Library of Philadelphia consists of 54 branches spread over 127 square miles in southeastern Pennsylvania, serving more than 1.5 million residents. The library had finished renovation on its branches and was set to renovate and expand the Central Library on the Benjamin Franklin Parkway. The plan was ambitious. They had a design from the world-famous architect Moshe Sofdie and was well on their way to raising the approximately $100 million they needed to:

> seamlessly add 180,000 square feet of space to the historic Beaux-Arts building. New and improved features [would] include: a Children's Library with a Preschool Center and a Craft Room; a first-ever Teen Center; a new 550-seat auditorium; two new Internet Browsing Centers, outfitted with 300 public-access computers; a new Business Department, with presentation space, online resources and a complete curriculum in business development; and a soaring, glass-enclosed pavilion with shops, a cafe and ample space for community gatherings.[24]

The library foundation, charged with fundraising and construction, was looking to have a new set of library services to match the facility. Rather than build a temple to books, the folks at the Free Library wanted to innovate and build a total library program for the future.

This, of course, was before the economic tsunami hit the country in the fall of 2008. Although the majority of funds for the central expansion were privately raised, it was deemed politically impossible to move ahead with the project when city budgets called for the closing of 11 branches (and a standoff between the mayor and the state threatened to close the library entirely). The proposed closing of the branches proved to be an interesting case study in and of itself in terms of social compacts.

With major budget cuts and a directive by the mayor to "do less with less," the library proposed closing 11 branches. They looked to ensure that, even with the closings, no member would be more than two miles from a library. However, the closings were blocked by the city council. As for the reason behind the push, was it lack of access? Diminished learning opportunities? Nope. It was this: Where would the kids go after school to be supervised?

21. http://www.oclc.org/reports/funding/default.htm
22. http://www.oclc.org/reports/funding/chapter4.pdf
23. Ibid.
24. http://libwww.freelibrary.org/expansion/

The librarians were operating with one set of values, whereas the politicians saw a different value equation. Yet rather than having an open and explicit conversation about library mission, it ended up in the courts under the aegis of mayoral power.

Although we can learn from the program plans of Philadelphia, we cannot avoid the obvious and painful lesson as well. We don't always get to win, and great ideas don't always rule the day. I worked with some outstanding librarians in Philadelphia. They were dedicated to making the city a better place. They were competent, inventive, and utterly professional. It pains me to see them battered and beaten in the winds of a financial and political storm. I'll talk about this more in the "Librarians" Thread in terms of change agents, but the sad truth is, no matter how good a librarian you are, you must learn grace in defeat. Never learn to like it, never learn to look for it, never take it as a final answer, but know it will come. As Craig Ferguson said, success is continuing to fail until you don't.

What follows, then, is not a description of what is but of what could be: a set of public library services developed in conjunction with the Philadelphia community to illustrate the ideas of new librarianship. The focus in these agreements is on topical centers with a curriculum.

*Entrepreneurium**

Public libraries are vital engines of economic development. They contribute to a skilled workforce, make the community more inviting for business and serve as the information source for small businesses. As the Urban Library Council stated:

> Public libraries build a community's capacity for economic activity and resiliency, says a new study from the Urban Institute. [The study] adds to the body of research pointing to a shift in the role of public libraries—from a passive, recreational reading and research institution to an active economic development agent, addressing such pressing urban issues as literacy, workforce training, small business vitality and community quality of life.

The question the Free Library had to answer was how to be an "active economic development agent." It turns out the answer came from an unexpected but, in hindsight, an obvious place.

Linda Johnson, the head of the Free Library's Foundation, had pulled together a technology advisory council. On that council, she

*See Agreement Supplement for an IMLS-format proposal for the Entrepreneurium.

had venture capitalists who funded technology companies, the founder of a tech company, and a few other consultants. In essence, she had a board of entrepreneurs. The original idea was to call these folks together and ask them to help plan the technology in the new library expansion. Almost from the first minute, however, they started planning how the library could incubate small business.

It was an organic shift. It started by talking about how the library could provide physical interfaces to digital retail. Netflix is great, but only if you have access to a computer to pick out your movies—the same goes for Amazon. What if the library provided physical storefronts for interested online retailers? This evolved into a discussion about public spaces and the library's relation to companies.

Interesting to note is that, when asked how the library helped the businesses represented on the board, the entrepreneurs admitted that it didn't. Most of them had library and information services of their own. However, they were quick to add, when they started their businesses, the public library was invaluable. Either they had no access to libraries (particularly expensive licensed databases) or they couldn't use them because they planned to leave their current employers.

That's when the Entrepreneurium started in earnest. What would be the ideal setup for the public library to support entrepreneurs and small businesses? Here's the list they devised:

- Services Offered

  - Mentoring and access to venture capitalists
  - A suite of computer tools and classes
  - Presentation space and video conference facilities
  - Organized programs of speakers and visits to local businesses and entrepreneurs
  - Access to business cases and a full business collection, including databases

- A Virtual and Physical Space

  - The center is a meeting point for the entrepreneurship community of Philadelphia, including board rooms and seminars
  - Access to online resources, plus a place to securely store presentations, business plans, and the digital backbone of a budding business
  - Workspaces for projects

- The Physical

  - Board room with smart board projection and video conference capability

- Work "pods" with networked computer, white board, and desk
- Small meeting spaces for mentoring and workgroups
- Fedex/Kinko's print center and a physical location for online-only stores such as Amazon and Netflix
- Hall of fame to recognize donors and success stories

- The Virtual

  - Online resource scheduling
  - Secure storage of digital files
  - Streaming video of presentations
  - Access to business databases
  - Ability to create online pitches with video and voice-over slides
  - Social network of mentors and entrepreneurs

- The Resource Collection

  - Business databases
  - Bloomberg, Gartner, Forrester, and so on
  - Journals and magazines
  - Fortune, inc., and so on
  - Business cases and business plans

- Management

  - Board of advisors consisting of business leaders and successful entrepreneurs provides strategic direction for the Entrepreneurium
  - Department head provides day-to-day operations and reference support

- Plan of Support

  - Business leaders provide support for recognition in the hall of fame and early access to entrepreneurs
  - Free library of Philadelphia annual budget for most of the collection
  - Pro bono volunteers in law, finance, marketing, and other related sectors

Note how many of these are centered on conversations and working with people, not just resources (meeting spaces, mentoring, etc.). One of the services I particularly liked was the organization of visits to successful small businesses. Not only can librarians leave the building, they can take their members with them.

What is not obvious from this list is that "Organized Programs of Speakers and Visits to Local Businesses and Entrepreneurs" is really

a curriculum. Members of the public would apply to be part of the program and go through the center in cohorts.

Also notice the "Management" section of the list. The business community I talked with not only pushed for co-ownership of the center, they wanted it formalized as a board with by-laws and all. This was not an invention of the librarians. In fact, the whole idea was driven by the business community. Once invited in, they were anxious to become part of the library.

A formal proposal for the Entrepreneurium can be found in the Entrepreneurium Agreement Supplement, which provides more details on the idea. In the "Improve Society" Thread, I spend a little more time on innovation versus entrepreneurship.

Writing Center

The success of the Entrepreneurium's planning process led to us to look for more places to build topical centers. Our eyes turned toward the successful lecture series the Free Library hosted. Every year the Central Library hosted famous authors, thinkers, and celebrities to come to Philadelphia and read from their books. Past speakers included Michael Palin, Joyce Carol Oates, Salman Rushdie, Orson Scott Card, and John Updike. The idea was to build on a writing reputation with a Writing Center. So a focus group was pulled together of published authors, poets, and avid local writers.

As before, we wanted to talk about how the library could help writers. This time, we prepared the list of services to jump-start the conversation. There were two notable entries on that list. The first was a sort of matching service where the library would build writing clubs so that writers could review each other's works. This was notable in that the focus group hated the idea. It turns out that writers' clubs are very much about the social dynamic, and personalities matter. People didn't want to be in a club until they had some serious conversations with each other.

The second notable list item, however, they loved: on-demand printing. Here the writers and the librarians had a sort of intellectual jam session. What started as a literary repository, where the authors (or anyone else) could print off copies of manuscripts on demand, quickly evolved into a social network of writers built around the concept of literary journals. The idea was that entries into the repository could be remixed with other writings to create unique compilations that could be printed or made available through the web. It was an idea that would come into play again.

When the idea of creating a Free Library imprint was raised, once again the writers balked. They wanted no restrictions on what went into the repository. They also wanted no form of established review criteria. The writing community had plenty of venues for publication with reviews and imprints; they wanted a more open and creative space.

In addition to the hybrid services (including writing workshops in person and on demand), the group talked about designing physical spaces. They envisioned two spaces. The first was quiet and full of power outlets for the actual writing. The second was a salon, or social space for writers, and those who were interested in writers.

The curriculum for the center would come through the writing workshops based on a successful poetry writing series earlier offered at the library.

When the question of governance was brought up, there was a considerably different approach to the Entrepreneurium. All the writers expressed confidence in the librarians to make the operational decisions. They thought an e-mail list for quick consultation with the writers as a whole would suffice for community governance.

Music Center

In 2008, sales of CDs and albums (including digital downloads) dropped 14% from the year before and 45% since the peak of record sales in 2000.[25] According to Recording Industry Association of America's (RIAA's) own statistics, the net value of music shipped in 2007 was $10.4 billion, down $4.2 billion from its peak in 1999. Although there are many possible reasons for this decline (some say piracy, some say competition of different media, some say bad business models, and some say a wider distribution channel for music), it is clear that the existing model of music publishing is in peril.

However, if you think that is bad, try writing classical music for a living. There are a few traditional classical publishers, but they're all on the brink, and most are being bought and sold between one conglomerate or another, so most composers self-publish.

We were told this by a focus group brought together to talk about a Music Center. Why music? First, it was a strategic desire to partner with cultural heritage institutions along a rejuvenated parkway cultural corridor. Next, the Free Library already had a special place in music in the form of the Fleisher Collection:

The Edwin A. Fleisher Collection of Orchestral Music is the world's largest lending library of orchestral performance material, with over 21,000 titles and growing.

It houses virtually the entire standard repertoire, and is also known for its many rare and out-of-print works available for lending around the world. It is a unique source of 19th- and 20th-century American music, and has a longstanding commitment to promoting new, noteworthy, and overlooked works.[26]

Add to this a vibrant arts scene in Philadelphia and a new performance space to be part of the expansion, and it was just a natural fit.

So what did the musicians want in their center? CDs and musical scores? Nope—they wanted two grand pianos on a stage. Why? Let's start with the pianos. If you recall in the discussion on language with all the L_0s and L_1s, the musicians wanted a way to communicate in their own L_1. It just so happens that it is in the form of musical notes instead of words. To have a meaningful musical conversation, they needed instruments and a place to perform together.

The stage, however, was not just a place to converse with other musicians. It turns out that downtown Philadelphia had a scarcity of performance spaces. For the musicians, it was performance that mattered. In fact, here the writer's remix repository idea was once again revisited. The assembled focus groups loved the idea of creating a repository for scores and performances—they had few other outlets. Also, they didn't worry about the sharing aspect because for them the value of having the work performed far outweighed the remote possibility of royalties. Unlike the writers, however, not everything the community wrote would end up in the repository. They wanted only performed music to be added to the repository system.

It is in the development of the Music Center that the idea of the Publisher of Community (see the "Facilitate" Thread) was formed. No longer would the community of Philadelphia come to the library to learn about other communities. Now, at least in music (and writing), other communities would come to the Free Library to learn about Philadelphia. The repository was also remarkable because it shows how centers can be birthplaces of ideas that can be incorporated into other centers.

25. http://www.nytimes.com/2009/01/01/technology/01iht-music.4.19032321.html
26. http://libwww.library.phila.gov/collections/collectionDetail.cfm?id=14

The curriculum for the center would be based on music appreciation built around the actual performances. Rather than focusing on creating musicians, the focus would be on creating informed listeners. As for governance, the musicians wanted a trusted curator to choose the performance schedule.

THE REAL VALUE OF CENTERS

So how does the center idea emerge from our understanding of knowledge? First, it facilitates:

- **Access:** It brings together conversants and appropriate resources to build knowledge.

- **Knowledge:** Through a curriculum, it helps novices quickly gain the requisite knowledge to participate in conversations.

- **Environment:** Through community-based governance systems, it ensures a feeling of ownership and trust with the community.

- **Motivation:** It allows interested community members to follow their intrinsic interests, as well as create publication systems based on the community's norms of recognition.

In terms of the fundamentals of learning, it concentrates conversants, supports their unique L_1 system of language, allows for guidance through existing agreements (the curriculum) as well as the creation of new agreements, and builds a memory of the conversations over time (the repository).

There is increasing talk of libraries being places of knowledge creation (e.g., such as this entire Atlas), but without real services and a proactive approach, the knowledge creation is diffuse. The center idea allows for focus and evaluation. By concentrating the efforts of the community and creating cohorts, the library can speed the development and diffusion of knowledge throughout the community and beyond.

It is not enough to hang out an empty canvas and expect art to occur. Aside from the tools of creation—paints and brushes—the artist needs a community from which to draw. The artist draws inspiration, learns new techniques, gets feedback, and ultimately develops an audience. Similarly, the library can't simply say it has arrayed a set of generic resources and services and expect great knowledge to occur. Rather, the community must be groomed, inspired, and given direction to achieve their aspirations.

ACADEMIC*

The drive to Albany from Syracuse can be spectacular. Early on a fall morning, the mists cling to the Erie canal, and the bright reds and yellows of the changing leaves frame a blue sky and oddly attractive rusting infrastructure. I took the drive at the invitation of New York State's Department of Education. The Office of Higher Education had a problem. They were getting requests to accredit graduate degree programs from out-of-state distance education institutions. The problem was that these institutions would not have physical facilities in the state, and one of the standards that had to be evaluated was the availability of library services.

You see, one of these universities argued that, by providing compiled readers for students, they were providing sufficient library services. Of course the standards were written in terms of collections:

> Describe traditional and electronic library holdings and access to them, indicating the approximate number of titles and periodical subscriptions in the present collection that would support the program.[27]

The universities argued that if the program needed a certain set of readings and they were provided, they had sufficient holdings to support the program. The Department of Education folks were more interested in how graduate students could explore their chosen disciplines beyond just a set of class readings. This is an example of how artifact-centricity can be problematic.

The standard was written around a model where the value of the library is in its artifacts and other things that can be counted. The intention was the richness of knowledge generation and, therefore, the richness of the conversations that could be had. Instead of asking what was the sufficiency of learning opportunities available to the student outside of direct class time, they had asked how many books and journals the institution had on a given topic.

Let's see if we can use our understanding of knowledge and facilitation to determine the sufficiency of library service:

- Conversants: Does the library service provide members of the academic community (faculty, students, staff) access to a range of conversants commensurate with the degree program?

*See Agreement Supplement for some ideas on better integrating academic libraries into the academy.

27. http://www.highered.nysed.gov/ocue/documents/progregprocedures.pdf

Figure 41

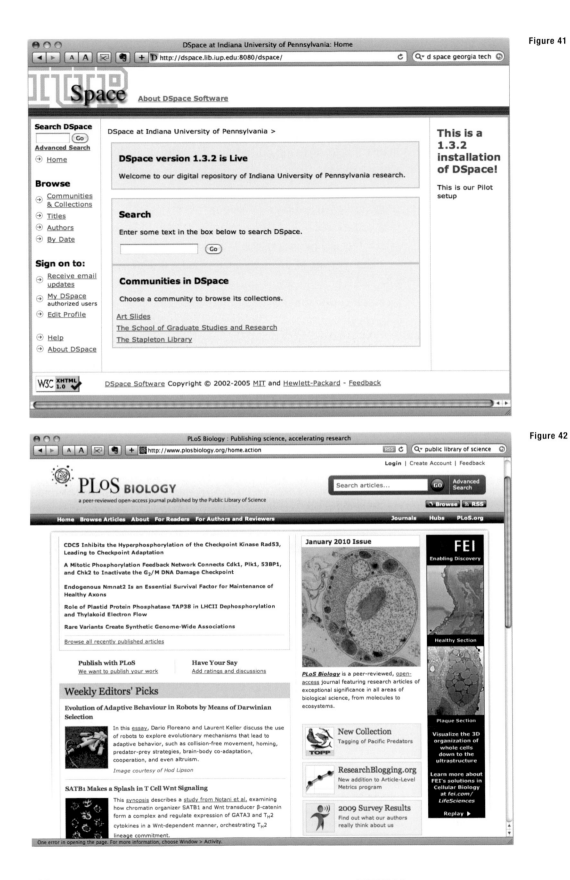

Figure 42

- Language: Do the librarians provide services at a sufficient level of expertise to the learning community (in other words, if you are teaching computer science, can the students access services and materials beyond simply "Java for Dummies")? Note that this means the facilitators of these conversations (faculty and librarians) need to prove expertise in the topic.

- Agreements: Do the librarians provide services aligned to the full range of understandings in a given academic program—is it mapped to the curriculum?

- Memory: Do the librarians provide a means to capture and retrieve new agreements developed by the academic community as well accurately represent and/or preserve the previous conversations?

To evaluate specific services, let's look at our four types of facilitation:

- Access: Can the academic community get to the necessary conversations?

- Knowledge: Do the librarians provide the necessary knowledge services and training to access and participate in conversations?

- Environment: Do the librarians provide sufficient safeguards for member privacy and academic freedom?

- Motivation: How do the librarians encourage knowledge creation in the domains taught, and are members of the community required to use library services?

Note how most of these questions are phrased in terms of librarians and not libraries. To simply provide materials is not providing library services. However, the standard as written in no way requires the skills of a librarian to fulfill the standard.

Also note that these questions are in line with the fact that accrediting agencies in higher education are shifting from an output model (things that can be counted, such as graduates, books, etc.) to an outcomes model (a measure of impact).

Of course, artifact-centricity pervades all sorts of library services. Take, for example, the last "next big thing" in academic libraries: the institutional repository.

Issues of Institutional Repositories*

Institutional repositories in the abstract make great sense in the future of academic libraries. They solve a key problem that libraries face in a connected world. If the role of the library is to collect materials outside of an academic community to make it more available to that community, the Internet presents some big problems. Instead of having to go through the library to acquire stuff, faculty and students can go directly to the provider of the information (or some alternative provider).

In this disintermediated world, it makes sense to collect things unique to the organization. By collecting the works of the academy, you are guaranteed relevance. More than that, you have the advantage of capturing the intellectual output of the institution and possibly save costs in terms of subscriptions and such. There's only one problem: All of this depends on a single big assumption (and you can see it coming from a mile away by now): The value resides in the artifacts being collected.

You see, this Atlas has no value if it just sits on my computer. It gains value when it is discussed in the community and when those conversations lead to impact. Although there are all sorts of shortcuts to measuring impact—citation counts, journal impact factors, and the like—impact still matters. Having a document sit in a repository helps no one.

This is the whole idea behind peer review. The peer review process acts as a moderator for a community conversation. Ideas are vetted, yes, but also refined through the editorial process. It is not that non-peer-reviewed materials are valueless; they simply enter a community conversation in a more raw form—they lack the credibility arrived at through reliable comments of peers—putting a greater burden on the reader to evaluate the credibility of the information. Peer review, although not alleviating the burden ("work" might be a better term) of the reader, places a large part of the burden on the editors, reviewers, and authors. It is a conversation among a subgroup of the community that precedes dissemination to the whole. So the question for academic librarians is: Does your repository capture the richness of this conversation or simply the artifacts?

Compare two repositories. The first, figure 41, is a DSpace implementation.[28] The second, figure 42, is the Public Library of Science Biology.[29]

The first tells you what is in the repository, and the second tells you what people are talking about. Note the "Editors' Pick," which

---

*See Agreement Supplement for an overview of institutional repositories and an annotated bibliography on the topic.

28. http://smartech.gatech.edu/handle/1853/6038
29. http://www.plosbiology.org/home.action

links to blogs and rating systems. The Public Library of Science Biology is about a community, and the DSpace repository is about a collection of stuff. As an academic, I am part of a community of scholars with borders beyond my own university. How can librarians help me with that?

To answer that question, we need to stop thinking of scholarly output and start truly supporting scholarly communications.

*Scholarly Communications**

Joan Bechtel was ahead of her time. In 1986, she wrote:[30]

> That these are challenging, often difficult, times for academic libraries is no news to anyone in the library world. Concern for professionalism, with its attention to accountability and responsibility, abounds. Unprecedented growth in technology provides vast new opportunities for communication, and the availability of information far outstrips most people's capacity to digest it all. In the face of this information explosion, it is ironic that academic librarians are casting about for an appropriate myth or model for library service.... While critics charge that academic libraries are not sufficiently integrated into the central concerns of the college or university and that librarians have their own, independent agendas, librarians responsible for present services as well as plans for the future are uneasy.
>
> Perhaps it is an overstatement to say that academic librarians are drifting in a vast sea of information and technological advances, searching for an appropriate course of action. Nevertheless, we appear to have lost the stabilizing rudder of confidence in who we are and what we are to do.
>
> As a more powerful alternative to the images of librarianship already available or proposed, I suggest that we begin to think of libraries as centers for conversation and of ourselves as mediators of and participants in the conversations of the world.

It is now more than two decades later, and still academic libraries have failed to fully incorporate these ideas.

I was at a meeting with a group of academic librarians discussing changes in scholarly communications. There was a general acknowledgment that just capturing journal articles and books was not enough. What was frustrating was that there was a general attitude that the scholars needed to figure it out so the librarians could go about the task of collecting and organizing the important stuff. OK, I'm a scholar—I don't trust myself to figure this out. I am proud and in awe of my colleagues' immense talent—I don't trust them either. We produce this stuff for lots of different reasons; we need help making sense of it all. If only there were a profession out there dedicated to making sense of resources in a knowledge environment—oh wait, that's you.

The academic librarian must not hold a shovel in one hand—heaping possibly related artifacts on a researcher at the beginning of his or her work—and a catcher's mitt in the other to "catch" the articles and artifacts published as a result of the research. Instead, librarians must facilitate the entire research process. In doing so, they not only provide better service, they become part of the scholarly conversation (I include teaching courses in this) and can build better knowledge discovery and memory systems. Let me give two examples: supporting funded research and the support of tenure.

There are a great number of disciplines where getting funding from a research project will result in the building of a website. Sometimes the website is just brochureware with the basics of the project. Sometimes it is a glorified blog with updates and initial results. In a growing number of cases, projects are requiring more interactive and social features. Large projects need to support many investigators working in different departments and universities. After the end of the project, results and communications need to be archived.

Right now, much of this responsibility is taken on by well-meaning faculty and graduate assistants. Why not instead see this as a service of the academic library? Librarians can bring considerable talent in information organization, social networking, and technical skills to use the web to support the project through its entire life cycle. Start with setting up a working space for proposal writing. Then post the initial project announcement, ensuring the announcement is also fed through university communication channels. As the project progresses, the librarian can aid in supporting the research activities through reference and identifying resources. As papers emerge, as well as blog posts, presentations, and software, this scholarly communication will make it to the project website as well as the library's growing scholarly repository. Finally, as the project winds down, the web space can be archived for future work.

---

*See Agreement Supplement for more thoughts on scholarly communications.

30. Bechtel, J. M. (1986). Conversation, a New Paradigm for Librarianship? *College and Research Libraries*, 47(3), 219–224.

What's more, the support for these services can be built directly into the grant. Faculty are more than willing to include dissemination costs as long as it is easy to include and well justified in proposal budgets. This doesn't even touch how such services provided solely as overhead (or indirect costs) make it clear to faculty and administration alike how the library is directly supporting the research of the institution. In the "Ability to Work in Interdisciplinary Teams" agreement supplement, I talk about some of these initiatives under the aegis of Cyber-Infrastructure Facilitator.

The second example of integrating librarian service into the scholarly life is in the tremendous opportunities around tenure.[31] Every year across the world, professors of every discipline go up for tenure. At a time known well in advance, professors compile amazingly detailed accountings of their research, teaching, and service. They put together boxes (or, increasingly, thumb drives) full of articles, syllabi, research reports, and more. At no other time in their careers are faculty members as highly motivated, organized, and desperate for help.

So what does every library that I know (save one) do with this opportunity? They wait for the faculty member to ask for a citation analysis as a reference question. Or worse, and I am not making this up, they wait for the request and then offer to teach the faculty member to do a citation analysis him or herself. That's right, faculty asking for help on bibliographic analysis, and we tell them they can learn everything they need to know in an hour or by reading a website.

Why not get a list of those going up for tenure a year in advance, go knock on their doors, introduce yourself, and offer to help (show up with an initial Web of Science search just to get their attention). Even better, have faculties write it into tenure guidelines that they ensure the validity of the process by having a trusted third party (you) do a citation analysis. This way you get access to the scholarly works of the faculty member, and, if they get tenure, you have made a friend for life. If they don't get tenure, they leave the university and can't badmouth you!

My point with both of these examples is that academic libraries must stop worrying about managing the stuff used in research (and teaching and service) and start improving the research (and teaching and service). If you facilitate the processes essential to the functioning of the academy, you become essential. Change the word "academy" for community, and it is a lesson we can all use.

31. For those keeping track, this is actually the second time I raise this idea. The first was in a slightly different context in the "Facilitating" Thread. I clearly think this is a good idea.

GOVERNMENT*

If public libraries are institutions funded by the public to serve the public, government libraries are funded by the public to support the agencies that serve the public. Although they often have an outward-facing set of services, they are often set up to first serve some governmental agency. Hence, the Library of Parliament in Canada serves the Senate and the House of Commons, the Library of Congress serves the U.S. Congress, and the National Library of Education in the United States has public services, but their main clientele is the Department itself.

Some of these libraries are huge. National Libraries can coordinate efforts at the national and international levels and house vital functions related to copyright. Some of these institutions are tiny, sometimes merely a room full of documents (which, to my mind, is not a library). Over the past few years, federal libraries in the United States have seen bleak times that often brought their public missions into direct opposition to internal missions.

However, not all U.S. federal libraries have public faces at all. This is the case within the U.S. Department of Justice.

Department of Justice*

Blane Dessy is a friend of mine. We met when he became the first director of the National Library of Education and I was part of the ERIC system that was made part of the new library. I used to joke with Blane that being a contractor to the Department of Education was no fun. There were no secret labs, no special forces, no cool James Bond spy things going on.

Then I went to visit Blane at his new job as the director of the U.S. Department of Justice Law Libraries. Oh sure, you had to wear an ID badge at Education, but you didn't have to go through a special enclosed detection system under the watchful supervision of armed guards. As Blane walked me to the library, he would point out interesting facts: "Turns out this is the best intersection for a biological attack on DC—crosswinds" and "That wall wasn't here last week." It was fun in a sort of worrying-about-whether-you-paid-all-your-parking-tickets kind of way.

*See Agreement Supplement for a discussion and links related to government libraries.
*See Agreement Supplement for a full report on the work I did at the Department of Justice.

However, once within the Department of Justice libraries, I found an amazingly dedicated group of librarians who were entrepreneurial and had proved their value well beyond the scope of their collections. Much of this is detailed in the "Department of Justice" Agreement Supplement, but that value for me was clearly demonstrated when they told me about their catalog system being down for three weeks. Yup, three weeks. The number of complaints in a Departmental staff of more than 105,000? Less than 20.

Now to be fair, not all 105,000 folks work in the DC offices of the Department. There are a lot in the FBI, Immigration, and such. Still, say there are more than 1,000 employees directly served by the Law Libraries. Why so few complaints? It is *not* because the Department of Justice doesn't use the Law Libraries. It is because the librarians have made themselves the main interface to library services. From finding a book (the lawyers don't care whether a book they need is on the shelf, down the street, or across the country), to searching for expert witness information, to becoming a part of litigation teams, the librarians of Justice (a great name for a band) understand their members: The librarians understand that most of those members want conversations and interactions, not interfaces and collection statistics.

An unintended result of these librarians developing new ways of serving their members was that traditional means of assessing their services did not work. Add to this an environment that was not always starved for resources, and the need for strong evaluation just wasn't there.

ASSESSMENT*

Don't be fooled by how we arrived at the "Assessment" agreement. Just because the method of assessment discussed was developed as part of work with the U.S. Department of Justice, assessment is a universal concern for librarians. Assessment is not just something tacked onto the end of a project or some time period to see what happened. Instead, it is a constant means to ensure the success of yourself and the members you serve.[32]

I have to admit that, at times, talking about assessment can give me a headache. There are smart people out there who can splice the difference between assessment and evaluation and spin massive complex webs of intentions and variables. However, I think, for most, we overcomplicate it (so we need to assess what a student learned, what the instructor thought the student learned, how both felt about how they learned, and align those to the standards set forth by the assessors, using evidence of performance, as well as process divided by the hypotenuse of the triangle). Assessment comes down to this: What needs to get done, how are we going to do it, are we doing it, and how can we do it better?

As I have mentioned before, new librarianship must be focused on outcomes rather than outputs. This comes from our mission not just current trends. Our ultimate effectiveness is through action and direct involvement: facilitation, not simply creating an environment; knowledge creation, not simply managing static artifacts. To measure the environment we create is insufficient. The number of volumes and their circulation don't mean anything if we can't tie them to their impact.

Assessment based on output is a functional approach. Just like our earlier examples with Wikipedia versus Encarta and MySpace versus GeoCities, outputs don't give you much insight into improvement. Without measuring our impacts and what the member has accomplished, we do not gain insight into how to evolve our services. Some of these ideas are addressed in the "Risks of Data" agreement and the "Improve Society" Thread, but let me give a quick example here.

Several public libraries I've worked with have had an effort to get all community members library cards. As a data point, this will show a huge spike in cards issued. However, what good did it do? Did it lead to more people actually using the library? One library targeted all incoming kindergartners in the city schools. Did it raise school test scores? Without these kinds of impact measures, all you know is that the library had to do a lot of work and spend more money on cards, but you have no idea whether it was worth it.

At least circulation is a measure of use, unlike measures such as number of volumes held. All this shows is that the library expended money, not that it has done so toward a purpose. In new librarianship, assessment must be centered on the conversations of the members, or in the aggregate, conversations of the community.

We already have two sets of criteria for assessment: one for the librarian and one for the member. For the librarian, we need to evaluate how well they facilitate:

- Access: how well did you provide access to service and conversations?

*See Agreement Supplement for more on the importance of library assessment.
32. Oakleaf, Megan. (2009). "The Information Literacy Instruction Assessment Cycle: A Guide for Increasing Student Learning and Improving Librarian Instructional Skills." *Journal of Documentation*, 65(4).

- Knowledge: how well did you instill the necessary knowledge to engage in these conversations?

- Environment: did you provide a safe environment?

- Motivation: how effectively did you motivate the member to create knowledge?

  For the member, we need to assess the knowledge-creation

  process and outcomes:

- Conversants: did the member effectively access conversant?

- Language: did the member's language move from L_0 to L_1?

- Agreements: did the member build a workable set of agreements to solve his or her problems?

- Memory: are these agreements integrated into their larger knowledge?

Obviously these are high-level criteria that need to be operationalized in a given community with a given service/conversation. There are also questions of formative and summative evaluation, quantitative and qualitative measures, and authentic and object evaluations, but I leave that to the experts.[33]

What I do now is show you a method I developed to both plan and evaluate librarian-developed service around conversations, which I call Mapping Conversations. It is important to see planning and assessment as part of the same process. You need to know what you want to do to know whether you accomplished your task. Likewise, you need to know whether you accomplished your task so you can plan your next steps.

Mapping Conversations

Mapping conversations is a way to identify community conversations and their priorities. It is a process I originally developed as part of my studies at the Department of Justice Law Libraries to make sense of the data I had gathered. It has since been tested at a small liberal arts college and several public libraries. I present it here more as an example of planning and assessment around conversations than a complete and ready methodology.

This process is strongly influenced by Lewin's Force Field Model.[34] Kurt Lewin was one of the most significant social psychologists of the twentieth century.[35] He spent a good amount of time studying how people and organizations change. He developed the force field approach to model how change decisions were made:

- Investigate the balance of power involved in an issue

- Identify the most important players (stakeholders) and target groups for a campaign on the issue

- Identify opponents and allies

- Identify how to influence each target group

We return to Lewin's work when discussing change management in the "Librarians" Thread.

Let me lay out the basics. First, it is important that this is a process that should be conducted with members and the community you seek to serve. Without such input, librarians are apt to see what they want to see, not necessarily what is really there.

STEP 1: IDENTIFY KEY MEMBER GROUPS (STAKEHOLDERS)

Here we want to identify the groups (subcommunities) of members to which librarians can be of service and converse with. One of these groups consists of the librarians or librarian. Recall that even if there is only one librarian serving a community, he or she still has an internal dialog (how am I doing, what more do I need to know, what can I do next, etc.). These groups form one of two axes, with time being the second as seen in figure 43.

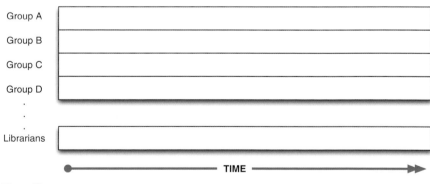

Figure 43

33. See, for example, Oakleaf, Megan. (2008). Dangers and opportunities: A conceptual map of information literacy assessment tools." *Portal: Libraries and the Academy*, *8*(3); and Oakleaf, Megan, and Kaske, Neal. (2009). Guiding questions for assessing information literacy in higher education. *Portal: Libraries and the Academy*, *9*(2).
34. Lewin, K. (1951). *Field theory in social science*. Chicago: University of Chicago Press.
35. Haggbloom et al. (2002). *Review of General Psychology*, *6*(2), 139–215.

Step 2: Identify Key Conversations Within and Across the Member Groups

Many of the key conversations are held within groups; that's why the groups exist in the first place. However, some conversations cross the groups. It is especially important to determine as best you can what the desired outcome of these conversations will be. Only by knowing the point of these conversations (realizing that recreation and socializing are important goals in and of themselves) can we truly provide facilitation. In figure 44, we add these cross-group conversations.

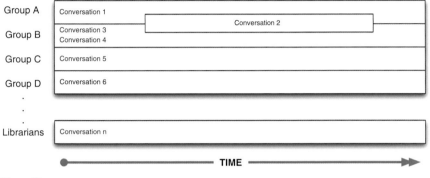

Figure 44

Step 3: Identify Regularities in the Conversations

Some conversations have a regular progression. These might be formally mandated (elections), historically driven (planning the traditional Fall Festival), or emergent (Professor Smith always assigns this paper in October). By identifying the structure of conversations (and mapping them like in figure 45), librarians can better support them. Where structure doesn't exist, it may be an opportunity for a librarian to assist members in developing one. However, you have to be careful not to overprescribe structure before the conversants are ready for it.

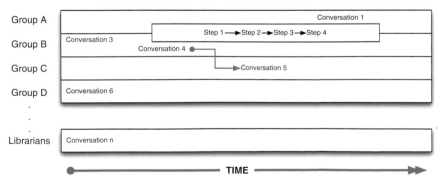

Figure 45

Step 4: Map Any Existing Librarian Services

In many cases, the community will already have existing library services. It is useful to identify these services for two reasons: to identify them for later value assignments, and to determine whether there are services that don't map to any of the identified conversations (such as Service C in figure 46).

Up until this point, the map is most useful as an assessment tool. We can identify orphaned services and attach other data to the conversations and services, such as resource usage, member satisfaction surveys, and more, and still capture a big picture. The next set of steps takes this baseline data into a planning process.

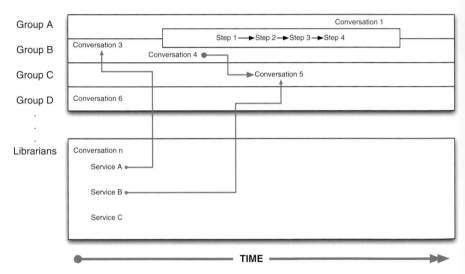

Figure 46

This is the first of two value steps. In this step, we see what value the librarians can bring to the conversations. This comes not only from the librarians' perspectives but from the community as well. However, these impacts will probably not be phrased as "my life would be sooooo much better if there was a librarian helping me with this." You need to understand what the conversants are trying to accomplish. In any case, here is a set of questions that will *not* help you figure this out.

"How do you use the library?" I hate to be the one to break this to you, but the universe does not revolve around you. It revolves around me. OK, so it revolves around the person who is answering the question, and he or she most likely has not taken the time to think about how every potential source of aid can help him or her out in detail.

"What do you want?" If the person knew that, he or she wouldn't need help. Members can't articulate what they want—they have a hard enough time trying to figure out just what they need. This is common knowledge in things such as interface design, where, to overcome a lack of people's ability to specify what they need, we regularly strap eye-tracking rigs on their heads and sit them in labs. We then ask them their questions and infer from there.

Although I will let smarter people talk about how to properly ask questions, I will state the obvious—it matters how you ask questions. My grandfather, God rest his soul, was possibly the worst salesman ever. He sold boxes, and every day he would walk into a customer's shop and ask, "You don't need any boxes today, do you?" Although this approach ensured he might be pleasantly surprised from time to time, it did not sell a lot of boxes.

But I digress. In this step, you, along with the members, assign a value from 1 (little potential for impact) to 5 (librarians can have a big and beneficial impact on this conversation). These values should be arrived at using the criteria for members' knowledge and librarian facilitation discussed earlier in the "Assessment" agreement. I've done this in figure 47.

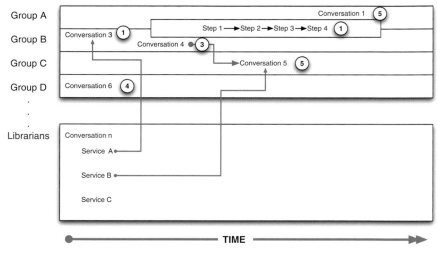

Figure 47

In Step 5, you asked how you could help out the conversations; in this step, you ask how they can help you out.

In the early development of this process, I was working with a small liberal arts college. The librarians dutifully identified the stakeholders, the conversations, and so on. One of the conversations they identified was the faculty discussing redoing the core curriculum. This was a big deal at the college because it involved all departments and was seen as important (and contentious). When I asked what the library was doing in that conversation, the answer was: "Nothing. Why?"

"It's the work of the faculty," they said.

"Won't a new core curriculum have an impact on the collections?" I asked.

"Absolutely. But what can the library add?" they asked.

"Is this the first college to redo the core curriculum? Can't you provide examples of revised curricula from like institutions? Can you create a home for ongoing comment by the faculty and eventually students online?" I asked.

The point is—and I know this sounds near mercenary—if the conversation is important to your community, you need to find a way to be a part of it. I have little doubt that in many cases you can find a way to be of great value, but in any case it is important to be engaged in the major conversations of a community, even if you are on the periphery. I've done this in figure 48.

To this point, we have really developed a needs assessment. We have a current status and a list of value targets. You can carry this needs assessment through a strategic planning process.

The final step, and it is a big one, is to bring the map of the conversation in line with the values arrived at in Stages 5 and 6. The easy part is to identify all the "1/1s": that is, low-impact, low-priority conversation/service pairings. Also easy to identify, although much more complex to fulfill, are all the "5/5s": high-impact, high-priority conversation/service pairings. The real work is in the middle ground. What high-potential impact conversations are you not serving or underserving? What do you do with high-potential impact conversations with a low priority for the planning group?

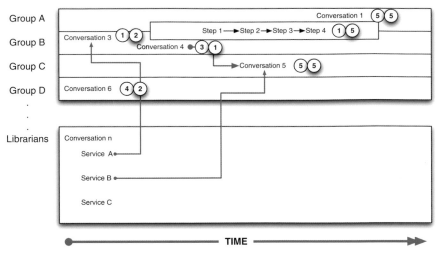

Figure 48

There are no magic answers here, nor does new librarianship provide any special solution to the delicate and often contentious process of picking and choosing needs. However, what must be avoided at all costs are services that do not meet the mission of librarians. There are boundaries for all professions, and although those boundaries may not be "only where books can help out," they are still there.

SPECIAL*

Perhaps no other type of library demonstrates the need for a common view of librarianship than the "special" libraries. The term itself, "special libraries," is a sort of lazy shorthand for libraries strongly affiliated with a given community. Yet in a medical context, legal, corporate, nonprofit, or any other domain, we are still talking about librarians serving the needs of their members.

In many ways, these librarians have helped form new librarianship before their counterparts in the academic and public domains. Corporate librarians have had to respond to community needs quickly under the pressure of a profit motive. Medical librarians learned long ago that they needed to be where doctors do their work.

To me the umbrella of special libraries demonstrates the importance of unity and diversity. Yes, I know that reads like a paradox, but let me explain. Diversity is vital in response to a community's needs; however, diversity of underlying values and skills undermines a profession.

Think about the web (and the Internet as a whole). Websites are certainly far from uniform. Each page has a different look and comes from a different source. Yet none of them would be of any use if they didn't conform to some basic standards (HTML, HTTP).

The key is to standardize (make uniform) the right parts. I would argue that attempting to create a standardized curriculum for LIS schools is choosing the wrong part to standardize. These attempts try to make librarians look alike at a functional level. This is a sort of Walmart approach, where if you walk into a Walmart anywhere in the world you feel at home. Nothing varies. This works well when you are emphasizing cheap stuff over professional competencies.

Contrast this to doctors. Doctors share a common set of knowledge and values but are hardly generic. There are generalists and specialists. In some communities, doctors make house calls; in other places, they work in big hospitals. In fact, much of the debate in health care reform is over what level of standardization we should bring to this field.

Part of the legacy of Melvil Dewey was an emphasis on standardization and efficiency. Dewey and his generation actually took out a great deal of diversity in librarianship. Add to this the advent of copy cataloging in the 1960s and 1970s and the generalist librarian was cemented. Our collections vary, but our tools and skills do not.

One of my goals in new librarianship is to recalibrate where standardization makes sense and where it does not. Ask librarians what they do, and you will get a consistent answer. Ask them what their value is, and it is all over the board. This is a result of functional views of the field and the exact opposite of what the field needs.

Within the rich mosaic that constitutes special libraries, we have librarians doing patent busting, helping prepare prosecution, performing meta-analysis of large-scale medical studies, pursuing policy changes in Washington, mining petabyte data sets, and helping to award grants. Often their tools are more like an HTML editor and an e-mail client than books and binders.

There is a sort of perennial debate at the Special Library Association about changing its name. All of these seem to focus on the word "library." I believe they should actually focus on the "special" part of their name. The words "library" and "librarian" may well have baggage, but they also have a lot of power. There is a fabulous book called *Don't Think of an Elephant* by George Lakoff.[36] Lakoff is a strategist for the Democratic Party in the United States and a cognitive linguist. His book talks about the power of words and how the Republican Party has been masterful in their use of language to frame debates. So instead of talking about inheritance taxes, it is death tax. Or, make sure to name a bill that eases regulation of pollution the "Clean Air Act." The title of his book refers to the fact that if I say (or you read) words, you can't help but create a mental structure with it. So if I say, "Don't think of the color red," guess what you think about? Or if I say "Don't think of an elephant," up pops the gray-skinned mammal.

What I like about his work is that he talks about, in a political tone, the ability to use this feature of human cognition and to shape how we see and think about issues. So if people think of you as a librarian, don't look for a new title, change the associations they have. There is a much better chance that you can change perceptions of the word "librarian" than to create meaning in terms such as "special" or create whole new concepts such as informationists.

---

*See Agreement Supplement for a discussion of special libraries.
36. Lakoff, G. (2004). *Don't think of an elephant! Know your values and frame the debate: The essential guide for progressives*. White River Junction, VT: Chelsea Green Publishing.

If there is any group reading this that should feel right at home, it is school librarians. Curriculum mapping, building knowledge, learning theory, and even meta-cognition are all familiar in a primary and secondary school setting. Gone are the days of simple clerks checking out books and overseeing study hall. Now the School Library Media Specialist (school librarian, teacher librarian) is a teacher of information literacy, partner to teachers to enhance their curriculum, and a part of the faculty. At my sons' elementary school, Andrew and Riley both receive a grade in library (they always score above grade level, I'll have you know). Yet even here we see opportunities for an expanded view of librarianship.

If we look at facilitating in a school context against our four means, we see a great deal of existing practice (the examples are not meant to be exclusive):

1. Access: Providing students and faculty access not only to relevant materials, but to online services and experts.
2. Knowledge: Provide students with an information literacy curriculum and map to the existing curricula of the school.
3. Environment: Uphold core values of intellectual freedom within a constrained policy environment (i.e., filters).
4. Motivation: Work with internally motivated students and faculty, as well as clear extrinsic motivation through assignments and possibly grading.

There is recognition that, just as in corporate settings, key contextualization has to take place to best serve the needs of the community. For example, the services and resources that librarians can provide to student members are bounded by an overall need to protect children.

There are also plenty of examples of school settings already acting on many of the key concepts presented in the Atlas. This is hardly a coincidence, as schools are also in the knowledge-creation business—mind you, with a different set of overall means of facilitation. Curriculum mapping is the creation of an entailment mesh. In fact, a major influence in the construction of this Atlas was the concept of Strand Maps that show the interrelations of key concepts in different curricular domains. For example, take a look at the NSDL[37] and the AASL Atlas of Science Literacy[38] in figure 49.

One of the primary shifts that school librarians, and indeed all librarians, need to make in new librarianship is in expanding the

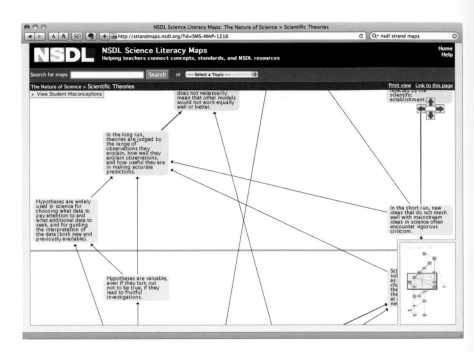

Figure 49

concept of access. Currently, the focus is on providing access to the outside world from the school community. However, an equal focus needs to be made on providing the world with access to the community. Certainly there are plenty of examples where this is happening (e.g., posting of student projects), but school librarians need to focus on building a two-way infrastructure.

Growing Importance of Two-Way Infrastructure

I was involved in many a project to get quality information (lesson plans, topical digests, etc.) into the classroom. As director of an ERIC Clearinghouse (when they still existed), AskERIC, the Gateway to Educational Materials, the Virtual Reference Desk Project (yes, it started as a K–12 project), and the National Science Digital Library, my job was to help teachers and school librarians get their hands on good quality information to do their jobs better. It turns out that my colleagues and I only had half the equation. You see, we made the mistake that most school librarians make—we think the problem is just getting good information into the classroom (or school), but what about helping good information escape?

*See Agreement Supplement for specific ideas on implementing new librarianship ideas in school settings.

37. http://strandmaps.nsdl.org/
38. http://www.project2061.org/publications/atlas/default.htm

This is a great example of how facilitation through access is not simply providing access to other people's conversations. Part of access is ensuring community conversations and information is made available beyond the community. Let me use the example of a lesson plan. School librarians are fantastic at finding good lessons on the Internet. But one thing we learned from the Gateway to Educational Materials project was that teachers rarely use lesson plans as written. They modify and often improve them (or at least tailor them to their classes). Why not help redistribute these modifications (where allowed by copyright and teacher permission of course)? This is similar to the open source concept: use what I provide but share improvements with the community.

There are other reasons that lessons need to escape from the classroom as well. In the United States, most districts and states require that lesson plans be provided to ensure that high-quality standards are being met. By building a one-way infrastructure to get lessons to teachers, you will require the construction of a second system for information flow out of the classroom and up to the state. Often this system will bypass the librarian. This means that you lose out on the ability to see what is being taught in the classroom (enabling things such as more seamless curriculum mapping). Just as in academic libraries where librarians would do well to make themselves a part of existing information flows, so too can the school librarian benefit from making it easier for teachers to find and information.

School Information Management Systems

One interesting result of mapping the conversations in schools is that you find that a great deal of information is flowing into and out of the school. The librarian is providing information to the teacher and working directly with the students. Teachers are talking to parents, administration to teachers and district officials, and so on. These are all conversations around the central concept of knowledge creation; this means they are all of potential import to the librarian.

In the early 1990s, there was a strong push to have school librarians take on the role of technology coordinators. It made sense because the tools librarians used were increasingly digital, and it made political sense as well. It increased librarians' visibility and gave them access to the classrooms. Some librarians took up this strategy, but many did not. Perhaps instead of trying to be the Chief Technology Officer, a better role would be Chief Information Officer. Look to how you can facilitate these flows of information in a School Information Management System. Already there are a number of disparate systems in play within the school environment: from curriculum management systems that map assessments and objectives; to communications systems that link students, teachers, and parents electronically; to library systems. There is a role for a librarian to bridge these systems around the students and faculty. What these types of systems look like will be strongly influenced by changing systems (see the Evolution of Systems in the "Knowledge" Thread for more).

This may seem like taking on too much—after all, we don't ask math teachers to do this, and increasingly school librarians are faculty with their own curricula. And it may well be for one person. You need a staff. The real question, and one only answerable by the community (the school) you seek to serve, is: What is the highest priority for your unique skills?

ARCHIVES*

For some, there has been an uncomfortable relationship between libraries and archives—are they the same or are they different? Many an archivist has felt like the odd man out within libraries. I have students who insist that, although libraries build collections (the first thing I correct them on—they do a lot more) for use in the here and now, archives build collections for the future. I then relate to them a conversation I had with an Ivy League Collections librarian about using reference data to influence acquisitions.

"What if we looked at the questions people ask to figure out what materials to buy?" I asked.

"We could do that, but I really see my job as building collections for future generations." What a gift! To know what future generations will need.

In any case, there are at the very least some fuzzy boundaries between archives and libraries. For me, there is also a clear and compelling connection. In the knowledge model at the foundation of new librarianship, we have conversants, language, agreements, and memory. Archivists are strong partners in memory (see the "Knowledge" Thread for more on memory).

Libraries also have a great deal to learn from archivists. Much of the field is about preserving the context of archives. The use of a curatorial voice, attempts to build linkages between artifacts, and the linage of artifacts to timelines, oral histories, and scholarship can be seen as a model for preserving context.

*See Agreement Supplement for an annotated bibliography on the archival community and literature.

For the end of this Thread, let me take all of the communities and environments and try to draw some general strategies that represent not only current trends but the increasing reality that conversations in almost all contexts are losing physical connections and barriers. This also means that librarians can increasingly cut themselves loose from physical places and go to the conversation.

I talk a great deal about librarians creating safe environments for knowledge creation. From meeting spaces to websites, a key means of facilitating knowledge creation is making a place for that creation to occur. However, there is no safer place for many than their own home. Not just their physical residence, but their intellectual home, their social homes, the physical and virtual locations that form their comfortable world. Librarians must be part of this world.

In some cases, that means being in a place (physical or virtual) the member frequents. Maybe some come to the library for quiet contemplation or for boisterous programs. Perhaps members regularly frequent the websites that librarians provide. In many, many cases, these locations will not be within the librarian's defined physical space. They will be in Facebook, their places of work, their schools, their offices, and their places of worship. Librarians must go to these places to facilitate conversations.

I was walking into the Free Library of Philadelphia with Linda Johnson, the former head of the Free Library's Foundation. She pointed out a sign at the entrance that said "No eating or drinking."

"I mean, isn't that ridiculous?" she said. "These folks are going to check out their books, take them home, and read them…while they are eating and drinking!" For me that moment says volumes about how librarians view their ability to control the contexts of conversation. They cannot.

Compare this to a program set up by the Onondaga County Public Library. There was state money to send nurses and early childhood specialists into the homes of the inner city. The librarians provided books for the nurse to take with him or her on the visit. Although it certainly wasn't the full range of services librarians could provide, it did make at least a symbolic gesture to the library being everywhere.

Academic librarians deserve a lot of credit for getting the academy online. By providing full-text databases and journals to the desktops of faculty, the librarians created a powerful incentive for faculty to get a desktop and then start using it for other things. The problem is, we sent the library online but in many cases left the librarians behind. This was a major push behind digital reference.

The same can be seen in school libraries. My doctoral advisor, Mike Eisenberg, used to rail at schools that would take old print encyclopedias and put them in the classroom when new editions were in the library: "You're providing better access to out-of-date information!" With the advent of online encyclopedias, librarians could provide the same level of access in the classroom as the library media center. However, have they provided equal access to the librarians?

One way in which librarians are going to the conversation can be seen in embedded librarians.

*Embedded Librarians**

As the doctor does his or her rounds with medical students, the medical librarian tags along. The librarian takes note of conditions mentioned and after rounds (or while on them) searches for new information on the conditions that may help the medical staff.

In the physics laboratory, scientists collaborate with colleagues around the world to sift through the masses of data from high-energy experiments. The librarian facilitates these cross-institutional sessions and ensures that the masses of data are accessible. The librarian ensures the effective and efficient flow of new discoveries and decisions throughout the team.

As the lawyers prepare their case, the librarian attends their strategy meetings. The librarian prepares dossiers of potential expert witnesses and works with paralegals to ensure proper citation of precedents. The librarian also provides background research on the matter of the case, such as chemicals involved in an illegal dumping case.

These are all real examples of embedded librarians. These librarians may have a connection to a physical library or simply an organizational library division; however, their real work happens in the field.

TRULY DISTRIBUTED DIGITAL LIBRARY

It is easy to send our stuff outside of the walls of a physical facility. However, we must become proficient at sending our true value, our facilitation, out of the walls as well. I cannot emphasize this point enough. If you have made a library a warm and inviting safe space but not visited the halls of your members, you have failed. If you have built an amazing social website but not allowed its features and functions to be embedded in other websites, you have failed. We must not

*See Agreement Supplement for a series of questions and links to more information.

be so arrogant as to assume that the world will come to us. Instead of insisting that the library is the heart of the campus or community, we must become the circulatory system. We must be the vital flow of knowledge and services that permeates our communities.

When you are in town hall, you are in the library. When you are in a classroom, you are in the library. When you are in the hospital, courtroom, coffee shop, or theater, you are in the library. In that way, and only in that way, do we become as indispensible as the blood that flows though our veins.

THREAD CONCLUSION

From time to time, I have heard questions and debates on the value of the term "librarian." Should we change it (to cyberarian, information professional, information consultant, informationist, etc.)? My response is always no. "But," they say, "we are one of the only professions named after the buildings we work in." To which I say, "No, they named the buildings after us." Now I realize that is not historically correct, but I also realize that the Latin root of library, "liber," was originally the word for the inner bark of a tree (that was used as paper), and librarians are not in the bark business.

No, the words "library" and "librarian" are powerful words. They evoke not only a romantic and long tradition, but they are entwined with the concept of knowledge and learning. Yet we all too often are willing to feed the perception that a library is about things and stuff in a place. When we build digital libraries, do we lock them up in a URL or allow them to move to the place of conversation through things such as APIs and RESTful interfaces? When we build digital libraries, do we include and make obvious that they are places for conversation and therefore true knowledge? Do we ensure that our online digital spaces are not the equivalent to a closet full of books? Do we send along the wisdom of librarians with the web pages and scanned images?

Never again let your value go unnoticed within the communities you serve, especially by you. Be of the community in both concept and action.

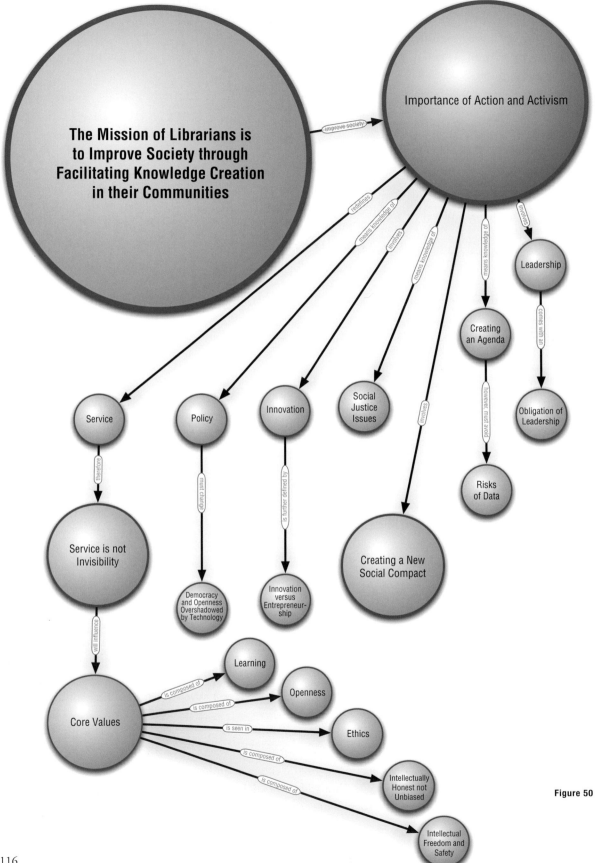

Figure 50

116

IMPROVE SOCIETY

> The eternal conflict of good and the best with bad and the worst is on.
> —Melvil Dewey

THE MISSION OF LIBRARIANS IS TO IMPROVE SOCIETY THROUGH FACILITATING KNOWLEDGE CREATION IN THEIR COMMUNITIES

If the previous Thread was about listening to the community and giving the members what they want, this Thread is about listening to your conscience and moving the community toward what it needs. It is about realizing that you have a voice in a conversation and a responsibility to guide conversations.

Look again at the mission (it is all about the mission). It has two parts. The "Knowledge," "Facilitation," and "Communities" Threads are related to the second part of the mission statement: facilitating knowledge creation in the community. "Knowledge" tells us how members (and we) create knowledge—through conversations that consist of conversants, language, agreements, and memory. Facilitation is all about how we can serve the members: through access, knowledge, environment, and motivation. The "Community" Thread is an exploration of the pressure for participation in different settings: digital, physical, hybrid, public, academic, and so on. Through these threads, I have consistently talked about co-ownership and focused on members.

But let us not forget the first part of the mission: to improve society. The first part is the ethical counterbalance to the second. It requires us not to simply do whatever the community wants but to ensure that our actions are for the betterment of the whole.

To talk of improvement, of "betterment," you must have a position—a baseline from which you work. As our means of facilitation help define us as librarians, our underlying worldview and general sense of direction—for "better" implies movement toward some goal—does even more so. This sense of direction and improvement comes ultimately from our values. It is our values, developed over centuries of tradition, that dictate how we should use our understanding of members' knowledge and the tools of facilitation.

Think of our tools and theory as a car: They define how the engine works, how we steer, how we accelerate, and so on. Our values define how we actually drive the car. Commercial search engines can provide access, baseline knowledge, and even policies that ensure some level of safety and take into account motivation. In essence, they have the same parts as us to build a car. However, these efforts are not grounded firmly in a mission to improve society and values developed with our communities that are embodied in a social compact. So although we may all be going down the road in cars, librarians are fundamentally concerned about the safety of our passengers (members) and getting them to the right destination, whereas others in the road are looking for exits to profit or fame.

However, the values of new librarianship are not simply taken whole cloth from our traditions. Some values espoused by librarians are simply incompatible with this new worldview. I would argue that, although librarians have been talking about concepts such as "unbiased," it has been impossible to enact. Further, librarians must come to terms with values that, when seen in the new realities of massive scale storage and computing, turn out to be at odds with each other. For example, how can we talk about intellectual freedom and the value of weeding a collection at the same time? Also, Dewey's unrelenting pressure on efficiency must be moderated to account for the messy reality of satisficing (the economic concept where people will take convenient information over optimal—we come back to this when discussing core values later.

Of course, values without deeds and action are nothing more than posturing. We must marry our beliefs and knowledge with action. Improving society is not as simple as believing you know how it could be better, but actually working to make it better. That is why this Thread combines core values with innovation and leadership.

That is the thrust of this Thread, then: to talk about our core values and the obligations we have as individual librarians and as a profession to lead and innovate—to make society better by making our voices heard.

IMPORTANCE OF ACTION AND ACTIVISM*

I had just given a lecture on participatory librarianship at the University of Boras in Sweden. I was having lunch with some of the lecture participants when one asked me, "So if two men are having a conversation about a topic they know little about, can we truly say that knowledge is created?"

"Yes," I said. "For those two people, if they are willing to act on the agreements they have developed, it is knowledge."

"But what if they are idiots?"

"It is still knowledge, although I would imagine that their knowledge would change if they tried out their agreement and it didn't work."

OK, I realize I have just lost most of the positivists in the crowd, but please give me a moment to explain. Let us take the case of the two men talking. Let us say they were talking about how to build an airplane. They had never flown an airplane, and indeed they had never even seen one in action. They held no degrees in aeronautical engineering—in fact, the most mechanical thing they had ever done was build a bicycle.

So these two men converse about how to build an airplane. They come to a set of agreements on how it is to be done. Is that knowledge? Yes. In fact, that's exactly how Orville and Wilbur Wright would have had to come to their agreements. They built the first airplane.

Here is the key to that story. Orville and Wilbur Wright had to test their knowledge through action. What's more, the knowledge they developed no doubt changed and shifted throughout their conversation, being constantly informed by what they did (or, in the case of early prototypes, what they didn't do—fly).

So it is too with our values as librarians. It is fine to have values and principles, but if they do not work in practice, they are useless. If librarians truly want to improve society, they must not only have their voices heard, but they must constantly work to improve society through action. In that way, librarians are activists—not liberals or conservatives but simply dedicated to real change through doing.

Let us revisit Orville and Wilbur around the table. Let's say that you were sitting there with them. As they talked, would you interrupt them and offer to help? If you did, and you provided them with plenty of information (books, journal articles, access to engineers, etc.) and they persisted in following an approach that by all contemporary measures was fool hardy, then what would you do? If they offered to write up their ideas (before the first flight), would you make it part of a collection for others? Realize that if you take the document you will bias the conversation around flight from then on (making this untested information more available). Now realize that if you do not take the document, you will also be biasing the conversation around flight as well.

Nothing in the apparatus of new librarianship up to this point directly addresses these issues. That is because knowledge and its creation don't equal absolute certainty or fact. Also, facilitation can help a member develop knowledge, but it does not ensure the "right" knowledge. So there must be an apparatus of new librarianship and part of our worldview that ultimately talks about ethical and appropriate knowledge and conversation. Further, this apparatus must be grounded in action. This reality influences how we view the core of all our values of librarianship: service.

SERVICE

Librarians seek to serve their communities—whether the goal of that community is money, happiness, well-being, learning, or governance. As such, librarians take on many of the values of their communities. This stems from the concept that librarians are of the community not for the community (see "Members Not Patrons or Users"). Being of the community means that you share something in common with your fellow community members. Being of the community also demonstrates that not all service is purely altruistic. Part of the reason you work to improve the community is to improve your own well-being—the better the community does, the better you as a member of that community do.

However, saying that the core value of librarians is based on service is far from sufficient to guide everyday decision making. I could use an obvious example, such as if a person were to ask for bomb-making information or a child were to ask for pornography. Would you give this out (serving the request) or not give it out (serving the larger needs of the community)? If your mission is simply to inform the community, not improve it, you could well answer yes, you would give it out.

But let me use a slightly more subtle example of how a dedication to service is insufficient for guidance. During the first Bush and then the Clinton administrations in the United States, there was an implicit policy around education information. This policy, best described as "the reflective practitioner," goes something like this: give classroom teachers access to a wide scope of information and the tools to navigate this information. In essence, turn teachers into practitioners who have the ability to analyze and evaluate resources (that's being reflective), not simply implement them. So the Department of Education set up or expanded projects such as the ERIC system and AskERIC, and it funded a large number of efforts to get source materials and lesson plans into the classroom. These were not approved or sanctioned lesson plans (the U.S. Department of Education is legislatively prohibited from endorsing curriculum), but all sorts of information. This was matched by an emphasis on teacher training.

This policy changed radically under the George W. Bush administration. Here the feeling was that teachers were simply too busy delivering instruction to wade through masses of digital resources. In fact, one informal study at the Gateway to Educational Materials project found that after teaching, grading, bathroom breaks, and lunch, teachers had on average 10 minutes a day for information-seeking. Further, it was thought that teachers should be trained to deliver instruction not get the equivalent of PhDs in education to figure out effective educational interventions.

To match this belief, the Department greatly curtailed their information dissemination projects and created the What Works Clearinghouse that would only disseminate information that had gone through significant peer review and only if the publisher of the information presented longitudinal evidence of effectiveness. Whereas ERIC was adding hundreds of documents a month, the What Works Clearinghouse was disseminating one to two documents per year. This approach is one of the main reasons that the ERIC system was pared down from a clearinghouse system to a single point article database.

Now, regardless of your political affiliations, you can see that both of these approaches were grounded in service and a desire to improve education. However, the underlying value systems and philosophies behind each approach differed radically. Librarians did not like the second approach, by and large. Why? Because there is a core value in librarianship, often mislabeled as "being unbiased," that dictates that the best decisions and the best knowledge come from working in the richest information environment possible. Librarians believe that more information from more sources will lead to better decisions.

Service Is Not Invisibility

What I hope is obvious throughout the Thread to this point is that, as librarians, the work you do has an impact on the community. As a librarian, you can't believe this and also believe that you are somehow a neutral force in the life of a member. We touched on this in the "Knowledge" Thread. Because we are engaged in a conversation, we influence that conversation.

I often have students who mistake the use of Dervin's "Neutral Questioning" in the reference interview with some sort of unbiased or neutral stance for the whole reference process. It is not. The minute you start to provide resources, the minute you start to choose where to look and how long to spend in those places, you begin biasing the process. As Joe Janes points out, if the first thing you do in answering a question is to reach for the keyboard or a book, you have biased the process.

In fact, this is the core of the pressure librarians exert within the community. I call it a pressure for improvement, but it is really just a special case of the pressure for participation talked about within the "Community" Thread. Librarians exert a force to guide members to

the best decisions possible. Most of the time, this pressure is in concert with the member and speeds the process of knowledge creation. However, there are times when this pressure is not directly aligned, and the librarian uses this force to try to move members and communities in a certain direction (cite more, read more, look at multiple perspectives, etc.). At times this force may be in direct opposition to the community's pressure for participation. Banned book weeks began this way, and the American Library Association's opposition to Patriot Act provisions is another example. This pressure for improvement comes from our core values as professionals.

CORE VALUES

Before we drop into the specific guiding values of librarianship, I have to point out one that is missing: efficiency. It is deliberately not there. Melvil Dewey had plenty of lasting impact on librarianship, but perhaps his biggest problem was his zealous drive toward efficiency. His belief in the ability to standardize not only collections but librarians as well may have worked in the relatively stable, information-scarce environment of the early twentieth century, but today it is showing not just cracks but huge gaping chasms.

We still live in a condition of scarcity, but it is no longer the information that is the scarce thing. It is our ability to absorb and make sense of information—to build knowledge—that is scarce. It is our attention and time that are scarce. In such an environment, a universal concept of efficiency is not just problematic, it is impossible. Don't take my word for it, take Herb Simon's—he won a Nobel Prize for figuring it out.

Herb Simon won that prize for something called satisficing. What Simon noticed was that people would take information that was most convenient over information of potentially higher quality. Now, many have misinterpreted Simon's observation for the so-called "good enough" argument. You know, where people will take "good enough" over high-quality stuff. The underlying statement is that people are lazy information gatherers (and often we as librarians must fix them).

The problem is, that's not what Simon meant. The problem Simon was trying to figure out was how to, in economic terms, optimize the system. Any system, technical or otherwise, can be optimized—made more efficient. For example, take a really mundane system such

1. http://projectinfolit.org/

as shipping books around a public library system. In most systems, you can take out a book from one library and return it to any other library. What's more, you can have any book at another library delivered to yours. That means the books have to be driven around the service area.

It can be a tedious task, and one with a lot of bottlenecks. You have to find the book, put it in a crate, pick up the crate, bring it to a central point to be sorted, ship it to the destination library, uncrate it, and notify the member. In a lot of library basements around the world, a lot of crates are stacking up. So you want to optimize this system as best you can. Does it make more sense to have the items presorted by the lending library? Does it make more sense to bring all the books to a central sorting facility? These are all empirical questions that can be tried and timed. Go with the shortest time at the lowest cost, and you optimize the system.

What Simon noted, however, was that such optimization assumes a static, controlled environment, and life just isn't like that. In our sorting example, how many books will you be working with on any given day? That can't be controlled. Are all requests equal in your community or do certain folks (lawyers in a law firm or doctors in a medical setting) get priority? How many of the requested books will be checked out already? What's the next best seller that will lead to a surge in demand? In such a dynamic environment, it is impossible to optimize with certainty.

Without such certainty, people make a tradeoff: They trade what is at hand against the uncertainty of whether they can do better. People do not choose a less appropriate resource simply because they are lazy; they choose it because that resource is the best they expect against the possibility that better ones are available.

Now think about this for a minute. Why does a member go with a full-text piece off of Google rather than getting a more appropriate resource from the library? The standard answer is convenience, but it is more complex than that. Do members know that the appropriate resource exists or is available from the library? If not, they have done their best to optimize the system. What about if they assume it does exist at the library, but they know what they have will suffice (the consequences of the decision are low)? They have optimized for their environment (take less time and expect nearly the same result—Dewey would be proud).

I had a school librarian who talked with pride about having taught her students to use only high-quality resources for assignments, such as full text databases. My question was, did this new information behavior extend to things beyond schoolwork? Look at it from Simon's point of view. Students need information to complete an assignment. They know the consequences of this decision are high (a grade and their GPA). They also have been made aware of a resource pool that exists, which will greatly improve the chances of success and still have acceptable costs (mostly in the form of time and mental effort). The students choose the library resources not because they are somehow universally best, but because they are the best bet to ensure success in that situation. They are still satisficing.

This is shown in the information literacy work of Head and Eisenberg.[1] They looked at undergraduates' information literacy behaviors. One of their findings was that Wikipedia was the "resource that shall not be named." Wikipedia was the first stop of a huge portion of the undergraduate population, but they never actually cited it in their final work. Wikipedia was their starting point, but they knew they had to cite more "acceptable" resources for the final work. They were optimizing as best they could. They weren't being lazy; they were making success calculations with the information available to them.

I take all of this time on efficiency because no matter how strong our principles are, they cannot overcome human nature. That's why I started with the mission and discussion of knowledge. Unless new librarians understand how people learn and their motivation, the application of values is a hit-or-miss proposition. It may be more efficient to catalog all materials in a single classification system, but is it more effective? Also, unless we understand deeply our mission, any measure of efficiency is arbitrary.

So if it is not "efficiency" or "unbiased," and "service" is not precise enough, what are the core values that librarians bring to any community? They are a dedication to learning, a commitment to openness, a provision of intellectual freedom and safety, and a dedication to intellectual honesty. Let's look at these values individually.

Learning

As a librarian, you value learning. This comes from our mission, as learning is defined as the acquisition of knowledge. We feel that all sectors of our community, from prisoner to prince, deserve the opportunity to learn. We also value learning in all of its varied contexts, from quiet solitary contemplation, to online learning, to informal investigations. The only thing that trumps the need to learn is the need to improve society.

Now that is really easy to say, and it rolls off the tongue. However, there are two aspects of the learning value I need to further articulate. The first is that learning is still very much in the hands of the individual. We cannot force someone to learn. The second is that we must model this value in our professional development. To become a librarian is to become a lifelong learner.

To be a true facilitator requires constant learning about the community, about the topics the community deems important, and about the process of facilitation. Your degree is not a ticket of completion but a lifelong commitment to devote yourself to constant study.

George Needham of OCLC once told me the secret to identifying a good conference. At a bad conference, librarians will preface their presentations with the date of their degrees (sometimes enumerated as "when dinosaurs walked the earth," "in the dark ages," or "in the time before the web"). At a good conference, presenters are so busy learning new things that the date of their degrees, or indeed the existence of the degrees, is irrelevant. One starts by looking back, whereas the other is always moving forward.

If service is the root of our values, learning is the trunk that holds everything together.

Openness

The importance of being a lifelong learner comes into clear focus with the value of openness. To be open is to be both transparent and available. This can be seen in current practice in things such as the reference interview, where librarians share process along with results. It can be seen in copy cataloging, where records are made available among libraries. We have also already seen it in the open source example, with a growing philosophy of sharing. In fact, libraries need to extend open source, with the sharing of completed code, with open effort.

"Open effort" is my phrase for an effort in which both the artifacts of developing a system (once again, software, policy, governance structure) and the development process are shared in an open fashion. There are plenty of technology examples of open efforts, such as the development of the Linux operating system. Perhaps the best one comes straight out of librarianship: legislative histories.

For those who don't know, legislative histories:

refers to the progress of a bill through the legislative process and to the documents that are created during that process. Attorneys, judges, and others often turn to these documents to learn why Congress enacted a particular law or to aid in the interpretation of a law.[2]

Within the United States at the federal level, a history includes the law, all the testimony that went into enactment of the law, amendments (both passed and failed) to the bill, and other evidence that tries to capture not only the process that went into passing the law, but also the intent of the legislators. This example also provides a great excuse to talk about possible limitations on openness.

As you might guess, the U.S. Department of Justice Law Libraries have an extensive collection of legislative histories. They are a beauty to behold: thick bound volumes. They do not lend them out. The reason? Because they worry that providing such information may end up helping opposing council. So openness is a core value, but it must still be guided by the community. Do librarians have an obligation to be completely transparent beyond the boundaries of their service community? I would say only insofar as it measurably improves society—for that clause of the mission must always trump service to community.

I would also have you note that this value or openness applies across the aspects of knowledge creation and facilitation. However, I would like to highlight the implications of openness on memory. When Bill Clinton came into office, he began a secret oral history project.[3] In secret throughout his administration, Clinton would sit with journalist and historian Taylor Branch and talk about current events and his presidency. The reasons for the project? According to Branch:

He [Clinton] asked…did I think that the records for his library would be good enough for future historians to bring to life what was about to happen in his. I was stunned that he would ask a question like that before he even took office, and told him that our historical records are indeed atrophied and make it harder and harder to do that. And as a remedial remedy project he initiated a diary, an oral history, that we ran secretly all through the eight years of the Clinton Presidency.

So to ensure memory and access, the leader of the free world had conversations. Although the project was secret at the time of implementation (to prevent subpoenas that would actually greatly close down the topics discussed), the ultimate purpose was actually to ensure openness over time.

This openness also necessitates the next core value of librarians: intellectual freedom and safety.

2. http://lib.law.washington.edu/ref/fedlegishist.html#intro
3. http://www.npr.org/templates/story/story.php?storyId=113269412

Intellectual Freedom and Safety

Where openness is about transparency, intellectual freedom is about a different type of openness—openness to other viewpoints. As I talked about in the U.S. Department of Education example previously in this Thread, librarians believe the best decisions and the best knowledge come from working with the richest information environment possible. This means the library must be a place not only for majority views but also the dissident voice.

Let's go back to our imaginary lunch with the Wright brothers. That crazy idea they were talking about wasn't really just about building an airplane. Many people were trying that. Their particular crazy idea was on how to control the airplane in the air. You see, the problem wasn't getting into the air—kites and balloons were commonplace. The real trick was how the pilot could control the plane. Now their basic idea is still in use in most planes today: You change the wing shape and thus the amount of lift to turn left and right and up and down.[4]

OK, pretty standard stuff, except that they didn't just use parts of the wing that flipped up and down like today's small aircraft; they actually distorted the whole wing. Why does this matter? The idea of reforming the wing as a whole structure turns out to have a lot of utility on jet fighters moving faster than the speed of sound where things such as ailerons can get ripped off by wind shear. So it turns out that these crazy people in the turn of the twentieth century actually had an idea that would come back into utility some 100 years later.[5] If the library didn't capture this kind of minority view, it may actually be hurting the community as a whole in the long term. Other crazy ideas that later gained mainstream acceptance? Plate tectonics, asteroid impact dinosaur extinction, democracy, and, of course, *Catcher in the Rye*.

There is no inherent contradiction with this reality and the act of guiding members to mainstream ideas or marking certain artifacts and conversations as out of step with accepted wisdom or outside of standard quality markers. The real problem is shutting out the views altogether. In fact, these member cues of quality and acceptability lead directly to the concept of intellectual safety.

Members, as I discussed in the "Facilitation" Thread, must feel safe to converse, learn, and participate. It is part of Maslow's hierarchy of need discussed in the "Mission" Thread. To truly appreciate freedom, one must first have stability and safety. To this end, you must ensure that members feel secure in their explorations of mainstream and minority views alike.

However, I cannot stress this enough: The means of providing safety and security, and even freedom, is not, I repeat, *not* to be unbiased. You can't be.

Intellectually Honest Not Unbiased

There we were, a crowd gathered around a large U-shaped table set up in the basement of Harvard's Gutman Education Library. The room was filled with librarians, folks who ran AskA services, technology vendors, government representatives, and professors. Our job was to develop quality criteria for digital reference services. My team—Abby Kasowtiz, Blythe Bennet, and Joann Wasik—had drafted a set of guidelines, and now they were being discussed, improved, and expanded. I remember this scene vividly because, not for the first time in my life (nor the last), Joe Janes, professor and creator of the Internet Public Library, said something so profound it totally changed my view of the profession.

We were going one by one through the standards and got to "digital reference services shall be unbiased." It was almost a throw-away line, so ingrained as it was in the library ethic. He said (OK, not so vividly that I don't have to paraphrase), "Wait a minute, that's not really right is it? In many ways, these different services provide value through their bias or point of view." He had a point, and here it is.

The quality standards were being developed not only for digital reference in general, but the AskA consortium, a group of digital reference services working with the Virtual Reference Desk project. These services consisted of some libraries but a lot of AskA services (they get their name from services such as Ask-A-Scientist, Ask-A-Volcanologist, etc.). Although these services had excellent reputations, they also had some built-in perspectives.

Take AskShamu, for example. The service was run by SeaWorld and answered questions about marine biology. The people providing the answers were credentialed marine biologists, and they had an outstanding reputation for quality. However, can you guess the kinds of answers they would give out if asked whether some animals should be kept in captivity? What do you think they would say if you asked whether it is good or bad to train whales to perform in shows?

As Joe started pointing to different services, his point became clearer and clearer. What do you think an Ask-A-Scientist site would say about questions on creationism? Volcanologists on plate tectonics? The Amish on religious life?

4. http://inventors.about.com/library/inventors/bl_wright_brothers.htm
5. http://www.thefreelibrary.com/Wings+of+change:+shape-shifting+aircraft+may+ply+future+skyways-a0111850337

Joe's point was that the network of these services can strive to be unbiased (really representative of multiple viewpoints), but the individual services aren't and shouldn't be. Did the consortium want to add a service for Ask the Ku Klux Klan? What about an AskA service for the North American Man/Boy Love Association? Even with values on intellectual freedom, are there limits?

I say that there are limits. And certainly in reality, librarians limit the types of resources to which they provide access. There are limits on the conversations that libraries seek to support, and it is not just a question of limited space, time, and/or budgets.

Bias, as I define it, starts in our fundamental understanding of knowledge. The entailment mesh of agreements predisposes human beings to certain ways of thinking and seeking new information. It has to. Can you imagine what your life would be like if you approached every situation without predispositions? You wake up in the morning and have to figure out how to get to work. You can't assume your car will work or the bus will come on time, so you must go test those options. You get up an hour early to do so. Once you get to work, you can't assume you are still employed, so you seek out your manager and ask him or her whether you can still work. While you're at it, you'd better ask your manager what you should do today because you can't assume that your job responsibilities haven't changed, and so on.

All this may seem silly, but they are obvious examples of where you have a bias—a predisposition that affects your behavior. When you started to read this Atlas, did you assume it would be a long discussion on how to do away with libraries (to be fair, some of you may think that is a consequence of the Atlas, but certainly not my intention)? Remember our word game in the "Knowledge" Thread with run, bank, and OMG? You had a bias to certain meanings of words. It is how our brain works: find a pattern, expect a pattern.

So if we are all biased, does that mean anything goes and it is OK? Being biased does not make you narrow minded or bigoted. Our biases can be overcome in service to a member's question, for example. Although the librarian at the table with Orville and Wilbur Wright may not have believed their approach to controlled flight would work, it shouldn't stop the librarian from still supporting them. Also, knowledge is dynamic, and there is always the ability to learn and come up with a new entailment mesh—a new set of predispositions.

For example, a doctoral student of mine, Sylvia Southwick, studied reference services at a university medical library. She found that the first thing librarians did when answering a reference question was to determine who asked the question. They wanted to know whether the question came from a doctor, nurse, staff member, or patient. The reason? Because if it were a nurse, they would print out any relevant information and send them a hard copy because nurses weren't as technologically advanced as the doctors. That is, unless you talked to the nurses, who asked why they would always send questions by e-mail but get paper back.

The librarians in this setting were making an assumption. They had a bias. Once they discovered a discrepancy, however, they started sending electronic files. They learned.

What you as a librarian must aspire to is intellectual honesty. You must be open to all voices but rigorous in their examination and dissemination. This concept of intellectual honesty arises out of rationalism and science. Science is both the accumulation of evidence and the rigorous development of explanations of the underlying processes that produced that evidence. Here is the centerpiece of science that rarely gets discussed in the popular media: All explanations are assumed to be refutable.

I know this may seem odd to some readers, but scientists do not claim evolution, relativity, or even Conversation Theory are fact. Instead they claim they are the best possible explanation of the evidence at hand and have yet to be disproven. Now that is still a pretty high bar of certainty, but it never rises to absolute confidence. It is impossible to say something for certain; it is only possible to disprove something with certainty.

To be intellectually honest works in conjunction with intellectual freedom, learning, and openness to say that as a librarian you will provide the best information available to you, make clear that you have a bias, and then be open to new evidence or approaches.

Before we leave this topic, however, we have to take on a few words: "best," "worst," "good," and "bad." In fact, all the comparatives need some rethinking. You see, in the world of intellectual honesty and few if any absolutes (ironically, the statement "There are no absolutes" is an absolutist statement), context is king. What is an appropriate conversation for one member may not be for another. A service or resource for one member may not be appropriate for that member in another context.

We saw this in our discussion of Wikipedia and college students. It was seen as an appropriate resource for starting a research process but not for the final assignment submission. Likewise, even if you personally hate Wikipedia, you have to admit there is no better resource for making your case than Wikipedia.

Life is complex and messy. As a librarian, your focus must be on context and the needs of the member, not the artifact or object. The artifact only takes on value and only has meaning in its use.

*Ethics**

So there are the core values of librarianship: coming from tradition, in line with our worldview and mission, and guiding our means of facilitation. However, they are only guideposts and factors in dealing with real situations, real members, and real communities. You will rarely face situations where they can be "cleanly" applied, because there are many cases where a community's values are far from consistent.

There is also a personal dimension that I have not touched. These are the values we bring to the profession from our own life experience. Bringing these in line with the professional values and community values into an ethical system used to evaluate and act in a situation is no easy feat. In some cases, you have to compromise a value to serve a larger value (e.g., the privacy of the reference interview over openness). In some cases, your community may transform a value from practice to advocacy, such as in the defense industry, where openness is curtailed by strict secrecy but where you as a librarian can push to be as open as possible. At the end of the day, it all comes down to doing good and doing well—in that order.

Just as we approach members as individuals, with their own unique take on ideas, artifacts, and the arrangement of agreements, so too are librarians individuals. The way they balance their professional values with the community's and with their personal value system is unique. The role of values in new librarianship is not as a set of absolutes where the profession seeks to enforce adherence to values, but rather as goals where the community provides a safe environment to discuss and examine the values in action.

The issue of values is in essence an ongoing conversation within the community of librarians. As such, it too needs to be facilitated. Although the recursive nature of this statement will no doubt make one's head hurt, a conversation on values must portray the values it is discussing. Of course, the conversation must be about creating new knowledge and learning from each situation to apply to the next set of ethical challenges.

SOCIAL JUSTICE ISSUES*

The obligation of librarians to know their values and act on them does not stop at organizational boundaries. Part of improving society is realizing that all parts of a community are entangled. Just as knowledge does not fit neatly into containers, the work of librarians cannot be limited to a single institution.

This is where I may be departing from some of my colleagues. I'm not asking you personally to become a political activist and "picket the power"—that is well beyond the scope of a professional responsibility. I have been careful to avoid a sort of personal mandate. What I am telling you is that, as a professional, you have an obligation to introduce your values in your professional conversations, including to members and other organizations outside the scope of a library. People must know what we believe and why.

For these kinds of views, I have been referred to as a "pragmatic utopian"—work for heaven by getting your hands dirty. I believe that values are not simply abstract but must provide utility. Take, for example, issues of diversity. It is a topic that has become charged in politics and cultural conflicts. I see diversity as an essential environmental condition for librarianship. If we value openness and individualism, and if we value the richest information environments for knowledge creation, we must value diversity. Diversity in culture, race, gender, religion, sexual affiliation, and worldview aids us in facilitating conversations. It may well be part of the value system in a community, but it is also eminently practical.

I was speaking at a staff development event at a large public library. The staff of the library assembled included librarians, folks from the physical plant, the branches, and coordinators of volunteers. I did my overview about the importance of conversations and engaging communities. In the question-and-answer period afterward, I received an excellent question: What if the community doesn't want to talk to us? My answer is that we had a responsibility to reach out to these communities, but we need to meet the community where they are not where we are. This is related to the idea of going to conversations I discussed in the "Communities" Thread. Except that it is not enough to go in a "locational" sense; we must also do our best to go to the conversation in terms of the values and norms of our engaged members.

Look at our means of facilitation again, but this time consider the cultural space surrounding the activity. To provide access means we must honor the norms of the conversations in terms of intellectual property and indeed propriety. For example, there are many cultures that have sacred rights, songs, and documents that are not to be shared beyond a specific set of cultural boundaries. The definition of necessary knowledge to engage in a conversation is often defined by

*See Agreement Supplement for a deeper discussion of the ethics of new librarianship.
*See Agreement Supplement for more thoughts on social justice issues and links to additional resources.

the conversant; likewise motivation. Let me give an example in terms of creating a safe environment.

One of the aspects of the academic culture that often intimidates students and newcomers is the concept of argument. There is a sort of unspoken assumption that in any conversation involving faculty, at least one person will take an affirmative stance and another a negative regardless of the true feelings of the faculty involved. In essence, there is always a devil's advocate in the room ensuring that any idea, proposal, or work is adequately scrutinized. From the outside, this process can seem unnecessarily combative and frankly inefficient. However, in the academy, the fitness of an idea only comes through a sort of Socratic dialog where we argue to the truth.

Coming into this environment unaware of the value of argument can kill conversations. Argument in this community is actually a means of providing a safe environment. There are rules (no personal attacks, the types of evidence to be inspected, etc.), and the community as a whole feels safe in that ideas communicated outside of a given conversation have been vetted and can be utilized.

The social justice obligation of a new librarian is to implement values within their communities, particularly around concepts of minority views. They must do so by understanding the value systems of the community and do their best to speak within that value system. However, once again the mission of "improving society" trumps the value norms of any one given community.

POLICY*

It was a magnificent, clear day in Phoenix. Better still, it was warm and sunny and March, and I was not in Syracuse. I was having lunch with a librarian from the Arizona State Library and the director of a suburban public library. One of the things I like to ask is, "What kinds of qualities are you looking for out of a library science program like at Syracuse?" The first answer I get is amazingly consistent, and that beautiful day in Arizona was no different: "Common sense." This then led into a conversation about library policy.

What I hear uniformly from library administrators was probably best put by Kathryn Deiss of the Association for College & Research Libraries: "Many librarians see policy as risk avoidance." In too many cases, we create policy to preempt decision making. If we have a policy, then we don't have to make personal decisions, we just implement the policy. Porn on a computer? Acceptable use policy. Disruptive teen in the reading room? Expulsion policy. Alien invaders from Mars

requesting a library card? Better put together a committee and work out a policy for our new green overlords (just checking whether you are still reading).

We could spend the next 100 or so paragraphs on policy horror stories. Although that would be cathartic, it is not the point of this agreement. The point is that librarians need to have a rich understanding of policy: the utility of policy, the limitations of policy, the role of policy in organizations, and the policy process. This richer understanding should lead to policy enabling good decision making, not preempting it.

Let me start with a definition of policy. Policies are formalized agreements that expedite decision making and seek to effect behavior. This definition closely parallels the definition of public policy put forth by Rick Weingarten:

> In general, "public policy" refers to laws, regulations, and other formal or informal rules governing individual or institutional behavior. The rules are established by some government authority (legislature, regulatory or executive agency, or court) at the federal, state, or local level; they cover some specific population of people or institutions; and they are usually accompanied by some form of sanctions—official consequences for subjects that do not obey the rules.[6]

Indeed, Rick even points out that policy developed at public institutions such as public libraries and public schools are public policy. A knowledge of policy is essential to enact our values, as well as part of our facilitation of knowledge creation.

As Gorman says, values are beliefs. They are not formulated from theory or necessarily mandated by our environment, but rather they are learned, debated, and either accepted or rejected. Beliefs are abstractions; when you encode them into "formal or informational rules governing … behavior," you create policy. Within contexts that the librarians control (the library as institution, the suite of services offered, etc.), these policies should be put forth sparingly because the world is complex and flexibility is essential. They should also be implemented at a high level and established to uphold values, such as ensuring minority voices are heard, ensuring transparency, and so on. Many organizations break policy up into two parts: the policies, high-level statements of belief that change slowly; and procedures,

---

*See Agreement Supplement for an annotated bibliography on policy in libraries.
6. http://www.mitpressjournals.org/doi/pdf/10.1162/dmal.9780262562324.181

the actual methods of implementing the policy that change as new circumstances arise.

Librarians would do well to adopt this approach. A policy to ensure access to a rich set of resources, for example, shouldn't talk about specific types of resources (books, etc.). That should be in the procedures because new formats pop up all the time. To conflate policy and procedure is to risk focusing on the trees at the cost of observing the forest.

Within the settings we control, policy is a key tool to build safe environments for our members. You will recall that a safe environment is one of our key methods of facilitation, as well as one of our core values in preserving intellectual freedom and safety. Our policies and procedures should not only work to ensure an open and safe community place (either physical or virtual) but communicate our intent to do so to the community.

Beyond the environments we control, policy becomes a way of ensuring social justice and improving the community. Be it laws of the land or rules of the corporation, librarians should be proactively engaged in the policy-setting operations of our communities. Nowhere is this more true than in the case of democracy.

*Democracy and Openness Overshadowed by Technology**

The United States is a liberal democracy. Canada is a liberal democracy. France, Germany, India, and Israel, too. The "liberal" part of liberal democracy has nothing to do with political party or even how socially progressive a country is; instead it refers to the belief that democracy is more than voting. A liberal democracy also includes protections of civil liberties and a constitutional protection from intrusive governmental power. It is an important modifier. Iraq under Saddam Hussein was nominally a democracy. Hussein was elected president with 99% of the vote. However, few would consider this a truly ideal democracy.

Why the quick civics lesson? First off, it is another example of how features and functions (in this case, voting) do not necessarily reflect the nuances of an underlying worldview. More important, however, it highlights the natural alignment of new librarianship with modern concepts of democracy. Liberal democracy, for example, is also referred to as participatory democracy.

In 1787, Thomas Jefferson wrote:[7]

The people are the only censors of their governors; and even their errors will tend to keep these to the true principles of their insti-

tution. ... The way to prevent these [errors] is to give them full information of their affairs through the channel of the public papers, and to contrive that those papers should penetrate the whole mass of the people. The basis of our governments being the opinion of the people, the very first object should be to keep that right; and were it left to me to decide whether we should have a government without newspapers, or newspapers without a government, I should not hesitate a moment to prefer the latter. But I should mean that every man should receive those papers, and be capable of reading them.

In 1822, James Madison wrote:[8]

A popular government without popular information, or the means of acquiring it, is but a Prologue to a Farce or a Tragedy; or perhaps both. Knowledge will forever govern ignorance; and a people who mean to be their own Governors must arm themselves with the power which knowledge gives.

As John Buschman[9] points out, these quotes serve as the foundation of the assertion that libraries are a necessary component of a democracy. This assertion certainly lay at the core of Andrew Carnegie's philanthropy in libraries.[10] Buschman further points out that this foundation has never been rigorously tested. Librarians and policymakers often invoke this assertion to get funding, but they rarely back up the idea with clear, predictable ways that libraries and librarians create a climate for democracy.

What's more, much of the rhetoric around participatory web technologies centers on a "democratizing" force. That is, blogs, Twitter, and Wikis give more people a voice and therefore extend power to the people. The problem with these statements is twofold. The first part is that, as Buschman points out, we don't have a clear idea what a democratizing force really is (did Saddam have a blog?). The second is that, although the rhetoric is there, much of the actual focus of librarians and these technologies is on the technologies. Take a look at any recent library conference program and count the number of sessions

*See Agreement Supplement for more on Buschman and democracy.

7. Jefferson, T. (1944). *The life and selected writings of Thomas Jefferson* (A. Koch & W. Peden, Eds.). New York: Modern Library.

8. Madison, J. (1973). *The mind of the founder: Sources of the political thought of James Madison* (M. Meyers, Ed.). Indianapolis, IN: Bobbs-Merrill.

9. Buschman, J. (2007). Democratic theory in library science: Toward an emendation. *Journal of the American Society for Information Science and Technology*, 58(10), 1483–1496.

10. http://www.carnegie.org/sub/about/pessay/pessay98.html

about how to X (blog, Wiki, Tweet) and then the number on bringing political power to the masses through distributed action.

All too often librarians talk a good game on democracy and empowerment, but most of their actual time is devoted to technology and procedure. We need to do a better job connecting our values, our work, and our communities into the policy conversations.

We also must be much more clear on how the work of librarians of all stripes contributes to an educated citizenry. Unless we take the value of learning seriously and back it up with real assessment and measurable impacts and outcomes, these lines ring hollow and do not help us.

INNOVATION

When you think of innovators, you might think of Steve Jobs, the iconic CEO of Apple. Perhaps you hearken back to someone like Edison, whose Menlo Park lab churned out light bulbs, phonographs, and moving pictures. In the sciences, you might think of Einstein, who changed our view of the universe; Madame Curie, who changed our understanding of radiation; Newton, who gave us a way of understanding gravity; or Rosalind Franklin, who was instrumental in the understanding of DNA. Perhaps your thoughts run to the political, with the governance innovation of John Locke or Susan B. Anthony. Although it is true that these people are all innovators, to hold them up as a sort of prototype makes innovation seem rare and nearly unattainable. When I think of innovators, I think of Danny Biasone.

Danny was the founder and owner of the Syracuse Nationals (now the Philadelphia 76ers) in the 1950s. He had a problem. At the time, professional basketball was a defensive game. Once one team was leading, the players would sit on the ball, dribbling and passing to keep it away from the other team to prevent them from scoring. It was slow to watch, and at the time the games often ended with scores like 30–20. Danny was looking for a way to make the games faster paced and more about scoring. He found it in an idea first proposed by Howard Hobson, a college coach. Hobson proposed limiting the time that one team could have the ball.

According to Biasone:[11]

I looked at the box scores from the game I enjoyed, games where they didn't screw around and stall. I noticed each team took about 60 shots. That meant 120 shots per game. So I took 48 minutes—2,880 seconds—and divided that by 120 shots. The result was 24 seconds per shot.

The results? The shot clock that limited a team to 24 seconds before they had to shoot. Also, the game became much faster and focused on scoring. This led to more elaborate scoring techniques such as the slam-dunk. The game was more fan-friendly, and television, with its success airing football, picked up on broadcasting professional basketball. This gave more money to the league, which led to the modern National Basketball Association and the billion-dollar industry we have today—all because Biasone was bored.

I want you to note a few things about this story. First, it's about basketball. It didn't reinvent the game, it just added a seemingly minor change. Innovation is not necessarily invention. To innovate is to do something that already exists (a process, service, or product) better. All too often we see innovation as having to fundamentally change the world when it only has to improve your life. It turns out that a minor tweak may have large repercussions.

At a recent presentation, a librarian asked when she was supposed to have time to innovate. After all the daily work of sorting and responding to e-mail and such, there wasn't time left over for innovation. Here's the thing: Those things that are taking your time are the things you should be looking to innovate. Innovation is not a time slot, it is an attitude.

The other thing I want to point out about Danny's innovation was that he didn't originate the idea of the shot clock. Rather, he saw its necessity, refined the idea, and implemented it. Innovation is not always—in fact, I would argue rarely—the result of individual genius working in isolation. More often, it is the result of taking a range of ideas, adding unique inspiration or application, and then implementing them.

I have talked to many library directors who say that they aren't innovative, but they are good at identifying and supporting good ideas. This is an important skill and an absolute necessity. When a librarian is in an organization, he or she must work to produce an atmosphere that fosters innovation.

Why is innovation so important for librarianship? It is not a way to continuously push ahead the field or merely a nice thing to foster in our members. No, innovation lies at the heart of librarianship. Is it a core value? Yes, it is part of learning and service. Think about this for a moment. Your knowledge is a dynamic and ever-changing combination of your agreements and their relationships. It circumscribes your

11. Pluto, T. (1992). *Tall tales: The glory years of the NBA, in the words of the men who played, coached, and built pro basketball.* New York: Simon and Schuster.

worldview. As you learn something new, it changes your world. This may be a fundamental shift in how you see the world (a revelatory moment when things click or fracture) or a minor shift in awareness (such as knowing Britney Spears' birthday). To learn is to change. Because we are in the knowledge field, we are in the change business (well, facilitating change through knowledge). Education and librarianship are about change, and our values tell us that we do change our communities and should do so for the better. Innovation is positive change.

Librarianship is not done yet. It wasn't finished when they built the Library of Alexandria. It wasn't done when they chained books to shelves or the Muslims built libraries in Toledo. It was not done when Dewey had his revelations or Ranganathan implored us to see that books were for use. It will not be done with the publication of this Atlas. If a field is done, it is dead. Remember Ranganathan's fifth law of librarianship: The library is a growing organism.[12]

How can you as a librarian expect to produce positive change agents from your members, and ask a community to change and improve, if you are not willing to do so yourself? Do you really think that a risk-averse, conservative community agency can fight for social change? Can a submissive collection of practitioners locked in practice by tradition and unquestioned practice change the world and society for the better?

Although I don't feel comfortable asking you to be a political activist, I have no problem telling you that you need to be a professional advocate and innovator. You must not wait for a chance for positive change to approach you; instead, you must ruthlessly and proactively scour the profession and your affiliated organizations for opportunities to create positive change. You must be merciless in questioning tradition: Uphold what works and innovate or eliminate the rest.

If you manage librarians, expect innovation. Create a safe environment for risk and experimentation. Give your staff time just to play. Reward attempts and failures as well as successes. *DO NOT* form an innovation committee. Innovations do not wait for committees. Do create a rotating innovation czar position where someone takes a month just canvassing staff and members for new ideas and works with them to prototype and try them out. The committee should be for deciding at three-month intervals what experiments get killed. The death of experiments is a vital role for any organization, and no one does it well.

Every librarian should also create a "crazy ideas" mailing list. This is a group of mentors, associates, fans, and resource folks who are will-ing to jump in and give you their opinion when a crazy idea comes to you. You would be surprised how many folks just need to get prompted and how many cross-institutional projects start out this way.

Last, do not sit in the back row of presentations and mutter about why things will not work. The two most important questions you need to ask every day are "Why?" and "Why not?" The "why" is what this Atlas is all about. Question tradition and the status quo and poke all procedures to see whether innovation is possible. The "why not" is all about an environment to innovate. It is why policies should be rare and high level. It is the first question you should ask of any new idea. Don't start out assuming it won't work; figure out how to make it work. If you can't, don't do it. If you could but you don't have the resources, try to find the resources. If it can work, do it. To sit back and simply "know" why something won't work and not contribute is a violation of an atmosphere of innovation.

Innovation versus Entrepreneurship

It is important to note a distinction I make between innovation and entrepreneurship. I make it because a brilliant librarian and former student named Meg Backus showed me the difference. What is brilliant about this idea is hers. Where it falls short is my fault.

Meg found the difference when she was examining the roles of public libraries in supporting entrepreneurship. She was looking for public libraries that had programs which supported entrepreneurs, defined narrowly as starting businesses. She didn't find much. She found some large programs with some impressive success and numerous smaller programs that had no way of determining whether they had success. None of the programs she contacted could tell her how many folks had used the library to start a business or how those businesses were doing.

The more Meg thought about this, the more she began to see a disconnect between the nature of public libraries and the entrepreneurial world. Were public librarians, for example, the best exemplars of entrepreneurship? How many of the librarians in public libraries had created their own businesses? Yet it was clear that a huge number of public librarians were innovators. Plenty of good ideas were also happening because of librarians.

Where she came down was that it was all about innovation. Tons of people with good ideas would use the library to help develop the

---

12. http://en.wikipedia.org/wiki/Five_laws_of_library_science

idea. Entrepreneurs were people who had a good idea but needed to get a hold of significant resources to implement it. So a woman with a great idea for a new invention would have to raise capital to prototype the idea, incorporate it, market it, and ultimately get a product to market. That capital might come from personal savings, loans, or venture capitalists, but in any case it would involve significant financial risk taking. Many of the people attending a session on entrepreneurship had great ideas, but they had no stomach for the risk.

Now, this is where it gets interesting. There are a lot of ideas in a community (once again, be that a community college, a city, a company, a hospital, etc.) that don't require a huge load of capital to be implemented. This is particularly true with ideas on the Internet. What may be required is not money but people's time and expertise. So if you have a great idea that can be made into a piece of software or a website, you now have access to millions and millions of Internet users, some of whom may be willing to contribute an hour here or there. This is the entire basis of the open source community. The Internet allows ready access to the masses, and the masses are a key to implementing innovation. Entrepreneurship, an important activity, needs access to capital and has a necessarily high bar of access.

Now, here's where it gets interesting. Although public libraries (I'm talking about institutions here, not individuals) may not be well equipped to support entrepreneurship, because they tend not to be venture capital firms, they are perfectly suited for supporting this type of innovation. Just as capital markets need regulation and organization, so too does the marketplace of ideas around innovation. What professional is well positioned to facilitate access to the multitudes, prepare innovators with baseline knowledge, mediate agreements among interested members, and then provide an ongoing memory of the innovation activity? Sounds like a spot-on definition of a librarian to me.

One last note. This does not abdicate your responsibility to support the needs of entrepreneurs in your community. If entrepreneurs are members, they have a right to service. If the community feels entrepreneurial conversations are important to support, then you should do so—just make sure you truly understand the impacts of your service.

CREATING AN AGENDA

There is not simply a gap between a good idea and implementation; there is a wide and treacherous chasm. We look at crossing this chasm in the "Curriculum of Communication and Change over Traditional Ideas of Leadership" agreement in the next Thread, but we need to talk about turning activism into action here. That is because our values must be married to innovation and leadership to make them meaningful. The mechanism of this translation is an agenda.

An agenda is "a list or program of things to be done or problems to be addressed."[13] For our purposes, it is a set of concrete steps that you need to take to achieve a goal—in this case, some means, minor or grand—to improve society. An agenda cannot be divorced from reality nor should it be fully bounded by it. This is not to say we all need to live in a bit of denial but rather that an agenda is about the future, and the future is not set.[14] As Alan Kay once said, "the best way to predict the future is to invent it."

So how do you stay true to reality, shape the future, and turn it from just an idea into a set of concrete steps? I'm glad you asked.

Start with a statement of the thing you want to change: a process to innovate, a community you need to influence, whatever. We'll call that "Today" as in figure 51.

Now, here's where methods, good data, and intellectually honest work matter. You need to predict what the future would look like if you did nothing. We'll call that the "Predicted Future" as in figure 52.

Now, a lot of folks stop there. If you read a lot of the "future of libraries" articles that pop up from time to time, most stop here. A great number of the doctoral students I work with stop here, thinking that research is all about prediction. However, I won't go back into all of this, but we live in a world where our very breathing changes it, so let us work to control that change. This is at the heart of new librarianship, so we need to add another point to our little timeline. We'll call it the "Ideal Future" as in figure 53, and it represents what we want to be and what we will work toward. Keep in mind Herb Simon's work on satisficing and how imperfect our estimation of ideal is, but for our purposes we at least have a target.

Today

Figure 51

13. *Oxford English Dictionary* entry.
14. If you are about to get into a conversation about fate and determinism now, you may well have missed the entire underpinning of the knowledge discussion.

Note that there will always be some "gap" between the Predicted Future and the Ideal Future. If there weren't, then we would have nothing to do. This gap may be quite small (if we keep doing the current process, we will take in $500 a year in revenue, and if we go with the ideal situation, we will make $600). It may be huge (current trends show library budgets decreasing on average 20%, and we would like to see an increase by a million billion percent—approximately). This alone may stop an innovation dead.

However, assuming the gap is seen as bridgeable, then we have a target and a sense of the difference we need to cover. For most innovations, the gap will be large enough that several steps or stages will be needed to bridge it. So we add a series of tasks needed to move us from the predicted to the ideal (like I've done in figure 54).

This is our agenda. It is grounded in the reality of the current, and a best guess of the future if our course is unaltered. It is not limited by this prediction, however, because we have a target change and steps to achieve it. Each step is a point of reflection where we can check our progress and adjust the agenda. Each point must also tie into assessment. This approach is just a more generalized conversation map like the one discussed in the "Communities" Thread.

This system can produce a research agenda:

Early digital reference literature predicted the system would fail because it lacked immediacy, but some saw the possibility of virtual reference being a widely available service. To do so, however, we needed to better understand what users wanted, how they would interact with librarians, what standards need to be put in place to allow scalability, means of determining quality and so forth.

It can be a personal agenda:

If I want to be an academic librarian, I need to get an MLS, within that I need to study about the academic context, I need to put together a portfolio, etc.

It can be a service agenda:

If we keep our current document delivery policy to the branches we will not be able to serve shut-ins, so we need to have a home delivery service. To do that we need to come up with a budget, to come up with the budget we need a good estimate of the population size, etc.

Today   **Predicted Future**

Figure 52

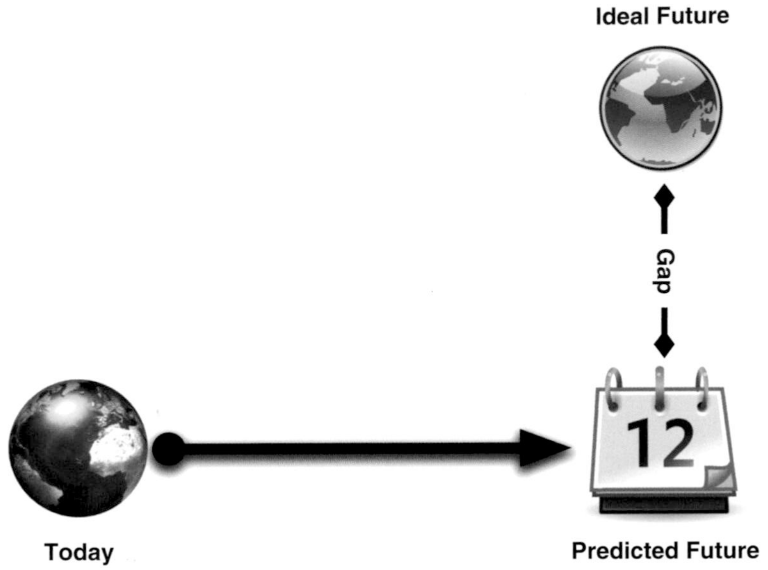

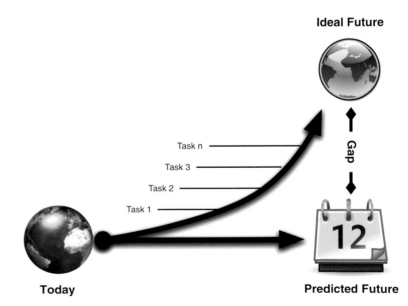

Figure 53

Figure 54

By the way, the process of developing an agenda? That's also a conversation. Was there such an agenda in participatory librarianship, now called new librarianship? Yup. Was part of it the production of an Atlas?

It takes leadership to implement any agenda. That is our next agreement. However, first I need to address an issue related to data.

Risks of Data

Any agenda needs good data. I learned this from Chuck McClure. There now exist large and diverse data sets on library trends and usage. Some of these include:

- U.S. Institute of Museum and Library Services (IMLS)/National Center for Educational Statistics (NCES) [academic, public, school, and state library data]. http://nces.ed.gov/datatools/

- Association of Research Libraries. http://www.arl.org/stats/annualsurveys/arlstats/

- Universal Service Administrative Company, School Library Division [E-rate data for schools and libraries]. http://www.universalservice.org/sl/tools/search-tools/

- American Library Association/Florida State University Information Institute, Public Library Funding and Technology Access Study. http://www.ii.fsu.edu/plinternet.cfm

- Association of Academic Health Sciences Libraries [Medical Library Data]. http://www.aahsl.org/Publications/about_stats.cfm

As Chuck points out, although there is a great deal of data, there has been too little effort in combining these data sets and making them easily accessible and usable by the library community. The result is that many librarian decisions made at all levels are done without data and evidence. This has made the library field in aggregate more open to personality-driven decisions and trends.

There, now that I've made Chuck happy (always important), it's time to piss him off (although I think he would probably agree with what I am about to say). The problem with data is that they are all about nouns, and life is all about verbs. That is a metaphorical way of saying that data can tell you what is but rarely tells you what should be.

Let me give you an example. I was at ALA midwinter in 1999 when Diane Kresh and Linda Arret of the Library of Congress tried to whip up support for a new digital reference idea that would become

known as the Collaborative Digital Reference Service (CDRS), which would later morph into QuestionPoint. They put up a graph on the decline of reference questions in academic libraries. It looked like the chart in figure 55 (although this is a more current version, which really makes the case for needing to rethink our value). It was a common practice to show this kind of chart and follow it up with, "So we need digital reference to go to the user and get these trends reversed."

Except after this line of reasoning was thrown out, an academic library director got up and said, "For the past 5 years, my reference staff has been asking for more resources to improve our website, do more instruction, and provide more databases. I look at this chart, and I see success. All that training, services, and interface work have helped our users find what they are looking for." Same data, different interpretations. Very different resulting agendas.

Take another story in the same vein. Intel had a help desk set up for engineers. Intel staff around the country could go to a website and enter questions. Consulting engineers and help desk staff would answer the questions. They noticed a lot of repeat questions, so they decided to add a new "sandwich" interface. This new interface would have the staff ask a question, parse apart the words in the query, and present them with probable answers to their questions. If the person asking the question didn't see an existing answer, he or she could then forward the question to the help desk staff. In the first month, questions dropped off by 90%. Success!

Except, when the folks who designed the system went back and compared the questions asked to the automated answers selected, they found 85% of them were not related. Yikes!

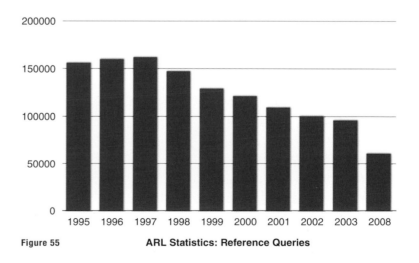

Figure 55   **ARL Statistics: Reference Queries**

In research methodology, we talk about two measures of quality. The first is reliability. This measures how consistent a piece of data (really a measurement) is. Do you get the same number if you do the same thing over and over again? So if you want to know the outside temperature with reliability, install two or three thermometers and see whether they all give you the same reliable answer.

The second quality measure is validity. This measures whether you have the right equipment to begin with. Did you, for example, put both of the thermometers right next to the dryer's vent so that every time you did laundry it miraculously got 20 degrees warmer? Although both are important, validity is much harder. As Suzanne Ripley of the National Information Center for Children and Youth With Disabilities once said to me, "I find people who ask for numbers rarely care which ones I give them." Data, no matter how "good," cannot replace asking the right question from the beginning.

LEADERSHIP*

As a kid, one of my favorite cartoons was the Super Friends. It was the Saturday morning cartoon of the Justice League with Superman, Batman, Wonder Woman, and the whole gang (including the addition of two teenagers and their dog Wonderdog and later the Wonder Twins and Gleep). You'd always see the superheroes seated around a conference table when an alarm would go off, and the Super Friends would spring into action and save the day. As I get older, I've started to think about what they were doing at the conference table before the alarm.

Superman: OK, let's call the meeting to order. Do I have a motion to pass the minutes of the last meeting?

Aquaman: I'll move that.

Wonder Woman: Second.

Batman: Wait, this says I used my Bat-a-rang on Manta on page three. That's not right. I used my Bat-Knock-Out-Gas. We need to change that.

Superman: OK, so, all in favor of passing the minutes?

Batman: …with amendment?

Superman: All those in favor of passing the minutes with the amendment?

All: Aye.

Superman: OK, first order of business…

Batman: What, no calling for the nays?

Robin: …or the abstentions?

*See Agreement Supplement for more on leadership in libraries.

Superman: Everyone said "Aye," There can't be any nays or abstentions.

Batman: OK, I'm just saying…

Superman: Moving on, first I'd like to hear from the subcommittee chair on Hall of Justice Facilitates and Grounds. Let's see…Aquaman, you chair that, right?

Aquaman: Yes, but all we really have to report on is the garden project, and that task force was headed up by Jayna of the Wonder Twins…

Superman: OK, the chair recognizes Jayna to report on the task force on gardening of the subcommittee on facilities and grounds.

Jayna: Gee golly, Superman, OK. Well, we planted the roses like everyone wanted, then Zan turned into a bucket of water, which I sprayed all over the roses in the form of an elephant.

Superman: Fine, fine, fine. You blew your brother out of your nose. Got it. OK, Wonder Woman, I see on the agenda that you have a report on membership?

Wonder Woman: That's right, Superman. As you all know, we've been thinking about expanding membership. I have compiled a list of possible recruits for you here…

Flash: Um… excuse me. This document was not circulated 24 hours in advance of the meeting. I thought we all talked about how we needed to distribute documents 24 hours in advance of meetings.

Wonder Woman: Well, technically I did, but since I sent the list from my Blackberry as I was sucked into a wormhole by Ares, it got caught in a relativistic time trap and won't arrive on Earth for 200,000 years, I thought I would cut the wait and just hand it out here.

Flash: Look, I'm just saying, you could have sent it again.

Batman: Come on Flash, you were busy with Gorilla Grodd all night, you wouldn't have had a chance to read it anyway.

Flash: Look, I know I can be a pain on parliamentary procedures, but why do we have rules…

Superman: OK, OK, let's step back for a minute. The whole 24-hour thing is an informal policy and hasn't even made it out of the policy subcommittee, much less been sent to the executive committee for approval, so…

Batman: Must not throw Bat-a-rang.

Flash: You know you're saying that out loud, right? Why do we always have to say what we're thinking out loud?!

BEEP BEEP BEEP BEEP BEEP BEEP BEEP BEEP BEEP

Superman: Great Scott! The Moon is being pulled out of orbit!

Robin: Holy Awkward Orbit Batman! Let's Go!

Flash: Wait!

Wonder Woman: What is it, Flash?

Flash: I didn't hear a motion to adjourn.

OK, this has been a gratuitous use of space for a simple point: No matter how super you are, committees and meetings can still suck the life out of the most exciting place to work. Also, I figured after all of that talk on social justice that you could use a break.

As a librarian, you must be constantly on guard against Daedalus' Maze. Daedalus was the mythical Greek engineer who created a maze so complex that even he couldn't escape it. All too often as librarians we have turned the tools we use to organize artifacts on ourselves. The same reductionist set of hierarchical boxes has all too often been employed in our organizational charts.

We see it in the constant need to type one another (I'm an academic reference librarian at a small liberal arts college in the Northeast who works from 12 to 8 during the week). We see it in our professional organizations (seriously, ALA has a standard for standards[15]). We see it in our policies (the Association for Library and Information Science Education had a policy against online proceedings three years before anyone actually proposed to produce online proceedings). There is even an old vendor joke: What do you call two librarians sitting at a bar? A consortium.

There is a word for this type of reductionist approach to management: bureaucracy. We know that word as a sort of pejorative noun meaning something too complex and rigid, but it was a term well explored by the German management scholar Max Weber.[16] Weber found a lot to like in bureaucracies. The idea is to keep subdividing an organization until the smallest possible area of the business can be well understood and analyzed. Once there is an employee or division keeping track of that area, it can report any variances, threats, or opportunities in that area up to the next level of management, who can then combine it with other areas and keep reporting things up until action can be taken. Sound familiar?[17]

In static environments, this system actually works quite well (assuming the communication up and down the chain of command can be made efficient). It also provides great stability and control. The problem is that there are few static environments around these days. What's worse is that all too often we drag this maze with us when we work with new communities.

Remember when I said in the "Social Justice" Thread that we need to bring our values with us? Leave the bureaucracy behind. I can't tell you the number of "third meetings" I have attended where I tried to do this (I'm a slow learner).

The scenario plays out like this. Two organizations decide to work together and have a meeting. In the first meeting, they decide they should share their stuff. The second meeting goes well until they real-ize that, although they have a lot in common, their naming conventions aren't among them. So they start trying to hammer out what to call things and how to pass information. If only there was some group who thought about these issues. Ah yes, librarians! Bring in the librarians. Third meeting, librarians show up.

Now, five years ago, I would go on to talk about how this is a great opportunity. It still is, but now I can tell you how I (and, I hate to say it, other librarians too) screw up this great opportunity. You see, I would come in, see the objective was to share stuff, pull out my box of librarian hammers, and begin pounding away at anything that might be a nail. "You say you have documents to share, no problem, that's a job for metadata!"

"What's that, you haven't defined a metadata schema yet? No problem, I have a Dublin Core hammer in here somewhere."

"You say you don't have a common taxonomy, wait a second. There's my thesaurus hammer."

And on it goes until at the end of the meeting everyone would be convinced they were in good hands. Then by Meeting 5, it would all go to hell. What happened? I thought the objective was to share stuff: It wasn't. The objective was to collaborate—quite literally to engage in conversation. While I was focusing on artifacts (and they were, too), the important stuff was not happening: facilitation. These groups needed to learn to trust each other. They needed to develop a common vocabulary, yes, but it was still in L_0 land, still negotiating real meaning. I was trying to jump to an L_1. These folks needed a lot less Dewey and a lot more Oprah. This is where librarians can provide real leadership and, in doing so, demonstrate their values (as well as their value) to members.

Todd Marshall and I were presenting ideas on participatory librarianship in Boras, Sweden. The session right after ours on conversations and participation was the great Birger Hjørland on "Arguments for the Bibliographical Paradigm." From some comments I received, I expect certain members of the audience were expecting the academic equivalent of a bar fight. After all, here was Lankes and Marshall with their member-oriented stuff and then Hjørland who clearly represented the old guard. Except we were all saying the same thing. Hjørland's main point was that the development of controlled

15. http://www.ala.org/ala/professionalresources/guidelines/standardsmanual/manual.cfm
16. Pronounced "Vaber" with a long A in case you want to impress your friends—I learned this the hard way.
17. It may also sound familiar if you read the footnote in the discussion of "Boundary Issues" earlier.

vocabularies and bibliographic schema was hard work, and he took focus on the process not just on the resulting standard (the artifact). What Hjørland was saying (among other things) is that things like the UDC classification system required the maintenance of a community engaged in conversation.

Now there are a lot of smart people writing a lot of smart things on leadership and management. I will let them provide the specifics behind leadership methods. I simply state that organizations are communities. Libraries are communities of members, librarians, staff, and volunteers. Within this community, librarians are needed not to structure and divide, but to facilitate and mediate. Communities of librarians must bring our values, our understandings of knowledge, our means of facilitation, and, most important, our mission to these communities. We must escape Daedalus' maze on wings of open learning organizations that value intellectual freedom and intellectual honesty and create a safe environment for discussion. Ultimately, these kinds of organizations, also grounded in service, will set us free.

Obligation of Leadership

So how does all this organizational talk apply to you? Improving society requires leadership. It requires someone or a group of people to stand up, point in a direction, and go. As Margaret Mead is quoted as saying, "Never doubt that a small group of thoughtful, committed citizens can change the world. Indeed, it's the only thing that ever has."[18] When your member is stuck, when your community seems frozen, it will come down to you to step up to the plate and lead.

Some may think service and leadership are somehow incompatible. They couldn't be more wrong. The key concept to keep in mind is stewardship. A steward is someone who is in charge for the good of the community. From a steward king, to elected officials being public servants, to the concept of libraries and museums as stewards of a community's cultural heritage, we have many models of leaders who point the way not for their own glorification but for the good of the community. Just as we lead members through a reference interview, we can lead whole communities to a better state.

This responsibility extends to our own organizations. I have heard too many librarians turn down larger administrative responsibilities because they don't want to lose contact with members, they prefer to work the desk, their greatest skill is in cataloging, or whatever. So they pass on increased leadership responsibilities and defer to the second-best choice. They may well serve themselves better, they may even serve a few members better, but they do not serve their mission. Our goal is an improved society, and that means that individual librarians must risk personal comfort and clearly defined boundaries for the greater good. Librarians must lead. They must do so not out of a desire for power, money, or a better parking spot, but because the better the leaders in the library community, the better the community as a whole can serve society.

I, for example, worry a lot about leadership in the LIS education community. I have seen too many brilliant researchers and fabulous scholars turn down deanships and directorships because they saw administration as a demotion from their research positions. So instead, schools bring in people outside of the LIS domain or promote more inexperienced faculty. With few schools large enough to have department chairs or associate deans, there is little to prepare the next generation for administration, only furthering the perception of administration as a trap.

Now don't get me wrong. Accepting leadership posts and stepping in front of a community is not a safe step. It is risky, and there is an excellent chance you will get hurt. As my father said, you can always tell the pioneer—he's the one with arrows in his ass. Remember the beginning lines of the Atlas:

> This atlas is written for you. It seeks to bolster the defiant who stands bravely before the crushing weight of the status quo, and seeks to give hope to those silenced by the chorus of the mediocre and resistant to change.

Those words, overcharged as they may be, did not come from nowhere. As I go around the country, I encounter too many librarians who see the vision, who embrace change, but who have grown too tired and discouraged to hope again. They are quieted by the scars of past optimism. These are the conversations with which I struggle the most. I want to "go all inspirational" and call them to action, but I too have those scars, and have plenty of times when I tried and failed. It is not a good feeling. I would like to avoid it, too. So I never want to fault others for their decisions.

18. http://empoweredquotes.com/2007/08/14/never-doubt-that-a-small-group-of-thoughtful-committed-citizens-can-change-the-world-indeed-its-the-only-thing-that-ever-has/

THREAD CONCLUSION

I was once asked after a presentation how anyone can stay optimistic. Between perpetually negative people of the world and the perceived resistance to change in the field, isn't it all just a lost cause? How can we overcome? How can we continue to step over the rubble of past initiatives and broken momentum and ignore the anticipation of disappointment while once again stepping into the firing line of positive change?

It may sound simplistic, but for me it comes down to needing some encouragement. We need to know that we are not alone. We are not. There is a whole pool of fellow librarians who "get it." We also need to realize that those who get it aren't just new librarians, but directors, managers, and policymakers. We have a lot of good examples to show the way as well. When I have those bad days, the first thing I have to do is decide to speak up. Then I have to do something. Even if whatever I decide to do is wrong, it is something. Finally, I listen to Shakespeare. Seriously.

For some people, when they need a pick-me-up, they turn to music; others prefer a movie. But for me, Shakespeare: Henry V's St. Crispen's Day Speech. I have to thank George Needham for introducing me to it.

I've said before that we live in Shakespearian times. I know it sounds grandiose. However, the issues we face today—from economic disaster to terrorism, to attacks on civil liberties, to uninformed policymakers, to simple apathy and ignorance—are so great they rival any other time in history. Think about the issues raised in this past presidential election. Global warming, the cost of energy, salary disparities as great as the gilded age of the 1920s, and all of it showing up right at the doorstep of our public libraries, schools, and colleges. If you don't know someone who has been laid off, you will soon. These themes and issues are not just fodder for book club conversations, they are real and now—and they are your problems to wrestle with as an essential social good. To think that somehow what we do today is of any less impact on the future of our children than anything in the past is simply wrong.

As I have said before, we too often undersell the importance and raw power of what we do. We are a noble profession. We don't shelve books and change toner cartridges—we maintain an infrastructure for social action. We don't reference resources and catalog artifacts—we teach and inspire. Whereas Henry's men were cloaked in armor and carried swords, we are wrapped in the trappings of intellect and wield the passion of knowledge. Henry faced an overwhelming and arrogant force, a seemingly insurmountable legion. Henry's men despaired. Yet Henry's army won—they won through superior technology (the long bow), experience, and superior tactics. They won also because they believed that they could. So, too, can librarians overcome the crushing forces of mediocrity and cynicism, but we must believe that we can.

Faced with the enormities of these tasks—terrorism, economic disaster, apathy—standing up at a meeting and speaking truth to power? Simple. In the face of the real issues we must face, I can take on the added committee assignment or backhanded comment. How do I stay optimistic? I realize first that the issues I face are miniscule to the good I can do. How do I get inspired to face intransigence, laziness, or ineptitude? I look right past them at the real goal and those who really need me.

Block me, and I will go around you. Build a wall, and I will build a door. Lock the door, and I will break a window. And if I don't have a leader to inspire me, I will lead. If I don't have a team that will support me, I will recruit a team from beyond the organizational boundaries—every policy has a loophole, every system has a hidden reward.

That's how I stay optimistic. As Henry said:

Let me speak proudly: tell the constable

We are but warriors for the working-day;

Our gayness and our gilt are all besmirch'd

With rainy marching in the painful field;

There's not a piece of feather in our host–

…
But, by the mass, our hearts are in the trim;

This is what inspires me. Let me speak proudly—we are librarians, and we have struggled and some dismiss us. We fight with meager budgets and outmoded structures. But our hearts are in the trim. This time, this information age? This is our age. Credibility, expertise, and compassion are our weapons, and we will fight ferociously for knowledge, for compassion, and for better communities in our towns, states, colleges, schools, and businesses. Every day we will fight in the hospitals, law firms, and classrooms. On the web or in the halls of power, we are the soldiers for a better day.

What inspires you?

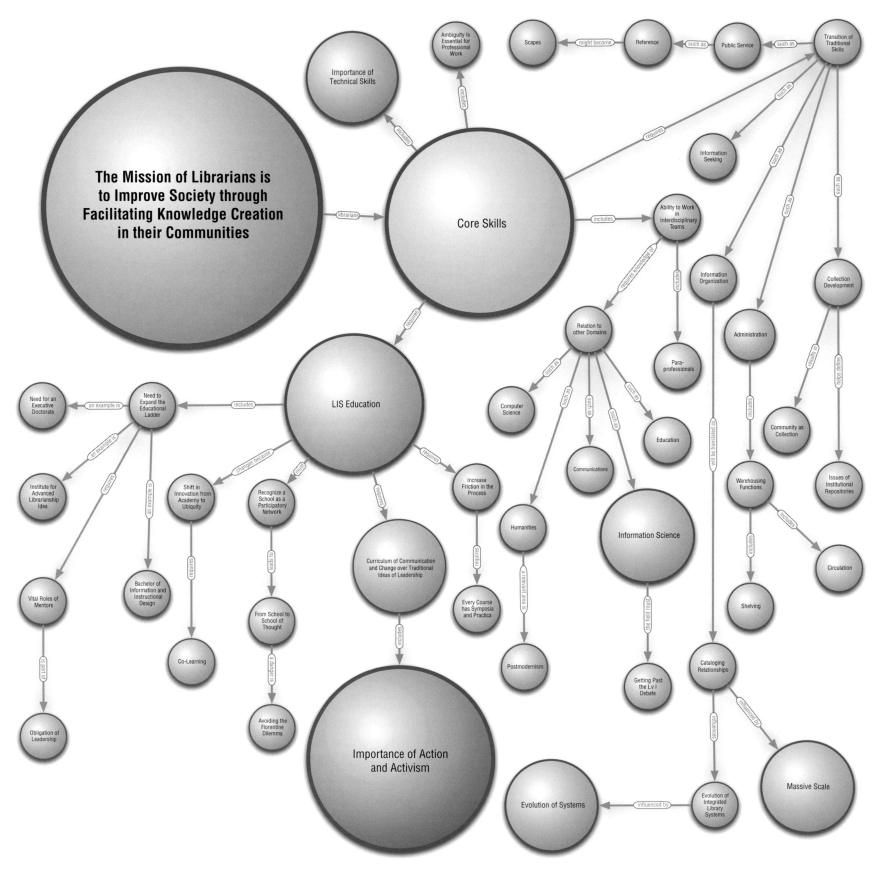

The Mission of Librarians is to Improve Society through Facilitating Knowledge Creation in their Communities

Core Skills

Importance of Technical Skills

Ambiguity is Essential for Professional Work

Scapes

Reference

Public Service

Transition of Traditional Skills

Information Seeking

Ability to Work in Interdisciplinary Teams

Information Organization

Collection Development

Administration

Para-professionals

Community as Collection

Issues of Institutional Repositories

Relation to other Domains

Computer Science

Education

Communications

Warehousing Functions

Circulation

LIS Education

Need to Expand the Educational Ladder

Need for an Executive Doctorate

Institute for Advanced Librarianship Idea

Vital Roles of Mentors

Obligation of Leadership

Shift in Innovation from Academy to Ubiquity

Recognize a School as a Participatory Network

Bachelor of Information and Instructional Design

Co-Learning

From School to School of Thought

Avoiding the Florentine Dilemma

Curriculum of Communication and Change over Traditional Ideas of Leadership

Increase Friction in the Process

Every Course has Symposia and Practica

Humanities

Postmodernism

Information Science

Getting Past the Lv I Debate

Cataloging Relationships

Shelving

Importance of Action and Activism

Evolution of Systems

Evolution of Integrated Library Systems

Massive Scale

136

Figure 56

LIBRARIANS

> We cannot have good libraries until we first have good librarians—properly educated, professionally recognized, and fairly rewarded.
> —Herbert S. White

THE MISSION OF LIBRARIANS IS TO IMPROVE SOCIETY THROUGH FACILITATING KNOWLEDGE CREATION IN THEIR COMMUNITIES

So why in an Atlas about librarianship do I tackle the Librarians Thread last? The answer is most likely obvious: Until we know what we are doing and why, we can't talk about the skills and preparation we need to do them.

There are many professions that share an interest in knowledge creation. Likewise there are many (most) professions that feel they are at least part of improving society. How do concepts of knowledge, communities, facilitation, and improvement come together to make a librarian? We have already talked about some of this in terms of values and mission, but the details of preparation, and the relation of you as a librarian to other professionals, hasn't been addressed square on… until now.

CORE SKILLS

Values endure, whereas skills come and go. If Ranganathan had lived in ancient Greece, we would all be talking about every scroll its reader and every reader his or her scroll. The concept of collection for use would still be the same. The point is that talking about core skills is not like talking about core values. "Core" in the case of skills is core for the moment. While we should fight for and hold dear our values, we should look at our skills as a means to an end.

This doesn't mean, however, that we should ignore skills—particularly in the preparation of new librarians. What we do, we must do well. When we build or find a tool, we should be committed to mastery. However, if we find another party who is simply better suited to those tools, we should partner with them.

The dilemma in writing this Thread is this: At what level do you discuss skills? Too specific and the writing is out of date by the time you read it; too broad and it provides little more direction than "know stuff." For the purposes of this chapter, let me present three broad categories of skills:

- Competencies: broad and durable approaches to fulfilling our mission.

- Skills: less broad, and less durable means of fulfilling competencies.

- Technologies and techniques: specific means and processes employed in the skills. These change often.

The competencies in this case are our means of facilitation: access, knowledge, environment, and motivation. Skills, as is explored in greater depth throughout this Thread, are familiar to most librarians—for example, information organization as part of facilitating through access. Technologies and techniques are specific ways of implementing the skills, such as the MARC record for information organization or the use of information-retrieval techniques to search a collection.

It should be noted that these levels do not form a strict hierarchy. In other words, a skill does not exclusively nest within a competency. As an example, information seeking applies to all four means of facilitation. We revisit the relationships between the skills and the techniques discussed in the following agreements. So let us start the discussion of skills by looking at the existing skill set of librarians and how they must evolve in light of new librarianship.

TRANSITION OF TRADITIONAL SKILLS

I begin with a reminder. You are not an accumulation of skills. Librarianship is not defined by how we do things—a functional view—but why we do things—a worldview. That said, librarians do some pretty cool things that have been successful for centuries. New librarianship does not refute skills such as information organization or information seeking. Instead it puts a different emphasis on the importance of these skills and the focus within the skill.

INFORMATION ORGANIZATION

So God calls a meeting, and to this meeting he invites Carl Linnaeus, the father of modern classification (he's the guy who gave out all the Latin names we had to memorize in biology), Melvil Dewey, and Penny, a rural library director who had just passed away the week before.

God says, "Well I've done it. I've called the rapture and brought up all the souls from Earth for judgment. In fact they're all behind that door over there. The problem is, when I came up with this plan, there were a lot fewer people on Earth—like two—and you folks have been busy. There are now a couple billion souls in that room, and I need some help in sorting the saved from the damned."

"No problem," says Linnaeus, who strides confidently through the door.

An hour goes by, then two, then five. Finally, at 7 hours, Linnaeus crawls back out of the door. His clothes are torn, and he is clearly shaken.

"I couldn't do it," he says. "I was doing OK until I came upon a goth Japanese teenager, and I ran out of Latin. It can't be done."

"I'm on it," says Dewey, who strides confidently through the door.

An hour goes by, then two, then three. Finally, 8 hours later, Dewey crawls out of the door covered in sweat.

"It can't be done! I had all the Christian denominations all sorted out, then I ran into a Jewish family and a couple of Muslims and I ran out of numbers."

Upon hearing this, Penny turns on her heals, marches through the door, and one minute later walks back out. "Done," she says.

"That's great," says God. "But how did you do it?"

"I just asked everyone who had ever voted to increase library funding to raise their hands and told the rest they could go to hell."

So what did Penny know that Linnaeus and Dewey seemed to have forgotten? There are an infinite number of ways to classify the world. Where Dewey and Linnaeus gained fame in seeking a universal classification system, the new librarian understands that by separating organization—and in an increasing number of cases, content—from physical containers, the full richness of multiple simultaneous classifications can be explored.

There is a great deal of brilliant work in the area of information organization. This is to be expected with the current and overwhelming focus on artifacts in the field. What's a shame is that much of the scholarship on information organization that examines the fundamentals of how humans organize things (artifacts, yes, but also ideas, concepts, and, in the language of new librarianship, agreements) gets lost in a flood of pragmatism and functional myopia. All too often information organization is viewed through the narrow lens of descriptive cataloging. The world is so much richer than what can be put into a MARC record or Dublin Core element.

Take as an example the article of Martha Yee:

There are two components of our profession that constitute the sole basis for our standing as a profession. The first is our expertise in imparting literacy to new generations, something we share with the teaching profession. The other is specific to our profession: human intervention for the organization of information, commonly known as cataloging. The greater goals of these kinds of expertise are an educated citizenry, maintenance of the cultural record for future generations, and support of research and scholarship for the greater good of society. If we cease to practice either of these kinds of expertise, we will lose the right to call ourselves a profession.[1]

I would obviously disagree with Yee's stance on what defines the profession (in fact I wrote a whole Atlas on the topic). Information organization and cataloging are skills and techniques and thus changeable over time. However, in the context of this agreement, it is her conflating information organization with cataloging that is the most problematic. By the way, I'm not picking on Ms. Yee in particular; rather I feel her comments represent ideas held broadly by librarians.

For example, web search engines use principles of information organization, while they do not use descriptive cataloging as defined by Yee. When Bing or Google crawl the web, they use the inherent structure of the web to create a broad topology of pages, words, and topics. This is stored as metadata in a series of large indexes that are optimized and searched.

There are plenty of examples of information organization that are not cataloging. Say you are in a doctor's office waiting to be seen. A song comes on the radio station being piped into the waiting area. You like it, but you have never heard it and don't know what it is called. No problem. As you are listening, you take out your iPhone, bring up the Shazam[2] app, and punch "tag now." The app records about 30 seconds of the song, uploads it to a central server that analyzes it, and in seconds you have a listing of the song title, artist, album, and even the ability to buy it on the spot through iTunes (or Amazon). How does it do this? Well, it has created special indexes of as many songs as they could get a hold of and simply compares your recorded clip with that index.

In the field of natural language processing and machine learning, a whole raft of techniques is used to find patterns in documents

1. http://www.slc.bc.ca/response.htm
2. http://www.shazam.com/music/web/home.html

and then match these patterns to queries. A lot of these techniques utilize something called a neural net. Here you feed a piece of software a sample of documents in a collection. The software looks for any pattern it can find. Some of these patterns you might guess: how many times does a given word occur, and how close to other words? However, a large number of rules the software creates have no direct human analog. It might find a pattern in the use of commas, the bit counts of numbers, or anything. The point is, you prime the software with some patterns, a bunch of documents, and then have at it.

If you own a Mac, you may have run into this in action. The new version of iPhoto introduced a feature called "Faces." iPhoto looks over a huge number of photos you have taken and looks for things that should be faces (two eyes, a nose, and a mouth). When looking at a photo, the software says, "Hey, I see a face, who is this?" If you give it a name, it then looks for all other faces that seem close and asks you, "Are these the same face?" You then say yes or no. The more of these yes and no judgments you make, the better iPhoto does at automatically recognizing that face. You are training a neural net.

All of these are examples of information organization that do not fit into the traditional approach of human-intermediated cataloging. In fact, you may say that these approaches don't have much to do with librarianship and seem more like computer science, and you would be right. Information organization is larger than human-created cataloging records and is not the exclusive domain of librarians.

There are three other points that need to be made from these examples. The first is that all of the mentioned tools are invaluable for a librarian to use. The second is that all of these examples combined dwarf the information organization work done by librarians. The third is that while the tools may be built by folks outside of librarianship, librarians' knowledge of information organization is a crucial skill that needs to be shared with other domains.

Concepts such as authority control, metadata record provenance, the differences between categorization and classification,[3] and development of taxonomies and ontologies all represent core skills of librarians that are extremely useful to other domains such as computer science. Yet note that these concepts, while they can influence the techniques and technologies of cataloging, are not bound by them.

Bottom line: Information organization is a current and long-standing skill for librarians much associated with the access means of facilitation/competency. As a librarian, you should be able to organize things and understand how to do so at a much deeper level than descriptive cataloging. As the world continues to evolve and as the concept of document devolves, your ability to bring contextualized structure for a given member or community is essential.

Why at a deeper level than cataloging? Well, for one thing, cataloging practice has been built around artifacts and the concept of document, and the new librarian needs to start with conversations and the realities of knowledge. The new librarian also realizes that the search for universal methods of information organization is misguided. At best we can create large-scale schemes (DDC, LOC, etc.), but they will never by truly universal. To that end, much of the current focus of the technologies and techniques of cataloging has been on the wrong things.

*Cataloging Relationships**

Today's catalogs are not finding aids; they are inventory systems. People encounter inventory systems all the time; however, they are normally not forced to actually use them. Let's say you go into a store, try on some shoes, and ask if they have a given shoe in a size 12. The salesperson will disappear to check the inventory system. He or she will either go look at the shelves in the back or hop on a computer (normally a black terminal with green text) and find out that, yes, they have one at their other store. They would never let you use the system because it is too arcane. What do we do as librarians? We turn the monitors around and tell the member, "I don't know if we have it—you find out."

Back in the "Knowledge" thread, I compared the results of library catalogs to Amazon when talking about the "Death of Documents." There I showed how Amazon records are much richer but also problematic: They contain a lot of contextual information, but this is squeezed into an artifact view. So while an Amazon user is talking about a series of books, he or she has to attach those comments to only one artifact.

Let's do another comparison between a library record and an Amazon one, in this case for the book *Healthy Sleep Habits, Happy Child*[4] as seen in figure 57.

Let's now look at the Chicago Public Library's record for the book in figure 58.

3. http://findarticles.com/p/articles/mi_m1387/is_3_52/ai_n6080402/?tag=content;col1
*See Agreement Supplement for some links to Semantic Web Technologies.
4. Weissbluth, M. (1999). *Healthy sleep habits, happy child*. New York: Ballantine Publishing Group.

Chicago Public Library

Amazon

Figure 57

Figure 58

Note that the majority of information on this book is about where it is (the listing at the bottom is holdings). Does where the physical item is placed help someone understand the content of the book? No, yet that is what we spend our time describing…because we are building an inventory.

To be sure, there is plenty of cataloging information that is about the book. Abstracts, indexes, and such. Classification information even tells us about the relationship between this book and other artifacts. However, it is a pretty paltry context, and it is not necessarily one that the member will understand. It is L_1 language, of most use to the librarian. It is the cataloging equivalent of a member asking for the time and you handing back a book on clocks. The question and answer are related, but the relation is not helpful in the context.

Rather than cataloging artifacts and assuming they are self-contained, we need to build systems that focus on the relationships. We have examples of this right now in the library world. The first is in the legal community. Legal information is all about conversations and relationships. From legislative histories that document debates leading up to legislation, to the rich corpus of case law that forms a fascinating chain of precedents and citations, legal information is organized around threads, conversation, and use. Westlaw is an invaluable tool to the legal profession not because it is a simple inventory of cases and outcomes, but because it is a set of important relationships.

In the scholarly world, we see the equivalent in the Web of Science. It is not enough to know whether an article exists. Scholars need to know how important that article is, and this is done through impact factors and citation. An article gains importance by how it influences the ongoing scholarly conversation in a field.

Even Amazon understands this. Figure 59 shows an excerpt of Amazon's listing of the *Healthy Sleep Habits* book. That's right—citations. Citations are one of the most pure representations of conversations in the written world. In law and in research, they are the most important information that can be provided outside of the content of a piece itself and, in some cases, more important. Yet in our catalogs, they are missing. It would be like taking the lines of a poem and randomly presenting them to a reader with a disclaimer that all of these lines are related.

By ignoring citation information where available and only paying attention to so-called front matter in cataloging, we are not only ignoring the vital flow of a conversation and stunting intellectual development, we are ultimately deceiving our members into believing that every artifact in a collection is of equal importance in all contexts. Context matters. Relationships expressed at simple topicality or fit in some "universal" classification system are insufficient. The relationships we capture and provide in our discovery systems should mean something to the members. These member-based relationships should live side by side with our classifications.

Take the simple example of "more like this." Those three words represent something of a holy grail in the organization of information. Those words are the basis for recommender systems and descriptive cataloging alike. We want to create meaningful groupings that will not simply let a member know that something exists, but that he or she can use that artifact (idea, agreement) to find other, related things. So how does your catalog or finding aid handle the concept of "more like this?"

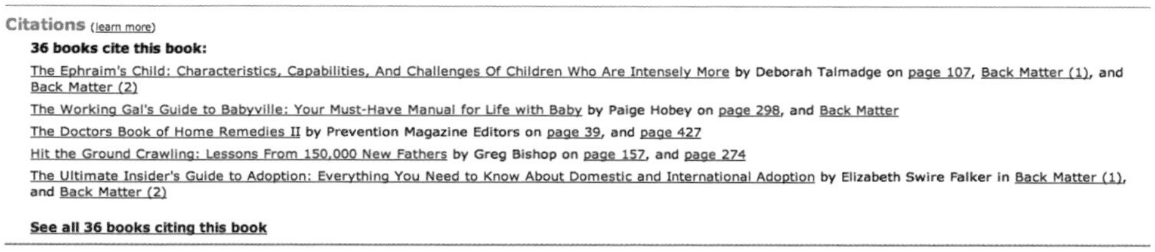

Citations (learn more)

36 books cite this book:

The Ephraim's Child: Characteristics, Capabilities, And Challenges Of Children Who Are Intensely More by Deborah Talmadge on page 107, Back Matter (1), and Back Matter (2)

The Working Gal's Guide to Babyville: Your Must-Have Manual for Life with Baby by Paige Hobey on page 298, and Back Matter

The Doctors Book of Home Remedies II by Prevention Magazine Editors on page 39, and page 427

Hit the Ground Crawling: Lessons From 150,000 New Fathers by Greg Bishop on page 157, and page 274

The Ultimate Insider's Guide to Adoption: Everything You Need to Know About Domestic and International Adoption by Elizabeth Swire Falker in Back Matter (1), and Back Matter (2)

See all 36 books citing this book

Figure 59

Take the Harry Potter series. What are "like" the series? More youth fiction? Other books by J. K. Rowling? Perhaps books on Magic? Dewey doesn't help here because this is fiction. So, what is it? For me the answer is *The Ultimate Lego Book*[5] and *Star Wars, Episode I: Incredible Cross-Sections*.[6] Why? Because those are the books that my eldest son and I really bonded over when he was age 6 and learning to read.

This is not a discussion of folksonomies versus classification. That is a false dichotomy. It is about open, multiple means of information organization versus limited, single classifications. It is not that Dewey or LC or Getty is bad. It is that they are not universal or enough. It is also not about building in a few schemas into a record or system. It is about realizing that a system must support an infinite number of categorization and classification systems. Even one member might have five or six major organizational systems (one for home, one for work, one for this hobby, one for this location, etc.). Tagging is not enough!

Take the central map of this Atlas. It is not enough to have all the agreements listed out alphabetically. The agreements gain value in their relationships. It is also insufficient to simply draw some lines between the agreements. A former colleague of mine, Chuck McClure, once said there are three ways to drive citations to your work: say it first, so that everyone cites your article as a seminal work; say it last, so everyone cites your work as a synopsis of a field or approach; or say it stupid, so that everyone has to cite you as they are telling you that you're an idiot. No, the relationships between agreements (artifacts, people) matter a lot and must be described.

There has been a lot of work on the concept of relationship among agreements. The whole of the semantic web and contextual linking world is devoted to these concepts. Semantic web developers must avoid, however, seeking a universal system to classify relationships. Such systems will face the same issues in the same way that all universal systems of classifications do. OWL, the Web Ontology Language, for example, focuses on the "crunchy" formal logic system that lends itself to computation. However, the real power is in the "squishy" qualitative connections between ideas.

Librarians must go back to the days of pathfinders and annotated bibliographies. In a real sense, the drive toward efficiency put in place by Dewey a century ago is going to greatly decrease the value of librarians. This drive has led to the equating of copy cataloging to information organization. Librarians are taking records focused on artifacts, developed in one context, and assuming they have universal utility to all communities. This is crazy. Just ask the parents who challenged Harry Potter as a book promoting witchcraft and devil worship.

New librarianship is all about context, all about communities, all about adding value through intellectually honest work. We gain value in our members' eyes, not by our ability to look like everyone else, but by looking like the community we serve. This is true in the services we offer, in the collections we chose to build, and in how we organize our information. Information organization remains a core skill of the new librarian, but cataloging as currently constituted is a technique and technology in desperate need of reexamination. If you want to see the urgency of this reexamination, look no further than the highways on which you drive.

MASSIVE SCALE*

Leni Oman is the best friend a library could have. She heads up the research division of the Washington State Department of Transportation. She is responsible for all of the environmental impact studies conducted as part of road and bridge construction, among other things. She is also in charge of the Department's library.

I met Leni while working on a National Academies panel investigating the management and dissemination of transportation information. The panel met for more than a year, exploring how to make transportation information, mostly at State Departments of Transportation and some university libraries, better integrated and more available. The panel focused on some pretty traditional approaches, such as union catalogs and expansion of a centralized gray literature database run out of the Transportation Research Board.

It wasn't until the end of the session that the real problem came into focus. All of the research reports and documents about transportation that we had been focusing on were just a drop in the bucket compared with the coming tsunami of transportation information. Those are data created by the infrastructure itself.

When you drive down the road today, you are generating data. First, your car, if it was made in the last 20 years, has a computer inside it monitoring your speed and engine performance. The road has sensors monitoring how many cars are passing, the ambient temperature, and even stresses on the asphalt. If you pass through a toll, there is an increasing chance that an RFID chip will automatically pay, creating a record of where you were and at what time. High above you, satel-

5. *The Ultimate LEGO book*. (1999). New York: DK Publishing.
6. Reynolds, D. W., Jenssen, H., & Chasemore, R. (1999). *Star wars, episode I: Incredible cross-sections*. New York: DK Publishing.
***See Agreement Supplement for a more comprehensive treatment of massive-scale librarianship.**

lites are monitoring the weather and aircraft the traffic. Perhaps you have a GPS that monitors where you are and, in some newer models, builds a peer-to-peer network of traffic and routing information. Off to the side of the road, more data are gathered on the environmental impact of emissions, salt, chemical seepage into the watershed, and even wildlife populations.

It is estimated that soon every mile of interstate highway in the United States will generate a gigabyte of data per day. It is assumed that this will become a gigabyte an hour as more and more technology finds its way into our vehicles and management systems (GPS data, real-time environment monitoring, etc.). Because there are 3.5 million miles of highways in the United States, that would be 3.3 petabytes of data per hour or 28 exabytes per year. Just in case you are wondering, 5 exabytes is enough to hold all words ever spoken by humans from prehistory to about the year 1995. Now imagine more than times that a year just on how the asphalt in the road is doing.

Transportation information is just one pot of data coming that will be of interest to our communities as they seek to learn. In Dubai, Cisco installed a "virtual concierge" in new high-rise buildings. This system not only records security video 24 hours a day but also monitors the temperatures in the different floors minute by minute, the efficiency of the elevators (so it can improve responsiveness as it learns traffic patterns over time), RFID-based location of cars and employees, and more. All of these data are simply dumped to massive storage farms off site until they figure how to wade through and turn them into better systems and living experiences.

Cisco is not alone. As the costs of computing and storage have dropped to ridiculous levels (like seven cents per gigabyte[7]), more and more organizations take a "save it to disk and figure out how to use it later" approach. The result is that librarianship needs to change radically.

Many of our concepts of information organization were originally conceived of in an artifact-centric, information-scarce world. The original collection of the Library of Congress was from one man, Thomas Jefferson, who needed to sell off his books to pay debts. Although Jefferson never would have claimed to have every significant book of his time, he was probably pretty close. Today, it is a person's attention span that is scarce, whereas the artifacts and information are plentiful.

How do we prepare librarians for a job that needs to organize terabytes of data produced every hour? How do we rethink the concepts of information organization in a massive-scale world? The way I see it, we have four options (these are discussed in greater depth in the Massive Scale Agreement Supplement):

- **Option 1: Ignore It**   No one said librarians had to take on every challenge presented to them. In fact, many criticize libraries for taking on too much. Perhaps the problem of massive-scale computing and storage is not a librarian problem. I argue that if librarians do not address these issues with their foundation of praxis and principles, the consequences for society and the field of libraries could be grave. The ultimate result may well be the commercialization of data stewardship in the massive-scale world. We have already seen how well that works with scholarly output and journals. To be sure, I am not arguing that librarians must do it all, but they must be a vital part of the massive-scale landscape. If we truly value our principles of privacy, access, and so on, we must see them as active not simply passive. We cannot, in essence, commit the sin of omission by not engaging the massive-scale world and allowing access and privacy to be discarded or distorted. We should be working to instill the patron's bill of rights throughout the information world, not simply when they enter our buildings or websites.

- **Option 2: Limit the Library**   A closely related strategy to ignoring the issue is to acknowledge the issue and redefine our mission around it. In essence, librarians are in the knowledge business, and that is now going to be defined as document-like objects, with some sort of elite provenance and well synthesized. However, there is a problem with this approach. Namely, it pits two longstanding practices and ideals in librarianship: selection and intellectual freedom. Selection and weeding are common practice. They grew out of resource limitations. Shelf space, book budgets, availability, use of jobbers, and the like are all about existing in a world of scarcity. All of these resources in the physical world constrain the size and scope of a collection. Not since the days of monks and illuminated manuscripts have libraries been convincingly able to collect it all. Yet with cheap storage, although they may not be able to collect it all, they certainly collect a lot more raw information. Can librarians choose what to collect and still say they are providing free and unencumbered intellectual access to these materials? In a massive-scale world, librarians will have to choose between these ideals.

7. http://www.everyjoe.com/thegadgetblog/hard-drive-cost-per-gigabyte-from-1980-to-2009/

- **Option 3: Catalog it All** It is a pretty commonsensical argument that the library field (or indeed any given field) is unable to provide the raw person power behind indexing the world of networked digital information. Ignore the problems of shifting pages and dynamic content for the moment and suppose for a minute that every page on the Internet was not only static but never changed its location. In 2005, Yahoo! estimated it indexed 20 billion pages.[8] If we had our 65,000 American Library Association (ALA) members spend one minute per record indexing these pages, the good news is that the entire Internet could be indexed in a little over seven months. The bad news is that those ALA members would have to work the seven months straight without eating, sleeping, or attending a committee meeting. At that same time, Google was claiming its index was three times as large.

- **Option 4: Embrace It** I obviously favor the option of engagement. In fact, I would further argue that it is the ethical responsibility of library and information science education to prepare librarians for the world of massive-scale computing. By not preparing future information professionals to deal with terabytes of data per second, we are limiting their ability to live up to the ideals of the profession and the needs of future (and many current) patrons.

To embrace massive-scale computing in libraries, we must:

1. Expand and Enhance Current Library Practice to include not only processing elite documents but real-time information as well.
2. Go Beyond a Focus on Artifacts and Items.
3. See Richness and Structure Beyond Metadata.
4. Change at the Core of the Library. All of this needs to be done at the core of library service, not as some new service, or by adding new systems and functions to an already labyrinthine array of databases, catalogs, and software.

The approach outlined in the Atlas, I believe, provides a firm foundation to explore these changes. By matching up massive-scale data to where it was created and used within a conversation (a knowledge development activity), we should be able to efficiently find the information again and understand in what contexts those data may be helpful. That is, instead of organizing the data set by inherent structures, we should be able to organize it more episodically, finding not a data point but a point in a conversation in which the data were created or used.

Evolution of Integrated Library Systems

Take our transportation information from the previous agreement. How exactly do we integrate 28 exabytes of data into our catalog? Would that be a single MARC record or do we want to do it comprehensively? The answer is, of course, we don't. It is time to stop all "next-generation" catalog conversations and ensure that this is the last generation of catalogs provided for public consumption. We need to separate inventory systems for librarian consumption from the discovery and knowledge representation systems that our members desperately need. I have already talked about some of the requirements for a new integrated library system throughout the Atlas, but let me see if I can bring them all together in a bit more coherent form.

The word "integrated" in ILS has come to mean monolithic: one code base driving circulation, searching, serials, acquisition, cataloging, and so on. Such large systems have become unwieldy. Such an approach, a remnant of mainframes and limited intermachine connectivity, comes at a big cost. Take, for example, the U.S. Department of Justice. They have a real problem with purchasing an ILS. You see, because of very strict computer security, they have to disable half the features of any system they purchase—and even then, they have to get a special waiver to put the application on the network. What's worse is that they still have to pay for and maintain the entire ILS. Meanwhile the ILS vendor is busily adding new features for their larger, more open customers, which only makes it more difficult to set up and maintain any system at the Department.

You end up with a vicious cycle. ILS vendors need to add new functionality to compete. They have to add this functionality to an ever-increasing (and aging) code base, which slows down the integration of new features. This means the ILS vendors must choose and add only features that satisfy its largest customers, who have the hardest time implementing new features.

What's very concerning to me is that I look at all the open source development around ILS systems and I see these folks trying to emulate the functionality of existing catalogs. Rather than breaking the cycle, open source ILS take a lot of new effort to end up with the same effect.

8. Battelle, J. (September 26, 2005). Google Announces New Index Size, Shifts Focus from Counting." Online posting, Sept. 26, 2005, John Battelle's Searchblog, http://battellemedia.com/archives/001889.php (accessed Sept. 15, 2007).

We need to break this cycle. You and I and all librarians need to step away from the ILS, and instead of looking for marginal improvements and cosmetic changes, we must start from scratch. There. I said it.

To begin with, we have to adopt modern development architecture and develop small sets of modular functions that can be rapidly combined. Instead of one ILS to rule them all, we need to build search modules, a bunch of circulation modules, serials modules, and so on. Then a librarian should be able to mix and match all of these modules to create their own custom ILS. If in three weeks a new and better circulation module is developed by a vendor, or the open source community, or internally, a librarian can just swap out the old module for the new. If a member comes up with a new way to visualize a collection, integrate a service with Google Maps, or geocode digital images using Flickr—click! It's in.

Vendors of library solutions then must compete on every feature and make their money from integration of innovations from around the web (like Red Hat has in the Linux world) and marketing innovations from their customers to new customers (like the Apple App store). This model will let folks from the Department of Justice get just the pieces they want and allow for small librarian-led operations to create systems that match their community needs, not their budgets. Why do you think LibraryThing has been so successful?

But Dave, you say, there are some things that every library needs, so why not just gain economies of scale by having a few players do it all? Because I don't believe there are things that *all* librarians need to serve their communities. Does the Glendale community library need serial prediction?

Part of this modularity needs to extend to the sources members, and librarians can integrate as well. Right now the ILS works as one massive artifact repository. This is the reason it is so awkward adding things that aren't very artifact-like (such as dynamic web pages, services like reference, and digital collections). By thrusting together the digital and the analog, the data and the metadata, we diminish the utility of systems that work with each system independently and simply confuse the member. It is absolutely essential that a member has one simple place to search all of this, but at the level of architecture and data, they should be segmented out like in figure 60.

OK, so we change the architecture of ILS to be modular market places. What other changes do we need to make? For one, we need to totally rethink the core item being managed by these systems. Right now every ILS begins with the assumption that you have a discrete artifact being managed (cataloged, circulated, shelved, etc.). Artifacts are not the core collections of librarians—members are. This one difference is why I have said that trying to tack social features onto an existing catalog is like trying to staple a satellite dish to a donkey.

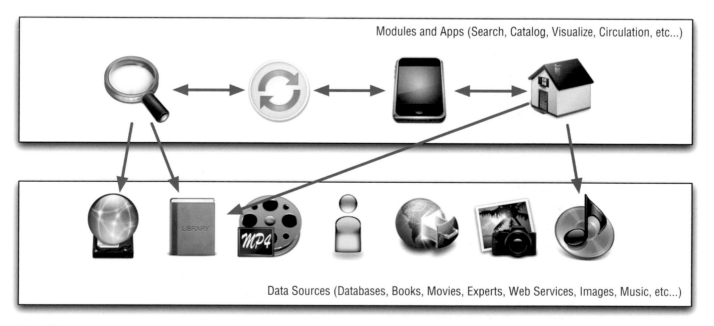

Figure 60

Artifacts are not social. Books don't sit around at night sipping martinis and talking about the silly patrons who couldn't work an index. So why is it that we think we can add social features to a catalog of things? Instead of looking at the library as a collection of collections of stuff like in figure 61, we need to see the library as a collection of member collections like figure 62.

To do this, we need to add another layer to our architecture: a knowledge layer. In this layer, the member and/or librarians organize ideas, agreements, services, and artifacts from our collection through our modules (or theirs) into a coherent view as in figure 63.

Sound abstract? Let me make it real. A group of students and I were asked to rethink how electronic reserves were being done at an

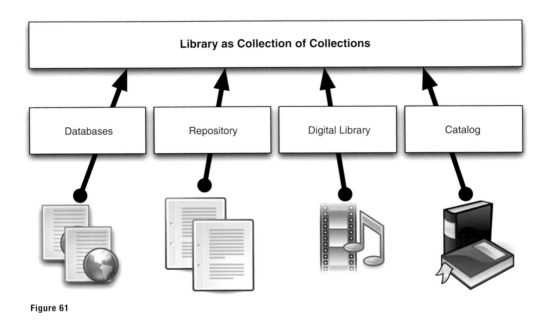

Figure 61

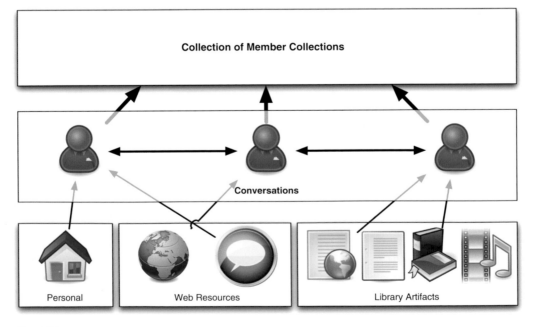

Figure 62

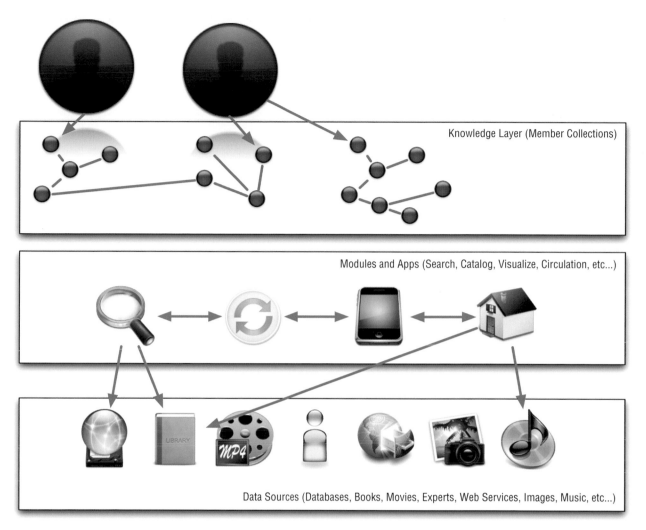

Knowledge Layer (Member Collections)

Modules and Apps (Search, Catalog, Visualize, Circulation, etc...)

Data Sources (Databases, Books, Movies, Experts, Web Services, Images, Music, etc...)

Figure 63

academic library. Students needed to get online and read the articles and items that professors had assigned them in class. The current system was based on the library's current catalog. You plugged in your class, and what came back was a simple list of associated artifacts like in figure 64.

We set about taking some of the early concepts of participatory librarianship and devising a prototype. We ended up with figure 65.

It reeks of Web 2.0. Every category was preceded with "My," you could have friends, there were a boatload of mashups (Amazon and LibraryThing), and you had a tag cloud. Clearly, we had succeeded. Except this screen represented a functional approach. We had looked at a bunch of "social" functions and thrown them together around stuff. In fact, we eventually called this the "PDF Glorification" screen. Although we kept using words like "My," there was nothing much here about "me" at all. What is the real difference between books and articles from the student's perspective? Why do I need friends in this space? It just doesn't hold together. So we went back to the drawing board.

Figure 64

What happens if we put members at the middle of these systems? Let's start with the collection of reserved items. Where did this list come from? The air? Did the instructor simply provide the students with a list of stuff to read? In most cases, it came from a syllabus, where the instructor lays out not only what is to be read, but in what order and in what context (the first subject of the class is X, and you need to read article Y on that topic). So why strip out all of these relationships and context? (The short answer is that existing catalogs can't handle the concept of "organized by instructor X.") In fact, a syllabus is the first statement in the learning conversation called a class. So let's start our system there.

Our first diagram, in figure 66, is of the syllabus, and it shows some sample connections to relevant artifacts.

Because this is the start of a conversation, it can be extended. In fact, the instructor has included assignments to help students do just that. So our system must include the ability for students to add to the conversation, as in figure 67.

If this starts to look like the Scapes system discussed in the "Knowledge" Thread, you are right. This is an early system that actually led to the Scapes concept.

Now that we have a conversation, one can imagine clicking on any item and adding notes on readings (annotations). If other students in the class choose to share their notes, you might see them as well. In fact, one could imagine seeing the notes from any class, student, or faculty member on a given artifact. A student might find that a text used in information studies is also used in anthropology. What an interesting connection to explore. In fact, now we understand what friends are doing here. This could be a way to group notes and annotations by people a particular member trusts or cares about.

Of course, this isn't the only conversation in which the student is involved. They have other classes, and they may want to use the system to keep track of their personal conversations—say, a book they are writing. So we add tools for the member to organize their own conversations like in figure 68.

Finally, we throw in some tools to add new items, search for items, and talk to a librarian to get help… and voila, figure 69.

Click on an item in this system and then the PDF Glorification screen up above might make sense because we have accounted for context and the member, not just the stuff (see figure 70).

But where do these items come from in the first place? The inventory system that we kept. Over time, however, as the conversations fill up and become richer and more diverse, members will spend less time

Figure 65

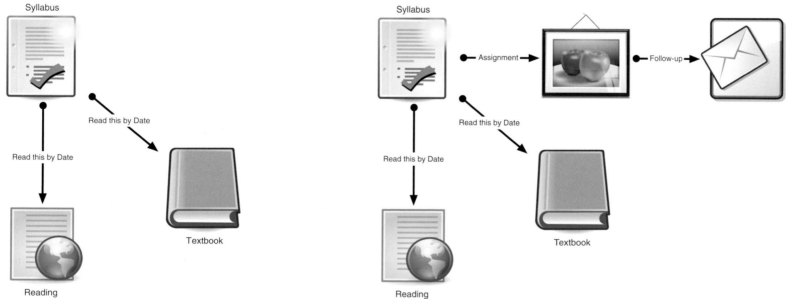

Figure 66

Figure 67

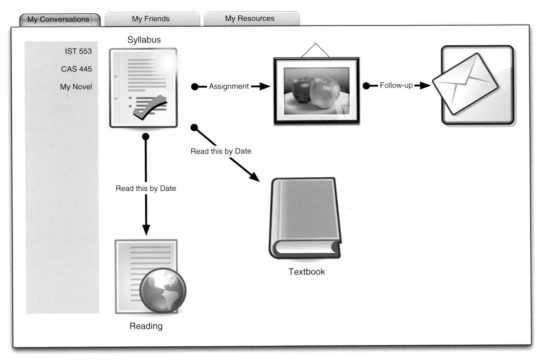

Figure 68

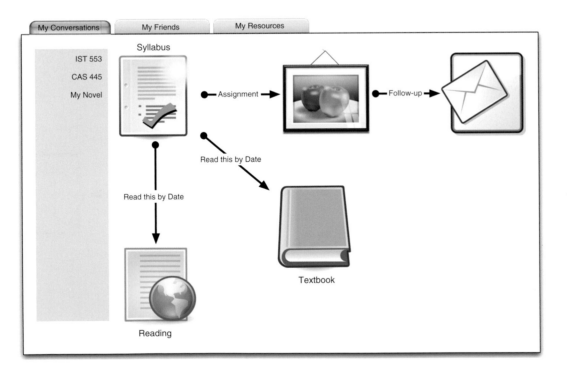

Figure 69

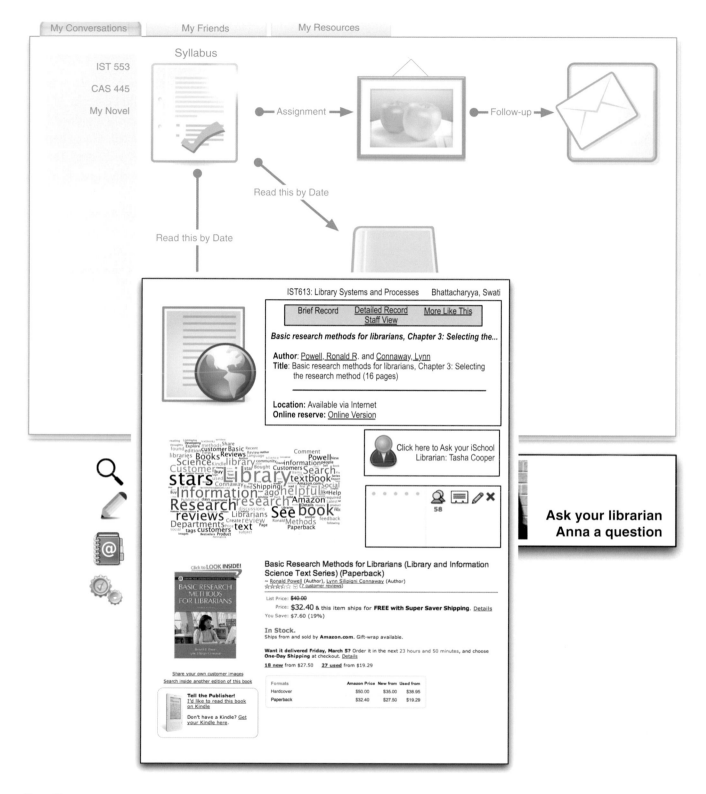

My Conversations   My Friends   My Resources

IST 553

CAS 445

My Novel

Syllabus

Assignment →

Follow-up →

Read this by Date

Read this by Date

IST613: Library Systems and Processes   Bhattacharyya, Swati

| Brief Record | Detailed Record | More Like This |

Staff View

Basic research methods for librarians, Chapter 3: Selecting the...

Author: Powell, Ronald R. and Connaway, Lynn
Title: Basic research methods for librarians, Chapter 3: Selecting
the research method (16 pages)

Location: Available via Internet
Online reserve: Online Version

Click here to Ask your iSchool
Librarian: Tasha Cooper

58

**Ask your librarian
Anna a question**

Click to LOOK INSIDE!

BASIC RESEARCH
METHODS
FOR LIBRARIANS

Basic Research Methods for Librarians (Library and Information
Science Text Series) (Paperback)
~ Ronald Powell (Author), Lynn Silipigni Connaway (Author)
★★★☆☆ (7 customer reviews)

List Price: $40.00
      Price: **$32.40** & this item ships for **FREE with Super Saver Shipping**. Details
You Save: $7.60 (19%)

In Stock.
Ships from and sold by **Amazon.com**. Gift-wrap available.

Want it delivered Friday, March 5? Order it in the next 23 hours and 50 minutes, and choose
One-Day Shipping at checkout. Details

18 new from $27.50   **27 used** from $19.29

Share your own customer images
Search inside another edition of this book

Formats	Amazon Price	New from	Used from
Hardcover	$50.00	$35.00	$38.95
Paperback	$32.40	$27.50	$19.29

Tell the Publisher!
I'd like to read this book
on Kindle

Don't have a Kindle? Get
your Kindle here.

Figure 70

in the inventory and more time in the knowledge system, thus giving us a migration path from our current catalogs to a new knowledge system as seen in figure 71.

I would also assume that librarians can prepopulate the knowledge layer with templates and pathfinders to jumpstart members. Imagine a school librarian having a curriculum map as the first interface a student or teacher sees. When teaching information literacy, why not have a Big Six template that walks a member through the research process?

Of course, this also fits in with our new modular architecture for integrated library systems. Want to add stuff from Amazon as well as the catalog? There's an App for that. Want to teach our knowledge system to do real-time video chat with colleagues and librarians? Plug it in. Initially, we want the new knowledge layer to speak MARC, but we can then add translation plug-ins for Dublin Core or the semantic web's Resource Description Framework (which would no

doubt be the initial scheme powering the knowledge layer). Don't like the graphical layout for aesthetic or disability reasons? No problem. Change out the visualizer for text or Braille.

Note what we have achieved in this transition. We have made the actual media type irrelevant. Those icons could be books, videos, content, or metadata, we don't care. What we have is a unified view of how artifacts, agreements, and ideas are connected. Going back to the idea of Reference Extract presented in the "Knowledge" Thread, we now have a unified topology to search against, thus getting us out of the horrific rut we are in with federated searching.

What's more, we have now created a knowledge management system or even a knowledge acquisition process—not just an inventory. Such a system starts to look much more like a learning management system or e-portfolio system than a catalog. All of this feeds into the Evolution of Systems agreement as well.

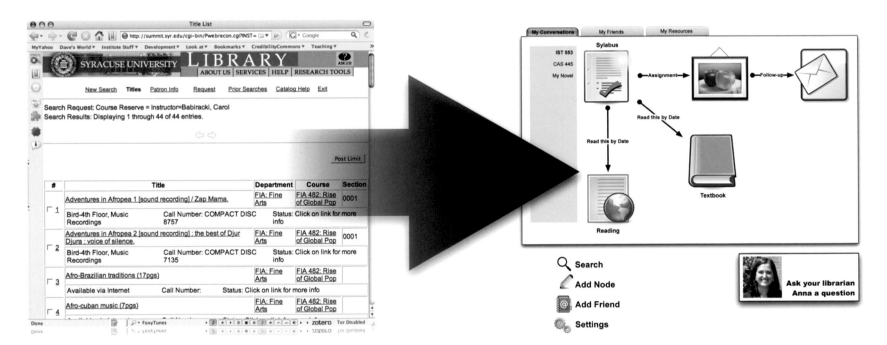

Figure 71

INFORMATION SEEKING

Information seeking and information organization go hand in hand. We organize to make things easier to find. As with information organization, it seems an inbuilt feature of being human to seek out information. Of course, as librarians, you and I have honed this skill to an art.

There has been a great deal of literature in the information science and library science domains about the ways in which members and librarians seek out information. From Herb Simons' concept of satisficing to our seeming obsession with the types of sources members turn to first (Wikipedia and Google—get over it), the field has made a core skill out of looking for information.

I will not spend much time on this skill because there is already so much good and relevant work done in the area.[9] What's more, this work has often focused on underlying human cognitive capabilities that make the skill durable over time. I would, however, like to throw one wrinkle into the discussion: It is insufficient to simply seek out information for a member.

First, realize that you as a librarian are part of the member's information-seeking process. You are simply another source in their ongoing conversation. As such, while you do your best to fully understand their information need, you never truly can (thank you Bob Taylor yet again). That means you must constantly touch back with the member to see how you are doing. It also means that the member is not simply absorbing the information you are bringing back into knowledge, they are processing it. This can take time.

By having a richer understanding of information seeking as a concept and the underlying cognitive function, and not simply as a set of technologies and techniques (I know Boolean, I know my databases, I know the Dialog commands), you will do your job better. Take Wilson's 1996 model of information-seeking behavior[10] as represented in figure 72.

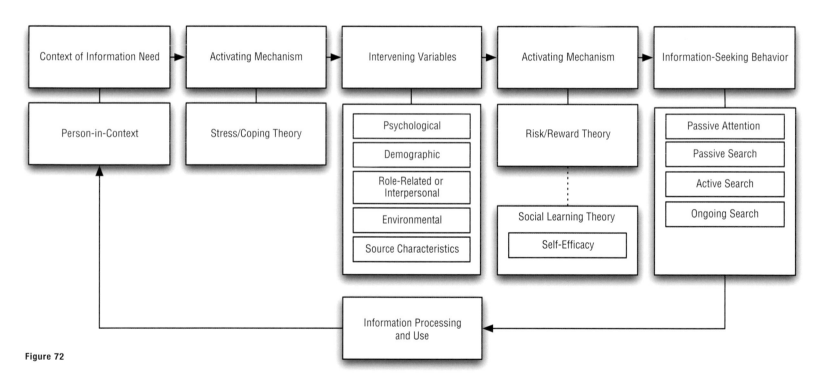

Figure 72

9. Such as Dervin, B. (1999). On studying information seeking methodologically: The implications of connecting metatheory to method. *Information Processing & Management*, 35(6), 727–750; and Wilson, T. D. (1999). Models in information behavior research. *Journal of Documentation*, 55(3), 249–270. Retrieved June 10, 2006, from http://informationr.net/tdw/publ/papers/1999JDoc.html
10. http://informationr.net/ir/11-4/paper269.html

Note that as a librarian seeking information on behalf of the member, you go through these steps. However, the member assimilating the information you have found also needs to go through them. That means that when you hand off the results, you are not done facilitating. How can you build systems and/or processes to do that? How can you evaluate how effectively a member is doing that?

The end result of a librarian's seeking out information is not presenting it to the member; it is facilitating knowledge within the member from what was found. This might be simple, such as confirming that the book you are handing to the member was the one that he or she asked for. It can be complex, such as the legal librarian sitting with the lawyer to debrief on a search. In any case, the results of an information-seeking process cannot be fire and forget. This is explored more in my discussion of reference below.

PUBLIC SERVICE

I hope that after this Atlas we can kill the phrase "public service." It is not helpful. There are plenty of libraries that have public service departments that don't actually serve the public (corporate libraries, a lot of academic libraries, etc.). What's more, everything that librarians do for members, from answering reference questions to organizing collections, is a service.

So the distinction between technical services that is all about getting and processing artifacts and public service—that is, their use—is a false dichotomy. Let's be honest: Public service is really anything in a library that isn't directly about artifacts and has become a sort of dumping ground for nonaccess functions. Because new librarianship is not about artifacts (it's about facilitation), this wall between "stuff" librarians and "people" librarians goes away. Librarians serve the community through access, knowledge, a safe environment, and motivation. The fact that artifacts may be used as tools in that process is beside the point.

Take the skills, technologies, and techniques most often lumped together into public service: reader's advisory, standing dissemination of information, instruction, story time, lecture series, and exhibits. What do these have in common? Well, most are about facilitating learning. These tasks actually map quite well to our core competencies/means of facilitation. For example, story hours, lecture series, and instruction are excellent means of facilitation through knowledge. Standing Dissemination of Information (SDI) is all about access.

What's more remarkable is that they also represent the underlying values and intuitive understanding of a community's pressure for participation in the field. Reader's advisory is a good example. How exactly can you say you are unbiased when providing a reading recommendation? Do you present all the fiction in your collection and say "good luck"? Of course not. Reader's advisory is an excellent current example of being intellectually honest, not unbiased. After reading *Walter the Farting Dog* at story hour, are you supposed to present some anti-flatulence point of view?

As librarians, we must stop the schizophrenia that public service represents. These are not offered on top of our core services. Public services are not extras or compromises of a mission; they are the mission. The skills we must retain from public service, and integrate throughout all librarian-provided services, are the ability to assess community needs and to be flexible in providing them. We must also take these services and incorporate them into a unified view of the library and take them outside physical walls to the community itself.

Reference

The director of the university library called her staff together. "I'm afraid I have bad news. Tuition revenue is down, fewer parents are sending their kids to our university, and there will have to be budget cuts."

A few hours later, the director decided to walk the building and get a sense of morale among her staff. In rare books area, she saw a group of librarians busily scanning books. "Why are you scanning all of those books?" the director asked.

"We're trying to increase the digital collection of the library so we can put a lot of great content on the website and make it more appealing to potential students."

The director went to the acquisition area and saw the librarians surfing Amazon. "What are you doing?" asked the director.

"We are looking to see if we can save money by buying directly from online retailers."

Finally, the director went to the first floor, where she saw the reference librarians pulling books off the shelf, tearing off the covers, and then randomly replacing them.

"WHY ARE YOU DOING THAT?!" cried the director.

"Job security."

Here's the question that this joke really raises: Is it the books being destroyed or the librarians present that made the first floor the reference area? A few years ago, I questioned whether there still would be reference librarians ten years from now. The question wasn't about the necessity of reference skills; it was more about whether reference skills should be constrained to only a subset of librarians.

Reference has always been an overloaded term. On the one hand, it means the human-intermediated process of answering questions. On the other hand, it also refers to a collection of artifacts that provide easy access to facts and figures. New librarianship helps inform both. Let's start with the human-intermediated process.

There is a lot in reference that as a new librarian you need to retain. For one, there is the entire concept of the reference interview or, as Marie Radford calls it, the reference encounter. The ability to work with a member to determine his or her information need is essential. However, the purpose of this interview is no longer to find out what artifact can be used to fulfill the need, but rather what conversations are necessary to build knowledge. These conversations may be prompted by artifacts, but increasingly you need to hook the member up with other members (with their permission of course).

Just as in my information-seeking discussion, providing the member with a pointer is also insufficient. You must facilitate the knowledge from access, to knowledge, to environment, to motivation. The interview is only the first step. This implies you will need a system to track a member through his or her knowledge-creation process. The idea of tracking members over several interactions requires a significant rethinking of privacy norms in reference interactions.

In addition to expanding the concept of a reference interaction through the entire knowledge-creation process, we must also expand the idea of the reference interaction as being solely a "one member to one librarian" situation. There is nothing even in the existing definitions of reference that limits interactions to one-on-one transactions[11]:

Reference Transactions are information consultations in which library staff recommend, interpret, evaluate, and/or use information resources to help others to meet particular information needs. Reference transactions do not include formal instruction or exchanges that provide assistance with locations, schedules, equipment, supplies, or policy statements.

Reference Work includes reference transactions and other activities that involve the creation, management, and assessment of information or research resources, tools, and services.

(The following bullets clarify what is meant by terms within the Reference Work definition.)

• *Creation and management of information resources* includes the development and maintenance of research collections, research guides, catalogs, databases, websites, search engines, etc., that patrons can use independently, inhouse, or remotely to satisfy their information needs.

• *Assessment activities* include the measurement and evaluation of reference work, resources, and services.

Nowhere in RUSA's definition does it say one librarian. Increasingly, as a librarian, you must be ready to work in teams to fulfill on-demand knowledge requests. These teams may be composed of several librarians, several experts, and any combination of members.

While I have RUSA's definition in front of me, let me put a new librarianship emphasis on parts of it. First, "information resources" must go beyond artifacts to services, people, conversations, and a whole host of "resources." Second, creation and management of these information resources is as important as answering questions. In fact, we need to adopt the concept of "reference authoring" prominently in how we conceive of reference. Reference authoring is the transformation of raw reference transactions into new information resources such as web pages, knowledge bases, and even textbooks.

Many of these concepts of reference are discussed in the "Scapes" and "Reference Extract" agreements and within the "Knowledge" Thread. These systems show the true task of a librarian during a reference interaction and indeed any member interaction: to weave together the entailment meshes of members. You will recall that an entailment mesh, from Conversation Theory, is the set of agreements and their relationships held by a person. These ideas strongly influenced the Development of Scapes (see the "Scapes" agreement).

Before we leave the reference process, there is a rather large white elephant sitting in the middle of the room that we must address. What exactly constitutes an answer in the reference process? You see, members and librarians don't agree. This is not about the famous 55% rule of Hernon and McClure, where we get factual answers wrong 45% of the time.[12] No, this is much more fundamental. By and large, members seek agreements, whereas librarians seek citations.

11. http://www.ala.org/ala/mgrps/divs/rusa/resources/guidelines/definitionsreference.cfm
12. Hernon, P., & McClure, C. R. (1987). *Unobtrusive Testing and Library Reference Services.* Norwood, NJ: Ablex.

I say "by and large" because there is certainly a host of corporate, legal, and medical librarians who would not have a job if all they provided were an unsynthesized list of artifacts in response to inquiries. Yet time and time again, normally in the name of being unbiased, we send out boatloads of citations and expect our members to thank us for increasing their workload. We need to give members what they perceive as answers, not what we do.

There are two issues often brought up at this point. The first is that as generalists, librarians may not know "the answer." The other issue is that simply giving out an answer may not help the member in the long term (such as in a school or academic setting). The response to the first question is that the librarian must engage the member's full knowledge-creation process, and so may be colearning the answer at the same time. This means spending more time with a member past when he or she approaches a desk or online form. Once again, we need to track members over time to solicit ongoing feedback and see how things are coming along. Note that this will not be a problem in the majority of reference interactions—we don't really need to track members on questions such as, "Where is the bathroom?" or "Can you locate X book?"

The answer to the second point—that of long-term good—is more complex. In the 1990s, I was part of a digital reference service for the ERIC system called AskERIC. Teachers, students, and policymakers from around the country would e-mail in questions about education, and information and education specialists around the country would answer these questions. Answers would include lists of citations and relevant resources. At a meeting of the ERIC directors, the question was raised of whether we should provide the same kind of answers to all questions. Education students, you see, could also e-mail in exam questions and use AskERIC responses as answers to their tests.

After much debate, we decided to give the same type of answer to all comers. Why? First, we couldn't be sure who was a student and who was a teacher. The second reason was that we wanted students to eventually use the AskERIC service when they became professionals. If students saw the service as unwilling to provide answers during their studies, why would they come back after they graduated?

Now, there are a lot of good reasons not to provide a typical answer, but rather to walk a member through a process. However, it is impossible to universally define a time when citations over facts or process over synthesis works. The somewhat unsatisfying answer is that this must be part of an ongoing social compact conversation with the community.

One more example to prove the point: As I mentioned, I was on a public library board. The board was full of folks with different backgrounds, knowledge of libraries, and agendas. At one board meeting, the reference function was raised. One board member asked what kinds of questions were asked. "Anything," replied the librarian.

"So I could call up and ask how to get a red wine stain out of a white table cloth?"

"Yes," replied the librarian.

"And my tax dollars are paying for that?"

The librarian was taken aback. There were some awkward statements of how if someone asks the wine stain question they would be more likely to ask questions about jobs or homework, but it was an unsatisfying exchange.

We must be ready to respond more affirmatively to these types of questions. Does the reference staff answer all questions? Do they stop at a given point because the teaching faculty of the school or academy doesn't want to make it too easy on the student? Do we provide tiered service to different segments of our community? These must be open and explicit conversations with the community. Expectations must be made clear. If not, you risk AskERIC's ultimate fate. It was shut down in large measure because a new administration at the Department of Education didn't think that librarians were qualified to answer the questions of teachers and evaluate the research needed in the answer.

Now let us turn our attention to the so-called reference collection and the genre issue. The genre issue revolves around how we teach reference. There is an ongoing struggle around the curriculum of reference courses. Some take a skills approach, where the focus is on the reference encounter and online searching. Others take a genre approach, where the focus is on the types of reference resources available (encyclopedias, dictionaries, gazetteers, etc.). The majority of courses seek some sort of middle ground, but that is rarely comfortable. A lot of this would be solved if we weren't restricting ourselves to a 2-year master's program, but we'll get there in a bit. For now, let me point out the inherent problems with a genre approach.

First, realize that a genre approach is an artifact approach. It seeks to teach structures and forms of certain artifacts for easier use. It would be beyond idealistic if I said that any such artifact knowledge is irrelevant. It isn't. Although artifacts are tools in conversations and are of secondary importance to the conversations, that doesn't mean they are unimportant. No, the real problem with genre-based education is the fluidity of the artifacts. What is this manuscript you are working with right now? Is it, in fact, an Atlas? It has a map. Is it an encyclopedia because it attempts to cover the whole of librarianship? Is it a textbook? Is it a long set of lecture notes? Does it matter?

The problem of genres is exacerbated by the growing, radical shifts in the publishing industry. With the growth of the Internet and self-publishing, traditional forms of editorial control are falling by the wayside. Why adhere to a given set of genre rules when you can add multimedia and hyperlinks to anything? Why conform to the notion of editions and versions when you can create living documents that can be changed by the minute? Is Wikipedia really an encyclopedia anymore?

Take the fabulous map collection of David Rumsey. Rumsey made his fortune in real estate and used a substantial part of this fortune to collect rare maps. He then hired on programmers to digitize the collection and put it on the web. However, he didn't simply put up images of maps in some geocoded scheme. Instead, he built Java applets and complex software to overlay maps, navigate topological maps in 3D, and basically blow apart the concept of an Atlas, changing it into an interactive experience.

We see millions of other examples of genre bending with mash-ups and living data. Students, enthusiasts, and the simply curious are combining data from a huge number of sources with interchangeable data and programming components to create whole new information objects. Thanks to "Goggles,"[13] you can now use Google Maps as an interactive flight simulator. With Wikipedia Vision,[14] you can see in real time the who, what, and where of Wikipedia edits. The Google Maps Directory[15] lists hundreds and hundreds of different mashups that directly challenge the concept of gazetteer and atlas alike. Do we expect every librarian to learn every one?

Genre approaches to reference are unsustainable. What is a reference book when every word of every page of every book is searchable? The world is too complex, and data are too malleable for us to know every significant resource ever again. We must now work with our members and communities directly to understand the types of resources needed to improve the community, and we must use our information-seeking skills to seek those resources out or, more likely, create them with the community.

13. http://www.isoma.net/games/goggles.html
14. http://www.lkozma.net/wpv/index.html
15. http://keirclarke.googlepages.com/directory.htm

COLLECTION DEVELOPMENT

So sell the books, right? Get rid of the videos and journals. Throw down some beanbag chairs and let the conversing commence! Right? Well, not quite. First, the collections that exist are important and need to be maintained. Just as in our catalog example, where we transitioned from inventories to scapes, we need to transition our focus from artifacts to conversations. This also does not mean the collections go away altogether.

The artifacts and collections that we have built up are part of an existing social compact that cannot simply be voided in expectation of new roles within our communities. Our members have come to depend on collections and will no doubt see them as an important part of any new compact for large institutional players such as academic and public libraries. That said, we should see the collection as part of a move forward, although in a secondary role. If we do not establish that any collection development in the future is at the service of librarians fulfilling their mission of knowledge creation, we will ultimately find ourselves out of a job.

Why such a bold statement? Because simply collecting materials does not require a professional; making sense and use of those materials does. I know this may seem an obvious statement to you, but politicians—and many members of our own communities—do not see that distinction. Furthermore, as the world becomes increasingly networked, the value of collecting is questionable.

Why not simply create something like an eBook or music subsidy built into every sale of every iPod or eBook reader, and then rather than paying to download individual items, we can get anything we want with some portion of the subsidy being redistributed to artists and publishers? Such a strategy would kill artifact-based librarianship, but it would be a huge boon to new librarians. Why a boon? Because then new librarians could build *ad hoc* collections based on the conversations they are supporting without concern for cost. If librarians are indeed about providing access to information (and I think they are so much more), then the idea of consumer cost subsidies for universal access should be greeted with cheers. Instead, librarians dread the idea because it directly cuts off the concept of collecting artifacts.

What you need to realize is that right now librarians exist in a nightmare middle ground between owned and leased collections. It is a nightmare because it is expensive and puts the fate of many library functions at the mercy of external forces such as publishers, vendors, and a fickle public.

You must also realize that the idea of the library as a group of artifacts that make up a collection has been a vanishing idea for more than four decades now. The most-used resources of the library are not owned by the library. They are leased. We have moved from an "own it and lend it" to a "lease it and view it" model. Either we get serious about ownership and stop our current practices or we accept this model and look to its logical conclusions.

The New York Public Library (NYPL), for example, has a copy of every issue of the *New York Times*. It also provides online access to the same resource. The difference is, the NYPL owns the physical newspapers and rents access to the online version. So when it came time to negotiate a new license for the online collection and the vendor asked for a huge increase in fees, the NYPL looked around and found NOVEL, the New York Online Virtual Electronic Library, a project of the New York State Library that provided statewide licenses to online databases, including the *New York Times* full text—except that it wasn't the full *New York Times* archive, just a more recent subset. So for a few months, while NYPL negotiated a new agreement with the vendor, the NYPL didn't have access to the full online archives of the *Times*.

What's more, as the vast majority of publishers have moved into the digital realm, they have adopted a licensing model over a sales model, meaning libraries can't even really buy new artifacts. Forget fair use: Licensing bypasses copyright altogether and goes to a contract model where the libraries have to give up their rights in order to have access.

We can teach collection development as a matter of selection and policy building all we want. It won't matter. Collection development skills these days are economic in nature. Instead of teaching how to compare book jobbers, we need to teach negotiation and cost analysis. If you want to retain an artifact-centric view, I suggest you also start teaching lobbying because the market for ownership versus licensing is not with you. This was beautifully summed up by On the Media's special episode on the music industry:[16]

RICK KARR: So if you're an online music entrepreneur, in the U.S., at least, even 10 years after Napster, it's still not such a good time. And if you work for a record label, if you manage to keep your job, that is, it's decidedly not a good time. And if you're a record retailer, it is emphatically not a good time!

But Tim Quirk of the music subscription service Rhapsody says the rest of us, fans and musicians, are better off than we were 10 years ago.

TIM QUIRK: Far better off; it's almost a paradise. As a listener, it means you've got access to almost anything you want to hear, almost anywhere you are, almost whenever you want. If you're an artist, labels are now an option, not a necessity. You can go direct to fans, if you want to. Even if you do opt to go with a label, you can get, depending on the label [LAUGHS], you can get much better terms than you used to be able to get because nobody's got a lock on distribution anymore.

The question in terms of collection—regardless of your take on new librarianship or whether you buy into the worldview I am presenting—is this: Do you think you can stand in front of the major shifts in the industry and the demand by consumers and side with the publishers? Or are you going to join the musicians and fans and make it a paradise of anything, anywhere?

In the Introduction to this Atlas, I wrote, "Seeing technology as the sole driver for change is short-sighted in the extreme." I stand by that. However, technological advancements are still a driver for change and an important one. We exist in a world where it is possible to be flying at 30,000 feet above the earth, carrying thousands of songs, tens of movies, and more computing power in our pocket than it took to put a man on the moon, while on our laptops we can videoconference with our children a continent away. From my home office, where I write these words, in the last week I have presented a keynote speech in Sweden, taught a class of students scattered around the globe, watched one of a thousand movies streamed to me, videoconferenced with colleagues in Europe, charted out a road trip using satellite imagery, purchased goods from California and Hong Kong, studied the archives of the New Alexandria Library, caught up on my favorite radio shows available on demand, kept abreast of the latest news from the BBC, CNN, and the *New York Times*, and for good measure downloaded Star Wars Jack-O-Lantern patterns for Halloween. What's incredible is how second nature this has become. We don't even think about how radically new a world that is for librarians and our members alike.

eBooks are not books. CNN's website is not the television station put online. Your smart phone is not a phone without a wire. Strip away the metaphor, and something truly radical is happening. All through this Atlas, I have downplayed these changes to a degree. That is because we are searching for the durable and looking to build

16. http://www.onthemedia.org/transcripts/2009/10/23/01

a bridge to the future from the success of the past. Yet in some areas—and our collections are the big ones—we simply must step back with fresh eyes and say, "This is new." This new world of spreading digital ubiquity is new. No, it is not universal. But it is not a question of the connected and the not connected: It is a question of the connected and the will be connected.

In a world of spreading digital-connected ubiquity, information is everywhere and from everywhere, and it is in every format. In such a world, librarians as facilitators of knowledge are invaluable. Collections of artifacts are only as valuable as the communities that use them.

Community as Collection

Remember in the evolution of the integrated library system agreement above, when I said, "We need to see the library as a collection of member collections"? There is an implication there that I didn't explore: If the collections belong to the members, what collection belongs to the librarian? The answer is, the members. Your community is your collection.

This is not just a nice little slogan, but it has real consequences, not least of which is that we need to understand our members better than we understand the artifacts we use to serve them. It also means that we should be willing to use members in answering questions and cultivating a collection. Not just asking teens what books they want in the teen space or having the local manga club assist in purchasing the right graphic novels. I mean really setting up systems so that you can refer other members and questions to the community at large, setting up standing arrangements with members to facilitate certain types of conversations, sharing shelves with members, and even locating some artifact collections at the members' locations.

In Syracuse, we just opened a children's hospital. In it, there will be a resource center that will include books, games, and magazines. What if the public library partnered with the hospital not just to create a children's collection but to have children's librarians make the rounds on a regular basis to see what questions the kids might have; to work with child life specialists and doctors to build programs around medical information, gaming, and more; to create a real bridge between the sick child and the community? We might have the library set up video conferencing with friends, for example. While at the hospital, because it is a member of the community, we might set up relationships with doctors and medical librarians to answer health questions for the community.

As I mentioned before, my wife is part of a moms' club in the Syracuse area. They run an electronic mailing list, and there are regular medical questions that get passed around the list: updates on the Swine Flu, discussions of vaccinations, doctor recommendations, and so on. Why not link the moms' club with the regional health information services run by the hospital? The idea would be for the library to tap into the medical community to keep kids out of the hospital in the first place. The doctors and the moms become part of the public library's collection (and the hospital's medical library collection as well).

Once again, I don't pretend this is a brand-new idea. In the Cleveland area, KnowItNow,[17] a virtual reference collaborative, has long partnered with local nurses to provide this kind of reference. In fact, virtual reference services are rife with these examples—connecting the legal services and the entire AskA community of scientists and historians. New librarianship isn't about "brand new" (nor thinking that only new is good), but rather understanding how this kind of innovative practice fits into the larger concept of librarianship and why it should be promoted.

What does collection development for a community look like? Quick, what is the poverty level of your community? How many of your students are on the honor roll? What are the specialties of your doctors? What cases are your lawyers working on? What is the big merger now afoot? Now, how many volumes do you have in your collection? What's your acquisition budget? Which of these sets of questions is easier for you to answer? Ultimately, collection development of a community looks like the assessment and planning process laid out in the "Communities" Thread.

Issues of Institutional Repositories

All of this "community is your collection" business brings us back briefly to the issue of institutional repositories. If you recall, that discussion was around how institutional repositories needed to look more like the academic community they serve. However, it is more than that for academic librarians. Scholars are your collections. They have titles, for sure, but each represents a whole little ecosystem of information. They have artifacts associated with them (their writings or works), they have activities (like teaching and presentations), they have expertise, and so on. A true institutional repository should be able to get at scholars, not just their artifacts.

17. http://www.knowitnow.org/

There are the equivalents to scholars in other settings as well. Community leaders, doctors, lawyers, partners, and politicians—all of these represent a sort of genre that has a unique structure and a set of associated systems and conversations. So while I said in the "Reference" agreement that we should abandon the genre approach to artifacts, perhaps we should revive it for people.

ADMINISTRATION

Year after year, students in Syracuse's LIS master's program complain about our management courses ("Why do I have to take this? This is all business stuff, it doesn't have any relevance to libraries"), and year and after year, our alums return to tell us how invaluable they are. Is "Administration and Management" a core competency as outlined by ALA?[18]

My unsatisfying answer is, "Sort of." I can see many circumstances when librarians will not have to manage other people or administer budgets. From a purely new librarianship worldview, there is nothing inherent about administration as part of a librarian's job. Administration and management as defined by ALA's Core Competencies is not really about librarians; it is about libraries as institutions. In essence, it is defining a core competency by what a lot of librarians do, not by why they do it (the functional approach rearing its ugly head once again).

With that said, administration and management are important skills to have when you are working within or running an organization of any size, be it a 1-person library or a 300-person staff in a Fortune 500 company. So would I advise students currently in an LIS program to take these courses? Yup. Would I make it a requirement? Yup. Do I think we need to do a better job of teaching these skills (particularly in an expanded educational system to be discussed later)? Absolutely.

To begin with, librarians must confront Daedalus' Maze, which I discussed as part of the Leadership agreement. Why the hell is the library community so hierarchical and segmented? After all, the whole key to the profession—and not just new librarianship, I mean the key for a century or more—has been about integrating all kinds of structures into a more accessible form. Yet we often make the profession impenetrable.

18. http://www.ala.org/ala/educationcareers/careers/corecomp/corecompetences/finalcorecompstat09.pdf

Librarians and the organizations they work for have created a maze of acronyms and organizations at the local, regional, state, national, and international levels, with a few hundred more in topical areas. What's more, we do most of our work behind closed doors, with most of our members clueless as to our real work.

It is time that we see the management of librarians as a conversation. Librarians working together, be it in formal or informal organization boundaries, are not some organizational chart but a participatory network, learning and building knowledge. Instead of turning our artifact-oriented systems of classification, categorization, and reductionism on ourselves, we must turn our facilitation skills loose on the profession. Rather than forming committees with subcommittees, with task forces, or with, I don't know, platoons or something, we need to organize around conversations. Instead of managers who enforce policies, we need facilitators who ensure rapid and effective communication.

There are some good models to look at within the library profession. Take the growth of digital reference cooperatives. As more and more libraries started offering digital reference, they sought to network with peer institutions. Sometimes these partnerships were around a given topic (Let's share legal questions), and sometimes they were around service considerations (I'll take morning questions because I'm on the East coast, you take evening questions because you're on the West coast, and we can both offer extended hours). So what, you say: more consortia. Except, it didn't happen that way. Most of these networks were informal. Most were created reference-librarian-to-reference-librarian. They grew peer-to-peer rather than as a set of tiered services with formal policies.

A lot of new initiatives start with passionate librarian advocates just jumping in and doing it. The barriers to these peer-to-peer exchanges have virtually disappeared. Where once we needed to set up organizations such as OCLC as a hierarchical system for copy cataloging or interlibrary loan, we can now just send an e-mail. Where once we had to travel to be together or pay long-distance charges (remember when there was such a thing as domestic long-distance charges?), now we can just IM, e-mail, or video chat.

This is not to say there is no cost involved in collaboration. There is. It has just shifted from logistics to coordination, from infrastructure to person hours, from fixed costs to opportunity costs. The problem that a librarian must manage, in an organization or otherwise, is no longer launching good ideas or projects but sustaining and shutting them down. This is best expressed by the phrase, "Death by Opportunity."

A good manager of librarians doesn't have to look at the costs of starting up an operation. Instead he or she has to look at two costs. The first is the cost of sustaining an operation—one that, as we discussed in the Innovation versus Entrepreneurship agreement, is increasingly being spread around a larger pool of people. Second is the potential loss of resources if you don't sustain the operation: so-called opportunity costs.

One consideration you have to make in terms of sustainability is the increased ease with which the librarians you manage can now bypass institutional resources and regulation. Time was that if a librarian had a good idea, he or she needed the resources, and therefore the OK, of an institutional party (like a library). So if a librarian wanted to build a service that allowed the community to upload their videos of the community, they would need server space, the time of IT, and so on. Now? YouTube.

Before, if a librarian wanted to start a blog and you said no, you had to manage the librarian's disappointment. Now? Librarians go and set up a free Blogger account and away they go. Now you have to manage their rebellion and potential impacts on the institution. With free accounts and ten minutes' time, a librarian in your employ can set up video sharing, music sharing (legal or illegal), discussion groups, blogging, a branded social network site, a Facebook page for your library, a place to review the faculty of your university, an anonymous Wiki, a real-time web conference, and about a dozen other services. The same awesome freedom that makes librarians invaluable makes them hard to say no to. This is power discussed throughout the Atlas, but for management it is a challenge.

So what can guide us? First and foremost are the facilitation skills that are the key to new librarianship. Just as we both facilitate our members and lead our communities (to improve), so too must we do these things for ourselves and our staff. Just as there is a pressure for participation exerted by the communities upon the library, so too there is a pressure among librarians upon the library. Just as the knowledge of the member is created through conversation, so too is the knowledge of any organization.

The other things that can guide us come from outside of librarianship. The concepts of flattening organizations, virtual collaborative work, learning organizations, and effective team dynamics from fields such as management, organization psychology, and economics can teach us to be better managers and administrators. These are not core skills of librarians, in that we do not seek to advance this knowledge per se; but it is vital that we know these techniques and skills.

So, is administration and management a core skill of librarians? No, but you had better know about it.

Warehousing Functions

Linda Johnson was heading up the Central Library expansion project for the Free Library of Philadelphia. She worked with funders, architects, and librarians to design an expanded facility that would last the library another hundred or so years. She had one rule for the new space: no compact shelving. The library was not going to raise a hundred million dollars and commission one of the world's leading architects so that members could be inspired by high shelves that moved on tracks.

This rule did not sit well with all the librarians. You see, in the century between the original construction of the library and the turn of the 21st century, when the expansion was designed, the library collection had grown: from 250,000 volumes in 1898 to more than 7 million items today.[19] The effect of this is pretty dramatic, as seen in the pictures of the Music Reading Room 50 years ago (figure 73) and a picture of today (figure 74).

What I want you to see is that much of our current vision of the library—as a place chock full of books—is not a universal image from our history, but of a recent history and the result of an artifact obsession. Dramatic cuts in production costs of artifacts led to a dramatic increase in their production, which led to our dramatic increase in their acquisition.

This accumulation of artifacts has, in many places, led to a nasty Catch-22. We'd love to offer new services, but we don't have room; we don't have room because we buy artifacts; people start to think of librarian-created places as places of artifacts; we need to buy more because that is what people want. This all leads to too many artifacts to try new services, and the cycle continues. In Philadelphia, there was little to no resistance to the idea of topical centers discussed in the "Topical Centers with Curriculum" agreement above; the resistance came in taking away new space for stuff.

19. http://www.freelibrary.org/about/history.htm

Figure 73

THREADS

Figure 74

This is why the future image of that music collection may well look like figure 75.

That is an image of an automated bin system. Artifacts are loaded into coded bins. You look up an item in an inventory system (where an inventory system makes a lot of sense), say go get it, and the system determines what bin it is in (which can have nothing to do with classification and co-location), and off the automated robotic system goes to pull the bin off a rack and deliver it to you. These systems are mostly used for off-site storage.

What's even better is that when something goes in one of these bins, it is often digitized first or right after it has been hauled off the rack. The document is then delivered electronically, making it even more convenient for the member even though it is off-site (because the digital document is delivered right to the member's phone or laptop). Plus the original artifact is preserved for those members who need to use the original item.

Once again this is actually not a new trend in libraries. As the web has exploded and libraries have offered up more and more services and content online, we have not crowded the reading rooms with the apparatus of storage. Rather we build back office server rooms or even outsourced server farms far away from our members. What we do put in the public spaces are not simply machines of access, but tools (computers) that can access the services and content, plus synthesize and create new knowledge.

So our physical member spaces end up looking like figure 76.[20] Where members are both accessing materials and acquiring baseline knowledge in a safe environment to satisfy their motivations. Not like figure 77[21]:

Once again, this is not an anti-book, anti-shelving rant. You must decide with your community whether you need a physical space or collection and how accessible that is. But it is a choice and an agreement around the tools librarians can use, not a decision about librarianship.

We are already seeing that when working closely with the community, often the social compact involves a lot less warehousing and a lot more conversation. We see this in the information commons movement where stacks of books are being cleared away for computers, meeting spaces, and shared service access points. We see this in new library construction with lofty public spaces and a mix of public and private enterprises co-located. We see a steady trend to deemphasize the idea of the library as a warehouse and as Bob Taylor said more than 40 years ago:

Figure 75

20. http://librarycommons.gatech.edu/images/0747001-P1-095.jpg
21. http://www.sourcecodesolutions.com/Pictures/ServerRoom001.JPG

Figure 76

Figure 77

not concerned with the usual library automation . . . routine automation is merely an extension of the control and warehousing functions of libraries. The work here is an early effort to understand better the communications functions of libraries . . . because that is what libraries are all about.

Shelving*

If you happened to be in a wheelchair in the 1920s and wanted to be a librarian, you never would have gotten into library school. You see, you couldn't have shelved books above a certain level. I point this out to show how sometimes functions and techniques can overshadow our deeper mission and values. Today turning away the disabled from library school is not only morally repugnant but illegal. Skills can (and in this case should) change over time to match our durable worldview in different times and contexts.

We have already seen in other parts of the Atlas how shelving can be used as a tool to facilitate conversations and build a sense of co-ownership in the library. We can give shelves to community groups. We can expand our shelves to include those in the members' homes.

We can also imagine using technology to overcome some of the perceived limitations of physical shelving. Imagine members with their cell phone walking through the stacks. As they pass by a rack of materials they hear a ding and see on the phone a list of items they might be interested in to their left. Imagine using the same technology to let members "paint" books on the shelves so their friends can follow the trail or see the annotations, reviews, and discussions of a physical item right at the shelf. It might look something like figure 78.

Using augmented reality techniques, we can create hybrid shelving that takes advantage of the browsing and collocation of physical shelves (that has never been fully duplicated online) with the richness of an online community. No cell phone? How about end cap monitors keyed to an RFID tag in the member's library card? It is important to think about the shelving of what artifacts we do choose to keep in our member spaces as browsing services and think if we can improve and augment that interface. One more thing: Stop putting the Dewey numbers on the shelves and a poster that translates the Dewey numbers into English hidden on a wall nearby. It's like hiding the secret decoder ring to break the librarian code.

*See Agreement Supplement for more on Augmented Reality.

Figure 78

Also, notice how things such as augmented reality, blogs, and digital tools are being used not because they are cool functions but because they enable us to fulfill our mission.

Circulation

At first glance, circulation is an area that sounds frighteningly mundane and artifact-oriented. Yet in the past few years, we have seen some real innovation in the space. Self-checkout and the circulation of audio books are some of the most obvious examples finding wide-scale adoption. Lending out ebook readers, iPods, and laptops are newer explorations. One of the coolest events I've now seen at multiple libraries is the idea of circulating experts. You "check out" a lawyer, accountant, or librarian for an hour or so. The member gets an hour or so of one-on-one attention. It's a nice play on the circulation metaphor. These examples reinforce the idea that innovation can happen anywhere and can have unanticipated and larger effects.

However, it also highlights an idea demonstrated in the Shelving agreement. Rather than thinking of the infrastructure we are deploying for circulation, shelving, and other warehousing functions such as artifact inventory control, we need to see it as being enabled for service development and conversation facilitation. So RFID is not (just) there to help circulation and theft prevention; it is there to enable hybrid services at the point of physical artifacts. Likewise, circulation is a gold mine of conversational data. People check out books for a reason. These data can be used to improve collection development and certainly identify hot topics and conversations ripe for service development.

Take, for example, the idea of floating collections. The idea of "floating" items between physical facilities (once again as part of a negotiated social compact with the community and as one of many tools you bring to the members to facilitate knowledge creation) has been around for a long time. Yet I think it is ripe for re-exploration. If you are part of a multisite system (branch libraries, distributed information centers, etc.) and you build collections at the system's facilities, the idea is to let those collections float between the sites. So if site A requests an item from site B, when the member returns the item to site A, it remains there rather than being sent back to site B. Over time, the collections at site A will "look" more like the community using that facility. This should also be true for site B.

Lots of libraries do this and have found that worries about any one site getting all the good stuff or smaller facilities being overwhelmed either don't play out or are easily managed through weeding, ensuring popular items exist at all facilities and even sharing only portions of the full set of collections. We should be able to do this even better these days by applying data mining and predictive algorithms to the process.

The point is that the use of artifacts in conversations leaves trails. It leaves trails online in blog posts and bulletin board messages. It leaves trails in the hybrid world with circulation records. Rather than ignoring the trails, we should use them, and to use them we must understand these trails don't come from concepts such as inventory control. They are rooted in conversations and knowledge development. Using this lens, these trails help us migrate away from an artifact-centric profession to one of knowledge facilitation, collections or no.

IMPORTANCE OF TECHNICAL SKILLS

Cliff Lynch had just finished giving the keynote at the third Virtual Reference Desk Conference in Orlando, Florida, and I was milling around with conference goers in the exhibit/breakfast area. Cliff had given an overview of standards, trends, and technologies that librarians should keep up with, and I was curious about how it had gone over. I approached two folks chatting over bagels and asked what they thought.

"Well, we're reference librarians," they responded.

"OK," I sort of skipped over the non sequitur and asked the question again. "So what did you think of the keynote?"

"We've been reference librarians for over 20 years."

I was now starting to wonder whether perhaps I wasn't the only one in the conversation, did a quick look around, found no one else, and said, "That's great, but what did you think of Cliff's talk?"

"Well, we just don't get all that Z9 whatever stuff."

It was then that I realized these folks defined reference librarian as a decidedly nontechnical portion of the profession. It wasn't the first and certainly has not been the last time that I have seen librarians exempt themselves from technical requirements. "That's for tech services" and "that's for academic librarians" are common phrases expressing this feeling.

Throughout this very Atlas, I have tried to temper my comments on technology, talking about physical and digital, trying to show that all that is "new" in new librarianship is not a direct result of technological functions or capabilities. So can there be a new librarianship without a strong technical background? Let me be clear here. No. Technical fluency is an essential skill in librarianship. In particular, librarians need a fluent knowledge of web service creation, databases (building them, not just searching them), and information retrieval (once again, how they work, not just how they are used).

Let me be even clearer. The Oxford English Dictionary defines *technology* as "the application of scientific knowledge for practical purposes." In that light, almost everything librarians do (new or old) is technology. Although technology has come to mean "digital/computer" technologies, we must remember that the card catalogs were technology. The binding process of artifacts uses technologies. The book itself is a form of technology. When we transform our concepts into applications and use some tool to do it (book, computer, pencil), we are using technologies.

So let me redefine the question: Is fluency in digital and computing technologies essential for new librarians? Yes. Does this mean that all interactions with patrons will be in a mediated digital environment? No. Does this mean that every service offered by a librarian has to have some technical component? No. Then why is it essential? Let me just take three big reasons:

1. Digital technologies, particularly network technologies, allow us to reach and interact with our communities in new and better ways. Because we are in the knowledge business, we must facilitate not only direct interactions but the memory of our members. This translates into things such as recommender systems and digital preservation of family and community heritage.

2. Increasingly, the tools at our disposal for facilitating conversations have a digital component, even if this is not immediately obvious. Take as an example the venerable library card. The bar code on a library card relies on a bar code reader, which relies on a computer. Increasingly, our analog world is monitored and managed with digital technologies.

3. Computing and network technologies allow for greater collaboration with more diverse partners. As discussed in a moment, the success of the new librarian is as much the result of partnership as individual effort. Digital and networked technology allows us to create and maintain partnerships with minimal regard to distance and even time. Now we can partner with organizations thousands of miles away at such a low cost that we can provide more services to more people.

The bottom line is that, although we may be in the knowledge business, we still live in the Information Age. If we don't maintain technical fluency, we limit our voice in issues involving privacy and policy. We limit our ability to create tools and thereby force ourselves to adopt tools from others solving other problems with other values.

One other note before we leave the topic of technology. Don't assume that all of this will be solved with the natural progression of age. There is a myth that the younger you are, the more proficient you are with technology. This just isn't true.[22]

For examples, the folks at CIBER at the University College London[23] in reviewing the literature found in the UK:

Only 27% of young people live up to the image of IT immersion

20% are "digital dissidents" ["that think computers are for dads"]

Frankly it has always escaped me why we think just because you are young you have a better grasp of digital and network technologies (yes, this may be me being a bit defensive). Look at the leaders of the digital revolution we hold in such high esteem. Steve Jobs was born in 1955. Bill Gates? 1955. The CEO of Google? 1955. There is no expiration date on computer skills. In fact, one of the fastest growing populations of online users is that of seniors over age 65.[24] Back to the CIBER literature review[25] that found: The over-65s spend four hours a week longer online than 18–24s.

The reason for this little interlude on the false assumption that youth equals tech savvy is not just about what you can assume about your members. It is also about what the field cannot assume about its younger librarians. Technology fluency in the profession, and knowledge of the essential tools to facilitate conversations, will not simply happen over time. We can't wait this one out. We must actively engage in proactive continuing education for all librarians. Today. Right now. What are you waiting for?

AMBIGUITY IS ESSENTIAL FOR PROFESSIONAL WORK

Here is how not to read this Atlas: "I am a cataloging librarian at a medium size liberal arts college in the Midwest…what page is that on?" You won't find it. I'm guessing if you have made it this far, you have noticed how the Atlas is structured as a funnel, with broad concepts at the beginning (such as "Knowledge is created through conversation") getting progressively more applied through the middle (examples from Philadelphia, screen shots), to the focused and applied (what was the last book on librarianship that actually focused on new ideas in shelving). But I mean, come on, it is still far from a workbook with detailed action plans and 12-point steps to a better library. Whenever we get too close to a prescription, I drop the whole "of course this will depend on your community" line.

In essence, there is a lot of ambiguity here. That is the nature of knowledge creation and conversations. They are not predetermined. They are about discovery, experimentation, and negotiation. It is your job as a librarian to ease that process as much as possible with your members and communities, but ambiguity will always remain.

Think about what it would mean if there were no ambiguity in the profession and the services we offer. It would mean that the field was dead. Scriveners do not have a lot of arguments about the nature of their profession, nor do charioteers or court jesters. These fields are finite. They don't need to evolve because they have gone extinct. Librarians are not there—you are not there. And you never will be so long as you continue to encounter novelty, which you will if you focus on knowledge creation, not artifacts.

22. https://connect.sunet.se/p39586246/
23. As a side note, this work is informative and worth some time to digest. It does a brilliant job of laying out the assumptions around the "Google Generation" and comparing it against data: http://www.jisc.ac.uk/whatwedo/programmes/resourcediscovery/googlegen.aspx
24. http://www.pewinternet.org/Reports/2006/Are-Wired-Seniors-Sitting-Ducks/Data-Memo.aspx?r=1
25. http://www.jisc.ac.uk/media/documents/programmes/reppres/ggworkpackageii.pdf

Now, here's where things get interesting (and a bit ambiguous). As a librarian—as a human being—you require both novelty and stability. Change is good, but constant change can devolve into chaos when there is no attempt at a routine or pattern. This is made clear when you study the process of change in organizations (which you should, but we'll get there). One of my favorite models of change comes from Kurt Lewin, and it is called the Freeze-Change-Refreeze model[26] pictured in figure 79.

Figure 79

Let's say you want to make a change. It might be a change in a process, an application, a job, whatever. Lewin says that you have to bring those affected by your change through three general stages. The first is the present state. People in the present state are frozen. They know what to do, and they do it. There is low ambiguity in their tasks. To implement change, you must first unfreeze these folks. That means you have to do two things: make them uncomfortable with their current situation, and make your alternative seem more attractive.

Half of that step is really easy, and library-land is full of folks making people uncomfortable with where they are. This was evident throughout the rise of the "Library 2.0" literature, where there seemed a strong vein of venom. Librarians rightly dissatisfied with the status quo looked toward technological innovations on the web (primarily social networking) and argued there was the reason to change. Unfortunately, there was a fair bit of hyperbole and an underlying belief that all the "old ways" were to be thrown out. The problem (besides the lack of guidance of a worldview) is that, after making folks uncomfortable with the present, the future state was often vague and limited. Blogging is not a strategy or a future state; it is a technology and a tactic.

After unfreezing your target comes a turbulent period of change. Here old structures break down, people are anxious, and there is un-

ease with the present. What is important to note is that this change stage is essential and *always* turbulent. No change comes without some sense of turmoil. Often we seek to smooth these waters, but we simply can't make change completely smooth and easy. People have to work for a new normal, and they must see the real difference between how things were and how things will be.

The change stage is also fraught with danger. Many who are unfrozen will seek out stability, and if you don't provide it, they will find it themselves. What's more, they will often go back to their original state to find stability. You must, in Lewin's terms, refreeze them.

This means that you (or your team) must create new structures for people to settle into. New forms of assessment, new stable technologies, and new training are all methods to refreeze. If you simply point the way or present a vision of the future without some stabilizing mechanisms, you will present to many an empty promise. People will begin to doubt.

Now, this is not to say that refreezing means the removal of all ambiguity. Rather it means creating a sense of stability to face new and ambiguous situations. Meaning, if you are going to replace your integrated library systems with a Scapes-like knowledge system, you must prepare your IT staff, your librarians, and, first and foremost, your members. Once you have made the move, you will discover gaps in what the system can do, whole new ways to use the system, and plenty that you do not expect. Without a worldview to address these issues, folks will quickly look to lock down functionality, create unnecessary procedures, and get a policy for everything. A work environment full of policies on every conceivable occurrence is frozen but lacks the ambiguity to see the new. It is also a sign of librarians seeking to avoid ambiguity.

This Atlas is an attempt to cover the stages of change in librarianship. It has elements to make you uncomfortable, and it presents a future vision to attract you. It also acknowledges there will be turbulence, and it tries to present some stabilizing ideas for the future state (mapping conversations, software, skills needed, and preparation programs). Yet, as we started off this agreement, ambiguity remains.

The future is uncertain. New opportunities and new threats will emerge that I can't even dream of in writing this. The only way you can be prepared is to have a strong sense of self and profession (a worldview based on durable concepts), a strong sense of values, a set of usable broad competencies to address the unexpected, and a healthy tolerance for ambiguity.

26. Lewin, K. (1951). *Field theory in social science*. Chicago: University of Chicago Press.

ABILITY TO WORK IN INTERDISCIPLINARY TEAMS*

OK, so let's just do a quick rundown of all the competencies, skills, and techniques/technologies you are now supposed to have as a new librarian:

- The four facilitation competencies: Access, Knowledge, Environment, and Motivation

- Information Organization with a focus on cataloging relationships between agreements and artifacts (as opposed to the artifacts themselves)

- The ability to organize and make sense of massive information stores

- The ability to re-invent the integrated library systems into one that is modular, a market place for new ideas, and focuses on knowledge

- Information-seeking skills, including assessing the impact of retrieved information on members

- Reference as a social process, focused on answers as commonly defined by the community and librarians

- Collection development where the collection is the community and its members, not things

- Administrative and management skills

- Understanding of warehousing functions where appropriate

- Digital and network technology fluency

- Appreciation of ambiguity and a firm understanding of change management

Of course there are plenty of skills and techniques hidden in that list and discussed elsewhere in the Atlas. For example, we know that memory is an important aspect of knowledge, and so therefore preservation is "hidden" in that competency. Also, because it is all about learning, we must include instructional skills. Also key to any librarian are the twin skills of planning and assessment, as well as mediation.

It's a long list. But wait, it's worse than that. As Isaac Asimov observed:

*See Agreement Supplement for an extended discussion of a team approach including the concept of Cyber-Infrastructure Facilitators.

Knowledge has a fractal like structure. No matter how much we learn, whatever remains, no matter how seemingly small, is infinitely complex.

What this means is that if you take any one of the skills mentioned, say information organization, you can study it forever at the highest level of intensity and devotion and still not find the "end" or the "answer." This is a real dilemma with artifact-centric librarianship. We can never, ever, finish MARC or the Dewey Decimal System. There will always be something else to learn. Serials acquisition? Always something new. If we continue a reductionist approach to constantly take something and continually break it down to understand it, we will never finish. In essence, it is a recipe to sit staring at a leaf on a tree while the forest grows around you.

This is where the importance of activism, a worldview, and a new social compact becomes so vital. These notions all present methods of saying, "I know enough to do some good, and I must get started."

But what if you don't know enough? What happens if you and the community determine it is important for a librarian to be part of something but you lack the requisite skill?

Well, the first answer is obvious: You will need to be constantly learning. Just as we are facilitating our members' knowledge creation, we must be constantly creating and caretaking our own knowledge. We come back to this in a moment under LIS Education.

The second answer to this, and indeed the fractal nature of knowledge, is to embrace the interdisciplinary nature of knowledge. You can never know everything, but you should get good at finding out who does. The only way we can facilitate knowledge creation is to work in teams and engage with our communities and with experts from outside fields. The new librarian realizes that part of facilitating knowledge for a member or community is putting together ad hoc and standing teams of experts of all sorts. Further, the role of a librarian in these teams involves the same core expertise they bring to the community: facilitation and mediation. The following sections begin to talk about some starting domains for us to look to for team members.

Relation to Other Domains

There is a sort of algorithm for academic success in today's universities (actually, there are two, and the first is to bring in a lot of research money, but we won't go there). It goes like this: divide the pond until you are biggest fish in it. So when I went up for tenure, I didn't just study libraries (too big a pond), I studied reference. Still too big? OK, I studied digital reference. Too crowded still? I studied digital reference systems…no the use of Commodore 64s in the digital reference on Tuesdays, and so on. This success through subdivision of fields of inquiry is a holdover from the reductionist philosophy that fueled most university growth over the past half century.

Things are now changing, in rhetoric, if not in fact. This comes from some major new findings (like paleontology + astronomy = dinosaur extinction) but mostly from a realization that problems of any serious consequence are too complex for a single perspective. That is the nature of knowledge—it is relationships, it is dynamic, and in many cases it is unpredictable. Knowledge may come from combining concepts in seemingly unrelated areas (it is said that Einstein developed some of his ideas on relativity by thinking about how to synchronize clocks along a rail road system[27]), and so the librarian must be adept at reaching across domains to seek support.

That said, there is clearly a cluster of "information professions" that form a natural (if not somewhat historical) cohort on which librarians can draw. In some cases, these disciplines have emerged from library science and forked off as the skills and techniques of librarians evolved. Other fields are so close as to cause friction as the scholars and practitioners in each seek to forge their own identities. It is worth our time to look at these fields as possible partners, yes, but also to use them as a comparison to better hone our identity of self (realizing that that too is fluid).

Boundaries, such as knowledge and conversations, are both fluid and unpredictable. The labels of a field are more a convenience for the conversants than representative of some absolute truth. For me, a field is defined by its primary conversations and conversants (often with an accompanying L_1). Just as we can map conversations within our communities, so too can we use the lens of conversation to map possible collaborations and means of supports with other disciplines. That will be our guide through the next several agreements: build a conversation map of the interrelations between closely aligned fields. It will not be a comprehensive map by any means.

Information Science

Let's just get this out of the way first. I think information science is different from library science, and that difference just doesn't matter. Why? Because library science as a conversation is historically centered on institutions (libraries) and is tightly bound to a value system. Information science, on the other hand, seeks universal concepts of information regardless of organizational types (indeed it can be organizational or personal) and often without a predetermined value system. Indeed, much of information science either assumes that information and the systems to manipulate it are neutral.[28] This is why we have no problem calling someone a librarian, but every time anyone tries to use the term "informationist," we either look at them oddly or roll our eyes.

Information science has its own need for a worldview. You can see this need in its constant seeking of boundaries and key definitions (what exactly is information?). However, this is beyond the scope of the Atlas, and there remains great value in a strong partnership with information science.

Getting Past the L v I Debate

Why doesn't it matter, the difference between information and library sciences? Well there are theoretical physicists and experimental physicists, and astrophysicists, particle physicists, geophysicists, and even econophysicists.[29] In fact, if you ask a physicist, he or she will tell you that chemistry is just applied physics. The point is that these foci are important, but the interrelationships between them are messy. An attempt to say that library science is contained within the larger field of information science or that information science is an offshoot of library science is just wrong. It's too simplistic, and such semantic escapades harkens back to a reductionist paradigm and the seeking of some universal classification system.

I, for example, am an information scientist and a library scientist. I am both because I choose to participate in both conversations. It is easy to participate in both because there is so much overlap (information seeking, information organization, systems, etc.). I value both conversations and the conversants within them. I care deeply about librarians and the institutions of libraries. I also know that I can take

27. Galison, P. (2003). *Einstein's clocks and Poincaré's maps: Empires of time*. New York: W.W. Norton.

28. For a brilliant discussion of this, see Batya Friedman's work on Value Senstive Design at http://depts.washington.edu/vsdesign/
29. Not really. http://en.wikipedia.org/wiki/Econophysics

what I learn in the library field and apply it to other fields. What I learn in corporations, government, and other communities I can apply within the context of librarians.

There is no debate here. The times when there are problems with the co-existence of information and library science are when one group excludes the other, or there is no respect between the two, or if information scientists seek to prepare librarians without understanding they must pass along a value system and worldview, not simply a set of functions.

There is a reason we talk about Library & Information Science or LIS. The "&" is important. It is much like the "and" of Boolean logic—a concatenation of common elements to form a larger set.

There is a debate coming, however. It will not be about "information" versus "library." It will not be about our name. It will not be about the names of our schools or buildings. It will not be an L v I debate. It will be an I v K and L debate: information versus knowledge and learning. Have no doubt that if you call yourself a new librarian, if you focus on conversations, and if you claim knowledge and learning as your main concerns, you will be taking a side.

There will be those outside of the library field that will be very confused, even angry. There will be members, politicians, and faculty alike who will see any deemphasis on books and artifacts as a retreat from a historic responsibility. That is why the explicit and very public conversation on a new social compact is so key.

However, these outside voices, they can be convinced. Those who see us as stereotypes and a sort of old guard can be convinced and shown the way. The real debate, and it is sure to be vicious, will come from within our own ranks. It will be from the annoyed librarians of the world who seek the status quo and see their mission as recorded knowledge, the collection of artifacts, and the maintenance of organizations labeled libraries.

There is and shall continue to be what Karen Schneider calls bibliofundamentalists. They are educated and dedicated to service. They will not show up in buns and comfortable shoes shushing like some stereotype. Rather they will come with calm voices and talk about tradition and social obligations. They will wave the OCLC Scan around where the word people most identify libraries with is books. They will cite rising circulation, and they will call for stronger standards. They will cry foul against relativism and new age ideas.

The voices of the bibliofundamentalists must not be silenced or dismissed. We must not look on them as enemies. Instead we must thank them for their service and ask them why. Why do we collect? Why do we classify? Why do we promote reading? Listen, then ask them, politely, isn't it so we can make society a better place? If we can agree on that, then we have only but to define our terms. Debate and challenge is only good for this profession. It means there is a conversation going on, and we are learning.

But listen to me. There will come a point when the debate must end—when, as we know from our understanding of Conversation Theory, we must agree to disagree. Then we will have to do something painful. We will have to leave them behind.

Communications

The kinship between conversations in library science and communications is growing. Conversations form a strong, wide bridge between the two. Folks in communications have been studying how people communicate at both the theoretical and applied levels.

In terms of theory, communications scholars can help us to better understand the process of conversations and the nuances of it. They can improve our understanding of the underlying psychology of language interchange.

In the applied world of communications, librarians have a lot to learn about message development and delivery. We can learn about marketing, media production, and ultimately how to communicate the impact of our services.

Librarians can also add to the field of communications. We can work with folks in communication on issues of long-term memory, the organization of communication artifacts (where appropriate), the description of relationships in agreements, and building systems that best serve a community's needs (translating underlying communication concepts into real tools).

Let us create a simple map of the research and applied conversations in communications and LIS. In figure 80, I've used a broad and somewhat generic set of steps for research and practice processes. There is much that could be learned by refining these steps in the different disciplines and seeing how we might improve such processes in librarianship.

Next we can link the conversations with some sort of relationship. For example, linking the "Deploy" step in the application of LIS with "Marketing/Advertising" in applied communications with a relationship like "utilizes." In a more readable form, it would be "use concepts of marketing and advertising from the field of communications to deploy our services." You can also see the obvious linkages

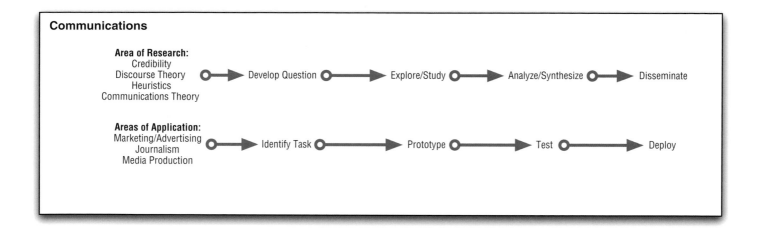

Communications

Area of Research:
Credibility
Discourse Theory
Heuristics
Communications Theory

Develop Question → Explore/Study → Analyze/Synthesize → Disseminate

Areas of Application:
Marketing/Advertising
Journalism
Media Production

Identify Task → Prototype → Test → Deploy

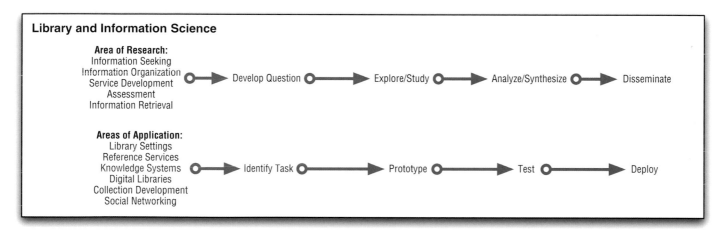

Library and Information Science

Area of Research:
Information Seeking
Information Organization
Service Development
Assessment
Information Retrieval

Develop Question → Explore/Study → Analyze/Synthesize → Disseminate

Areas of Application:
Library Settings
Reference Services
Knowledge Systems
Digital Libraries
Collection Development
Social Networking

Identify Task → Prototype → Test → Deploy

Figure 80

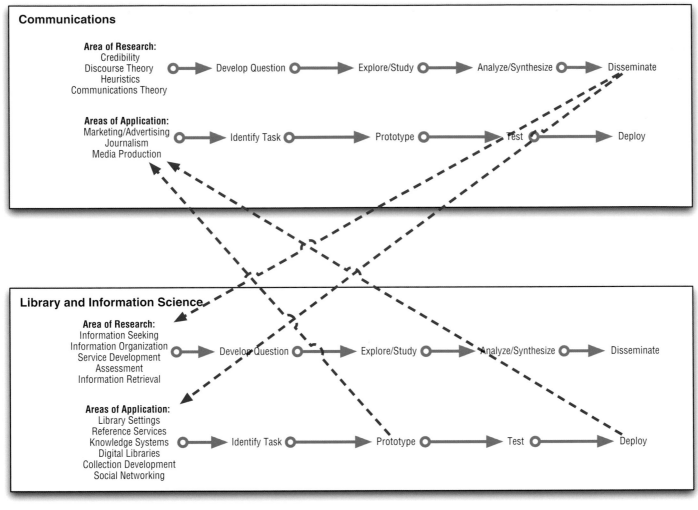

Communications

Area of Research:
Credibility
Discourse Theory
Heuristics
Communications Theory

Develop Question → Explore/Study → Analyze/Synthesize → Disseminate

Areas of Application:
Marketing/Advertising
Journalism
Media Production

Identify Task → Prototype → Test → Deploy

Library and Information Science

Area of Research:
Information Seeking
Information Organization
Service Development
Assessment
Information Retrieval

Develop Question → Explore/Study → Analyze/Synthesize → Disseminate

Areas of Application:
Library Settings
Reference Services
Knowledge Systems
Digital Libraries
Collection Development
Social Networking

Identify Task → Prototype → Test → Deploy

Figure 81

between prototyping and deployment of services with "Media Production" in communications.

We could keep this exercise going and show how the results of communications research in credibility will affect information-seeking research in LIS. Likewise, the dissemination of communications research, or at least the form it takes (venue, genre, artifact type), will affect the application of LIS like in figure 81. We would expect many such linkages because communications and LIS, particularly new librarianship, have so much in common. After all, the heart of both is conversations.

Computer Science

I can create a simple conversation map between LIS and computer science just as I did for communications like figure 82. You can also see the same types of relations that existed between LIS and communications in terms of the output of research from Computer Science feeding the LIS' areas of applications. In fact, you can imagine this particular type of relationship between LIS and any area, although the context difference is still worthy of investigation.

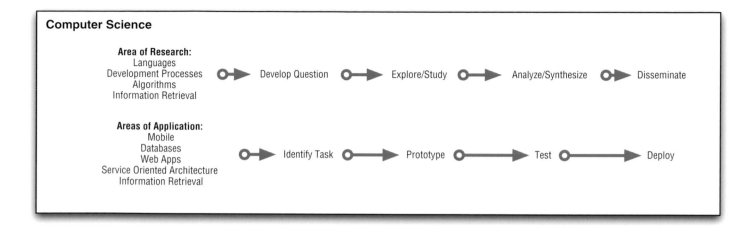

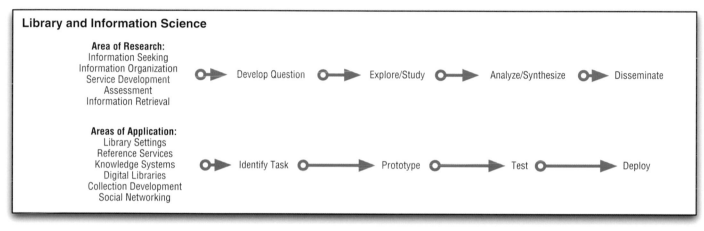

Figure 82

I won't bother you with the messiness of all the lines connecting these areas. To do so would be beyond the scope of the Atlas (now mapping out the fields of librarianship, computer science, communications, etc.) and lead to a map much more complex than the Map at the center of this Atlas.

Instead, let me simply highlight some key areas of investigation in computer science that can benefit librarians, as well as where librarianship can be of great benefit to computer scientists. The first is the study of the software development process.

Computer scientists are examining concepts such as agile development, rapid prototyping, and all manners of improving the efficiency and effectiveness of software development. These techniques are currently being applied in large library organizations such as OCLC, but there is much every librarian can learn from them as well. Librarians should look to these studies not simply in terms of tool building but all manner of service building.

Also note that "Information Retrieval" is a common area of investigation. What used to be the primary domain of information science—some might even say the area that created information science—is now shared, increasing both the potential cooperation and competition between our two fields. In fact, many of the applied areas of computer science need to become applied areas of librarians as well. Maybe not to the same depth, but certainly enough so that librarians should be able to develop web applications, have a strong background in databases, and understand mobile applications. Even if you partner with computer science, you need to know the baseline of these technologies to engage in meaningful conversations.

One last shared conversation opportunity before I leave computer science: digital libraries. There is no conversation that better exemplifies the role of worldview than digital libraries. For the past decade, both fields have seen the importance of digital libraries, and both have shared an overwhelming obsession with artifacts. However, the forums where they have worked together have often been full of strife and downright hostility. We saw this in the two definitions discussed in Digital Environments in the "Communities" Thread:

> Digital libraries are organizations that provide the resources, including the specialized staff, to select, structure, offer intellectual access to, interpret, distribute, preserve the integrity of, and ensure the persistence over time of collections of digital works so that they are readily and economically available for use by a defined community or set of communities. —Digital Libraries Federation, 1998[30]

and

> Digital library is a managed collection of information, with associated services, where information is stored in digital formats and accessible over a network. —Arms, 2000

Now computer scientists need us to build digital libraries. We understand concepts such as authority control and our values to service. They also need to learn how to run organizations and methods of sustainability.

We have something to learn from computer scientists as well. We can learn about appropriate forms of automation, and methods such as semantic web tools for creating more responsive digital library services. In truth, library scientists and computer scientists working on digital libraries need each other. They also need to have respect for each other's conversations.

Humanities

The library tradition in the humanities is long and strong. Library directors used to be historians and textual scholars. This relationship has been strained over the past decades as librarianship as a discipline began crafting itself as a social science. The increased focus on services and digital resources has been met with resistance from humanities scholars as they see it as a diminished focus on their core scholarly materials.

Yet much of humanities studies are dedicated to an ongoing conversation about what it is to be human and the nature of our cultural heritage. Humanities scholars understand the idea of the society as a grand conversation taking place over all of human history. Further, they understand this at a deeper and much more complex level than the social or physical sciences. Indeed, it is from the humanities that the idea of postmodernism emerged.

In our discussion of a social compact, it is the humanities that can provide a rich perspective on the concept of social compact and context in how it moves forward. We should actively engage humanities scholars on these topics. We must move them from the idea of artifacts and the library as temple to librarians and aiding their discoveries.

Education

OK, if you don't see the links between new librarianship and education, you just haven't been paying attention. Clearly we have much to learn from education in terms of learning theory, constructivism, motivation, and just about everything else core to librarians. Librarians are educators in that they are in the learning business. They are not, however, teachers. School library media specialists are librarians and teachers, much like I am a library scientist and information scientist.

What is the distinction? Just as librarians have a strong relationship with information science but have a strong value system and awareness of a strong institutional context, so too teachers have a strong value system and are prepared for a given institutional context (which school librarians are also conversant in).

30. http://www.diglib.org/about/dldefinition.htm

Paraprofessionals

There is one special class of partners we need to take some time with: the paraprofessional. Let's face it: This is another big "other bucket" we have created within the field. Some paraprofessionals are clerks; others are librarians in all but title. Some are masters of technology, others masters of shelving. The problem is, across the profession they are often discounted and underappreciated.

I was invited to speak at a staff development day for paraprofessionals at Penn State. I was told that the hardest thing about organizing the day was finding librarians to staff the reference desks. In library after library, I find that desk time in particular is being handled by paraprofessionals. In some cases, 60% of member contact time is with paraprofessionals.

Far from finding this a disturbing trend, I think it is great, but only if done for the right reason. If paraprofessionals are being brought in to replace librarians because they are cheaper, this is not the right reason. In contrast, if paraprofessionals are brought in for their expertise, or even to relieve librarians from some task (noting that these are two different populations), this can be beneficial.

In all cases, you must see the paraprofessionals you work with as partners and equal members of a conversation. Too often I have talked with library staff who are literally irreplaceable, and yet they don't get the keys to the librarian club. It is reprehensible for a profession about service to create a class system within their services and institutions. To replace a meritocracy, where people rise in status and responsibility based on performance, with some sort of degree-based "librocracy" where only accredited librarians count, is not only against our professional ethics, it shows real insecurity.

We should be looking for any means to identify talented people who can help the library and bring them into the library fold. We need to do this with our education system. We need to do this with our administrative systems. Yet first and foremost, we need to do this with our cultural system. Just as traditional librarians wouldn't think twice before they adopted a useful artifact into the collection, a new librarian does the same with members and experts.

LIS EDUCATION

Let us end these Threads and examination of new librarianship with where it should all begin: how we prepare new new librarians (say that five times fast). The issue of the conversation around how we prepare librarians is second in importance only to how we best serve our members. It is in education that we instill our values and our worldview, in addition to the skills needed by communities.

As with many things in librarianship, the conversation of LIS education has become formalized and at times confrontational. The high-stakes accreditation process seeks a fine balance between allowing for diversity among the LIS programs and ensuring some level of uniformity in new librarians. There is a built-in tension between scholars who are rewarded with discovering the new and practitioners who have an obligation to satisfy the demands of the now.

In this set of agreements, I do not directly take on the questions of accreditation and the formal processes of curriculum development. Rather I try to take the foundations of new librarianship and apply them not only to the content of LIS education (what new librarians need to know) but also the process itself (how LIS education can embrace and utilize the foundations of new librarianship).

Before we jump whole hog into this, I have to be clear on a few matters. The first is that as I write this, I am not only a professor in an accredited LIS program; I am taking the reins as director of that program at Syracuse. That does not mean that the program I facilitate will look exactly like this. There are many voices and pressures that ultimately decide a curriculum, and I am as much accountable to them as anyone else.

The second thing to point out is that my comments and perspective do not concern only one program. The following is based on extensive site visits and conversations with LIS faculty and students at all sorts of library schools in North America. There are all sorts of programs out there. There are progressive ones and conservative ones. There are small programs and big programs. There are also, frankly, programs that can prepare new librarians and those rooted deeply in the past.

To my fellow faculty I say to you what I say to the practitioners: How can we expect a risk-averse conservative institution to produce radical change agents who can improve society? How can we educate librarians founded on conversation, change, and leadership if we do not model these behaviors ourselves? Just as librarians have become increasingly fixated on artifacts, we have become increasingly fixated on technology and data. Although library science and information schools have traditionally served as facilitators in field-wide examinations of the profession, our effectiveness in this role has been blunted. There are several reasons for this:

- A Greater Emphasis on Research Funding: The economic realities in higher education drive any discipline in today's universities to greater emphasis on research funds, and greater pressure to grow existing degree programs and to start new ones. The need to expand budgets through research funds means a greater emphasis on applied research in "hot areas." Today, with information being central to so many endeavors, those hot areas are in defense, telecommunications, and economic development. Further, although many universities are trying to reverse the trend, career success for research faculty still comes through increased specialization, making the results of research harder to translate into boarder settings, including libraries.

- Pressure to Expand Enrollment in Degree Programs and Start New Degree Programs: Although research dollars are an expanding part of a school's budget, in most programs tuition pays the bills. Add to this the pressure of growing college enrollments and a societal pressure for more universal postsecondary education, and classes are getting bigger. Where more library science students may not be found, new programs at the master's and undergraduate levels are leading to larger schools with more diverse foci. In some universities, information science is being cast as an essential curriculum, and schools are being asked to take a greater role on curricula throughout a university or college's offerings.

- The Increased Shifting of Boundaries in the Information Professions: As more and more industries are awakening to the value of effective information utilization, they are seeking the graduates of library and information science schools. The realities of higher salaries, and in some students' minds greater chance for change, are putting pressure on schools to deliver more transferrable skills. As such, many classes teach vital skills but without the values so essential to librarianship.

- The Lack of a Continuing Education Model: The main problem that library and information schools face is the lack of a continuing education model for the field. There are few requirements for ongoing engagement between schools and professionals beyond the initial master's degree. What's more, with a wide variety of conferences and workshops offered by a vast range of non-university organizations, it is nearly impossible to maintain a long-term dialog between the schools and the profession. So while universities have much to offer in terms of new models, missions, and skills to the library profession, their most efficient corridor to the field is through new graduates who enter an organization with little cultural knowledge and low professional status.

Far from being seen as universally negative, the ability of the library and information science schools to adapt and, in many cases, thrive in the current higher education market place is a good thing for library science as a whole. There are more students enrolled now in library science programs than ever before, and they are graduating with new and valuable skills. However, there are few if any places where librarian innovation is being examined in a holistic way.

The bottom line is that just as our new mission must change the worldview and activities of librarians, so too must it change library schools. Just as librarians must recognize and adapt to growing pressure for participation from their communities, so too must LIS schools respond to pressure from the field and their students. If a librarian facilitates knowledge creation, so too must library schools. If we expect librarians to improve the society through action and activism, so too must we expect library faculty.

Shift in Innovation from Academy to Ubiquity

Time was when you went to library school to learn about the cutting edge of the field. This was particularly true in terms of technology. Universities were not only inventing new approaches and tools, they were given access to them by vendors eager to influence future customers. Today, however, with the wide availability of the Internet, innovations not only in technology, but business models, services, and processes are now a click away. Open access journals, online case studies, open source software repositories, and streaming lecture series all have allowed librarians to bypass the academy to learn about the new and the innovative.

By and large, this is a good thing. However, it does call for a significant shift in the thinking of LIS curriculum. Now instead of focusing on new technologies and skills, we can focus on concepts and how to implement these new elements in a broader context. Instead of teaching folks how to use Google (or Bing, or Yahoo!, or Ask, etc.), we can focus on how to form strategic partnerships with search companies or how to take advantage of these technologies within our community.

Don't get me wrong. It is imperative that faculty in LIS schools continue to do research and discover the new and innovate and invent. It is just now we can also present a much bigger and richer set of innovations to our students than the sweat of our own brow.

Co-Learning

A direct result of this richer world of innovation is that faculty no longer have the time (or even the ability) to fully understand an innovation or new practice before it needs to come into a classroom. For example, the semantic web is far from a finished concept or tool set. Yet if librarians are going to both utilize semantic web technology and, more important, positively influence the development of the semantic web, we cannot wait until it is all done to put it into courses. What's more, XML, RDF, SOAP, RESTful interfaces, and linked data could make up a career to truly understand, and we should be teaching it now.

How can this happen? Well, faculty need to walk into the classroom and be able to say, "I only know half of what we are going to learn this semester; we'll be learning the other half together." In order to do this and not hear howls from students like, "How much per credit am I paying for you to learn?", faculty also need to forge a new social compact with their members, the students. Faculty also need to continue the transition from professor as lecturer to professor as facilitator, understanding that the value of faculty is not knowing all the answers but knowing how to find the answers when needed.

A current student of mine, Heather Highfield, put it best when she said, "When I asked a question as an undergraduate, the professor would give me the answer. As a master's student, he or she will tell me, 'Great question, go figure that out.'" Of course now it should be, "Great question, let's go figure it out together."

LIS classes need to become more studio-like with a series of guided investigations and a lot of whole-class synthesis time. This is a model very familiar in the arts and architecture. The first part of classes is covering concepts and examples, plus mapping out the uncertain terrain. As the class progresses, these more broadcast portions get smaller and are replaced with projects (more on this in a moment). The end of class then looks like a sort of group-think, where each student comes back and the instructor facilitates a synthesis session where new ideas are explained, and the class as a whole seeks to integrate the new knowledge back into a map that will help guide the next class.

Modeling co-learning doesn't just let us get important topics into the classroom faster, it builds a stronger sense of ownership in the learning from the student perspectives and solves a major issue with faculty: gaining time to learn new things. The irony of faculty-life in a university setting is that people are so busy discovering the new that they don't have time to learn new things. I'll explain that in a bit when we get to Recognizing a School as a Participatory Network. For now, let's look at how we can do a better job preparing librarians by making their lives harder.

INCREASE FRICTION IN THE PROCESS

A student takes a reference class. The student thinks of a brilliant idea to buy laptops with 3G network cards and go into the community: roving reference neighborhood-wide. The instructor thinks it is a great idea, it fits all of the requirements, and the student gets an A. The student graduates, gets a job in a public library, and tells the director he or she has a great idea for roving reference community-wide. The director says there is no budget, their insurance won't cover the librarian out of the building, and the county has put a freeze on new cell phone accounts. Idea dies.

Now you can say the instructor should have known better, that it wasn't the point of the exercise to predict all possible challenges, or simply that some things are unpredictable. Fair enough, but there is also the fact that a classroom, no matter how rigorous, will always be an artificial setting and miss the friction that comes from the community in which the librarian finds him or herself (coming in large part from the community's pressure for participation).

This is why it is so vital that practitioners and faculty team together. By using real projects with the input of real practitioners in the classroom (and indeed placing the classroom in the real setting), there is a greater chance of providing students with the needed reality check.

Also, as a side note, the new librarian shouldn't let the idea die so easily.

Every Course Has Symposia and Practica

However, and I cannot stress this enough, the point of an LIS education is not to replicate the real world (see the Florentine dilemma in a moment). The point is not to build an apprenticeship program where every LIS graduate knows exactly the same thing as someone in the field. After all, all librarians are going to encounter a different context when they graduate.

Furthermore, it is important that librarians in training gain the worldview and values that can often be lost in the daily tasks of simply getting through the day. That is why each class needs to have both a symposia (theory, conceptual) component and a practica (practice, application, project) component. Students need to understand an idea and to explore the idea unencumbered by the compromises of the situational. They then need to apply it in a context and see where and why compromises are made, and they need to see whether the idea holds up to application. Finally, students need time to reflect, synthesize, and debrief on the idea.

I must make two points. First, this should happen in every class. Library science is still a professional discipline, and every good theory needs some empirical data. Waiting for some end-of-study experience like an internship is not as helpful. The emersion of internship is extremely valuable, but even here there should be scholarly guidance to make sense of the environments in which library students find themselves.

The second point is that not every practica component has to be linked to an organization formally known as a library. Students need to see how librarianship works in many different settings. Librarianship, as I remind you once again, is not about buildings and org charts but knowledge and action. Knowledge-creation facilitation happens in banks and barber shops, hospitals and hotels, libraries and laundry mats. The point is to show new new librarians (you think that's awkward to read, try writing it) that they have impact and a role outside as well as inside places called libraries.

Now it turns out this is much easier said than done. As a professor, I get a number of people who call me during the year with a project they think would be perfect for a grad student. The problem is, schools are not, and frankly never will be, consulting agencies. Because the focus of the LIS school is on education over a set of externally defined deliverables, schools find it difficult to take on a number of high-priority projects. Further, when they do, it is often supplemental to an external organization's key mission. So they're great to generate ideas or do that project someone was always meaning to get around to, but not so good for mission critical development or operations. What's more, the overhead of finding these projects, finding the students, and incorporating them into curriculum and assignments often relegates to "real-world" projects to internships or some experiential class.

So how do we overcome these barriers to projects but accommodate real problems in the classroom? I'm going to steal an idea that Richard Katz of Educause and I talked about at a recent meeting. What if the school identified a set of "grand challenges"? These large-scale challenges could be identified through ongoing conversations between the academy and practice and in sufficient time to be incor-

porated into curriculum. Throughout students' course of study, they could do projects around a grand challenge, and instructors could use cases and examples to illustrate the challenges or use the challenges to illustrate some other point. Better still, practitioners and external organizations that helped identify the challenges could list projects and opportunities (including a willingness to come into the real or virtual classroom) that relate to the challenges. Now students can pick from a waiting set of sandboxes, projects, and professionals in their existing coursework. Faculty would have a menu list of guest speakers and case studies they could use as well.

Note, this is not a brand-new idea by any means. Several business schools use it to create cohorts. However, it is not a model often seen across an entire LIS curriculum often because there is so little effort and substantive worldview to indentify a grand challenge beyond "What is the future of libraries?" (once again, a bad question). Also, it is important that the grand challenge approach be done with external organizations and professionals to add some much needed realism. It is all well and good to come up with a solution, but if that solution depends on technology yet to be invented, or a few billion dollars, it isn't much of a solution. This sense of realism in innovation leads right to our next agreement about the ultimate focus of new librarianship curriculum

CURRICULUM OF COMMUNICATION AND CHANGE OVER TRADITIONAL IDEAS OF LEADERSHIP

What impacts do librarians have in a community? Well, back to the mission: to improve society. That means librarians must change the community and society for the better. To this point, an awful lot of focus in LIS education has been on leadership. Yet traditional aspects of leadership focus on visioning and management. We need for newly minted librarians to be prepared to lead but also to be able to bring about change. It is one thing for Martin Luther King, Jr., to have a dream but quite another to speak on the steps of the Lincoln Memorial and orchestrate social change.

We need to teach students tactics of change. How to plot and scheme, cajole and convince. How to map power and gain power to put behind a vision. I realize that sounds mercenary, and you are right. We are back to Saul Alinsky's rules for radicals, and that is only fitting because that's what a library school should be: a caldron and training ground for activists and radicals. Look at what I am asking you to do: go into a community with a strong set of values and a strong sense of better. Map and organize the community through their conversations. Empower the members of a community through knowledge so that they may make positive social change. Is there anything more radical than being a librarian? That is why this agreement is linked to the Importance of Action and Activism in the "Improve Society" thread.

Of course our schools must model what they teach and a dedication to values, innovation, and leadership. To do that, they must be more than a conglomeration of faculty; they must be participatory networks and schools of thought.

Recognize a School as a Participatory Network

A professor and his family move to a new house near campus. Realizing that her husband is absent-minded, the professor's wife writes the new address on a piece of paper and hands it to the professor, who goes into work.

While working in his lab, the professor has a startling thought, reaches into his pocket, takes out that paper, and scribbles notes all over it, putting it on his desk afterward.

After work that night, the professor returns to his former house and only then remembers that he has moved and realizes he no longer has his wife's note with his new address. He looks around and sees a small girl on the sidewalk and asks, "Excuse me little girl, but do you happen to know where the former occupants of this house live now?"

The girl takes the professor's hand and says, "Yes I do, and mommy sent me here to bring you home, dad."

The stereotype of the absent-minded professor is almost as ingrained as the bookish librarian.[31] As I mentioned before, the reward system of a university is still dominated by specialization. It is one of the real factors that often prevent library scientists from working at the macrolevel of "librarianship" and instead focus on some aspect of it (note please that the Atlas is being written after I'm tenured). It is the trap of the fractal nature of knowledge. We keep digging and digging in hopes to understand, and we keep finding more and more dirt at the bottom of the hole.

There is nothing inherently wrong with this as long as it is balanced with colleagues digging other holes and reporting back. This notion has been referred to as an invisible college: a set of scholars working on an area bound by topic not institutional boundaries. We

31. Of course what's worse is the older I get, the more true it becomes.

must work to make these colleges more visible and expand the concept to not only include faculty research areas but teaching and service areas as well.

Just as librarians are being called on to facilitate knowledge in communities of geography and institution, faculty must also understand that facilitation is needed to efficiently and effectively create knowledge around questions of teaching and service. In fact, this would be an excellent role for academic librarians in faculties of all sorts.

The idea is not simply to use technology to disseminate research or to ease collaboration of geographically separated scholars, but to constantly scan for innovations in teaching and service (as well as research opportunities) and feed this back to the faculty as a whole. Rather than waiting for some annual faculty retreat, faculty should look to social networking technologies and participatory technologies such as blogging to keep each other apprised of activities, new ideas, and innovations.

From School to School of Thought

Seeing the faculty as a participatory network also requires the development of a common worldview among them. In essence, there has to be a reason to be together and bother to keep up with each other.

Schools of library and information science have to make the transition from school to school of thought. A school is simple. It means there is some organizational recognition within a university. A school of thought, on the other hand, is amazingly difficult. It requires the members of a school to come together and answer the question, "Why is the world a better place because we are here, at this moment?" Answers like the number of students graduated or the amount of research dollars acquired are not adequate answers to this question.

An LIS school (college, department) needs an entrepreneurial attitude that is demonstrated as a faculty and as individual researchers. The school should have a broad research profile. However, faculty must take a common intellectual framework and seek out opportunities for impact. So although natural language processing, data mining, motivation, grid computing, Internet policy, e-commerce, document genres, virtual reference, metadata, evaluation, human computer interaction, group collaboration, and security may seem to some as a disconnected collection of investigations, at their heart they seek to understand and empower the member as active creator and user of services in an environment of constant change and scarcity. Whether it be software to sort through massive piles of data, interfaces that make sense of information processes, polices that enable institutional structures to support the member, or even how systems can protect members, these investigators share a common core that allows the faculty to not only communicate with each other but to truly collaborate as an integrated school of thought. This integration and seamless focus is forged in action and shown in research, service, teaching, and governance.

A school must believe that it is not enough to articulate problems, but that it must illuminate problems along with potential solutions. Any solution, any approach, any theory posited by the faculty must be tested in relation to members and their contexts. Truth is forged in action, in the member. It is in action that concepts from our varied perspectives are fused. This key focus influences a faculty's need for impact, their research, and their active learning processes. Impact is achieved through partnership with members and communities, not as a missionary task where solutions are imposed. In research, the faculty must be devoted to rigor and excellence but agnostic with respect to methodological orthodoxy.

Avoiding the Florentine Dilemma

There is one problem that each school of thought with a co-learning curriculum must avoid, and that is the Florentine Dilemma. The name comes from a trip I took to Florence. While there, I went to visit the Galleria dell'Accademia that houses Michelangelo's David. The Accademia, or Academy of Art in Florence, is considered the epicenter of Renaissance art, and as a holder of a Bachelor of Fine Arts, it is sort of a cultural Mecca you have to see.

While I was there, I noted a group gathered by a locked gate. They were listening to a guide talk about the art of the walls. The guide unlocked the gate, and as the group entered I tagged along. We entered a long rectangular room with high ceilings. Down the center of the room were plaster sculptures the masters had used to create the final marble sculptures we are familiar with. Up one wall was a series of shelves filled with busts, one on top of the other. Flanking the room on either end were huge Renaissance-era oil paintings. You can see it in figure 83.[32]

I was, frankly, a little awestruck. Then I heard the guide, while pointing to a painting, saying, "…and here you can see the problem."

32. Source Wiki Commons.

Figure 83

I missed the rest, but as she walked us around the room, she pointed to the busts along the wall.

"The busts at the bottom are those of the masters—the teachers of the Academy. Every row up to the ceilings holds the work of the students. They were, in essence, their final projects. They couldn't graduate until their work was indistinguishable from that of the masters. Which, of course, is the other problem." By the time the tour guide made it to the other end of the room and was talking about another painting, I got it.

"You can see from this painting that the Academy had become stuck. Their style dictated a near photographic representation of their subjects. So they became limited to what they could see. And as the busts show, if the masters were stuck, so too became their disciples, for they couldn't graduate unless they could replicate the work of the master. Such a cycle, where to succeed you had to do exactly what the masters did, and the masters could not evolve into new styles, set back art in Italy after the Renaissance for a century."

This is what schools, and librarians in general, must avoid in LIS education: They must not teach only what they know and create exact duplicates of themselves. LIS programs should never be apprenticeship programs. Instead, faculty and librarians alike must endeavor to produce a next generation of librarians who go beyond what we know and beyond the limits we set on ourselves. This is why the tolerance of ambiguity is so essential for faculty, practitioners, and students alike.

By the way, if anyone from Florence is reading this, I'd love the chance to come and talk about this in person.

NEED TO EXPAND THE EDUCATIONAL LADDER

Still looking for the radical quote about LIS education? How about this one: "The 50-year experiment with master's level education for librarians has failed." That's not from me, that's from a dean I interviewed as part of a MacArthur project on the future of libraries. His or her point (see what I did there to protect the dean's identity?) is that a master's degree was supposed to build greater respect for the profession and garner better pay. The only problem here is that it is actions and perceived value, not degrees, that lead to this outcome. No, I'm not telling you who said it, but I agree. That might not sound right coming from a professor of library science, but here's how I see it.

My colleagues and I (mostly my colleagues) do a great job of preparing librarians given the time we have. But we all want to do so much more. I hear librarian after librarian bemoaning all the things that are not taught in library school, and they're right. Librarians need to know more (although I don't often agree with what we should be teaching with the extra time). But it is worse than that. The idea that librarians can learn everything they will ever need to know as librarians in two years at the beginning of their careers is simply insane.

Simply adding more time won't help. There are things librarians need to know at the beginning of their careers, different things they need to know if they assume management positions, and still different things if they seek to be true librarian leaders.

Some of this slack can be made up with field-initiated continuing education, but the current disjointed nature of conferences, classes, workshops, webcasts, seminars, and in-service days are far from providing a coordinated and accessible suite of options. If librarians work for an organization that happens to have enough funding to send them to a conference and they happen to pick the right session (with no guidance), then they might get something useful?! Insanity. Barbers and accountants have tighter continuing education requirements.

Don't get me wrong. I applaud professional organizations and consortia for taking on the task of continuing education, one all too often shunned by universities due to a lacking business model (yeah, $1,000 a credit hour for a three-credit course in the middle of the day—that will work). They have done as well as can be expected in an artifact-centric profession that has lacked a cohesive worldview. But we can do better. We must marry expanded formal educational levels with coherent professional development activities directed by a new social compact with our communities. What is your 10-year learning plan?

We must also look for ways to co-opt the best people regardless of their educational background. Just as education has created intensive education academies to bring talented second-career folks into the classroom, we must find a way to promote the best from other fields (including paraprofessionals from our own) to librarian status.

If you think that will somehow diminish the value of the degree, I ask you to look throughout the southwest United States where low population has led to a raft of high school-educated library directors who do a great job of serving their communities.

In essence, LIS schools in partnerships with libraries, librarians, accreditors, states, and professional associations should aim to craft a seamless education ladder that prepares librarians all along the way from their first job to CIOs (and CEOs) of industry and the nonprofit sector. To abuse the metaphor, we currently have a series of step ladders arranged randomly around one big ladder that doesn't go all the way to the top.

Let me continue with a focus on the formal degree part of the seamless ladder. There are two clearly missing parts of formal LIS education, at least in North America: the bachelor's degree and the doctorate. However, we need something more than simply having a BS in LIS, and we need something different than the current dominant "faculty in training" research-oriented PhD. Let's take a look.

Bachelor of Information and Instructional Design

Who in the world would want an undergraduate degree in library science? Even assuming that professional associations were willing to accredit them, what 18-year-old says, "I want to be a librarian"? Well, we'll just ignore the fact that there are plenty of countries where they already do, including the United States.[33] Instead, let's rephrase the question.

What 18-year-old would want a degree that taught him or her how to organize large data sets and build social networking web applications? The degree will prepare you for a career in web development,

33. http://collegesearch.collegeboard.com/search/servlet/advsearchservlet?buttonPressed=viewResults&navigateTo=9&viewpage=1&odbparam=major:797&AffiliateID=MCP_Major&BannerID=LibraryScience

corporate training, government information, medical information, law firms, broadcasting, and more. The focus is on technology not only to attract younger students but that needs to be the focus of the undergraduate: skills, technology, and techniques (in addition to the worldview). The list of job opportunities comes not just from where libraries currently exist but where there is a need for the skills of new librarianship.

This includes places in need of instructional design and training support. Because the core of new librarianship is facilitating knowledge creation, in essence learning, it makes sense to include these skills at the undergraduate level.

But, you say, there are some pretty high-level skills in mediation, theory, and management that are simply master's-level concepts. I agree. That is why we are adding a bachelor's degree, not transforming the library degree from a master's. For example, teachers in many states in the United States get a provisional certification with an undergraduate degree but require a master's degree for permanent certification. Having an undergraduate degree frees up those precious two years of master's education for the higher level concepts and more project/symposia work.

If you think it is crazy and think no one will take it, I'd ask you to look at the explosion of undergraduate programs at iSchools. Syracuse, Washington, Texas, and more have exploded (and fueled an expansion of these schools). In many cases, we simply need to make the linkage between the undergraduate and master's levels more obvious and ensure that the values and worldview of librarianship are taught at the undergraduate level.

But, you say, these undergraduates are all getting information technology degrees and wouldn't be interested in working in libraries. They can make a lot more money elsewhere. To which I say, who said librarians had to work in a library? In fact, if you want the reputation of librarians and libraries to grow, isn't it better to demonstrate how these skills are valued outside of libraries? Not all lawyers work in law firms. Not all doctors work in hospitals, and I wouldn't say these professions are undervalued. Remember, it is about librarianship and improving communities, not about buildings and preserving institutions.

As an interim step, before we even have to change accreditation, we should put in place a 4+1 model. A student does a 4-year undergraduate program and with an extra year of study is also certified as a librarian. This model works with existing information science undergraduates as well as content areas such as physics, history, and more.

Need for an Executive Doctorate

There are plenty of doctoral programs around in library and information science. Yet most of them are geared toward "faculty-in-training" models. That is, they seek to prepare students for life as a professor. This makes sense in the world where a master's degree is the terminal degree. However, there are all sorts of places where a doctorate would be helpful as a librarian not wanting to be a faculty member. For example, in both academic and school libraries, a doctorate is increasingly necessary to join administration.

What we need is an executive or professional doctoral equivalent to Education's ED (doctorate of education), which is focused on deeper concepts and understanding research but in the context of application and a work environment.

The curriculum of the executive doctorate (and full disclosure here, Syracuse offers a Doctorate of Professional Studies) would be around theory and deep concepts. Special attention would be placed on administration and management. Also students would be focused on interpreting research results, putting data in context, and the future of the profession.

Institute for Advanced Librarianship Idea*

To this point, I haven't really spent any time on the format of delivery or the structure of the school. I frankly don't plan to do so other than to say as a general rule I think in-person delivery makes sense at an undergraduate level for reasons of socialization, and distance delivery makes sense for the executive doctorate because ideally the students would remain in their current positions throughout the program.

However, one thing I do want to emphasize is the importance for heterogeneity in the education landscape. It is a good thing for different contexts to provide different foci and means of education. It matches the central tenets of new librarianship, a common core applied in a mosaic of contexts and communities. Please note that the common core I am talking about is in terms of worldview, mission, and means of facilitation, not specific courses and subject areas.

As an example of this, working with the folks at the Free Library of Philadelphia, I put together a proposal for the Institute for Advanced Librarianship. It would bring together a cohort of advanced students from the different LIS programs around the world in their second year

*See Agreement Supplement for an Institute proposal.

of study to work as a cohort in a place like the Free Library (or the New York Public Library, the Harvard Library, etc.) on a large-scale project. During their year of study, the cohort would get a mix of intensive practica and symposia working to innovating library services.

You can find the full proposal in the Agreement Supplements. I present it to you not as the model of LIS education of new librarianship but to show how some of the ideas in this thread could be put into action.

Vital Roles of Mentors

Before we leave the world of LIS education and bring the Threads to an end, I have to say to librarians already done with their formal education: You are not off the hook. The only way we will reform LIS education, ensure the initiation of new librarians, and indeed guarantee that there will be a next generation of librarians is if the entire profession sees itself as part of the education of new librarians. If we learn through conversations, we need good conversants to talk with.

I have been blessed with some amazing mentors in my life. Mike Eisenberg, Ray von Dran, Jeffry Katzer, Stuart Sutton, Ruth Small, and Chuck McClure showed me a profession essential to society and instilled in me an analytic eye and an evangelical soul to try and make the profession even better. I also learned from them what makes good mentors: People who work hard to ensure those they mentor will do better than themselves.

OBLIGATION OF LEADERSHIP AND THREAD CONCLUSION

Librarians have many good mentors and role models from which to choose. However, librarianship is also prone to the cult of personality. Those who are willing to stand up and who can speak well tend to get a lot of attention. You must be on guard against the visionary without reality and those who put mottos in place of intellectual signatures. You must beware the bibliofundamentalists and their seductive call to simpler times. They promise security, but you can't live in the past. Beware the flexible revolutionary who says, as Alexandre Ledru-Rollin wrote, "There go my people. I must find out where they are going so that I may lead them."

Facilitation, mentorship, and learning are all cut from the same cloth. All of these tasks are the new collection development of new librarianship. We tend to our members, our colleagues, our partners, our staff, our administration, and the society at large. We mediate their disputes, aid their learning, and ultimately lead them to a better place. We do so through facilitating knowledge creation driven by our values and implemented with our skills. We provide access to conversations, we instill the baseline knowledge needed to engage in these conversations, we do this in a safe and inspiring environment, and we do this in line with their motivations.

No one skill or tool defines us as librarians. Instead, it is our mission and an accompanying worldview. Code, shelves, artifacts, and even degrees: These are the armor and weapons of our fight against ignorance and intolerance. But it is the mission that beats strong in our hearts and takes us every time into the fight. In time the tools of today will fade, and the skills we hold so dear will evolve, but the mission? The mission remains. It endures. And with it we too endure. The best days of librarianship are ahead of us.

It is with faith that we look to the future: faith in ourselves, faith in our colleagues, and an abiding faith in our communities. Through the lens of faith, we see where our communities have chosen knowledge over ignorance, the greater good over savage greed, openness over narrow-mindedness. But we are not blinded by faith. We know these choices do not come easily, nor every time. We know that our communities sometimes need our hands to pull them from the darkness. Yet we will stand bravely before that darkness of ignorance and apathy. We will scream as a chorus together into the void, "No further, enough, and no more." And then, together we will fight to dispel the night. We can do it. I have faith in us.

THREADS POSTSCRIPT

That was a lot to absorb, and you may be swimming a bit. I also can't end the narrative section of the Atlas without addressing the question I get at the end of every presentation on new librarianship: What exactly should I do now? OK, standard caveats apply here about how your context and your community will ultimately dictate the answer to that, but here is a plan of action to at least get you started. I'll break down my advice by the potential readers I outlined in the introduction.

PRACTITIONERS

Practitioners, the first thing you should do is start mapping the conversation as outlined in the Assessment Agreement in the "Communities" Thread. Ideally, this should be part of a larger strategic planning process where you build a demographic profile of your service community to identify the stakeholder groups in the community (so students, faculty, staff or teens, seniors, businesses, etc.). With this map in hand, you can begin a substantive dialog (read: have meetings and focus groups) first with internal staff (if you have any) and then with representatives of the identified stakeholder groups (who you have already engaged and identified as part of mapping their conversations) to ask the question, "How can we help make this community a better place?" This is the first real step to developing a new social compact.

The central point of this discussion should be the map, but it should also make clear your mission and values. The map of the conversations should be as expansive as possible, directly linking to usage data of existing services, artifacts used as part of the community conversations, census data, transcripts of the focus groups, and so on. In fact, my hope is that these maps would be made widely available online so that they can be linked across communities and types of libraries.

Bottom line, don't just sit there; start looking for conversations.

LIBRARY AND INFORMATION SCIENCE SCHOLARS

On the research side, scholars need to do what they do best. Poke and prod at the framework. Where you find an acceptable generality, fill in the detail in terms of theory, method, and results. Where you find error or can disprove an assertion, do so. I would only ask that if you negate a portion of the Map, you suggest an alternative or a replacement. The field needs the big picture and not just for target practice.

For my colleagues in LIS schools, let us begin in earnest a conversation of curriculum and accreditation with the accrediting agencies. This debate should not be about developing some universal curriculum. Rather, it should be on general principles of preparation (symposia and practica, best practices in co-learning, the formal education ladder, etc.). We must also directly engage with professional library associations and consortia to bring some coherence and sense to continuing education. Note, I did not say bring coherence and sense to the consortia, but rather partner with them so the lines between learning and practice, school and profession, and professor and mentor melt into a rich tapestry of opportunities.

To make that concrete, I recommend creating a central service where providers of instruction can register their opportunities and learners can seek out these opportunities. The system should allow the creation of recommended learning plans that a learner can adopt and annotate. The system should also allow materials, webcasts, podcasts, and the like to be added and from the service embedded into websites and learning management systems. I, of course, would recommend these materials be organized around the Atlas concepts of core values and skills, but not exclusively. For those who prefer, say, ALA's core competencies or SLA's competencies, the materials should be mapped to this system.

Of course such a system should not be just a set of links to artifacts but should allow real ongoing conversations about the things librarians need to know and the sequence in which they need to learn them. Such a system could be used as part of accreditation statements as well.

STUDENTS

Demand more. Demand more input into your classes. Demand more and continued access to the field. Demand more than an apprenticeship program. The reason you need to encounter more friction during your education is not so you get worn down but more finely honed.

Just as innovation in librarianship is no longer confined to the academy, neither are you. The work you do, your assignments, can now form a working service, a living portfolio. Take an interest you have (reading, NASCAR, science fiction, knitting, whatever) and go out and build a community to serve. Maybe you will do this as a place-based service in your local community, but increasingly you can go online.

Identify the potential members and their conversations. Then build services around that community to facilitate conversations. Don't worry about the collection; remember the community is your collection. Use open source software, or the plethora of hosted solutions (or build it in Facebook), and provide real services to real members every day. Refine the services with every class. Once it has a substantial level of use, either make it your job or take it to a potential employer. Instead of asking for a job with a transcript, you can make the hiring institution a proposal: Hire me and I come with experience and a community for your organization.

MEMBERS

Demand more. Your library should be staffed by the most amazing information professionals you can imagine. If all they do is organize a collection, you are losing out. As a member, you should have a voice in how the library is run and the services it offers. Of course this comes with the responsibility to be part of those services. Offer to answer questions in your area of expertise. Offer to share a collection that will be of use to the larger community. Translate interfaces and build foreign language guides if you're fluent in another language. Invite the librarians into your communities. Host an "Ask a librarian" night at your church, temple, mosque, business, or school.

Most important, when the librarian asks you what you are talking about or asks about the biggest problems you are dealing with, tell them. Don't just tell them the ones you assume the librarians can help you with because you never know.

THE WHOLE COMMUNITY OF LIBRARIANSHIP

Our next task, yours and mine, is to seek out those who share our views and together form a movement. With that movement we will engage those who disagree. We shall sit and listen and adopt their best ideas, hoping that as we do so, they will adopt ours. Then we will work hard to refine our ideas, seek out best practices, and all the time continue talking and informing each other, becoming a participatory network.

This doesn't mean we need a new conference because every conference should be about new librarianship. We don't need a new organization, a new mailing list, or a new journal. Instead, every journal on librarianship should be about new librarianship; every list, every organization. We will assume roles of leadership when offered. In time, we will discard any modifiers like "participatory" and "new" and simply be librarians, part of a better society, respected by our communities, and devoted to our members.

WEB CITATIONS

To talk about librarianship in this day and age requires a great deal of citing the web and Internet-accessible resources. This of course poses a challenge to librarians and scholars alike as we seek to accurately (or at least credibly) preserve memory and help create new knowledge. To that end, I present table 1 as one means of battling the link rot so rampant in today's conversations.

The list is a simple column of the original footnote number and an archival version of that page archived at WebCite (http://www.webcitation.org/), a service of a consortium of publishers seeking to bring some permanence to web citations. Please note that not all pages are equally well archived, and some URLs in the Atlas were not archived at all (due to limitations set by the page authors). A lot of the archived pages retain the original content but definitely miss the look and feel of the original. Still, it is a start and a nice challenge to librarians to do better. Why not just put the archived URL in the footnotes? I think the original URL contains a lot of information folks use to make credibility decisions, and so the originals are retained for readability.

INTRODUCTION

1	http://www.webcitation.org/5mSSCuqVl
2	http://www.webcitation.org/5gxG3k8hg
3	http://www.webcitation.org/5mSSLan4R

MISSION THREAD

6	http://www.webcitation.org/5mVfSzyes
7	http://www.webcitation.org/5gxG3k8hg
13	http://www.webcitation.org/5eBIPrwc60
14	http://www.webcitation.org/5mSSdpw3h
21	http://www.webcitation.org/5mSShjASM
31	http://www.webcitation.org/5mSSkUD2N
32	http://www.webcitation.org/5mSSnObz4
32	http://www.webcitation.org/5mSSpfzk3
32	http://www.webcitation.org/5mSSrcrNN
33	http://www.webcitation.org/5mSStrPdm

KNOWLEDGE

37	http://www.webcitation.org/5mVipTfXY
39	http://www.webcitation.org/5mX5BMSOY
39	http://www.webcitation.org/5mSTQkAgn
44	http://www.webcitation.org/5mVgJeu0Qw
45	http://www.webcitation.org/5mVglph7V
46	http://www.webcitation.org/5mSTxsDOB
47	http://www.webcitation.org/5mSU28G0n
48	http://www.webcitation.org/5mSU63IiF
49	http://www.webcitation.org/5mSU7g3AB
50	http://www.webcitation.org/5mVgx939T

FACILITATING

51	http://www.webcitation.org/5mSW446G8
52	http://www.webcitation.org/5mVhYiiZD
53	http://www.webcitation.org/5mVhgO0tm
55	http://www.webcitation.org/5mSW91uA6
56	**NO ARCHIVE ALLOWED**
57	http://www.webcitation.org/5mSWCd0ZY
58	http://www.webcitation.org/5mSWE8rMT
59	http://www.webcitation.org/5mSWGhXZK
60	http://www.webcitation.org/5mSWHnOxM
62	http://www.webcitation.org/5mSWLGQts

FACILITATING

64	http://www.webcitation.org/5mVi0ctL1
66	http://www.webcitation.org/5mSXD4Q33
67	http://www.webcitation.org/5mVi5xD6j
68	http://www.webcitation.org/5mVi8LFio
72	http://www.webcitation.org/5mViY5Sew
73	http://www.webcitation.org/5mVibmZN1
74	http://www.webcitation.org/5mVievash
77	http://www.webcitation.org/5mVihFm2e

COMMUNITIES

78	http://www.webcitation.org/5mVk68HwL
80	http://www.webcitation.org/5mVk8D3Nv
81	http://www.webcitation.org/5mVk9yGVc
82	http://www.webcitation.org/5mVkBjjks
83	http://www.webcitation.org/5mVkD3cHR
84	http://www.webcitation.org/5mVkKJqfW
85	http://www.webcitation.org/5mVkMB92I
86	http://www.webcitation.org/5mVkOq8mJ
87	http://www.webcitation.org/5mVkQqGgL
88	http://www.webcitation.org/5mVkSdXir
89	http://www.webcitation.org/5mVkUyL6H
90	http://www.webcitation.org/5mVkWxX1u
91	http://www.webcitation.org/5mVkZD8o5
92	http://www.webcitation.org/5mVkaz3LY
93	http://www.webcitation.org/5mVkd5hnt
94	http://www.webcitation.org/5mVkequ8d
95	http://www.webcitation.org/5mVkgkD2U
97	http://www.webcitation.org/5mVkizXv3
98	http://www.webcitation.org/5mVkoPj99
99	http://www.webcitation.org/5mVkmxrLf
101	http://www.webcitation.org/5mVkq64wd
102	http://www.webcitation.org/5mVksJetB
103	http://www.webcitation.org/5mVkuFlz1
104	http://www.webcitation.org/5mVkwQVOi
105	http://www.webcitation.org/5mVky9woK
106	http://www.webcitation.org/5mVkzlql8
114	http://www.webcitation.org/5mVl3dOZf
115	http://www.webcitation.org/5mVl5GzYq

IMPROVE SOCIETY

116	http://www.webcitation.org/5mVtqwMJb
117	http://www.webcitation.org/5mVttLalD
118	http://www.webcitation.org/5mVtvfp2o
119	http://www.webcitation.org/5mVtxOJxV
120	NO ARCHIVE ALLOWED
121	http://www.webcitation.org/5mVu8ETQa
125	http://www.webcitation.org/5mVuAHZfG
127	http://www.webcitation.org/5mVuBv2qc
130	http://www.webcitation.org/5mVuEQUL1
133	http://www.webcitation.org/5mVuH9Fon

LIBRARIANS

134	http://www.webcitation.org/5mVuaTB5W
135	http://www.webcitation.org/5mVucjamb
136	NO ARCHIVE ALLOWED
140	http://www.webcitation.org/5mVukYkLh
141	http://www.webcitation.org/5mVumxChr
143	http://www.webcitation.org/5mVuqHa0c
144	http://www.webcitation.org/5mVusLafK
146	http://www.webcitation.org/5mVuuXsmz
147	http://www.webcitation.org/5mVuxQGQ9
148	http://www.webcitation.org/5mVuzjW82
149	http://www.webcitation.org/5mVv1wdTT
150	http://www.webcitation.org/5mVvHzyzf
151	http://www.webcitation.org/5mVvJVBE1
152	http://www.webcitation.org/5mVvL79r1
153	http://www.webcitation.org/5mVvMdEwm
154	http://www.webcitation.org/5mVvOo5dp
155	ARCHIVE UNAVAILABLE
156	http://www.webcitation.org/5mVvTKE8E
157	http://www.webcitation.org/5mVvc8GzG
158	http://www.webcitation.org/5mVveSGCC
161	http://www.webcitation.org/5mVvjYoAZ
162	http://www.webcitation.org/5mVvhzU6p
163	http://www.webcitation.org/5mVvlUq4C
166	http://www.webcitation.org/5mVvwYKIA

AGREEMENT SUPPLEMENTS

Every agreement of the Map was covered at some level in the Threads section of the Atlas. However, for the purposes of space and creating a narrative flow, information on some agreements was left out. This is also due to the fractal nature of knowledge first raised as part of the "Ability to Work in Interdisciplinary Teams" agreement in the "Librarians" Thread, where any agreement could be explored to an almost infinite depth. The end result is this set of supplements, where additional information, citations, thoughts, and/or examples are given.

These supplements serve three purposes. The first is as an index for the Atlas. Looking up each agreement, you can find out where it is on the Map, as well as where it is discussed in the Threads. The second purpose is as appendices to the Threads, with additional ideas, citations, examples, and, in some cases, whole essays related to some agreements. The third purpose, and perhaps the most important in the long term, is as a conversation starting point. As new ideas, studies, examples, questions, and answers are developed throughout the life of the Atlas, they can initially be added to the Agreement Supplements and later, if appropriate, into the Threads.

Not all agreements in the Threads or this supplement are equally fleshed out or of equal weight. I'll remind you that the Atlas is not an encyclopedia of librarianship. If anything, the supplements are more like Wikipedia—stub records waiting for further discussion and elaboration.

These agreements are not written to be read in a linear way. There is no attempt to have one agreement flow into one another—that is accomplished through Threads. In fact, I have organized agreements alphabetically specifically to avoid the resemblance to some sort of hierarchical classification system. You could, and should, take these agreements and organize them in your own system (technically an entailment mesh) and even swap out my agreements with your own. This structure also allows me (or you) to add new agreements or refined agreements as this new view of librarianship evolves.

Each agreement supplement will have:

- **Title** The agreement title used in the Map and the Threads.
- **Map Location** Coordinates to the agreement on the Map.
- **Thread Location** Page numbers that point to a discussion of the agreement in the threads.
- **Scape** A graphical representation of the context of the agreement. Related agreements are shown centered on the current agreement.

In addition, some supplements will contain more information such as:

- **Author/Contributor** The author of a supplement or the person who provided the bulk of the content for the agreement. If there is no one listed, I am to blame for the content.
- **Agreement Description** A narrative discussion of the agreement.
- **Conversation Starters** Questions to consider related to the agreement.
- **Related Artifacts** Articles, books, presentations, data-collection instruments, and other materials that relate to the agreement or can deepen the understanding of the agreement. *Take special note that not all resources cited agree with positions in the Atlas.* They are provided as general background.

So the best way to proceed from this point is to read through the Threads if you haven't already. When you hit an idea in the Thread that either doesn't make sense or needs a more thorough discussion, look it up in these agreements. Within the Threads, you'll have a sense of what is waiting for you here by looking for the symbol "*" and the accompanying **bolded footnote.**

ABILITY TO WORK IN INTERDISCIPLINARY TEAMS

MAP LOCATION

C, 9

THREAD LOCATION

Page 170

SCAPE

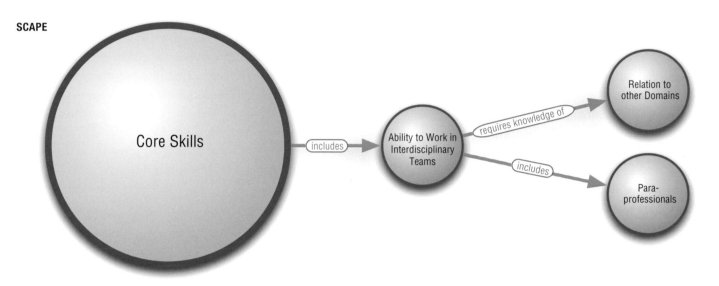

Figure 84

AUTHOR

R. David Lankes

AGREEMENT DESCRIPTION

This Atlas centers on librarians and the organizations they build and support. As such, it focuses on what librarians can and should do. This focus might leave the reader with the impression that the role of librarians is the only necessary role to build knowledge in communities. This is far from the truth. Improving decision making, building knowledge, and improving communities are complex tasks. They require a multitude of perspectives and skills and individuals. Librarians must be ready to not only work with other problem solvers, but to step in and coordinate these people.

Why leave it to librarians to facilitate multiskilled teams? It fits their core skills and values. Librarians are facilitators and are therefore prepared to aggressively put forth both their principles and their voice while still being able to put their own agenda aside for the good of the community and their problems.

NO LIBRARIAN IS AN ISLAND

Learning theory, policy, legal issues, technology, and information organization—these are just some of the skills outlined within the Atlas. To advocate that one person (with one type of degree) could be a master of all of these skills is ludicrous. While a librarian should be aware of these areas (and master some), the ultimate answer to bringing an expanded, participatory skill base to the library is a team approach. Librarians must work with lawyers, technologists, educators, and content experts to choreograph the necessary facilitation within their communities. By working in functional teams, a librarian can bring necessary resources to a community beyond simple artifacts and materials.

Often when the idea of an interdisciplinary team approach is proposed, several obstacles are quickly identified. Almost all of these are based on the assumption that the whole team is organizationally and physically located within the library. Certainly there have been issues with nonlibrarians (e.g., technologists) feeling like second-class citizens or lacking a peer group. Libraries often complain about a lack of resources to attract highly qualified specialists or point out how salary discrepancies caused by a competitive marketplace can alienate librarians. These are real concerns.

However, nothing says that all team members must be under the egis of the library. Crossing administrative lines is possible. In fact, there is an advantage to pulling teams from across these boundaries, such as leveraging resources, gaining advocates in other organizations, and more.

There is, however, one essential factor in effective teams: clear respect and identification of the value of team members. Effective teams require a team member to feel valued and to value their team members. All too often in the library profession, facilitation is seen as a primarily passive and often invisible task. The goal seems to be to interject as little of the librarian's voice as possible to avoid bias.

This realization—that facilitation is a proactive shaping activity—also provides a foundation for a team approach to service and for technological innovation. Teamwork requires a strong sense of identity.

Without a strong sense of purpose, method, and underlying conceptual frame, librarians can have great difficulty working in teams. It is, in essence, a form of professional insecurity that often sees other skill sets and conversants as competition. This realization points out the dangers of using technological landmarks outside of the library profession as a pointer to some preferred future. It leads to a sort of schizophrenia whereby members of the profession are looking externally for innovation and, when they find it, see the innovators as competition and a threat.

This situation was apparent in much of the discussion of the library in relation to Google, Yahoo!, and Amazon over the past decade. It was not unusual to go to conferences where Google was described as a great threat to libraries in an era of "good enough" information ("Google will put us out of business because people would rather have it quick than right") and in the next session a discussion of using a simple single search box to search library Web sites, catalogs, and databases ("All library search has to look like Google because that is what they expect"). Before Google "forced" libraries to adopt simple search boxes, Yahoo! forced us to fit all of our services and resources into 13 categories on a homepage. The truth is that if libraries continue to try and be a better Google, a better Yahoo, or a better Amazon, the best they can ever achieve is coming in second. Adopting innovation without a matching mission is a follower's game.

Instead of competition, librarians must see other expertise (and other organizations) as resource pools—see creating teams of expertise as a new form of collection development. Librarians need to have strong relationships, both professional and interpersonal, with folks from other fields. This way they can quickly call on these resources to solve a given problem. Rather than seeking to build a large centralized scheme for gathering experts, librarians need to facilitate flexible and permeable groups. Because facilitation is a core skill of librarians, it makes sense for them to take the lead in this process.

A SPECIAL NOTE ON DIVERSITY

This agreement is clearly about the power of diverse skill sets brought together to solve problems. There are all kinds of diversities beyond professional competencies. These include religious, social, ethnic, and so on. There is a great body of literature on the importance of all of these types of diversities, and I do not seek to repeat it here. Rather I would emphasize that the more diverse the team, on all levels, the greater its ability to respond and solve problems.

AN EXAMPLE

An example of the facilitating role that librarians can play in interdisciplinary teams is currently under study at Syracuse University. The National Science Foundation has funded the development of a curriculum for Cyber-Infrastructure Facilitators (CI Facilitators). The curriculum is being developed in response to the growth of e-science or the use of networked technologies in the so-called STEM[1] disciplines. As physicists are crunching terabyte datasets from particle collisions on another continent, as astronomers are using telescopes thousands of miles away, and as meteorologists are simulating weather patterns on shared terascale grid computing platforms, it is becoming increasingly difficult for scientists to understand both their field of expertise and the increasingly sophisticated technology infrastructure.

CI Facilitators are envisioned as individuals who do not master all the technology but who coordinate teams of scientists and technologists. Much of the curriculum being developed draws on traditions in library science and is based on cases where librarians have become part of labs and research teams and increased efficiency and funding.

One can also see the increasingly powerful roles that librarians are playing as part of legal teams in the discussion of the Department of Justice (see Department of Justice).

1. Science, Technology, Engineering, and Mathematics.

CONCLUSION

There is power in librarianship. Yet this power, as it is called on in wider and wider contexts, can become diffuse. The solution is not to avoid such contexts but rather to armor ourselves with the company of experts. By working with the scientist, the writer, the technologist, and the community leader, we amplify our effect and help forward the mission. Further, by engaging and valuing our brothers in the common good, we better serve our members. To stand in this company of experts, we must have a firm belief in our own value.

CONVERSATION STARTERS

1. Librarians need to be able to work in interdisciplinary teams because the community problems they are seeking to solve are increasingly complex and multifaceted.
2. Librarians can play the key role of facilitators in these teams because of their focus on core skills and values.

RELATED ARTIFACTS

Documents

Lankes, R. D. (Forthcoming). Innovators wanted: No experience necessary? In Walter, S., Coleman, V., & Williams, K. (Eds.), *The expert library: Staffing, sustaining, and advancing the academic library in the 21st century.* Chicago, IL: Association of College & Research Libraries.

Lankes, R. D., Cogburn, D., Oakleaf, M., & Stanton, J. (2008). *Cyberinfrastructure facilitators: New approaches to information professionals for e-Research.* Oxford e-Research Conference. Retrieved from http://ora.ouls.ox.ac.uk/objects/uuid:392876bd-5d9f-40b0-822f-269332643e6b.

Presentations

"Cyberinfrastructure Facilitators: New Approaches to Information Professionals for E-Research" Oxford e-Research'08 Conference, Oxford, UK.

Abstract: This paper introduces the concept of a CI Facilitator defined as a vital member of the research enterprise who works closely with researchers to identify extant tools, datasets, and other resources that can be integrated into the process of pursuing a research objective. To prepare CI Facilitators to evolve with e-Research endeavors, they must be grounded in deep conceptual frameworks that do not go out of date as quickly as any given cyberinfrastructure technology. One such framework, that of participatory librarianship, is presented here and explored in terms of tackling the issue of massive-scale data in research. Participatory librarianship is grounded in conversation theory and seeks to organize information as a knowledge process rather than as discreet objects in some taxonomy.

Slides: http://quartz.syr.edu/rdlankes/Presentations/2008/Oxford.pdf

Audio: http://quartz.syr.edu/rdlankes/pod/2008/Oxford.mp3

Video: http://ptbed.org/downloads/Oxford-Record.mp4

ACADEMIC

MAP LOCATION
D, 5

THREAD LOCATION
Page 101

SCAPE

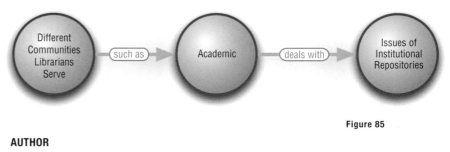

Figure 85

AUTHOR
R. David Lankes

AGREEMENT DESCRIPTION

Academic libraries have been steadily migrating from warehousing artifacts to being more directly integrated into the educational missions of colleges and universities. This can be seen in the push of services to the desktop of students and faculty. This began with a massive increase in the expenditures on full-text databases. This made the artifacts of the library more accessible outside of the physical facility. This was later matched by the wide availability of digital reference services to make the librarians also accessible from the academies' desktops (and laptops and increasingly mobile phones).

Academic libraries are also working hard to retask their physical spaces. They are moving collections offsite in favor of more meeting and commons space. This transition has been met by quite a bit of resistance from some faculty and academic disciplines, most notably the humanities.

Academic libraries are, however, well situated for their next step of evolution to conversations and new librarianship. The ideas of knowledge, conversation, and learning are far from new in this arena. Joan Bechtel said[1]:

> That these are challenging, often difficult, times for academic libraries is no news to anyone in the library world. Concern for professionalism, with its attention to accountability and responsibility, abounds. Unprecedented growth in technology provides vast new opportunities for communication, and the availability of information far outstrips most people's capacity to digest it all. In the face of this information explosion, it is ironic that academic librarians are casting about for an appropriate myth or model for library service. . . . While critics charge that academic libraries are not sufficiently integrated into the central concerns of the college or university and that librarians have their own, independent agendas, librarians responsible for present services as well as plans for the future are uneasy.
>
> Perhaps it is an overstatement to say that academic librarians are drifting in a vast sea of information and technological advances, searching for an appropriate course of action. Nevertheless, we appear to have lost the stabilizing rudder of confidence in who we are and what we are to do.
>
> As a more powerful alternative to the images of librarianship already available or proposed, I suggest that we begin to think of libraries as centers for conversation and of ourselves as mediators of and participants in the conversations of the world.

This quote always startles me when I look at the date, 1986, because it feels amazingly contemporary.

The academic library used to be seen as the heart of the campus. Unfortunately, too many academics are starting to see it more like the spleen (somewhat hard to find, and they could probably get along without it). I think that the college library needs to move from the heart of the campus to the circulatory system, moving vital ideas around the different schools and departments.

Think about how well the library is situated in these days of multidisciplinary initiatives. What other part of the academy is better able to engage and interconnect the intellectual work of the faculty than the library? Imagine engaging with faculty (and students, administration, and staff) to not only provide services to their intellectual endeavors but to also connect them with other academics working on related issues. Rather than trying to simply capture and archive the intellectual output of the academy (see Issues of Institutional Repositories on page 103 and the corresponding agreement supplement), librarians need to be knitting it together—knitting it together not simply through classification or pathfinders but mediating an interdisciplinary meeting of the minds and ongoing conversations on intellectual efforts.

One example might be arranging for interdisciplinary symposia or summits between faculties. Take topics identified of mutual interest, link them to like conversations happening in the wider world (through identifying resources, conversants, etc.), and then moderate the symposia, seeking out next steps and new initiatives. The librarian acts as honest broker, a neutral ground of intellectual camps, seeking new conversations.

This will only happen if the library is constantly engaged with faculty. This can be done through becoming involved in tenure support services, attending faculty meetings, and/or being embedded in the schools. The bottom line is that, rather than trying to capture the output of research and teaching, make yourself indispensible in terms of outcomes and the process of discovery.

RELATED ARTIFACTS

Documents

Bechtel, J. M. (1986). Conversation, a new paradigm for librarianship? *College and Research Libraries, 47*(3), 219–224.

Presentations

"Library Science and the Ivy League," Cornell Libraries, Ithaca, NY

Abstract: A discussion of the intellectual contributions libraries make to the academy.

Slides: http://quartz.syr.edu/rdlankes/Presentations/2008/Cornell.pdf

Audio: http://quartz.syr.edu/rdlankes/pod/2008/Cornell.mp3

Video: http://ptbed.org/downloads/Cornell.mp4Instruments and Data

---

1. Bechtel, J. M. (1986). Conversation, a New Paradigm for Librarianship? *College and Research Libraries, 47*(3), 219–224.

ACCESS

MAP LOCATION

D, 3

THREAD LOCATION

Page 67

SCAPE

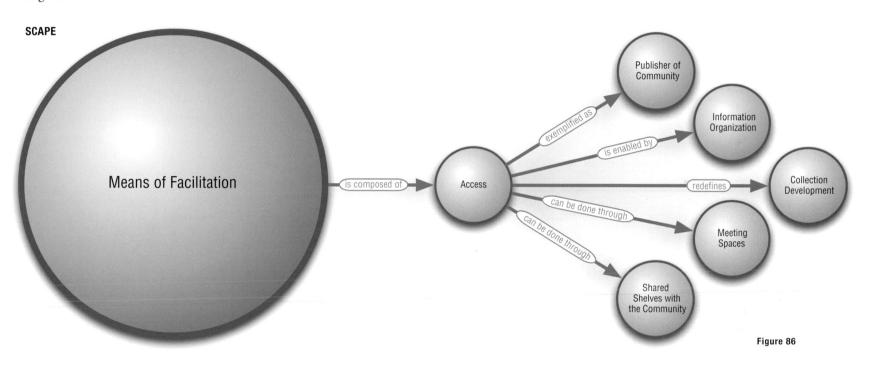

Figure 86

ADMINISTRATION

MAP LOCATION

E, 7

THREAD LOCATION

Page 160

SCAPE

Figure 87

AGREEMENTS

MAP LOCATION
E, 2

THREAD LOCATION
Page 39

SCAPE

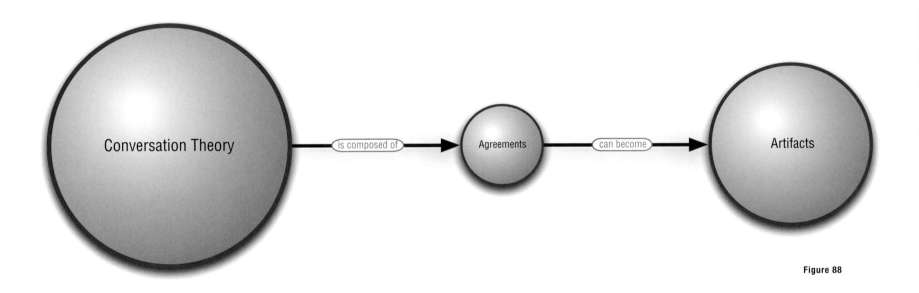

Figure 88

AGREEMENT DESCRIPTION
See Conversation Theory Agreement Supplement

AMBIGUITY IS ESSENTIAL FOR PROFESSIONAL WORK

MAP LOCATION

C, 9

THREAD LOCATION

Page 168

SCAPE

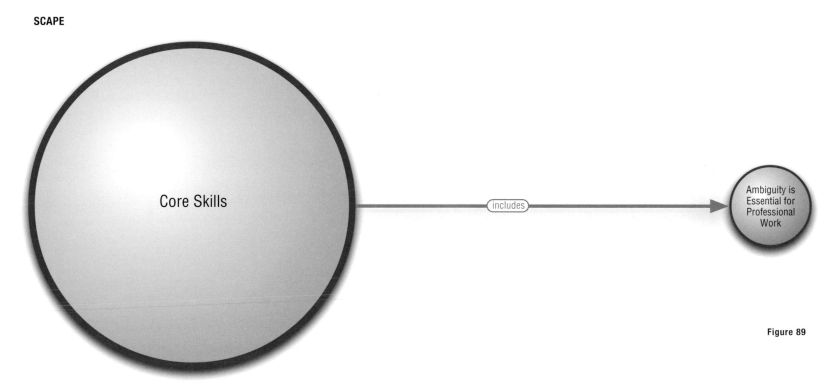

Figure 89

ANNOTATIONS

MAP LOCATION

F, G, 2

THREAD LOCATION

Page 49

SCAPE

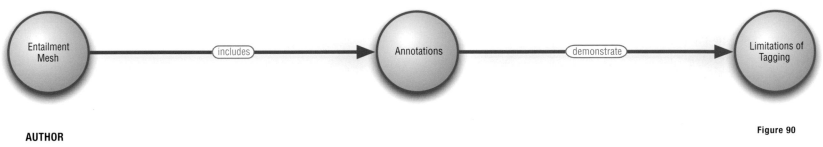

Figure 90

AUTHOR

Nancy Lara-Grimaldi

AGREEMENT DESCRIPTION

Annotations are a mechanism whereby users can document their contexts (relationships and agreements). This is an important function that began back in the dark ages with glossing text and continues to this day with lists and tagging.

An annotation is a summary of the contents of a particular book, article, or other document and is traditionally created by the author or publisher of the work. Library catalog records include concise summaries, or abstracts, of library holdings and system resources, which aid in locating appropriate resources. These metadata describe the contents of a particular item, whereas annotations may cover a wide range of notations. Annotations allow users to put documents into context relevant to their topic or subject area. Annotations may include personal observations, reactions, insights, interpretations, or any other type of notation for that matter. Similarly, wikis and blogs provide a means for users to add individual annotations to documents created by others.

If libraries developed a client-side tool for members to create and share annotations, whose responsibility would it be to monitor it? Will this information be stored on library servers, and what policies must be developed for access and privacy? In her article, "Unlocking the Museum: A Manifesto," Corinne Jorgenson proposes a new concept in the creation and distribution of annotated contents to allow "information consumers to become information producers." She notes that a "revolutionary reconceptualization of practice which provides flexibility in the concept of the locus of authority in the description of documents could not only offer hope for tangible solutions to these problems of descriptions, but could facilitate the creation of new knowledge...."

CONVERSATION STARTERS

1. How can the use of annotation facilitate knowledge creation?
2. Would users find value in creating, sharing, and reading annotations with friends, individuals, or groups of people?
3. What are the implications for libraries in providing this service to their members?
4. How can degrees of annotations at L_0 and L_1 benefit different users?
5. How do you organize the many different levels of annotation into a single, searchable format?

RELATED ARTIFACTS

Robert, C. A. (2009). Annotation for knowledge sharing in a collaborative environment. *Journal of Knowledge Management, 13*(1).

Han, L., & Yan, H. (2009). A fuzzy biclustering algorithm for social annotations. *Journal of Information Science, 35*(4), 426–438. Retrieved September 27, 2009, from doi:10.1177/0165551508101862

Jörgensen, C. (2004). Unlocking the museum: A manifesto. *Journal of the American Society for Information Science & Technology, 55*(5), 462–464. Retrieved September 27, 2009, from Library, Information Science & Technology Abstracts database.

Pomerantz, J., & Marchionini, G. (2007). The digital library as place. *Journal of Documentation, 63*(4).

Quint, B. (2009). The foresight of searchers, or how I love being right. *Information Today, 26*(5), 7–8. Retrieved September 27, 2009, from Library, Information Science & Technology Abstracts database.

Verhaart, M., & Kinshuk (2006). A dynamic personal portfolio using web technologies. *Encyclopedia of Human Computer Interaction.*

Wu, P., Heok, A., & Tamsir, I. (2007). Annotating eb archives—structure, provenance, and context through archival cataloguing. *New Review of Hypermedia & Multimedia, 13*(1), 55–75. Retrieved September 27, 2009, from doi:10.1080/13614560701423620

Yang, S. (2008). An ontological website models-supported search agent for web services. *Expert Systems with Applications, 35*(4), 2056–2073. Retrieved September 27, 2009, from doi:10.1016/j.eswa.2007.09.024

APPLICATION BUILDERS

MAP LOCATION

E, 6

THREAD LOCATION

Page 87

SCAPE

Figure 91

AUTHOR

R. David Lankes

AGREEMENT DESCRIPTION

Application builders are the agents devoted to software development on the Internet. An application produces software that uses the infrastructure to produce, provide, capture, and organize information on the Internet.

Software, for the purpose of this agreement, is considered content free. That is not to say that this software does not provide information to the user. Rather, the information provided does not directly match the information needs of the member. The member utilizes these applications as a means to access other information. Applications created by application builders are a means to an end. For example, when someone uses the Firefox web browser to access a weather report, he or she is interested in the weather not the Firefox software.

Not all the software created by these agents, however, is visible to the member. Software used to provide and organize information within organizations is also included in this category. Servers, for example, are vital to the client/server paradigm used in today's Internet information services. It is the server's ability to remain invisible to the member that makes the client/server model so powerful.

See also Internet Model Example Agreement Supplement

RELATED ARTIFACTS

Lankes, R. D. (1998). *Building & maintaining Internet information services: K-12 digital reference services*. Syracuse: ERIC Clearinghouse on Information & Technology.

ARCHIVES

MAP LOCATION

D, 4

THREAD LOCATION

Page 113

SCAPE

Figure 92

CONTRIBUTOR

Michael Luther

RELATED ARTIFACTS

Bastian, J. A. (2009). Flowers for homestead: A case study in archives and collective memory. *American Archivist, 72*(1), 113–132. Retrieved October 20, 2009, from the American Archivist eJournal database.

> Annotation: This article gets at the issue of memory as a feature of archives.

Galloway, P. (2006). Archives, power, and history: Dunbar Rowland and the beginning of the State Archives of Mississippi (1902–1936). *American Archivist, 69(1)*, 79–116. Retrieved October 21, 2009, from http://archivists.metapress.com.libezproxy2.syr.edu/content/m462n0564g87jqm0/?p=459438df7ded4576b1e1a15b30826834&pi=0

> Annotation: Also dealing with memory, this article takes the issue one step further: the power to be had by influencing memory through collection practices.

Pederson, A. (n.d.). Basic concepts and principles of archives and records management. *Understanding Society Through its Records.* Retrieved from http://john.curtin.edu.au/society/archives/management.html

Society of American Archivists. (n.d.). Provenance. In *A Glossary of Archival and Records Terminology.* Retrieved from http://www.archivists.org/glossary/term_details.asp?DefinitionKey=196

Society of American Archivists. (n.d.). Original order. In *A Glossary of Archival and Records Terminology.* Retrieved from http://www.archivists.org/glossary/term_details.asp?DefinitionKey=69

Roe, K. (2005). *Arranging & Describing Archives & Manuscripts (Archival Fundamentals Series II).* Chicago: Society of American Archivists.

Schellenberg, T. R. (1988). *Management of Archives.* Washington, DC: National Archives and Records Administration.

Schellenberg, T. R. (1968). *Modern Archives, Principles and Techniques.* Chicago: University of Chicago.

Yakel, E., & Torres, D. A. (2007). Genealogists as a "Community of Records." *American Archivist, 70*(1), 93–113. Retrieved October 21, 2009, from http://archivists.metapress.com.libezproxy2.syr.edu/content/ll5414u736440636/?p=a558f0aa51814906b05acf6bcc6a8d34&pi=5.

> Annotation: I felt this article touched nicely on matters of memory, community, sense making and conversation in terms of archives.

ARTIFACTS

MAP LOCATION

F, 2

THREAD LOCATION

Page 41

SCAPE

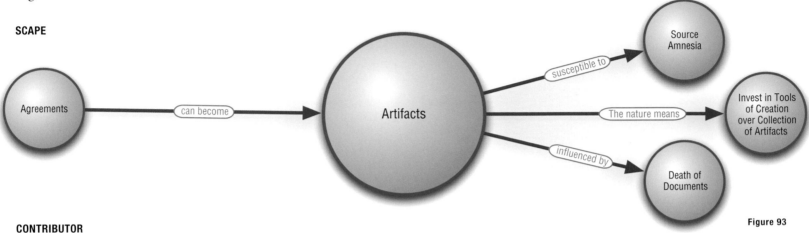

Figure 93

CONTRIBUTOR

Michael Luther

CONVERSATION STARTERS

1. What is the role of the library in preserving cultural heritage?
2. To what extent do different library types (public, academic, corporate, etc.) have a preservation responsibility?

RELATED ARTIFACTS

Bee, R. (2008). The importance of preserving paper-based artifacts in a digital age. *Library Quarterly,78*(2), 179–194. Retrieved September 24, 2009, from the Library Literature and Information Science Full Text database.

> Annotation: Bee reminds us that the artifact—let's say a book—carries a lot more information than can be contained within the textual content between its covers. Artifacts provide insight into their own construction, their creators, and the time and place from which they come. As librarians use their precious space less for artifact storage and more for interaction, it might be wise to consider the potential costs to a reliance on digital or otherwise reformatted content.

Lewis, D. W. (1998). What if libraries are artifact-bound institutions? *Information Technology and Libraries, 17*(4), 191–197. Retrieved September 25, 2009, from the Library Literature and Information Science Full Text database.

> Annotation: In this grim and somewhat dated article, Lewis informs us that the ship is going down; rather than saving it, we should direct our efforts toward the safety of the passengers. Monographs and serials first! Lewis has a similar premise to the Atlas in some ways. He exhorts us to focus not on what libraries have done

(the functional view) but rather on what they are for. It is here that the Atlas diverges somewhat. Lewis says libraries provide information to the public easily and affordably. I think this is a far more humble view of librarianship than that put forth by the Atlas.

MacPherson, D. L. (2006). Digitizing the non-digital: Creating a global context for events, artifacts, ideas, and information. *Information Technology and Libraries, 25*(2), 95–102. Retrieved September 25, 2009, from the Library Literature and Information Science Full Text database.

> Annotation: This article, if I understand it, might be a bit of a stretch to our discussion. I mention it because it relates well to some of the other abstracts and annotations provided here. Context-Driven Topologies is a system that recognizes the value of an artifact's context as well as its content. Tracking relationships between artifacts and people could provide valuable information. It also notes the human dimension—that artifacts are connected to people. I find all of this relevant and interesting to our discussion of the artifact in librarianship.
>
> It brings to my mind the observation that an artifact can have a digital context in its digital state as well as a natural context in its natural state.

Smiraglia, R. (2008). Rethinking what we catalog: Documents as cultural artifacts. *Cataloging and Classification Quarterly, 45*(3), 25–37. Retrieved September 24, 2009, from the Library Literature and Information Science Full Text database.

> Annotation: Smiraglia speaks of the cultural value of artifacts from the cataloger's perspective. He states that it is part of the essence of librarianship to comprehend and transmit the cultural milieu along with the artifact. In a sense, catalogers are curators. This line of thinking is at odds with the Atlas in that it understands this essence not as conversation but as dissemination. Curators are storytellers. They tell us what all the stuff means. For an utterly contrarian view on the much-loathed "recorded knowledge," see section two, paragraph one of this article.

ASSESSMENT

MAP LOCATION

F, 6

THREAD LOCATION

Page 106

SCAPE

Figure 94

AUTHOR

Megan Oakleaf

AGREEMENT DESCRIPTION

Library assessment is not an optional activity; assessment is a librarian's professional obligation. Assessment enables librarians to articulate member needs and organizational goals and allows them to know whether both are met effectively and efficiently. Librarians who assess also maximize opportunities to demonstrate library value and impact to their stakeholders—and they are ready with evidence to bolster requests for additional resources as needed.

Assessment, like many library activities, is not a single event. Rather, it is an ongoing cyclical process. The process begins with the **identification of goals or expected outcomes** of a library service or collection. Historically, librarians have focused on "input" or "output" measures, such as the number of books circulated, the cost of databases per use, or the percentage of students receiving information literacy instruction. While critical for managing library services, collections, and other activities, such measures do not provide librarians with the information they need to assess library impact. In contrast, outcome measures reveal information about library value in many forms, such as the effect of circulated resume books on job seeker success, the role of medical journal articles in patient care, or the increased ability of students to select and use credible information resources. Librarians seeking to investigate outcomes, rather than input and output mea-

sures, should consider writing goals in the language of educational objectives: "The member will be able to + ACTION VERB PHRASE."

The member will be able to articulate the impact of library resources on his or her job search.

The member will be able to identify journal articles relevant to diagnosis of patient health issues.

The member will be able to locate credible online information.

The member will be able to engage in face-to-face conversations about new fiction publications.

The member will be able to contribute new information to online discussion forums.

Taking the time to craft explicit outcomes enables librarians to articulate the value they provide to their members. Once librarians have clearly stated their outcomes, they **enact the services, collections, or other activities** that are necessary to achieve them.

In the next step of the assessment process, librarians **collect, interpret, and analyze evidence** to ascertain whether their activities are achieving the intended outcomes. Evidence collection can take many forms, and most of them involve members in an assessment "conversation" either directly or indirectly. For example, surveys, interviews, and focus groups allow members to self-report how they have felt the impact of the library. Artifact analysis is another method for collecting evidence; librarians can observe or evaluate member-created documents, such as blog posts, multimedia presentations, or bibliographies to determine the ways in which the library facilitates information use and knowledge creation.

Finally, librarians **use evidence analysis to make decisions and take actions** to achieve the main purpose of assessment—to increase library impact on members. In this step, sometimes called the "closing the loop" stage, librarians use assessment evidence to improve library activities and increase library value. In addition, librarians can use assessment evidence to **"tell the story" of the library to stakeholders**, either to celebrate successes or leverage problem areas to gain additional resources.

With so much benefit to be gained from assessment, why do some librarians avoid it? Librarians commonly cite these barriers: lack of time or resources, lack of a coordinated structure, lack of experience or knowledge of assessment processes, and fear of negative results. Although challenging, these assessment barriers are not insurmountable. They can be addressed using a few key strategies: prioritize, coordinate, educate, and communicate. Librarians who are short on time or resources for assessment must **prioritize**. What is important must be accomplished. Thus, if librarians acknowledge the importance of assessment, then they must minimize, reassign, or eliminate another work duty or resource cost. Fortunately, assessment often reveals which library activities are most valuable and which may be terminated without a significant decrease in library impact. Librarians who need supportive structures can **coordinate** with others who engage in assessment within the library, in other areas of their overarching institution, or in a professional association. If know-how or experience is a barrier, librarians should **educate** themselves by identifying professional development opportunities focused on assessment, participating in assessment communities online, or seeking out seminal readings on the topic. Finally, communication is the best way to address librarians who fear negative results. Librarians who conduct assessment must **communicate** with their colleagues and stakeholders clearly—not only about how assessment results will or will not be used but also about what information will be shared beyond library walls.

Armed with these strategies and the steps of the assessment cycle, librarians are well prepared to engage members in library assessment and use the results to continuously improve library services, collections, and other activities. This is the professional obligation of all librarians—to increase library value.

QUESTIONS/CONVERSATION STARTERS

1. What outcomes do our libraries seek to achieve? Are we being ambitious enough?
2. What tools will enable us to know whether we have achieved our outcomes? Do they actively involve members in the process?
3. What does achievement of our outcomes look like? What does a member who has been impacted by our library look like?
4. What will we do if we find out we have not yet achieved our outcomes? What do our next steps look like?
5. How do we articulate library value to members?

RELATED ARTIFACTS

ALA Connect. (2010). *Assessment and evaluation.* Retrieved January 25, 2010, from http://connect.ala.org/taxonomy/term/9133

American Library Association. (2010). *Selected outcomes assessment resources.* Retrieved January 25, 2010, from http://www.ala.org/ala/educationcareers/education/accreditedprograms/resourcesforprogramadministrators/outcomesassessment.cfm

Association of Research Libraries. (2010). *Library assessment conference.* Retrieved January 25, 2010, from http://www.libraryassessment.org/

Association of Research Libraries. (2010). *Statistics and assessment.* Retrieved January 25, 2010, from http://www.arl.org/stats/

Harada, V. H. (2005). Working smarter: Being strategic about assessment and accountability. *Teacher Librarian, 33*(1), 8–15.

Horowitz, L. (2009). Assessing library services: A practical guide for the nonexpert. *Library Leadership Management, 23*(4), 193.

Kyrillidou, M. (2010). *Library assessment blog.* Retrieved January 25, 2009, from http://libraryassessment.info/

Maki, P. L. (2004). *Assessing for learning: Building a sustainable commitment across the institution.* Sterling, VA: Stylus.

Oakleaf, M. (2009). The information literacy instruction assessment cycle: A guide for increasing student learning and improving librarian instructional skills. *Journal of Documentation, 65*(4).

Oakleaf, M., & Kaske, N. (2009). Guiding questions for assessing information literacy in higher education. *Portal: Libraries and the Academy, 9*(2), 273–286.

Rubin, R. J. (2005). *Demonstrating results: Using outcome measurement in your library.* Chicago, IL: ALA Editions.

AUTHORITATIVE VERSUS AUTHORITARIAN

MAP LOCATION

F, 3

THREAD LOCATION

Page 91

SCAPE

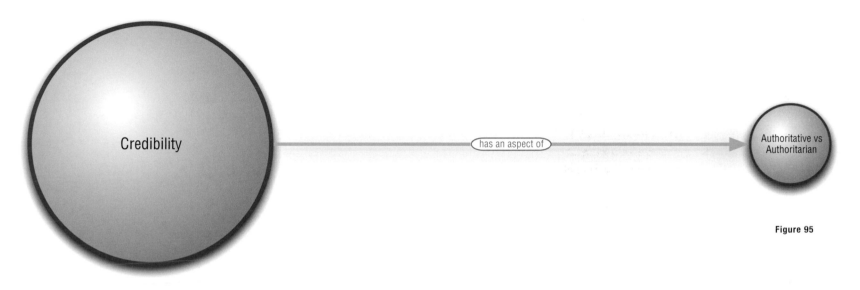

Figure 95

AVOIDING THE FLORENTINE DILEMMA

MAP LOCATION

F, 9

THREAD LOCATION

Page 182

SCAPE

Figure 96

BACHELOR OF INFORMATION AND INSTRUCTIONAL DESIGN

MAP LOCATION

E, 8

THREAD LOCATION

Page 183

SCAPE

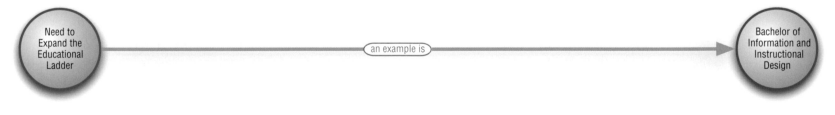

Figure 97

BOUNDARY ISSUES

MAP LOCATION

C, 5

THREAD LOCATION

Page 85

SCAPE

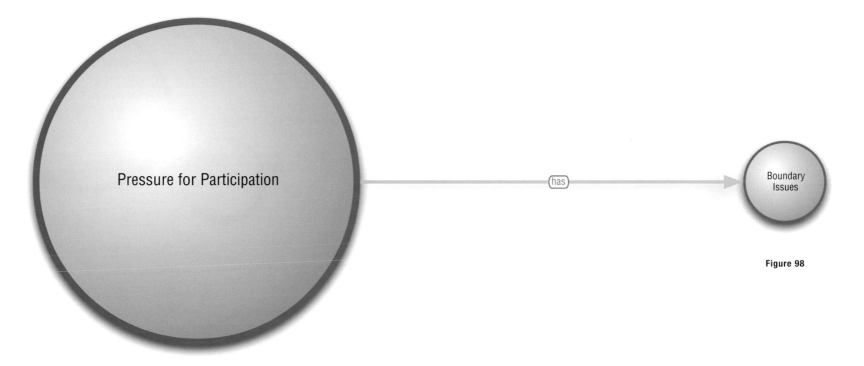

Pressure for Participation — has → Boundary Issues

Figure 98

CATALOGING RELATIONSHIPS

MAP LOCATION

G, 2

THREAD LOCATIONS

Pages 44, 53, 139

SCAPE

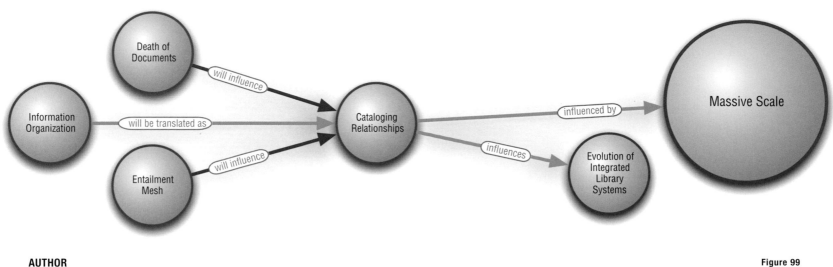

Figure 99

AUTHOR

R. David Lankes

AGREEMENT DESCRIPTION

Much of the reasoning and ideas for cataloging relationships is well covered in the Threads. The underlying technologies to do so are not. There is an active set of projects, communities, and research going into building the necessary infrastructure for this work. Most of it falls under the rubric of the semantic web. Although not all the concepts of the semantic web are in line with new librarianship (there seems to be a much more optimistic vision of data without context), the standards being put forth such as the Resource Description Framework (RDF) and registries and service-oriented architectures hold great promise.

RELATED ARTIFACTS

Main Page. (n.d.). In *Semantic Web*. Retrieved from http://semanticweb.org/wiki/Main_Page.

OWL 2. (n.d.). In *Semantic Web*. Retrieved from http://semanticweb.org/wiki/OWL.

RDF. (n.d.). In *Semantic Web*. Retrieved from http://semanticweb.org/wiki/RDF.

CIRCULATION

MAP LOCATION

F, G, 8

THREAD LOCATION

Page 166

SCAPE

Figure 100

CO-LEARNING

MAP LOCATION

E, 8

THREAD LOCATION

Page 179

SCAPE

Figure 101

COLLECTION DEVELOPMENT

MAP LOCATION

F, 4

THREAD LOCATIONS

Page 157

SCAPE

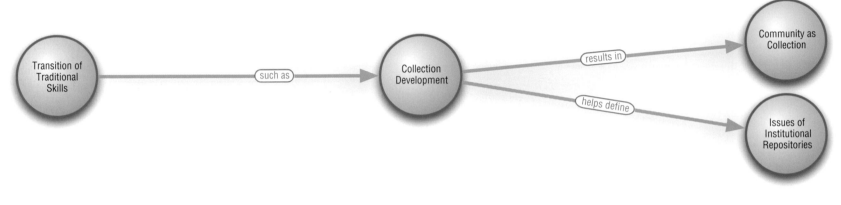

Figure 102

COMMUNICATIONS

MAP LOCATION

E, 9

THREAD LOCATION

Page 172

SCAPE

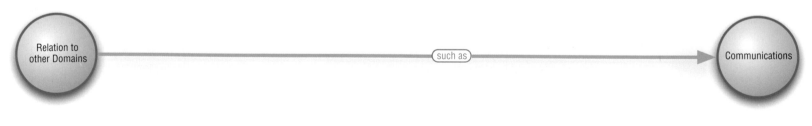

Figure 103

COMMUNITY AS COLLECTION

MAP LOCATION

F, 4

THREAD LOCATION

Page 159

SCAPE

Figure 104

COMPUTER SCIENCE

MAP LOCATION

E, 9

THREAD LOCATION

Page 174

SCAPE

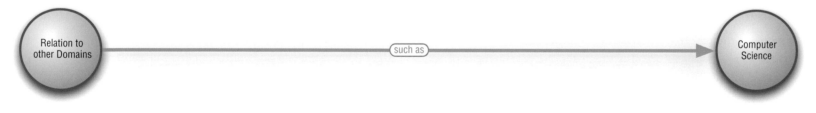

Figure 105

CONSTRUCTIVISM

MAP LOCATION

E, 3

THREAD LOCATION

Page 27

SCAPE

AUTHOR

Jocelyn Clark

Figure 106

AGREEMENT DESCRIPTION

From the agreement "Importance of a Worldview," we move along the mission Thread to "The Importance of Theory and Deep Concepts" to "Learning Theories" and then to "Constructivism." Exploring constructivism as a learning theory as relevant to the mission of librarians leads us to the development of constructivism as a theory of knowledge creation. Constructivism postulates that knowledge is created within a person, not communicated from the outside (i.e., knowledge is internally constructed based on interpretation of our experiences). Cooperstein and Kocevar-Weidinger (2004) give a great summary article on the application as a learning theory. Thanasoulas (n.d.) also gives an excellent overview of the topic.

Psychology, philosophy, educational theory, sociology, and other schools of thought have contributed to the development of constructivism as a learning theory. The credit for the development of educational constructivism is generally credited to Jean Piaget and his work on childhood learning. Other names that are associated with this field are Ernst Von Glaserfeld, John Dewey, Jerome Bruner, and Lev Vygotsky. Vygotsky developed the theory of "social constructivism," which affirms that social interaction plays an essential role in cognitive development. Three particular reference Web sites are listed below with extensive bibliographies of these theoretical works (Ryder and Marsh, Barrie, & McFadden, Jean Piaget Society).

Constructivism is generally agreed to be the process where individual knowledge is created internally through a person's interaction with an external world. "Learners construct their own knowledge by looking for meaning and order; they interpret what they hear, read, and see based on their previous learning and habits" (Thanasoulas). This contrasts with the objectivist philosophy that learning is transmitted from teacher to student directly. Social constructivism acknowledges the roles that social interaction and culture have on that knowledge creation.

There are critics of constructivism. They argue that it denies the existence of a true reality—that philosophically there are issues with creating a worldview of complete relativism. They take issue with statements like that of Tobin, "A constructivist perception acknowledges the existence of an external reality, but realizes that cognizing beings can never know what that reality is actually like." Critics of constructivism as a learning theory suggest that constructivists want to teach that there are no objective facts to be learned; that constructivists want people to reinvent the wheel repeatedly. In addition, there exists an ongoing debate between encouraging self-discovery of science and mathematical relationships through constructivism versus teaching the principles objectively (Chakerian). Despite the ongoing philosophical debates, many constructivist principles are employed routinely and successfully but perhaps are not representative of pure constructivism. In the context of new librarianship, we do not necessarily have to enter into the philosophical debate about constructivism because we are looking more narrowly at its concrete applications as a learning theory and at its application within the cosmos of librarianship.

In the classroom, constructivist theories are applied through a learning model that includes opportunities for active questioning, interpreting, and problem solving (Marlowe). The work of Jean Piaget is used extensively in developing programs that support active learning. Solomon provides some concrete principles to guide the use of constructivist principles in the classroom. Cooperstein and Kocevar-Weidinger also discuss constructivism in library education. Many other resources are available that discuss the implementation of constructivist principles in a classroom environment. Some are listed below. However, a classroom is not the same thing as a library, and a librarian is not the same as a classroom teacher.

In a library, the concept of facilitating knowledge creation is closely tied to the principles associated with developing an independent-learning, inquiry-based, project-based classroom. However, the question relative to the mission of librarians isn't about classroom studies so much as it is about use of the theory of constructivism to build a model of librarianship that enables people to create their own knowledge. How do we create an information environment that facilitates personal knowledge creation? In most of the classroom applications, we still have a situation with a teacher designing a lesson and then administering it using constructivist principles. The teacher has an agenda for the students, and although students are experiencing some freedom to explore, in the end, the teacher has defined learning objectives. That type of instruction may work in school library media centers but is not a model we can use for auto-didactic activities, as those in a public library, or anywhere outside a formal learning environment. In librarianship, we are often less an instructor than a guide. In physical libraries, we are often inherently creating an environment for personal knowledge creation without defined learning objectives. One example is the creation of learning commons in academic libraries. Another might be the integration of a discover layer tool onto a traditional library catalog. In addition, many of the social library and Web 2.0 library tools are based on interactive knowledge construction and align with the theories of Vygotsky.

One interesting question about the application of constructivism in the library goes back to Ranganathan's principle of saving the time of the reader. Sometimes we are involved in accessing multiple sources, creating theories, exploring topics, and creating knowledge. Sometimes we just want to know a quick answer to help us on our way; we don't want to be involved in an additional protracted journey of self-discovery. It reminds me of a conversation I had with my mother in about the eighth grade:

Me: Mom, what does "didactic" mean?
Mom (giving the appropriate mom response): Well, why don't you look it up in the dictionary?
Me: Mom, I know how to use a dictionary, can you just tell me what the word means?

Sometimes having your mother tell you the answer is all you really need if the objective is an external fact so you can carry on with your other activities. At the reference desk, we might send a student on a quest with just some guidance, or we might just hand a user the answer. Which one really depends on the situation, the library, and the question. In the process of constructing knowledge for themselves, people might need anything from a quick fact, to a formal lesson on identifying credible sources, to an uncensored Internet connection, to a room to work on a group project. Identifying those tools is the challenge of applying constructivism in libraries.

To go in the opposite direction, if we have a librarian with an Internet connection (and no library) standing between an information-seeker and the knowledge, can we really be implementing constructivism? Perhaps we need to get out of the chair and let them use the computer to facilitate their exploration. The question changes to: How do we create tools to facilitate knowledge creation in the virtual world? Constructivism as a learning theory encourages us to look at all the ways people create knowledge and understanding for themselves and then challenges us to explore those tools in our redefinition of librarianship.

RELATED ARTIFACTS

Documents

Bruner, J. S. (1966). *Toward a theory of instruction*. Cambridge, MA: Belknap Press of Harvard University.

Chakerian, G. D., & Kreith, K. (n.d.). *The Pythagorean Theorem*. Retrieved from http://www.mathematicallycorrect.com/pythag.htm

Cooperstein, S. E., & Kocevar-Weidinger, E. (2004). Beyond active learning: A constructivist approach to learning. *Reference Services Review, 32*(2), 141–148.

Glaserfeld, E. V. (2002). Radical constructivism in mathematics education (Mathematics education library). In *Mathematics education library, v.7*. New York: Kluwer Academic.

Glasersfeld, E. V., Larochelle, M., Ackermann, E., & Tobin, K. G. (2007). *Key works in radical constructivism (Bold visions in educational research)*. Rotterdam: Sense.

Marlowe, B. A., & Page, M. L. (1998). *Creating and sustaining the constructivist classroom*. Thousand Oaks, CA: Corwin Press. Retrieved from http://www.mathematicallycorrect.com/pythag.htm

Solomon, P. G. (2009). *The curriculum bridge: From standards to actual classroom practice*. Thousand Oaks, CA: Corwin Press.

Talja, S., Tuominen, K., & Savolainen, R. (2005). "Isms" in information science: Constructivism, collectivism and constructionism. *Journal of Documentation, 61*(1), 79–101.

Thanasoulas, D. (n.d.). *Constructivist learning*. Retrieved from http://www.seasite.niu.edu/Tagalog/Teachers_Page/Language_Learning_Articles/constructivist_learning.htm and http://dimitristhanasoulas.com/wordpress/?page_id=8

Tobin, K. G. (1993). *The practice of constructivism in science education*. Hillsdale, NJ: Lawrence Erlbaum Associates.

Resource Material

Piaget

Jean Piaget Society. http://www.piaget.org

Resources for Students. (n.d.). *Jean Piaget Society*. Retrieved from http://www.piaget.org/students.html

Classroom Examples

Here are some Web sites and videos that give concrete examples and discussion of constructivism in a classroom:

Constructivism as a paradigm for teaching and learning. (n.d.). *Concept to classroom*. Retrieved from http://www.thirteen.org/edonline/concept2class/constructivism/index.html

tbed63. (2008, October 11). *Constructivist math correcting method*. Video posted to http://www.youtube.com/watch?v=Xe1Ei4wYR3E

tbed63. (2008, October 5). *Constructivist social studies lesson*. Video posted to http://www.youtube.com/watch?v=p6pFMPSWBds

Constructivism, (n.d.). In *Information Age Inquiry*. Retrieved from http://virtualinquiry.com/scientist/constructivism.htm

Other Videos

changelearning. (2008, January 31). *Building knowledge: Constructivism in learning*. Video posted to http://www.youtube.com/watch?v=F00R3pOXzuk

Kliegman, K. (2007, November 5). *Constructivism in the library*. Message posted to http://wlteam.blogspot.com/2007/11/constructivism-in-library.html

Koltzenburg, T. (2006, April 1). Rock on! Celebrating the library and learning. *ALA TechSource*. Retrieved from http://www.alatechsource.org/blog/2006/04/rock-on-celebrating-the-library-and-learning.html

Possible Constructivist Tools

Discovery Layer Interfaces. (n.d.). In *Library Technology Guides*. Retrieved from http://www.librarytechnology.org/discovery.pl

Digital Learning Commons (n.d.). *Washington State*. Retrieved from http://www.learningcommons.org

Five Weeks to a Social Library. (n.d.). Retrieved from http://www.sociallibraries.com/course

Library Wikis. (n.d.). Retrieved from http://librarywikis.pbworks.com

Wikis. (n.d.). In *Library success: A best practices wiki*. Retrieved from http://www.libsuccess.org/index.php?title=Wikis

Reference Websites: *These Web sites contain a multitude of writings on constructivism. The Emtech site contains writings in opposition to constructivism in addition to other writings.*

Marsh, G., Barrie, J. P., & McFadden, A. C. (n.d.). *Constructivism, Instructivism, and Related Sites. Emerging Technologies*. Retrieved from http://www.emtech.net/construc.htm

Jean Piaget Society. (2008). *Internet Resources*. Retrieved from http://www.piaget.org/links.html

Ryder, M. (2009). *Constructivism*. University of Colorado School of Education. Retrieved from http://carbon.ucdenver.edu/~mryder/itc_data/constructivism.html

CONVERSANTS

MAP LOCATION

E, 3

THREAD LOCATION

Page 32

SCAPE

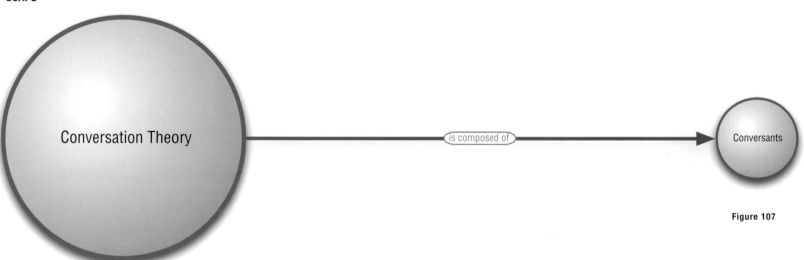

Figure 107

AGREEMENT DESCRIPTION

See Conversation Theory Agreement Supplement

CONVERSATION THEORY

MAP LOCATION

D, 2, 3

THREAD LOCATIONS

Pages 23, 31

SCAPE

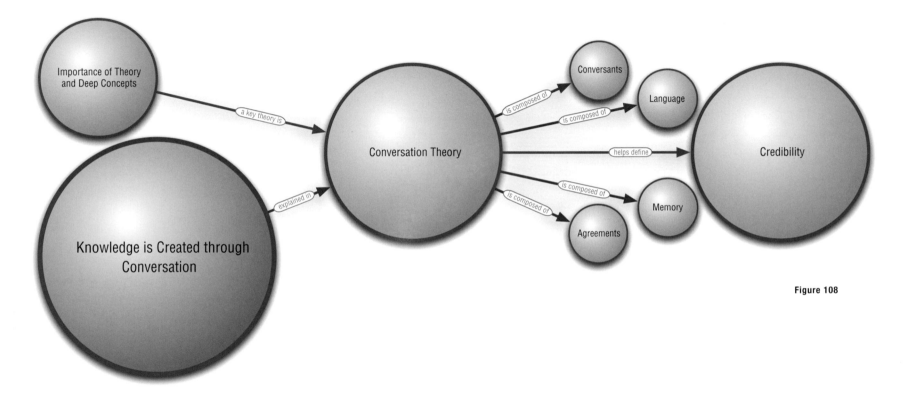

Importance of Theory and Deep Concepts

a key theory is

Knowledge is Created through Conversation

explained in

Conversation Theory

is composed of

Conversants

is composed of

Language

helps define

Credibility

is composed of

Memory

is composed of

Agreements

Figure 108

AUTHOR

R. David Lankes

AGREEMENT DESCRIPTION

In an interview with an Italian library journal, I was asked,

> "The conversation" is a brilliant metaphor, since The Cluetrain Manifesto, but somehow vague. According to you, which forms can the conversation take?

I responded that conversation is not a metaphor. When I say "knowledge is created through conversation," I mean that at least two parties are actively going back and forth in an engaged manner and language is being exchanged. Why "parties" and not people? What do I mean by the notion that language is exchanged? Let me start at a basic level. This is all grounded in Pask's Conversation Theory (although he does it at a *much* deeper level).

A conversation has four parts:

1. Conversants: at least two parties,
2. Language: sets of meaning going back and forth,
3. Agreements: shared understandings between the conversants arrived at through language, and
4. An Entailment Mesh: a collection and relation of the agreements.

Conversants: Parties to a Conversation

In a conversation, you have at least two parties or "agents." Why not call them people? Because agents are a scalable notion, that is to say, it can be two people (you and I), two groups (say a teacher and his or her students), two organizations (like a library and a vendor negotiating a contract), two countries (a treaty), or even two societies (the great conversation on the meaning of life).

Likewise, these agents can be within a single person. In fact, it is the basis of a lot of instruction and education theory. Call it metacognition or critical thinking skills, or simply arguing with yourself, you have these conversations all the time. If you just asked yourself, "What does he mean by that?!," who are you asking? Pask, in about 100 pages of dense prose, says that you are in a conversation with different aspects of yourself set up to come to some agreement about a concept. Waking up in the morning and deciding what to wear ("This makes me look fat, this is too dressy…") is a conversation.

Also, this conversation can happen over a great period of time and through a series of media. So, you read this book (my part of the conversation), think about it, and send me an e-mail about how you agree, or disagree, or simply want clarification. That is a conversation (to be precise, if you are reading this book, you are having a conversation with yourself; it is only if you start sending me feedback that I get involved).

Language: Talking at Their Level

So what are these two or more agents doing? They are exchanging language. This may seem obvious, but it has a lot of implications. There is a large body of research about how people exchange language. For example, there is a discussion on how people know how to take turns in a conversation. There is active research in how people determine things such as power relationships in a conversation (e.g., who is in charge). All of this research is relevant here and can be (and has been) applied to conversations in libraries.

However, Conversation Theory does not directly examine these aspects of conversations. It omits them for several reasons, not the least of which is that much of Pask's work predates discourse theory. More important for us, however, is that Pask wasn't just dealing with language between two people. Conversations can also be between two organizations or two parts of one individual. So he approached it in a much more general way. It is also a way that has great implications for how libraries work on a day-to-day basis.

When two agents are sharing language, they do so at one of two levels. The first level is directed and pretty low level. This kind of language is used when at least one of the conversants doesn't know much about a topic. Take, for example, a librarian walking a patron through a database. It might be a simple set of exchanges, such as "click here, then click here, then type in your query." The patron's part of the conversation may be a series of clicks and "OK, now what?" Because the patron doesn't have much knowledge about what he or she is doing, the language is not rich. Pask calls this kind of language L_0. L_0 language is used to set up the conversation.

In contrast, L_1 is language exchanged between two agents when they both share knowledge of a topic (or domain as Pask would call it). In these exchanges, language is used to build a common understanding of a domain, mutually expand domain knowledge, or clarify some part of the domain. Imagine two librarians debating the finer points of classification, for example.

It is easy to say the patron/librarian example from before was an example of bad instruction ("Don't just teach where to click, teach why"), but that is a bit simplistic. Good instruction (and Pask would argue, good systems) attempt to raise the conversation from L_0 to L_1.

However, you have to start somewhere. Furthermore, there are many times when L_0 is just fine. Think driving directions (I just want to get to the library. I don't need a lesson in city planning).

Agreements: Agreeing and Agreeing Not to Agree

So we have a conversation where information is being exchanged in a sequence between two agents (people, organizations, countries). That alone does not create knowledge; that is simply a process between two black boxes.

If a conversation is at its heart simply a back and forth exchange, what's the point? For example, I could say "1," you could say "2," then I say "3," and so on. Are we really learning anything? Not really because we already know what we are doing (counting up by one), and that means we already know this. No, to learn something, we must seek agreements. That is, we go back and forth making an assertion and seeing what the response is. If I say something and get back an unexpected answer, I need to figure out why. So if I say "1" and you say "3," I might ask, "Are we counting up by 2s?," and you might say, "Yes." I might then say "fine" (meaning I have learned what our task is) or even "5," and we can continue. This is a pretty minor case of learning, I grant you.

Once we've been doing this for a while, we build a whole host of agreements, on which we can seek new ones in new conversations. So if I say "libraries are cool," for that to mean anything to you somewhere in the past you had to have had a conversation on what the words "library" and "cool" mean. If not, I could just as well have said that we need to turn up the heat in libraries, or, to a C programmer, sets of precompiled functions I can include in my software are really neat. In truth, this book and your internal and external debates are seeking agreement on what we mean by the word "librarian."

Already you can glimpse some of the implications of Conversation Theory. There are many libraries that claim an educational mission. If learning is an active set of agreements and conversations, then simply providing access to information is insufficient to fulfill our mission! Acquiring materials, organizing materials, and presenting materials may aid in conversations, but they are insufficient to educate. We must present a forum, tools, and opportunities for agreement and conversation. Further, librarians need to actively engage communities in seeking agreements.

So, we have a process of information interchange in sequence that seeks out agreements. It should be noted that an agreement can include "We will never agree on this." The collection of these agreements is kept in a memory that can be represented in something Pask calls an entailment mesh.

Memory and Entailment Meshes: Pask's Tangles

Your memory constitutes what you know about the world. It is the sum of agreements we retain after our conversations. However, it is not a simple list or blob of these agreements. As we just discussed, agreements build on themselves. Memory is the agreements and the relationship of these agreements. If you want to impress your friends, you could call memory a "knowledge representation" system like ontologies and semantic networks. If you have no friends, think of it like a map of the stuff you know.

The important thing you need to know is that your memory is all about relationships. That is to say, Conversation Theory talks about the fact that you understand the world not as a series of isolated events or facts but as a dynamic network of agreements and understandings. So to "learn" (Pask talks about "knowing"), a person needs to actively relate new information to what is already known.

Because we're in the thick of theory, I have to introduce another important phrase: entailment mesh. An entailment mesh is a method of representing the relational nature of one's memory. It is related to a whole host of visualizations like concept maps or brain maps. Why bother with a fancy phrase? Well, for one thing, to keep us in line with Conversation Theory, but more important, for precision. What's in your head stays there. Although there is a lot of good research from cognitive psychology to neuroscience that attempts to understand precisely how memories are stored in the brain, Conversation Theory does not. It is much more concerned with how these relationships are expressed, particularly in analog and digital systems. Whenever you create a representation of the memory (try to show how things are connected), you are creating an entailment mesh.

RELATED ARTIFACTS

Wikipedia entry on Conversation Theory: http://en.wikipedia.org/wiki/Conversation_theory

Todd Marshall has put together this bibliography on Conversation Theory and the works of Gordon Pask:

Bechtel, J. M. (1986). Conversation, a new paradigm for librarianship? *College & Research Libraries, 47*(3), 219–224.

Bernard, S. (1980). The cybernetics of Gordon Pask. *International Cybernetics Newsletter, 17*, 327–336.

Fisher, K. M. (2001). Overview of knowledge mapping. *Mapping Biology Knowledge*, pp. 5–23.

Ford, N. (2004). Modeling cognitive processes in information seeking: From Popper to Pask. *Journal of the American Society for Information Science and Technology, 55*(9), 769–782.

Ford, N. (2005). "Conversational" information systems: Extending educational informatics support for the web-based learner. *Journal of Documentation, 61*(3), 362–384.

Glanville, R. (1993). Pask: A slight primer. *Systems Research, 10*(3), 213–218.

Lankes, R. D., Silverstein, J. L., & Nicholson, S. (2007). *Participatory networks: The library as conversation.* Technical Report. Information Institute of Syracuse, Syracuse, NY.

Lankes, R. D., Silverstein, J. L., Nicholson, S., & Marshall, T. (2007). Participatory networks: The library as conversation. *Information Research, 12*(4). Retrieved from http://InformationR.net/ir/12-4/colis/colis05.html

Laurillard, D. (1999). A conversational framework for individual learning applied to the "learning organization" and the "learning society." *Systems Research and Behavioral Science, 16*(2), 113–122.

McKeen, J., Guimaraes, T., & Wetherbe, J. (1994). The relationship between user participation and user satisfaction: An investigation of four contingency factors. *MIS Quarterly, 18*(4), 427–451.

Pask, G. (1975). *Conversation, cognition and learning: A cybernetic theory and methodology.* Elsevier: Amsterdam.

Pask, G. (1996). Heinz von Foerster's self organization, the progenitor of conversation and interaction theories. *Systems Research, 13*(3), 349–362.

Patel, A., Kinshuk, & Russell, D. (2002). Implementing cognitive apprenticeship and conversation theory in interactive web-based learning systems. *Sixth Multi-Conference on Systemics, Cybernetics and Informatics. International Institute of Informatics and Systemics*, 523–528.

Pimentel, D. M. (2007). Exploring classification as conversation. In Tennis, J. T., Eds., Proceedings North American Symposium on Knowledge Organization, 1, 1–8, Toronto, Ontario. Retrieved at http://dlist.sir.arizona.edu/1893/

Scott, B. (1993). Working with Gordon: Developing and applying conversation theory (1968–1978). *Systems Research, 10*(3), 167–182.

Scott, B. (2001). Cybernetics and the social sciences. *Systems Research and Behavioral Science, 18*(5), 411–420.

Thomas, L., & and Harri-Augstein, S. (1993). Gordon Pask at Brunel: A continuing conversation about conversations. *Systems Research, 10*(3), 183–192.

Wenger, E. (1998). *Communities of practice: Learning, meaning and identity.* New York: Cambridge University Press.

CORE SKILLS

MAP LOCATION

B, 8

THREAD LOCATION

Page 137

SCAPE

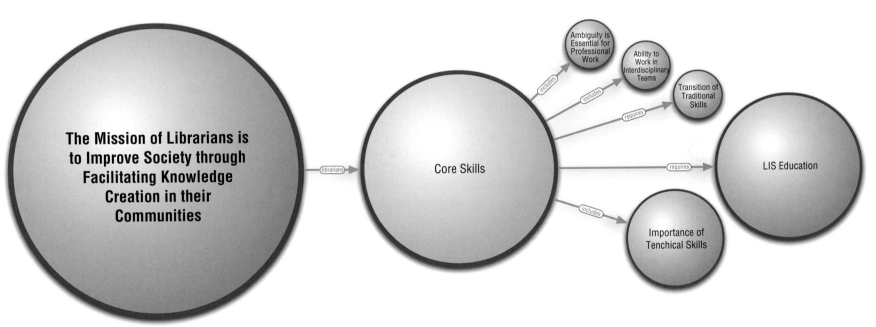

Figure 109

CORE VALUES

MAP LOCATION
G, 3

THREAD LOCATION
Page 119

SCAPE

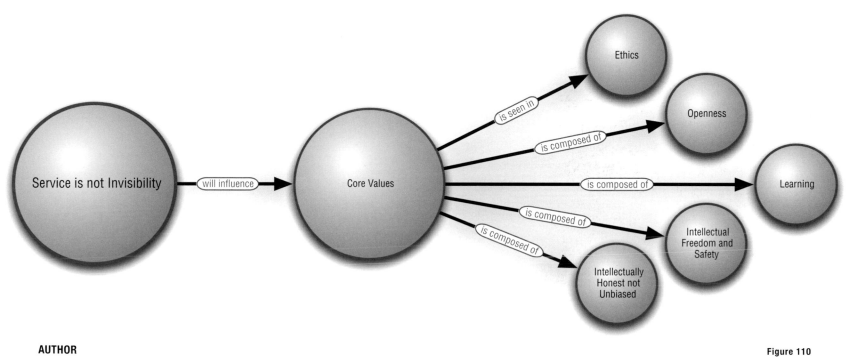

AUTHOR
Kelly Menzel, Nancy Lara-Grimaldi

Figure 110

AGREEMENT DESCRIPTION

The Atlas states that we still live in a condition of information scarcity, but it is no longer that information that is the scarce thing—it is our ability to absorb and make sense of information that—to build knowledge—that is scarce. Michael Goreman (2000) mirrors this statement when he speaks of the relative differences between today's society and American society in the late 19th century. He speaks of the proliferation of materials, the sudden and numerous technological advances, the question of what to do with all of the new materials, how to catalog them, how to provide access, and so on.[1] "In all probability," he states, "the largest single difference in a late 20th-century life, compared with a late 19th-century life, is lack of repose and opportunity for repose."[2] Many of the questions asked are about how to run a library. He argues that the core values should be the same as those asked in the latter part of the 19th century.

Many letters, communications, and editorials in the *Library Journal* in the earliest years of the 20th century were concerned with new techniques, methods, and applications of machinery. The same articles and pages also carry much rumination on the implications of what they saw as a great rate of change in the profession and in service to the growing and changing population.[3]

Regardless of the point in time, librarians have always struggled to accomplish the same things and held the same things as core values. So, what has changed since then? According to Goreman, we simply have less time to wade through all of the information being produced. Without "the opportunity for repose," people are bombarded by too many items to look at and often too many to even keep track of. That is when people give up. The question, then, is how we as librarians should apply our age-old core values to today's society to help a society with too much information and not enough time. Should we add efficiency as a new core value despite that, as the Atlas points out, it was deliberately not included in it after Dewey's obsession with the topic?[4] Being more efficient would certainly aid in slogging through all of the information and making it easier for our members to find what they need when they want it. Such a core value, however, would likely interfere with other core values, such as service. The most efficient service is often not the same as the best service.

RELATED ARTIFACTS

American Library Association. (2004). *Core Values of Librarianship*. Retrieved from http://www.ala.org/ala/aboutala/offices/oif/statementspols/corevaluesstatement/corevalues.cfm.

Andrew L, Bouwhuis Library. (n.d.). *Andrew L. Bouwhuis Library*. Retrieved November 7, 2009, from http://library.canisius.edu.

Goreman, M. (2001). Human values in a technological age: A librarian looks 100 years forward and backward [Electronic version]. *Logos, 12*(2), 63–69.

O'Gorman, J., & Trott, B. (2009). What will become of reference in academic and public libraries? *Journal of Library Administration, 49*(4), 327–339. Retrieved from doi:10.1080/01930820902832421.

Special Libraries Association. (2003). *Vision, Mission and Core Value Statements*. Retrieved from http://www.sla.org/content/SLA/AssnProfile/slanplan/index.cfm.

Tolley-Stokes, R. (2009). Try on a new pair of sensible shoes. *College & Research Libraries News, 70*(5), 288–291. Retrieved from Library, Information Science & Technology Abstracts database.

Vargas, M. (2009). Aligning core values to a philosophy of service. *Catholic Library World, 79*(4), 276–278. Retrieved from Library, Information Science & Technology Abstracts database.

---

1. Goreman, M. (2001). Human values in a technological age: a librarian looks 100 years forward and backward [Electronic version]. *Logos, 12*(2), 63–69.
2. Goreman, M. (2001). Human values in a technological age: A librarian looks 100 years forward and backward [Electronic version]. *Logos, 12*(2), 67.
3. Goreman, M. (2001). Human values in a technological age: A librarian looks 100 years forward and backward [Electronic version]. *Logos, 12*(2), 67.
4. Atlas, 155.

CREATING A NEW SOCIAL COMPACT

MAP LOCATION
F, 6

THREAD LOCATION
Page 28

SCAPE

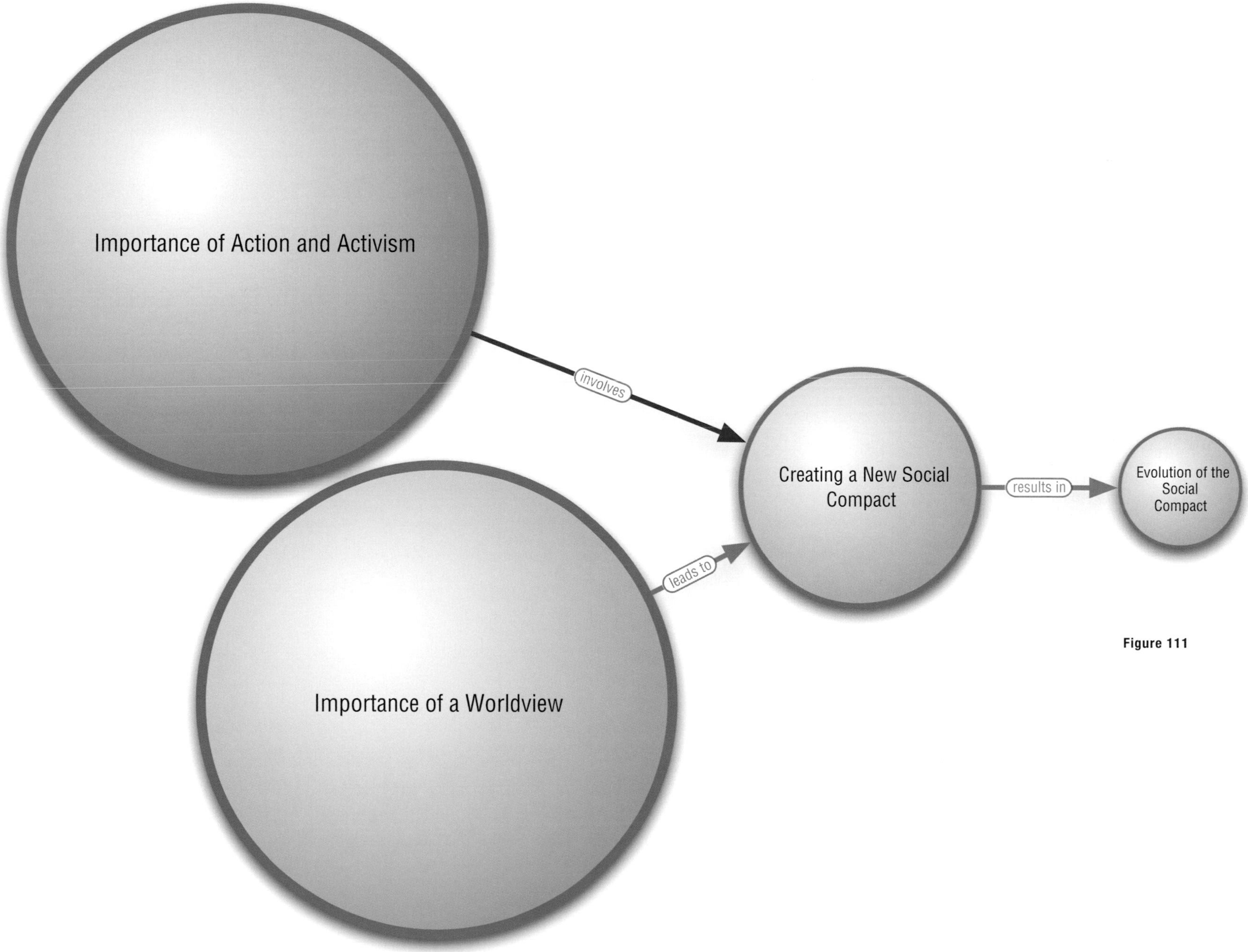

Importance of Action and Activism

involves

Creating a New Social Compact

results in

Evolution of the Social Compact

leads to

Importance of a Worldview

Figure 111

CONTRIBUTOR

Amy Leigh Edick

CONVERSATION STARTERS

1. Who gets to pick what the social compact will be?
2. Is it the right choice?

RELATED ARTIFACTS

Andrews, J. G. (2006). How we can resist corporatization. *Academe, 92(*3), 16–20.

Anonymous. (2004). What is the future of the social compact? *The Presidency, 7*(3), 13.

Cherwitz, R. A. (2005). A new social compact demands real change. *Change, 37*(6), 48–49.

Gargarella, R., & Gilabert, P. (2008). Lectures on the history of political philosophy. *Social Theory and Practice, 34*(4), 640–647.

Stone, D. (2009). Single payer—Good metaphor, bad politics. *Journal of Health Politics, Policy and Law, 34*(4), 531.

CREATING AN AGENDA

MAP LOCATION

F, 7

THREAD LOCATION

Page 129

SCAPE

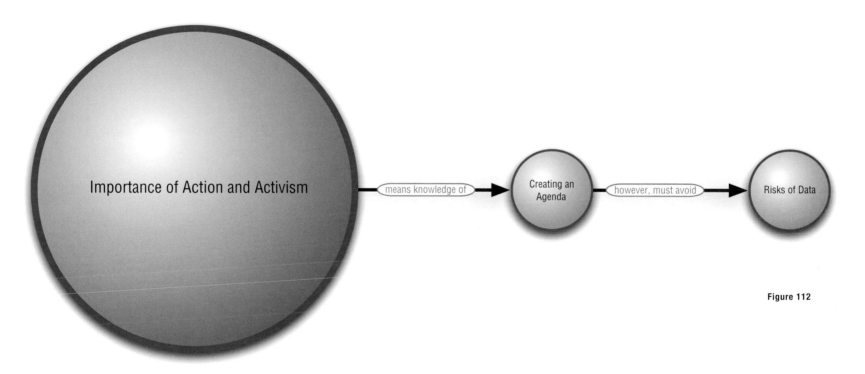

Figure 112

CREDIBILITY

MAP LOCATION
F, 3

THREAD LOCATIONS
Pages 24, 90

SCAPE

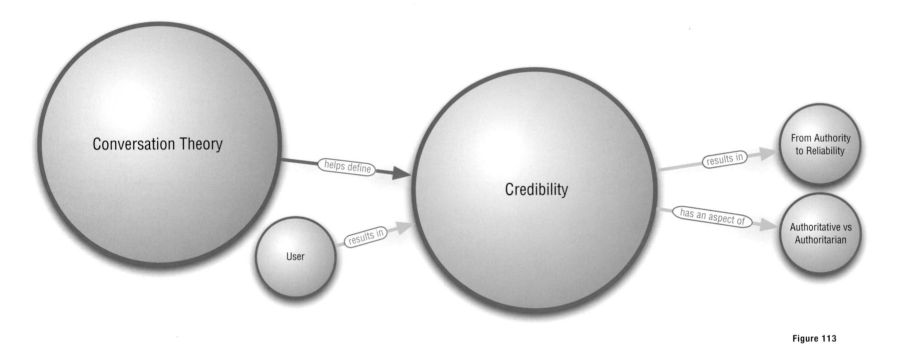

Figure 113

CURRICULUM OF COMMUNICATION AND CHANGE OVER TRADITIONAL IDEAS OF LEADERSHIP

MAP LOCATION

D, 7, 8

THREAD LOCATION

Page 180

SCAPE

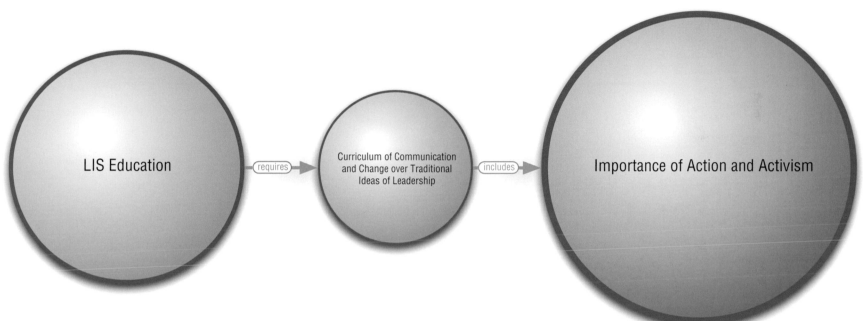

LIS Education —requires→ Curriculum of Communication and Change over Traditional Ideas of Leadership —includes→ Importance of Action and Activism

Figure 114

DEATH OF DOCUMENTS

MAP LOCATION

F,G, 2

THREAD LOCATION

Page 44

SCAPE

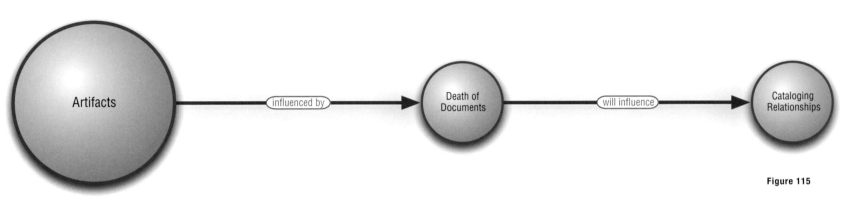

Figure 115

AUTHOR

Jocelyn Clark

CONVERSATION STARTERS

1. What kind of tools are we using to store memories and communicate ideas?
2. As our recorded world becomes more fluid, how do we capture snapshots of it for documentation, memories, or communication of ideas?
3. What is a document anyway?
4. Is the document dying or are certain characteristics of the document dying?

RELATED ARTIFACTS

Documents

What is a document and is it even a useful definition? Two theoretical views of the definition of a "document" are found in the following sources:

Frohmann, B. (2009). Revisiting "What is a document?" *Journal of Documentation, 65*(2), 291–303.

Stone, D. (1997). What is a "document"? *Journal of the American Society of Information Science, 48*(9), 804.

THE CHANGING WORLD OF PUBLISHING

There is a lot of discussion in the world about the decline of newspaper publishing, the decline of the independent bookstore, and the growth of self-publishing on blogs, wikis, social media, and bulletin boards. Many journal articles are now accessed more frequently online through fee-based databases. In addition, the world of direct access publishing is increasing.

DECLINE OF NEWSPAPERS

kxan. (2009, April 17). *Paul Steiger addresses the future of newspapers.* Video posted to http://www.youtube.com/watch?v=fwA2Ego5BW0.

Perez-Pena, R. (2008, October 28). Newspaper circulation continues to decline rapidly. *New York Times.* Retrieved from http://www.nytimes.com/2008/10/28/business/media/28circ.html.

Who killed the newspaper? (2006, August 24). *The Economist.* Retrieved from http://www.economist.com/opinion/displayStory.cfm?Story_ID=7830218.

Change in Publishing

Rich, M. (2009, January 28). Self-publishers flourish as writers pay the tab. *New York Times*. Retrieved from http://www.nytimes.com/2009/01/28/books/28selfpub.html.

Predictions of the Death of the Book or the Ultimate Failure of the eBook

There seem to be dueling theories about the ultimate success or failure of the paper-based book as an artifact. Will the paper or the ebook win out in the end? Does it matter? How does the business model of publishers change as the format changes?

Gomez, J. (2008). *Print is dead: Books in our digital age*. London: Macmillan.

> Contends that printed books will be replaced by digital books and that book distributors and readers should actively support the transformation by encouraging digital book creation and the standards required for storage and delivery.

jlaccetti (2007, April 18). *Digitise or die: Margaret Atwood*. Video posted to http://www.youtube.com/watch?v=5GUJ4uA7G2w.

Levy, D. M. (2001). *Scrolling forward: Making sense of documents in the digital age*. New York: Arcade.

Marsh, S. D. (n.d.). *The death of the book*. Retrieved from http://www.marshillreview.com/extracts/mash.shtm

Weinberger, D. (1998, March 19). The death of documents and the end of doneness. *Journal of the Hyperlinked Ogranization*. Retrieved from http://www.hyperorg.com/backissues/joho-march19-98.html#death.

Changing Permanence

Documents that exist in the digital world can be much less permanent than paper-based documents. Related concepts include: perpetual beta, living (or evergreen) documents, and continuous improvement. All of these ideas point to the concept of impermanence. Content that exists in a particular form one day may not exist in that format the next day. Efforts to increase permanence such that accessibility to ideas is maintained require that time is stopped occasionally such that a snapshot can be kept as a record. More important is that today's library cataloguing routines are difficult to apply to documents that won't stand still. How do you catalog an artifact that won't remain in existence?

Bowker, G. C. (2005). *Memory practices in the sciences (Inside technology)*. Cambridge, MA: MIT Press.

Internet Archives: Wayback Machine. Retrieved from http://www.archive.org/web/web.php.

Business Document Management Systems

Although paper books, newspapers, and other printed material may be decreasing, the business world is turning to digital document and content management systems to augment their communication and documentation processes. For years, there have been Paperless Society/Paperless Office utopia theories. In contrast, requirements for record-keeping seem to be increasing.

Ragnet, F. (n.d.). *The future of documents*. Retrieved from http://futureofdocuments.blogs.xerox.com.

Document Management Software for Project Managers and Business Examples

Ademero. (n.d.). Retrieved from http://www.ademero.com.

Knowledge tree. (n.d.). Retrieved from http://www.knowledgetree.com.

Other Topics of Interest Relative to Document Management in the Business World

Content management, digital documentation, knowledge management systems, information delivery systems, and more.

Increasing Access to Digital Resources and Digital Archives

Services like Google books and the Project Gutenberg are increasing digital access to archival materials at the same time that current book publishing is decreasing. Access to these documents is no longer facilitated by or dependent on the library archives. In contrast, these archives are now partly dependent on commercial ventures, which have both benefits and costs.

American Libraries. (n.d.). In *Internet Archive*. Retrieved from http://www.archive.org/details/americana.

Google Books. (n.d.). Retrieved from http://books.google.com.

Main Page. (n.d.) In *ProjectGutenberg wiki*. Retrieved from http://www.gutenberg.org/wiki/Main_Page.

Materiality of Communicative Practices

Researchers in communication theory are also dealing with the impact of technology on established communication practices. The idea of "boundary objects" is explored.

Osterlund, C. (2008). The materiality of communicative practices: The boundaries and objects of an emergency room genre. *Scandinavian Journal of Information Systems, 20*(1), 7–40. Retrieved from http://iris.cs.aau.dk/index.php/volume-20-40200841-no-1.html.

DEMOCRACY AND OPENNESS OVERSHADOWED BY TECHNOLOGY

MAP LOCATION

F,G, 6

THREAD LOCATION

Page 126

SCAPE

Figure 116

AUTHOR

Andrea Phelps

AGREEMENT DESCRIPTION

In this Thread, Lankes (2009) compares the idea of participatory librarianship to that of liberal (or participatory) democracy. "Liberal democracy" is defined by Encarta as "a political system that has free elections, a multiplicity of political parties, political decisions made through an independent legislature, and an independent judiciary, with a state monopoly on law enforcement." A similar definition for participatory democracy can be found on AllWords.com. Two excellent and well-known quotes from Thomas Jefferson and James Madison highlight in particular the importance of knowledge and access to information to a liberal democracy. The potential for library involvement, then, should be fairly obvious.

The biggest problem, Buschman argues, is that librarians aren't really doing anything to capitalize on this opportunity. Librarians are generally calling on the grand ideals of Jefferson and Madison to show their importance in a democratic nation but not actually concerning themselves with ways to bring the idea into action (Buschman, 2007, p. 1484). To start librarians thinking more about how they can bolster democracy, Buschman presents a few ideas put forth by scholars in a number of fields that can help guide librarians to doing more for democracy than just providing access to information.

The first idea is heavily tied to the Atlas's focus on conversation and is also the easiest concept to incorporate into a library setting. Buschman claims that Jürgen Habermas presents democracy as rooted in conversation, and that public places are where these important discussions happened and continue to happen. Further, he claims that some of these previously existing places for discussion, namely mass media, are no longer the freely public forums they once were (Buschman, 2007, p. 1487). The other big concept presented by Buschman is that "an institution cannot foster democracy without practicing it" (p. 1493), which echoes the Atlas' discussion of the importance of community interaction and decisions in libraries.

As Michael Buckland (2008) points out in response to Buschman's article, libraries aren't important just for developing a democracy but also other political structures and beliefs (p. 1534). Does a library need to practice all modes of government in some way to appropriately foster those methods? Not to do so is another form of bias on the librarians' part, and there are plenty of people who feel there are better forms of government out there than democracy.

It is not only impossible to be completely unbiased as a librarian; it may be harmful in building trust with library members. Jill Hurst-

Wahl (2009) recently wrote about how the key to earning trust in a social network setting is to behave normally and be yourself; it makes sense that the same thing may be true for in-person interactions. Yet the same is certainly true for the other extreme. If we let ourselves get too involved or become too fanatic in our jobs, we may lose that hard-earned respect and trust.

There are ways in which librarians can encourage democracy and debate without getting too deeply involved, and the Progressive Librarians Guild can be a great resource for ideas. Michele Sipley (2003) presents a number of ways to covertly encourage discussion in a school library setting, including working with teachers to set up debates by students, holding question-and- answer sessions, teaching critical thinking, and more. These ideas can be translated to other settings, such as public libraries, where there can be space for local politicians or groups to debate topics.

There are also ways for librarians to actively take a stand, the best examples of which are tied to the PATRIOT Act. Emily Drabinski (2006) looks at a number of ways in which librarians were affected by the PATRIOT Act and what they did to fight back. For more aggressive activism for democracy, Chris Gaunt (2004) describes her personal experiences with nonviolent dissent outside of the librarian setting.

CONVERSATION STARTERS

1. How should librarians move beyond the idea that libraries support a democracy by supplying information? What else can we do to create a democratic space?
2. What shouldn't we do (or what is too much and too biased and should be avoided)? How far can we go before it is considered not our place or that we are opening an unnecessary can of worms that is making things worse? Can we ethically do more than provide a place for a discussion by participating heavily in the conversations?
3. Is activism such as Gaunt's appropriate within a library setting? Or is that something only to be pursued as an individual? Can your personal activism really be separated from you as a librarian? Too much activism may have a negative effect on trust and respect from the community and could seriously impact a library's role in the community.
4. What should be the role of technology in promoting democratic environments in libraries? Is technology in this instance any dif-

ferent than it is normally? The same sorts of downfalls mentioned here are common in any instructive use of technology: too much focus on the tool rather than the material and ideas behind it, not using the right tool for the purpose, not marketing it appropriately to the audience, and so on.

RELATED ARTIFACTS

Buckland, M. K. (2008). Democratic theory in library information science. *Journal of the American Society for Information Science and Technology, 59*(9), 1534. Retrieved from doi:10.1002/asi.20846.

Buschman, J. (2007). Democratic theory in library information science: Toward an emendation. *Journal of the American Society for Information Science and Technology, 58*(10), 1483–1496. Retrieved from doi:10.1002/asi.20634.

Definition of participatory democracy. (n.d.). *AllWords.com*. Retrieved November 8, 2009, from http://www.allwords.com/word-participatory+democracy.html.

Drabinski, E. (2006). Librarians and the Patriot Act. *Radical Teacher, 77*, 12–14. Retrieved from Omni File Full Text Mega database.

Gaunt, C. (2004). Jailed for dissent "in these times." *Progressive Librarian, 24*, 41–49. Retrieved from http://libr.org/pl/24_Gaunt.html.

Hurst-Wahl, J. (2009, October 31). *Lose control & gain credibility*. Message posted to http://www.enetworking101.com/blog/2009/10/lose-control-gain-credibility.html.

Liberal democracy definition. (n.d.). *MSN Encarta Dictionary*. Retrieved November 8, 2009, from http://encarta.msn.com/dictionary_1861696490/liberal_democracy.html.

Sipley, M. (2003). Operation–Patriots Act: The role of school libraries in promoting a free and informed society. *Progressive Librarian, 22*, 52–62. Retrieved from http://libr.org/pl/22_Sipley.html.

DEPARTMENT OF JUSTICE

MAP LOCATION

E, 6

THREAD LOCATION

Page 105

SCAPE

Figure 117

AUTHOR

R. David Lankes

AGREEMENT DESCRIPTION

The following report is based on a series of visits to the Department of Justice (DOJ), February 13–15, 2008. During these visits, several conversations took place among the researcher, librarians, and library clients within different sections of the DOJ and in several DOJ libraries. An initial draft of this report was then provided to the Department for feedback. This revised report briefly outlines the observations in each of these conversations. It attempts to highlight opportunities and provide an outsider's reaction to these conversations given a narrow window of engagement. The emphasis in all of this is on the ability/role of DOJ librarians to facilitate these conversations.

What emerged from the visits was the beginning of a planning process based on participatory librarianship and conversations. Although the principles of participatory librarianship have been used to present an overall vision of library systems (Lankes et al., 2007) and to develop library software (Lankes, 2008) and services, a clear method for planning and evaluating library services holistically has yet to be developed. Although this case does not directly present such a methodology, it does point to one. From the case, the approach would be to:

1. Identify major participatory communities within the service community.
2. Identify and describe the major conversations within and across these communities.
3. Identify the services and resources provided by the library to these conversations (later this needs to be refined into means of facilitation).
4. Look for gaps (where the library could but is not providing facilitation), dead ends (where the library is providing a service not linked to conversations within a community), and opportunities (where the library could provide service to a community's conversation but is not).

In the case example below, three participatory conversations were identified. Within a key community (legal staff), a high-level conversation was identified (the "life of the law"). A basic mapping was done (figure 1). Certain opportunities to provide better facilitation were identified as well (e.g., the "In Search of" process for lawyers and the extranet for the librarians).

This initial approach was used as part of a strategic retreat process at a small academic library with some success. Although clearly great specificity and data are needed to firm up this planning process, this case study serves as a first step.

CAVEATS AND LIMITATIONS

Several caveats are important to note. Three days and a handful of focus groups are far from adequate to capture the richness of any organization. The best that can be hoped for are initial observations and to capture broad themes and ideas. Although much of this report is written in an authoritative tone (i.e., making assertions and generalizations), that is simply a device to prompt further discussion. The idea is to prompt and provoke. This often leads to richer conversation rather than a more cautious and nuanced tone. So although there aren't many "the research thinks," "it might be," or "one would guess" phrases within, they are implied.

The initial result of this visit was a chart of the "A Participatory View of the Department of Justice Libraries" in figure 118. This chart seeks to capture the different conversations occurring from the library perspective. It is far from complete, but it attempts to capture broad areas of understanding.

PARTICIPATORY COMMUNITIES

There appears to be four major participatory communities. These communities represent groups of people talking about similar things in similar fashions. They share processes and concerns. Certainly within the communities there are a lot of different voices with different roles (lawyers, managers, paralegals). Also, there are certainly communities not addressed in the visit (policymakers, IT, etc.). Why bother talking about communities? Why not simply use the standard breakdown of library and patrons? Because in a participatory approach, the library's role is to facilitate communities' conversations. They must understand the dynamics of the communities regardless of whether those interactions are with the library. Also, in any attempt to increase the quality of participation (conversations) within the communities, and thus improve the knowledge of these communities, one must respect the norms, cultures, and structures of these communities. Simply put, why would lawyers want to participate in library systems when they are part of a different community altogether? If libraries want to build effective conversations, they must do so in as close alignment to com-munities as possible (including building systems within the communities rather than within the library).

For example, within the legal staff, there is not much discussion or concern with how case files are managed. It seems that most lawyers keep a set of files in a series of folders on their desktops. There is no standardized way of storing these data. Clearly, how these files are stored is of great interest to librarians. From a library perspective, capturing these data, organizing them, and providing them back to customers is of high priority, but to the legal staff it is not. Thus, if librarians were to attempt to capture these data to build new services, they would find great resistance on the part of legal staff. Why? Because to the legal staff, once all of these data are used to file a formal courts document (such as a brief), the world of documents around that formal document becomes nearly irrelevant. If it is not in the brief, it is not important. If the library deems it important to capture and organize this information, it does so by having a conversation internally to its own community. If it wants to get lawyers on board, it will have to make a strong case based on the norms and in the language of the legal staff.

In the site visits, five communities became apparent:

1. *Legal Staff* Lawyers and support staff are well versed in the formal conversations of the law. From formal filings to informal searching on databases, there is a high-level understanding of a general process: understand the legislative intent of a given law, build a brief that captures both the facts and the theory of the case, and understand the life of the law including precedents, decisions, and related legislative action. The conversations of the legal staff are in many cases formal and regulated. Not every case will include "Legislative Intent" formally. There are also many informal conversations happening between litigators.

2. *DOJ Librarians* The librarians in the Department of Justice form a community that regularly exchanges information, techniques, and resources. However, although there is a clear desire to provide outstanding service, much of how this service should be delivered remains an open question. With little to no data on actual service utilization, service priorities and decisions are often based on individual success, anecdotes, and personal philosophies. This makes it difficult to truly gauge the effectiveness of services.

3. *Database Vendors* Hein, Westlaw, and LexisNexis constitute the core databases for the legal profession and are clearly needed across the enterprise. However, each section has its own key re-

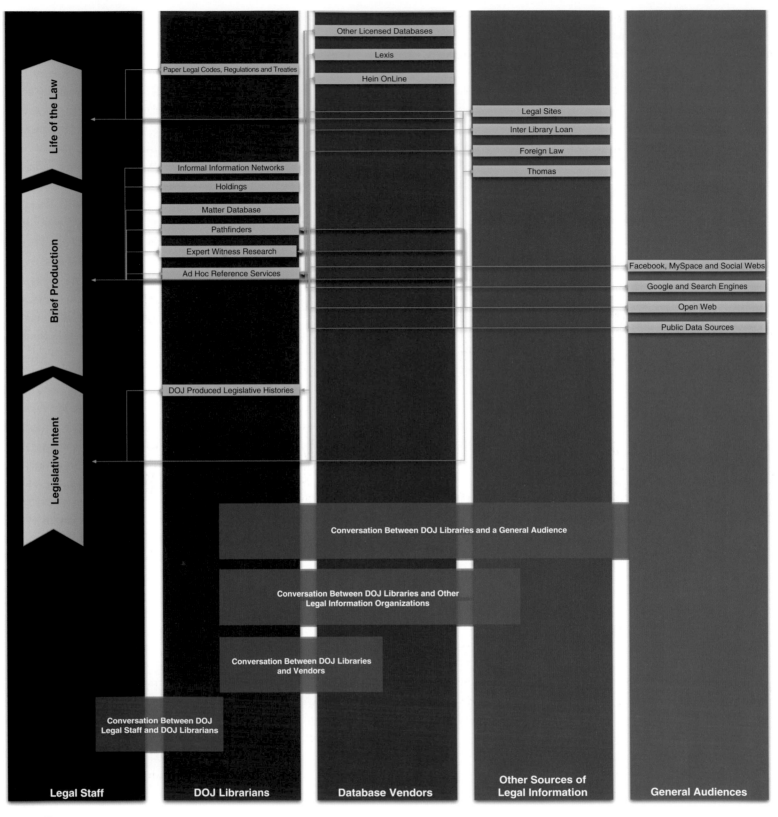

Legal Staff

DOJ Librarians

Database Vendors

Other Sources of
Legal Information

General Audiences

Life of the Law

Brief Production

Legislative Intent

Other Licensed Databases

Lexis

Hein OnLine

Paper Legal Codes, Regulations and Treaties

Legal Sites

Inter Library Loan

Foreign Law

Thomas

Informal Information Networks

Holdings

Matter Database

Pathfinders

Expert Witness Research

Ad Hoc Reference Services

Facebook, MySpace and Social Webs

Google and Search Engines

Open Web

Public Data Sources

DOJ Produced Legislative Histories

Conversation Between DOJ Libraries and a General Audience

Conversation Between DOJ Libraries and Other
Legal Information Organizations

Conversation Between DOJ Libraries
and Vendors

Conversation Between DOJ
Legal Staff and DOJ Librarians

Figure 118

sources. There is great competition between these vendors with little information sharing.

4. *Other Sources of Legal Information*   This disparate group consists of other law libraries, legal research centers, other law firms, and a wide variety of other players. There are some formal means of communications, such as AALL, but there are also structural issues in creating formal connections (privacy of case matters, competitive advantage, proprietary information, and billing structures).

5. *General Audiences*   This is not a formal community by any means. Rather, it is the open information environment that the Department of Justice exists within. It is constantly changing and has little coherence.

Within these communities, there are opportunities for the library to improve service and to better facilitate knowledge building. Which, if any, of these opportunities the libraries pursue is a matter of internal priorities and resources, although a few recommendations are made.

It should also be noted that it is in the intersection of these communities (and of conversations across communities) that most of the opportunities for improved library service lie. Therefore, in the discussion of the communities, special note shall be made of these cross-community collaborations.

Legal Staff (A Litigating Section)

There is an interesting dichotomy of knowledge creation and capture that occurs within litigating sections. On the one hand, there are formal processes of documenting knowledge and conversations. Legal rules of disclosure, brief production, and case filings force lawyers to make most knowledge explicit. On the other hand, there is a much larger volume of information or "research" that is gathered and created in the process of brief development. Along the process of creating a brief, there seems to be an accumulation of information until a "theory of the case" is developed. Once this is developed, materials are loosely organized into folders and subfolders. Some of this material might make it into an archiving process, but much remains in the heads of lawyers and other legal staff. It also seems that most information organization is case-oriented. All data are gathered and associated with cases with little larger topical-oriented organization.

It would appear there is a great need for an organizational system for lawyers to keep case-oriented information, plus the rich world of research around a case. Right now librarians capture some of this in

pathfinders and informal files on experts but only when the legal staff comes to the library for information and assistance.

This is not to say that there aren't some attempts at a more section-wide organization of cases and knowledge. One litigating section talked about their "In Search Of" ("ISO") process. ISO is a means of section lawyers asking for information from others in their section. Throughout the day, legal staff send requests for information (who has dealt with topic X, has anyone used X as an expert witness, etc.) to a secretary. Twice a day, the secretary bundles up the requests and sends out a section-wide e-mail with the questions. Answers are then sent from legal staff to legal staff with no attempts to match questions with answers section-wide. Mid-level supervisors also serve as repositories of organizational knowledge/history. Another mechanism to share knowledge within a division is a "matter" database. This informal system attempts to capture cases and legal matters currently under consideration by a division.

The informality and patchwork nature of these section-wide conversations seems to be the result of several factors. The first is the need for confidentiality in the cases under consideration. Some cases and issues are too sensitive to be made known widely (indeed topics may not go beyond the lawyers directly involved in the topic). However, this need varies widely across sections, with many sections having virtually no such prohibitions. The other factor relates to the nature of the cases under consideration. Some sections work on a relatively small domain of issues where sharing information yields great dividends, whereas a section dealing with a wide variety of cases would find little overlap in lawyer knowledge.

Librarians as Investigators

It is worth noting an interesting idea that emerged in how some of the legal staff saw the role of librarians. Clearly, librarians have gained great success in specializing in research concerning expert witnesses. Librarians also appear to have a great opportunity in situating themselves directly into the legal process. Several times the idea of librarians working closely on a case—whether in terms of providing direct evidence or aiding the development of case theory—was mentioned. In these circumstances, lawyers attributed the success of cases directly to the aid of library staff. In the case of anti-trust, this even developed into real staff resources.

The idea of librarians as civil investigators was raised several times. Whereas in criminal cases DOJ provides investigatory staff or agents, in civil cases this is not always the case. Civil lawyers mentioned using librarians in this capacity to discover evidence and materials pertinent to the case. This seemed to go beyond expert witness research and was seen as a much closer relationship between lawyer and librarian. It seems this kind of relationship is worth special scrutiny (and promotion) in any follow-up activity.

Recommendations

There is a great opportunity for the librarians in the department-wide case management initiative. Although development and implementation of the electronic case management system may well be beyond the resources, expertise, and authority of the DOJ libraries, they should be a part of the overall process. By having librarians "at the table" in the development of this system, the libraries can ensure a presence in the system likely to become the most used interface in the Department. Beyond this tactical concern, librarians have a great deal to offer system creators in terms of information management and reuse. By both better understanding the processes lawyers must use, being more visible to litigators in this process, and helping ensure good information practice, DOJ librarians can have a large and positive impact on the system. One approach might be to create an institutional repository that looks like a law review journal or some other format lawyers would use on a regular basis.

Such a system would also allow for new services to provide feedback into the legal community. For example, the "Brief Bank" currently offers exemplary briefs to lawyers. It would be interesting to analyze these briefs and return the results to litigating sections. One could imagine a sort of reverse citation analysis where litigators get feedback on which items are cited the most in briefs (legal codes, cases, but more important, bodies of evidence and current thinking). Analyzing the information sources and people DOJ lawyers use might provide interesting data back to divisions. They could see what sources they depend on regularly, detect any biases in sources, learn about new resources, and identify seminal cases in the making. This might be a good partnership with the Bureau of Justice Statistics. Such an initiative also aligns to the purpose of the Brief Bank. If DOJ is concerned with consistency in approach, policy, and documentation, the library can provide a vital bibliographic check toward this end.

DOJ Librarians

The DOJ librarians have an excellent reputation among the groups participating in the visit. They are proactive and engaged. They are also clearly dedicated to service. There are, however, three areas for improvement that stood out when looking at them as a group. Librarians appear to be risk averse, manually oriented, and data poor. Once again, this is an aggregate view with individual exceptions. Let us take each in turn.

By and large, DOJ librarians are risk averse. This is a result of the DOJ culture and the nature of the practice of law. It is natural and right for all members of a legal enterprise to be acutely concerned with disclosing too much information. Librarians naturally do not want to be the source of a leak, to make their legal clients look bad, or to be accused of undermining the core litigation activities. Far from being a negative, this shows keen understanding of the culture. However, it clearly creates some conflict between librarian principles of openness and the large DOJ culture. Librarians also seem to fail to take into account that the lawyers act as the gatekeepers and either make the necessity of confidentiality clear to librarians or do not disclose confidential information in the first place. The result is that the librarians are hesitant to share anything outside of the firewall even when they have clear ability to do so. Currently, librarians default to not sharing and going outside the firewall without formally examining the issues.

These issues have been brought up in terms of sharing legislative histories, but the more interesting case might be expert witness databases. DOJ librarians have been successful in building their reputations and utility by becoming master searchers in terms of expert witnesses. Librarians scour the web, databases, and other information sources for an expert's documents, thoughts, and profile. The result is information that then goes to legal staff. However, experts are often used repeated times or by multiple parties. One could imagine capturing all of these expert resources into a central repository for a section. A strategy might be the development of a high-level expert database that does little more than identify an expert, a general area of expertise, and a case they were associated with. This way a lawyer could quickly find out whether an expert had been used before and by whom without the risk of maintaining extensive files of citizens. However, librarians are wary to create such a database, worried that it could be requested under FOIA and might reveal legal strategy. They may well be right, but has the question ever been formally asked? By defaulting to an "If in doubt, don't" default position, the librarians may be holding back useful services unnecessarily.

The second characteristic found was a reliance on highly manual processes. This can be most clearly seen in terms of the DOJ Virtual Library and the pathfinders on the site. These pages are static and require manual link checking, editing, and updating. This results in a lot of extra labor in maintaining the site and lost opportunities that a more sophisticated technical approach might bring (such as SDI-like services or alerts on new/changed resources for interested parties). It is ironic that some of this manual processing stems from the departmental use of PHP. PHP is a web-scripting language created for the explicit purpose of integrating dynamic elements into web pages. The root cause for this manual orientation seems to be a distrust of the IT staff and services. The IT infrastructure is seen as highly buttoned down and antithetical to innovation. This problem seems exacerbated by a near absence of a library IT authority and a previously failed attempt to build a custom acquisitions system. IT authority is not simply technical knowledge that is certainly present in the library but the ability for the library staff to directly control the IT being used. This topic is addressed more deeply in the recommendations.

The last characteristic of DOJ librarians worth noting is the data-poor environment in which they work. This poverty does not relate to the data and information sources used in the practice of librarianship (databases, holdings, etc.), which are vast. Clearly DOJ librarians have done an excellent job making a case for resources. Rather this refers to the evaluative data of service use. Use of data in terms of evaluation, utilization, and even size of patron base simply is not part of the everyday workings of the librarians.

Although there are many good reasons for this near absence of data (lack of time to gather statistics, absence of a circulation system, poor tools to track Web site usage), the end result is that discussions on service priorities come down to persuasiveness of personal arguments and reliance on authority. In other words, when deciding what services to enhance and which to cut, decisions are made by how well someone argues a position, not on actual use and projected impact of the services. In a collegial environment like that of DOJ libraries, these methods can work, but they can also cause friction and division in staff over time.

An example of how all three of these characteristics come into play can be seen in the current discussions around a new integrated library system. The two current ILS systems must be replaced. The question on the table is how to replace these systems. There is currently a perception that the technical service staff and the reference staff have different priorities in terms of replacing these systems. The reference staff sees a need for a different approach to holdings and feels the technical services staff is being too traditional. However, in conversations with the technical service side of the house, the exact

same desires are put forth. No one sees an "off-the-shelf" ILS as ideal. They are cumbersome, lack innovation, are inherently not secure, and take a great amount of effort to maintain. The only thing that all agree on is the value of a good acquisitions system because of the universally agreed-on value of efficiently and effectively licensing resources for the entire agency (not coincidentally, the acquisitions service has the most data available in terms of usage, costs, and overall value to the agency).

In the debate on replacing the catalog, risk aversion, manual process, and data poverty are quickly apparent. There is a strong desire to buy an off-the-shelf solution by the technical staff. Not because these are seen necessarily as the best solutions, but off-the-shelf ILS solutions are the safest in terms of guaranteed delivery of functionality, support of the system, and experience. The technical staff was burned by trying to build custom solutions in the past, and that lesson still remains front and center in the consideration of a new system. In response to the universally perceived deficiencies with the current catalog solutions, librarians have been using manual processes to make up the difference. The Virtual Library is a product of manual work around an inadequate catalog. Yet there is a real question as to the true value of the catalog in the first place. Without data on who is using the catalog, for what, and how often, how can the group make a real plan? It would seem that the primary interface to DOJ holdings for lawyers is the reference librarians. Outside of a few notable exceptions, lawyers ask librarians for materials and don't know or care whether these resources come from a collection, interlibrary loan, or, in some cases, librarians using their own public library cards. By knowing the reality of who uses the catalog versus who uses the Virtual Library, one could decide where to invest resources. If the catalog is indeed used beyond librarians as an inventory system, then using resources to enhance the underlying ILS to be more portal-like makes good sense. However, if it is primarily for librarians, buy the easiest to maintain with a good acquisitions module and be done with it.

Recommendations

One could make a whole host of recommendations to address some of the concerns. However, the fact is that there is a culture in the libraries, and by and large that culture seems to be working. The questions are not really about how to make libraries less risk averse, nor are they about how to gather more data on service utilization (that only helps if someone will attend to the data). What participatory librarianship tells us is that, to further a conversation, people must participate in something that has a useful context and meaning in their daily lives.

So the point is to take something the community already considers important and address issues in that context. The ILS makes an interesting starting context.

First, take the areas on which there seems to be agreement. The new ILS must act more as a portal to a wide range of information beyond physical holdings. Patrons and librarians alike must be able to see a more holistic picture of the services and resources available. What's more, such a system must provide robust backend systems for acquisitions. Further agreed on is that current ILS systems are inadequate or, at the least, represent the priorities of different library types. Current ILS systems already present a security nightmare for the Department and the librarians who have to certify and maintain them. Add to this the complexity of maintaining a full ILS system when only a fraction of current functionality is needed. Plus ILS vendors are busy adding new features in a proprietary manner that will be inapplicable to the DOJ setting, thus increasing the maintenance needs without increasing the system's functionality.

The obvious alternative to purchasing an existing ILS is to build a custom solution, meeting just the needs of DOJ, much as the first OPACs were developed by academic libraries dissatisfied with commercial alternatives. However, past experience has shown how difficult that proposition is (in terms of building custom software for DOJ and in terms of building new library systems in general). There is a third option, and one that might work well for the DOJ setting. Because holdings information is not seen as sensitive data and can be made publically available (indeed, it already is within WorldCat), one could see a hosted solution being utilized. This system would reside outside a firewall and simply be pointed to by DOJ. The acquisitions function could remain a separate function hosted within DOJ.

Several hosted systems are worth looking into, the most notable being OCLC's WorldCat Local. Other possibilities would be to externally host an open source ILS, such as Evergreen or Koha. However, once the idea of hosting a system externally becomes viable, the possible benefits and nature of the system become much more interesting—interesting particularly in terms of addressing questions of risk aversion, manual labor, and data poverty.

What if the librarians evaluated all of their resources in terms of what could be externally hosted? What portions of the Virtual Library, digitized legislative histories, pathfinders, whatever, could safely sit outside of the DOJ firewall? This would be done in conjunction with clearance officers to make policy and boundaries clear, lowering the risk that librarians feel they are taking by sharing information.

Once a sizable external collection can be created in terms of information resources, the infrastructure used to host this library extranet becomes wide open, outside the purview of DOJ IT, allowing the libraries to utilize their own IT skills. With the raft of hosted web solutions available, DOJ librarians could create sophisticated and interactive systems (RSS feeds, blogs, streamed instruction, multimedia pathfinders, shared bookmarks, group wikis) without the constraints of firewall-level lockdown. With today's widely available hosted solutions and open source software, librarians can now build sophisticated web tools with minimal technical knowledge, thus mitigating the issues of manual tool building and maintenance. Further, such tools can have built-in tracking and statistical systems (such as Google Analytics) that will provide rich data on actual use.

These rich reference tools can then be combined with the hosted catalog to create a useful portal system for DOJ staff. Further, given that these resources are already cleared for public consumption, the DOJ libraries can reap the added benefits of better serving tax payers and be seen by peer institutions as taking a leadership role.

Imagine the DOJ extranet: a web-accessible service contributed to and used by law libraries across the country. An extranet is an internally focused web presence hosted outside of the organization—like an "intranet" hosted beyond the firewall. A DOJ lawyer could get onto the site and quickly search across catalog, pathfinders, and database locator materials (and using technologies such as Open URL, perhaps licensed resources) from inside or outside of the firewall. The same lawyer could set up an alert system so as to be notified by e-mail or RSS feed of new materials in their area of practice. Furthermore, law libraries from across the country could add their own pathfinders and materials because they too can benefit from sophisticated hosted solutions outside of their own firewalls. They might also add their holdings information to a true union legal catalog.

Aside from the obvious service benefits of the extranet to the DOJ lawyers and librarians, DOJ libraries take a highly visible leadership position in the legal community. It could also be spun into a great giveback to taxpayers and help address the Department's reputation for secrecy. The project also creates a new continuing innovation opportunity for DOJ librarians. The site can be a testing ground for new services and help teach librarians about new technologies. These technologies may not be directly implemented in the extranet, but they would still have utility.

Take, for example, social networking sites such as MySpace and Facebook. Although it is highly doubtful that DOJ law libraries would build and run a successful social networking site for DOJ lawyers (they don't have the time, the confidentiality of their work precludes participation, etc.), by learning how such sites work, DOJ librarians can enhance their expert witness searching repertoire and teach lawyers how information from such sites can be gathered for use in briefs. The system becomes a context for continuing education. More on this concept is detailed in "Key Recommendations" later.

Database Vendors

Another obvious community that DOJ librarians must be aware of is the loose collection of vendors that create, combine, and sell licensed resources such as databases to DOJ. There is fierce competition among these vendors and little in terms of cooperation. The nature of this community makes it difficult for easy integration of these resources into any portal solution and will necessitate the continued role of librarians in navigating these resources on behalf of the legal staff. However, with the obvious buying power of DOJ and the ability to bring attention to issues in legal information, there may be levers that DOJ libraries can use to prompt vendors to aid DOJ libraries in their work.

Recommendations

The first thing DOJ libraries should do is press database vendors to provide better and more regular statistics in terms of resource use. Although "pay-for-use" databases provide clear data, flat-fee databases do not necessarily provide common and comparable statistics.

It would also be useful to include database vendors in the discussion of the extranet. By allowing vendors to participate in the project, they will gain attention and have the ability to develop general-purpose tools (such as OpenURL resolvers, web services, XML-layer exchanges) that they can use to enhance their own product offerings.

Other Sources of Legal Information

There are many sources of legal information beyond the DOJ and the database vendors. Courts, state agencies, and university law libraries are only a few examples. These examples tend to have well-established communities unto themselves and are easily discoverable. However, there are a host of less formal legal sources, many commercial, that seem to be of value to DOJ librarians in their daily work. In fact, a great deal of effort seems to be spent in locating and evaluating these disparate legal sources.

Recommendations

It would be worth keeping track of which external legal sources are referred to and how often. Beyond interlibrary loan requests, how often do librarians seek out these sources on behalf of legal staff? Such work is the basis of pathfinder development, but more formal examination of these sources may yield interesting patterns of use. Such patterns would be helpful in an extranet project. In this context, such sites could be described and included and also invited to directly contribute information and data once vetted by library staff.

General Audiences

This broad category is a loose community that in reality constitutes the open web and various disciplines from which DOJ staff draw information. It is only seen as a coherent community in that major trends, fads, and technologies emerge in this space that impact DOJ. One need look no further than the rise of large-scale digitization efforts such as Google books. Such a project creates new resources for DOJ to use, but it also creates impressions on the part of some DOJ staff that libraries are becoming less relevant. Such notions are based on a fundamental misperception of what a library is. On several occasions, lawyers raised the idea that libraries are less useful because of increasingly available digital information and the redundancy of print materials. Such cases stood out and the individuals discussed are exceptions, but it does raise the question of how prevalent this idea is beyond the core patrons the library has won over. This of course goes back to issues of measurement data in terms of patron use of resources and how wide the libraries user base truly is within DOJ.

Recommendations

The bottom line is that DOJ libraries are not immune from pressures, misperceptions, and fads promulgated on the open Internet. By knowing its constituency well and being seen as a player on the open web, the DOJ libraries have an excellent opportunity to proactively address and shape these pressures.

Key Recommendations

This report made several recommendations. Some are straightforward: They develop and track more usage data to better aim services and inform decision making of DOJ librarians. This includes DOJ library services (such as reference, Virtual Library usage, catalog usage), as well as external resources usage like use of vendor databases. The other recommendations are more ambitious.

DOJ librarians should look to support informal information networks within the litigating divisions. Replicating the success of the ISO e-mails and matter databases across litigating divisions cam make lawyers more successful and will allow librarians to support and insinuate themselves into these networks to provide better service.

Certainly a much more ambitious project would be to address the need for better case management and knowledge management by lawyers in the litigating sections. Such a system must take into consideration that lawyers often do not realize the utility of research that does not make it into formal briefs and should be made easy for them to use. Rather than building this institutional repository as a sort of "bit bucket," where documents are accessible by author and/or date, the library should look to the format and norms of law journals. Lawyers understand the format, organization, and importance of these document types.

Perhaps the recommendation with the greatest opportunity for immediate impact and service improvement would be the creation of an extranet. By creating an externally hosted and cooperative virtual library with DOJ legal resources and pathfinders (those clearly approved for public consumption), the libraries can raise their visibility, provide more innovative services to their clients, and gain an invaluable testbed for their librarians. The next section details a proposed process for such an initiative.

Building the DOJ Extranet

A librarian logs into a hosted site outside of the DOJ firewall. He or she quickly scans any broken or updated links they are responsible for. By correcting a link, it is instantly corrected in every page using that resource. The librarian can then review any outstanding questions posed by the network of law librarians around the country. The librarian can also quickly see any answers for questions he or she has posed. After a quick read of announcements, he or she uses point-and-click tools to put together a pathfinder on recent legislation. The pathfinder links to public data, a new online legislative history, and links to proprietary information that only patrons with licenses will be able to see. Once the pathfinder is complete, the librarian logs into the DOJ library blog and writes a quick post on the new resource that is put on the home page as well as disseminated via an RSS feed. Finally, the librarian checks in on the online class he or she is taking on ethics and anti-trust.

A few moments later, a DOJ lawyer receives an e-mail alert that a new pathfinder in his or her area is available. The lawyer brings up the new pathfinder and clicks through to a preformulated Westlaw query. Westlaw automatically detects the lawyer is within DOJ's firewall and executes the query seamlessly (had the lawyer been at home, he or she would have been prompted for a password). Finding some relevant additional sources, the lawyer sends an e-mail to his or her librarian, where an ILL request will be done.

The preceding scenario is within reach of the DOJ. Using open source software, existing web services, and minor development effort, such a system can be put in place without substantial investment into custom software development. Further, such a system can be built in conjunction with a number of high-profile partners. What is required? An organizational effort on the part of DOJ libraries, an experimental philosophy, and some resource investment.

The necessary components of such a system would be a hosted open source infrastructure outside of the DOJ firewall. A university would be an ideal home for such as system, but AALL might also provide a home or some other noncommercial, nonadvocacy institution. In any case, it would require a supported piece of hardware with adequate bandwidth and backups.

The DOJ libraries would need to review their existing Virtual Library for a substantial base of resources that could initially populate the public site. Significant work would also need to go into specifying and implementing a hosted inventory/catalog system for the DOJ collections.

The whole project would be presented as an ongoing experiment, seeking reliable service, but stressing innovation over fortification (key documents and resources could be duplicated as static files within DOJ for unexpected downtime). Once this initial base of resources and infrastructure is in place, partners should be sought out to be part of the experiment. States, universities, and other non-commercial legal entities could be prioritized, with vendors being invited to develop new products to enhance and integrate with the public site (much like PubMed).

To explore the possibility of the extranet, a few initial steps should be taken:

1. *Technical Readiness* In most cases, technology should follow needs assessment and concrete planning. However, in the DOJ case, librarians need a better sense of what technical capabilities exist in the open web environment as a means of stimulating

their brainstorming and thinking. Technical readiness will both expose librarians to the possibilities of new technologies as well as establishing their confidence in using and incorporating these technologies. They need to be more at ease with technology development. This could be done online, but perhaps a series of intensive one-day hands-on workshops would be a better idea. In these workshops, they would build technologically enabled pathfinders, blogs, and full-blown sites, increasing their confidence.

2. *Brainstorming*   After technical readiness, librarians can spend time thinking about conversations going on within the library (and externally where applicable) and come up with a vision and mission for the extranet.

3. *Inventory and Policymaking*   With vision in hand, librarians can scour the existing Virtual Library and other library resources to determine what can and cannot reside outside the firewall. In parallel, work needs to begin on implementing a hosted solution for DOJ holdings.

4. *Experimentation*   With a mission in place, a project team can begin work with an external partner or partners on developing functional prototypes of the extranet. These implementations should show the advantages and disadvantages of a hosted open approach. It will also give library staff and clients real systems to react to.

5. *Implementation*   Once prototyping determines the baseline of the extranet, DOJ and partners can go about building and previewing the system. Librarians should be an integral part of the building process, not simply clients consuming someone else's work. They should be given time to work as part of the development team.

6. *Ongoing Education*   Once the system is in place, librarians exploring new or existing technologies and service models can learn and build within the extranet.

While the priorities and realities of the DOJ will dictate the actual timeline, the above steps could be accomplished in 12 to 18 months.

CONCLUSIONS

The DOJ clearly enjoys great library service. The librarians are skilled, dedicated, and committed. However, they are also constrained in their abilities to innovate by a chasm between the services they provide and the tools to provide them. Good librarians, no matter their titles, are tool builders. Pathfinders, ILS's, databases, and even standing files are tools. The current IT environment makes it difficult for librarians to build effective tools. This, more than an environment of confidentiality, is holding the libraries back from innovation. To this point, it is the librarians who sense this frustration, and they have been able to shield lawyers from this reality through a lot of manual effort.

The good news is that, in participatory library terms, DOJ libraries are exemplars. They have a strong understanding of the communities they serve and are facilitating and improving them. However, it is difficult without better evaluative data to say how far that support extends within the DOJ organization. If DOJ does nothing more than document its successes, it is in an excellent position. However, if it wants to continue to be a leader and be seen in that leadership role beyond DOJ, it must come to terms with the technical tools available to it. By using hosted solutions in the guise of an extranet, it can provide better service to its clients, solve its immediate ILS problem, feed into the current library staff's thirst for innovation, and position itself in the larger legal information community.

RELATED ARTIFACTS

Lankes, R. D. (2008, January 12). *"Scapes" OCLC symposium on reference and social networking, Philadelphia, PA*. Message posted to http://quartz.syr.edu/rdlankes/blog/?p=459

Lankes, R. D., Silverstein, J. L., & Nicholson, S. (2007, December). Participatory networks: The library as conversation. *Information Technology and Libraries, 4.*

DIALECTIC THEORIES

MAP LOCATION

D, 3

THREAD LOCATION

Page 25

SCAPE

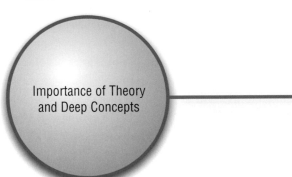

Importance of Theory and Deep Concepts — a relevant theory is → Dialectic Theories

Figure 119

AUTHOR

Jaime Snyder

AGREEMENT DESCRIPTION

Other Theories of Conversation

LIMITATIONS OF PASK'S CONVERSATION THEORY

When looking to theory for support of the basic principles of participatory librarianship, as discussed above, Pask's Conversation Theory provides a link to the foundations of library and information science by referencing the information theory and system applications research of the 1950s and 1960s. However, Pask's primary concern was to provide instructional guidelines for implementing his learning system. Pask's writing style is reminiscent of system specifications, and he focuses on describing and supporting a set of rules that define the core of his proposed educational interface. His perspective is indicative of his times and reflects a confident belief in the ability of the machine to surpass human cognitive limitations if we can only learn to harness that power.

While the intention of Conversation Theory resonates with the spirit of participatory librarianship, the technical aspects are, in fact, over thirty years old, and Pask's specifications do not necessarily help us put our ideas into action today. Nor does Pask's theory reflect the subsequent decades of communications research that would follow after he originally introduced his system.

Here we provide a brief overview of additional theories that address the study of conversation, coming from a range of fields. Our intention is to enrich our definition of conversation and attempt to connect Pask's work to the present.

UNDERSTANDING CONVERSATION IN A WIDER CONTEXT

Generally, theories of human communication that address conversation can be grouped into five broad and potentially overlapping categories: structural/functional, cognitive and behavioral, interactionist, interpretive, and critical (Littlejohn, 1996). All of these categories attempt to explain or describe some aspect of the structure of exchanges between individuals; however, they differ in their level of analysis (individual, group, culture), their unit of analysis (signal, word, utterance, message), and their filters (systems, linguistics, politics).

STRUCTURAL/FUNCTIONAL THEORIES

Conversation research in the structural/functional realm looks at patterns of exchanges and utterances with a goal of constructing frameworks based on the mechanics of verbal communication. Structuralism is based on linguistics and stresses the organization of language and social systems. Functionalism grew from biology and seeks to understand the ways that organized systems sustain themselves. Functional models assume that the world is comprised of systems that consist of variables in a network of functions (Littlejohn, 1996). This family of theories includes structural linguistics and discourse analysis. Pask's Conversation Theory also falls under this category, a unique example of system theory built on principles of conversation.

BEHAVIORAL AND COGNITIVE THEORIES

Primarily focused on the individual, theories of communication influenced by behavioral psychology look at stimuli–response relationships, whereas more cognitive theories look into the information processing that lies beneath these relationships, often taking into account the physiological basis of human perception. Like structural/functional approaches, these theories also try to identify the most important variables associated with communication. However, in addition to focusing on the person over the text for evidence regarding these variables, this approach also focuses on individual human thought rather than collective experiences (Littlejohn, 1996). Hence, the residue of conversation (or participation) in the form of knowledge is not as important as the behavior of individuals. Other approaches refer more directly to socially constructed knowledge, such as interactionist theories discussed below.

INTERACTIONIST THEORIES

Interactionist theories involving conversation take a slightly more sociological perspective, looking at the influence of actors and environment on outcomes to better understand human communication. Because of the situational nature of this approach, the research tends to focus on specific social groups and cultures and is less generalizable than structural/functional theories (Littlejohn, 1996). Pragmatics is the branch of discourse linguistics that looks at the larger social context of conversation. Conversation analysis, although structural in some aspects (i.e., examination of turn-taking), also seeks to identify social and cultural influences on the content of conversation.

INTERPRETIVIST AND CRITICAL THEORIES

Explanations of conversation-based communication can also be analyzed through an interpretivist lens that seeks to identify power dynamics between actors. These dialectic theories have grown from foundations in interpretivist and critical theory and are, for the most part, outside the scope of our current investigation as they stress the political and social implications of personal exchanges over the potential for knowledge creation.

Two Approaches to be Considered in More Detail

We have identified two approaches to the study of conversation that we feel may complement Pask's Conversation Theory as we move forward to refine and implement participatory librarianship: discourse analysis and conversation analysis. Although these approaches overlap in theory, method, and goals, each offers a distinctive point of view to the study of conversation.

DISCOURSE ANALYSIS

Discourse analysis is the examination of the structure of language as it occurs above the sentence level. Grounded in the tradition of structural linguistics, which primarily focuses on the use of language at the sentence level, discourse linguistics studies the structure of messages as expressed in groups of sentences, paragraphs, and passages. Discourse analysis is not strictly limited to dialog but can focus on the text of a single speaker. Depending on the context and application, the analysis of messages can lean more toward a traditional linguistic basis for structure (more highly ritualized contexts) or can take a more sociological perspective (more informal or less predictable situations) that is more dependent on knowledge regarding culture and social context. Regardless, discourse analysis always starts with the concepts and terminology of linguistics and seeks to overlap this framework onto naturally occurring text (Cutting, 2002). This is in contrast to the more interpretive methods used in conversation analysis, discussed below.

The subject matter of discourse analyses is most often natural language, although this research is also useful when working with computer-generated text, such as that produced by question-answering systems. It is important to note, again, that discourse analysis is dependent on the examination of actual examples of natural language, being interested in description over prescribing maximally optimal conversation practices.

Pragmatics, also an extension of structural linguistics, can be described as being one level of language analysis higher than discourse analysis. Pragmatics is considered to be interdisciplinary in its approach to language (Verschueren, 1999). Beginning with a structural framework, when compared with other linguistic areas, pragmatics gives greater importance to the social principles of discourse (Cutting, 2002), addressing the cultural aspects of language use, the social aspects of human behavior related to the communication of messages, and roles played by speakers, including issues such as social distance between speakers and rules of politeness.

Further investigation of discourse analysis principles and methods would involve examining Speech Act Theory (Searle, 1969), which seeks to describe rules governing the act of speech, with the utterance being the base unit of analysis; and propositional coherence (vanDijk, 1979), an extension of discourse studies that looks at the ways in which people create cohesive messages in speech. Neither of these theories directly addresses conversation specifically, although because of the importance that Speech Act Theory places on the intention of the speaker, either or both could enrich our examination of conversation as participation.

Conversation Analysis

Often used in ethnographic studies to closely examine the sequential order and content of conversations between members of a specific group or culture, conversation analysis has roots in both sociology and linguistics. Focused on naturally occurring dialog, this is where the more conventional notion of conversation as talk comes into play (Wardhaugh, 1985). Through careful analysis of text (usually spoken), this approach seeks to catalog interactional features (such as turn-taking, silences and gaps, and overlaps) of a given conversation (Littlejohn, 1996), in addition to identifying evidence of more general conversational rules to better understand why people say what they say.

Conversation analysis often takes an interpretivist format, building a code from repeated and careful reading of a body of text rather than applying an already existing structure to the text. Because conversation analysis looks so closely at a particular example of conversation to generate a model of the communication, it is more difficult to generalize from this approach (Cutting, 2002).

Philosopher H. Paul Grice developed a fundamental theory of conversation involving so-called Gricean Maxims that describe general principles of interaction that humans follow when engaged in most conversations. When involved in conversation, we assume (unless provoked otherwise) that, among other things, others will be telling us the truth, that they will tell us only the things we need to know, that what they say will be meaningful to us, and that they will be polite (Wardhaugh, 1985). Conversation analysis can be used to look for violations of rule like these and to explain how these violations affect the outcome of the communication as evidenced by turn-taking, silences, and interruptions.

When both Pragmatics and conversation analysis are used to describe the organization of conversational groups, it is called Interactional Sociolinguistics (Cutting, 2002). This is also an area that might be generative for future research, as it might allow us to view conversations within context and provide a more flexible (possibly too flexible) framework for defining the mechanisms of knowledge creation through conversation.

CONVERSATION STARTERS

1. Libraries are traditionally quiet spaces. Can we retain this while encouraging two-way conversations within the library?
2. Two-way conversations already occur between library staff. How can the library facilitate conversations between patrons and between patrons and staff? How can these conversations be retained so as to enrich the library?
3. Librarians are traditionally in the business of vetting sources for patrons, making sure the information they provide access to is accurate. How can this be negotiated in a conversation with no sources to check?

RELATED ARTIFACTS

Cutting, J. (2002). *Pragmatics and Discourse: A Resource Book for Students.* New York: Routledge.

Dijk, T. A. V. (1979). Relevance assignment in discourse comprehension. *Discourse Processes, 2,* 113–126.

Littlejohn, S. W. (1996). *Theories of Human Communication* (5th ed.). New York: Wadsworth Publishing Company.

Searle, J. (1969). *Speech Acts: An Essay in the Philosophy of Language.* Cambridge, UK: Cambridge University Press.

Verschueren, J. (1999). *Understanding Pragmatics.* New York: Arnold.

Wardhaugh, R. (1985). *How Conversation Works.* New York: Blackwell Basil.

DIFFERENT COMMUNITIES LIBRARIANS SERVE

MAP LOCATION
C, 5

THREAD LOCATION
Page 95

SCAPE

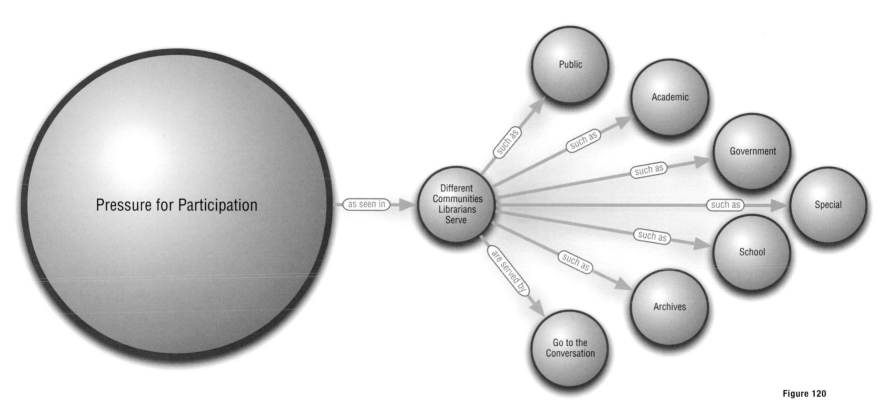

Figure 120

DIGITAL ENVIRONMENTS

MAP LOCATION
C, 6

THREAD LOCATION

Page 86

SCAPE

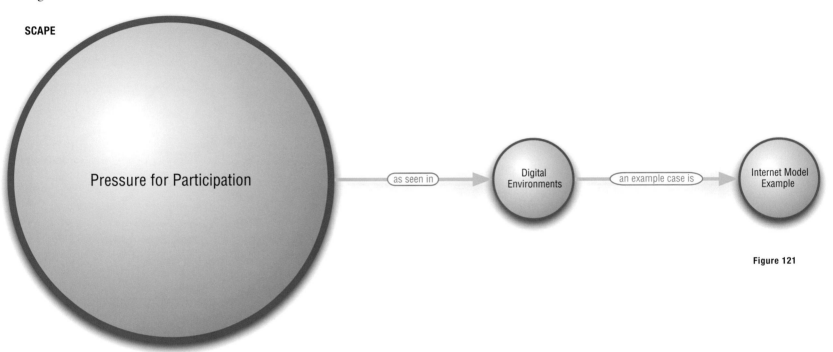

Figure 121

EDUCATION

MAP LOCATION
E, 10

THREAD LOCATION
Page 176

SCAPE

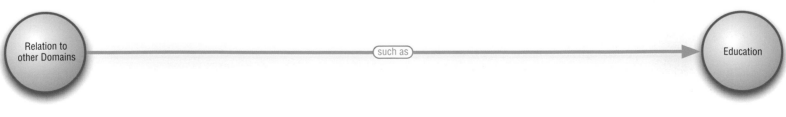

AGREEMENT SUPPLEMENTS

Figure 121a

EMBEDDED LIBRARIANS

MAP LOCATION

E, 5

THREAD LOCATION

Page 114

SCAPE

Figure 122

AUTHOR

Nancy Lara-Grimaldi

AGREEMENT DESCRIPTION

Embedded librarianship is an excellent descriptor for defining the changing role of librarians. It's not just about decentralized service, as Gary Freiburger and Sandra Kramer (2009) discuss in their article titled, "Embedded Librarians: One Library's Model for Decentralized Service," but about a change in mindset and the need for librarians to market their expertise.

As embedded librarians, we need to become visible experts in proving valuable information. This requires an understanding of our users' needs and a working knowledge of the quality and availability of resources that can best meet their needs.

Whether we are organizing entrepreneurial, writing, or musical services, as embedded librarians we are attempting to identify a need, facilitate a conversation, and inform or solve a problem.

CONVERSATION STARTERS

1. How do we become embedded librarians?
2. Do we take up kiosks at the mall?
3. Do we set up a table outside our local Shoprite?
4. Do we send flyers home through the schools or pay for advertising on the back of supermarket receipts alongside $3.00 discount coupons for the local carwash?

RELATED ARTIFACTS

Freiburger, G., & Kramer, S. (2009). Embedded librarians: One library's model for decentralized service. *Journal of the Medical Library Association, 97*(2), 139–142. Retrieved October 26, 2009, from Library, Information Science & Technology Abstracts.

Shumaker, D. (2009). Who let the librarians out? *Reference & User Services Quarterly, 48*(3), 239–242. Retrieved October 26, 2009, from Library, Information Science & Technology Abstracts.

ENTAILMENT MESH

MAP LOCATION
F, 2

THREAD LOCATION
Page 49

SCAPE

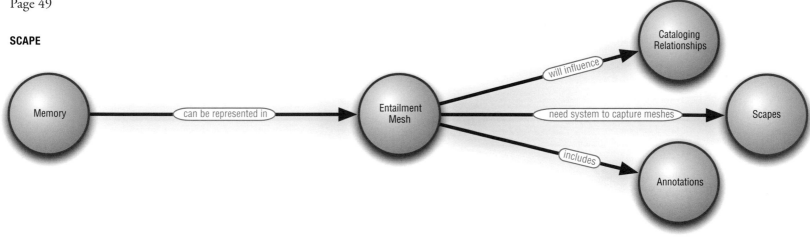

Figure 123

ENTREPRENEURIUM

MAP LOCATION
F, 4

THREAD LOCATION
Page 98

SCAPE

AUTHOR
R. David Lankes

Figure 124

AGREEMENT DESCRIPTION

The Entrepreneurium: Building a Research-Based Model for Serving Small Businesses and Entrepreneurs

ASSESSMENT OF NEED

Syracuse University and the Free Library of Philadelphia propose to investigate the roles and opportunities for public libraries in the support of entrepreneurs. This study is a direct result of the Free Library of Philadelphia engaging the business community and seeking to better serve the entrepreneur, a key driver of economic development, an effort that has been named the "Entrepreneurium." Rather than simply build a new center or replicate existing efforts of other libraries, the Free Library feels there is great value in developing such services from grounded research. It also feels that such research is invaluable to the rest of the public library community.

Increasingly, public libraries are seen as stakeholders in the economic development of their communities, as was highlighted in a recent report by the Urban Libraries Council:

> Public libraries build a community's capacity for economic activity and resiliency, says a new study from the Urban Institute. [The study] adds to the body of research pointing to a shift in the role of public libraries—from a passive, recreational reading and research institution to an active economic development agent, addressing such pressing urban issues as literacy, workforce training, small business vitality and community quality of life.[1]

Because small and new businesses currently constitute 45.1% of the payroll[2] in the country, an increased focus by libraries on the startup, in addition to the more established library role in job searching, is warranted.

Public libraries have long been involved in providing service to entrepreneurs. From print and electronic resources that are so critical to this constituent to workshops and one-on-one assistance, libraries are attempting to fill gaps in services available to entrepreneurs. Libraries are often invaluable resources to the startup, offering the Gale Virtual Reference Library, ReferenceUSA, Dun & Bradstreet's Million Dollar Database (whose usage at the Free Library has almost doubled), and Business and Company Resource. The Free Library

1. http://www.urbanlibraries.org/jan1006makingcitiesstronger.html.
2. http://www.sba.gov/advo/research/rs314.pdf.

alone spends more than $100,000 each year on 12 databases useful to entrepreneurs and small business owners. This dollar figure doesn't count the extensive one-to-one assistance, workshops, and reference activities that libraries are offering. The Free Library is hardly alone in its current outreach to entrepreneurs, with notable programs at the Brooklyn Public Library, the St. Paul Public Library, Middle County Public Library, and even the British Library.

However, librarians create many entrepreneurial offerings with little direct involvement in startup operations. Further, libraries may emulate existing entrepreneurship programs in the not-for-profit sector without deep consideration of the library's role beyond the provision of resources. In essence, a great deal of money is being spent on an important activity but with little concrete research and evaluative data on which to build their programs.

If public libraries are to play an important role in entrepreneurship, thereby enhancing their communities and the libraries' role within the community, they need evidence-based guidance in creating, operating, and governing entrepreneurship centers. This research project will provide such guidance grounded in the real world, with real data, and with real resources.

NATIONAL IMPACT AND INTENDED RESULTS

The overall aim of this proposed research activity is to increase and promote the ability of public libraries throughout the country to stimulate entrepreneurship in communities. The Entrepreneurium, an umbrella project concept, will do this through data, actionable plans, and shared resources. The resources and findings of this project will strengthen the public library's role in economic development by creating mechanisms to engrain the public library in the entrepreneurship communities throughout the country.

The emphasis on entrepreneurship and the startup comes directly from the mission of public libraries to enhance their communities. Entrepreneurial activities not only form a major part of the U.S. economy, but they also are directly relevant to traditionally underrepresented populations. According to the Public Forum Institute, 600,000 to 800,000 new businesses are started in the United States each year:

> These small businesses are the foundation for our employment growth. They allow their owners to work for themselves and be self-sufficient.... Firms of fewer than 20 employees generate the majority of net new jobs in the U.S. New jobs from start-ups are an immediate and significant boost to the economy. New dynam-

ic theories of the economy suggest that the prevalence of small firms provide a constant tide of new ideas and experimentation vital to the health of the economy as a whole.[3]

A recent article in the *Journal of Leadership and Entrepreneurial Studies* brought some interesting statistics together:

> 74 million Americans stated they plan to start a new venture within the next five years while an additional 199 million Americans plan to start a venture someday. (The Small Business Economy, 2006) Women-owned ventures increased from 5.4 million in 1997 to 7.7 million in 2006. (Center for Women's Business Research, 2007) The non-profit Tax Foundation reports that entrepreneurs pay more than 54% of all individual income taxes. Approximately one new firm with employees is established every year for every 300 adults in the United States. As the typical new firm has at least two owners-managers, one of every 150 adults participates in the founding of a new firm each year. Substantially more—one in 12—are involved in trying to launch a new firm. The net result is that the United States has a very robust level of firm creation. These numbers make it clear that entrepreneurial ventures are dominating the US economy . . . truly an entrepreneurial economy.[4]

Other studies show that "immigrants far outpaced native-born Americans in entrepreneurial activity last year while African Americans were the only major ethnic or racial group to experience a year-to-year increase in the rate of entrepreneurship."[5]

The realities of American entrepreneurship—that it is wide scale and diverse—make it an excellent lever point for public libraries to directly impact the welfare of their communities. However, the simple act of collecting entrepreneurial materials, while valuable, is far from realizing the true potential impact of the library. What is needed is a proactive set of programs based on best practices in the governmental, corporate, and not-for-profit sectors. This project will identify these best practices. It will create a firm research foundation of best practices, programs, and resources that can be replicated at libraries around the country. It will also seek to build a lasting, if informal, network of public libraries engaging entrepreneurs.

At the end of the project, a public library shall:

- have a comprehensive inventory of the resources and services necessary to start an entrepreneurial center/activity;

- be able to best evaluate the readiness of the library's patrons for the startup enterprise,

- have a ready set of empirically tested interventions to build the entrepreneurial skills of its community, and

- have a network of other libraries interested in entrepreneurship it can share with and learn from.

PROJECT DESIGN AND EVALUATION PLAN

Participatory librarianship forms the conceptual basis for the design and evaluation of this project. Simply put, participatory librarianship, based in large part on Conversation Theory,[6] recasts library and library practice using the fundamental concept that knowledge is created through conversation.[7] Libraries are in the knowledge business and are, therefore, in the conversation business. Participatory librarians approach their work as facilitators of conversation. Be it in practice, policies, programs, and/or tools, participatory librarians seek to enrich, capture, store, and disseminate the conversations of their communities.

Participatory librarianship provides a set of theoretically derived principles for engaging key library constituencies in projects such as these. First, the library serves as a facilitator of conversation. Second, true engagement with the community means shared management responsibilities. Third, investment in tools for knowledge creation is preferred over the collection of artifacts from previous knowledge-creation processes. Preliminary engagement with the business community in the Philadelphia area using these participatory concepts has already identified the importance of an entrepreneurial focus (vs. a focus on general business or job skills). It has also identified a rich set of areas for investigation in terms of services and needed skills of entrepreneurs.

Although there is no strict relationship between the participatory theoretical approach and a suite of methods, qualitative techniques shall be employed due to the exploratory nature of the project and to provide the richest dataset possible to allow for later discussions of

---

3. http://www.publicforuminstitute.org/nde/entre/index.htm.
4. http://www.allbusiness.com/human-resources/employee-development-leadership/4501619-1.html.
5. http://www.kauffman.org/items.cfm?itemID=704.

6. Pask, G. (1976). Conversation theory: Applications in education and epistemology. New York: Elsevier.
7. More information on participatory librarianship can be found at http://www.ptbed.org.

model transferability into new settings. Each phase of the research, as outlined below, will employ mixed methods, including interviews, document analysis, and focus groups. The researchers will also employ a validity cycle, where emerging concepts and findings are fed back to participants (in this case, site visit organizations and a panel of entrepreneurial experts) for confirmation and additional data gathering. The end result of this naturalistic inquiry shall be specific interventions and understandings tied to higher level concepts.

This three-year study will create a firm, empirical, and replicable foundation for entrepreneurship centers in public libraries. It will do so in four phases detailed in table 2.

PHASE 1: DEVELOP A SKILLS ASSESSMENT FOR PATRONS BASED ON SUCCESSFUL PRACTICES	YEAR 1	RESPONSIBILITY: SYRACUSE	
DESCRIPTION	THE NECESSARY SKILLS FOR ENTREPRENEURS WILL BE DEVELOPED BY CANVASSING THE ENTREPRENEURSHIP AND LIBRARY LITERATURE, AN ADVISORY BOARD OF SUCCESSFUL ENTREPRENEURS AND SUCCESSFUL ENTREPRENEURSHIP CENTERS (INCLUDING THOSE IN LIBRARIES). CANDIDATE SKILLS INVENTORIES AND INSTRUMENTS WILL BE TESTED IN PILOT GROUPS TO ASSURE VALIDITY OF THE INSTRUMENTS.		
OUTCOME	SKILLS INVENTORY THAT A LIBRARY CAN USE WITH THEIR PATRONS TO DETERMINE FUTURE PROGRAMS AND TOOLS NEEDED WITH VALID INSTRUMENTS; LITERATURE REVIEW OF ENTREPRENEURSHIP IN LIBRARIES; SITE VISIT REPORTS OF CENTERS.		
PHASE 2: ADMINISTER THE SKILLS INVENTORY	YEAR 1	RESPONSIBILITY: FREE LIBRARY	
DESCRIPTION	THE RESEARCH TEAM WILL WORK WITH THE FREE LIBRARY OF PHILADELPHIA'S PATRON POPULATION TO DETERMINE GAPS IN CURRENT PATRON KNOWLEDGE IN TERMS OF ENTREPRENEURSHIP. THE CURRENT PATRON POPULATION INCLUDES A LARGE NUMBER OF ENTREPRENEURS AND ENTREPRENEURSHIP PROGRAMS.		
OUTCOME	AN "ENTREPRENEURSHIP" PROFILE OF THE FREE LIBRARY COMMUNITY, PLUS A TEMPLATE FOR SIMILAR PROFILES AT OTHER LIBRARIES.		
PHASE 3: TEST PROTOTYPE PATRON INTERVENTIONS TO INCREASE ENTREPRENEURIAL SKILLS	YEAR 2	RESPONSIBILITY: FREE LIBRARY, SYRACUSE	
DESCRIPTION	WHILE PHASES 1 AND 2 WILL DETERMINE THE NEEDS A LIBRARY MUST MEET IN TERMS OF SUPPORTING ENTREPRENEURSHIP, THE REMAINDER OF THE STUDY FOCUSES ON HOW THE LIBRARY CAN MEET THOSE NEEDS. IN ORDER TO DETERMINE THIS, DIFFERENT SERVICES AND TOOLS, IDENTIFIED EITHER IN THE SITE VISITS, THE LITERATURE, OR FROM THE RESULTS OF THE ASSESSMENT WILL BE TESTED. INTERVENTIONS MIGHT INCLUDE TRAINING SESSIONS, ONLINE NETWORKING TOOLS, AND/OR NEW COLLECTIONS OF MATERIALS (SUCH AS BUSINESS PLANS).		
OUTCOME	PROTOTYPE INTERVENTIONS WITH EMPIRICAL EVIDENCE TO THEIR EFFECTIVENESS; METRICS TO DETERMINE THE SUCCESS OF INTERVENTIONS; SPECIFIC PHYSICAL NEEDS OF A GOOD CENTER.		
PHASE 4: DETERMINE SUSTAINABILITY AND TRANSFERABILITY MODELS OF ENTREPRENEURSHIP CENTERS	YEAR 3	RESPONSIBILITY: FREE LIBRARY, SYRACUSE	
DESCRIPTION	INTERVENTIONS ARE OF NO USE IF THEY CANNOT BE SUSTAINED. NO PROGRAM CAN BE SUSTAINED IF IT DOES NOT FIT INTO THE OVERALL STRUCTURE OF A LIBRARY. THE RESEARCH TEAM WILL DEVELOP SUSTAINABILITY AND MANAGEMENT MODELS FOR USE WITH ENTREPRENEURSHIP CENTERS. PARTICULAR ATTENTION WILL BE GIVEN TO HOW DIRECT OWNERSHIP OF THE CENTER AND ITS GOALS CAN BE SHARED BETWEEN THE LIBRARY AND THE ENTREPRENEURIAL COMMUNITY. THE FREE LIBRARY WILL ALSO HOST A SYMPOSIUM ON THE TOPIC OF "ENTREPRENEURSHIP AND THE LIBRARY" TO GAIN FEEDBACK ON THE WORK PRODUCTS OF THE GRANT AND DISSEMINATE WHAT WAS LEARNED.		
OUTCOME	SUSTAINABILITY MODEL; OWNERSHIP PLAN BETWEEN THE LIBRARY AND ENTREPRENEURS; SYMPOSIUM AND SYMPOSIUM REPORT		

Each of these phases seeks to employ mixed methods, but all depend on testing concepts and models in real situations with real clients. Throughout the study, the research team will draw on the expertise of a board of successful entrepreneurs and key stakeholders, including members of the banking sector. The overall goal is to create a toolkit that public libraries can use nationwide.

Table 1 also forms the basis of both ongoing and summative evaluations of the project and the model. Evaluations will be conducted throughout each phase to ensure only valid outcomes are achieved and passed to the next phase. For example, in phase 1, the "skills inventory" will be validated in terms of data gathered, as well as in terms of the instrument itself (e.g., language use). Only once the inventory has been validated will it be passed on to phase 2, where the entrepreneurial profile of the community developed corresponds to the overall service population of the Free Library's Central Library.

Dissemination

Disseminating the findings of this research is seen as a priority task for the research team. The importance of entrepreneurship exists not just in Philadelphia but across the nation. A primary motivation in conducting research is that it is transferable, not simply building a set of services at a single library as a demonstration project. To that end, the research team has three strategies for the dissemination of the findings of this research.

The first strategy is ensuring that the instruments and materials generated as part of the research (such as the skills inventory, literature reviews, and site visits) are produced for national consumption. The second strategy is the use of http://entrepreneurium.org, a planned participatory Web site that will allow for immediate and easy access to the materials and findings of the study. The site will also allow for profession-wide input and commenting, thus serving as the foundation for an informal network of libraries interested in entrepreneurship programs. The building of the site will utilize best practices in community web development. The third strategy is the offering of a national symposium in phase 4 of the study. This symposium will provide for immediate input and feedback in a face-to-face fashion. The symposium will take advantage of the participatory features of the Web site to allow for distance participation in the symposium as well.

Sustainability

As a research project, the end of the grant is the end of the effort. However, exploring the sustainability of entrepreneurship programs at public libraries is a key effort within the scope of work. Further, a number of the entrepreneurship activities identified through this research project will be incorporated into the Central Library's current Business Department, and the Free Library's plans to expand the Central Library and construct a new Business Department offer the potential to sustain the project's results well into the future. The Free Library is excited to incorporate a full spectrum of services, resources, and facilities necessary to support entrepreneurs and small business owners in its new Business Department. As one of the largest urban libraries in the country, in a world-class city that attracts and supports entrepreneurs, the Library will continue to serve Philadelphia's growing base of new business owners with the resources identified in this research project.

Conclusion

Public libraries have an opportunity in the area of entrepreneurship to improve their communities and their position within those communities. Entrepreneurs and public libraries share an aspirational nature. Both activities are seen as means to advance the best of a community. Public libraries serve as instruments that support the public's ability to overcome their current limitations to succeed, be it in literacy, school, vocations, or the business world. It is vital that public libraries are equipped to court, support, and advance a vital sector of our economy, the entrepreneur. Further, libraries must be able to both justify their means of supporting the entrepreneur and evaluate their effectiveness in this support. Such a research foundation will give any interested library a compelling story to tell in the boardroom, city hall, and business community. By supporting innovation and personal initiative, public libraries not only contribute to the bottom line of their municipalities, but model themselves as a place of leadership for the community. It is now time for libraries to go beyond simply providing resources for the intrepid few and actively promote services to empower all. The research from this project will help libraries, and those libraries will in turn improve their communities.

ENVIRONMENT

MAP LOCATION
D, 4

THREAD LOCATION
Page 77

SCAPE

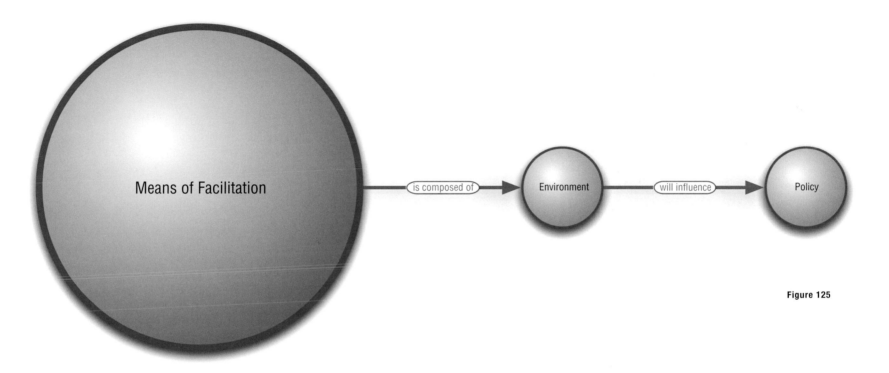

Figure 125

ETHICS

MAP LOCATION

H, 3

THREAD LOCATION

Page 124

SCAPE

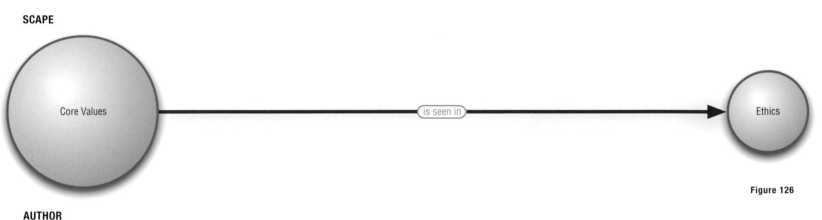

Figure 126

AUTHOR

R. David Lankes

AGREEMENT DESCRIPTION

It was 1999, and the AskA consortium was meeting at Harvard's Graduate School of Education. The panel of librarians, library instructors, AskA services, and government officials were discussing a set of quality standards in virtual reference (Kasowitz et al., 2000). When the standard stating that services should be without bias was brought up, an interesting discussion ensued. Joseph Janes observed that the biases of a given AskA service were in many ways the strength of the service. Take AskShamu (http://www.seaworld.org/ask-shamu/index.htm), for example. AskShamu was a service of SeaWorld that answered questions on marine biology and was considered an exemplary service. "What kind of answer do you think they will give when asked whether keeping animals in captivity is a good thing or bad?" asked Joe. Likewise, one could ask a library about the benefits of fair use.

The point was not that these services were without bias, but whether their biases were obvious, and more important for the consideration of a virtual reference consortium, whether the network of all the services achieved a neutral stance. This may seem like a fine distinction, but it highlights an inherent struggle in the ethics of a profession that is situational but seeks universal approaches. Take the ALA code of Ethics (American Library Association, 1995). The first code states, "We provide the highest level of service to all library users through appropriate and usefully organized resources; equitable service policies; equitable access; and accurate, unbiased, and courteous responses to all requests." Here the professional librarian should be neutral and unbiased. Yet in the sixth code, librarians "…do not advance private interests at the expense of library users, colleagues, or our employing institutions." So, as in the case of AskShamu, what happens if the employing institution has a bias? I argue that all organizations and all individuals have inescapable biases. The best one can do, from an ethical perspective, is to disclose those biases as much as possible. At the least, this allows our patrons to be aware of potential distortions in service.

Such a disclosure is an essential part of conversation. Conversation Theory and later theories on discourse and communication talk about a sometimes subtle negotiation process that takes place between parties in a conversation. Issues of status, language, and experience all factor into an interaction. These interactions and negotiations ultimately end up in a series of agreements that form the basis of knowledge creation. The library profession is quick to point out such biases in service populations—the public thinks books are all the library offers, the patrons think the library is stuffy, and so on. Sometimes these biases are elicited through research and found in data, but often they are actually perceptions/biases the professional holds about the public.

With this more situational approach to ethics, where biases and ethical constraints are negotiated as part of knowledge creation, it also becomes clear that the inevitable biases of librarians will shape the conversations of the community. This is far from a bad thing. Librarianship is a principled profession. That is to say, it is a profession that has taken the time and effort to make explicit its principles and ethics. As such, it is seen as an honest broker in many conversations and information-seeking processes. It has become a respected and credible voice because it is so forthright about its ethics and principles.

However, such a principled approach can degenerate into a sort of paternalism when not guided by adherence to some larger goal. In librarianship, this ultimate goal is service, and it should prevent paternalism. Without this drive to serve and be part of a community, the library can seek to shape the community based on a narrow and elite view. This can easily be seen in the early American library movement when the promotion of literacy became the promotion of the "right" literacy as defined by the library (most often Christian white men). One can still see such paternalism in reactions to the rise in gaming programs at the library. Stocking public library shelves with science fiction and romance novels is acceptable, but promoting video games somehow does not rise to the bar of propriety. Worse, public libraries that may have story times and knitting groups shy away from game nights because teens should somehow be engaged in more educational programs, such as knitting and puppet shows?

The bottom line is that ethical neutrality is a myth. Everyone and every organization have a stance and a set of biases. The best it can do is to make such biases known. Further, it is only by grounding a field's ethics and principles in the ultimate goal of service that librarians avoid separation from the community and promotion of their ethics over those of the community.

Obligations to the Community

The flip side of paternalism toward a community is surrender to that community. A comment to the Ann Arbor District Library asked for "free prostitutes and pie" (http://www.flickr.com/photo_zoom. gne?id=74201588&size=o). Although this would be sure to attract some new patrons, many would question whether prostitution and pies belong in a library. Some would base these questions on the ethics of a library that would trade in human desire and promoting obesity, even in communities where both might be legal. Clearly, although the library is of the community, it does not have to reflect the full range of ethical positions of that community.

How can the library have it both ways—reflecting the community's ethics while maintaining its own? The answer comes again through Conversation Theory. In a conversation among individuals or community members, such as the library and its patrons, there is a negotiation occurring between two sides. Each actor in the conversation is working toward an agreement that includes what information, actions, and the like are "in bounds." Libraries and librarians must reflect the ethics of their community, but they must also shape them. In many cases, the libraries have negotiated an understanding that intellectual freedom and fair use, for example, are ethical imperatives that enrich a community, although in other agents of the community they are suppressed. In some cases, however, libraries have failed in these negotiations, such as in CIPA, and they must resign themselves to operating the best they can within the boundaries the community has set.

What we see in these often subtle negotiations is that sometimes libraries and librarians actively promote their ethical frames, sometimes they simply make such frames and biases explicit, and sometimes they actively suppress them in the service of a higher ethical burden—service.

Consider again the issue of filtering Internet access. At first, it seems to go against the basic principle of free and unencumbered intellectual access to information. However, let's take the situation of a public library that turns off filtering of public access computing for adults on request. Now let's say that the police, aware of this practice, start patrolling the library and looking over people's shoulders, in particular watching for parole violations by sex offenders. One can well imagine that such observation might have a chilling effect on Internet usage. Is it ethical to require filtering of all terminals to remove the police presence, thereby allowing the greatest access to the greatest number of people? The ultimate answer to this question can only be derived by actively engaging the service community in conversation. It may sound like this approach rules out ethical stands or that the lowest ethical common denominator shall win, but this ignores the power of a principled profession that in most cases already holds credibility and the good faith of the community. Put plainly, negotiations can be active and spirited, and sometimes people agree to disagree.

Inclusion of Communities

Another community aspect of our new approach to librarianship and the question of ethics is direct inclusion of the patron into the library's processes. As the technology brief states[1]:

1. Lankes, R. David, Silverstein, J. L., & Nicholson, S. (2007). Participatory networks: The library as conversation. For the American Library Association's Office of Information Technology Policy [available at http://quartz.syr.edu/rdlankes/ParticiaptoryNetworks.pdf].

How can such a traditionally rigid system [the catalog]… be made more participatory? What if the user, finding no relevant information in the catalog, adds either the information or a placeholder for someone else to fill in the missing information? Possibly the user adds information from his or her expertise. However, assuming that most people go to a catalog because they don't have the information, perhaps the user instead begins a process for adding the information. The user might ask a question using a virtual reference service; at the end of the transaction, the user then has the option to add the question, along with the answer and associated materials, to the catalog. Or perhaps, the user simply leaves the query in the catalog for other patrons to answer, requesting to be notified when an answer is posted. In that case, when a new user does a catalog search and runs across the question, he or she can provide an answer. That answer might be a textual entry (or an image, sound, or video), or simply a new query that directs the original questioner or new patrons to existing information in the catalog (user-created "see also" entries in the catalog). (Lankes et al., forthcoming)

This idea of community inclusion directly into library processes has also included ideas of offering community organizations shelving space for them to house (and maintain) their own documents. Other ideas discussed as part of ongoing conversations with the Free Library of Philadelphia include the library publishing works by community authors and musicians or accessioning video of local events and town meetings.

Although such ideas raise questions of quality, expertise, and the like (to be answered in an ongoing and active conversation with the community), there are ethical issues raised as well. As we have just discussed, libraries are not required to represent the full range of ethical norms of their communities in their offerings, just as a community's churches, courtrooms, or classrooms are places with strong ethical boundaries. What is interesting about all of these settings is that, at their best, they invite open discussion and instruction on ethical conduct.

This idea that a library can be a proactive cauldron to instruct ethical behavior is far from a unique concept. Discussions on intellectual freedom, copyright, and the role of libraries in digital divide issues are at their heart as much about ethics as they are about policy, technology, or practice. Even the ALA Code of Ethics prescribes action:

We strive for excellence in the profession by maintaining and enhancing our own knowledge and skills, by encouraging the professional development of co-workers, and by fostering the aspirations of potential members of the profession.

"Striving" and "fostering" imply moving beyond a simple unbiased or neutral approach to work. Instead, they imply actively biasing conversations. Note the fifth code of the previously mentioned ALA code of Ethics, which states that librarians should "advocate conditions of employment." Or look at the third code where librarians "protect each library user's right." This has translated into a pronounced bias and position with regard to things such as the PATRIOT Act. By inviting the community into the library as partners, we also have a chance to invite the community to learn and share (and continuously shape) our ethics. Librarians are free to do so because they understand that it is impossible to enter into any relationship (including a service relationship) without biases.

A Biased and Principled Profession

Knowledge is created through conversation. As an individual or community seeks to learn, it seeks to engage in a process of communications that lead to a series of agreements. Ethics plays a two-part role in this knowledge-creation process, and both are vital. The first is in the belief that librarians must act ethically in these interactions. They must be dedicated to service, dedicated to providing the best information available to them, and doing so in a way that best represents the community within which the librarian is situated. The second role of ethics is in the communication act. Librarians must make their ethical stance clear and discoverable. This includes being upfront about potential biases held by the librarians, the library, and the profession as a whole. It is only by being up front and honest about existing ethical stances that the profession can continue to be a trusted member of the community and broker of information.

Librarians are biased toward disclosing more information than less, providing more viewpoints than fewer, and doing so in a way that biases personal privacy over institutional supervision. In essence, librarians believe in private interactions with public information. Librarians must understand these are biases founded in ethics and that the span and scope of their ethical behavior must be constantly negotiated within the community of which they are a part.

RELATED ARTIFACTS

This Agreement Supplement was derived from Lankes, R. D. (2008). The ethics of participatory librarianship. *Journal of Library Administration, 47*(3/4), 233–241.

EVERY COURSE HAS SYMPOSIA AND PRACTICA

MAP LOCATION

E, 9

THREAD LOCATION

Page 179

SCAPE

Figure 127

EVOLUTION OF INTEGRATED LIBRARY SYSTEMS

MAP LOCATION

H, 2

THREAD LOCATION

Page 144

SCAPE

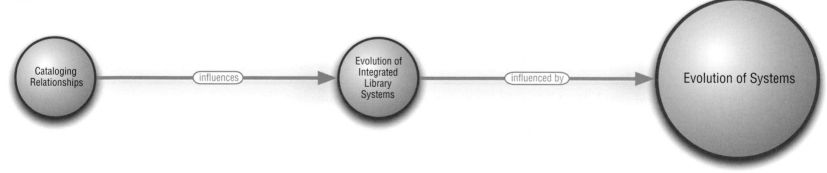

Figure 128

EVOLUTION OF SYSTEMS

MAP LOCATION

H, 3

THREAD LOCATION

Page 35

SCAPE

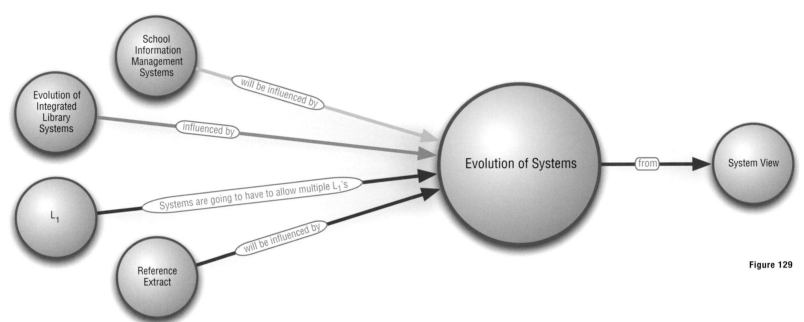

Figure 129

AUTHOR

Andrea Phelps

RELATED ARTIFACTS

Documents

Bertalanffy Center for the Study of Systems Science. (n.d.). *General System Theory: Origins of General System Theory (GST)*. Retrieved from http://www.bertalanffy.org/c_26.html.

Commentary: Describes not just the origins of GST but also what it entails and some of the effects it has had on science and other fields.

Drack, M. (2008). Ludwig von Bertalanffy's Early System Approach. *Proceedings of the 52nd annual meeting of the ISSS*. Retrieved from http://journals.isss.org/index.php/proceedings52nd/article/view/1032/322.

Commentary: Discusses the biological aspects and uses of GST. Another good look at why the theory was necessary and where it came from, even though it only applies to the uses of the theory in biology.

Drack, M., et al. (2007). On the making of a system theory of life: Paul A Weiss and Ludwig von Bertalanffy's conceptual connection. *The Quarterly Review of Biology*, *82*(4), 349–373.

Commentary: Reviews the early beginnings of the GST and the drive of Weiss and Bertalanffy's desire to fix the mechanical nature of study in biology in the 1920s. A helpful look at what brought about the various system theories that Bertalanffy and his friends and colleagues worked on.

Jiménez-López, E. (n.d.). System science: Is it necessary? *Bertalanffy Center for the Study of Systems Science*. Retrieved from http://www.bertalanffy.org/c_39.html.

Commentary: Most useful for its definition of open system, this essay does help prove the lasting use and relevancy of Bertalanffy's theories.

von Bertalanffy, L. (1950). An outline of General System Theory. *The British Journal for the Philosophy of Science, 1*(2), 134–165. Retrieved from http://www.isnature.org/Events/2009/Summer/r/Bertalanffy1950-GST_Outline_SELECT.pdf.

Commentary: Bertalanffy's presentation of his theory and what led to the creation of GST. Not only does he describe the trends in biology but similar trends in the other sciences. This may be satisfactory for the context of the Atlas, but if there are more librarian-specific trends and systems that would help enlighten the reader, those might be of more use in this arena.

Zadeh, L. A. (1962). From circuit theory to system theory. *Proceedings of the IRE. May 1962.* Retrieved from http://ieeexplore.ieee.org/xpl/freeabs_all.jsp?arnumber=4066785.

Commentary: Explains the reason that System Theory became adopted by electricians and some of the problems the field has with System Theory. Compounded with the information on what drove Bertalannfy to create the theory in his own field of biology, this gives a slightly better picture of what GST evolved from.

Presentations

Lankes, R. D. (2008). *If they build it they will come.* Paper presented at the Rethinking Access to Information IFLA Satellite conference, Boston, MA. Retrieved from http://quartz.syr.edu/rdlankes/blog/?p=523.

EVOLUTION OF THE SOCIAL COMPACT

MAP LOCATION

F, G, 6

THREAD LOCATION

Page 29

SCAPE

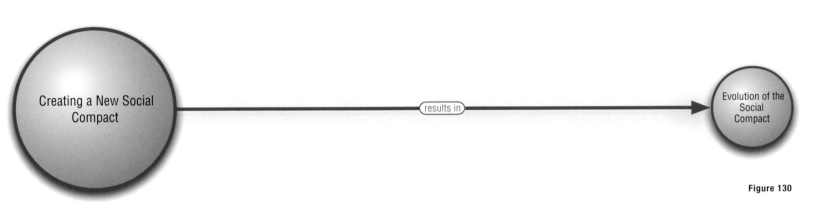

Creating a New Social Compact

results in

Evolution of the Social Compact

Figure 130

AUTHOR

Elizabeth Gall

AGREEMENT DESCRIPTION

The community a library serves, and society as a whole, are quickly changing. Ranganathan's 5th law of librarianship states that the library is a growing organism. Because both the library and its surroundings are changing, the relationship between them is also in a constant state of flux. As the social compact among the library, librarians, and members evolves, libraries and librarians must constantly reevaluate their missions. Before considering the mission statements, however, we must first examine how the social compact has changed and how that change has affected members' expectations of the library and librarians.

The already prevalent and still-growing dependency on technology has had a large impact on the social compact among the library, librarians, and members. This has presented libraries and librarians with the opportunity to effect change as they attempt to work within the new social compact. The challenge comes not in recognizing

the need for change but in determining the best way to forge ahead. Libraries and librarians have different mission statements. However, neither can be effective unless it is compatible with the other.

Librarians have informally operated within the new social compact as it has evolved with the changing needs of members. However, the current mission statements of the libraries in which they function limit them. It is much easier to change the mission statement of the librarian than that of the library because it is less formal and subject to fewer obstacles. Where a library mission statement is subject to discussion and approval by boards, committees, librarians, members, and so on, a librarian's mission statement is much more personal. As librarians interact with patrons in their daily lives, they are exposed to changes in the social compact as they occur. Once they have learned of the changes, librarians can immediately refocus their mission statements to meet them.

Libraries, in contrast, must go through an official process to change their mission statement. I have never heard of a library that allowed patrons, librarians, or administrators to access and edit its mission statement in real time. Even as the library adjusts to meet the community's changing needs by increasing online services, adding computers with Internet access, developing new programming, and so on, it is unlikely that the mission statement has been amended to reflect these changes. By the time the mission statement has been changed, it is likely that a whole new social compact will have developed. One could argue that a broad, theoretical mission statement would give both librarians and libraries room to adapt to new social compacts as they form because it imposes few limits. Conversely, a broad, generalized mission statement might cause confusion and inhibit growth because it does not give enough direction.

A more specific, detailed mission statement carries its own set of problems. In their article, "Revisiting Library Mission Statements in the Era of Technology," Svenningsen and Cherepon argue that library mission statements should include all kinds of formats. Is referencing specific formats a good idea? Changing technology plays a large role in reshaping social compacts; however, not all technologies are going to stand the test of time. Ten years ago, a library may have argued for the inclusion of zip disks, a technology that is rarely used today, in their mission statement. A specific mission statement, especially regarding technological formats, will need to be revised much more frequently than a more general one. Library mission statements are much more effective if they are outcome-specific. It is up to the librarians and their mission statements to ensure these outcomes are achieved given the current social compact.

The most important element of both library and librarian mission statements is an emphasis on the user. This is especially true as we make the shift to web-based resources. Children, teens, and young adults turn to the Internet for many of their information needs. They are less likely to seek out help from a librarian even when visiting library Web sites. Librarians and libraries must be vigilant not only in fulfilling evolving social compacts but also in educating and supporting members. Many members are unsure of the librarian's ability to effectively utilize new technologies. Ultimately, they fear that librarians are evolving at a slower pace than the institutions in which they work. This is the exact opposite of reality. Librarians must reassure members that their mission statements and abilities are effectively evolving as they reach out and embrace the new social compact.

RELATED ARTIFACTS

Atkinson, R. (2004). The acquisitions librarian as change agent in the transition to the electronic library. *Library Resources & Technical Services, 48*(3), 216–226. [Reprinted from *Library Resources & Technical Services, 36*(1), January 1992.]

Bales, S. N. (1998). Technology and tradition: The future's in the balance. *American Libraries, 29*(6), 82–83+.

Bertot, J. C., McClure, C. R., & Jaeger, P. T. (2008). The impacts of free public internet access on public library patrons and communities. *The Library Quarterly, 78*(3).

Chowdhury, G., Poulter, A., & McMenemy, D. (2006). Public library 2.0: Towards a new mission for public libraries as a "network of community knowledge." *Online Information Review, 30*(4), 454–460.

Cunningham, J., & Stoffel, B. (2004). The campus web portal: Is there a channel for the library? *College & Undergraduate Libraries, 11*(1), 25–31.

Hsiung L. (2007). Expanding the role of the electronic resources (ER) librarian in the hybrid library. *Collection Management, 32*(1/2), 31–47.

Janes, J. (2003). The next best thing to being there. *American Libraries, 34*(9), 70.

Mielke, L. (1995). Short-range planning for turbulent times. *American Libraries, 26*, 905–906.

Svenningsen, K., & Cherepon, L. (1998). Revisiting library mission statements in the era of technology. *Collection Building, 17*(1), 16–19.

EXTRINSIC

MAP LOCATION

F, 1

THREAD LOCATION

Page 79

SCAPE

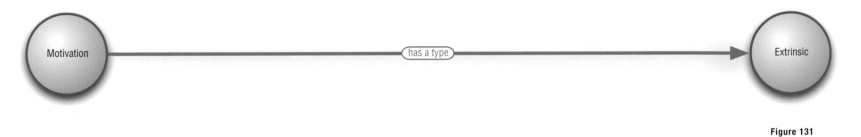

Figure 131

FREE LIBRARY OF PHILADELPHIA

MAP LOCATION

E, 4

THREAD LOCATION

Page 97

SCAPE

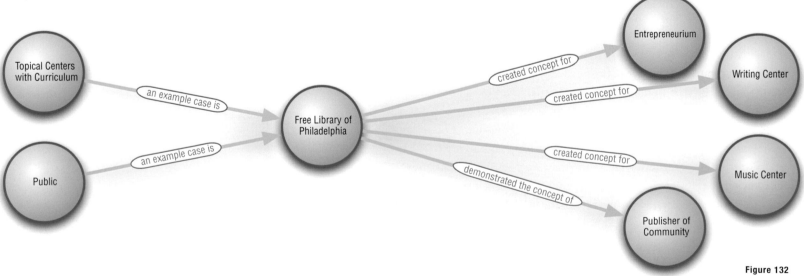

Figure 132

FROM AUTHORITY TO RELIABILITY

MAP LOCATION

F, G, 3

THREAD LOCATION

Page 91

SCAPE

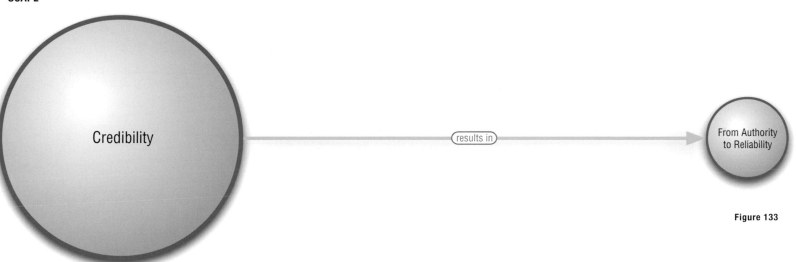

Figure 133

FROM SCHOOL TO SCHOOL OF THOUGHT

MAP LOCATION

E, 9

THREAD LOCATION

Page 181

SCAPE

Figure 134

GAMING

MAP LOCATION
F, G, 1

THREAD LOCATION
Page 75

SCAPE

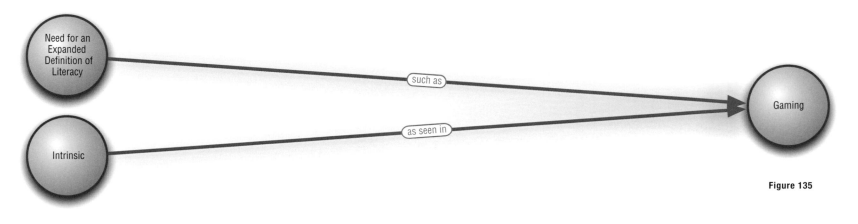

Figure 135

AUTHOR
Scott Nicholson

AGREEMENT DESCRIPTION

In the context of the Atlas, "games and gaming" encompasses many forms of structured play—board and card games, computer games, video and console games, role-playing games, war and combat-focused games, and even alternate reality games. Just as librarians support a variety of member interests and age ranges, the librarian should support all types of games that are appropriate for the needs of the specific group of members.

Games, like movies, music, and even fiction, are a form of popular media that the librarian supports. As the role of gaming in society has grown, the role of gaming in libraries has also grown. Sometimes this draws a critical eye from the public in the same way that, over the years, movies, popular music, and even recreational reading has drawn as the library supported these services. The "penny dreadfuls," inexpensive popular serial fiction from the late 1800s and early 1900s, drew the same kind of questioning as gaming does today (Dyson, 2008). Over the years, the library has changed to reflect the changing recreational interests of the public that it supports. Currently, at least for electronic games, "the average game player is 35 years old and has been playing games for 12 years" (Entertainment Software Association, 2009), and "sixty-eight percent of American households play computer or video games" (Entertainment Software Association, 2009). Therefore, it makes sense that librarians support games for a growing portion of their population.

There are two primary ways through which a librarian supports games and gaming—through collections and services. Many librarians have created collections of games, and in this way the game is treated just like any other artifact in the library. Games are selected according to a selection policy to develop a collection that meets a specific need and audience. School and academic librarians build collections of games to support the curriculum either through games that teach other subjects or games that are used to teach courses about gaming. A growing number of special collections of games and game-related materials are in libraries and museums. These games can be accessed by users in the same way that other forms of media are accessed. In many cases, they are circulated and played either at home or in the libraries. Supporting games as collections falls in line with a more traditional view of librarianships and can neatly fall underneath policies that dictate other collections.

In line with new librarianship is the support of gaming as a service. With these gaming services, patrons are able to play games in the library. There are several ways that gaming goes in libraries. Most librarians allow patrons to use computers for whatever they would like for a certain period of time. This means that while patrons can use the computers for database searching and web browsing, they can also use them for personal e-mail, social networking, and gaming. Some librarians do ask that while others are waiting, those using computers for personal enjoyment limit their use. Another common implementation of gaming in libraries is as part of a summer reading program or other program for children. One traditional sight in many libraries is public domain games, such as chess or checkers. In fact, U.S. libraries have supported chess since the 1850s (Mechanics' Institute, 2009).

The growing area of gaming as a service is a formal gaming program. These programs could be focused on one game, such as a Scrabble tournament, or one type of game, like the Nintendo Wii, or a variety of board, card, and video games in a mixed session. These gaming programs may be an open play event, where players come and engage in games with each other with no other structure, or a tournament, where players play within a structure with the goal of providing competitive play and recognition. These programs could be focused on one age group, such as teens or seniors; could be explicitly intergenerational, such as a family game day; or could be open to all. Programs could be one-time or ongoing, and they vary in size from a Pokemon regional tournament that draws hundreds or an ongoing Dungeons and Dragons game that brings six players per week.

Surveys done by the Library Game Lab of Syracuse have unearthed three common reasons for gaming programs. The most common reason is to provide a service for those who are not served as well as other groups by the libraries; typically, these are teen-focused programs designed to draw teens into the library. Another common reason is to create an activity that allows members of the community to engage with each other in a participatory manner (compared with more passive programs where the audience comes together to watch something but not engage). The third common reason for gaming programs is to extend existing library programs; summer reading gaming is a good example of this. Because games engage and motivate, gaming programs can create new dimensions to book talks and other traditional library programs (Nicholson, 2009).

One of the problems that librarians can have in starting gaming programs is making decisions about which games to use based on personal gaming interests. Just as librarians should not make decisions about which books to purchase for the library based on their own reading interests, librarians need to be careful to represent the needs and interests of their target community in selecting games. Librarians should start with their mission and goals and use these to inspire development of gaming experiences. The games selected should be justifiable as the most appropriate choice for the patron group and the librarians' missions. The programs can then be assessed to demonstrate how they fulfill the librarians' goals. These assessments are then valuable for those needing to answer the critics of gaming programs.

When used with the librarians' goals and missions in mind, gaming programs can be motivating ways to bring people to the library on a regular basis to engage with each other through shared activities. They easily fit into the model of new librarianship as interactive and exciting activities that fit the interests of a growing group of the population.

RELATED ARTIFACTS

Dyson, J. P. (2008, November 2–4). *The power of play today*. Presentation at the ALA Techsouce Gaming, Learning, and Libraries Symposium, Chicago, IL.

Electronic Software Association. (2009). *Industry facts*. Retrieved December 28, 2009, from http://www.theesa.com/facts/index.asp.

Mechanics' Institute Library & Chess Room. (2009). *About us*. Retrieved September 29, 2008, from http://www.milibrary.org/MI_about_us.pdf.

Nicholson, S. (2009). Go back to start: Gathering baseline data about gaming in libraries. *Library Review, 58*(3), 203–214.

For more information about gaming in libraries, Dr. Nicholson taught a 30-video course through YouTube on Gaming in Libraries, which can be accessed at http://gamesinlibraries.org/course. In addition, Dr. Nicholson has written a book on the topic called Everyone Plays at the Library, which is coming out by Information Today in 2010.

GETTING PAST THE L V I DEBATE

MAP LOCATION

F, 10

THREAD LOCATION

Page 171

SCAPE

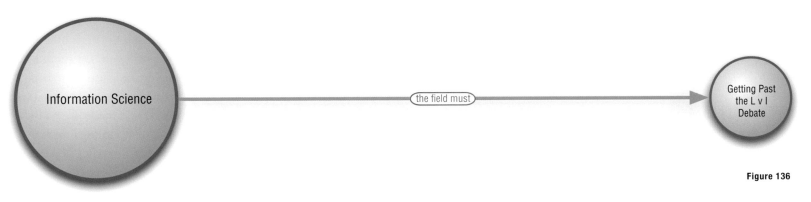

Figure 136

GO TO THE CONVERSATION

MAP LOCATION

D, 5

THREAD LOCATION

Page 114

SCAPE

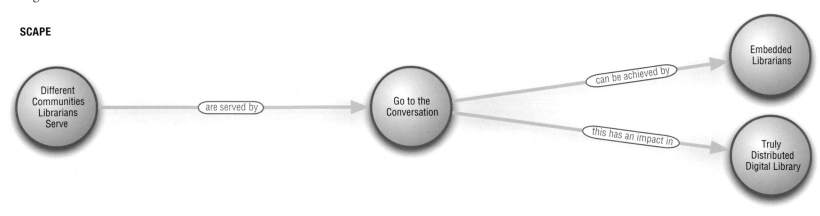

Figure 137

GOVERNMENT

MAP LOCATION

D, 6

THREAD LOCATION

Page 105

SCAPE

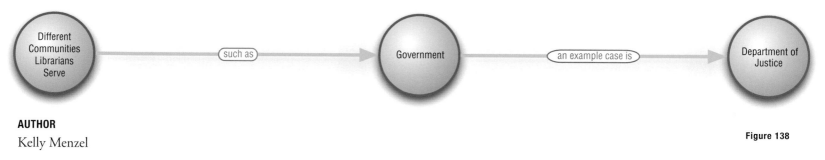

AUTHOR

Kelly Menzel

Figure 138

AGREEMENT DESCRIPTION

Government libraries vary just as much as public and academic libraries do in terms of size and audience.[1] Some are tiny and have a narrow scope, such as the apparently volunteer-run NCTC Conservation Library, whereas others, like the Library of Congress, are large.[2] Still others function more as academic or public libraries. Military base libraries, for example, are meant to support active duty members, their families, base staff, retired military members, and even military school students and local people in all their information and entertainment needs. In fact, a large number of public and academic libraries serve partially as government libraries through their function of federal depositories. Therefore, it makes sense that each has a radically different membership to serve. A university that functions as a federal depository may serve students, faculty, and researchers of its usual community, but the depository also serves the general public of the area, local government, and other libraries. Meanwhile, the NCTC serves NCTC staff, students, Aramark employees, FWS employees, and visiting scholars, although some of the collections and services are available to the general public as well.[3] Each, however, shares the common goal of attempting to serve its particular communities as well as possible.

This is obviously a wide range of member communities to deal with, even for a single library. What skills can unite such a wide range of member needs and library types? In other words, what does one need to be able to serve these communities? The Federal Library and Information Center Committee (FLICC) has produced a document of federal librarian competencies, which attempts to outline this.

The paper's sections for "Program Development and Outreach" and "Customer Education and Training," which are most relevant to basing services off one's community, suggest that an expert (the highest level of competency) should be able to do the following:

1. To see the range, see http://www.usa.gov/Topics/Reference_Shelf/Libraries.shtml#U.

2. U.S. Fish and Wildlife Service Conservation Library. "National Conservation training Center." National Conservation Training Center. 15 July 2009. http://library.fws.gov.

3. U.S. Fish and Wildlife Service Conservation Library. "About the Conservation Library." *National Conservation Training Center.* 15 July 2009. http://library.fws.gov/About.html; U.S. Fish and Wildlife Service Conservation Library. "FWS/Open Access Publications." *National Conservation Training Center.* 15 July 2009. http://library.fws.gov/FWSOpenAccess.html.

Program Development and Outreach

- Demonstrates ability to evaluate and adapt the principles and practices of program and event planning and development.

- Demonstrates ability to evaluate and adapt the principles and practices of outreach to existing and potential clienteles.

- Demonstrates ability to develop, evaluate, and support alliances and collaborative relationships in program development and outreach.

- Demonstrates ability to evaluate and stratify existing and potential clienteles to customize programs and outreach.[4]

Customer Education and Training

- Demonstrates ability to evaluate bibliographic instruction outcomes and adapt delivery methods.

- Demonstrates ability to evaluate information literacy programs' outcomes and adapt them.

- Demonstrates ability to evaluate and select standard or emerging training and instructional techniques.

- Demonstrates ability to evaluate and select or design the library's instructional materials.

- Demonstrates ability to evaluate and select or create education and training delivery methodologies.

- Demonstrates ability to create and evaluate the library's education and training products, services, and programs.

- Demonstrates ability to apply understanding of diverse learning styles to evaluate efficacy of education and training programs.

- Demonstrates ability to plan, implement, evaluate, and adapt library educational and training programs.[5]

All of these skills are about tailoring current practices elsewhere in the field to the librarian's particular environment and customer base. Unfortunately, the FLICC does not see the ability to create something entirely new to fit what the "customers" need, and to jettison current best practices elsewhere if they do not fit the members' needs, as an important skill. The biggest problem I see with these competencies, however, is that they do not mention discussing changes or decisions with the members at all, but merely applying theory of learning styles to what is done; and are focused solely on programming and teaching styles. It lists no changes of how the library works as a whole to accomplish these goals.

At the same time, these skills are basic enough to be listed as the core competencies for librarians in *any* setting. This is understandable because federal libraries alone are so diverse. The document recognizes this, stating, "The expectation is that the competencies will be helpful to others beyond the federal librarian community including human resource professionals, information technology peers and partners, executive level management, policy-makers, product developers and the vendor community, educational institutions, and certifying entities, as well as other information professionals."[6] Yet there is no mention of creating a dialog with the library members to discuss how to best change things. This seems to fly in the face of what the Department of Justice Law Libraries did because to know what their members needed, much conversation was required; even more was required to reach the point where the members relied heavily on what the librarians could find and trusted them to find the right information without even checking the catalog resources. Nor is there mention of working with other library types to create better services for shared communities despite the fact that government libraries often share the same audiences as local, public, academic, and special libraries—and despite the document's own mention of borrowing best practices. Without a dialog, how will those best practices be properly implemented in the first place, and how will anyone know how they were tweaked so that the profession as a whole can seek out better "best" practices? Essentially, the basic skills of serving a populace are in place within these core competencies, but the issue of communication and creating services when needed, rather than tailoring them out of old best practices, are ignored.

4. FLICC. "Federal Librarian Competencies October 2008." FLICC. October 2008. http://www.loc.gov/flicc/publications/Lib_Compt/Lib_Compt_Oct2008.pdf, 10–11.
5. FLICC, 13.
6. FLICC, 2.

Example Libraries

So, how do other libraries stack up against this document and against the Atlas' call for wholly serving one's community? To check, the Web sites of several different government libraries were examined to see how each library is currently working to actively serve its members.

The Muir S. Fairchild Research Information Center for Air University is, obviously, academic in nature.[7] It appears to be doing a good job of targeting its audience and getting conversations started even in the online sphere. There is a section entitled, "Featured New Books," directly on the homepage, which shows the book's cover and gives a short description. Clicking on the item unfortunately leads to only the catalog record for the book, which doesn't exactly invite discussion. However, the featured new books are each about main topics the students deal with and are a way of making the library relevant to their needs outside of the classroom. In addition, there are links on the side for the Text a Librarian and downloadable audio book projects, both of which show an attempt to connect to the members on their own level and through the means of communication they most often use. There's also a main sidebar for members to "make a comment," which leads to a short online form for making suggestions.[8] Unfortunately, every line must be filled out for the form to be processed, and there is no ability to remain anonymous. These requirements make it harder for people to quickly point out issues they have with the library or a simple service they wish was there. They also dissuade sending in complaints or asking for new services because the member's name and rank is on file. Programming is not advertised or even mentioned in any detail, leaving the library's services beyond the basic (book circulation, practice rooms, ILL) in question.[9]

The Wirtz Labor Library serves both Department of Labor employees and the general public with information regarding labor, both current and historical. The main page is simple and direct, stating what the library does and whom it serves, along with how members can use the online Web site, with major topics hyperlinked for easy access. The main resource sections (labor law library, law tips archive, Internet bibliographies, etc.) are also hyperlinked in a side bar; each leads to a more specific catalog or information regarding that service/collection. Although this is a traditional library portal, it seems to do a good job in serving its members by providing clear directions on how to access the information they are looking for. Unfortunately, the in-house services are not mentioned on the Web site, so people are more likely to simply use the Web site rather than seek out the physical location.

RELATED ARTIFACTS

Air University. *United States Air Force Muir S. Fairchild research information center.* Retrieved from http://www.au.af.mil/au/aul/lane.htm.

Federal librarian competencies. (2008, October). *FLICC.* Retrieved from http://www.loc.gov/flicc/publications/Lib_Compt/Lib_Compt_Oct2008.pdf.

U.S. Department of Labor. (n.d.). *Wirtz Labor Library.* Retrieved from http://www.dol.gov/oasam/library.

U.S. Fish and Wildlife Service Conservation Library. (2009). About the conservation library. *National conservation training center.* Retrieved from http://library.fws.gov/About.html.

U.S. Fish and Wildlife Service Conservation Library. (2009). National conservation training center. *National conservation training center.* Retrieved from http://library.fws.gov.

U.S. Fish and Wildlife Service Conservation Library. (2009). FWS/open access publications. *National conservation training center.* Retrieved from http://library.fws.gov/FWSOpenAccess.html.

7. Air University. Muir S. Fairchild Research Information Center. United States Air Force. 10 August 2009. http://www.au.af.mil/au/aul/lane.htm.
8. Air University. Muir S. Fairchild Research Information Center. "Make a Comment." United States Air Force. 10 August 2009. http://www.au.af.mil/au/aul/forms/comment.asp.
9. Air University. Muir S. Fairchild Research Information Center. "Maxwell-Gunter Community Libraries." United States Air Force. 10 August 2009. http://www.au.af.mil/au/aul/commun.htm.

GROWING IMPORTANCE OF TWO-WAY INFRASTRUCTURE

MAP LOCATION

E, 6

THREAD LOCATION

Page 112

SCAPE

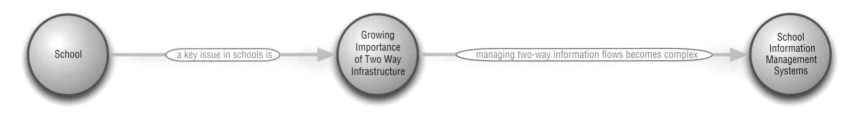

Figure 139

HUMANITIES

MAP LOCATION

E, 9

THREAD LOCATION

Page 176

SCAPE

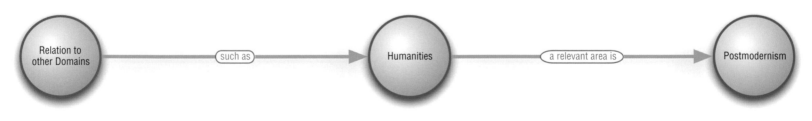

Figure 140

HYBRID ENVIRONMENTS

MAP LOCATION
C, 5

THREAD LOCATION
Page 94

SCAPE

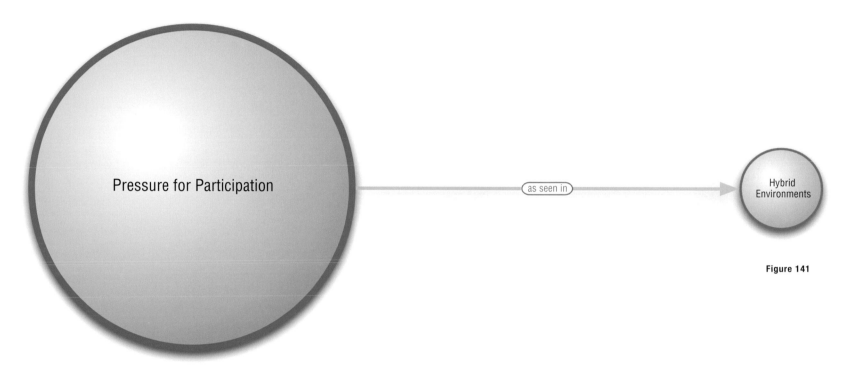

Pressure for Participation

as seen in

Hybrid
Environments

Figure 141

IMPORTANCE OF A WORLDVIEW

MAP LOCATION
B, C, 4

THREAD LOCATION
Page 15

SCAPE

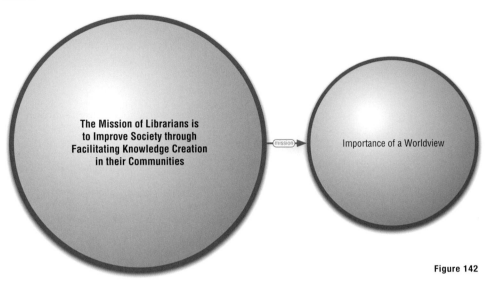

The Mission of Librarians is to Improve Society through Facilitating Knowledge Creation in their Communities

mission

Importance of a Worldview

Figure 142

AUTHOR
Kelly Menzel

CONVERSATION STARTERS

1. Where do programs fit into the current worldview of librarians? Although not artifacts, programs are often based on artifacts (books, games, even people in the case of guest speakers) and are usually highly focused on the tools used to accomplish a specific program's overarching goal. For example, your typical book club may be created to increase critical reading of books within a community, to create a sense of togetherness by having a large number of people read and think about the same thing (or talk about topics vaguely related to the book, more often), or even just to broaden people's horizons by having them read something they usually wouldn't. These same reasons, with slight tweaks, often drive other programming, such as gaming programs, film showings, and cultural events. However, librarians usually become so focused on the program (reading, showing a new film, inviting traditional storytellers) that the original meaning behind the program is lost and the reason becomes "to get people to show up" or "to have a neat program." In addition, programs vary widely by the type of library, as do the reasons behind them. An IL program may be created at a school media library to help students learn how to research effectively for classes, while the same program may be required by a college and integrated into the school curriculum or required for new employees at an office. So, do programs ultimately fit into the current artifact-based worldview, and where would they fit in a new, integrated worldview?

2. Once a uniform worldview is created, how do we go about making others aware of it from an outsider's point of view? Hopefully, having one will make the profession more unified in general and libraries will work "better" from the eyes of the patrons and other professions, which will in turn draw the attention of others. But is marketing the worldview to others advisable or even feasible? Worldviews are hard to explain, especially to those who aren't a part of them. At the same time, though, library members (and potential members) have a right to know what the worldview is behind their libraries, just as other professions and scholarly fields do. Placing the worldview by a library's mission on the Web site is one thing, but truly showing others the librarian's worldview is entirely different.

RELATED ARTIFACTS

Agre, P. (1997). The end of information & the future of libraries. *Progressive Librarian, 12/13*. Retrieved September 15, 2009, from http://libr.org/pl/12-13_Agre.html.

Annotation: This short article gives an overview of several previous worldviews in the information world. It also provides a potential future worldview for librarians to look to and touches on how such a worldview may affect how librarians and libraries work. It's interesting not only for the worldview it posits, which is similar in many aspects to that the Atlas appears to be calling for, but for the fact that it recognizes and explains changes in worldviews. The author recognizes the dialectical nature of today's society and the current lack of this in libraries, as well as sees communities as tied by common threads but still vastly different from each other. He feels that librarians need to reach out and help support the "collective cognition" of their communities. It also illustrates how changes in a worldview affect the world right down to terminology. Although it is from 1997, the ideas it puts forward are still valid and worth looking at.

Ewbank, A. D., & Moreillon, J. (2007). Is there a teacher-librarian worldview? This we believe.... *Knowledge Quest, 36*(1), 12–15. Retrieved September 11, 2009 from http://vnweb.hwwilsonweb.com.libezproxy2.syr.edu/hww/jumpstart.jhtml?recid=0bc05f7a67b1790e9e8f8b7ba4031106752adafc22c2fd52af2cee9acbb2cf74f54dfc0a779c119f&fmt=P.

Annotation: This article explicitly looks at the possibility of a specific teacher-librarian worldview, asking early in the article:

It is clear that all the authors in this issue feel a responsibility to go above and beyond their immediate work environment to advocate for the profession at large. We wonder if this sense of responsibility emanates from a shared worldview. Do we, as teacher-librarians, have a collective set of beliefs and values that underpin our work? How does our worldview influence our work as advocates? (Ewbank and Moreillon, 2007).

The authors give their own ideas as to what that particular worldview is, which, coupled with similar testimony from librarians in other specialties, could be helpful in determining what is similar and different about the various library positions. The authors' conversation also highlights issues stemming from the current lack of common worldview. The article is also helpful from a more basic standpoint, in that it gives a clear definition of worldview and how individuals form their worldviews, complete with examples.

Herring, J. (2008). Teacher librarian world view (2) and fish pie. *James Herring's Blog, September 3, 2008, 9:28 am.* Retrieved September 10, 2009, from http://jherring.wordpress.com/2008/09/03/teacher-librarian-world-view-2-and-fish-pie.

Annotation: The author references Ewbank and Moreillon's article and brings up several points it misses, including the fact that worldviews vary based on culture and geography, making the united worldview they propose unlikely. He uses an interesting analogy about fish pie recipes. Although he then digresses into actual recipes rather than introspection, he does make a valid point. This, however, could not easily count as a stand-alone piece; it needs to be used in reference to the article it discusses.

Sager, D. J. (2001). The search for librarianship's core values. *Public Libraries, 40*(3), 149–153. Retrieved from http://vnweb.hwwilsonweb.com.libezproxy2.syr.edu/hww/jumpstart.jhtml?recid=0bc05f7a67b1790e9e8f8b7ba40311065dd3b371894a6ac68637f934888a21db0d7125b2136a4d16&fmt=P.

Annotation: The article examines a set of "core values" that can help librarians recognize and articulate their beliefs, as well as providing new library students with a strong foundation. Although this is slightly different from a common worldview and more explicit (he is also only looking on a national level), his ideas as to why this is needed are similar to the reasoning behind a common worldview. They articulate the need for librarians to have something concrete in common from which to frame their decisions and help the public (and, likely, themselves) understand what librarians stand for. At one point, he states, "it is important to remember that without common values, we are not a profession." This statement seems worthwhile to look at in more depth. The core values, as created by the ALA Core Values Task Force, may be useful to look at when searching for wording and components of a common worldview.

Weissinger, T. (2003). Competing models of librarianship: Do core values make a difference? *The Journal of Academic Librarianship, 29*(1), 32–39. Retrieved from http://vnweb.hwwilsonweb.com.libezproxy2.syr.edu/hww/jumpstart.jhtml?recid=0bc05f7a67b1790e9e8f8b7ba40311062afd1711b1b0ce79b27b9492958d48aebc961c77f8e36b2e&fmt=P.

Annotation: This article contends that "cultural diversity and recruitment practices within academic libraries are limited by the profession's worldview." Although the author's comments on the hiring of minority librarians aren't relevant to the Atlas' goal, the article does contain some interesting points. The author is against the "distillation" of what librarians do and stand for into even the eight core values Sager references and proposes for enduring values rather than common values to be listed. There is an interesting list of historical librarian positions based on culture, and the author brings up questions regarding the worldview American libraries promote (i.e., a Western one). He comments on the limitations such a worldview creates, both in terms of space, and in the concept of who is a proper librarian. In addition, his philosophical connections may be worth looking into in more depth.

IMPORTANCE OF ACTION AND ACTIVISM

MAP LOCATION

D, E, 7

THREAD LOCATION

Page 117

SCAPE

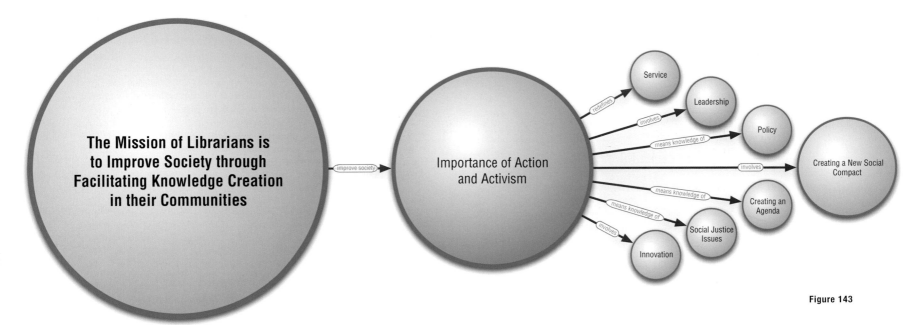

Figure 143

AUTHOR

Elizabeth Gall

AGREEMENT DESCRIPTION

In "Facilitating Knowledge Management and Knowledge Sharing: New Opportunities for Information Professionals," Marshall (1997) discusses the difference between information and knowledge. She explains that, "information is transformed into knowledge when a person reads, understands, interprets, and applies the information to a specific work function" (Marshall, 1997). The librarian's goal is to facilitate this process. This agreement examines what action and activism are necessary for librarians to facilitate knowledge creation in members.

A recurring theme throughout the Atlas and our discussion of new librarianship is that of knowledge creation. This theme is at the root of action and activism by librarians. The "Importance of Action and Activism" section in the Atlas argues that knowledge is created even when those having the conversation know little or nothing about the topic. Lankes explains that knowledge must be tested through action. But what action should be taken? The Atlas says that any action will impact knowledge creation, but it will also skew the conversation surrounding the topic. How can we as librarians know that our actions are not skewing the conversation for the worse?

Ojala (2004) believes we must tailor information to the audience. She argues that information professionals can take action not only by analyzing or summarizing information but also in how they present it. The first or boldest item in a list of resources is likely to have a greater impact than the last. Ojala champions this fact as a means to better serve members and to better market services. At no point does she discuss or even mention the ethical implications of skewing the conversation. Lankes concludes the "Importance of Action and Activism" section with a call for "a new apparatus of librarianship," a part of our worldview that ultimately talks about ethical and appropriate knowledge and conversation. Ojala's stance highlights just how important that is.

In addition to the call for a new apparatus, Lankes argues that simply having values and principles is not enough. Librarians must work to improve society through action. It can be argued that this is possible through the skewing of conversation. For example, if a librarian highlights the results of an online search that come from reliable, safe Internet sources, they are skewing the conversation to promote the creation of knowledge through responsible, safe web navigation.

A classmate, Jocelyn Clarke, shared an example regarding a search for information on mixing illegal drugs. She found the sites written by enthusiasts to contain more complete and helpful information than the neutral sites. Is it ethical and appropriate to encourage knowledge creation from a source that promotes breaking the law through illegal drug use? It may depend on the member. It would be more appropriate to share these sites with a mother worried about her wayward child than with a preteen working on a report for school. The student is most likely looking for facts while the mother is looking for a way to help her child.

As librarians we are taught not discriminate based on age, religion, socioeconomic status, and so on. Is skewing the conversation for members a method of discrimination? I don't think it is, but I do think it is a good question for librarians to keep in mind when taking action. If we are going to skew the conversation (we are), we must work to stay aware of how knowledge creation is changed. "Information professionals need to refrain from evaluating or 'improving' upon internal information" (Marshall, 1997). Librarians must be sure that they are not skewing the information in the process of skewing the conversation.

We cannot have a discussion on the importance of action and activism without also considering service. Librarians strive to serve the communities to which they belong. They also believe "the best knowledge comes from working in the richest information environment possible." What impact will "the richest information environment possible" have on knowledge creation? This includes proven as well as faulty information. Eventually, the Wright brothers figured out how to build a plane that would fly, but first they went through many plans and models that did not work. The richest information environment possible would include these faulty plans. A member is unlikely to learn how to build a plane from them, but they might gain a deeper understanding of the principles of flight. Librarians must be sure to keep a record of failures along with successes if they want the "best knowledge" to be created in their library.

Ultimately, only through action and activism can librarians ensure that members gain information in the manner that suits them best and determine which information is most valuable. Only through action and activism can librarians develop the richest information environment possible where the best knowledge can be created. Rowley (2006) argues that data become information, which becomes knowledge, which becomes wisdom. By taking the above actions, librarians will not only improve knowledge creation in their community but also encourage the creation of wisdom.

CONVERSATION STARTERS

1. What is ethical and appropriate knowledge and conversation?
2. When a librarian provides a member with several resources from different publishers, media, schools of thought, and so on, how is knowledge creation impacted? Does it discourage the creation of new knowledge?
3. What role do librarians play in documenting knowledge creation within their community? Should all knowledge creation be recorded even if the knowledge it creates is faulty?

RELATED ARTIFACTS

Marshall, L. (1997, September/October). Facilitating knowledge management and knowledge sharing: new opportunities for information professionals. *Online, 21*. Retrieved from http://vnweb.hwwilsonweb.com/hww/jumpstart.jhtml?recid=0bc05f7a6 7b1790e9e8f8b7ba403110609cab8641d5a38367839d243c98f8570bc64e3bd8603d eae&fmt=H.

Ojala, M. (2004). Information creation. *Online, 28*(2). Retrieved from http://vnweb. hwwilsonweb.com/hww/jumpstart.jhtml?recid=0bc05f7a67b1790e9e8f8b7ba40311 06684a178ede8d7997e16ba217d69bf64bba73fb0643bf74b7&fmt=P.

Prekop, P. (2002). A qualitative study of collaborative information seeking. *Journal of Documentation, 58*(5). Retrieved from http://www.emeraldinsight. com/10.1108/00220410210441000 doi: 10.1108/00220410210441000.

Rowley, J. (2006). Where is the wisdom that we have lost in knowledge? *Journal of Documentation, 62*(2). Retrieved from http://www.emeraldinsight. com/10.1108/00220410610653332 doi: 10.1108/00220410610653332.

IMPORTANCE OF TECHNICAL SKILLS

MAP LOCATION

C, 8

THREAD LOCATION

Page 167

SCAPE

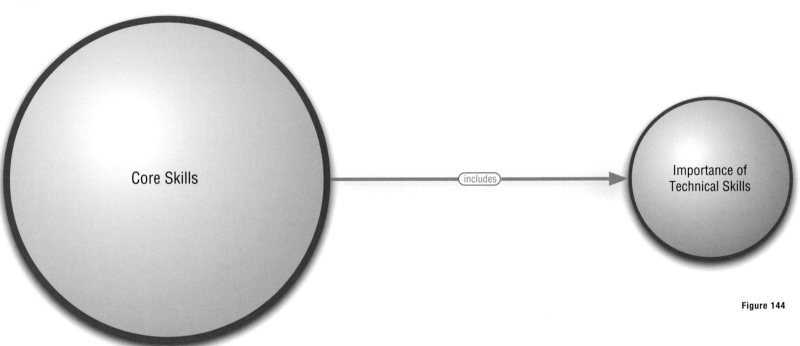

Figure 144

MAP LOCATION

C, 3, 4

THREAD LOCATION

Page 18

SCAPE

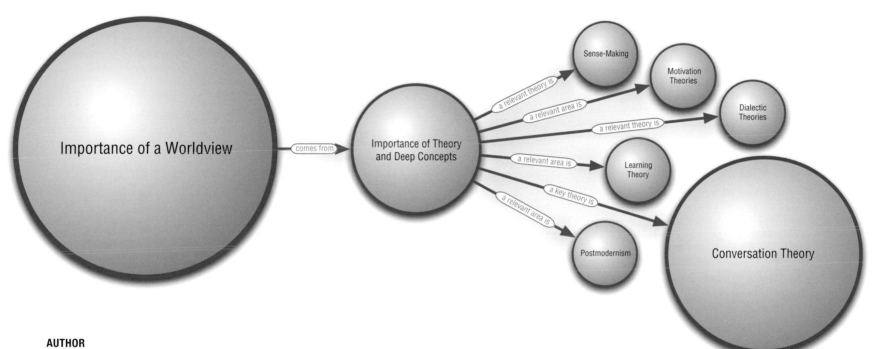

AUTHOR

Michael Luther

Figure 145

CONVERSATION STARTERS

1. Institutions have missions and Associations have missions, but do broad fields such as Sociology or Psychology have missions?

RELATED ARTIFACTS

Brooks, M. (2008). *13 things that don't make sense: The most baffling scientific mysteries of our time*. New York: Doubleday.

> Annotation: The basic idea is that every problem is an opportunity, and sometimes what can seem an unsolvable problem is actually potential for a giant advance. But the prologue of this interesting book says it far better than I can, so I will let the book speak for itself.
>
> "In Science, being completely and utterly stuck can be a good thing; it often means a revolution is coming."
>
> "The Things that don't make sense are, in some ways, the only things that matter."
>
> There has been so much talk of the imminent cataclysm within librarianship—that the field is obsolete, and it is merely a matter of time. Although the last decade has been a period of great creativity and experimentation in libraries, I don't know that we are any less stuck. Our relevance is still very much on the table. What librarians have shown is their perseverance and creative thinking. Maybe the time is ripe for our own revolution.

Crowley, B. (2005). *Spanning the theory-practice divide in library and information science*. Lanham, MD: Scarecrow Press.

> Annotation: This is a review of Crowley's book. The idea of cultural pragmatism is introduced as a means of bridging the wide gap between the academic and the practitioner. Cultural pragmatism is "an aid to researchers in both camps for its inclusion of context specificity and the need for testing a theory's usefulness through continually analyzed experience." Theory cannot just be an exercise for furthering one's academic career; it must be applicable in the real world.

Jones, B. (2005). Revitalizing theory in library and information science: The contribution of process philosophy. *Library Quarterly, 75*(2), 101–121. Retrieved from Library Literature and Information Science Full Text Database.

> Annotation: With a focus on theory and knowledge and an emphasis on "the library in the life of a person," this article seems particularly relevant to our discussions of the importance of theory.

Kim, S., & Jeong, D. Y. (2006). An analysis of the development and use of theory in library and information science research articles. *Library & Information Science Research, 28*(4), 548–562. Retrieved from Library Literature and Information Science Full Text Database.

Annotation: This article ties into the Atlas nicely by helping the library community to understand the current state of theory development and use. Analytical articles like this one will help us see where we are and where we should go, perhaps by seeing which are the most hopeful theories to follow or merging theories into a more unified theory of librarianship.

Perrone, V. (2009). Theory and practice in the library workplace. *LIS News*. Retrieved from http://www.lisnews.org/taxonomy/term/17.

> Annotation: Perrone points out that the purpose of theory is to tell us why we are doing things. Library school is an ideal place to engender this "shared theoretical basis." Although these theories are not eternal, such systems of values can become internalized and therefore deeply entrenched. Managers should also lead occasional theoretical discussions to draw out competing theories within an organization. Perrone notes the shift that has occurred in the way libraries are perceived and suggests that change has come so fast that we should not make assumptions that everyone has the same understanding of our field.

Qvortrup, L. (2007). *The public library: From information access to knowledge management: A theory of knowledge and knowledge categories*. Retrieved from http://informationr.net/ir/12-4/colis/colis17.html.

> Annotation: This article investigates a topic that should be very important to our current discussions in New Librarianship: knowledge. The author presumes that the job of the library is not to provide access to limitless quantities of information (as he claims it once was) but to provide knowledge management. After discussing a number of past theories of knowledge, he offers a new one: "Knowledge is confirmed observations." This confirmation can take place on a personal level (by oneself) or on a social level (by someone else). Knowledge is broken into four categories, and functions are assigned to each category. This, the author hopes, will help to organize the modern library.

Thompson, K. M. (2009). Remembering Elfreda Chatman: A champion of theory development in library and information science education. *Journal of Education for Library and Information Science, 50*(2), 119–126. Retrieved from Library, Literature, and Information Science Full Text database.

> Annotation: Thompson, by using Chatman's extended work in theory and theory building as an exemplar, hopes to aid in teaching the "practical use of theory and theory building" in library and information science. Chatman was interested in "information poverty" and applied various social theories to shine light on user behavior and information poverty specifically. Four social theories are examined: Diffusion Theory, Opinion Leadership Theory, Alienation Theory, and Gratification Theory.

INCREASE FRICTION IN THE PROCESS

MAP LOCATION

D, 9

THREAD LOCATION

Page 179

SCAPE

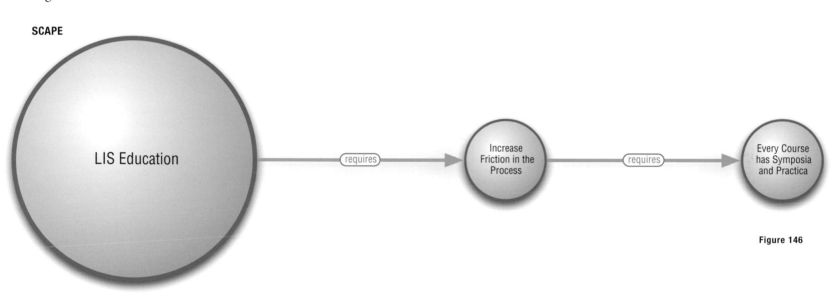

Figure 146

INFORMATION ORGANIZATION

MAP LOCATION

E, 3

THREAD LOCATION

Page 137

SCAPE

Figure 147

INFORMATION SCIENCE

MAP LOCATION

E, 10

THREAD LOCATION

Page 171

SCAPE

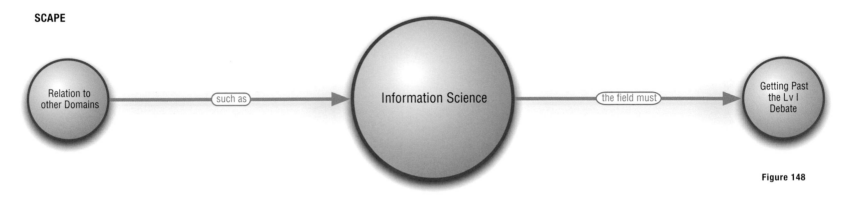

Figure 148

INFORMATION SEEKING

MAP LOCATION

E, 4

THREAD LOCATION

Page 153

SCAPE

Figure 149

INFORMATION SERVICES

MAP LOCATION

E, 6

THREAD LOCATION

Page 88

SCAPE

Figure 150

AGREEMENT DESCRIPTION

See Internet Model Example Agreement Supplement

INFRASTRUCTURE PROVIDERS

MAP LOCATION

E, 5

THREAD LOCATION

Page 86

SCAPE

Figure 151

AGREEMENT DESCRIPTION

See Internet Model Example Agreement Supplement

INNOVATION

MAP LOCATION

F, 6

THREAD LOCATION

Page 127

SCAPE

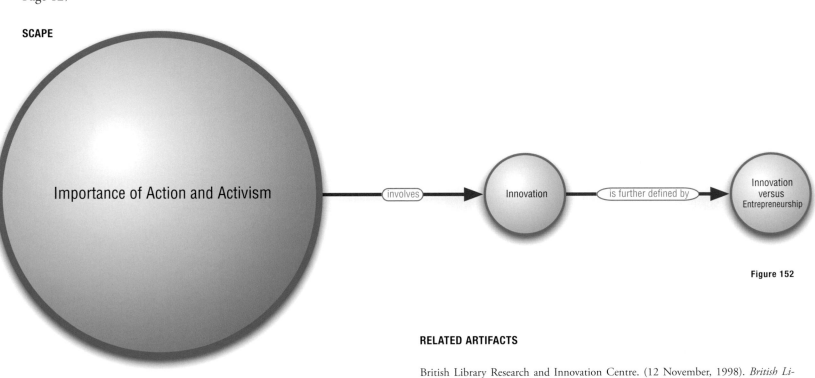

Importance of Action and Activism → involves → Innovation → is further defined by → Innovation versus Entrepreneurship

Figure 152

CONTRIBUTOR

Jennifer Recht

CONVERSATION STARTERS

1. We should innovate because any organization can stagnate and eventually fail without change. But we should also innovate because it's a buzzword that looks great on resumes and library mission statements. How do we tell the difference between innovating because we have to, in a good way, and innovating because we have to, in a bad way?

2. How can we get around the creativity-killing anxiety that arises when we are told we must innovate (now!)?

3. Is there ever a time when something is going so well that we should stop innovating for a while? How can we tell?

RELATED ARTIFACTS

British Library Research and Innovation Centre. (12 November, 1998). *British Library Research and Innovation Centre*. Retrieved from http://http://www.ukoln.ac.uk/services/papers/bl.

Eventective, Inc. (2009). *Westville Library and Innovation Centre*. Retrieved from http://www.eventective.com/Canada/Nova+Scotia/Westville/212465/Westville-Library-Innovation-Centre.html.

Journal of Library Innovation. (n.d). *Journal of Library Innovation*. Retrieved from http://www.libraryinnovation.org/index.

Public Library Association. (n.d.). *Highsmith Library Innovation Award*. Retrieved from http://http://www.ala.org/ala//pla/plaawards/highsmithlibrary.cfm.

River John. (n.d.). *River John Library and Innovation Centre*. Retrieved from http://www.riverjohn.com/index.php?option=com_content&task=view&id=19&Itemid=33.

Sloane, P. (3 November 2009). *21 great ways to innovate*. Retrieved from http://www.innovationtools.com/Articles/EnterpriseDetails.asp?a=473.

Town of New Glasgow. (2008) *Public library: New Glasgow Library and Innovation Centre*. Retrieved from http://www.newglasgow.ca/index.php?Itemid=137&id=54&option=com_content&task=view.

INNOVATION VERSUS ENTREPRENEURSHIP

MAP LOCATION

F, G, 6

THREAD LOCATION

Page 128

SCAPE

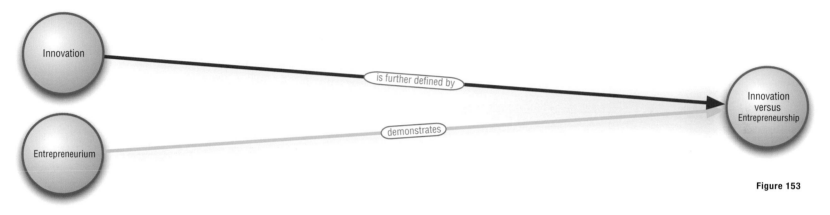

Figure 153

INSTITUTE FOR ADVANCED LIBRARIANSHIP IDEA

MAP LOCATION

E, 8

THREAD LOCATION

Page 184

SCAPE

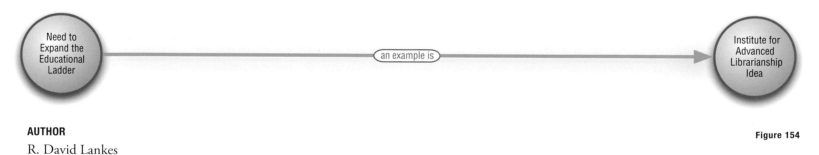

AUTHOR

R. David Lankes

Figure 154

AGREEMENT DESCRIPTION

A Note about the Description

Developed initially as part of ongoing dialogs with the Free Library of Philadelphia and other library and information science schools, the Institute is an example means of expanding the educational ladder (see "Need to Expand the Educational Ladder"). The ideas within this example could certainly be replicated at any prestigious and/or progressive library (academic, public, special, governmental, etc.).

The following description is a slightly modified version of a proposal prepared for the Free Library of Philadelphia. It has been slightly modified to make it more generic, but it is still a proposal and reads as such.

Concept

The Institute for Advanced Librarianship is envisioned as an elite clinical teaching and research environment that seeks to innovate current library practice and invent the future of the field. It shall prepare future leaders in information science and technology with world-class academic and research programs that emphasize innovation and real-word impact. The Institute shall be a shared effort of the library science community, housed at one of the nation's leading universities and located at the world-class library. Rather than competing with other library science programs, it will work with and enhance the current offerings of these programs.

Each year the Institute will offer 10 fellowships to current LIS students who have completed their basic or core instruction (normally their first year of a full-time program). These students will be in residence at the partner library for two semesters, where they will study as a cohort, improving and innovating real services for real users. They will gain invaluable technical and organizational skills (marketing, change management, risk assessment, budgeting) from full-time faculty, experts from industry, visits to policymakers, and top practitioners all in the framework of innovation and change. They will then return to their home schools to graduate.

Detailed in this agreement are the concepts, structure, and aspirations for the Institute. It is divided up for easy access to the particulars, but taken as a whole it is a vision for harnessing the strengths of partners and location to improve libraries and, ultimately, the communities they serve. The Institute is a place to prepare change agents in the academy, industry, government, schools, and towns throughout the continent.

The Need

Libraries in North America are seeking a new mission. Beyond the advances in technology and the explosion in information production, the communities they serve are changing, forcing libraries to adapt. These communities are changing as a result of the increasing capabilities of and reliance on a digital information infrastructure. This digital transformation shows up not only on the Internet but in areas as diverse as entertainment, where digital distribution of media is changing television and music distribution alike; government, as essential services such as tax payment and even voting are becoming digitally enabled; banking; and health care. Whether a community member interfaces with this new digital world through a computer, cell phone, or mediator such as a bank, the digital pressure is changing nearly all aspects of daily life. In such a world of connected massive stores of diverse data, no wonder libraries that seek to serve these communities are facing a challenge of identity, resources, and mission.

While library science and information schools have traditionally served as facilitators in such field-wide examinations, their effectiveness in this role has been blunted. There are several reasons for this:

- A Greater Emphasis on Research Funding: The economic realities in higher education drive any discipline in today's universities to greater emphasis on research funds; there is also greater pressure to grow existing degree programs and start new ones. The need to expand budgets through research funds means a greater emphasis on applied research in "hot areas." Today, with information being central to so many endeavors, those hot areas are in defense, telecommunications, and economic development. Further, although many universities are trying to reverse the trend, career success for research faculty still comes through increased specialization, making the results of research harder to translate into broader settings, including libraries.

- Pressure to Expand Enrollment in Degree Programs and Start New Degree Programs: Although research dollars are an expanding part of a school's budget, in most programs tuition pays the bills. Add to this the pressure of growing college enrollments and a societal pressure for more universal postsecondary education, and classes are getting bigger. Where more library science students may not be found, new programs at the master's and undergraduate levels are leading to larger schools with more diverse foci. In some universities, information science is being cast as an essential curriculum, and schools are being asked to take a greater role on curricula throughout a university or college's offerings.

- The Increased Shifting of Boundaries in the Information Professions: As more and more industries are awakening to the value of effective information utilization, they are seeking the graduates of library and information science schools. The realities of higher salaries—and, in some students' minds, greater chance for change—are putting pressure on schools to deliver more transferrable skills. As such, many classes teach vital skills but without a library-centric view.

- The Lack of a Continuing Education Model: The main problem that library and information schools face is the lack of a continuing education model for the field. There are few requirements for ongoing engagement between schools and professionals beyond the initial master's degree. What's more, with a wide variety of conferences and workshops offered by a vast range of nonuniversity organizations, it is nearly impossible to maintain a long-term dialog between the schools and the profession. So while universities have much to offer to the library profession in terms of new models, missions, and skills, their most efficient corridor to the field is through new graduates who enter an organization with little cultural knowledge and low professional status.

Far from being seen as universally negative, the ability of the library and information science schools to adapt and, in many cases, thrive in the current higher education marketplace is a good thing for library science as a whole. There are more students enrolled now in library science programs than ever before, and they are graduating with new and valuable skills. However, there are few if any places where library innovation is being examined in a holistic way.

This has led to the profession forming a series of leadership programs. However, as Jana Varlejs (2007) of Rutgers University states, "Leadership institutes for librarians have proliferated recently in the United States, yet there has been little evaluation to show whether they are effective in producing leaders." These programs tend to be short term, with a week or two attendance, and uncoordinated. However, such programs have shown success. The goal of the Institute for Advanced Librarianship would be to build on these programs designed for mid-career professionals by preparing leaders earlier in the process and concentrating on change management and innovation.

As the library science schools expand and succeed, there is an increased need for a program that can concentrate their success and learning to the library as an institution. As the library profession forms leadership programs, there is a need to concentrate their lessons earlier in the career and in a greatly expanded format. The proposed Institute is presented as a means to these ends.

By proactively engaging the next generation of leaders and giving them the skills to enter, innovate, and, most important, institute lasting change in organizations, the Institute shall prepare libraries for the changing world they exist within. Furthermore, the Institute shall create a dedicated cohort of change agents that will position libraries as leading institutions within their communities, where they can garner greater support and respect through excellence in service.

Institute Impacts

Margaret Mead is quoted as saying, "Never doubt that a small group of thoughtful, committed citizens can change the world. Indeed, it's the only thing that ever has." It is this sentiment that shapes the Institute to be small in terms of people but large in terms of impact. This plan lays out a program with 10 students per year and three full-time faculty. These numbers are unheard of in a field where full-time faculties can be as large as 45, and schools can graduate more than 200 students a year. The size does not represent a lack of ambition but instead a strong desire for focus. In essence, this program seeks to create Mead's small group of "thoughtful, committed citizens" who shall change the world. This impact approach is based on the realities of the library field.

Librarianship is a profession that is diverse in its settings but coherent in its membership. One can reach a large percentage of the library profession efficiently through the Internet and conferences. Once you reach this core of engaged individuals, one can have enormous impact. For example, presentations at the American Library Association's annual conferences reach provosts at universities, school librarians in K–12 schools, public librarians, and even Chief Information Officers in industry. Furthermore, rightly or wrongly, individuals have been shown to have a large impact on the thinking of the profession. From Melvyl Dewey to F. W. Lancaster, the field is often primed for dynamic individuals with a compelling mission.

The potential for impact can be seen in the rise of virtual reference. In a little less than 8 years, a relatively small group of researchers and practitioners were able to transform answering reference questions online from a novelty to a broadly implemented basic service in public, academic, and corporate settings. Similar experiences can be recounted in the metadata and public access computing communities.

The Institute shall have the following short- mid-, and long-term impacts:

- Short Term: The Institute will be quickly positioned in a leadership role within the library practice community, given its home at both a library and a prestigious university.

- Short Term: Library and information science programs will seek partnership with the Institute due to its position within a prestigious university and the ability to highlight their own contributions to library science.

- Mid Term: The Institute shall highlight the utility of library and information science through an expanding network of partnerships with industry and clinical faculty.

- Mid Term: The experiences of the Institute in working with students from a diverse set of LIS programs will aid partnering schools in refining their curricula by providing direct feedback on student preparation by comparing students across programs.

- Mid Term: Projects of the Institute will improve service offerings at the Free Library of Philadelphia and partnering practice environments.

- Long Term: The growing cohort of Institute graduates will take on leadership positions within library science, thus providing a greater platform for library innovation and positive change.

- Long Term: Libraries will improve and increase their benefits to their communities.

The Institute shall not be simply a school but a school of thought. It shall have a focused and integrated intellectual signature that will diffuse throughout the field through its research, students, and operations.

The Curriculum

The curriculum of the Institute shall be an equal mix of practica and symposia taught by some of the nation's leaders in information science, marketing, technology, and librarianship. Rotating hands-on practica shall place students in direct contact with the subject matter and the community. Students shall learn customer service skills from reference librarians, vice presidents, and marketers. They shall learn information organization from catalogers, metadata specialists, and digital library researchers. They shall learn technology from IT staff running libraries, corporate CIOs, and university provosts. They will learn policy from visits to Congress and participation in legislative days. This experience-based learning shall be complemented by symposia—highly interactive classes with scholars, business entrepreneurs, and thought leaders from around the world. The net effect will be a continuous cycle of ideas and innovation matched to the realities of real-world institutions.

Structured Outcomes, Unstructured Courses

The Institute curriculum shall take advantage of the small number of students, the focus of innovation, the location at a world-class library, and ready access to a deep pool of expertise in the region by not using a traditional 3-credit hour topical structure. Instead, the structure of the courses will be highly fluid, with only a few structural components consistent from year to year:

- A standing daily symposium for the cohort and faculty to exchange ideas, plan new experiences, and jointly explore topics.

- A year-long practicum where the student explores an area of librarianship and produces a functional system (piece of software, service, collections, or process) that has been implemented and is appropriately sustainable.

- A colloquium on the topic of their practicum that the student organizes and is delivered to the library community.

In place of formal classes and traditional structure, the Institute's curriculum shall be founded on the growing model of assessment in high education: outcomes. Through the course of planning and launching, the overall goal and objectives of the Institute in technology, innovation, and change will be refined into a rubric. This rubric constitutes a sort of contract between the Institute and its academic partners. To provide real evidence and outcomes, the Institute shall use a series of mid-semester reviews and a portfolio to ensure student achievement.

The actual content of the curriculum will come from a variety of sources:

- The Faculty: Full-time faculty, clinical faculty, and faculty of practice will work one on one with students and as a cohort to explore aspects of librarianship and information industries. They will share their own expertise and craft practical engagements to cement concepts.

- Directed Readings: Each year, with the input of the faculty and the Board of Visitors, a reading list shall be constructed. The readings shall form a common core of information that students and faculty alike shall use in their interactions and projects.

- Field Experiences: Visits from and to libraries, information science schools, government, and industry located throughout the region.

The core of the Institute's educational program lies in a practicum experience. The students, working with the faculty, shall devise a year-long project that they will have to plan, execute, and evaluate. This project (practicum) shall incorporate outcomes from across their experiences, and they shall reach out to experts at their home schools, other LIS programs, industry, government, and the not-for-profit sectors.

The bottom line is that with a strong focus on outcomes over courses, the Institute shall be responsive to current events and able to take advantage of new opportunities as they arise. In many ways, the Institute's curriculum shall reflect highly successful PhD and management programs.

Research in the Curriculum

A heavy dependence on faculty for a curriculum centered around innovation requires that the faculty involved are engaged in innovation activities. To that end, core faculty are expected to have active research agendas. These agendas shall include funded research activities from multiple sources. They are also expected to include cohort students in these projects. In fact, student practica may be portions of these funded research projects.

Faculty Model

A diverse and fluid Institute requires multiple types of faculty to serve differing purposes, including providing consistency across cohorts, direct guidance on research, library-centric viewpoints, and broader information perspectives, as well as highly specialized expertise in areas such as marketing and economics. The faculty model of the Institute breaks out each of these roles and their responsibilities.

Core Faculty

The key personnel of the Institute are three tenure-track professors who run the Institute, have the most contact with students, and provide the scholarly underpinnings of the program. Because the primary aim of the program is innovation and re-invention of a vital field, the scholarly core is essential. True, lasting innovation must be derived from core principles and theory. The core faculty must be academically rigorous to ensure a strong conceptual foundation for this new approach to librarianship.

Core faculty are seen as innovative, with excellent reputations and research skills, yet they are in the middle or even early phases of

their careers to provide long-term benefit to the Institute. They shall have PhDs in the library and information science domain and would be expected to actively seek external funding for research and projects. The three core faculty would each have distinct roles:

- Director: Oversees the Institute, is the interface between Institute partners, and provides overall vision and leadership for the program.

- Associate Director for Research: Is tasked with seeking out and creating funded research opportunities, provides methodological guidance to other faculty and students, and interfaces with research funders.

- Associate Director for Academics: Oversees other faculty types, works to bring in the highest quality clinical faculty, and structures and schedules curricular activities.

All faculty would be expected to be on the tenure track and comply with tenure requirements at the university partner. This is vital not only to ensuring the quality of the faculty (and making that quality evident to those outside of the Institute), but also in terms of recruiting and sustained performance. It will be nearly impossible to recruit top-tier faculty to the Institute without the protection of tenure. The market for LIS faculty is currently competitive, with existing information and library science faculties growing rapidly. Given the choice between a tenure-track position and a non-tenure-track spot, the natural inclination will be to a school offering tenure.

Clinical Faculty

Clinical faculty members are affiliated experts in their disciplines who teach symposia and aid students in their practica. They are expected to have full-time careers outside of the Institute and to maintain outstanding reputations in those outside endeavors. These are not the traditional "adjunct" faculty who are brought in to teach regularly taught courses, but rather leaders in industry, government, and librarianship who share their valuable time once or twice a semester.

Faculty of Practice

Faculty of practice are full-time employed staff at the partner library and partnering organizations that provide direct oversight of students as part of their regular duties. Examples might include the head of the Business and Industry Department who will work with students and show them how to manage such an operation, much as an internship supervisor might. It should be noted that not all staff at the library would be considered a faculty of practice—only those staff members who show excellence in their operations, dedication to the mission of the Institute, and great engagement in their interaction with students.

Plan Partners

Partners are essential for its creation and continued success. While the list of partners will grow as the Institute moves from planning to implementation to continued operation, the types of partners needed at this point are clear:

- A Setting for the Institute
- Library and Information Science Schools
- Libraries
- Academic Home
- Funders

Each of these broad categories is addressed in greater depth below.

The Setting

The Institute shall be physically housed in a large library with ready access to regional resources in commerce, government, and nonprofit sectors. The size of the library matters in that it must provide many rich opportunities for experimentation. The physical location of the library is also important in that it should provide access to multiple library types for student projects. So while Institute students may meet in a public library, for example, they may be doing their project work across town in an academic or a school library.

Not an Apprenticeship Program

It needs to be made clear that the Institute is not envisioned as an apprenticeship program or some sort of superinternship. This is not intended to bring the best students to the library to learn existing practices and spend their days mastering the tools of present librarianship. Although some hands-on work is needed as a basis to launch innovative services, the focus is on developing new and better practice. This development will be done through scholarship and experimentation, not replication and praxis. In this way, the Institute does not represent a step back to the days when library schools were simply

outgrowth of library training programs, but a new paradigm where outstanding scholarship is done at the point of impact, much like a university hospital where new treatments are developed.

Schools

There are 56 ALA-accredited library programs in North America.[1] These programs represent a wide variety of institutions—from the small and specialized to the large and diverse. The LIS programs are vital partners for the Institute in three ways:

1. Shapers of the Innovation Curriculum: Participating schools will be a large source of the initial and ongoing shape of the Institute's curriculum. Through consultation with standing bodies of LIS programs like ALISE and the iSchool conference, as well as members of the Institute's Board of Visitors, the experiences of LIS programs will help shape the offerings of the Institute.
2. Pool of Applicants: As of 2004,[2] there were nearly 17,000 master's students working toward a degree in library science (Wisser & Saye, 2004). This represents the pool from which 10 shall be chosen.
3. Partners in Research: Just as the Institute seeks to be highly collegial in its educational offerings, so too does it seek to collaborate widely in terms of research. It is important that the Institute's core faculty (and students) remain active and visible members of the LIS research community and not become a boutique operation.

The Institute shall actively work to make these programs official partners. Partnership can be at a variety of levels. At the most basic, LIS schools and the Institute shall make arrangements for the transference and assignment of credits earned by cohort students (this shall be discussed in greater detail below). Each school with an accepted student shall also receive regular feedback on that student's performance, as well as a comparative analysis of the student's competencies versus students from other programs (without identifying these other programs). The report can be used as part of an LIS program's performance for accreditation. Beyond the sharing of students, the Institute shall seek to constantly engage partnering schools in matters of trends in librarianship and research.

---

1. http://www.ala.org/ala/accreditation/lisdirb/alphaaccred.cfm.
2. The latest data available online from ALISE.

Target the Top

As previously stated, there are a wide variety of LIS programs. It will take time to reach out to all of these programs. Therefore, the Institute shall target the top-ranked LIS programs according to *U.S. News and World Report* in the prelaunch phases. With these schools on board, the Institute is guaranteed top-quality students and an excellent reputation.

With the reputation of a high-quality university partner and the vision of the Institute, it should be possible to quickly get these schools on board. However, if the Institute is seen as regressive or a retrenchment of traditional librarianship, these programs will not be interested in participating. One mechanism to get these programs on board and seed the Institute's academic program would be to grant these programs a slot for the first class.

The Power of Visiting Faculty

A challenge for this program will be ensuring credits and information flow smoothly from the Institute to the home college of a student. Simply transferring in half of a student's master's degree, even from a prestigious university, is problematic at best. While each partnering school may have its own method to do this, some initial models might involve naming core Institute faculty as visiting or adjunct faculty within the home school. Another model might be to have a faculty member within the home school act as a sort of supervisor for the student and issue credit within the home school as independent studies or internships (or a combination of these). In any case, it would be an exception if more than a student per year were selected for the Institute's programs, so the administrative burden on partnering schools should be minimal.

Not a School

There are some substantial reasons why the Institute shall not offer a fully accredited library degree program and, further, why the Institute should not be placed within an existing school (or university with a school). By focusing on the second year of existing degree programs, the Institute avoids ALA accreditation. Such accreditation would mean the offering of basic LIS courses, a job well handled by existing programs. It would also put the Institute into competition with existing LIS programs for students and ranking. Once in a competitive stance, the Institute's ability to draw the best students from other

programs is severely limited. The same logic applies to locating the Institute within an existing LIS school. Although it may be possible to set up a firewall between an existing program and the Institute, it would be difficult to demonstrate independence to other schools and universities.

Libraries

If schools represent the supply of students, libraries represent the bulk of the demand. Libraries of all sorts must see the value in the Institute; in particular, they must seek out the graduates of the program. This enthusiasm must be maintained in continuous engagement and through the net effect of Institute alums and research.

Libraries must have a place on the initial advisory board and in subsequent Boards of Visitors. Institute faculty and students shall also be highly visible within library associations and meetings. Furthermore, a variety of library types (public, academic, school, special, etc.) must be represented.

It should also be noted that not all graduates shall be destined for libraries. Innovation, change, and technology skills are highly prized throughout the information industry. Non-library participation in hiring, clinical faculties, and projects should be seen as a sign of success, and the Institute shall constantly seek to bridge a strong core of librarianship to other fields. However, librarianship does remain the core focus.

Several large libraries and library organizations have been informally consulted on the Institute concept. Those consulted voiced universal enthusiasm for the project, and it is reasonable to work toward endorsements from these organizations.

Academic Home

The ideal home for the Institute for Advanced Librarianship shall be a university with a stellar reputation and a strong mission in terms of intellectual rigor and a practical outlook. The academic home must aid the Institute in fostering innovation, entrepreneurship, and excellence in both students and faculty.

The benefits to the university partner are both tangible and large scale. A portion of the Institute's operating income shall be fed back to the university in the form of a standing overhead agreement. Furthermore, indirect income from sponsored research plus tuition revenue that may be generated in later expansion projects would go to the university from the Institute. The Institute shall also bring attention to the university from the library and information communities beyond the institution's own existing library operations.

There are also intangible benefits to the university housing the Institute. The first is that the Institute will be tackling issues of great interest to higher education in terms of participatory learning and technology (implementation as well as policy). The Institute shall act as a pool of information scholars—ready consultants working collaboratively with existing university programs.

The Institute shall also be an asset to the partnering university in exploring interdisciplinary opportunities between academic programs. Few areas are as well positioned to advanced interdisciplinary initiatives as library and information science. In many ways, a university's libraries serve as a vital connective tissue between scholars. Librarians work across disciplines and have the opportunity to seek common goals and complementary projects. The Institute can be an invaluable think tank, influencing how the university forward interdisciplinary research working with the university's libraries. Library and information science as a scholarly discipline has been described as inherently interdisciplinary. In addition to core concepts in information organization and services, the field draws from computing, communications, education, sociology, economics, and public policy. Look today at an information school, and you will find scholars with a wide variety of backgrounds, forging new understandings by coming together through action and application.

Library and information science belongs at a prestigious university as a discipline. As the elite schools redefine science and the humanities in the modern age, LIS skills and insight can assure wide adoption and integration of the underlying information infrastructure. Today's LIS scholars, professionals, and facilitators can identify user needs, appropriate technologies, and maximize both the efficiency and effectiveness of information. The Institute, drawing from the best of these scholarly and interdisciplinary traditions, can become an asset to the partnering university as it continues to evolve in today's market place of ideas, increasingly competitive research environment, and increasing social mission.

Funding

Vital partners of the Institute shall be its source of income. A mix of private and public funders shall fund the Institute in the form of an endowment and also continuously through research and special projects.

Governance

Institute governance will maximize the benefits of partnership while mitigating any potential conflicts between partners. The ideal governance structure is one that allows for all partners to have a voice but also allows the Institute to act decisively and formulate its own vision. Internal governance mechanism and policies will need to be developed by the Institute faculty once they are on board. To help shape the program to that point, a board of advisors shall be established.

Role of Advisor Board

The board of advisors represents the major partners of the Institute and provides input to the director, the Free Library, and the university partner as the Institute is formed. They shall advise of curricular issues, structural aspects of partnerships (how academic credits can be moved across institutions, for example), and help promote the Institute and its mission. Upon the formal launch of the Institute, the board of advisors shall become the Board of Visitors that provide ongoing guidance to the Institute.

The initial structure of the board will be co-chaired by a representative of the university home and a representative from the housing library. Other board positions shall be taken up by LIS school representation, representation from the practicing library sector, and members, where appropriate, of funding agencies.

RELATED ARTIFACTS

Varlejs, J. (2007). The New Jersey Academy of Library Leadership: What impact has it had? In A. R. Saur (Ed.), *Continuing professional development: Pathways to library leadership in the library and information world* (Vol. 126, pp. 183-198). IFLA Publications.

Wisser, K. M., & Saye, J. D. (2004). *ALISE library and information science educational statistical report 2004.* (ALISE, Producer) Retrieved February 4, 2008, from http://ils.unc.edu/ALISE/2004/Contents.htm.

INTELLECTUAL FREEDOM AND SAFETY

MAP LOCATION

H, 3

THREAD LOCATION

Page 122

SCAPE

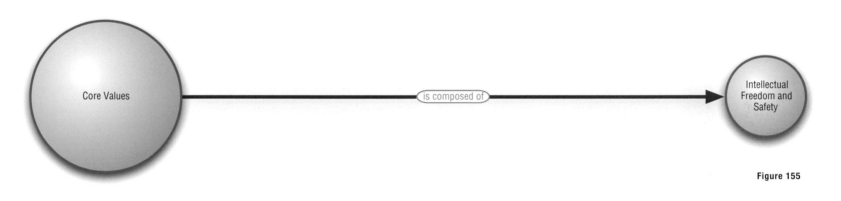

Figure 155

AUTHOR

Sarah Schmidt

AGREEMENT DESCRIPTION

The American Library Association (2009) defines intellectual freedom as: "the right of every individual to both seek and receive information from all points of view without restriction. It provides for free access to all expressions of ideas through which any and all sides of a question, cause or movement may be explored." The ability to access a diverse body of information is a core value of librarianship. In this agreement, we will see its importance throughout the library: at the service desk, in collection development, and even in technical services. The literature reviewed here supports the Atlas' ideas on intellectual freedom.

Providing a safe place for the access and expression of a wide range of views is one area the Atlas emphasizes for librarians (Lankes, 2008). In an article on the trend of media conglomeration, the authors agree ("Fostering Media," 2007). They note that in 2003, the Federal Communications Commission changed its regulations on media ownership so that it allowed for the increased consolidation of media sources. They observe that librarians responded by officially condemning such consolidation and setting out to study what they could do to ensure that a multiplicity of resources could survive in such a climate. Additionally, the librarians decided to try to bring more public awareness to the issue of resource diversity. This sense of awareness of problems with access is echoed in another article on the issue of patron privacy ("Model Policy," 2007). The authors consider the consequences of the renewal of the Patriot Act in 2006, focusing on librarians' vexed position of being forced by federal investigators to hand over their patrons' records. They note that librarians, seeking a solution that would ease the minds of librarian and patron alike, created a standard policy for librarians to lean on when pressed on privacy issues.

Self-examination of one's own assumptions and biases is another area the Atlas emphasizes for librarians. In his study of what guides librarians' approaches to their work with patrons, Olsson (2009) agrees. He argues that librarians need to shift their focus from systems to users. This new approach would require a more integrated method to coordinating their work with resources and patrons, one with increased attention on emotion, relationships, and how people comprehend information. But such a goal can only be achieved if one examines one's understanding of and relationships with patrons. Olsson holds that librarians must rethink their concept of users. Similarly, Marcoux (2009) touches on this notion of self-analysis. Marcoux

took part in a pilot program for educators on improving instruction for diverse populations. The course asked participants to explore their position on issues like identity, prejudice, cultural differences, and value systems. As a result of the program, Marcoux personally felt better equipped to teach to students from a wide range of backgrounds.

CONVERSATION STARTERS

1. We review and evaluate our performance fairly frequently; why don't we give more thought to what lies beneath what we do? How can we ensure we stay ethically "sharp"?

RELATED ARTIFACTS

American Library Association. (2009). *Intellectual freedom.* Retrieved November 13, 2009, from http://www.ala.org/ala/aboutala/offices/oif/basics/ifcensorshipqanda.cfm.

Fostering media diversity in libraries: Strategies and actions. (2007). *Newsletter on Intellectual Freedom, 56*(5), 177, 218–226. Retrieved November 6, 2009, from Library Lit & Inf Full Text database.

Marcoux, E. (2009). Diversity and the teacher-librarian. *Teacher Librarian, 36*(3), 6–7. Retrieved November 6, 2009, from Library Lit & Inf Full Text database.

Model policy: Responding to demands for library records. (2007). *American Libraries, 38*(8), inserts 1–4. Retrieved November 6, 2009, from Library Lit & Inf Full Text database.

Olsson, M. (2009). Re-thinking our concept of users. *Australian Academic & Research Libraries, 40*(1), 22–35. Retrieved November 6, 2009, from Library Lit & Inf Full Text database.

INTELLECTUALLY HONEST NOT UNBIASED

MAP LOCATION

H, 3

THREAD LOCATION

Page 122

SCAPE

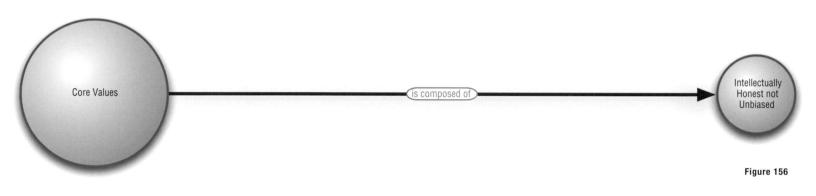

Figure 156

INTERNET MODEL EXAMPLE

MAP LOCATION

D, 6

THREAD LOCATION

Page 86

SCAPE

AUTHOR

R. David Lankes

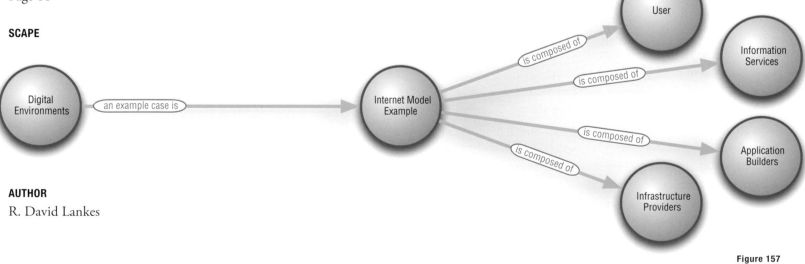

Figure 157

AGREEMENT DESCRIPTION

The Lankes/Eisenberg Architecture (Lankes, 1999) divides the Internet and, by extension, digital networks into four distinct layers: infrastructure providers, application builders, information services, and users. The following sections define these layers and provide examples of how each level, aside from the use level, can manipulate information in a way that is completely transparent to the user.

Infrastructure Provider

Infrastructure is composed of hardware, such as routers, and protocols, such as the Internet's Transmission Control Protocol /Internet Protocol (TCP/IP) suite used to move bits from one place to another on the Internet, and the organizations, such as Internet Service Providers (ISPs) that provide and maintain these mechanisms. This layer is often the most invisible to end users yet can have a profound impact on the information being provided to users for credibility assessments. Infrastructure providers can easily block traffic to and from certain destinations. What many people do not realize is that such blocked traffic can be made invisible. For example, when a library blocks access to certain Web sites, it may post a message to a patron's browser stating that the site is blocked. However, there is no technical barrier to that library only providing a "site not found" indication to a user's browser…the same error it would send if the user misspelled a URL. Further, ISPs can block access to any application, disabling software such as Instant Messaging (IM) at the network layer. The user, not aware of such a block, would only know that their IM program did not connect to a server and may assume the error lies in the remote server, thus affecting a user's credibility assessment of the remote server, not the infrastructure provider.

Application Builders

Applications on the Internet are software that allows information to be exchanged between different actors on the Internet. Applications include web browsers and IM clients, as well as high-level protocols such as the HyperText Transfer Protocol (HTTP) that transfers web pages. This broad category covers everything from e-mail applications that automatically mark incoming messages as "junk mail" to the Simple Mail Transfer Protocol (SMTP) that enables e-mail over the Internet, including spam. Spam filters are excellent examples of technology affecting credibility in a nearly invisible way. Many schools have implemented spam filters based on opaque and often proprietary algorithms at the organization level, discarding numerous e-mail messages before any human eyes ever see them.

Information Services

Information services are organizations that use applications and infrastructure to meet users' needs on the Internet; examples include Google, Facebook, or a library Web site. There are ample studies that look at how information services such as Google skew results in their search engines (for an example and further citations, see Choo & Roy, 2004). For example, top results tend toward shopping and technology services in Google (Mowshowitz and Kawaguchi, 2002). Without knowing this, users may assume that top results are the "best" regardless of context.

Users

The use layer is comprised of individuals and groups, such as teachers and patrons, who primarily consume information and seek to meet their own information needs on the Internet.

RELATED ARTIFACTS

Choo, J., & Roy, S. (2004). Impact of search engines on page popularity. In *International World Wide Web Conference: Proceedings of the 13th international conference on World Wide Web* (pp. 20–29). New York: ACM Press.

Lankes, R. D. (1999). *Building and maintaining Internet information services: K-12 digital reference services*. Syracuse: ERIC Clearinghouse on Information & Technology.

Lankes, R. D. (2008). Credibility on the Internet: Shifting from authority to reliability. *Journal of Documentation, 64*(5), 667–686. [2009 Literati Outstanding Paper Award]

Mowshowitz, A., & Kawaguchi, A. (2002). The consumer side of search: Bias on the web. *Communications of the ACM, 45*(9), 56–60.

INTRINSIC

MAP LOCATION

F, 1

THREAD LOCATION

Page 79

SCAPE

Figure 158

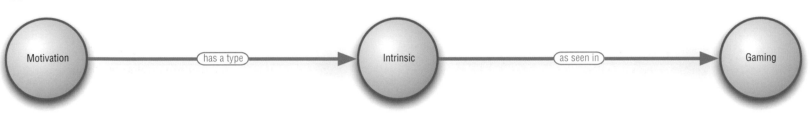

AUTHOR

Jennifer Rose Recht

AGREEMENT DESCRIPTION

None of these articles is relevant to intrinsic motivation:

Dunnewind, S. (2006). Dos and don'ts for getting kids to read. *Teacher Librarian, 34*(1), 28–29.

> Abstract: A reprint of an article that appeared in the *Seattle Times*, July 1, 2006, is provided. It provides parents with advice on encouraging their children to read.

Mcpherson, K. (2007). Harry Potter awet of motivation. *Teacher Librarian, 34*(4), 71–73.

> Abstract: The writer examines some of the key research on reading motivation and suggests instructional approaches aimed at fostering strong reading motivation in students.

Vent, C. T., & Ray, J. A. (2007). There is more to reading than fiction! Enticing elementary students to read nonfiction books. *Teacher Librarian, 34*(4), 42–44.

> Abstract: The writers report on an action research project that aimed to increase fourth-grade students' interest in reading nonfiction. The project implemented four strategies—nonfiction book displays, book talks, book pairings, and book passes. All these strategies proved to be successful in enticing the students in Grade 4 to read nonfiction.

So why aren't these articles relevant? First, they are reminiscent of the thread's discussion of "read" posters. How to get kids to read. How to get kids to read better things. How to get adults to read. How to get readers to read more things about reading more. Teach your dog to read.

Second, they have little to do with intrinsic motivation. Motivating people to read has nothing to do with what those people's motivations are, motivations that could shape productive library membership.

Motivating people to read is about motivating people to do what the library thinks they should do, wants them to do, or needs them to do.

Librarianship, as a profession, needs to stop fetishizing books. Sure, they look really nice lined up all pretty on the shelf, and half of us getting into the profession probably did so because we love books, we grew up reading and went to library story time, and we love the smell of books (at least until we start to sneeze). Perhaps we need a new name; perhaps we should all put "information professional" on our business cards because we are no longer simply caretakers of books. We are caretakers of information. And when we focus all our energy on the fraction of information that is contained in books, it's as if the whole richness of programming to be found in a library can be ignored or reduced to the question of whether, on the way out, someone checked out a book.

The knowledge the person gained at whatever activity he or she participated in does not count because it didn't come from something with a barcode on it.

Intrinsic motivation: Let's find what people really want and then put barcodes on that.

Mardis, M. A., & Perrault, A. M. (2008). A whole new library: Six "senses" you can use to make sense of new standards and guidelines. *Teacher Librarian, 35*(4), 34–38.

> I may have included this article just because the abstract actually mentioned intrinsic motivation, and I was really excited. However, I think the idea of education driven by students' intrinsic motivations, and not by correct answers on multiple-choice, standardized tests, is analogous to the Read problem. Reducing the success of the library to something easily quantifiable, like circulation statistics, tells us nothing about the real mission of the library. Is the community learning? Is the community creating knowledge? We don't know, but circulation is up 10% from last year.

INVEST IN TOOLS OF CREATION OVER COLLECTION OF ARTIFACTS

MAP LOCATION

F, G, 1, 2

THREAD LOCATION

Page 42

SCAPE

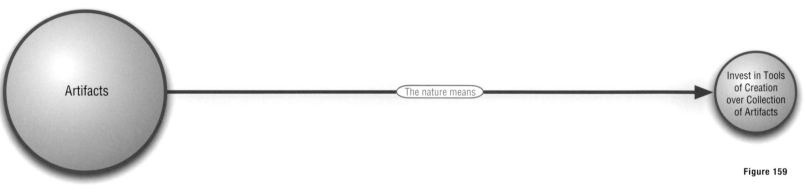

Figure 159

ISSUES OF INSTITUTIONAL REPOSITORIES

MAP LOCATION

F, 5

THREAD LOCATION

Page 103

SCAPE

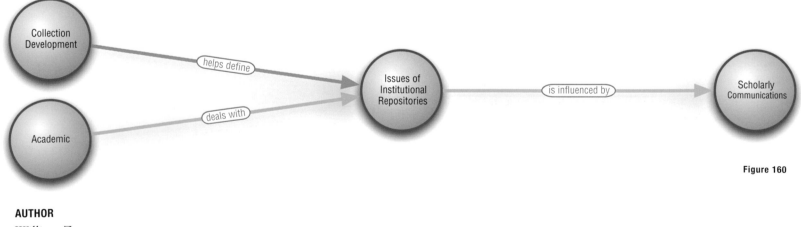

Figure 160

AUTHOR

William Zayac

What Are Institutional Repositories?

Slowly becoming more popular around the world, Institutional Repositories are open access databases of the works created by the people who work in or study at the repository's host institution. One major survey of Institutional Repositories, the University of Michigan MIRACLE[1] Project, found that research institutions were more likely to develop Institutional Repositories than universities and colleges that catered only to master's and baccalaureate students. It also found, however, that there was a "sleeping beast of demand" among these master's and baccalaureate institutions. That said, the concept of an Institutional Repository (at least in the digital context in which it is now used) is still in its growth phase, and its benefits and weaknesses cannot accurately be understood or assessed on a larger scale because of its limited expression in the real world. However, that has not stopped researchers from searching for and discussing these benefits and weaknesses or at least expressing their views concerning them.[2]

Why Create an Institutional Repository?

The main purpose of an Institutional Repository is to provide on-line access to essays, papers, presentations, and other digital works created by the faculty at a specific institution or school. One of the most important jobs of a library is to provide its users with access to a wealth of knowledge relevant to their interests and needs. Therefore, one would assume that the wealth of knowledge preserved in an Institutional Repository has a significant audience, at least for those who started the trend. It should come as no surprise, then, that many of the earliest developed collected the works of workers at research-focused institutions and that one large set of institutions following suit is comprised of universities and colleges. The access granted by these institutions allows many people to gain access to scholarly works to which they may not normally have access, whether it is because they are not in the databases to which they have access on their own or through their own respective institutions due to budgetary constraints or for whatever reason. Librarians, often focused on the transfer of information and the creation of knowledge through this communication, will immediately recognize these benefits in Institutional Re-

positories. However, there are other qualities that can help justify the existence of Institutional Repositories.

For one, certain repositories are more affordable to host and easier to create than they have been in the past. Several pieces of open source software for the creation and management of Institutional Repositories have been developed and are available to whichever institutions are willing to host them. Items can be more easily found with greater standards regulating metadata and its use. Items can be labeled accurately and then disseminated from a central resource. This saves faculty members time and effort as the maintenance of labels, formats, and thoughts concerning a work becomes increasingly complicated.[3] And, of course, trends change and so do the opportunities for outside thinking. Scholarly works that would not normally fit into certain standard database groups may be difficult to find through "normal" resources.[4] On a more basic level, Institutional Repositories provide libraries with the opportunities to develop new strategies and standards for digital collection management[5] and have even expanded the perception of the library as a "viable research partner" in institutions.[6]

What Issues Must Still Be Addressed with Institutional Repositories?

As with any good library, the interface providing access to works must be appropriate for its patrons. In the Communities Thread, Lankes points out that there are many Institutional Repository home pages that only begin to provide access to works. However, the aim of librarianship is no longer to simply match people to a resource or a set of resources for which they are searching; it is (as the Atlas emphasizes) to encourage the creation of knowledge through conversations, and most Institutional Repositories do not yet do this. While looking at the initial interfaces of six different Institutional Repositories, I encountered none that came as close to providing conversation as the PLoS Biology

1. Making Institutional Repositories a Collaborative Learning Environment.
2. Smith, K. (2008). Institutional repositories and e-journal archiving: What are we learning? *Journal of Electronic Publishing, 11* (1).
3. Lynch, C. A. (2003). Institutional repositories: Essential infrastructure for scholarship in the Digital Age. *ARL* (226), 1–7.
4. This is mostly in reference to my own experiences searching for respectable resources for a term paper on the music of *Buffy the Vampire Slayer*. I was able to find several essays in books about *Buffy* and several Web sites which seemed to host respectable-enough resources. Having a set of databases which may not be as restricted to significant and traditional scholarly works, as some Institutional Repositories may eventually be, would have been incredibly helpful in this endeavor. Of course, this only helps if one knows where to look or has a centralized search available covering multiple repositories.
5. Lynch, C. A. (2003). Institutional repositories: Essential infrastructure for scholarship in the Digital Age. *ARL* (226), 1–7.
6. Smith, K. (2008). Institutional repositories and e-journal archiving: What are we learning? *Journal of Electronic Publishing, 11* (1).

Repository did in the Communities Thread, and only two even began to feature any information not simply for searching the database (those of Brandeis University and the Massachusetts Institute of Technology).

Institutional Repositories result from interdisciplinary work and the cooperation of many parties. Of course, sometimes certain parties cooperate more than others, and the balance of power may not be stable. There have been times when Institutional Repositories have been overcome by administrative control and policy requirements. Although administrative support is good, an overbearing administration can limit enthusiasm and growth and reduce the effectiveness of the enterprise. There may even be the tendency to treat the repository as if it were a standard journal, but "the institutional repository isn't a journal, or a collection of journals, and should not be managed like one."[7]

Finally, although it provides works in an "open access" form and may use open source software in its development, a well-structured Institutional Repository requires quite a bit of work and maintenance along with people who know how to run it. Creating an Institutional Repository is not cheap or easy and will require staff members to dedicate some hours to it. It may not even be helpful to all institutions, especially if not advertised correctly to the members of their communities. As with other programs, it must be kept relevant and up-to-date to ensure that people will use it. In the case of a school where the library is not visible and does not see much use from the students or faculty, it might not even be worth considering creating this type of collection.

CONVERSATION STARTERS

- What are the limitations of Institutional Repositories?

- Do the benefits of being able to centrally locate all the works by individuals from a specific institution outweigh these limitations?

- When considering relevancy to a community, should a librarian working on creating or maintaining an Institutional Repository focus on making it helpful for the university's community or for the world as a whole?

- How might one's work differ to address these two potentially different groups?

- If Institutional Repositories provide such great access to work, how can a library maintain its status in the community? That is, if it actually is all on the Internet, why would someone come in to use the library (outside of to gain access to the Internet)?

RELATED ARTIFACTS

American Society for Information Science and Technology. (2009, April). *Bulletin of the American Society for Information Science and Technology April/May 2009.* Retrieved October 31, 2009, from ASIS&T: The American Society for Information Science and Technology: http://www.asis.org/Bulletin/Apr-09/index.html

> Annotation: This issue of the ASIS&T Bulletin provides a strong look at the many debates focusing around Institutional Repositories, including whether all universities should have one, how they should be created, how they should be maintained, and what is required for repository success. Both sides of each debate are presented by various authors with experience in large institutions, encouraging and displaying a true conversation on the topics.

Harvard launches DASH repository. (2009). *Advanced Technology Libraries, 38*(10), 1, 10–11.

> Annotation: This article describes the history of the development of the DASH repository at Harvard University, including school policy and copyright issues addressed during the DASH's development. Although there is strong support for the idea of allowing open access to all scholarly works through the repository, the university has created an opt-out policy to ensure that there is choice for the scholars to grant or not to grant permission for their work to go into DASH. Faculty authors' names, when included in search results, are linked to their main profiles. By employing several unique ideas, DASH is growing and providing a good example of what Institutional Repositories can become.

Palmer, K. L., Dill, E., & Christie, C. (2009). Where there's a will there's a way? Survey of academic librarian attitudes about open access. *College & Research Libraries, 70*(4), 315–335.

> Annotation: This article explores the results of the 2006 MIRACLE Survey concerning librarians' opinions on open access resources, how well their actions support or contradict these results, and the potential repercussions of expanding open access resources too much. They cite several experts who question the limitations of open access resources and their growth, both in terms of where emphasis is placed (should we really be doing this simply because it might save money in the long term?) and how effective the movement actually is (will Institutional Repositories replace the library?).

7. Lynch, C. A. (2003). Institutional repositories: Essential infrastructure for scholarship in the Digital Age. *ARL* (226), 1–7.

KNOWLEDGE

MAP LOCATION

D, 1

THREAD LOCATION

Page 72

SCAPE

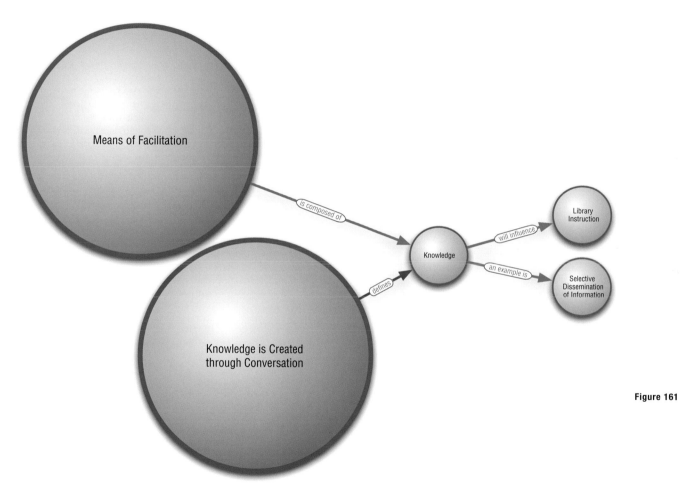

Figure 161

KNOWLEDGE IS CREATED THROUGH CONVERSATION

MAP LOCATION
C, B, 2, 3

THREAD LOCATION
Page 31

SCAPE

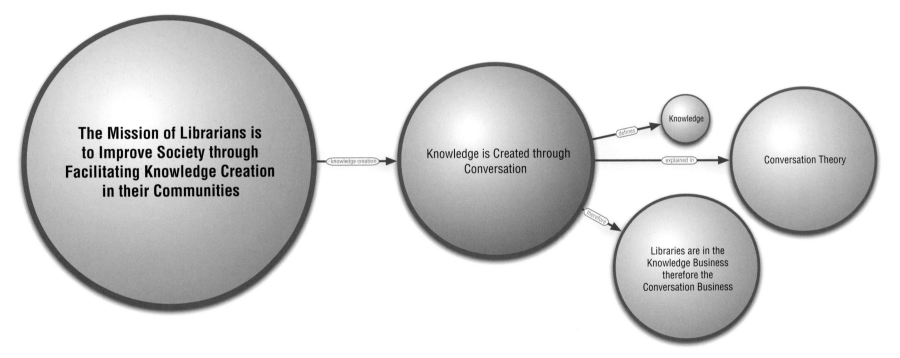

Figure 162

L_0

MAP LOCATION

F, 2

THREAD LOCATION

Page 33

SCAPE

AGREEMENT DESCRIPTION

See Language Agreement Supplement

Figure 163

L_1

MAP LOCATION

F, 2

THREAD LOCATION

Page 34

SCAPE

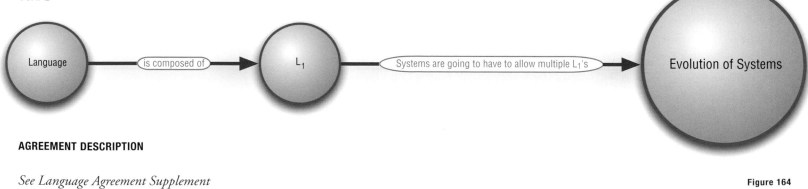

AGREEMENT DESCRIPTION

See Language Agreement Supplement

Figure 164

LANGUAGE

MAP LOCATION

E, 2

THREAD LOCATION

Page 33

SCAPE

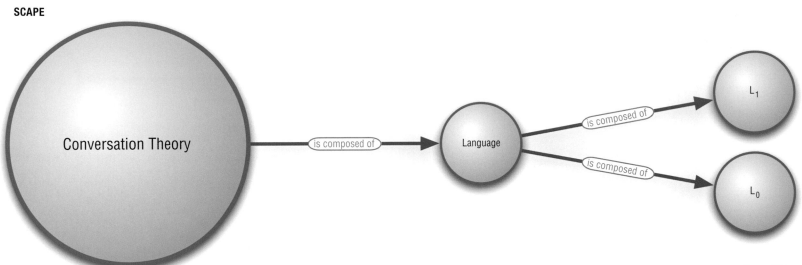

Figure 165

AUTHOR

R. David Lankes

AGREEMENT DESCRIPTION

New librarianship, based on conversation theory, concerns itself with two levels of language being exchanged between conversants: L_0 and L_1. L_0 is the language exchanged between two conversants where at least one of the parties has little knowledge of the domain being discussed. It tends to be very directional (do this, now do this). Most of the discourse is negotiating meanings and terms at a very simple level. L_1, in contrast, is exchanged between two parties with a high understanding of the domain discussed. Here conversations tend to use special language, explore more "why" questions, and establish structural relationships between concepts.

Let's use a simple example to illustrate the difference in language levels. Take the following sentence:

"Our catalog uses MARC to present our users with a great searching experience."

If you are a librarian, this is a meaningful sentence. You might even ask "how can MARC impact a user's experience?" However, if you are not a librarian, this sentence is a jumble. Are we talking about catalogs like from a store where I pick out sweaters—who is Marc and why is he so helpful—do we really want to make it easy for users—that is people who use drugs? As we saw in our previous word game, preexisting structures and contexts to words matter a lot. The more relationships and contexts of words that are shared by conversants (what we will call agreements), the higher the possible level of discourse. A high level of shared contexts equals L_1.

These levels of language have real implications for the systems we present to users. Systems can either attempt to work at differing levels of language, to bring users from L_0 to L_1, or bring the system from L_0 to L_1 (see the example of a search engine interface in figure 166).

It does little to educate the user about how to interact using high-level language. It is built around an assumption that users will be communicating their needs in L_0. The system will use complex algorithms and information-retrieval techniques to make up for the fact

Figure 166

that the search engine will probably be getting a very anemic query. If you do take the time to learn the language of this system, you can actually use some rather advanced language to improve your results (in this case, using a query language with +, −, ~, and quotes).

Help desks and search are often used in systems where there is an anticipated difference in the languages of the users and the system builders. In libraries, for example, reference as a function came about because indexes and classification systems were too complex for many library users. The idea was to provide a human intermediary as a sort of bridge between a person with a question and the complex language used by library systems.

The second approach is what Pask would refer to as learning systems that systematically bring users from L_0 to L_1. One of the best examples of increasing language levels in systems can be seen in modern games. Where once games came with long and in-depth manuals, today complex games actually incorporate learning into the game itself. The first level is often a form of in-game tutorial, familiarizing players with the basic mechanics of the game while still advancing the game's narrative.

Of course the approach of raising the user's language level is founded on the rather dubious assumption that a system can change the user. It is also antithetical to the user-centered paradigm dominant in today's system development world. A third approach is to assume the user is at L_1 and it is the system that needs to catch up. The use of tagging and annotations in web systems demonstrates this approach. Here users incorporate their own language. Systems can then look for patterns in language use to provide information.

Nobody Is Born Speaking Dewey

It is worth stopping here for a moment to explore the real implications of these different languages. Think about the basis of a great deal of library work: classification or, more broadly, information organization. To make things easier to find, we have developed a whole host of common languages: the Dewey Decimal Classification and the Library of Congress Classification (LC), just to name two. The idea being that by mapping a body of knowledge to one system of terms, we can collocate items on shelves and make it easier (at least more efficient) to find something. We are using language to do this. In fact, Dewey and LC are the end result of an ongoing conversation centered on the question, "How can we organize the world's knowledge?"

So why, then, doesn't this approach always work? To be more precise, why does it work so well for librarians and so poorly for a mass of patrons? This is a great example of L_0 versus L_1. When patrons try to navigate Dewey (or LC), particularly in catalogs, they are working at or pretty close to a simple directed "click here" level. Once they get a call number, off they go to the shelves. Librarians, in contrast, understand the worldview of these classifications and so can manipulate the system much more effectively. So one conclusion that one could reach is that we need to bring patrons up from an L_0 to an L_1 conversation. How? Well, one wide-scale approach has been library instruction. Another approach, the one Pask spent most of his effort on, was building capabilities in the system to teach patrons domain knowledge and transition them to L_1 use of systems. Never thought of your catalog as a learning system? It shows.

There are big implications in terms of digital systems and language. One approach to the L_0/L_1 gap is in interface design. By doing a good job of anticipating the user's needs, we can have the system do sophisticated things with little input from the user. Google is a great example of this. The old way of doing search was to provide two interfaces: simple search and advanced search. L_0 users go to simple, and L_1 users head to advanced. Google even combined this into one interface. If you are at an L_0 level, just type a term and Google uses clever algorithms like Page Rank[1] to assume that simple use of language can be best answered by the most popular information. If you are an L_1 user, in the same box you can add cool things like quotes, ~, +, −, and so on. The more sophisticated your knowledge, the more sophisticated interaction you can have with Google. However, note that the interface does not teach users or help them to transition from L_0 to L_1.

Another approach to the language divide is to build learning systems. This is an interface that attempts to teach as it works. Librarians attempt to model this behavior. Good reference librarians in person or online don't just provide an answer; they help users understand how they found an answer and impart the skills to the users so they can self-serve. This approach also inspires things like "tool tips," where little explanations pop up when you hover a mouse over a button in Microsoft Word. Word also shows how just trying to instruct is insufficient… think "Clippy." Perhaps the most effective demonstration of this learning approach can be found in videogames as mentioned before.

A great number of Web 2.0 sites point to another approach all together. Minimize the functions and interfaces of the system to allow users to use their own language and domain understandings. This is the allure of tagging. By letting the users add their own terms or letting users link differing information in their own way (think mashups or FaceBook pages), users create their own L_1 systems. Of course, these can create a sort of Tower of Babel, but it is effective in circumstances when there is already a set of common terms or agreements. At the least, by exposing the process of language development, users have a better chance to come up to an L_1 level and become more effective and efficient users of systems.

LEADERSHIP

MAP LOCATION

F, 7

THREAD LOCATION

Page 132

SCAPE

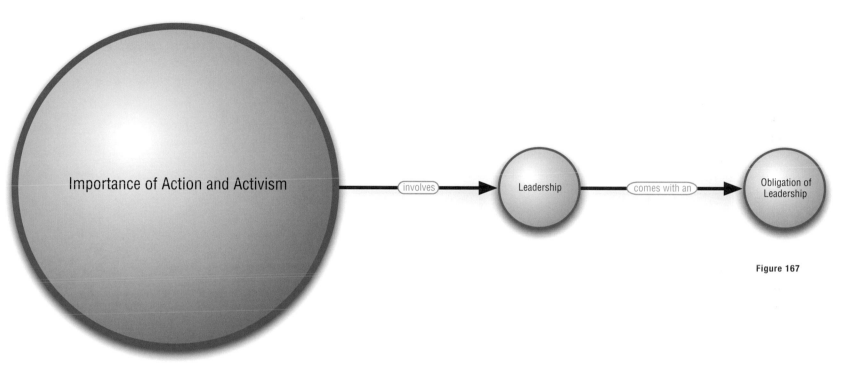

Importance of Action and Activism — involves → Leadership — comes with an → Obligation of Leadership

Figure 167

AUTHOR

Michael Luther

AGREEMENT DESCRIPTION

Lankes makes the point in this Thread that much of what we do as librarians is about process, not product. Because process takes time and because protracted journeys provide a lot of opportunity for distraction and wrong turns, one or more professionals need to lead the party from point A to point Z. Enter librarians. Leadership is presented as a duty of librarians. Duty or not, Christopher Raab (2009) says leadership is a skill that does not come naturally to many librarians. Our skills of organization make us natural managers, but "librarians sometimes have difficulty inspiring people and recognizing opportunities to lead." Raab continues by describing the R.O.L.L. Matrix, a device intended to aid academic librarians in the identification of leadership opportunities.

In the forest/trees debate, a leader has to come down squarely in the camp of the forest. A leader has to see the big picture and care for the overall health of the vision. Accordingly, a leader must be concerned with individual practices (trees) insofar as these practices affect the larger forest. Maybe deforestation is a practice or maybe another practice leads to blight, but in the end the concern is for the whole. Others may care for individual parts.

Ammons-Stephens et al. (2009) contribute to the discussion of leadership in libraries by breaking leadership down into its component parts. They argue that libraries are successful if they are run by successful librarians, and so they propose to look at outputs and competencies as a means of developing leadership. The authors identify the core competencies as cognitive ability, vision, interpersonal effectiveness, and managerial effectiveness. Each core competency is then subdivided and the attribute itself defined. For example, one attribute of interpersonal effectiveness is accountability, defined as:

- Instills trust in others and self

- Leads by example

- Assumes responsibility for decisions made

It is hoped that competency models will help to cultivate leadership skills in librarians.

Because leadership is so important, to what extent do librarians, particularly young librarians, want to take on leadership roles? DeLong (2009) asked just this question of new professionals in Canada. She conducted a study with statistically significant findings showing that young librarians are interested in leadership roles. DeLong concludes that the profession should recognize and tap this interest.

CONVERSATION STARTERS

Where does personality stop and duty start?

RELATED ARTIFACTS

Ammons-Stephens, S., Cole, H. J., et al. (2009). Developing core leadership competencies for the library profession. *Library Leadership & Management, 23*(2), 63–74.

DeLong, K. (2009). The engagement of new library professionals in leadership. *Journal of Academic Librarianship, 35*(5), 445–456.

Frost, C. (2005). Library leaders. *Knowledge Quest, 33*(5), 41–42.

Mosley, P. A. (2009). Perspectives on leadership in LLAMA: A round table interview with Paul Anderson, Teri Switzer, and Nicole Cavallero. Library *Leadership & Management, 23*(2), 60–79.

Raab, C. (2009). Recognizing opportunities for library leadership. Library *Leadership & Management, 23*(2), 80–84.

LEARNING

MAP LOCATION
H, 3, 4

THREAD LOCATION
Page 120

SCAPE

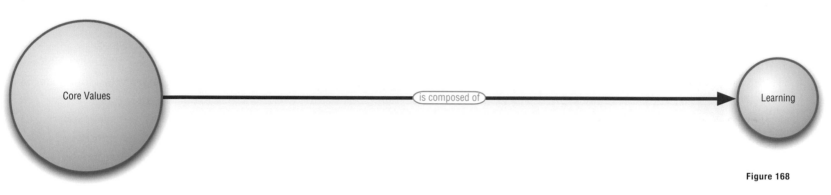

Figure 168

LEARNING THEORY

MAP LOCATION
D, 3

THREAD LOCATION
Page 27

SCAPE

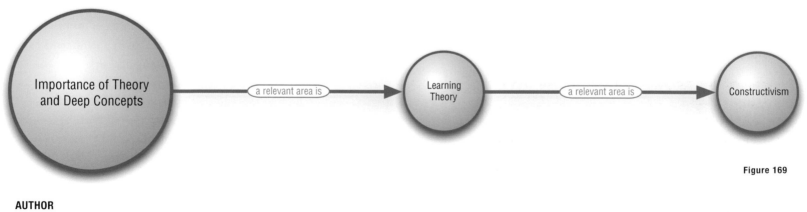

Figure 169

AUTHOR
Angela Usha Ramnarine-Rieks

Learning theories are closely associated with motivation. The question that we wrestle with is not only how our library members seek information and learn, but also what motivates them to do so. Although there are a number of motivation theories discussed (for example, intrinsic–extrinsic orientation theorizes that some people create their own rewards, such as satisfaction of curiosity or simply interest in a given topic). This type of reward is intrinsic, which are satisfaction, feelings of accomplishment, and control. Rewards such as praise or a receipt of a prize are typically regarded as less effective than intrinsic rewards (Small et al., 2004).

Given the ubiquity of online content and the increasing number of entry points into the digital information "universe," it has become necessary to move beyond existing models of librarianship and address the unanticipated issues that are emerging both inside the profession and within the members that the library serves. As noted earlier in the Atlas, our mission must accommodate learning theories and therefore individual learning. However, there is a pronounced absence in understanding learning in preparation as a librarian. Dempsey (2006) noted that libraries must co-evolve with the changing research and learning behaviors that exist within the myriad electronically networked spaces. The problem is that, as librarians, we tend to focus on the impact of technology on libraries; the real long-term issue is how technology will influence the learning behavior of our members, as well as expectations for the ways in which information is created, codified, accessed, and distributed. By successfully establishing a role supporting learning, libraries will increase the potential of expanding their community.

Critical use of information resources is fundamental to education; therefore, we stress on members abilities to use libraries and information resources critically. With the new generation of computer-literate members and the vast amount of information available in both print and electronic formats, the necessity to develop the ability to use authoritative information resources in the library is paramount. Consequently, we find that academic libraries now assume a far greater role in assisting students to locate and evaluate information critically by teaching information literacy. As Kwon (2008) notes, there is immense emotional challenges that students—the Millennials or Generation Y who are considered to be competent and comfortable about their online-networked environment using blogs, Facebook, and integrated activity with technology every day—are uncomfort-

able, confused, and intimidated in an unfamiliar, huge academic library. However, I tend to agree with the musings of Weiler (2005) that academe, libraries, and indeed the entire world are currently in the middle of a massive and wide-ranging shift in the way knowledge is disseminated and learned. We cannot just blame it on technologies negatively impacting the development of students' cognitive skills but recognize and embrace the change.

Recently, we have been seeing increasing research showing that games can provide a rich experience while providing the ability to navigate virtual worlds, in which complex decision making and the management of complex issues might resemble the cognitive processes that they would employ in the real world (Ducheneaut et al., 2006; Squire, 2005; Stokes, 2005). Games are engaging because they give us enjoyment and pleasure; give us intense and passionate involvement; give us structure; give us motivation; give us doing; give us flow; give us learning; give us ego gratification; give us adrenaline; they spark our creativity; give us social groups; and give us emotion (Prensky, 2001, p. 144). There are many studies on the use of games in educational activities, and they indicate that it has the potential to support learning. This will be covered in greater detail in the Atlas. However, there seems to be a limited understanding of how learning takes place and how that learning can inform the design of effective educational games and aid its integration into contemporary environments like libraries. There are many learning theories that can be used as underpinnings for exploration of libraries as facilitators of learning.

Overview of Learning Theories

Human learning and the importance of social structures has long intrigued scientists involved in the development of learning theory (e.g., Bandura & Walters, 1963; Durkheim, 1893/1984; Miller & Dollard, 1941; Tönnies, 1887/2001; Vygotsky, 1978; Weber, 1922/1978; Wellman & Berkowitz, 1988). As the understanding of human learning became more refined, theorists began to explore the impact of the social environment on an individual's learning and development. At the time it was conducted, much of this research was rooted in the psychological school of thought that confers primacy to the learner's mind. In essence, these psychological conceptions of learning focused on the premise that learning is an individual cognitive process (e.g., Pavlov, 1927; Piaget, 1954; Skinner, 1938; Thorndike, 1901; Wundt, 1897). This individual-centered perspective of learning persisted as the central dogma of learning theory well into the 20th century.

Social Interpretations to Learning

In the early part of the 20th century, an alternative interpretation of learning emerged; instead of considering learning as predominantly an individual psychological process, research supported the notion that learning happens within, and as a result of, social interactions. The idea of learning based on personal experiences is attributed to Dewey and Lindeman. Dewey's (1916) contended that "the social environment is truly educative in the effects in the degree in which an individual shares or participates in some conjoint activity. By doing his share in the associated activity, the individual appropriates the purpose which actuates it, becomes familiar with its methods and subject matters, acquires needed skills, and is saturated with its emotional spirit" (p. 26). Similar to Dewey's comments, Lindeman (1926/1961) proclaimed that "the resource of highest value in adult education is the learner's experience," and "if education is life, then life is also education" (p. 6). Likewise, he predicted "the approach to adult education will be via the route of situations, not subjects" (p. 6), and, finally, "experience is the adult learner's living textbook" (p. 7).

This shift in the conceptual understanding of learning eventually paved the way for the development of a social learning theory (Bandura, 1977). Presently referred to as social cognitive theory (Bandura, 1986), the emphasis of this learning paradigm is that most human learning is derived from social engagement and is therefore integral to the sociocultural context in which that learning transpires. In recent years, social cognitive theory has been extended and applied to a number of related disciplines, such as organizational research (Argyris & Schön, 1978; Brown & Duguid, 1991; Senge, 1990), educational issues (Cunningham, 2000; Jarvis, 1987), and social anthropology (Lave, 1988; Suchman, 1987).

Sociocultural Model

As we see, novel ideas on learning began to gain momentum, and this subsequently ushered in new areas of research on human learning. Significant developments emphasized the importance of the external environment on one's learning; namely, that learning is a dynamic interplay between one's sociocultural setting and one's psychological processes. Vygotsky and Bandura played seminal roles in the further development of this perspective of learning research. Russian theorist named Lev Semyonovich Vygotsky (1978) developed a sociocultural theory of learning that emphasized the role that social institutions and culture play in a child's learning. Vygotsky's sociocultural model

of learning asserted that society and culture not only influence what an individual learns, but they also impact the patterns of thinking that govern the learning processes; in other words, the social environment impacts how a person learns.

Related and somewhat contemporaneous to Vygotsky's work was the creation of social learning theory (SLT) by Bandura and his colleagues in the 1950s and 1960s. As an extension of the psychological theory of learning that focused primarily on the mind of a solitary learner, SLT (Bandura & Walters, 1963) broadens the psychological paradigm by taking into consideration the influence of other individuals, as well as the sociocultural context in which the process of learning transpires. Bandura (1977) emphasized that learning takes place in social settings where individuals learn through the processes of observation, imitation, and modeling. The work of these researchers substantiates the idea that learning is a dynamic phenomenon that involves the complex social arenas in which humans interact.

Situated Learning

Standing on the theoretical groundwork of Bandura, Vygotsky, and others (for example, see also Akers et al., 1979; Miller & Dollard, 1941; Piaget, 1969; Sears, 1951), Lave (1988) extended the work on SLT by advancing the notion that the majority of learning (cognition) is "situated" in the activity, context, and culture in which it occurs. Brown, Collins, and Duguid (1989) further developed this concept of "situated learning" by explaining that, "the activity in which knowledge is developed and deployed ... is not separable from, or ancillary to, learning and cognition. Nor is it neutral. Rather, it is an integral part of what is learned" (p. 32).

Social anthropologists first connected the concepts of social cognition and practice by introducing the premise of "situated learning" (Hanks, 1991, p. 14). According to Lave (as cited in Wenger, 1998, p. 281), social practice is the means to understanding the complexity of human thought that is situated in real-life settings. Lave and Wenger (1991) explicated this connection by contending that "a person's intentions to learn are engaged [situated], and the meaning of learning is configured through the process of becoming a full participant in a sociocultural practice. This social process includes, indeed it subsumes, the learning of knowledgeable skills" (p. 29).

Over the years, this interpretation of practice has become more intertwined with SCT. Addressing this progression, Barton and Tusting (2005) explained that "practice has become more central as a concept, and there is a definite shift from a cognitive psychological framing to one which is more in tune with social anthropology" (p. 4). In short, practice is the convergence of social engagement and human thought; it serves as the cultural context underlying, as well as the outward manifestation of human cognition and learning.

Lave and Wenger described situated learning as an active endeavor in which the interaction of a community of individuals generates, not only the fundamental content of what is learned, but also the context, culture, and activities that govern this learning process. This perspective on learning provides a number of opportunities for theorists to apply and expand the situated learning construct regardless of the environment.

Legitimate Peripheral Participation

Lave and Wenger (1991) extrapolated the situated learning theory to develop several corollaries. They broadened the theory through the conception of legitimate peripheral participation (LPP). They explain LLP as "to draw attention to the point that learners inevitably participate in communities of practitioners and that the mastery of knowledge and skill requires newcomers to move toward full participation in the socio-cultural practices of a community." "Legitimate peripheral participation" provides a way to speak about the relations between newcomers and old-timers, and about activities, identities, artifacts, and communities of knowledge and practice (p. 29). In other words, LPP explains that as new members participate more fully in the sociocultural practices of a group, they go through, not so much an apprenticeship, but rather a process of social integration and enculturation. In explaining this concept further, Wenger (1998) pointed out that the term "legitimate" is used to establish an entryway for belonging that is extended to newcomers and also that the meaning of the term can take many forms, such as "being useful, being sponsored, being feared, being the right kind of person" (p. 101), and so forth. They used the term "peripheral" to address the fact that initially new members learn at the periphery of the community before gaining in competence and participating more richly in the group's experience. According to Wenger (1998), members learn not so much from the acquisition of knowledge, but from the process of legitimate social participation. Thus, social dynamics and context are paramount to learning within the confines of a community.

Communities of Practice

Another extension of the situated learning paradigm is Lave and Wenger's (1991) formulation of the community of practice (CoP) model. In an attempt to rectify further the relationship between social learning and practice, Lave and Wenger (1991) conceived the notion of CoP. There are many success stories of CoP in industry and business organizations. In advancing the CoP construct, Lave and Wenger (1991) conceptualized learning as a form of participation in a "culture of practice" (p. 95). That is, as individuals engage in life's activities, they are learning in association with others engaged in common pursuits. Lave and Wenger (1991) pointed out that together the terms "community" and "practice" constitute a new concept that transcends the meaning of each of these terms considered in isolation. Wenger, McDermott, and Snyder (2002) asserted that a CoP is a specific type of social structure with a specific purpose; that is, at its core a CoP is an action-oriented "knowledge structure" (p. 41). Since its conception, the CoP concept has been a consistent topic of interest. In general, a CoP can be defined as an association of individuals who share a common interest or concern that they collectively negotiate, learn about, and undertake.

Drawing on his work with Lave, Wenger (1998) contended that CoPs are formed by a group of action-oriented individuals who share a unified history, identity, and sense of purpose. Considering this description, CoPs can emerge in almost any setting in which common interests or concerns exist. Accordingly, CoPs can function within, or be applied to, a vast number of contexts, even libraries. In fact, Wenger (1998) made explicit the ubiquity of CoPs by pointing out that everyone belongs to at least several CoPs, and that they (CoPs) are widely distributed. Furthermore, some CoPs are transitory and ephemeral, whereas others are permanent and fixed. Wenger (1998), and later supported by Wenger, McDermott, and Snyder (2002), state that these informal associations of people (CoPs) have existed since the dawn of humankind, and, furthermore, that these enterprises are so pervasive that sometimes the very group that created them hardly notices them.

Facilitating Collaborative Learning

As early as 1977, Dervin stated that the core standards and practices of the library profession need to move toward a new model that will help librarians facilitate interactions among individuals, groups, and "information through more informed perspective." Libraries typically still tend to locate users at the end of their process flow, where they are offered carefully mediated information given to them by professionals well versed in identifying "authoritative sources." In keeping with Dervin observations, the notion of carefully parsing out authoritative information to "end users" needs to be overturned in such a way that the primary focus of library professionals is directed toward the users themselves as the source of problem contexts that can then be addressed by the reappropriation of existing resources to meet a specific emergent need. In the same manner in which individual-centered perspective of learning persisted, libraries need to address the individualist focus that currently exists in the library environment. Buschman (2003) notes that customer-driven librarianship presents information as a commodity and "abandons the notion of the library as a sharer of information and a place of creativity . . . where information's value does not erode because it is shared, and in fact, can sometimes increase in value" (p. 120). The concept of library member as customer privileges the individual over the social and undermines our role in sustaining and enhancing the democratic public sphere. A common thread that unites these observations challenges the individualist model and more effectively theorizes, supports, and assesses the social aspects of librarianship. Providing physical spaces where people can do collaborative work is but just a first step toward a new future for libraries.

Learning Styles and Multiple Intelligences

One can argue that the individual cognitive process is important, and collaborative structures should not ignore these important theories. I agree that the concept that conceives of knowledge as individual mental states is important, but is that the end of the learning facilitation? As highlighted by Hjørland (2004), the "individual's knowledge structure" is not the starting point, but instead we also need to "look at knowledge domains, disciplines, or other collective knowledge structures." Therefore, individualistic perspectives such as learning styles and multiple intelligences should not be tossed out of the mix but incorporated.

Consider this: Would you say that you learn better by visually seeing something, by hearing, or by acting out the information you receive? Everyone has different learning styles and learns by a combination of ways, but one type is usually dominant in each individual. The concept of people having different learning styles was initiated in 1921 by the work of psychologist Carl Jung, who proposed the theory of different "personality types." This theory was expanded to education by determining that these individual personality types have varying ways of learning. Gardner (1993) developed the theory of multiple intelligences. His work is closely related to Jung theory but more specifically addresses intelligence rather than personality. He identifies seven intelligences: verbal–linguistic, logical–mathematical, visual–spatial, body–kinesthetic, musical–rhythmic, interpersonal, and intrapersonal. And there are more that he did not identify. Interestingly enough, traditional education emphasizes only two of these areas: verbal–linguistic and logical–mathematical. Educators have recognized that only a small percentage of the general population prefers to learn by reading. These discoveries have helped tremendously in establishing continued interest in active learning techniques that attempt to capture the learning abilities of students relying on other intelligences.

While learning styles and intelligences affirm the need for instructors and training to recognize the importance of individual learning differences and to use methods that help create a climate that increases the potential learning for all trainees, human concepts and human knowledge are a result of human cooperation and communication. Hjørland (1997) sees that individual knowledge structures can only be understood based on a group-oriented analysis of language users (p.122). As Epperson (2006) noted, librarianship must negotiate a delicate, dynamic balance. He noted that, on the one hand, dialogic education is predicated on an understanding of, and engagement with, the learner's social context, needs, interests, and capabilities. On the other hand, education and, by extension, librarianship cannot be bound or limited by the marketplace expectations of the learner or member.

RELATED ARTIFACTS

Akers, R. L., Krohn, M. D., Lanza-Kaduce, L., & Rodosevich, M. (1979). Social learning and deviant behavior: A specific test of a general theory. *American Sociological Review, 44,* 636–655.

Argyris, C., & Schön, D. A. (1978). *Organizational learning: A theory of action perspective.* Reading, MA: Addison-Wesley.

Bandura, A. J. (1977). *Social learning theory.* Englewood Cliffs, NJ: Prentice Hall.

Bandura, A. J. (1986). *Social foundations of thought and action: A social cognitive theory.* Englewood Cliffs, NJ: Prentice Hall.

Bandura, A. J., & Walters, R. (1963). *Social learners and personality development.* New York: Holt, Rinehart & Winston.

Brown, J. S., & Duguid, P. (1991). Organizational learning and communities of practice: Toward a unified view of working, learning and innovation. *Organizational Science, 2*(1), 40–57.

Buschman, J. E. (2003). *Dismantling the public sphere: Situating and sustaining librarianship in the age of the new public philosophy.* Westport, CT: Libraries Unlimited.

Cunningham, P. M. (2000). A sociology of adult education. In A. L. Wilson & E. R. Hayes (Eds.), *Handbook of Adult and Continuing Education* (pp. 573–591). San Francisco: Jossey-Bass.

Dempsey, L. (2006). The (digital) library environment: Ten years after. *Ariadne, 46*. Retrieved April 15, 2009, from http://www.ariadne.ac.uk/issue46/dempsey/

Dervin, B. (1977). Useful theory for librarianship: Communication, not information. *Drexel Library Quarterly, 13*(3), 16–32.

Dewey, J. (1916). *Democracy and education: An introduction to the philosophy of education.* New York: Macmillan.

Ducheneaut, N., Yee, N., Nickell, E., & Moore, R. J. (2006). "Alone together": Exploring the social dynamics of massively multiplayer online games. In *Proceedings of the SIGCHI Conference on Human Factors in Computing Systems* (pp. 407–416). New York: ACM Press.

Durkheim, E. (1984). *The division of labor in society* (W. D. Hall, Trans.). New York: Free Press. (Original work published 1893)

Epperson, T. W. (2006). Toward a critical ethnography of librarian-supported collaborative learning. *Library Philosophy and Practice, 9*(1). Retrieved December 17, 2009, from http://www.webpages.uidaho.edu/~mbolin/epperson.htm

Gardner, H. (1993). *Multiple intelligences: The theory in practice.* New York: Basic Books.

Hjørland, B. (1997). *Information seeking and subject representation: An activity-theoretical approach to information science.* Westport, CT: Greenwood Press.

Hjørland, B. (2004). Social and cultural awareness and responsibility in library, information and documentation studies. In W. B. Rayward (Ed.), *Aware and responsible: Papers of the 2001 Nordic-International Colloquium on Social and Cultural Awareness and Responsibility in Library, Information, and Documentation Studies (SCARLID)* (pp. 71–92). Lanham, MD: Scarecrow Press.

Jarvis, P. (1987). *Adult learning in the social context.* London: Croom Helm.

Jung, C. G. (1971). *Psychological types.* Princeton, NJ: Princeton University Press. (Original work published 1921)

Kwon, N. (2008). A mixed-methods investigation of the relationship between critical thinking and library anxiety among undergraduate students in their information search process. *College & Research Libraries, 69*(2), 117–131.

Lave, J. (1988). *Cognition in practice.* Cambridge, England: Cambridge University Press.

Lave, J. (1991). *Situated learning: Legitimate peripheral participation.* Cambridge, England: Cambridge Univ. Press.

Lindeman, E. (1961). *The meaning of adult education.* Norman: University of Oklahoma. (Original work published 1926)

Miller, N., & Dollard, J. (1941). *Social learning and imitation.* New Haven, CT: Yale University Press.

Pavlov, I. P. (1927). *Conditioned reflexes.* London: Routledge & Kegan Paul.

Piaget, J. (1954). *The construction of reality in child.* New York: Basic Books.

Piaget, J. (1969). *The mechanism of perception.* London: Routledge & Kegan Paul.

Prensky, M. (2001). Digital natives, digital immigrants. *On the Horizon, 9*(5), 3–4.

Sears, R. R. (1951). A theoretical framework for personality and social behavior. *American Psychologist, 6,* 476–483.

Senge, P. M. (1990). *The fifth discipline: The art and practice of the learning organization.* New York: Doubleday.

Skinner, B. F. (1938). *The behavior of organisms: An experimental analysis.* New York: Appleton-Century.

Small, R.V., Zakaria, N., & El-Figuigui, H. (2004). Motivational aspects of information literacy skill instruction in community college libraries. *College & Research Libraries, 65*(2), 96–121.

Squire, K. (2005). Changing the game: What happens when video games enter the classroom? *Innovate, 1*(6).

Stokes, B. (2005). Video games have changed: Time to consider "Serious Games." *Developmental Education Journal.* Retrieved December 5, 2009, from http://www.netaid.org/documents/DEJ_article-Games_and_Development_Education-June05.pdf

Suchman, L. (1987). *Plans and situated actions: The problem of human-machine interaction.* Cambridge: Cambridge University Press.

Thorndike, E. L. (1901). *The human nature club: An introduction to the study of mental life* (2nd ed.). New York: Macmillan.

Tönnies, F. (2001). *Community and society* (J. Harris & M. Hollis, Trans.). Cambridge: Cambridge University Press. (Original work published 1887)

Vygotsky, L. S. (1978). *Mind in society: The development of higher psychological processes.* Cambridge, MA: Harvard University Press.

Weber, M. (1978). *Economy and society* (T. Parsons, Trans.). Berkeley: University of California Press. (Original work published 1922)

Weiler, A. (2005). Information-seeking behavior in Generation Y students: Motivation, critical thinking, and learning theory. *The Journal of Academic Librarianship, 31*(1), 46–53.

Wellman, B., & Berkowitz, S. D. (1988). *Social structures: A network approach.* Cambridge: Cambridge University Press.

Wenger, E. (1998). *Communities of practice.* Cambridge: Cambridge University Press.

Wenger, E., McDermott, R. A., & Snyder, W. (2002). *Cultivating communities of practice: A guide to managing knowledge.* Boston, MA: Harvard Business School Press.

Wundt, W. M. (1897). *Outlines of psychology* (C. H. Judd, Trans.). Leipzig, Germany: Wilhelm Engelmann.

LIBRARIES ARE IN THE KNOWLEDGE BUSINESS, THEREFORE THE CONVERSATION BUSINESS

MAP LOCATION

D, 2

THREAD LOCATION

Page 63

SCAPE

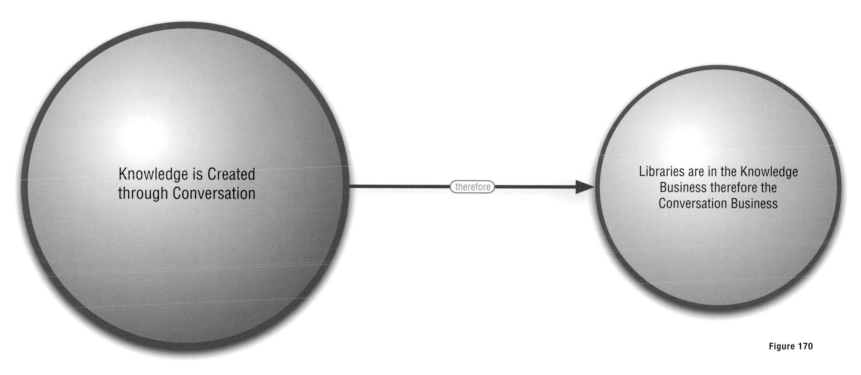

Figure 170

LIBRARY INSTRUCTION

MAP LOCATION

E, 1

THREAD LOCATION

Page 72

SCAPE

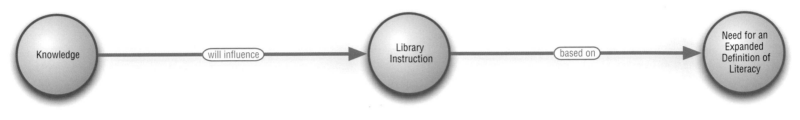

AUTHOR

Andrea Phelps

Figure 171

CONVERSATION STARTERS

Should library instruction always focus on information literacy?

RELATED ARTIFACTS

Characteristics of programs of information literacy that illustrate best practices: A guideline. (2003). *ACRL*. http://www.ala.org/ala/mgrps/divs/acrl/standards/characteristics.cfm.

Eisenberg, M. B. (2005). Evaluation—Checking it all out. *Library Media Connection, 24*(3), 22–23. http://search.ebscohost.com.libezproxy2.syr.edu/login.aspx?direct=true &db=bsh&AN=18773458&site=ehost-live.

Everhart, N. (2007). Information literacy assessment: Putting the cart before the horse. *Educators' Spotlight Digest, 2*(1). http://www.informationliteracy.org/users_data/admin/V2I1_Guest_writer_Everhart_1002.pdf.

Miller, J. (2008). Quick and easy reference evaluation: Gathering users' and providers' perspectives. *Reference & User Services Quarterly, 47*(3), 218–222. http://vnweb. hwwilsonweb.com.libezproxy2.syr.edu/hww/jumpstart.jhtml?recid=0bc05f7a67b1790 e9e8f8b7ba4031106dfcade1ff4ccd482a9befdd21c05c3f2d4643937b6a9325a&fmt=P.

Small, R. V. (2006). Transforming research into practice. *Educators' Spotlight Digest, 1*(1). http://www.informationliteracy.org/users_data/admin/Volume1_Issue1_Guest_writer.pdf.

Smith, L. L. (1991). Evaluating the reference interview: A theoretical discussion of the desirability and achievability of evaluation. *Reference Quarterly, 31*(1), 75–79.

Zabel, D. (2006). Is everything old new again? Part two. *Reference & User Services Quarterly, 45*(4), 284–289. http://vnweb.hwwilsonweb.com.libezproxy2.syr.edu/hww/jumpstart.jhtml?recid=0bc05f7a67b1790e9e8f8b7ba4031106dfcade1ff4ccd48 2491250c366664c215ee2406ce722912b&fmt=P.

LIMITATIONS OF TAGGING

MAP LOCATION

G, 2

THREAD LOCATION

Page 51

SCAPE

CONTRIBUTOR

Elizabeth Gall

Figure 172

RELATED ARTIFACTS

Mendes, L. H., Quinonez-Skinner, J., & Skaggs, D. (2009). Subjecting the catalog to tagging. *Library Hi Tech, 27*(1), 30–41. DOI: 10.1108/07378830910942892.

Furner, J. (2008). User tagging of library resources: Toward a framework for system evaluation. *International Cataloguing and Bibliographic Control, 37*(3), 47–51.

Sanders, D. (2008). Tag—You're it! *American Libraries, 39*(11), 52–54.

Rethlefsen, M. L. (2007a). Chief thingamabrarian. *Library Journal (1976), 132*(1), 40–42.

Rethlefsen, M. L. (2007b). Tags help make libraries del.icio.us. *Library Journal (1976), 132*(15), 26–28.

LIS EDUCATION

MAP LOCATION
C, 8, 9

THREAD LOCATION
Page 177

SCAPE

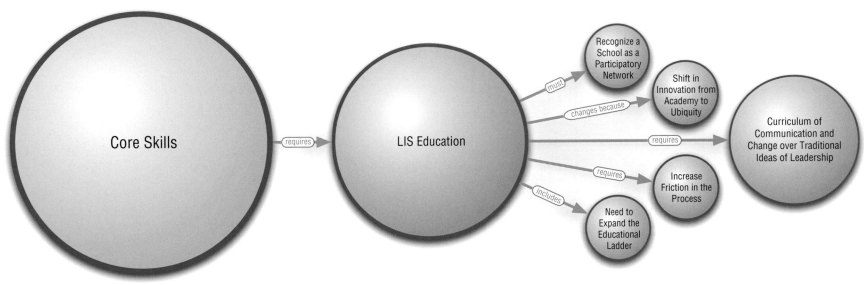

Figure 173

LONGITUDE EXAMPLE

MAP LOCATION

C, 4

THREAD LOCATION

Page 16

SCAPE

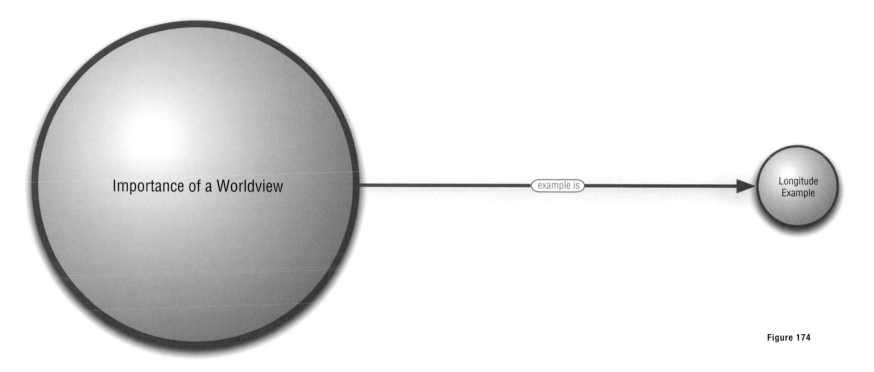

Importance of a Worldview

example is

Longitude
Example

Figure 174

MAPPING CONVERSATIONS

MAP LOCATION
F, G, 6

THREAD LOCATION
Page 107

SCAPE

Figure 175

MASSIVE SCALE

MAP LOCATION
G, H, 2

THREAD LOCATION
Page 142

SCAPE

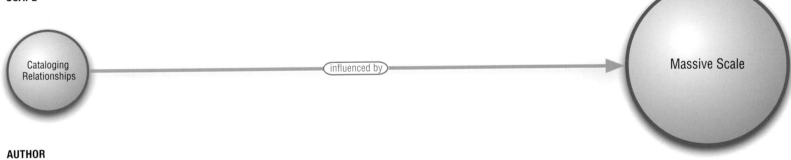

AUTHOR
R. David Lankes

Figure 176

In the process of a Transportation Research Board study on information management in the transportation industry, several panel members observed that soon every mile of road will generate a gigabyte of data a day.[1] These data will come from road sensors embedded into asphalt to detect temperature for winter salting, real-time traffic data from roadway cameras, weather information, toll data from Radio-Frequency Identification (RFID) expressway systems, car black boxes, and a myriad of other data sources. It is assumed that this will become a gigabyte an hour as more and more technology finds its way into our vehicles and management systems (GPS data, real-time environment monitoring, etc.). Because there are 3.5 million miles of highways in the United States, that would be 3.3 petabytes of data per hour or 28 exabytes per year.

Some readers may not be familiar with an exabyte. It is the name for a large volume of storage like megabytes, gigabytes (1024 megabytes), and terabytes (1024 gigabytes), technically 2^{60} bytes. Table 3[2] will give the reader some sense of the scale involved.

BYTE	1 BYTE: A SINGLE CHARACTER;
KILOBYTE	2 KILOBYTES: A TYPEWRITTEN PAGE;
MEGABYTE	2 MEGABYTES: A HIGH-RESOLUTION PHOTO-GRAPH;
GIGABYTE	2 GIGABYTES: 20 METERS OF SHELVED BOOKS
TERABYTE	2 TERABYTES: AN ACADEMIC RESEARCH LIBRARY
PETABYTE	2 PETABYTES: ALL U.S. ACADEMIC RESEARCH LIBRARIES;
EXABYTE	5 EXABYTES: ALL WORDS EVER SPOKEN BY HUMANS.
ZETTABYTE	
YOTTABYTE	

What the reader needs to realize is that each succeeding row in the table, from megabyte to gigabyte to terabyte and so forth, is an exponential increase. By and large, people do not think in exponential terms. Gladwell uses the analogy of folding paper to demonstrate just how big the shifts involved in exponential change are. Imagine you have a huge piece of paper.[3] Although the paper is large in terms of its width and height, it is only 0.01 inches thick. You fold it in half. You then fold it in half again 50 times. How tall would it be? Many people might say as thick as a phone book or get really brave and predict as high as a refrigerator. The actual answer is approximately the distance between the earth and the sun.

How can this be? Certainly if I stack 50 pieces of paper on top of each other the stack would not be that large. However, stacking separate sheets is a linear progression, and that is not what you accomplished by folding the paper. With every fold, you doubled the thickness of the paper. With one fold, the paper is twice as thick as when you started. With the second fold, the paper is four times as thick—the next fold is eight times as thick, and so on. In the first few folds, you do not see a major increase, but at about fold 40 you are doubling a mile. We are not used to thinking in terms of exponential growth because most things we deal with grow linearly. However, technology is not.

Predictable Change

In 1965, computer pioneer Gordon E. Moore predicted that the number of transistors that could be fit on a chip (roughly equivalent to the speed at which the chip could process information) would double every eighteen months.[4] The prediction has become so reliable it is referred to as Moore's Law. The law is an exponential change just like the paper folding. Computers have not just gotten faster over the past decade, they have gotten exponentially faster. What is more, currently, makers of storage technologies—hard drives, solid-state flash memory, and the like—are exceeding Moore's Law. The emergence of massive-scale computing in our every day lives is a predictable change unlike the web.

1. Transportation Research Board, Committee for a Future Strategy for Transportation Information Management (2006). Transportation knowledge networks: A management strategy for the 21st century. TRB Special Report 284, Washington D.C. www.trb.org/news/blurb_detail.asp?id=5789 (accessed Sept. 15, 2007).
2. University of Berkeley (2000). How much information? http://www2.sims.berkeley.edu/research/projects/how-much-info/datapowers.html (accessed Sept. m16, 2007).
3. Malcolm Gladwell (2002). *The Tipping Point: How Little Things Can Make a Big Difference.* San Francisco: Back Bay Books.
4. Gordon E. Moore, "Cramming More Components onto Integrated Circuits," Electronics 38, no. 8 (April 1965), http://download.intel.com/museum/Moores_Law/Articles-Press_Releases/Gordon_Moore_1965_Article.pdf (accessed Sept. 16, 2007).

The web and associated widespread Internet penetration was a discontinuous event. No one could truly predict a world where URLs come with every can of soda or where an online search company would become one of the biggest corporations on the planet. Libraries can be excused for taking some time to adjust their service models to such an unpredictable and disruptive force. Yet libraries, by and large, have adapted to the new reality. Be it providers of access, guiding online research, supporting distance education, providing virtual reference, or developing metadata schema, libraries have adapted to this change and continue to do so.

The question now lies before the library community: Will massive-scale computing be another disruptive force or, as it is a predictable change, will libraries proactively engage in the massive-scale computing world? This question is neither theoretical nor a question that can long be delayed. Consider that following quote from *Wired Magazine*:

> Ask.com operations VP Dayne Sampson estimates that the five leading search companies together have some 2 million servers, each shedding 300 watts of heat annually, a total of 600 megawatts. These are linked to hard drives that dissipate perhaps another gigawatt. Fifty percent again as much power is required to cool this searing heat, for a total of 2.4 gigawatts. With a third of the incoming power already lost to the grid's inefficiencies, and half of what's left lost to power supplies, transformers, and converters, the total of electricity consumed by major search engines in 2006 approaches 5 gigawatts . . . almost enough to power the Las Vegas metropolitan area—with all its hotels, casinos, restaurants, and convention centers—on the hottest day of the year.[5]

Consider also that many universities, companies, and even primary and secondary schools have run out of power to add new computing equipment. Either their own electrical infrastructure cannot handle the load of computing or their municipalities literally have no more power to send.

Options?

So how can the library community respond to the emerging reality of massive data stores, unimaginable processing power, and super-fast networks? In particular, how will libraries respond when the limitations of storing the world's information indefinitely disappears and the production of new data and information grows exponentially from today? Let us explore some options.

Option 1: Ignore It

No one said the library has to take on every challenge presented it. In fact, many criticize libraries for taking on too much. Perhaps the problem of massive-scale computing and storage is not a library problem. Certainly for those who argue that libraries are in the business of literacy and cataloging, there is plenty to do with published documents.[6] After all, libraries are plenty busy with published documents and digitizing historical documents. Why add the problem of real-time information stores and digital items that don't remotely look like documents? Furthermore, there are already plenty of other disciplines lining up to tackle this issue. From e-commerce to computer science to individual industry, sectors like transportation and medicine many have begun to acknowledge the problem of massive-scale computing. The National Science Foundation and the National Endowment for the Humanities alike have begun "cyberinfrastructure" initiatives. In addition, the computing industry has certainly taken care of these problems to date. With faster processors, smarter software, and bigger hard drives, no doubt Apple, Microsoft, or the other industry players can solve these issues.

The answer to "why not ignore it," I argue, comes down to a simple ethical consideration. If libraries do not address these issues with their foundation of praxis and principles, the consequences for society and the field of libraries itself could be grave. Look at the largest portal and search engine companies. When they partner with libraries, such as in large-scale digitization efforts, these commercial organizations gain credibility and have negotiated safeguards of the material they are digitization (e.g., scans being redeposited with libraries). However, look at the data these organizations store on users. How comfortable is the library profession with these data stores when search engine providers cooperate with governments (domestic and abroad)? Will principles closely aligned with civil liberties and privacy be preserved? Will data stores of unique resources beyond the current library collec-

---

5. George Gilder, (October, 2007) The Information Factories. www.wired.com/wired/archive/14.10/cloudware.html?pg=1&topic=cloudware&topic_set (accessed online Sept. 14, 2007).
6. Martha M.Yee, with a great deal of help from Michael Gorman, "Will the Response of the Library Profession to the Internet be Self-immolation?" online posting, July 29, 2007, JESSE, http://listserv.utk.edu/cgi-bin/wa?A2=ind0707&L=JESSE&P=R14797&I=-3.

tions be made widely accessible? The answer is obvious—only as long as the business model is served.

The ultimate result may well be the commercialization of data stewardship in the massive-scale world. We have already seen how well that works with scholarly output and journals. To be sure, I am not arguing that libraries must do it all, but they must be a vital part of the massive-scale landscape. If we truly value our principles of privacy, access, and so on, we must see them as active not simply passive. We cannot, in essence, commit the sin of omission by not engaging the massive-scale world and allowing access and privacy to be discarded or distorted. We should be working to instill the patron's bill of rights throughout the information world, not simply when they enter our buildings or Web sites.

OPTION 2: LIMIT THE LIBRARY

A closely related strategy to ignoring the issue is to acknowledge the issue and redefine our mission around it. In essence, libraries are in the knowledge business, and that is now going to be defined as document-like objects, with some sort of elite provenance and well synthesized. In fact, arguments have been made that sound close to this approach. The distinction is sometimes subtle, as in this quote from Crawford and Gorman:

> Libraries and librarians serve their users and preserve the culture by acquiring, listing, making available, and conserving the records of humankind in all media and by providing services to the users of those records.[7]

Here, although the mission sounds expansive, the key comes in defining what a "record of humankind" is. Do large-scale datasets fit into this category? What about blog entries or reference inquiries? Certainly they appear not to in Gorman's later essay, "Web 2.0: The Sleep of Reason."[8] Here Gorman bemoans "an increase in credulity and an associated flight from expertise."[9] The problem, of course, has always been in defining and agreeing on an expert. Such notions are almost always situational.

However, there is a much deeper problem in this line of logic. Namely, it pits two longstanding practices and ideals in librarianship: selection and intellectual freedom. Selection and weeding is common library practice. It grew out of resource limitations. Shelf space, book budgets, availability, use of jobbers, and the like are all about existing in a world of scarcity. All of these resources in the physical world constrain the size and scope of the collection. Not since the days of monks and illuminated manuscripts have libraries been convincingly able to collect it all. Today, the concept of "comprehensive" is often limited to a serial run or manuscript series.

Yet in a truly digital world, the growing prospect of cheap storage makes digital artifacts different. Although licensing and cost may still restrict access to some items, collecting massive, effectively limitless, digital items makes the selection due to scarcity argument all but moot. Imagine an academic or school library collecting every paper (including every draft and note) ever written by all of its students. Imagine every public library collecting video and minutes and audio from every public meeting held. The old arguments of not enough room to accomplish such tasks are clearly disappearing.

Certainly by having a library collect and disseminate such information we are providing free and open access to information. Whether we should, whether it is worth doing so, is no longer a selection from scarcity debate. It becomes a selection by choice debate. Can libraries choose what to collect and still say they are providing free and unencumbered intellectual access to these materials? In a massive-scale world, libraries will have to choose between these ideals.

OPTION 3: CATALOG IT ALL

Some have argued that cataloging lies at the heart of librarianship.[10] Although many take issue with the argument equating "human intervention for the organization of information" solely to cataloging, including myself, it is hard to refute the more general concept that information organization lies at the heart of the profession. Why not then extend the current praxis of the field (i.e., metadata generation) to the growing mass of digital information?

It is a pretty commonsensical argument that the library field (or indeed any given field) is unable to provide the raw person power behind indexing the world of networked digital information. However, we also have some pretty good empirical reasons to show this is not an acceptable means of proceeding. The first is that, as a field, we

7. Walt Crawford and Michael Gorman (1995). *Future libraries: Dreams, madness and reality*. Chicago: American Library Association, 120.
8. Michael Gorman, "Web 2.0: The Sleep of Reason. Part I, " online posting, July 11, 2007, Britannica Blog, http://blogs.britannica.com/blog/main/2007/06/web-20-the-sleep-of-reason-part-i/ (accessed Sept. 15, 2007).
9. Ibid.
10. Yee, "Will the Response of the Library Profession to the Internet be Self-immolation?"

have already tried this. From early OCLC experiments with CORC (Cooperative Online Resource Catalog) to the Librarians Index to the Internet (claiming more than 20,000 sites indexed), librarians have tried to selectively catalog the net. They all cite problems of timeliness and a rapidly changing Internet environment (catalog it today, the page will move tomorrow) in trying to catalog the world.

Ignore the problems of shifting pages and dynamic content and suppose for a minute that every page on the Internet was not only static but never changed its location. In 2005, Yahoo! estimated it indexed 20 billion pages.[11] If we had our 65,000 American Library Association (ALA) members spend one minute per record indexing these pages, the good news is that the entire Internet could be indexed in a little more than seven months. The bad news is that those ALA members would have to work the seven months straight without eating, sleeping, or attending a committee meeting. At the same time, Google was claiming its index was three times as large.

The fact is that the Internet is, however, very dynamic. Blogs, gateway pages, news outlets, and other dynamic content represent a growing portion of the web. If all of those ALAers did decide to spend seven months cataloging the web, they would have to start in the eighth month doing it all over again. Of course, they might also want to spend sometime on the four billion new pages created each year also (using a conservative estimate from OCLC's growth data).[12]

All of this debate, however, ignores the most interesting aspect of massive-scale computing—the invention of whole new records that defy traditional cataloging. Take, for example, gigapixel images. According to the Gigapxl Project:

> It would take a video wall of 10,000 television screens or 600 prints from a professional digital SLR camera to capture as much information as that contained in a single Gigapixil exposure.[13]

Imagine a historian creating a directory of gargoyles on the facade of the Notre Dame cathedral. Instead of taking a series of images of each sculpture, the historian simply takes four gigapixel images (one for each face of the building). Any user of the directory can zoom in from the entire front of the cathedral to any individual gargoyle at high resolution from a single image. How does one catalog that image? As Notre Dame? A Cathedral? A collection of gargoyles? What about a later scholar who uses the same image to explore the stained glass, construction, weathering of the facade, or any number of other details that can be explored in the image? At such high resolutions, what is foreground, what is background, what is predominant, or what is detail becomes messy at best.

OPTION 4: EMBRACE IT

I obviously favor the option of engagement. In fact, I would further argue that it is the ethical responsibility of library and information science education to prepare librarians for the world of massive-scale computing. By not preparing future information professionals to deal with terabytes of data per second, we are limiting their ability to live up to the ideals of the profession and the needs of the future (and many current) members.

To embrace massive-scale computing in libraries, we must:

- Expand and Enhance Current Library Practice. As previously discussed, librarians must become conversant in not only processing elite documents but real-time information as well.

- Go Beyond a Focus on Artifacts and Items. As is discussed, books, videos, and even web pages are simply artifacts of a knowledge-creation process. To concentrate on containers and documents is to be overwhelmed. By focusing instead on knowledge creation and directly incorporating patron knowledge, librarians should be better able to manage and add value to the tsunami of digital data being created.

- See Richness and Structure Beyond Metadata. To move from processing containers to capturing and organizing knowledge means going beyond traditional methods of classification and cataloging. Too often librarians enter a discourse community and drive it to taxonomy creation when the vocabulary, the very concepts, of the discourse community are still formative. Instead, librarians need to look to other structures in knowledge products and the creation process such as provenance, linking (citations), and social networks to provide a useful method of information discovery and enrichment.

- Change at the Core of the Library. All of this needs to be done at the core of library service, not as some new service, or by adding new systems and functions to an already labyrinthine array of databases, catalogs, and software.

11. Battelle, John (September 26, 2005). Google Announces New Index Size, Shifts Focus from Counting," online posting, Sept. 26, 2005), John Battelle's Searchblog, http://battellemedia.com/archives/001889.php (accessed Sept. 15, 2007).
12. OCLC, Size and Growth Statistics, www.oclc.org/research/projects/archive/wcp/stats/size.htm (accessed Sept. 15, 2007).
13. Gigapxl, The Gigapxl Project (August 2007). http://www.gigapxl.org (accessed Sept. 15, 2007).

If our new model of librarianship is to be of any use, it must address these issues. We can see from the Atlas' treatment of artifacts one way to approach the massive-scale issue.

The other implication of this approach is that books, videos, and documents are by-products of conversations. That is not to say they are unimportant, rather acknowledges they are only a pale reflection of the knowledge- creation process. By the time you read this article, for example, it has already been rewritten and edited numerous times. By the time the ideas are encoded into words, they have been debated and discussed by a wide spectrum of people. The citations at the end give only an idea of the resources used to develop these arguments (the ones written down and easily addressed). The article also no doubt leads to a few discussions and disagreements after it is published. Yet it is this written document that will be indexed in the databases. The rich conversational space around it is lost.

The idea of conversation in librarianship or a "conversational space" around articles is not all that new. Bechtel talked about how scholarly communications should be taught as an ongoing conversation in information literacy programs.[14] Conversational organizational approaches can also be seen in citations and scholarly communication, law and precedents, bibliometrics, Web of Science, reference, and special collections, and it plays a large role in collection development. In many ways, libraries have been in the conversation business; they have simply developed technologies centered on items—so much so that we are now struggling to recapture the conversation in initiatives such as federated searching and Functional Requirements for Bibliographic Records (FRBR).

Now turn this problem around for a moment. Let us say that we could capture this conversational space. We would have audio files of class conversations, video of presentations, the full text of the articles cited (including the citations used in those articles hot linked), drafts, and editor's notes—the whole work. Approached as items, each would need a catalog record, and all might be available in the catalog. Yet what holds all of them together as a conversation? In fact, the conversational aspects of this collection of artifacts exist between the catalog records. It is the relationship among the items, not the items. This is the kind of information we capture in an annotated bibliography.

If, in addition to capturing the items, we captured the relationships, how might that work? Imagine now finding this article online. Once there, you should be able to instantly find the rest of the items.

14. Bechtel, Joan M. (1986). Conversation: A new paradigm for librarianship? *College & Research Libraries, 47* (3), 219–224.

Click—you see a previous draft. Click—there is a citation. Click—here is another article by that author. You are now surfing the conversation. It also allows you to rapidly find lots of heterogeneous data. Click on this article and see the text, find a graph, and click on it. Up pops access to a large dataset. Run some new analysis on the data and post it. Now someone finding your article can find both the original dataset and the original article that was published. It is in the relationships among the items that we gain navigation, not in the items themselves.

As a field, we must think in threads. The way to handle a terabyte of data per second is not to try and catalog items in less than a second; it is to know what thread the new terabyte extends. "Oh, this is more weather data from NOAA, I'll attach it to my NOAA thread." Once available, scientists, students, and the general public can use that new dataset as a starting point for yet a new thread.

Take our gigapixel image of Notre Dame. The image is simply one item in a thread about gargoyles as created by the author. The same item, however, can also become the starting point for threads by the architect, historian, theologian, and so on. Furthermore, by finding any point in the conversation about Notre Dame, be it architectural, historical, or spiritual, you can find any other conversation.

If this begins to sound like the web, you are right. However, imagine imbuing the web with the ideals and tools of librarianship. These threads we create can incorporate fundamental concepts such as authority files. The search tools and "thread" (annotation) tools can both preserve privacy and provide new structures for the library community to capture and add value to.

Conversations: It Takes Two

So by organizing materials into threads and capturing and adding value to the relationships among items, the library can begin to approach massive scales of information. However, just as with trying to catalog the world of digital information, creating and capturing threads can quickly overwhelm the resources of professional librarians. More to the point, with networked technology, we want to capture these threads at the point of knowledge creation with the authors of ideas. In order to do this, we must expand our systems and services to truly incorporate our patrons into them.

In the library science field, we have seen an evolution in thinking about the relationship between systems and users. Early computer systems were designed by programmers and more reflected the system designer than those the system was intended for. This so-called system view was challenged and eventually supplanted (at least rhetorically) by a user-based design paradigm.[15] In the user-based approach, the user's needs and habits needed to be well understood and then reflected in the systems we created. However, today, we see a further evolution to truly user systems. In today's spate of social Internet tools, the systems only provide a sparse framework of functionality for users to populate and direct. Wikis, blogs, video-sharing sites, and the like have shown that when users construct the system around themselves, they gain greater ownership and utility. We call these participatory systems.

Participatory systems and participatory librarians do not seek to construct a system of functions and information and then bring the users to them, but rather seek to support users as they construct their own systems and information spaces. Once again, rhetorically, this fits well with the rhetoric of librarianship. After all, from reference to collection development to cataloging (in the concept of literary warrant), we claim the users direct our services. Yet look at the systems we use to instantiate these ideals. The catalogs we provide only accept queries from users not actual documents. In reference, we have a conversation between librarian and patron, not patron and patron. It is time to take our ideals and make systems that reflect that the library is an agent of the community not simply a service to it.

In other venues, these ideas are much more fully developed, and I recommend to the interested reader seeking the more fleshed-out discussions of participatory librarianship. For now, let me simply state that to be of the community means that you have trust in your patrons and they have a voice. To be a service to a community implies a paternalistic relationship and a separation.

Recommendations and Conclusion

Libraries must be active participants in participatory networking. This must be done at the core of the library not on the periphery. Anything less simply adds stress and stretches scarce resources even further. The reason we should be looking at technologies such as blogs and Wikis is to get closer to the community and knowledge generation and to make all of our library systems more inclusive of community. By thinking in threads and using the social intelligence of our service community, the library profession is actually well poised to take on the world of massive-scale computing.

15. Dervin, Brenda and Nilan, Michael Sanford (1986), Information needs and uses. *Annual Review of Information Science and Technology, 21*, 3–31. .

However, the library field will only thrive in the massive-scale world to engage the ideas and current massive-scale stakeholders. To ignore the implications of massive-scale computing is dangerous. It abdicates serious decisions and consequences to others who do not have our experience and firm principles. Participatory librarianship is an opportunity not only to enhance the mission of the library, but proactively to position librarians at the forefront of the information field . . . where they belong!

MAP LOCATION
C, 1, 2

THREAD LOCATION
Page 66

SCAPE

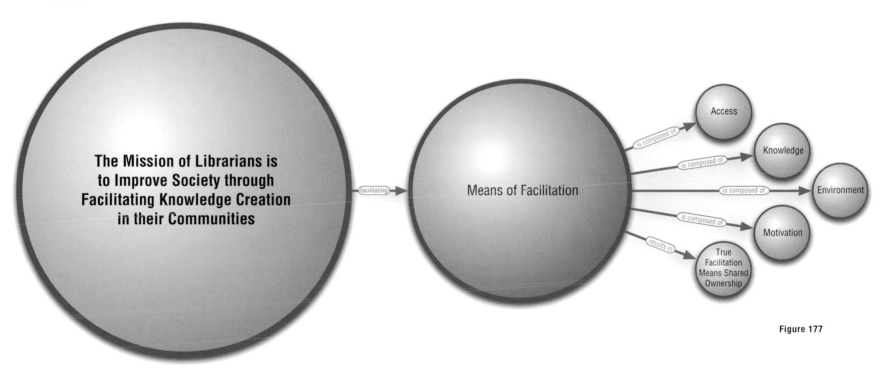

Figure 177

AUTHOR
Amy Edick

AGREEMENT DESCRIPTION

The Atlas covers four primary means of facilitating knowledge creation:

- Access: Providing access to a member's conversation or providing access for a member to others' conversations.

- Knowledge: Providing baseline or foundational knowledge (skills, concepts, history) so that a member may fully participate in a conversation.

- Environment: Providing a place of safety (physical, cultural, emotional, legal) for members so they will not be penalized by participating in a conversation.

- Motivation: Providing the appropriate incentives and disincentives to encourage members to engage in conversations.

CONVERSATION STARTERS

1. How does one know whether one is facilitating correctly?
2. Does it really depend on varying scenarios?
3. Is the process of the facilitation unsuccessful if the person fails on the receiving end?

RELATED ARTIFACTS

David, V. L. (2009). Access to technology in transition. *Teacher Librarian, 36*(5), 46–47.

> Annotation: This article dealt more with different types of facilitation linked with schools and filters. It shows the different extremes that schools vary. I feel that this is a good depiction of facilitation, even though it is only focusing on a small example. It shows how facilitation can change depending on each school's values, morals, and atmosphere.

Ellen, M. (2009). More search smarts. *American Libraries, 40*(6/7), 94.

> Annotation: This article could be a great resource to help librarians further or broaden their skills in the field. I find this one to be more fitting than the first article because it is not as specific. It could pertain to many different situations.

Howe, E. (2009). Using pathfinders to facilitate collaboration and teach information skills. *Learning & Media, 37*(1), 5–7.

> Annotation: This article clearly stated the different steps and processes to good facilitating practices. This seems like it would be a good tool to use, yet it may be a little misguided. Not all situations are going to be alike enough to use the same set of rules each time. There are going to be different types of people and topics involved in each situation.

MEETING SPACES

MAP LOCATION

E, 3

THREAD LOCATION

Page 69

SCAPE

AUTHOR

Jocelyn Clark

Figure 178

AGREEMENT DESCRIPTION

Meeting spaces are the places where people can come together to hold a conversation, share ideas, and create knowledge. The librarian's role in facilitation of these meeting spaces can take a number of forms. We can design good physical spaces, create virtual spaces, help people to use these spaces, and help people hold the meetings. There are facilitation methods for the spaces and the meetings themselves. Mostly I have discussed the spaces because the discussion of means of facilitation is a huge topic.

Initially, I did some brainstorming of all the different kinds of spaces for people to meet. There are dozens, and they can be defined in different ways. Some are formal and some are informal, virtual or physical, voice-based, text-based, video-based, and so on. The rough division falls along physical spaces versus virtual (or distance) spaces. The list is below.

In the library literature, there is a lot of discussion about physical meeting rooms and their role in library service. Many libraries have separate meeting rooms available to the members or groups. Usually, there has to be a clearly defined policy regarding who can use the meeting room, how it can be used, and the access and reservation procedures. This type of space is clearly different from the more informal spaces that are used for smaller meetings—tutoring sessions, study dates, and so on. There is also quite a bit about the transition to a "learning commons" that many academic libraries are undergoing. Transforming physical spaces into collaborative spaces include changes such as:

- Creation of multiple collaboration areas where people can converse without disturbing other library members.

- Computer terminals where multiple people can gather and be noisy.

- Supplies and technologies that can be checked out and used in meeting rooms (whiteboards, laptops, projectors, speakerphones [gasp]).

- Flexible spaces that can adapt to different groups and uses.

In the virtual world, there are an enormous number of venues where people are interacting and discussing: everything from Facebook to SecondLife to blogs to bulletin boards to chat rooms. They can be synchronous or asynchronous. Even document services such as Google Docs can be a type of meeting space or collaboration space. The numbers of collaboration spaces are increasing dramatically. Web-based productivity tools are allowing businesses and individuals to collaborate while located all over the world. Google now has a beta version of its online collaboration space: Google Wave.

In thinking about meeting spaces, we think about access to the physical space within a library, the types of physical spaces provided, access and use of virtual spaces, and facilitation of the use of those spaces.

Types of Spaces

Below is the result of a brainstorming session on types of meeting spaces that are used by people. Some have examples, some do not, but the idea is to begin to grasp the variety.

- Physical Spaces
  - Private Meeting Rooms
  - Instructional rooms
  - Learning commons
  - Public social spaces (coffee shops, etc.)
  - Privately held meeting spaces (my living room, corporate conference room, etc.)
  - Performance space
  - Repurposed or flexible space (dorm lounge, empty classroom, etc.)
- Virtual Spaces
  - Social networks/social spaces
    - Facebook, mySpace, ning, LinkedIn, etc.
    - Voice Thread http://voicethread.com/
    - Twine http://www.twine.com
    - Second Life
    - Massive multiplayer games
  - Wikis
    - http://pbworks.com/
  - Bulletin Boards
  - Document Services (and others)
    - http://docs.zoho.com/jsp/index.jsp
    - http://docs.google.com/
  - Chat rooms
    - http://www.chatmaker.net/
    - http://www.100topkid.com/?cat=Chat
  - Virtual and web-based conferencing technology
    - http://www.dimdim.com/products/what_is_dimdim.html
    - http://www.onlinemeetingrooms.com/
    - http://www.microsoft.com/windows/windows-vista/features/meeting-space.aspx
  - Digital Centers
    - Columbia University Libraries Digital Social Science Center http://www.columbia.edu/cu/lweb/indiv/dssc/index.html
  - Collaboration Software
    - BaseCamp http://basecamphq.com/
    - Google Wave http://wave.google.com/help/wave/closed.html
    - Convos http://www.convos.com/
- Environments (both physical and virtual)
  - Conversation environments
  - Collaborative learning environments
    - Cornell University Collaborative Center http://mannlib.cornell.edu/rooms-labs/collaborative-center
  - Informal social spaces
  - Community of practice/interest spaces

Where Do Librarians Fit In?

Ideas include teaching, moderating, embedding in spaces, roving reference, and others. Teaching others how to collaborate, communicate, and create knowledge within these spaces seems to be key. The physical meeting space services provided by libraries vary with the type of library. Academic libraries have been moving toward learning commons and more collaborative spaces designed for students. Public libraries generally provide public meeting rooms with tables and chairs but not much else. There is not much of a presence for librarians as facilitators in the virtual collaboration world outside of some academic applications. There is still a lot of room in these meeting spaces for librarians to be facilitating knowledge creation, but the question of how to do it hasn't been answered. Do we keep to our information island in Second Life? Or do we roam through World of Warcraft as a librarian? It gets back to access not being enough. Particularly in virtual spaces, people don't need librarians to get access, so our role has to be something different. Our role becomes one of true facilitation and teaching.

RELATED ARTIFACTS

Association of Research Libraries. (2009, November 13). *New thinking on space & facilities*. Retrieved from: http://www.arl.org/rtl/space/index.shtml.

> Annotation: This is a collection of recent articles, tools, and other resources gathered by ARL.

Balas, J. (2007). Physical space and digital space—librarians belong in both. *Computers in Libraries, 27*(5), 26–29.

Barton, E., & Weismantel, A. (2007). Creating collaborative technology-rich workspaces in an academic library. *Reference Services Review, 35*(3), 395–404.

Bennett, S. (2008). The information or the learning commons: Which will we have? *Journal of Academic Librarianship, 34*(3), 183–185.

Fernandez, S. (2008). Premium space. *Public Libraries, 47*(6), 18.

Gabbard, R., Kaiser, A., & Kaunelis, D. (2007). Redesigning a library space for collaborative learning. *Computers in Libraries, 27*(5), 6–11.

Hill, N. (2008). Meeting rooms: All for one and one for all? *Public Libraries, 47*(6), 17.

McLeod, K. (2008). Blessing or curse? *Public Libraries, 47*(6), 17–18.

Pollard, D. (2005, March 18). *Virtual collaboration: If you can't work side-by-side*. Retrieved from: http://blogs.salon.com/0002007/2005/03/18.html.

Stuart, C. (2009). Learning and research spaces in ARL libraries: Snapshots of installations and experiments. *Research Library Issues, 264*, 7–18.

MEMBERS NOT PATRONS OR USERS

MAP LOCATION

E, 1

THREAD LOCATION

Page 66

SCAPE

Figure 179

MEMORY

MAP LOCATION

E, 2

THREAD LOCATION

Page 48

SCAPE

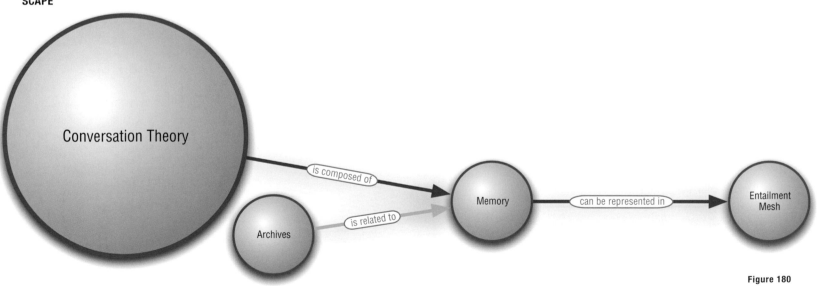

Figure 180

MOTIVATION

MAP LOCATION

E, 1

THREAD LOCATIONS

Pages 26, 78

SCAPE

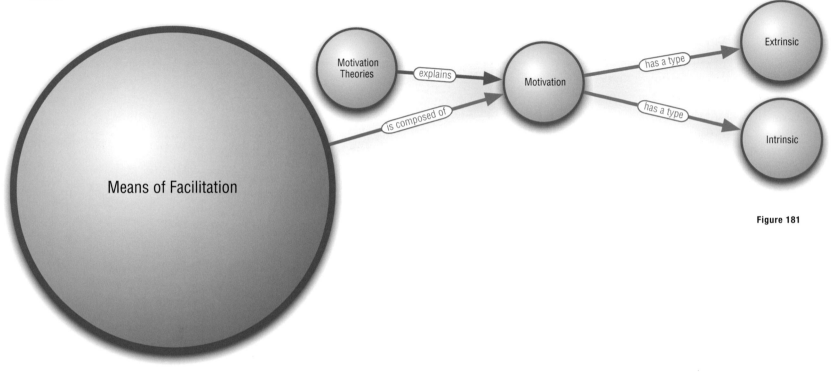

Means of Facilitation

Motivation Theories — *explains* → Motivation

is composed of →

Motivation — *has a type* → Extrinsic

Motivation — *has a type* → Intrinsic

Figure 181

AUTHOR

Andrea Phelps

AGREEMENT DESCRIPTION

A library existing solely on intrinsically motivated members can bring about the end of a library if the community is in hard times. That is not to say that intrinsic motivation is a bad thing and should somehow be discouraged, but rather that some forms of extrinsic motivation can help bolster intrinsic.

Although it may be out of scope of the Atlas or this Thread, it may be worth noting that motivation has to start within the librarian. If the library staff is not motivated about their job in any way, motivating members will be a huge challenge. Any lack of motivation among staff is a hurdle that should be explored and addressed in some way before any real progress will be made outside of the library. A reference interview performed by an unmotivated librarian will be a bad experience for the member and librarian. A good place to start is to think about what motivates you and then ask members of your staff the same thing.

Motivation is at the core of everything librarians do and work toward. Libraries and librarians are supposed to be community focused; without understanding what motives drive the community they are a part of, fulfilling the needs of the community and serving their members is a tall order. Understanding motives can help with more than adjusting advertising to get new members into the library, it can help librarians conduct reference interviews, plan better programs and events, purchase appropriate technology, build better spaces, and acquire actually useful materials.

RELATED ARTIFACTS

Among the many articles on Maslow's Hierarchy of Needs, the following two directly relate to librarians:

Anderson, S. (2004). How to dazzle Maslow preparing your library, staff and teens to reach self-actualization. *Public Library Quarterly, 23*(3/4), 49–59.

> Annotation: Although focused on a specific age group, Anderson's article addresses how librarian's can map Maslow's Hierarchy of Needs to the services they provide. It provides a good example of a smaller scale incorporation of the Hierarchy of Needs into a library setting and a more intellectual approach to the Hierarchy.

The Chronicle of Philanthropy. (2006, December 16). Philadelphia library offers jobs to the formerly homeless. Retrieved from: http://philanthropy.com/news/philanthropytoday/1679/philadelphia-library-offers-jobs-to-the-formerly-homeless

> Annotation: As mentioned above, the Philadelphia Library took a more literal view of the Hierarchy of Needs and took steps to solve the basic needs expressed by the population of homeless, incorporating some of Maslow's ideals on a much larger scale.

The following two articles look closer at intrinsic and extrinsic motivation.
Antoni, G. (2009). Intrinsic vs. extrinsic motivations to volunteer and social capital formation. *Kyklos, 62*(3), 359–370.

> Annotation: This article discusses some of the effects of actions based on intrinsic versus extrinsic motives. We discussed in Blackboard how extrinsic motivation can carry negative connotations and have a lasting effect on members, but intrinsic motivation can be easily swayed. This article looks at some other effects of intrinsic and extrinsic motivation in volunteer work and may have some really interesting insights into how to leverage both forms of motivation in a library setting.

Wiechman, B., & Gurland, S. (2009). What happens during the free-choice period? Evidence of a polarizing effect of extrinsic rewards on intrinsic motivation. *Journal of Research in Personality, 43*(4), 716–719.

> Annotation: This article looks at the harm to intrinsic motivation that can occur when an activity is given an extrinsic reward as well. The analyses of these phenomena among college students seem central to how librarians should advertise and extrinsically motivate their members.

Last, these two articles look more specifically at children and young adults, and how they are motivated:

Roeser, R., & Peck, S. (2009). An education in awareness: Self, motivation, and self- regulated learning in contemplative perspective. *Educational Psychologist, 44*(2), 119–136.

> Annotation: Roeser and Peck present Contemplative Education as a means of motivating students. A few of the subcategories worth looking at in depth are those involving community membership and teacher–student relationships (which in many ways compare to that of a librarian and student, particularly in a reference interview). Although very conceptual, the article has some really interesting ideas about intrinsic motivation and how to spark intrinsic motivation in children.

Tatar, M. (2009). From bookworms to enchanted hunters: Why children read. *The Journal of Aesthetic Education, 43*(2), 19–36.

> Annotation: Tatar looks at what attracts children to books and reading. Although not a broad look at how people are motivated, it is certainly an interesting look at what librarians should take into account for reader advisories and ways to interest children in reading.

MOTIVATION THEORIES

MAP LOCATION

D, 2

THREAD LOCATION

Page 26

SCAPE

Figure 182

MUSIC CENTER

MAP LOCATION

F, 3, 4

THREAD LOCATION

Page 100

SCAPE

Figure 183

NEED FOR AN EXECUTIVE DOCTORATE

MAP LOCATION

E, 8

THREAD LOCATION

Page 184

SCAPE

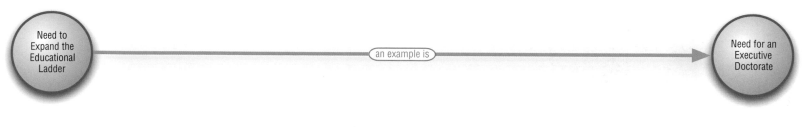

Figure 184

NEED FOR AN EXPANDED DEFINITION OF LITERACY

MAP LOCATION

F, 1

THREAD LOCATION

Page 73

SCAPE

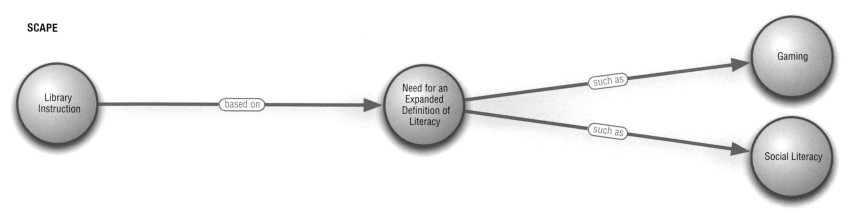

Figure 185

NEED TO EXPAND THE EDUCATIONAL LADDER

MAP LOCATION

D, 8

THREAD LOCATION

Page 183

SCAPE

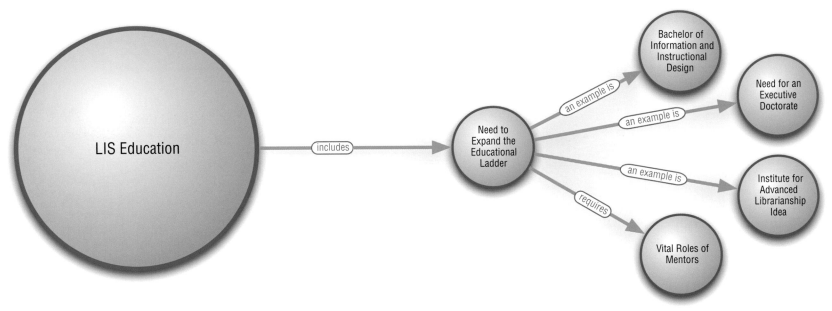

Figure 186

OBLIGATION OF LEADERSHIP

MAP LOCATION

F, G, 7

THREAD LOCATION

Page 134

SCAPE

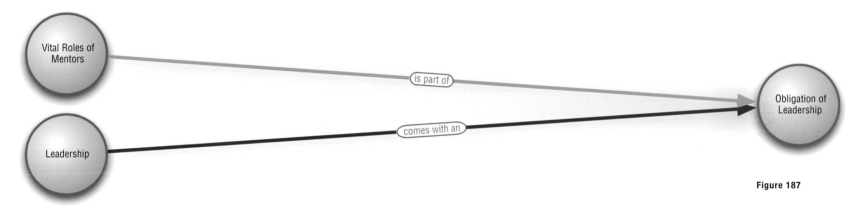

Figure 187

OPEN SOURCE

MAP LOCATION

F, 5

THREAD LOCATION

Page 87

SCAPE

Figure 188

OPENNESS

MAP LOCATION

H, 3

THREAD LOCATION

Page 121

SCAPE

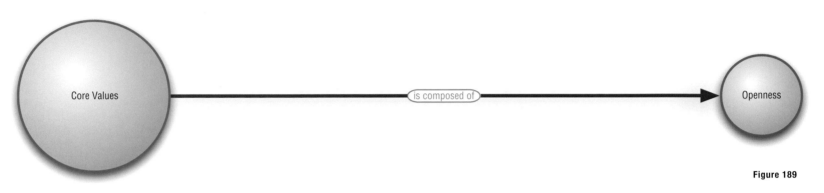

Core Values — is composed of → Openness

Figure 189

PARAPROFESSIONALS

MAP LOCATION

D, 9

THREAD LOCATION

Page 177

SCAPE

Ability to Work in Interdisciplinary Teams — includes → Para-professionals

Figure 190

PHYSICAL ENVIRONMENTS

MAP LOCATION

C, 4, 5

THREAD LOCATION

Page 93

SCAPE

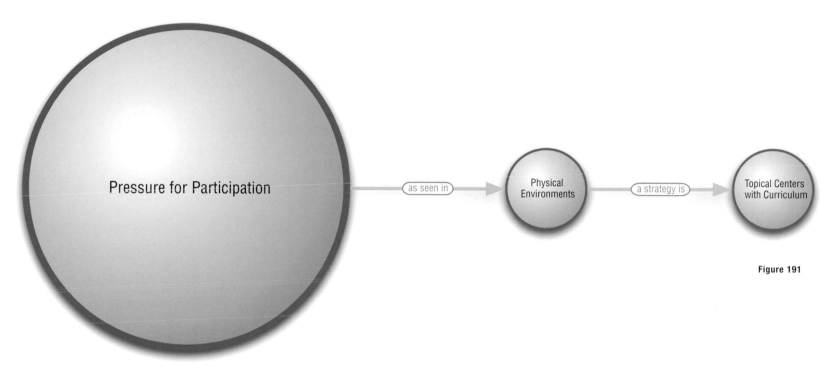

Figure 191

MAP LOCATION
F, 6

THREAD LOCATION
Page 125

SCAPE

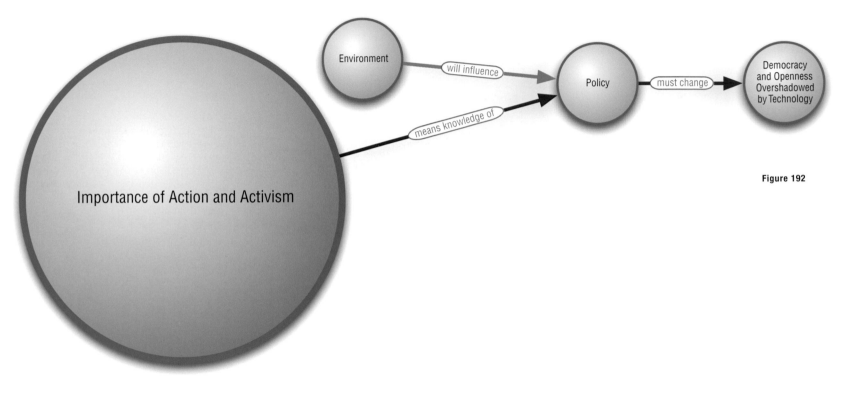

Figure 192

AUTHOR
William Zayac

CONVERSATION STARTERS

1. How much should policies change over the years? How often do changing circumstances actually require policy changes?
2. How should policies initially be set? Should they reflect a current culture of the library, past trends among the library, future possibilities within the library, or the trends in the library world? Should they be preventative, proactive, or reactive? Where would the balance lie?

RELATED ARTIFACTS

Anonymous. (2005, August). Library policies on the web. *Municipal Research and Services Center of Washington*. Retrieved November 7, 2009, from http://www.mrsc.org/Subjects/InfoServ/publiclib/libpolicy.aspx.

Annotation: This website includes links to several library policy websites (general policies and specific policies) for public libraries in the Washington, DC, metro area. Sadly, some of the specific policy links are outdated and others are incomplete. These do, however, include a variety of types of policies (from comprehensive policies to display and grievance-reporting policies) from these websites. Certain libraries, such as Richland Public Library, simply state the policies and provide little information about reporting occasions when the rules have been broken, whereas others explain the contextualization of such policies and the policies concerning policy address (as with the Spokane County Library District).

Anonymous. (2006). American Association of law libraries: AALL government relations policy. *Louisiana Libraries, 68*(3), 19.

Annotation: This article simply includes two examples of AALL policy concerning Intellectual Freedom and Information Management, providing examples of the policies of a large nongovernment library group.

Hitchcock, L. A. (2006). A critique of the new statement on labeling. *The Journal of Academic Librarianship, 32*(3), 296–302.

Annotation: Hitchcock traces the various changes in the ALA's policy on labeling from the 1948 version of the Library Bill of Rights to the 2005 revision of the position document and their effects on the strength of the idea. Some of the changes seem to have been purely superficial (stemming from a feeling of the statement being "dated"), whereas others have focused on the changing labels already provided on materials and constantly used otherwise in culture (such as the MPAA film ratings). The latest revision proves itself to be problematic because the wording could be construed to mean that catalog records are improper labels.

Magi, T. J. (2007). The gap between theory and practice: A study of the prevalence and strength of patron confidentiality policies in public and academic libraries. *Library & Information Science Research, 29*(4), 455–470.

Annotation: Trina Magi designed and executed a nonrandomized survey of 213 library directors in Vermont concerning the strength of their libraries' patron confidentiality policies and practices when they have one (of which 149 returned surveys were studied and compiled for their results); 46% of the libraries had received one request for patron information from various groups, although more may have been addressed from government agencies but suppressed by gag orders. Overall, 48% of responding libraries stated that they had written policies or procedures concerning this, whereas 35% of libraries without written policies were planning on developing them within a year. Also, the libraries with MLS-holding directors were nearly twice as likely as those whose directors did not hold these degrees to have patron confidentiality policies. Why did so many libraries not have patron confidentiality policies? What made these differences? Magi does not explore these questions; she only reports on the studies.

Terry, J. (2009). ALA testifies on access to copyrighted works for the blind. *College & Research Libraries News, 70*(7), 416–423.

Annotation: This article provides an example of an actual conflict in policies that occurred, prompting the U.S. Copyright Office and the U.S. Patent and Trademark Office to call a public meeting about the applicability of copyright legislation on works for the disabled. It also addresses the problem with this decision and its lack of addressing the potential for accessible copies created for international users, which are restricted by trade laws. Another example of public policy explained within this article is the ALA support for the Digital Millennium Copyright Act 1201 exemption for faculty members concerning audiovisual copying to make compilation tapes to be used in physical classrooms.

Wilson, A. (2009, November 8). Child protection or censorship? Library employees lose jobs over book. *Kentucky.com*. Retrieved November 11, 2009, from: http://www.kentucky.com/latest_news/v-print/story/1011029.html.

Annotation: This article explains the problem of little-visible library policy or, at least, one that seems to be seldom enforced. Sharon Cook and several other library workers at the Jessamine County Public Library decided to circumvent the normal book-removal policies and removed the graphic novel *The League of Extraordinary Gentlemen, Volume IV: The Black Dossier* from circulation themselves, one worker even removing a hold that had been put on the book by an 11-year-old (whom she did not believe should be exposed to the "explicit sexual content" of the graphic novel). The two ladies were fired for their actions, but they claimed that they were unaware that they were doing anything wrong.

POSTMODERNISM

MAP LOCATION
F, 9

THREAD LOCATION
Page 27

SCAPE

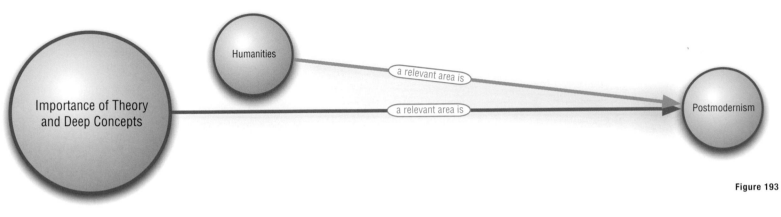

Figure 193

AUTHOR

William Zayac

AGREEMENT DESCRIPTION

Although experts in postmodern theory cannot agree on a strict definition of the term "postmodern," many aspects of postmodernism appear in different cultures. As stated in the Mission Thread section of the Atlas, some postmodern thought may be recognized in the reference interview. According to the Stanford Encyclopedia of Philosophy, two main roles in postmodernism are the "expert" and the "philosopher," both of which serve roles within the reference interview. The expert knows both the breadth and limitations to his knowledge, while the philosopher learns what is known and must be gained through questioning.[1] By seeking to better understand these roles, the librarian can become more comfortable and adept in the reference process and in the creation of searching tools and guidance

1. Aylesworth, G. (2005, September 30). Postmodernism. *Stanford Encyclopedia of Philosophy*. Retrieved from: http://plato.stanford.edu/entries/postmodernism.

tools. Understanding how people seek information is also integral to creating good cataloging and classification systems for its constantly changing users, especially considering the increasingly global community many large libraries now serve.

Appropriately, the growing trend of postmodern thinking in overall academia are leading to further research and rethinking of traditional librarian tools. Postmodernism reinforces the idea of constant change and adaptation to increase knowledge in people and to improve the process by which people can gain access to appropriate information. As such, American librarians are looking into how they can better adapt systems of organization (such as the Dewey Decimal Classification system) and reference transactions to serve increasingly diverse patrons. Many academic libraries are beginning to form research help areas such as Bird Library's Learning Commons at Syracuse University, where students may find guidance and help in learning to better search for and identify appropriate resources for projects. As the world changes, the reflective and adaptive nature of postmodern thinking encourages libraries to adapt to better serve their patron base.

CONVERSATION STARTERS

- Where in the library can postmodernism most appropriately be applied? Are there good systems in place in certain facilities that may not benefit from "overanalysis"? In certain libraries or societies, many patrons may have adapted well enough to the current system that they could navigate it better than they would be able to with such a severe change.

- How does one introduce postmodernism appropriately and accurately to "traditionalist" librarians? Might there be those, like a former English student, who are frightened by the very word? What kind of "cushioning" might one use to prevent fear? "Postmodernism" is a broad concept and presents quite a few problems with definition and presentation. In fact, most of the Web sites I consulted to find a basic definition of the term were either too broad or were so full of philosophical jargon that they were difficult to understand. Most librarians may become confused if the concepts are not presented correctly.

RELATED ARTIFACTS

Bodi, S., & Maier-O'Shea, K. (2005). The library of babel: Making sense of collection management in a postmodern world. *The Journal of Academic Librarianship, 31*(2), 143–150.

> Annotation: Bodi and Maier-O'Shea explore the repercussions of postmodernism in the organization and management of academic library collections, from providing multiple access points to providing a more information-centered environment in libraries because of the changing culture of universities and colleges and the increased movement toward an experience-based management philosophy. When academic libraries shift toward postmodernism, should they still simply support the school's curriculum or should these libraries also change toward the overall learning outcomes emphasized by the school (if the two differ)?

Cullen, R. (1998). *Measure for measure: A post-modern critique of performance measurement in libraries and information services.* Proceedings from the IATUL '1998: The 27th International Association of Scientific and Technological University Libraries Conference. The challenge to be relevant in the 21st century, University of Pretoria, Pretoria, South Africa.

> Annotation: Cullen uses postmodern theory to analyze how most modern libraries perform assessments and deconstruct the traditional modes of assessment available to librarians, asking whether the "tried-and-true" methods of the past are providing enough accurate data and whether libraries are making vital enough changes called for by the data collected. She also makes suggestions on how to bring current evaluation practices up to a greater and more effective standard for libraries and information services, including tailoring the library's mission to reference the need it serves in the community before considering how well the library lives up to its community's expectations.

Deodato, J. (2006). Becoming responsible mediators: The application of postmodern perspectives to archival arrangement & description. *Progressive Librarian, 27*, 52–63.

> Annotation: Deodato attempts to explain the growing influence of postmodernism on the archival community. He acknowledges the effect of the postmodern mindset on selection and appraisal of new artifacts and attempts to further the incorporation of these values into the description and arrangement of artifacts through addition to traditional finding aids and expanded records concerning them. Deodato also provides some beginning guidelines for creating a more comprehensive record of the artifacts in a collection that not only acknowledges the social conditions under which the writer of such a record created it but also allows for future changes that may help users understand the collection and artifacts more thoroughly because artifacts can seldom be objectively identified due to their socially constructed identities.

Taylor, M. J. (2002). I'll be your mirror, reflect what you are: Postmodern documentation and the downtown New York scene from 1975 to the present. *RBM, 3*(1), 32–52.

> Annotation: Taylor discusses the nature of the contents of libraries as a reflection of culture, questioning the nature of such a reflection of culture. By deconstructing the concept that a library is the repository of culture, Taylor explores the quality of the cultural reflection through possession of artifacts, asking whether the significance or meaning of the artifact is affected by its incorporation into a larger collection. When looking into the reflection of a culture, he says, one must remember that the viewer is reflected as well, and the view of an item by any one person (or group of people) is inherently biased. Ensuring that both the archive (or library) workers and the patrons of an archive (or library) understand and recognize this idea is the only way to provide a better understanding of the artifacts contained there.

MAP LOCATION

B, C, 5

THREAD LOCATION

Page 84

SCAPE

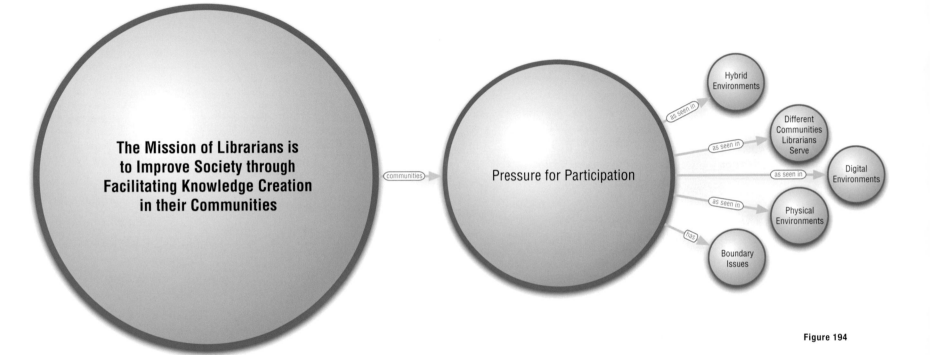

Figure 194

PUBLIC

MAP LOCATION
D, 4

THREAD LOCATION
Page 96

SCAPE

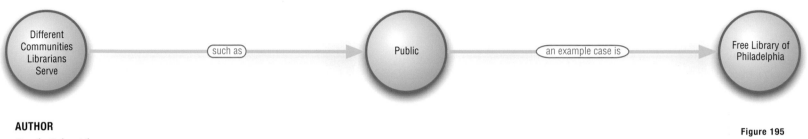

Different Communities Librarians Serve — such as → Public — an example case is → Free Library of Philadelphia

AUTHOR
Sarah Schmidt

Figure 195

AGREEMENT DESCRIPTION

The Atlas notes that although public libraries come in a variety of shapes and sizes, their unifying function is to be the intellectual glue of a community. In this agreement, I look at some of the efforts made by libraries to understand and respond to their communities' needs. The literature discussed here is in agreement with the Atlas' ideas on surveying the community and creating innovative services and spaces.

Evaluation of the community's satisfaction is one area the Atlas emphasizes for public libraries. Lankes notes, "When determining whether or not to deploy a given feature you must do careful analysis of what users are trying to accomplish." In his study of Australian public libraries, Bundy (2006) agrees. He found that the proportion of primary and secondary students using the public library was quite high, and those numbers are only increasing. He discovered that users were generally satisfied with the libraries' wide range of services—but that they also needed more IT support and study space. He also finds there needs to be more libraries in less developed places. Fisher (2003) also concurs with Lankes and Bundy on the importance of surveying the community. She examined how members of a school library community thought of and used the local public library. Unfortunately, she found a high level of dissatisfaction with the library. But, she notes, this information is important in deciding how the library should plan for the future.

The results of surveys like these have an impact on how the library serves the community. In the Atlas, Lankes calls for libraries to create a "seamless interaction of digital and virtual, with physical spaces feeding into digital worlds, and vice versa." He also notes that participatory tools are popular not simply because people "love" technology but because they fulfill a social need for people to connect with one another. Public libraries are adapting to this new reality in an increasingly electronic world. In this same vein, Cook and Ellis (2008) write of their own experiences updating their public library's Web site and learning of its teen population's deep dissatisfaction with it. They found that the teens wanted a more progressive Web site to connect with the library. To investigate their need, Cook and Ellis began exploring tools such as del.icio.us and Flick. Cook and Ellis found that by applying these tools, they were able to encourage participation by members of the community. Buhmann et al. (2009) agree with the work of Lankes, Cook, and Ellis. Buhmann and his colleagues write of their experience with Skokie Public Library's creation of SkokieTalk, a Web site that allows patrons to interact with one another and add their community-related information. It started in 1994 when members of the community bemoaned the lack of a central source for community information such as child-care options, grocery stores, public transportation, medical facilities, and so on. It began as a simple directory of links and has since grown into a much richer collaboration among participating members of the community, one that more efficiently directs patrons to library resources.

Public librarians have also applied their knowledge of the community to create more innovative uses of library space. As Lankes argues in the Atlas, spaces must be organized "to aid like conversations to progress from agreement to agreement… [towards] the topics that your community sees as crucial not simply to support, but to showcase and move forward." Blumenstein (2009) is of the same opinion. She documents how the Pearl Avenue Branch Library in San José, California, was able to incorporate environmentally friendly art and architecture in the San Jose libraries. The city of San Jose has a citywide green building policy. Because of the constituents' commitment to environmentalism, the community was deeply engaged with the building of the library. Similarly, the people of Eckhart Public Library in Auburn, Indiana, rallied to transform a dilapidated garage (originally to be used for library vans) into a space for expanded children's services (Bushnell, 2009). The library radically changed its construction plans for the garage. Later the community asked that it be environmentally sustainable as well. Following the community's wishes, today the garage is a certified green building.

Keeping an eye toward the community's needs also affects the services the public library offers. In the Atlas, Lankes argues that increased member usage comes from members being able to influence their educational system. In documenting the story of Studio I at the Public Library of Charlotte and Mecklenburg County, Czarnecki (2009) finds this to be true. Open since 2005, Studio I uses several forms of technology to allow teenagers to tell new kinds of stories using video cameras and animation software. At Studio I, adolescents are allowed to shape their own learning experience and even contribute to the department by interning or volunteering there. Echoing this idea of pioneering services is the work of the teen services department at the County of Los Angeles Public Library (Delatte, 2009). The theme of the summer reading program of 2008 was "metamorphosis." Going off the beaten trail, the department created a program that went beyond reading and more toward creating. It created "Project Morph." Modeled after the television show "Project Runway," teens brought old clothes to the library and had an hour to reinvent their clothing. Afterward, they walked a catwalk to simulate a fashion show. The project meant that the library had to buy nontraditional items—like fabric markers, assorted trim, and gems—but the program was such a hit that 30 libraries followed suit.

CONVERSATION STARTERS

1. Fisher finds that the surveying library is disturbed to discover that the community is unsatisfied with its level of service. I think this is why more libraries don't evaluate themselves. It's a fear a lot of libraries have—they are afraid of what they might find. How can libraries overcome this fear? Is there a strategy to accepting negative results and moving on from there?

2. Buhmann et al. describe how SkokieNet has become an impressive platform for community members to connect and learn from one another. But how does this tool differ from Facebook, or other social networking applications that are now in existence? Does SkokieNet better meet the community's needs? If so, does the fact that it's locally made—by and for the people of Skokie— have anything to do with its success?

RELATED ARTIFACTS

Blumenstein, L. (2009). San Jose's Green Art. *Library Journal (1976)*, 24–25. Retrieved October 24, 2009, from Library Lit & Inf Full Text database.

Buhmann, M., Greenwalt, T., Jacobsen, M., & Roehm, F. (2009). On the ground, in the cloud. *Library Journal (1976), 134*(12), 35–37. Retrieved October 24, 2009, from Library Lit & Inf Full Text database.

Bundy, A. (2006). Supporting students: The educational contribution of Australia's public libraries. *Australasian Public Libraries and Information Services, 19*(3), 126–136. Retrieved October 23, 2009, from Library Lit & Inf Full Text database.

Bushnell, S. (2009). Library's green annex brings acclaim, growth. *Library Journal (1976)*, 32. Retrieved October 24, 2009, from Library Lit & Inf Full Text database.

Cook, K., & Ellis, J. (2008). Getting started with Library 2.0: No PhD required. *Tennessee Libraries (Online), 58*(2), 1–8. Retrieved October 23, 2009, from Library Lit & Inf Full Text database.

Czarnecki, K. (2009). Mentoring over movies and music: Studio i-Style. *Voice of Youth Advocates, 32*(3), 198–199. Retrieved October 24, 2009, from Library Lit & Inf Full Text database.

Delatte, M. (2009). Project morph: Bringing fashion rehab to Los Angeles Library teens. *Young Adult Library Services, 7*(4), 11–12, 18. Retrieved October 24, 2009, from Library Lit & Inf Full Text database.

Fisher, H. (2003). A teenage view of the public library: What are the students saying? *Australasian Public Libraries and Information Services, 16*(1), 4–16. Retrieved October 23, 2009, from Library Lit & Inf Full Text database.

PUBLIC SERVICE

MAP LOCATION

E, 4

THREAD LOCATION

Page 154

SCAPE

Figure 196

PUBLISHER OF COMMUNITY

MAP LOCATION

F, 3

THREAD LOCATION

Page 67

SCAPE

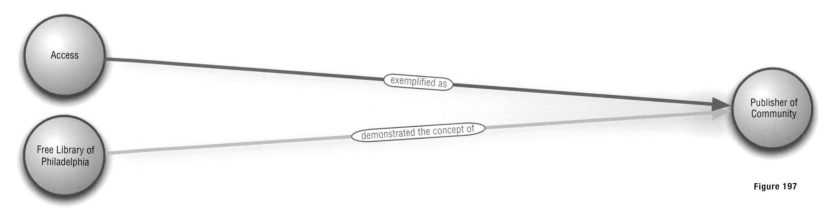

Figure 197

RECOGNIZE A SCHOOL AS A PARTICIPATORY NETWORK

MAP LOCATION

D, 9

THREAD LOCATION

Page 181

SCAPE

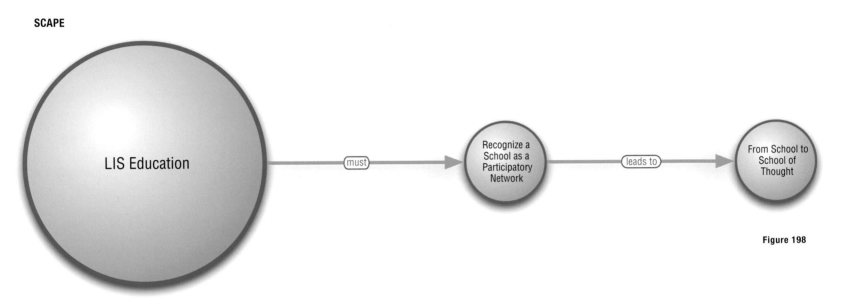

Figure 198

REFERENCE

MAP LOCATION

F, 4

THREAD LOCATION

Page 154

SCAPE

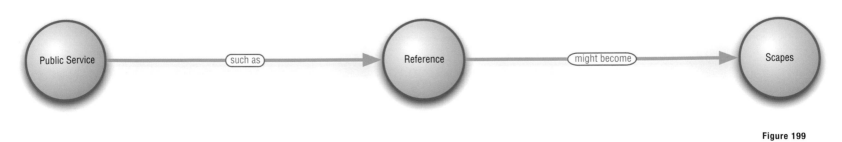

Figure 199

REFERENCE EXTRACT

MAP LOCATION

G, 4

THREAD LOCATION

Page 60

SCAPE

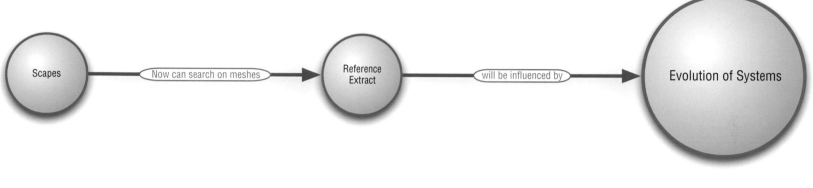

Figure 200

RELATION TO OTHER DOMAINS

MAP LOCATION

D, 9

THREAD LOCATION

Page 170

SCAPE

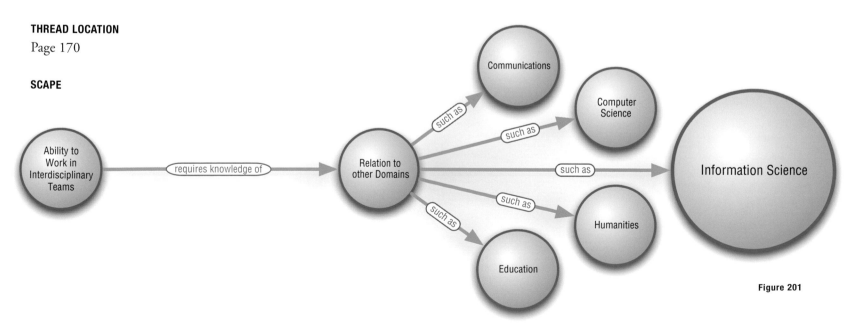

Figure 201

RISKS OF DATA

MAP LOCATION

F, G, 7

THREAD LOCATION

Page 131

SCAPE

Figure 202

SCAPES

MAP LOCATION

F, G, 3

THREAD LOCATION

Page 53

SCAPE

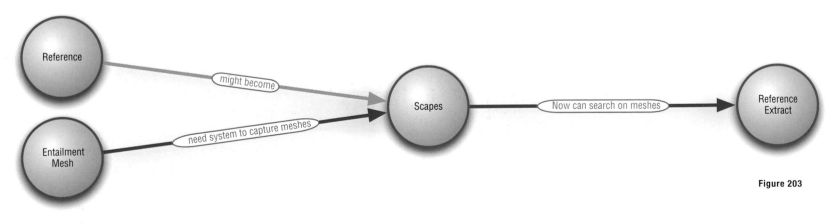

Figure 203

AUTHOR

R. David Lankes

AGREEMENT DESCRIPTION

The following questions and answers about Scapes development are derived from a consideration of a proposal before the MacArthur Foundation. There are two answers to each question. The first is the quick answer, followed by a more in-depth response that contains more technical detail. It should be noted that these questions and answers, although useful generally, were focused on a single development effort for Scapes.

Who do you see as your primary audience for Scapes?

> *Quick response:* The initial audience for Scapes[1] will be library learners—those individuals using library services for formal (e.g., K-12 and college students) and informal education (e.g., members of the general public engaged in research).

> *More Detail:* This population is chosen for a few reasons:

- The library community is a coherent and easily engaged partner in the process. Initial discussions of the Scapes concept within this community have generated enthusiasm, and it is believed that libraries will be willing to provide input, testing, and resources into all phases of development. Further, libraries have experience in evaluating software.

- Libraries have a known need for this type of software. Libraries know they need better systems to engage users in their learning processes. There is wide discontent with current catalogs and virtual reference software. Scapes can help fill these needs.

- Libraries represent a diverse user population. Although the library community is coherent (it shares an education base, it has a lot of professional structures such as conferences and associations), their reach is diverse. Libraries can test Scapes in populations of students, government workers, lawyers, scholars, and more.

- Libraries have resources that can seed initial user-generated scapes. Libraries not only hold a large and diverse set of materials, they have well-structured metadata for these collections that will make inclusion in Scapes relatively easy.

---

1. Throughout this document "Scapes" with a capital S is used to refer to as the software product; "scapes" with a small s is referred to as a document types (so *Scapes* produces *scapes*).

For these reasons, libraries are seen as an ideal target audience and initial set of partners, but that does not mean that the utility of Scapes is limited to libraries. Once the initial infrastructure is in place, Scapes is seen as general-purpose software that is functionality useful in any knowledge representation endeavor.

Some examples might be useful. It should be noted that the illustrations are just simple ideas—sketches really. The final interface will be determined by the specification and implementation processes.

K–12 Example

Riley is doing a report on global warming. In his school library, he searches the catalog for books on the topic. He finds a few promising titles and adds them to a new scape right through the catalog's web interface. He then checks out the books. At home, after reading the books, he opens his web browser and brings up the scape he started at school (he also has scapes for personal projects and other classes). Right now it is little more than a scattered collection of "nodes," each representing the books he checked out.

Riley now deletes a text that wasn't relevant and begins to sort the remaining books. He puts all the books on weather effects into one pile. He draws a line from that pile to another book that refutes global warming and labels the line as such. Now he begins searching his library's online databases through the web-based Scapes interface for articles on the topic. As he finds relevant articles, he drags them into the scape he is working on and connects them with links such as "Global Warming in Politics" and "The Science of Global Warming." He ends up with a Scape that looks like the one found in figure 204.

At this point, Riley could simply add his teacher to the list of those authorized to see his Scape and submit it as his assignment; however, his teacher wants a written report. Riley exports the Scape as an outline. The links become major headers in the report, and each node (book, article, etc.) is listed as a citation. He opens the outline in his word processor and begins to write.

The use of a tool like Scapes in K–12 education is not completely without precedent. Scapes is similar to mind mapping already in wide use in K–12 education. There are, however, some key differences. These differences range from the model of representation—mind or concept mapping requires a "root node" from which all ideas must stream—to the technical—most mind mapping applications do not work with computationally useful nodes, rather focusing on visual maps.

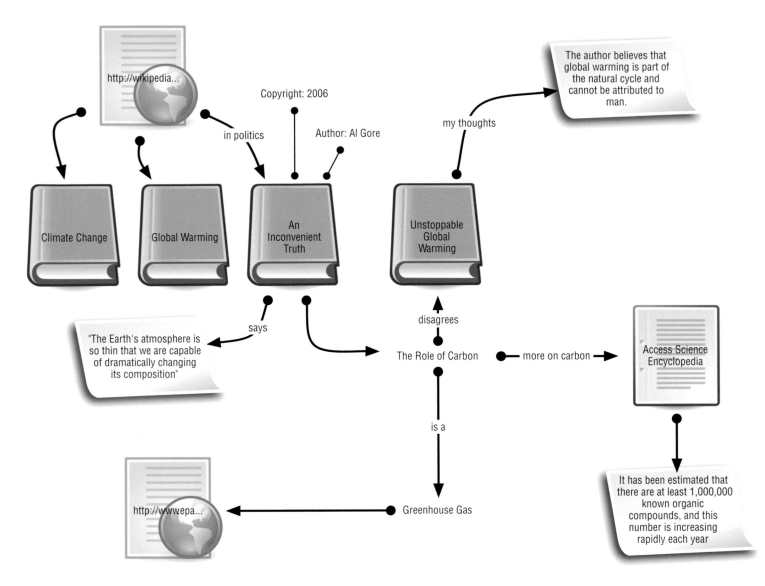

Figure 204

College Course

Sue is a college professor preparing a course on global warming to be offered during the next semester. The normal procedure would be to write a syllabus with a course introduction and list of readings, put the readings on reserve with the college library, and upload additional materials in an online course management system like Blackboard. This setup already requires students to go to three separate sources for course information.

Instead, Sue creates a Scape for the course, linking in her content, as well as readings on reserve at the library and on the web. This Scape is not a simple list of readings but a connected system that shows how the readings and course content are related. Also, since the Scape will be made available to Sue's students, it is interactive. The students can connect the course Scape to their own Scape with assignments, discussions, and reactions. Sue can also use the chat functionality of the Scapes software to work with students remotely.

So the initial Scape might look like the screenshot in figure 205 from an early mockup.

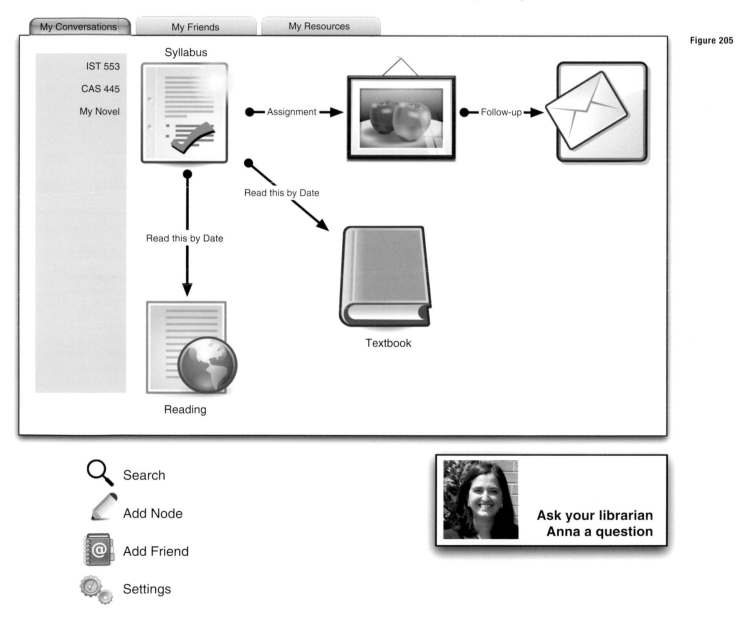

Figure 205

One of Sue's students can then connect his or her own Scape (using the previous K–12 example) to the class scape found in figure 206.

What's more, all of these scapes can be made public[2] within the college to represent what the college community knows and its approach to a given topic. Now anyone who finds Sue's course syllabus can also see examples of student work (if the students give permission). This would allow for better program accreditation and evaluation.

Community Organizing

Syracuse, like many urban centers, has a youth violence issue. The mayor has task forces, community groups are involved, and the University wants to help. One of the first steps to combating any problem is understanding what it is. When combating a problem requires multiple groups to be involved, a shared understanding of the problem is essential.

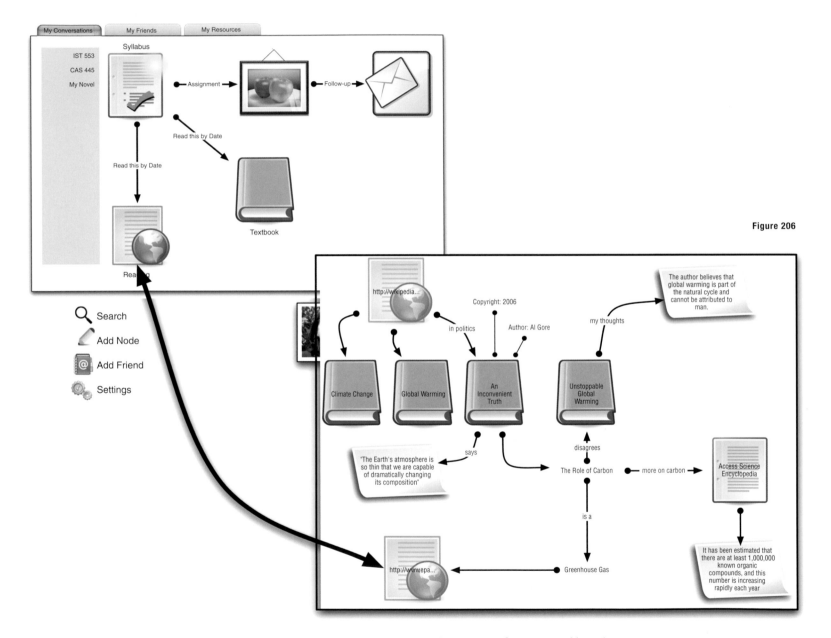

Figure 206

2. See question 3 for more on public and private scapes.

The public library creates a scape of the youth violence issue. The librarians pre-populate it with articles and books that might be helpful. Experts are asked to contribute to the scape, and community groups are asked to join in mapping the issue and possible solutions. Governmental agencies add information on existing programs. Community foundations add the outcome of their funded work, as well as information on possible resources available to combat youth violence. Where disagreement occurs, new scapes are created to represent divergent views. Over time, these differences are discussed, and most of these alternatives are incorporated into a common view.

As a plan emerges, it is tied back to the literature, best practices, community agencies, and planning documents. Videos of town hall meetings are added to the scape to provide a crucial memory for the long-term plan. As new services are created, tried, and evaluated, they too are pointed to from within the community scape.

This could have all been done with a wiki of course. However, a wiki would not allow the visual representation, or, more important, the intelligent use of objects such as materials, ideas, people, and organizations. Because this information is within a scape, other communities tackling the youth violence issue can reuse it. Agency names and contact information can easily be changed, with Syracuse acting as a template for other urban centers. Other tools can also be used with the scape, for example, placing agencies and resources on a map or exporting portions of the scape for grant applications or reports.

The scape on youth violence can also be linked into other community-wide efforts in economic development, beautification, education, transportation, and so on. Although this can be done with today's web-based tools, the links are one way, as opposed to bi-directional, and would require a multitude of interfaces and systems. Scapes can act as not only a high-level view of a problem but a sort of glue to a vast variety of resources.

Can you expand on how people would use/access Scapes? We're having trouble understanding how this would be implemented.

Quick Answer: The initial deliverable will be a website where users can log in and create their Scapes. This website will present users with a view of (1) all the public Scapes being created, (2) the Scapes that the user is working on (individually, as part of a group, or simply public Scapes the user contribute to), and (3) finally the actual interface for building and editing Scapes. This can be seen in figure 207.

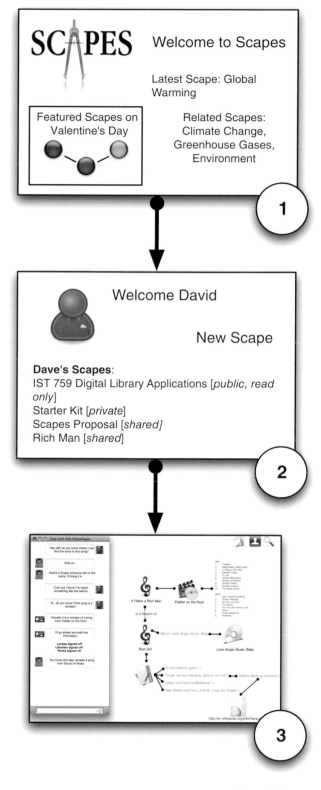

Figure 207

This centralized site will also allow organizations to integrate Scapes' functionality in their own sites like they can now include maps from Google and videos from YouTube. For example, a library might include a link to the Scapes site right in its catalog. A user clicking on the link would be taken to the Scapes site and shown a set of all the scapes containing the object selected in the catalog (see figure 208).

Once a user creates a scape, he or she can embed an interactive version of it in his or her own site with a simple cut and paste (just like YouTube). With this embedding capability, just about anywhere a user can cut and paste HTML code, he or she can include a fully interactive version of the scape. For instance, a user could paste it into a blog entry (see figure 209).

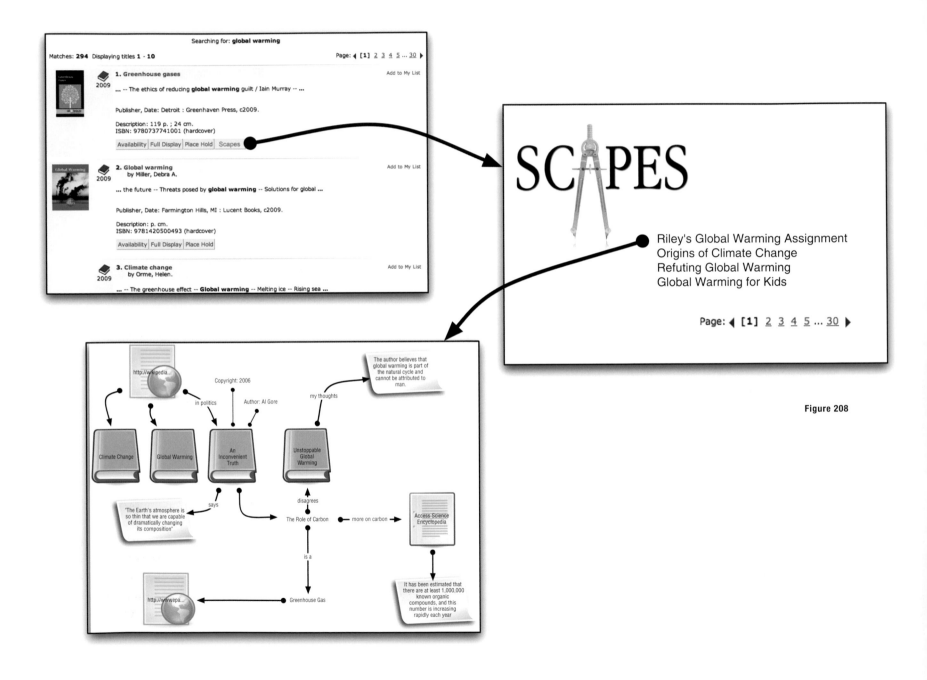

Figure 208

Figure 209

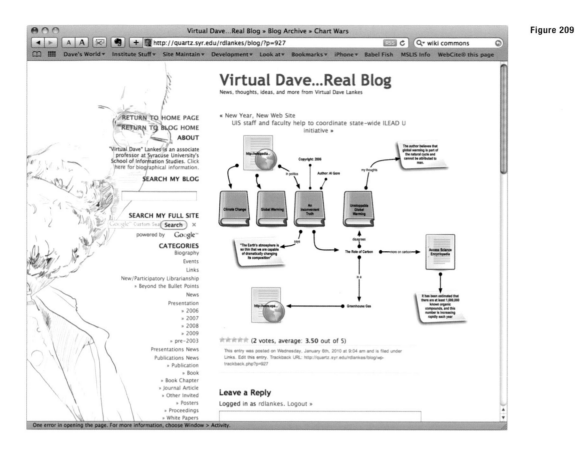

So the community group from the previous example could include its joint scape on its team's webpage, or MacArthur could create a scape of all its grants and grantees in a given area (say on credibility) and include it in a listing of the grants.

The Scapes server software will also be offered as a download so that anyone can download and create his or her own scapes site (or integrate scapes into his or her own site). Like the web, which creates a set of connected pages on different sites, the Scapes specification and software will enable easy linking between sites. This arrangement will allow organizations concerned about security or reliability to set up internal Scapes systems.

A good analogy would be Wikipedia. Users create accounts and contribute to the Wikipedia site, but anyone can download the software used to build and maintain Wikipedia, called MediaWiki.[3]

The Scapes specification can also be used so that people could write their own software that can create interconnected scapes. Thus,

one might imagine a Scapes desktop system that would allow users to create scapes when disconnected from the Internet, say on a plane.

More Details

Scape implementation consists of really four parts: a specification, a reference server implementation, a reference user interface, and a facilitating infrastructure. Each is explained below.

Specification

When the web was initially developed, it was little more than a multipage document of specifications. These specifications outlined the basics of how to mark up documents (HTML) and a protocol for sending data across the Internet (the HyperText Transfer Protocol [HTTP]). It was this specification developed by Tim Berners-Lee that was adopted by the National Center for Supercomputing Applications (NCSA) and used to create Mosaic and the first web server.

3. http://www.mediawiki.org/wiki/MediaWiki.

Today, it is the specifications that underlie thousands of different web servers (with Apache and Microsoft's Internet Information Server being the most widely deployed) and the various web browsers (Internet Explorer, Chrome, FireFox, Farari, Opera, etc.). It is the web specification that enables Google and MacFound.org. It is the specification that will ultimately dictate the success and shape of Scapes.

The Scapes specification will need to define the file format of a Scape. It is currently assumed that this will involve RDF and an XML application. Think of this as the file format of a Scape that could be copied onto a hard drive and e-mailed around. This format will have to accommodate node descriptions, bidirectional linking (so both an object pointing and being pointed to are aware of the link—this allows for the easy identification of dead or altered links as well as enhanced search).

The specification will also have to define minimal interactions with Scapes such as adding a node, adding a link, describing a link, deleting nodes, and so on. The idea is to, like HTML, keep the specifications simple and allow for rich interactions through combining interactions.

Perhaps the most important part of the specification will be in how Scapes work in a networked environment. This part of the specification will have to link up the different anticipated Scapes servers together. The initial thought (described more fully under infrastructure) is a central registry system. Here the different Scapes servers would communicate what Scapes are available and where to find them. The network part of the specification will have to handle questions of unique identifiers for Scapes and nodes within a Scape. This portion of the specification is also, frankly, where much of the lessons learned about the deficiencies of the web standards can be addressed in terms of searching across Scapes and dead links.

Reference Server Implementation

However good a specification is, without real software and real examples, it will go nowhere. From experience with many projects such as AskERIC, the Gateway to Educational Materials, and the Virtual Reference Desk, the team behind Scapes has learned some valuable lessons that will be brought to Scapes. The first is the need for real software that is functional from the start. It is much harder to convince anyone else to implement specifications without having done it yourself. There is a need for examples. What's more, there is no sense in low-balling the example. That is to say, the example should strive to

be the best in class. This way if there are initially few others building servers, the one built by the project is more than adequate for satisfying user needs. Also, the first mover in a given space on the web tends to gain a large user base, so you want the majority of users using the best software.

For this reason, the reference server implementation will strive to be the best central system for creating Scapes. It will need to provide for user accounts (including sophisticated identity management as discussed in question 3), rich interactions, embedding of Scapes within other systems and pages (as discussed in the "Quick Answer"), powerful searching across Scapes, and easy expansion (via APIs as discussed in question 4). The server is anticipated to be a LAMP implementation (LAMP is short for Linux, Apache, MySQL, and PHP and describes a widely available server environment so that people can easily implement Scapes on their own servers).

Reference User Interface

The interface developed by this grant will be web-based. These days highly interactive and "desktop-like" user interfaces through a web browser are attainable through the use of technologies like AJAX. AJAX (short for Asynchronous JavaScript and XML) is a set of existing technologies that allow users to drag and drop objects, as well as manipulate interface elements through a web browser just as they would in a drawing program or a word processor. If you have ever panned and zoomed a map through the web, you have experienced AJAX.

The user interface for Scapes will consist of the construction space of the Scapes (adding, linking, and describing nodes), as well as a means of managing multiple Scapes by a single user and millions of Scapes for the entire web community. In essence, all of the diagrams used in this addendum are simplified initial guesses at what the user interface will look like. It is also assumed that others using the Scapes specification can create a whole raft of new user interfaces including interfaces for mobile phones, differing operating systems, and more.

Infrastructure

To fully realize the potential of Scapes, there must be not only several implementations but a way of tying an active development and implementation community together. To maximize the diffusion of Scapes, there must be infrastructure to keep the differing scapes connected. As alluded to under specifications there will need to be some technical infrastructure in place to stitch together Scapes. This includes a registry of Scapes implementations, a system to assign unique IDs to Scapes and their objects, and a sort of interchange for linking. This link interchange will monitor the objects being linked across all Scapes and notify users (and servers) if either end of a link has changed. This will allow for services like leak deletion, creating cached version of objects to maintain the integrity of Scapes, and search services.

All of these parts are represented in figure 210 with the deliverables of this grant outlined in the dotted line.

Other infrastructure will not be technical. This will include a clearinghouse on Scapes development and implementations, an ongoing body to discuss extensions and alterations to the Scapes specification, a directory of Scape extensions, and other ways of tracking a community engaged with Scapes.

All of this detail may seem burdensome or grandiose. The philosophy is to plan for success but guarantee initial utility. That is to say, build a tool that can be used right away. If a community of developers and other Scapes implementations do not emerge, the central site will still have great functionality. If the community does develop, the growth can be managed.

Could there be a "public Scapes"—one that you share with others—and a "private Scapes"—one that you use only to organize your own research/work/relationships?

Quick Answer: The short answer is yes. Scapes files can be private, shared with a group, or public. Likewise, a Scape can be shared in full or read-only.

More Detail: To do this, the Scapes specification will have to include a common way of handling "identity management." Every Scape will have to have an identity or identities associated with it. This will allow functionality such as notifying Scapes creators of changes to items and other Scapes they might have pointed to (thus avoiding the dead link problem or pointing to outdated URL's in the current open web).

It is worth noting that "identity" is not the same as "person." Identities may be as simple as a username or an e-mail address. However, as they get more complex, they can allow for greater access to resources. For example, if a Scape author provides a university ID, he or she can get the full text of articles in a Scape, whereas an anonymous user may simply receive the bibliographic information.

Are there challenges around interoperability and content access (some people have access to certain databases and others do not, how would Scapes deal with this)?

Quick Answer: Much of the interoperability challenges are alleviated initially by working with links to objects, as opposed to manipulating the objects itself (i.e., linking to book records, not editing the records or creating them). This is much like how a user organizes files and folders on his or her computer. The software creating the folders and letting the user drag files around does not have to open and/or edit these files, just know their locations and what piece of software to use to actually open and work with the file.

More Detail: There are always interoperability challenges to face in terms of software systems. The initial plan to address them consists of four approaches.

1. High-Level Pointers

Scapes, like the web, are based on a pointer system. It connects objects with contextual links creating a set of relationships. As such, it does not have to be able to manipulate the related items (documents) directly. Think of how you organize your files on your computer. File Explorer in Windows or the Finder in the Mac Operating System needs to know some basic information about the file (its size and its type) and its location. It does not need to edit PDF files, just know that they are PDF files and where they are. It doesn't need to understand all the objects it encounters, just link to them. Scapes are the same way. As long as they know an object's location and some basic details, they do not need to get bogged down in all the intricacies of the file formats and features. What they do need to be able to do is read and manipulate metadata (descriptive information about the files). Also, as the product matures, it can add greater item-level functionality (just as in operating systems that have evolved to provide previews of file contents or quick printing).

2. Adherence to Metadata Standards

What Scapes will need to do is intelligently read and manipulate a variety of object metadata. The most obvious is the MARC standard to make incorporating library objects easy. They will also need to understand Dublin Core and HTML metatags—widely used metadata

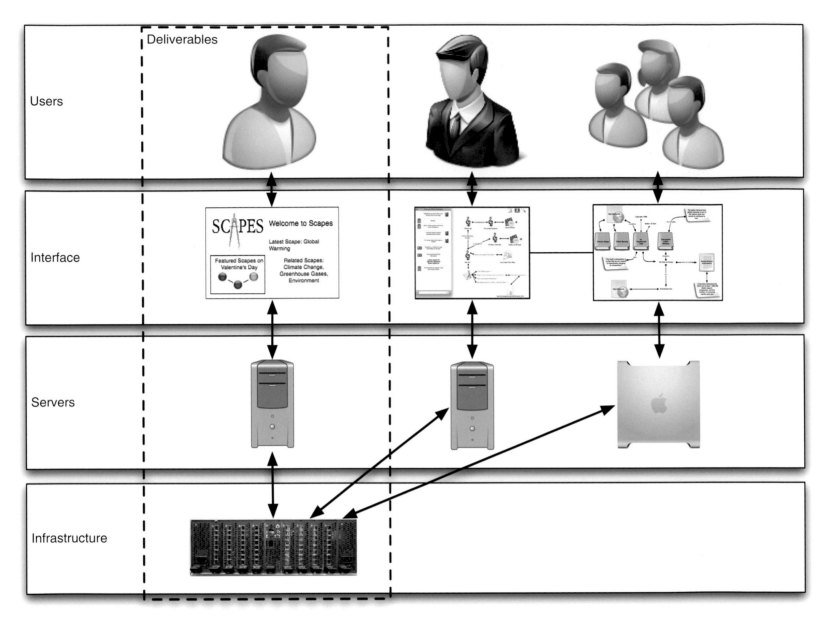

Figure 210

standards. This basic functionality will allow Scapes to take advantage of existing metadata in objects today. However, most of the objects that Scapes will encounter will have no metadata. This means the user will be adding metadata as he or she links objects together but in a different way from today's object-centric approach to describing digital objects.

A normal approach to metadata is to use some separate editing program to describe an object—entering fields like title, author, and so on. This approach can take time, and the person describing the object has to anticipate all the potential uses of that object. Many people don't realize this, but programs like Microsoft Word have this capability built in. Figure 211 is the screen that Word brings up when editing a file's properties.

Figure 212 is the same functionality implemented in Adobe Acrobat.

The reason that people don't realize these screens exist is because it is an often unused capability. There are many reasons for this, but this is territory well covered in the original proposal. The point of this response is that if someone takes the time to enter these data, Scapes will use it. If not, Scapes will create metadata from the linking between objects. This is more useful because it is all about context.

3. Adherence to Web Standards

The area of interoperability on the web has come a long way in the past five years. There are several widely available and followed standards that will aid in tying objects together in Scapes. The first is the suite of Semantic web standards such as the Resource Description Framework (RDF) and the extensible Markup Language (XML). These two standards provide a clear way of linking together a disparate set of resources without a great deal of customization. XML will allow records to be read out of proprietary databases and library catalogs, for example. RDF is a way of describing relationships among objects, terms, and even people. Open-source RDF tools will allow for rapid development of Scapes, as well as the reuse of Scapes data in other applications.

4. Building an Open Platform for Expansion

The last approach to interoperability will be the extensive use of good Web 2.0 practices. That is, making it easy for people to add new functionality to Scapes and to include Scapes functionality into their own applications. The primary mechanism for this interoperability

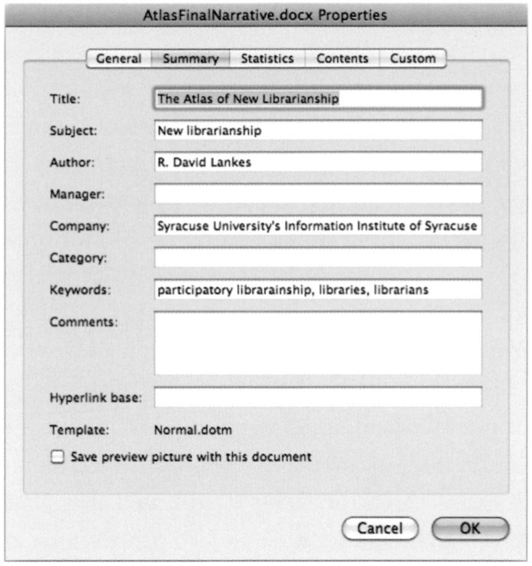

Figure 211

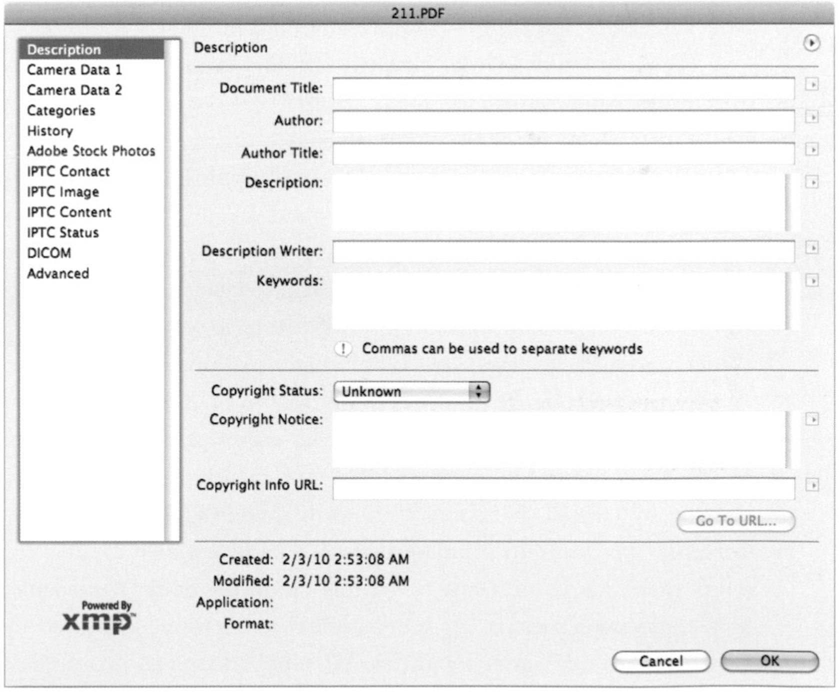

Figure 212

approach is the use of well-documented and web-accessible Application Programming Interfaces (APIs). An API is little more than a URL where another program (or web page) can send a request. For example, Google Maps has an API so that, with the use of a single piece of cut-and-paste HTML code, you can include a map on your web page. With a simple piece of HTML, you can also include a book cover from Amazon, a song title from Apple's iTunes, book information from OCLC, and more. It is the API that will allow people to embed a web version of Scapes in whatever page they want.

APIs will also be used to handle issues of authentication into proprietary databases and access into for-fee resources. This is not an approach unique to Scapes. This will build on efforts throughout the academic and library world built up over the past decade—technologies such as OpenURL and Z39.50, for example. APIs will also allow users to embed different search engines directly into Scapes such as Google or the proposed Reference Extract product.

Examples

In many cases, the real story can be hidden behind an alphabet soup of standards. The best way to show how interoperability can be achieved with existing technologies is to show an example.

The Ann Arbor District Library's Catalog, found at http://www.aadl.org/catalog, might look like a standard catalog application, but it is not. It is actually a piece of open source software called Drupal. Drupal sits between the user and the actual catalog. When the user searches for a book, Drupal sends the request via an API to the catalog (a proprietary piece of software). The results of the search are then processed by Drupal and presented to the user with additional features such as tags, user annotations, full-text page scans from Google Books, and other reviews. These additional functionalities come from all over the web but are presented seamlessly to the user using APIs.

Figure 213 shows (1) the listing the user sees from his or her search—it is information from the library catalog but presented to the user by Drupal that also adds links to (2) a program the Ann Arbor librarians wrote to simulate a physical card in a card catalog, (3) a link that takes you directly to the full text of the book (if available) in Google Book Search, (4) user-supplied annotations produced by Blackwell's Book Services, and (5) user-supplied tags and comments stored by Drupal.

If you are having a hard time following my diagrams, all you need to know is that at least five different systems are being utilized for this one book, and the user does not have to know. What's more, the five different services don't have to know anything about the other applications (in other words, Google has no idea that the Ann Arbor Library is pointing to its books). It would be a simple matter for the library to add a link to any Scapes that included this book, for example.

CONCLUSION

I hope these responses were clarifying. If not, please let me know, and I can try again. What I hope is that the core of the Scapes idea is not lost in the important details. Yes, there are many challenges to developing Scapes, but there are huge pieces of existing software and interoperability standards already available on which to build. As with any new software project, there are sure to be challenges and unanticipated problems. However, the core idea that we need systems that allow us to represent knowledge, not things, remains. The true mission of Scapes is not to demonstrate the power of APIs or the intricacies of metadata. The true mission is to unlock the knowledge present in our communities. The mission is to build tools that can begin to capture the conversations and contexts of people. The mission is to break from the strangle hold of things and objects and move to knowing and action. These may seem like grand missions, but that is the point. The web has shown us the emergence of social knowledge. Wikipedia, Google, Amazon, and more thrive in a world of connected ideas. The web did not create the notion of linking; it simply made the links evident. In the same way, Scapes does not seek to invent or change how people know; they simply make it easier to share that knowing. The Scapes concept is a result of theory, practice, and hard-won experience.

RELATED ARTIFACTS.

Lankes, R. D. (2008, January 12). *Scapes*. Retrieved from http://quartz.syr.edu/rdlankes/blog/?p=459.

Lankes, R. D. (2009). New concepts in digital reference. *Synthesis Lectures on Information Concepts, Retrieval, and Services, 1*(1). doi: 10.2200/S00166ED1V01Y200812ICR001.

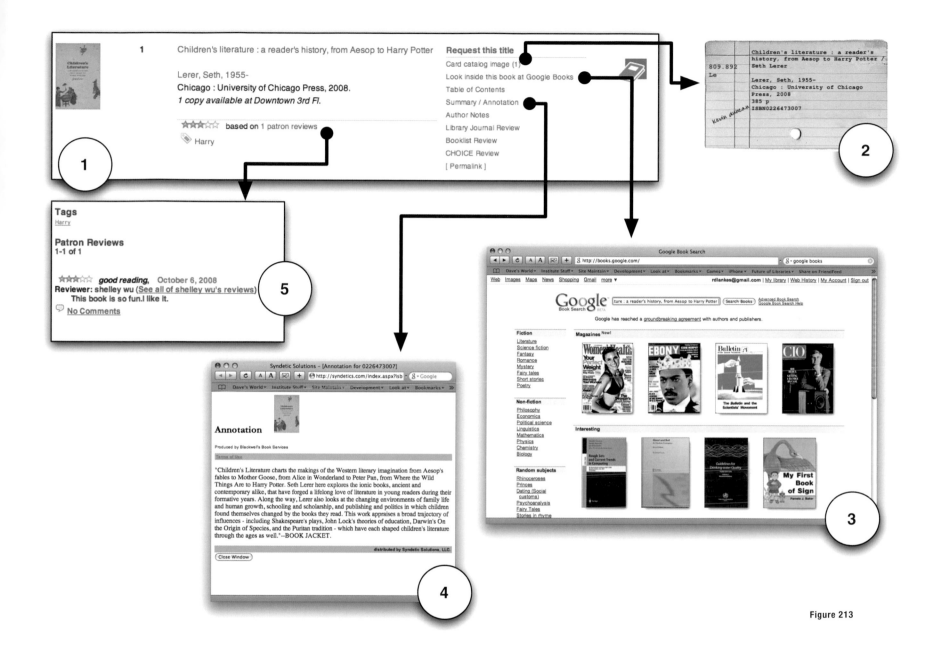

1

1   Children's literature : a reader's history, from Aesop to Harry Potter

Lerer, Seth, 1955-
Chicago : University of Chicago Press, 2008.
1 copy available at Downtown 3rd Fl.

★★★☆☆ based on 1 patron reviews

🏷 Harry

Request this title

Card catalog image (1)
Look inside this book at Google Books
Table of Contents
Summary / Annotation
Author Notes
Library Journal Review
Booklist Review
CHOICE Review
[Permalink]

2

Children's literature : a reader's
history, from Aesop to Harry Potter /
Seth Lerer

809.892
Le

Lerer, Seth, 1955-
Chicago : University of Chicago
Press, 2008
385 p
ISBN0226473007

Kevin duncan

5

Tags
Harry

Patron Reviews
1-1 of 1

★★★☆☆ *good reading,* October 6, 2008
Reviewer: shelley wu (See all of shelley wu's reviews)
   This book is so fun.I like it.
💬 No Comments

4

Syndetic Solutions – [Annotation for 0226473007]

http://syndetics.com/index.aspx?isb

Annotation

Produced by Blackwell's Book Services

Terms of Use

"Children's Literature charts the makings of the Western literary imagination from Aesop's fables to Mother Goose, from Alice in Wonderland to Peter Pan, from Where the Wild Things Are to Harry Potter. Seth Lerer here explores the ionic books, ancient and contemporary alike, that have forged a lifelong love of literature in young readers during their formative years. Along the way, Lerer also looks at the changing environments of family life and human growth, schooling and scholarship, and publishing and politics in which children found themselves changed by the books they read. This work appraises a broad trajectory of influences - including Shakespeare's plays, John Lock's theories of education, Darwin's On the Origin of Species, and the Puritan tradition - which have each shaped children's literature through the ages as well."--BOOK JACKET.

distributed by Syndetic Solutions, LLC.

Close Window

3

Google Book Search

http://books.google.com/

Google has reached a groundbreaking agreement with authors and publishers.

Fiction
Literature
Science fiction
Fantasy
Romance
Mystery
Fairy tales
Short stories
Poetry

Non-fiction
Philosophy
Economics
Political science
Linguistics
Mathematics
Physics
Chemistry
Biology

Random subjects
Rhinoceroses
Princes
Dating (Social customs)
Psychoanalysis
Fairy Tales
Stories in rhyme

Magazines New!

Interesting

My First Book of Sign

Figure 213

SCHOLARLY COMMUNICATIONS

MAP LOCATION

F, G, 4, 5

THREAD LOCATION

Page 104

SCAPE

Figure 214

AUTHOR

Elizabeth Gall

AGREEMENT DESCRIPTION

In the section on Scholarly Communication in the Atlas, Lankes charges that librarians must participate in the scholarly pursuits driving academia rather than standing by and cataloging the results. He argues that librarians must take control of their role rather than wait for professors to approach them for help, input, and so on. Right now librarians are waiting to be invited to the table instead of pulling up a chair and inserting themselves into the conversation. The idea that librarians must redefine their role has come up again and again in the Atlas. Academic librarians can do so by becoming an essential part of scholarly communication at their university. As Lankes points out, it will benefit the librarian in multiple ways. It will not only integrate them into communities they previously had not been a part of, but it will also help librarians keep a better, more complete record of knowledge creation at the university. Hahn (2008) argues that this change is already happening, and librarians must be more aggressive in defining their new role. The Atlas discusses several areas where there is potential for librarian involvement in scholarly communication.

One way that librarians can get involved in scholarly communication is to take an active role in the process and documentation of funded research. By facilitating documentation of a project from start to finish, librarians can provide a valuable service to the research team while they build a collection of in-house research and findings. This prospect is especially appealing because the funding for these services could be written into the research proposal. It is a way for the librarian to become part of the conversation without requiring the library to take on a financial risk.

What can librarians do to break into the conversation? Courtois and Turtle (2008) discuss the success of faculty focus groups at Kansas State University. The focus groups at Kansas State were part of a scholarly communication program that was focused on issues surrounding journal publishing and included faculty from a variety of disciplines. These groups helped the librarians understand the needs of the faculty. In addition, areas where the faculty were confused and those library services they were unaware of were highlighted. Focus groups on scholarly research could be an effective way for librarians to enter the conversation.

Support of professors going through the tenure process is another area where librarians can easily enter the scholarly conversation. As Lankes points out, professors are more motivated and in need of help at this point in their career than at any other time. If librarians reach out to these professors, and if faculty support librarian involvement in the process, a myriad of benefits could follow. By performing a citation analysis for the professor, libraries can validate the results. Hopefully, professors who are successful in their bid for tenure will remember the librarian who helped them along the way and become advocates for library service. So many of the examples we have seen in our discussion of the Atlas suggest that face-to-face interaction is one of the keys to getting members to use library services. Let's get professors hooked at the start of their career so they will continue to use, and facilitate the use of, library services.

CONVERSATION STARTERS

1. Is there also a responsibility on the part of the professor to reach out to librarians and acknowledge the importance of the services they provide?
2. Do the professors need to reassess their perception of the status of librarians in order to take full advantage of what librarians have to offer them?
3. How can librarians insert themselves into scholarly communication when an increasing amount of research is done virtually?
4. Is this another argument for the embedded librarian?

RELATED ARTIFACTS

Courtois, M., & Turtle, E. (2008). Using faculty focus groups to launch a scholarly communication program. *OCLC Systems and Services, 24*(3), 160–166.

Hahn, K. (2008). Talk about talking about new models of scholarly communication. *The Journal of Electronic Publishing, 11*(1).

Vassallo, P. (1999). The knowledge continuum: Organizing for research and scholarly communication. *Internet Research, 9*(3), 232–242.

SCHOOL

MAP LOCATION

D, 6

THREAD LOCATION

Page 112

SCAPE

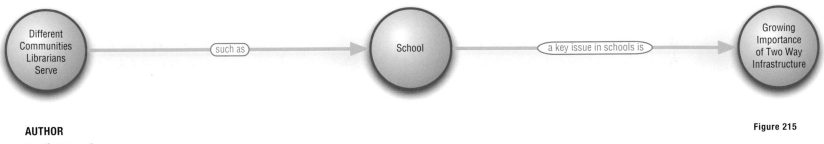

Figure 215

AUTHOR

Buffy Hamilton

AGREEMENT DESCRIPTION

How are contemporary school libraries inviting and creating spaces for rich conversations that lead to learning with students? How can expanding the concept of information literacy act as a catalyst for knowledge construction? How might school librarians get away from the traditional emphasis on "information objects" in the library space and instead posit the facilitation of learning as the primary mission of the school library? If school librarians are in the change business, how can we disrupt a standardized test-driven culture in favor of an inquiry-driven paradigm that is directed by conversations rather than knowledge consumption? The concepts of new librarianship support school libraries' efforts to achieve these program goals.

Creating Conversations for Formal Learning

The four major standards for 21st Century Learners from the American Association of School Librarians include:

- *Standard 1* Inquire, think critically, and gain knowledge

- *Standard 2* Draw conclusions, make informed decisions, apply knowledge to new situations, and create new knowledge

- *Standard 3* Share knowledge and participate ethically and productively as members of our democratic society

- *Standard 4* Pursue personal and aesthetic growth

These standards can be a vehicle for an inquiry-driven school library program that privileges questions and conversations. How do we use a framework of participatory librarianship to create conversations around these standards for learning with students?

One way that school librarians can create conversations about information evaluation and social scholarship is through the active creation and integration of research pathfinders into library instruction. By integrating traditional forms of information sources, such as widgets for databases and for the card catalog as well as emerging forms of social scholarship, such as RSS feeds from Twitter and blogs, or embedding YouTube videos, school librarians can open up conversations with students about the concept of authority. The use of both traditional and nontraditional information sources in research pathfinders provides a springboard for questions and discussions about when and how to use particular information sources for a range of information-seeking tasks.

School librarians can also create conversations about collaborative knowledge building using wikis and inquiry based activities that engage students through collaboration, cooperative construction, and knowledge sharing. For example, I created and facilitated a wiki to support tenth graders' exploration of how individuals and groups are using social media for social good. Through this wiki, students could share links to articles, videos, and blog posts that discussed ways that people are using social media for charity and social justice; through the wiki, students could dialog with each other about the ideas they were discovering in their research. School librarians can also integrate face-to-face learning experiences that support an inquiry stance on information literacy. To reinforce the discussions taking place on the class wiki, I borrowed an activity from Dr. Bob Fecho, professor of Language and Literacy Education at the University of Georgia, to spark conversations among students. The "speed dating" article activity involved students working in small groups to do rotating three-minute interviews of each other about the "social media for social good" information sources they had posted to the class wiki. As students interviewed each other, they took notes on the ideas that stood out in the interviews; the culminating activity was to then share these interview notes on the class wiki. This activity gave students the opportunity to converse and construct knowledge as they shared their findings and reflections on the ideas from their research.

School librarians can help students create conversations about adaptability and research strategies by teaching students blogging skills and strategies. As part of extended inquiry into issues facing Africa, students blogged multiple times each week. Some blog entries were reader response journals for the book they and their literature circle were reading; these books, fiction and nonfiction works, reflected one or more issues related to Africa and were selected from a menu of texts by each group. In addition, students engaged in conversations with themselves as well as their peers through weekly research reflections. In these blog entries, students wrote about challenges, successes, and questions they were encountering as they researched their chosen issue.

The school library is the perfect place to engage in conversations about digital citizenship and ethical use of information. If you are teaching presentation zen skills, ways to share and create new knowledge through new media tools like video, Glogster, or Voice Thread, seize these learning experiences to create conversations about fair use or Creative Commons licensed media. If you are facilitating the traditional research paper, create conversations about giving appropriate credit and ethical use of information through citation support tools like Noodletools or Zotero.

A participatory philosophy can support school librarians' efforts to convey ideas about alternate representations of knowledge, organizing knowledge, sharing learning reflections, and sharing resources. Multimedia medium, such as VoiceThread, student-created videos, and Glogster, are tools that students can use to create learning artifacts that are not text-centric and allow for alternate ways of representing key information. Students can use music, images, and other sounds to represent and create conversations about learning. Video and VoiceThread can also be used for students to verbally share what they are thinking and to verbalize their reflections or thoughts about their knowledge-creation process. The use of cloud computing tools like Google Sites allow students to leave comments and develop conversational threads on specific web pages they create for learning and research portfolios; on a larger scale, they may invite conversation from the community because their Web sites are viewable worldwide.

Social bookmarking tools also create opportunities for conversations about knowledge and authority. At the Unquiet Library, I work with teachers to create class groups for research projects using Diigo; students can share bookmarked resources—whether they be videos, database articles, Tweets, blog posts, or web pages—with their peers in the group. Diigo also allows students to leave comments and indicate whether they "like" a bookmarked resource. Students can even share their sticky notes with their annotations of the web page with the general public, or they can share them within the class group. This form of note-sharing can be a conversation starter as students compare ideas and information.

Skype is another tool that has great potential for creating conversations within and outside of the physical library space. Many authors are now offering virtual visits via Skype in which they re-create their traditional physical visit. Students and the author can easily interact through verbal discussion via a webcam in real time, creating conversations about reading and writing. In addition, Skype can be a window to a world of experts on issues that students may be researching in which conversations can take place between students and scholars.

Creating Conversations for Community

One of the most popular tools for conversations I have used to create conversations about books, reading, and genres in my library is the use of book displays. Creative and attractive book displays not only draw foot traffic to specific collections or genres of books, but they also provide an opportunity for students to engage in conversations about books and authors with each other as well as adults, including teachers, administrators, and library staff. Physical arrangement of collection, such as bookstore-style shelving strategies, can also engage students in conversations about books and favorite topics, genres, or authors of interest.

Displays don't have to be just about information objects for students. The display of student work, such as poetry and artwork, can be a catalyst for conversations about learning in the school library. Each spring, we support and host poetry readings in collaboration with classroom teachers that we record and share via podcasts and/or slidecasts to highlight student work. In addition, we have a "poetry clothesline" that we have in the commons area of our library featuring student-created poems as well as student-selected poetry of famous (and not so famous) poets. Inevitably, students are engaging in conversation with each other about their work and with library staff about the poems. We also host rotating displays of student-created artwork to celebrate student creativity while encouraging conversations about the artwork.

Celebrating student passions is another way to create conversations in the school library. We have adapted the *Geek the Library* campaign as a way of making what students "geek" or love visible in the library. Students can share what they "geek" with silver Sharpie pens and black construction paper; once they have completed their "geek" flyer, they hang it from our display clothesline in the library. The "geek" flyers are frequently the center of inquiry and discussion among students and teachers who visit the library.

Physical space also plays a significant role in supporting a conversation-friendly environment in the school library. Café-style tables, comfortable lounge seating, and strategic placement of seating can create spaces for learning that are conducive to collaborative work and discussions, whether students are simply hanging out, using our library laptops, or working in small groups. Students are encouraged to share suggestions for furniture purchases and physical arrangement; their input has been instrumental in the physical space we have today in our library and, consequently, the rise of our library as a popular gathering spot for informal and formal learning.

The library's web presence and use of social media are important mediums for supporting and igniting conversations. Our patrons can dialog with us and with each other about resources, announcements, and library activities on our blog, Twitter, Flickr, Slideshare, Friendfeed, and our Facebook fan page. In addition, we host a Meebo chat room three nights a week to answer any reference questions students may have. Our YouTube channel also features student and teacher interviews, in which participants share ideas and reflections about library program activities and learning experiences. Students and teachers can also complete a Google form to submit materials requests for items they would like to see in circulation. I also frequently incorporate polls, such as PollDaddy, into our research pathfinders to get student feedback on the resources we are using and to know what is working for them as learners. Text-based polls with Poll Everywhere always get discussions started when used to introduce an information literacy lesson.

Play is another way of engaging conversations in the school library. One of our most popular areas is the puzzle table; at any given time, you will usually find a hive of activity and conversation happening here, whether it be students, teachers, or a combination of the two. We also use playful learning activities, such as Readers' Theater, to help students learn and converse about information literacy topics through fun and creative student-performed skits. Lunch trivia sessions, complete with food, also bring in students and stimulate animated conversations as well.

Transparency of the library program is also vital for creating conversations with library stakeholders. Whether we are posting and blogging our monthly report in traditional text format or with video, the sharing of monthly reports can be a springboard to cultivating collaborative partnerships with faculty, administration, and partners in education, as well as district officials and fellow librarians around the world. Our social media presence is also an important vehicle for communicating what our library does for our students and school and to invite conversation about those happenings.

By establishing a climate of participation, risk-taking, acceptance of "messy" learning, and inquiry, we can create conversations that in turn create school libraries that are responsive and organic. A participatory approach to librarianship can ultimately lead to learning experiences that, in the words of Steve Jobs, "make a dent in someone's universe."

SCHOOL INFORMATION MANAGEMENT SYSTEMS

MAP LOCATION

G, 6

THREAD LOCATION

Page 113

SCAPE

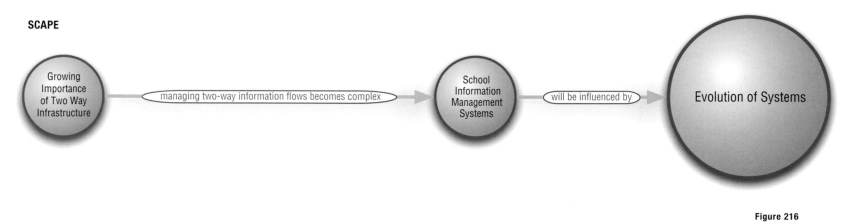

Figure 216

SELECTIVE DISSEMINATION OF INFORMATION

MAP LOCATION

E, 1

THREAD LOCATION

Page 72

SCAPE

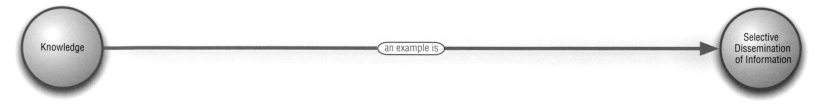

Figure 217

SENSE-MAKING

MAP LOCATION
D, 4

THREAD LOCATION
Page 25

SCAPE

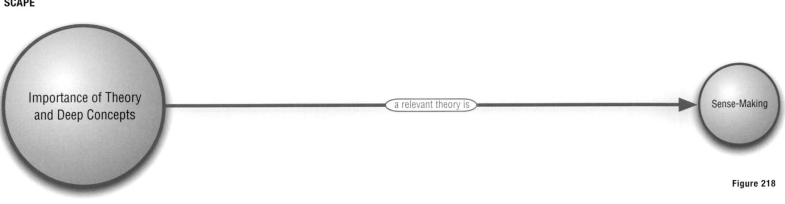

Importance of Theory and Deep Concepts

a relevant theory is

Sense-Making

Figure 218

AUTHOR
Todd Marshall

AGREEMENT DESCRIPTION

"Sense-making" and "sensemaking" may be pronounced the same, are almost written the same, and are based on similar constructivist perspectives, but they are not the same. When speaking about individuals making sense of their world and their environment, two prominent ideas lead this discussion. The first is "Sense-Making" as championed by Brenda Dervin (Dervin & Nilan, 1986), and the second is "sensemaking" by Karl E. Weick (Weick, 1995).[1] Sensemaking according to Weick will be the adopted approach, but because of the similarity in terminology and to remove the possibility of confusion, Dervin's approach deserves a brief overview first.

Dervin's Sense-Making focuses on the individual as he or she moves through time and space. As this happens, gaps are encountered where the individual must "make sense" of the situation to move, physically or cognitively, across the gap. The key components in this process are the situation, gap, and uses. The situation is the context of the user, the gap is that which prevents movement, and the use is the application of the sense that is constructed (Dervin, 1999). In this sense, Dervin's approach is monadic because it focuses on the individual and the sense that the individual makes as he or she is trying to cross the gap. This is in contrast to Weick, who focuses on group sensemaking as at least dyadic but more often triadic or polyadic. In other words, Weick focuses on multiple people working together to make sense. Although this contrast between the group and the individual is significant, Dervin's approach has the same philosophical roots as Weick's. Dervin (1999) states: "I have described Sense-Making as a constructivist approach, while now I describe it as post-constructivist, or postmodern modernist" (p. 730). Although Weick and Dervin have both been associated with constructivism, Dervin does not directly link Weick's sensemaking with her own Sense-Making but as one of many "parallel approaches" (Dervin et al., 2005).

---

1. Because the wording of Dervin and Weick's terminology are so close, "Sense-Making" will be used when referring to Dervin's concept and "sensemaking" will be used when referring to Weick's concept. This follows each author's conventions.

There are many uses of the term sense making as phenomena in the literature (spelled myriad different ways) which have no relationship to Sense Making Methodology. For example Weick's (Weick, 1995) Sensemaking in organizations looking at organizational life by examining the phenomenon [of] sensemaking. (Dervin, 1999, p. 729)

Although Dervin does not link Weick to her work, they both follow a constructivist approach. This is demonstrated especially by Weick's conceptualization of equivocality (Weick & Sutcliffe, 2001, p. 10). In contrast to Dervin, Weick's major works do cite Dervin or trace his conceptualizations to her work (Weick, 1969, 1993, 1995, 2003, 2005, 2006, 2007; Weick & Roberts, 1993; Weick & Sutcliffe, 2001; Weick, Sutcliffe, & Obstfeld, 2005; Wenger, 1999, 2001, 2005a, 2005b; Wenger, McDermott, & Snyder, 2002; Wenger & Snyder, 2000; Wenger, White, Smith, & Rowe, 2005). There are other constructivist approaches that one could consider, such as Habermas. However, as one researcher under the supervision of Brenda Dervin stated: "I suggest that current theory based upon Habermas' theories of communicative action and the public sphere may be too limited for describing grounded communicative practice within online environments" (Schaefer, 2001, p. ii). In summary, Weick's view of sensemaking as a group activity is more relevant for library communities than Dervin's monadic approach, which focuses on individual Sense-Making. Therefore, the discussion now focuses on Weick.

The theoretical framework for the organizational perspective of this study will be that of sensemaking as described by Karl E. Weick in *Sensemaking in Organizations* (Weick, 1995) and *Managing the Unexpected: Assuring High Performance in an Age of Complexity* (Weick & Sutcliffe, 2001). These works were foreshadowed in his first book, *The Social Psychology of Organizing* (Weick, 1969). Sensemaking had its foundations in several significant case studies where Weick investigated complex situations to understand how human beings tried to make sense out of seemingly contradictory information. The majority of Weick's work was in "public sector organizations," with only a few in "commercial" organizations (Weick, 2006, p. 1733). Unfortunately, he has not written about the nonprofit sector or libraries. Two significant examples of his approach are studies of the flight deck of an aircraft carrier (Weick & Roberts, 1993) and a firefighting disaster (Weick, 1993). Sensemaking does not have a strict definition per se, but here are several examples from Weick.

The basic idea of sensemaking is that reality is an ongoing accomplishment that emerges from efforts to create order and make retrospective sense of what occurs. (Weick, 1993, p. 635)

Sensemaking is about the enlargement of small cues. It is a search for contexts within which small details fit together and make sense. It is people interacting to flesh out hunches. It is a continuous alternation between particulars and explanations with each cycle giving added form and substance to the other. (Weick, 1995, p. 133)

To talk about sensemaking is to talk about reality as an ongoing accomplishment that takes form when people make retrospective sense of the situations in which they find themselves and their creations. There is a strong reflexive quality to this process. People make sense of things by seeing a world on which they already imposed what they believe. In other words, people discover their own inventions. This is why sensemaking can be understood as invention and interpretations understood as discovery. These are complementary ideas. If sensemaking is viewed as an act of invention, then it is also possible to argue that the artifacts it produces include language games and texts. (Weick, 1995, p. 15)

Sensemaking is about authoring as well as interpretation, creation as well as discovery. (Weick, 1995, p. 8)
Organizational sensemaking is first and foremost about the question: How does something come to be an event for organizational members? Second, sensemaking is about the question: What does the event mean? (Weick et al., 2005, p. 410)

The constructivism is in part revealed in Weick by his emphasis on using gerunds as opposed to nouns (Gioia, 2006) and not using the term "is" but rather by giving descriptive statements about something or someone (Weick, 2007). Describing Weick's perspective, Dervin says: "There is no such thing as organization. There is only organizing" (Dervin, 2003, p. 116). The point in both cases is to move away from viewing reality as a collection of static, fixed entities (nouns) to viewing reality as ever-changing entities. "It is about the 'process of becoming' rather than the 'states of being' " (Gioia, 2006, p. 1711). "Now when you think in terms of verbs and gerunds, it changes the way you talk about and understand phenomena. ... The conversation changes when you emphasize verbs and gerunds. And that's one of the main reasons why, when you take a 'Weickian' view, you cannot help but see things differently" (Gioia, 2006, p. 1711).

These descriptions of sensemaking speak of creation, sharing, interacting, cyclical activity, and people engaging each other to create a better understanding of their world and their work. Weick identifies seven distinguishing characteristics of the sensemaking process:

1. Grounded in identity construction
2. Retrospective
3. Enactive of sensible environments
4. Social
5. Ongoing
6. Focused on and by extracted cues
7. Driven by plausibility rather than accuracy (Weick, 1995, p. 17)

Having provided a brief overview of sensemaking, it's time to examine the constituent parts of sensemaking.

Identity Construction

The issue of identity begins with Weick's iconic question: "How can I know what I think until I see what I say" (1995)? In this statement, all four pronouns are all "I." Sensemaking begins with the individual and the sense that the individual makes of a situation.[2] This discussion with one's self is the first step that then allows one to make sense with others. Sensemaking is a complex process by which the individual, through interaction with self and others, defines the self. "The trap is that the sensemaker is singular and no individual ever acts like a single sensemaker. Instead, any one sensemaker is, in Mead's (1934) words, 'a parliament of selves'" (Weick, 1995, p. 18). This follows the logic of Pask and conversation theory as described in the Thread on conversation. This is the conversation with self. Likewise quoting Knorr-Cetina (1981, p. 10), Weick identifies with the understanding that "the individual is a typified discursive construction" (Weick, 1995, p. 20). Even when individuals are "alone," they are engaging themselves because every individual is a collection of selves. In other words, no individual is truly a lone sensemaker. Although this may seem to simply lead to schizophrenia, the "more selves I have access to, the more meanings I should be able to extract and impose in any situation," and "the less the likelihood that I will every find myself surprised" (Weick, 1995, p.

24). "Thus, identities specify relationships that are central to the social nature of sensemaking among diverse actors" (Weber & Glynn, 2006, p. 1646). Identity construction is about making sense of the entities, individuals, and organizations in the sensemaking situation. These identities are constructed by looking back on what has been said, as the initial questions implies. There can be no sense before the conversing begins. In Weick's terminology, this aspect of sensemaking is retrospective.

Retrospective

Sensemaking is ongoing and retrospective, making sense of what has happened (Gioia, 2006; Weber & Glynn, 2006; Weick, 1995). It is not a prospective activity. Individuals make sense of what people have said and done and therefore cannot make sense about what has not yet been said or done (i.e., the future). "Sensemaking involves the ongoing retrospective development of plausible images that rationalized what people are doing" (Weick et al., 2005, p. 409). In summary, individuals consider and contemplate the conversations, artifacts, and happenings and try to make sense of them. It is the process of attending to that which has occurred, looking back from the now to the past, recognizing that it is subject to the fallibility of memory, and can be very misleading (Weick, 1995). Although this process may seem hopeless, humans are nevertheless able to navigate the world despite the weakness of the incompleteness of the individual's ability to understand what has happened. This leads to the need for other voices to assist in sensemaking as described above. The "more selves I have access to, the more meanings I should be able to extract and impose in any situation" and "the less the likelihood that I will every find myself surprised" (Weick, 1995, p. 24).

Enactive of Sensible Environments

Sensemaking is a combination of "action and cognition together" (Weick, 1995). Weick refers to this as "enactment." This speaks to the fact that individuals participate in their environment. As they are creating their environment, they are also making sense of it. People are making sense of dynamic environments "*not* some kind of monolithic, singular, fixed environment that exists detached from and external to those people" (Weick, 1995, p. 31). The individual is part of the environment through the process of co-constructing it with fellow sensemakers. This is why sensemaking is not just interpretation. Interpretation is about reading a "text." Sensemaking involves not only understanding the text but also creating the text.

2. While this may parallel Dervin's idea, Weick does not relate this to her work. While the reader may see the similarity between Sense Making and sensemaking, this discussion will not pursue this line of reasoning since Dervin and Weick themselves do not.

Enactment is the stubborn insistence that people act in order to develop a sense of what they should do next. Enactment is about two questions: What's the story? Now what? When people act in order to answer these questions, their acting typically codetermines the answer (Weick, 2003). Sensemaking is not simply interpretation because it also includes "the ways people generate what they interpret" (Weick, 1995, p. 13). The sensemaker makes the environment, and the environment makes the sensemaker. From this perspective, individuals can never fully be neutral or objective about themselves or their sensemaking process. "If this is ontological oscillation, so be it. It seems to work" (Weick, 1995).

Social

Sensemaking is "both an individual and social activity," and it is unclear whether these are separable because this activity is "a durable tension in the human condition" (Weick, 1995, p. 6). It is an individual and a collective process at the same time. Sensemaking recognizes that "the social context is crucial … because it binds people to actions that they then must justify, it affects the saliency of information, and it provides norms and expectations that constrain explanations" (Weick, 1995, p. 53). As Weick says, "Sense may be in the eye of the beholder, but beholders vote and the majority rules" (Weick, 1995, p. 6). "What is especially interesting is that she tries to make sense of how other people make sense of things, a complex determination that is routine in organizational life" (Weick et al., 2005, p. 413). This is essentially second-order cybernetic systems as described by Pask, systems of observing systems (Pask, 1975a, 1975b, 1976). This is the individual conversing with self about the conversing of others. In every case, conversation is at least dyadic because two or more parties are involved. From this perspective, sensemaking is most significant (as opposed to Dervin) for the organizational context that affects the sensemaking process in the library. The organization or library affects sensemaking because: "(1) institutions prime sensemaking by providing social clues; (2) institutions edit sensemaking through social feedback processes; (3) institutions trigger sensemaking, posing puzzles for sensemaking through endogenous institutional contradiction and ambivalence" (Weber & Glynn, 2006, p. 1648). Because libraries consist of individuals who are constantly making new "sense" of their situations, the whole process is ongoing. This takes place in the context of the library among its staff, members, and other stakeholders.

Ongoing

"Sensemaking never starts. The reason it never starts is that pure duration never stops" (Weick, 2006, p. 43). The sensemaker can only live in the here and the now. For the sensemaker, the "now" never really began, and as long as there is consciousness, it never really ends. One is always in the process of making sense. From this standpoint, sensemaking has no past tense. People were making sense, are making sense, and will be making sense but have never totally made sense of something. "Sensemaking is clearly about an activity or a process…" and not just an outcome (Weick, 1995, p. 13). As people are making sense, there are always new stimuli that affect the process and the sense. "The contrast between discovery and invention is implicit in the word sense. To sense something sounds like an act of discovery. But to sense something, there must be something there to create the sensation. And sensemaking suggest the construction of that which then becomes sensible" (Weick, 1995, p. 14). Although life provides the stimulus for sensemaking, the reason that sense must be made is because there is a continual gap, problem, or cognitive dissonance. As Weick says, "My one contact with the real seems to have been my dissertation in 1961 on cognitive dissonance" (Weick, 2006, p. 1734). That is, "the interruption, the inconsistent, the inexplicable," which causes one to have to make sense of the situation (Weick, 2006, p. 1734). Because this dissonance is a recurring event, it leads to a "reciprocal interaction of information seeking, meaning ascription, and action" (Thomas, Clark, & Gioia, 1993, p. 240). Problems are "constructed from the materials of problematic situation which are puzzling, troubling, and uncertain" (Weick, 1995, p. 9). For the sensemaker to resolve the dissonance or problematic situation, he or she will look for clues in the environmental context as part of the sensemaking process. This is a continuing process because the problems forever present as long as there is movement through time and space.

Focused on and by Extracted Cues

When applying sensemaking, it is essential to look not at the act of deciding itself but the circumstance or context that resulted in that action. Understanding the contextual circumstances leads one to asking "how" the situation came to be rather than "why" a decision was made (Weick et al., 2005). This will help identify the clues that informed the sensemaking process. The context not only provides the cues, it contains the patterns of cue usage. The organizational culture may emphasize certain sources for cues and ignore others. In this way, the organization tells the sensemaker where to look for cues. In Wenger's terms, the sources of cue location are the result of reification as patterns are built through participation. To put it another way, "the social context is crucial for sensemaking because it binds people to actions that they then must justify, that constrain explanations" (Weick, 1995, p. 53). The context helps one determine where people are directing the focus of their intention, where the cues are coming from. In the library, these clues are created through classification schemes, signage, metadata, library catalogs, and all the other means that libraries use to guide, direct, and instruct their members.

Plausibility over Accuracy

When looking at the sensemaking process from extracted clues, one must remember that "sensemaking is driven by plausibility rather than accuracy" (Bansler & Havn, 2006, p. 61). Accuracy is secondary to plausibility for several reasons. First, people are constantly filtering the cues that affect their decision making. Next, people tend to link present cues with previous cues and build present sense on sense made in the past. Third, people often lack the time necessary for accuracy before they act. Their sense just needs to be good enough for the next step. Finally, accuracy is more relevant for short durations and for specific questions than for global circumstances (Weick, 1995). In short, the explanation of the sensemaking process must "make sense" not necessarily "be accurate."

> Sensemaking is about accounts that are socially acceptable and credible.... It would be nice if these acceptable accounts were also accurate. But in an equivocal, postmodern world, infused with the politics of interpretation and conflicting interests and inhabited by people with multiple shifting identities, an obsession with accuracy seems fruitless, and not of much practical help either. (Weick, 1995, p. 61)

While sensemaking, people "read into things the meanings they wish to see; they vest objects, utterances, actions and so forth with subjective meaning which helps make their world intelligible to themselves" (Frost & Morgan, 1983). When people are sensemaking, they are not striving for accuracy but rather plausibility and sense. If it seems plausible and is sufficient to provide the necessary meaning to take the next step, that is accurate enough for the person to act. Whether that is the "correct action" is a separate question. This was seen in the Mann Gulch fire. One plan of escape made sense to most of the firefighters. Although the plan for escape made sense to them, it was inaccurate and led to their deaths. The accurate plan did not make sense. This is a prime example of individuals acting on sensibility, what makes sense, instead of accuracy (Weick, 1993). So, when trying to understand what happened, one must consider what was plausible to the sensemakers even if their sense was or is inaccurate.

Summary

Sensemaking in organizations and libraries is an ongoing process that never begins and does not end as long as the organization continues. "First, sensemaking occurs when a flow of organizational circumstances is turned into words and salient categories. Second, organizing itself is embodied in written and spoken texts. Third, reading, writing, conversing and editing are crucial actions that serve as the media through which the invisible hand of institutions shapes conduct ..." (Weick et al., 2005, p. 409).

Through this process of sensemaking, decisions are made leading to behavior. However, sensemaking and decision making are not the same. The difference between decision making and sensemaking is that "the former prompts us to blame bad actors who make bad choices while the latter focuses instead on good people struggling to make sense of a complex situation" (Eisenberg, 2006, p. 1699). The goal of the library then should be to help the member make sense of the resources that the library contains, whether those resources are human, digital, or artifactual. This is an ongoing process that never ceases and requires conversing among all the library stakeholders. The requires librarians to embrace this dynamic, conversational process and understand that librarianship is about facilitating sensemaking and not about achieving a static state where every item finally has "the right label" and is "in the right place."

RELATED ARTIFACTS

Bansler, J., & Havn, E. (2006). Sensemaking in technology-use mediation: Adapting groupware technology in organizations. *Computer Supported Cooperative Work, 15*(1), 55–91.

Dervin, B. (1999). On studying information seeking methodologically: The implications of connecting metatheory to method. *Information Processing and Management, 35*(6), 727–750.

Dervin, B. (2003). Given a context by any other name: Methodological tools for taming the unruly beast. In B. Dervin, L. Foreman-Wernet, & E. Lauterbach (Eds.), *Sense-making methodology reader: Selected writings of Brenda Dervin* (pp. 111–132). Cresskill, NJ: Hampton Press.

Dervin, B., Fisher, K. E., Durrance, J., Ross, C., Savolainen, R., & Solomon, P. (2005). Reports of the demise of the "user" have been greatly exaggerated: Dervin's sense-making and the methodological resuscitation of the user-looking backwards, looking forward. *Proceedings of the American Society for Information Science and Technology, 42*(1).

Dervin, B., & Nilan, M. (1986). Information needs and uses. *Annual Review of Information Science and Technology, 21*, 3–33.

Eisenberg, E. M. (2006). Karl Weick and the aesthetics of contingency. *Organization Studies, 27*(11), 1693.

Frost, P., & Morgan, G. (1983). Symbols and sensemaking: The realization of a framework. In L. R. Pondy, P. J. Frost, G. Morgan, & T. C. Danderidge (Eds.), *Organizational symbolism* (pp. 207–237). Greenwich, CT: JAI Press.

Gioia, D. A. (2006). On Weick: An appreciation. *Organization Studies, 27*(11), 1709–1721.

Knorr-Cetina, K. (1981). The microsociological challenge of macro-sociology: Toward a reconstruction of social theory and methodology. In K. Knorr-Cetine & A. V. Cicourel (Eds.), *Advances in social theory and methodology: Toward an integration of micro-and macro-sociologies* (pp. 1–47). Boston: Routledge & Kegan.

Mead, G. H. (1934). *Mind, self, and society: From the standpoint of a social behaviorist.* Chicago, IL: University of Chicago Press.

Pask, G. (1975a). *Conversation, cognition and learning: A cybernetic theory and methodology.* New York: Elsevier Publishing Company.

Pask, G. (1975b). *The cybernetics of human learning and performance: A guide to theory and research.* Hutchinson, KS: Hutchinson Educational.

Pask, G. (1976). *Conversation theory: Applications in education and epistemology.* New York: Elsevier.

Schaefer, D. J. (2001). *Dynamics of electronic public spheres: Verbing online participation.* Unpublished dissertation, Ohio State University, Columbus, OH.

Thomas, J. B., Clark, S. M., & Gioia, D. A. (1993). Strategic sensemaking and organizational performance: Linkages among scanning, interpretation, action, and outcomes. *Academy of Management Journal, 36*(2), 239–270.

Weber, K., & Glynn, M. A. (2006). Making sense with institutions: Context, thought and action in Karl Weick's theory. *Organization Studies, 27*(11), 1639.

Weick, K. E. (1969). *The social psychology of organizing.* Reading, MA: Addison-Wesley.

Weick, K. E. (1993). The collapse of sensemaking in organizations: The Mann Gulch disaster. *Administrative Science Quarterly*, 628–652.

Weick, K. E. (1995). *Sensemaking in organizations.* Thousand Oaks, CA: Sage Publications.

Weick, K. E. (2003). Enacting an environment: The infrastructure of organizing. Debating organization: Point-counterpoint in organization studies. In R. Westwood & S. R. Clegg (Eds.), *Debating organization: Point-counterpoint in organization studies* (pp. 184–194). Oxford: Blackwell Publishing.

Weick, K. E. (2005). Managing the unexpected: Complexity as distributed sensemaking. *Uncertainty and Surprise In Complex Systems: Questions On Working With The Unexpected, 51*.

Weick, K. E. (2006). Faith, evidence, and action: Better guesses in an unknowable world. *Organization Studies, 27*(11), 1723–1736.

Weick, K. E. (2007). The generative properties of richness. *The Academy of Management Journal, 50*(1), 14–19.

Weick, K. E., & Roberts, K. H. (1993). Collective mind in organizations: Heedful interrelating on flight decks. *Administrative Science Quarterly*, 357–381.

Weick, K. E., & Sutcliffe, K. M. (2001). *Managing the unexpected: Assuring high performance in an age of complexity.* San Francisco: Jossey-Bass.

Weick, K. E., Sutcliffe, K. M., & Obstfeld, D. (2005). Organizing and the process of sensemaking. *Organization science, 16*(4), 409.

Wenger, E. (1999). *Communities of practice: Learning, meaning, and identity.* New York: Cambridge University Press.

Wenger, E. (2001). *Support communities of practice: A survey of community-oriented technologies.* San Juan, CA: Self-published report.

Wenger, E. (2005a). *Communities of practice in 21st-century organizations: Guide to establishing and facilitating intentional communities of practice.* Quebec: CEFRIO.

Wenger, E. (2005b). *Communities of practice: A brief introduction.* Retrieved May 5, 2009, from http://www.vpit.ualberta.ca/cop/doc/wenger.doc.

Wenger, E., McDermott, R. A., & Snyder, W. (2002). *Cultivating communities of practice: A guide to managing knowledge.* Boston, MA: Harvard Business School Press.

Wenger, E., & Snyder, W. M. (2000). Communities of practice: The organizational frontier. *Harvard Business Review, 78*(1), 139–146.

Wenger, E., White, N., Smith, J. D., & Rowe, K. (2005). Technology for communities. In E. Wenger (Ed.), *Communities of practice in 21st-century organizations: Guide to establishing and facilitating intentional communities of practice.* Quebec: CEFRIO.

SERVICE

MAP LOCATION

F, 5, 6

THREAD LOCATION

Page 118

SCAPE

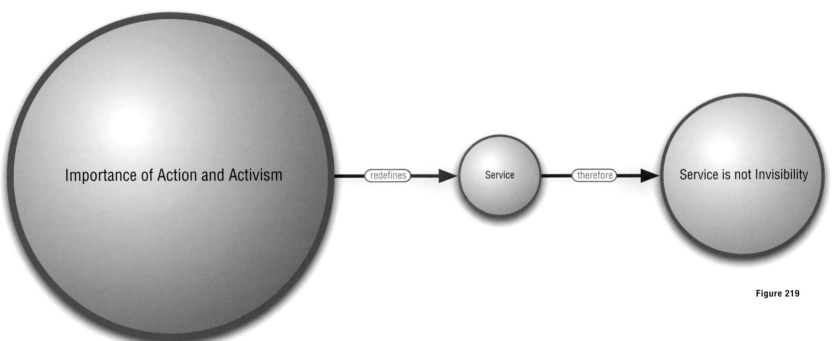

Figure 219

SERVICE IS NOT INVISIBILITY

MAP LOCATION

F, G, 3

THREAD LOCATIONS

Pages 33, 119

SCAPE

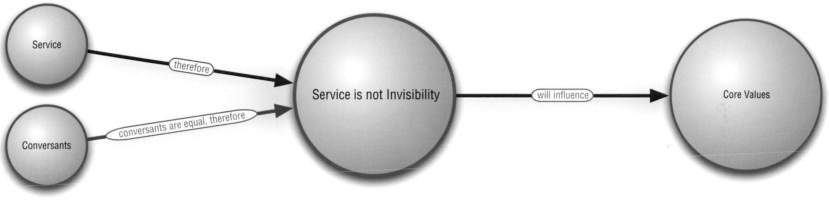

Figure 220

SHARED SHELVES WITH THE COMMUNITY

MAP LOCATION

E, 3

THREAD LOCATION

Page 68

SCAPE

Figure 221

SHELVING

MAP LOCATION

F, G, 8

THREAD LOCATION

Page 166

SCAPE

Figure 222

AGREEMENT DESCRIPTION

See also Shared Shelves with the Community

RELATED ARTIFACTS

Augmented Reality Wikipedia Entry: http://en.wikipedia.org/wiki/Augmented_reality.

Layar [an Augmented Reality platform]. http://layar.com.

Pegoraro, R. (2009). "Augmented reality" fuses the web and the world around you. http://www.washingtonpost.com/wp-dyn/content/article/2009/11/20/AR2009112001318.html?hpid=sec-tech.

MAP LOCATION

D, 8

THREAD LOCATION

Page 178

SCAPE

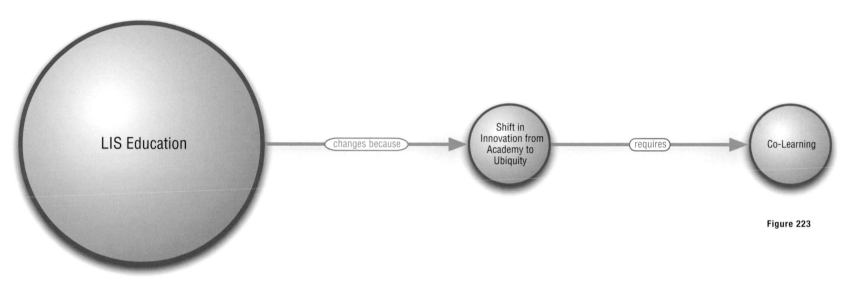

LIS Education

changes because

Shift in Innovation from Academy to Ubiquity

requires

Co-Learning

Figure 223

SOCIAL JUSTICE ISSUES

MAP LOCATION

F, 7

THREAD LOCATION

Page 124

SCAPE

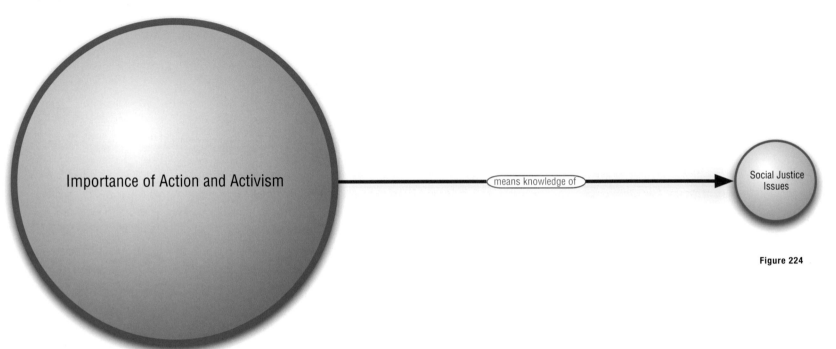

Importance of Action and Activism

means knowledge of

Social Justice Issues

Figure 224

AUTHOR

Jocelyn Clark

Broadly speaking, social justice issues reflect movements that push for greater voice and more representation for underrepresented or underpowered communities. Because libraries and librarians are tasked to serve all communities, we are inherently involved with and must be aware of issues of social justice. Ideals near to the heart of social justice advocates are egalitarianism, balance of power, social advocacy, public service, and diversity awareness. All of these issues are reflected in the work that librarians do to serve our communities. Specific social justice issues encompass many areas, and I list a few here just to help guide our thinking: racism, poverty, ageism, immigration policy, sexism, civil rights, mental health activism, homelessness, labor law, environmentalism and environmental justice, and so on. There are many ways in which librarians can address social justice needs with community, and I present some of them below.

Promoting awareness of social justice issues is one way to "improve society" because awareness of an issue is the first step to education and change. However, discussions around social justice can be fraught with controversy. Clearly, not everyone agrees with the basic assumption of creating a more egalitarian society, and even if they do, the methods to achieve change are controversial. You can start by discussing Spanish-language services and services to undocumented immigrants to see the sparks fly. However, the existence of controversy does not release us of responsibility to address issues of social injustice, provide services to ALL of the community, and maintain awareness of the impacts of our work.

One of the traditional ways to support social justice in a library is collecting and providing access to materials that specifically address social justice issues. People often look to the libraries when researching topics such as immigration policy. To effectively support a debate or conversation about a social justice topic, librarians can provide access to conversations, thoughts, and materials with multiple viewpoints. Libraries and librarians have a responsibility to be knowledgeable about the current social issues such that they can provide access to materials that represent the debate. This is more or less the traditional role of the librarian, to provide access to all viewpoints without inserting oneself in the debate. We have to keep reminding ourselves that only with access to ALL material can we truly understand the issue. Yes, both the Rush Limbaugh book, *The Way Things Ought to Be,* and Al Franken's, *Rush Limbaugh Is a Big Fat Idiot,* should be in the library—despite with whom you agree. Librarians engaged in social

justice issues, such as Kathryn de la Peña McCook, advocate developing information resources around legislation and political action as another method of furthering social justice. To engage in conversation around social justice issues, the conversants should have access to up-to-date information on the current political situation.

School library media centers have gained a lot of attention lately as vehicles to address social justice issues. Bush (2009) gathers a number of writings together from American Association of School Library's journal, *Knowledge Quest.* These articles address issues of civic responsibility in school libraries. Moffat (2005) also addresses integrating social justice programs and resources into a school media center.

Another method to support social justice is through reference work and research. Topics around social justice are rife with inaccuracies, hearsay, rumor, and propaganda—just like many other topics. Providing authoritative and reliable materials to dispel inaccurate information is essential to supporting social justice. The conversation on a particular topic should be based as much as possible on fact rather than propaganda. Inaccurate and unsubstantiated resources do not necessarily have a place in the discussion, and it is up to librarians to decide which resources will be made most accessible and to encourage our members to choose resources appropriate to the discussion.

One of the more active ways that librarians can engage in social justice activities is by designing outreach services that meet the needs of underrepresented communities. In-home delivery service to seniors, non-English-language services, even Internet access services can all be argued to be services for communities with unique needs. Stoffle (2007) addresses the use of new digital technologies to address the needs of underserved populations.

To take this a step further, by abandoning the role of unbiased mediator and taking positions on issues of social justice, we can use our roles to work for change. Several professional organizations support librarians who choose to combine their professional and personal political beliefs. I've listed at least some below, including the Progressive Librarians Guild and Radical Reference.

Last, I'd like to call attention to one individual who led the way in activist librarianship: Sanford Berman. I've listed only one of his many writings in the Resources section (Berman, 1993), but there is a Web site, http://www.sanfordberman.org/, which has an interesting biography and collection of works. Sanford Berman is an activist librarian/cataloguer who worked on revising the Library of Congress Subject Headings to remove bias. McCook and Phenix (2007) prepared a list of other activist librarians and their contributions to human rights through their professional actions.

CONVERSATION STARTERS

1. How do librarians promote issues of social justice while also promoting a balanced perspective?
2. Can and should you keep your own moral/ethical/religious values from influencing the goal of knowledge creation?
3. What is the difference between taking a position advocated by a profession versus a personal position? How do librarians determine whether to represent their own moral position or that required by the responsibility of the position/profession? Are guerrilla librarianship tactics ethical?
4. Does taking a position on social issues help or hinder the ultimate goal of knowledge facilitation in the community? How does the perception of a librarian as activist change how a community might view his or her work?
5. Is it our job to see both sides of a debate and represent each equally? What does it mean to represent a fair and balanced perspective on an issue?

RELATED ARTIFACTS

Abilock, D. (2006). So close and so small: Six promising approaches to civic education, equity, and social justice. *Knowledge Quest, 34*(5), 9–16.

Berman, Sanford. (1993). *Prejudices and antipathies: A tract on the LC subject heads concerning people.* Jefferson, NC: MacFarland & Co.

> Annotation: Discussion of the life-long efforts of Sanford Berman to rid the Library of Congress subject headings of those with historical or social bias. There are many of Sanford Berman's writings available in other forms and places.

Bush, G. (2009). *School library media programs in action: Civic engagement, social justice, and equity.* Chicago, IL: American Association of School Librarians.

Canadian Association for School Libraries. (2004). Intellectual freedom and social responsibility. *School Libraries in Canada Journal, 24*(4). Retrieved from http://www.clatoolbox.ca/casl/slic/SLICVol24issue4.pdf.

Canadian Association for School Libraries. (2007). Intellectual freedom and social responsibility: Building understanding. *School libraries in Canada Journal, 26*(2). Retrieved from http://www.clatoolbox.ca/casl/slic/vol26issue2.html.

McCook, K. (2009). *Selected publications.* Retrieved from http://shell.cas.usf.edu/~mccook/selectedpublications.htm.

McCook, K., & Phenix, K. J. (2007). A commitment to human rights: Let's honor the qualities required of a librarian dedicated to human rights. *Information for Social Change, 25.* Retrieved from http://libr.org/isc/issues/ISC25/articles/A%20COMMITMENT%20TO%20HUMAN%20RIGHTS.pdf.

> Annotation: A collection of mini-biographies of various librarians involved in working for human rights and social justice.

Mehra, B., & Braquet, D. (2007). Library and information science professionals as community action researchers in an academic setting: Top ten directions to further institutional change for people of diverse sexual orientations and gender identities. *Library Trends, 56*(2), 542–565.

> Annotation: A study of the academic experiences of lesbian, gay, bisexual, transgender, and questioning (LGBTQ) individuals and an examination of the role that LIS professionals can play in forwarding institutional change using the following LIS roles and services: (1) collection and resource development, (2) social and community information sharing, (3) social justice representation and advocacy, (4) outreach and community building, and (5) information dissemination.

Moffatt, L. (2005). Working for social justice in the school library: Exploring diversity, culture and social issues through children's literature. In R. Doiron & M. Asselin (Eds.), *Literacy, libraries & learning: Using books and online resources to promote reading, writing and research.* Markham, Ontario, Canada: Pembroke.

> Annotation: This chapter provides some specific ideas about methods of bringing social justice issues into a school library. She also provides lists of resources on particular topics.

Morrone, M., & Friedman, L. (2009). Radical reference: Socially responsible librarianship collaborating with community. *Reference Librarian, 50*(4), 371–396.

Roberto, K. R. (2008). *Radical cataloging: Essays at the front.* Jefferson, NC: McFarland & Co.

Stoffle, C. (2007). Social equity and empowerment in the digital age: A place for activist librarians. In R. Feinberg (Ed.), *The changing culture of libraries: How we know ourselves through our libraries.* Jefferson, NC: McFarland & Co.

Resources

Peace Project list of DVDs. http://peaceproject.com/books/av.htm
Social Justice Journal. http://www.socialjusticejournal.org/
Social Justice Lecture Series/District of Columbia Public Library
Teaching Tolerance Magazine. http://www.tolerance.org/magazine/archives

Blogs

Banned Librarian. http://bannedlibrarian.wordpress.com/
Librarian at the Kitchen Table: http://librarianoutreach.blogspot.com/
List of Social Justice Blogs. http://socialjusticemedia.ning.com/profiles/blogs/2152681:BlogPost:101
Social Justice Librarian blog. http://sjlibrarian.wordpress.com/
Union Librarian: http://unionlibrarian.blogspot.com/

Library Activist Groups

Information for Social Change http://libr.org/isc/

> Annotation: From website: "Information for Social Change is an activist organization that examines issues of censorship, freedom, and ethics among library and information workers. It is committed to promoting alternatives to the dominant paradigms of library and information work and publishes its own journal, *Information for Social Change.*"

This group is in liaison with the UK library organization: Chartered Institute of Library and Information Professionals (CILIP).

Librarians for Peace. http://libr.org/peace/

Annotation: From website: "Librarians for Peace is an ad hoc group of librarians and library workers, mainly Americans but also people of other nations, using the internet to organize and lobby against armed conflict where we consider it unnecessary, with a focus on our own country and its allies."

Library Underground—a guide to alternative library culture. http://www.libraryunderground.org/

Progressive rians Guild. http://libr.org/plg/index.php

Annotation: The development of public libraries was initially spurred by popular sentiment, which for one reason or another held that real democracy requires an enlightened citizenry and that society should provide all people with the means for free intellectual development. Members of PLG do not accept the sterile notion of the neutrality of librarianship, and we strongly oppose the commodi-fication of information that turns the "information commons" into privatized, commercialized zones. We will help to dissect the implications of these powerful trends and fight their anti-democratic tendencies.

Radical Reference. http://www.radicalreference.info/

Annotation: Mission statement from website: "Radical Reference is a collective of volunteer library workers who believe in social justice and equality. We sup-port activist communities, progressive organizations, and independent journal-ists by providing professional research support, education and access to informa-tion. We work in a collaborative virtual setting and are dedicated to information activism to foster a more egalitarian society."

Social Responsibilities Round Table of the ALA. http://libr.org/srrt/

Annotation: "SRRT is a unit within the American Library Association. It works to make ALA more democratic and to establish progressive priorities not only for the Association, but also for the entire profession. Concern for human and eco-nomic rights was an important element in the founding of SRRT and remains an urgent concern today. SRRT believes that libraries and librarians must recognize and help solve social problems and inequities in order to carry out their mandate to work for the common good and bolster democracy."

The Network: Tackling social exclusion in libraries museums, archives and galleries http://www.seapn.org.uk/

Annotation: Mission from website: "To assist the cultural sector, including li-braries, museums, archives and galleries, heritage, and other organizations, to work towards social justice."

SOCIAL LITERACY

MAP LOCATION

F, G, 1

THREAD LOCATION

Page 76

SCAPE

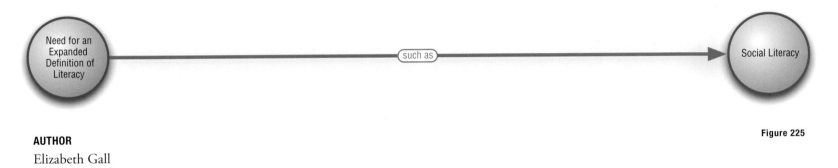

Figure 225

AUTHOR

Elizabeth Gall

AGREEMENT DESCRIPTION

The Atlas defines Social Literacy as (i) the power of identity in groups, and (ii) the process of defining and expanding social groupings to further our aims (p. 93). Although the recent emergence of online social networking tools has reminded us of the need for librarians to facilitate social literacy, it is an issue that has been present and in need of attention in libraries much longer than Facebook has been around.

The Atlas argues that literacy is a radical topic and librarianship is a radical profession. The truth of this statement shines through in the argument that librarians must work to facilitate social literacy within the profession in the same way they facilitate the social literacy of members. There are some serious issues with social literacy in libraries, and librarians cannot ignore them if they want to facilitate social literacy among members. In the library, there are librarians and nonlibrarians, and the groups are clearly defined. This division affects members, nonmembers, paraprofessionals, and librarians alike. If social literacy

is the power of identity in groups, the social literacy of libraries is divided and ineffective. If the librarian and nonlibrarian groupings identify themselves as separate groupings that simply function in the same space, neither will be able to clearly define themselves or their aims. Ultimately, the library will not function in a way that serves the needs of its community.

As librarians define their identity as separate from the rest of the library staff, members, and nonmembers, they deny those groups' input in defining their identity. Let's return to the Atlas' other definition of social literacy, the process of defining and expanding social groupings to further our aims. If librarians want to play a role in this process as they facilitate other groupings' social literacy, they must open their own grouping first so they can learn what their new role is and embrace it.

If librarians are to facilitate social literacy, must they participate in defining member groups? Can they define these groups if they are not a part of it? Reason says no. How can you define a group if you do not have intimate knowledge of it from within? Imagine defining a word after seeing it written alone, without a context. Instead of defining librarians based on their title, libraries are beginning to define their role based on the groupings they serve. As their role is redefined, librarians are becoming a part of these member groupings. Instead of reading one word, they are reading a paragraph.

One example of active library participation in member groupings is embedded librarianship. Kesselman et al. (2009) define embedded librarians as those who provide information services as a part of the group. They further explain, "Embedded librarians are, first and foremost, integrated into their settings, be they traditional or nontraditional" (Kesselman et al., 2009). They argue that, for librarians to find their place in our increasingly digital and constantly changing world, they must actively engage with the populations they serve regardless of their location, purpose, or aims. Embedded librarians can function in a range of intensities. They may manage a grouping's online presence and provide digital resources to meet their needs. They may attend regular meetings or simply read a group's monthly newsletter. No matter what, they must become a part of the groups they serve to facilitate social literacy.

Forrest (2005) discusses a library that took a different approach to librarian involvement in member groups. The Generals Libraries at Emory University found that it is better able to serve the university community by creating market councils for different member groups. By becoming directly and continuously involved in the groups, librarians are better able to define them and provide services that best suit their needs. Two years after the implementation of market councils, the General Libraries at Emory University found they are an effective way to respond to and serve different member groups. Regardless of the setting, librarians must redefine their own grouping and become a part of other groupings if they want to facilitate social literacy.

RELATED ARTIFACTS

Forrest, C. (2005). Segmenting the library market, reaching out to the user community by reaching across the organization. *The Georgia Librarian, 42*(1), 4.

Annotation: The General Libraries at Emory University realigned its organizational structure along functional processes. It created market councils for different segments of the university population. The population was divided by area of study as well as certain demographics, undergraduate, international, and so on. The councils' goal is to ensure that the functional units of the library are aligned with the needs of the subset of members the council serves. As a result, the functional units define themselves according to, or dare I say as a part of, the member group it serves. As a result the library is user-focused and better able to define and serve the needs of different groups on campus.

Kesselman, M., & Watstein, S. (2009). Creating opportunities: Embedded librarians. *Journal of Library Administration, 49*(4), 383.

Annotation: Kesselman et al. first define the embedded librarian, next examine the role of the embedded librarian in higher education, and finally discuss the practical implications of embedding librarians. A librarian can be embedded in any kind of library, within any community, and part of any group. An embedded librarian is one for whom a regular part of work is to provide information and information services as part of a group. Embedded librarians function as part of member groups on an increasingly frequent basis. These librarians facilitate social literacy as parts of the groups they are defining. Some librarians are extremely involved in the groups and others are less active participants, but they are all developing the social literacy of librarians along with that of the groups to which they belong.

SOCIAL NETWORK SITES

MAP LOCATION

H, 5

THREAD LOCATION

Page 39

SCAPE

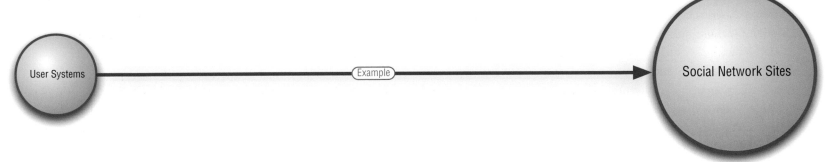

User Systems

Example

Social Network Sites

AUTHOR

Kelly Menzel

Figure 226

One way that libraries can look at social networking is to see how the business world is beginning to utilize social networking, and how they wrangle with the issue of language levels, because businesses each have their own specialized L_1 language, just as libraries do. However, they also have to be able to talk with other businesses and to people outside of their realm of business who are likely to have a different L_1 language, just as libraries and librarians need to be able to communicate to other libraries with different "dialects" (especially internationally) and to members whose language capabilities range significantly.

From the business side of social networking comes a few NPR shows: Conan's "Social Networking Grows Up" (*Talk of the Nation*) discussion of social networking sites between businesses and individuals in different business (Yelp, LinnkedIn) serves as a nice counterpoint to "When Is Social Networking Kosher in the Office?" (*All Things Considered*). Although both deal with how business language and communication styles are being enhanced by social networks, each discusses radically different uses of the sites and even, for that matter, radically different styles of social network sites. The twitter-like Yammer used by the businesses featured on *All Things Considered* illustrates an already-standing group using previously known language with people they already know in some context. In this case, the program, by its very nature, allows for use of L_0 language (when addressing those outside of your department) or sophisticated L_1 language depending on how the users wish to utilize the tool. Essentially, each company that uses the Yammer can use its own specialized L_1 language within the L_0 language of the tool to create a sophisticated in-company social/business network. The social networking tools mentioned in *Talk of the Nation*, in contrast, apply standard L_1 language for businesses to connect new people, create conversations that likely otherwise wouldn't occur due to lack of connections, and enhance those that would have taken place in a traditional setting (What does everyone candidly think about Person X as a worker? What are your skills?). The online forum actually encourages new connections to be formed and for members to discuss items candidly.

In both cases, the user's experience can, to an extent, be customized. The Yammer users can decide who to ignore and even who they wish to "follow" while being placed in/joining specific groups based around their company's current organization structure (which I am sure creates real-life conversations and informs others about people's proclivities), whereas the Yelp and LinkedIn users have relatively the same level of experience customization as Facebook users. They can decide to only search those people they already know, or they can find others based on experience, skills, and so on, to increase their known web of people on the site. What is interesting about the business-oriented tools is that they all have "tiers" of customization based on whether you pay for extra capabilities. A tiered style based on whether you pay for it may not be useful to librarians, but one based on how much you wish to share or a member/librarians' level in the organization could be useful if a social network of libraries were to be set up. In the more public realm of Facebook, a customized L_1 "tier" (group) could be created to allow librarians to talk to each other using their specialized language without flooding the members' accounts with so much techno-jargon.

Olwen's article about LibraryThing brings up a different idea worth looking at—that of deliberate use of language to achieve a certain effect. Here, it is the act of bringing people together through casual connections that is emphasized, rather than the specific connections the NPR shows seem to focus on. It also displays how language helps you learn and form connections more so than the other two. In contrast, Rolla's article, "User Tags Versus Subject Headings: Can User-Supplied Data Improve Subject Access to Library Collections?," provides a more scholarly look at LibraryThing and the differences in language use in the tags the site allows uses to add to titles. More than the other articles, it discusses the user's ability to customize the site and add knowledge to it—in this case, through the use of tagging. Unlike Olwen, Rolla sees LibraryThing's deliberate rejection of library "rules" as something that libraries should consider trying themselves or at least figuring out how to add members' contributions to the system to help facilitate knowledge generation, conversations, and build wider networks of people searching for similar items. These two articles may have radically different views about the merits of tagging and the use of social network ideas/usage in a library setting, but both question how language use affects the users of the site. Also, both lead to the question of how a learning space can be created, which appeals to all members just as much as it does to librarians. L_0 language is universal but may lack the specificity required, especially when searching for particular editions on LibraryThing. Also, the same "tag" can mean many different things to many people; even if typically recognized as L_0, much vocabulary plays into individuals' L_1 languages, making a "standard" the ideal. But whose standard should be used to satisfy all users? Should a new L_1 be created or an already existing one be put in place? The same questions apply to libraries using sites such as LibraryThing to add, show, and share information to other library professionals and the public, as well as to libraries considering adding such features to their own Web sites (see limitations of tagging section).

Kanuka and Anderson's article provides the theory behind the concepts the other articles look at but never mention. Dated though it may be, it provides a different, more scholarly, look than the other articles on what forms relationships and where people go within and without their social networks for information. The tenets of their work are played out in the *Talk of the Nation* show, although there are several notable differences, including the willingness of people to seek help outside of their already-established, real-life social networks and how learning is different in the online sites versus a personal network. Kanuka speaks of people's unwillingness to look outside of current networks, whereas the online social networks of today encourage such behavior to the point where it is almost the norm. Yet the same things are often at stake, and the person still puts him or herself "out there" when a question is asked or any information is shared. As is noted in *Talk of the Nation*, "You can build your own network of contacts through a social network in the way that you couldn't with use in other traditional bulletin boards. You can amass a friends' list. You can join groups within the network. You can share photos. It's much more of a personal experience." Within the traditional sphere of social networks, so much information was rarely given out even to those within the sphere, let alone to contacts outside of it.

CONVERSATION STARTERS

1. How different are the actual conversations that occur on a business-based social networking site, a site for your business, or a purely social site for something that interests you? Is it merely the language level (or what L_1 language you use) that differs or does the entire learning process change?

2. Does entering a site for, say, equestrian fans demand an L_1 knowledge of the subject, or can anyone figure out what's going on with a little time?

ARTIFACTS/CITATIONS

Anderson, T. (1998). Online social interchange, discord, and knowledge construction. *Journal of Distance Education, 13*(1), 57–74.

> Annotation: This article is a bit older than would be preferred, and it doesn't mention social networking sites as we know them today and instead focuses on an online forum. However, it does provide a good summary outline of the basic

research behind how people learn in an online space. However, I do wonder whether it is too dated to be of use.

Block, M. (Host). (2008, November 24). When is social networking kosher in the office? *All Things Considered*. Washington, DC: National Public Radio.

> Annotation: This brings up a new mode of communication at use in office situations. The offices have applied social networking forms of communication (specifically, Twitter) to the office situation as a way to cut down on e-mail. Interestingly, although it's a very "unofficial" mode of communication, most of the posts given out are related to the office and in the L_1 language of the office as well. A few posts still come in about what employees are eating, showing a lingering disconnect between tool and language (and perhaps workplace etiquette), but those are the exception.
>
> Interoffice conversations are now sent out to everyone, rather than a select few, which may seem confusing, but it eliminates the problem of deciding who (and in what order) to send an item to people, along with reducing e-mail boxes (which was the point in the first place). The conversations are both larger and smaller. People can, and likely are, ignoring a good deal of the posts that come to them in this way, but every conversation posted is open to a much wider number of conversants than before. What was once strictly a two-person dialogue "Do you happen to know X?" becomes a much larger conversation that all employees can note. Even the log of messages becomes part of an internal dialogue for each person because they can see what their coworkers are up to. One of the interviewees, for example, mentioned that he can use the log to see what each of his employees is doing when, bringing what may not have been noticed before or just internally noted up front where he can examine it.
>
> I found this interesting because of the application of social networking styles of communication to the business world and how easily most of the employees seemed to take to it. I also found the few irrelevant posts interesting because they were the now stereotypical posts about what someone was eating or what they were doing on their free time. I wish that the show had gone on to talk about how it changed the way the offices in question worked, beyond smaller e-mail in-boxes.

Conan, N. (Host). (2007, June 27). Social networking on the web grows up. *Talk of the Nation*. Washington, DC: National Public Radio.

Catherine Holahan, a staff writer for *Business Week*. Tom Watson, the publisher of OnPhilanthropy.com.

> Annotation: The host and guests discuss social networking sites as allowing users to create their own spaces with larger ones, using their individualistic L1 languages. It goes into specified sites for certain interests, business-oriented sites, and the customization available in large sites, such as MySpace and Facebook. Knowledge is formed both online and offline in these sites, with people meeting people they "know" from the sites to continue conversations about their topic of choice, as well as to enhance knowledge about each other. People post items related to shared interests, sparking dialogue and informing others. Although, technically, most of the conversation is internal (Person Y reads Person X, Z, and B's notes on an upcoming dressage competition on an equestrian site and then, with that information, questions whether he should go), there is a lot of dialogue created in bulletin boards, walls, etc.... One of the guests brings up the effect of this level of customization: "I think that one of the biggest differences between the old bulletin boards and the newer social networks is the fact that you can build your own network of contacts through a social network in the way that you couldn't with use in other traditional bulletin boards. You can amass a friends' list. You can join groups within the network. You can share photos. It's much more of a personal experience."
>
> Here's one anecdote I found particularly interesting:

MARCY: Well, I am the online publisher and editor-in-chief of a magazine called *Root Magazine: Global, Dance, Culture, Where Humanity Comes Together in Movement*. And our address is rootmag.typepad.com. And I find my writers, my musicians and dancers through MySpace and TribeNet, online forums and chat rooms and…

CONAN: Wait. You find dancers on MySpace?

MARCY: I do. I find dancers online. There's a huge network of dancers that talk about their trials and tribulations of the business, costumes…

CONAN: But how do you audition a dancer online?

MARCY: Oh well, that's very easy. A lot of dancers are uploading videos and specifically on their MySpace pages. So I can see what their troupe does, what they look like, solicit them for possible articles in magazine, find about their influences, their loves, their travels, everything. And I've got connections in Africa, Amsterdam, South America, you name it.

[….]

CONAN: And so this has changed the way you do your business.

MARCY: Exactly. It's absolutely incredible and I find to talk this (unintelligible) as well. So I have to say that without social networking sites, I would be a little bit in the dark on research. And, you know, answers that I have regarding, you know, certain things that might be culturally sensitive, I can immediately go to these online forums and networking sites and ask these questions and get answers (unintelligible).

Marcy uses MySpace as a research center, finding out more about the dance troupe she hires through their sites than she would through a visit to the studio or a traditional interview. It is all information that the troupes readily give, but she feels as though she's able to learn answers to "culturally sensitive" questions more easily through posting on their websites or forums than she would otherwise. I believe that she, as many others, feels more comfortable soliciting potentially uncomfortable information via these networks than through something as "personal" as a telephone call or e-mail. At the same time, however, she is interacting more personally with the troupes she looks at and may be able to gauge how to ask such a question in a more sensitive manner (or even find the question already answered for her).

Rolla, P. J. (2009). User tags versus subject headings: Can user-supplied data improve subject access to library collections? *Library Resources & Technical Services, 53*(3), 174–184.

Annotation: The differences between the controlled vocabularies of libraries and the very different (L_0 and L_1) languages of library members is discussed, as well as the implications for library catalogs. It provides a very nice review of recent library literature dealing with tagging and brings the user's ability to customize and control information on social networking sites to the foreground.

Terris, O. (2009). A quizzical look at LibraryThing. *Multimedia Information Technology, 35*(3), 84–85.

Annotation: This article provides an interesting example of the deliberate use of L_0 language in a social networking site. LibraryThing, used by many libraries and librarians, rejects L_1 library language, and in fact some practices, to embrace a wider audience. At the same time, however, it uses the British Library's bibliographical data and makes joyful use of library cataloging standards. What is most interesting to me is not that it chooses to reject such language and conventions, but that it states that it is doing so on purpose. Although the author is a cataloguer who finds the whole affair slightly sinful, LibraryThing's choices are deliberate. They were created to aid the average user with creating his or her own collections, as well as to make the site more of a true social network than place with individual lists of books. I question whether, up to some point, LibraryThing's refusal to "use the library's rules," as it were, actually harms rather than hurts it because it's harder to search for specific editions or covers with their search terms.

Yammer.com. https://www.yammer.com/

Annotation: Yammer's website. The About and Product sections reveal yammer to be much like Facebook and Twitter but applied in a single company rather than over multiple companies.

SOURCE AMNESIA

MAP LOCATION
F, G, 2

THREAD LOCATION
Page 42

SCAPE

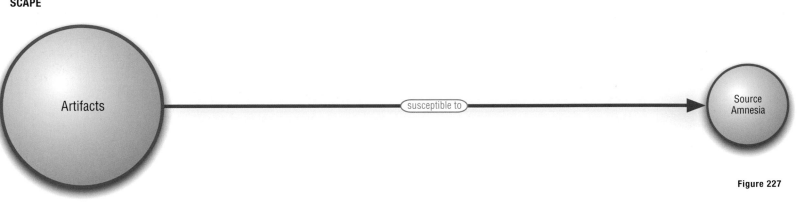

Figure 227

AUTHOR
William Zayac

AGREEMENT DESCRIPTION

Source amnesia is something that most, if not all, people experience in their lifetimes. Because of how the human brain works, repetition becomes one of the most effective ways to emphasize an idea over time, and unless it is thought of in relation to the original context enough, it may lose the connection to how it was learned, often leading to the idea that "I think I read it somewhere...." In some cases, facts may be misremembered or the source may be misremembered. In other cases, pure fiction may become part of someone's memory or false memories may be created because of the strength of the repetition and the emphasis on the actions.[1]

In fact, this is how many urban legends are started and maintain a presence in the cultures in which they exist: Somebody hears something—or thinks they do—and attributes it to an obscure relation through which it may or may not be able to be verified.[2] Another

important qualification to the development of an urban legend is that it must make sense in the culture and to those who spread the information—if it is truly unbelievable, it will not be believed and will not be passed along.[3] A common attribute with information that falls victim to source amnesia as well.[4] Other misattributions may take place as well: One might even confuse what a famous person had said with something an imitator of that person said (specifically citing the power of Tina Fey's mocking of Sarah Palin on many *Saturday Night Live* skits during the 2008 election season).

1. Sugimoto, H. (nd.). Source amnesia, fantasy blends reality. *Evl: electronic visualization laboratory*. University of Illinois at Chicago. Retrieved September 27, 2009, from: http://www.evl.uic.edu/sugimoto/memSrc.html.

2. Whipps, H. (2006, August 27). Urban legends: How they start and why they persist. *LiveScience: Science, Technology, Health & Environmental News*. Retrieved October 2, 2009. from: http://www.livescience.com/strangenews/060827_urban_legends.html.
3. Ibid.
4. Want, S., & Aamodt, S. (June 27, 2008). Your brain lies to you. The *New York Times*. Retrieved from: http://www.nytimes.com/2008/06/27/opinion/27aamodt.html.

Many political figures use source amnesia to help spread ideas helpful to themselves or harmful to their opponents that may or may not actually be true.[5] This approach may be particularly effective because of the potential for memory manipulation that occurs even when refuting the idea. As with R. David Lankes' personal story in the Knowledge Creation Thread, this may occur even with the most astute of researchers and students while performing research, and they may not notice the error until it has been pointed out by other people. At this point, the citation may have already been seen by others and has already become a resource that may, in the future, be further cited with the same incorrect information and citations. While the citations may be checked by some researchers, others may simply take the researcher's reputation for granted and assume that the citations are correct. In this way, source amnesia can become contagious and may, in fact, spread through even the best-intentioned members of a field.

CONVERSATION STARTERS

With the rise of electronic resources, can librarians and database managers help monitor and correct erroneous citations caused by source amnesia? It may be one of the few ways to prevent the spread of the erroneous information and incorrect citations. Perhaps if an author or a publisher is notified and a retraction is printed it could be annotated to the original article's citation in the database. If this does not work, how else could the external effects of source amnesia be limited?

What obligation do librarians have to prevent source amnesia from affecting academic writings? Whose responsibility is it to teach this carefulness to students without overstepping the boundaries of standard librarian values? Whose responsibility is it to monitor retractions and corrections so erroneous citations do not pass through another level of writings?

RELATED ARTIFACTS

Anonymous. (2009, April 4). Source amnesia and its political pertinence. *Politics, Religion, Science, Philosophy, Health: The Fact of My Ignorance*. Retrieved September 27, 2009, from http://thefactofmyignorance.com/politics/source-amnesia-and-its-political-pertinence

> Annotation: This blog post, as it says in its entry title, examines the political ramifications of source amnesia manipulation and political tactics that utilize the tendency toward source amnesia. It even describes how harmful it may be for news reports and articles to present controversial ideas in sensationalistic ways and then refute them at the end of the article.

Bornstein, R. F. (1999). Source amnesia, misattribution, and the power of unconscious perceptions and memories. *Psychoanalytic Psychology, 16*(2), 155–178.

> Annotation: This article explains the power of source amnesia and unconscious images and why it is difficult to counteract these types of misattributions. Although psychoanalysts may be able to break through previous mental blocks against memories, the power of repeated information remains distinctly powerful, and implicit memory may affect preference and recognition.

Source amnesia. (2003, March 23). Retrieved September 27, 2009, from http://everything2.com/title/source+amnesia

> Annotation: This website gives a basic definition of source amnesia while also describing the courtroom science implications of how a person's distant memories can be manipulated through suggestion. For example, a clinical therapist may be able to "uncover" a person's "repressed memories" through repeated sessions with intense questioning, but there is also a good chance that the "victim" has become susceptible to suggestion and the questioning led him or her to believe he or she was abused in some way. This may be good reason to be careful wording interview questions and have even larger implications for how librarians may present information to patrons.

5. Barber, T. (July 2, 2008). Sarkozy and source amnesia. *Brussels Blog. Financial Times.* Retrieved September 27, 2009, from: http://blogs.ft.com/brusselsblog/2008/07/sarkozy-and-source-amnesia.

SPECIAL

MAP LOCATION

D, 6

THREAD LOCATION

Page 111

SCAPE

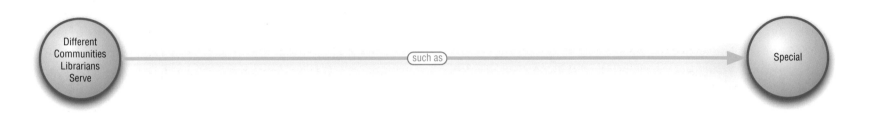

Figure 228

AUTHORS

Jill Hurst-Wahl, Assistant Professor of Practice, Syracuse University
Ruth Kneale, Systems Librarian, National Solar Observatory

AGREEMENT DESCRIPTION

This Atlas agreement is focused on special librarians. In 1909, John Cotton Dana and 26 other librarians decided that there was a need for a type of librarian who focused on special topics and interests. The event, which has become known as the "Veranda Conference," laid the foundation for the Special Libraries Association and for the terms "special librarians" and "special libraries." The term "special librarian" has come to define librarians and information professionals who work in a wide range of institutions and environments, including corporate, government, judicial, science, military, and academic settings. Although many special librarians work in departments that resemble "traditional" libraries providing library services, many others work as information analysts, chief information officers, researchers, trainers, records managers, social media consultants, web developers/webmasters, and more. A study completed for the Special Libraries Association in 2008 found that its members had more than 2,000 job titles, which is a testament to the variety of positions that special librarians hold. Because of the breadth of positions, some feel that the term "special librarians" no longer applies, and so the term "information professional" is often used to describe this type of librarian. That term, however, can be used more broadly to describe many other positions where an MLS is not preferred.

What are the characteristics of a special librarian? These librarians usually have a focus on a specific area that may be broadly or narrowly defined (e.g., transportation, legal, sports, or geography) yet is outside the areas typically covered by (for example) public or general academic librarians. Some special librarians are focused not on a topic but on the needs of the parent organization. For example, a corporation might include a business or technical librarian who provides information to corporate employees for use in their work no matter what that work may be.

For many special librarians, their users aren't just those who visit the library physically; they also interact with the library and its staff via telephone, e-mail, fax, and an increasing number of social media tools. Understanding the needs of their users—including resources, types of interaction, information-seeking skill levels, etc.—helps special librarians ensure their continued relevancy. It is important that special librarians be relevant to their users both today and in the future. Therefore, understanding user requirements is vital for their continued existence.

A special library may house physical and digital resources that will be important to its users but is trending more toward the virtual. The ability for users to access materials virtually has led special librarians to use an increasing number of digital resources that can be accessed from any location to meet their users wherever they are. An unintended result of the ability for users to share digital resources and to use library staff physically located at other locations has been the closure of some special libraries. Organizational budget tightening led some to encourage users to rely on library resources housed elsewhere. In some cases, those resources were made available through third-party companies (e.g., information brokers or independent information professionals). In some cases, although the physical library may have closed or been reallocated, the librarian was integrated into the user base so the organization didn't lose the skill set of the special librarian.

Although special librarians will certainly continue to exist, how they operate will continue to change, possibly dramatically. Technology will continue to have a major influence on how users interact with library materials and alter user expectations. The need to be subject-focused will continue, but there will be an even more increased need for these practitioners to work virtually, embed themselves into organizational units, and meet user requirements no matter where that user is.

How can Special Librarians Make a Difference?

Every organization is drowning in information, even those that do not feel they have enough. It has become easier for organizations to capture as well as acquire information and to do so more quickly than ever. This, however, does not mean it is useful to the organization; while they are drowning in information, they lack knowledge. Knowledge can be described as synthesized information. It is information that a person has ingested and merged with other known information and then finally put into context with that person's specific spin. Although it can be effective to use information to build your own knowledge, most organizations do not have the time or resources to do that. Instead they need to tap into the knowledge of others.

Special librarians, whether embedded or in a separate library, can help their organizations acquire information as well as connect the organization to people who already have the needed knowledge. Organizations value those who are seen as "connectors." Although librarians are generally seen as connecting people to information, special librarians also need to connect people to people; people who want knowledge to those who already have it. This is a skill that is not taught in library science programs, yet special librarians learn quickly that it is a skill they must have. Special librarians dive into topics that are important to their organizations, learn the resources and the people behind those resources, and then create networks that will allow them to locate the right knowledgeable expert when needed. They are, if you will, the keepers of the organizational memory net.

Why Should You be a Special Librarian?

It is while studying for a master's degree in library science that most LIS students encounter the idea of a being a special librarian. But why would someone decide not to pursue being a school or public librarian or a general academic librarian? Consider the impact that a special librarian has. The special librarian doesn't just impact another person, but impacts an entire organization. A special librarian provides information as well as connections to knowledgeable people who help the organization make decisions about new products, markets, inventions, directions, and more.

Special librarians:

- Provide research to doctors that help them develop new forms of treatment

- Connect attorneys to case law that can be used in litigation

- Locate experts who can assist a company with new product development

- Help an architect uncover the history of a building before it is renovated

- Work with legal counsel to locate reasons (prior art) that a patent should not have been granted

- Help organizations ensure that they do not spend time "reinventing the wheel" (products and services that already exist)

- Connect the research of two parts of the organization that may speak different languages (e.g., engineers and scientists)

- Administer the centralized engineering database for a construction project

- Investigate (and play with!) new technologies and new applications of existing technologies to see how they can be used to benefit an organization

- Ensure that their organizations know who the movers and shakers are in their industry

QUESTIONS/CONVERSATION STARTERS

1. What skills do institutions require in order to organize their knowledge? Where do those skills reside in the institution?
2. How do special libraries advance the mission of their institutions?
3. What activities occur in a special library that do not occur elsewhere in an organization?
4. Rather than being their own entities, how are organizations embedding the functionality of special libraries into their structures?
5. How do special librarians differ from other information professionals? What unique skills and values do they embody?

RELATED ARTIFACTS

Haycock, K., & Sheldon, B. E. (Eds.). (2008). *The portable MLIS*. Westport, CT: Libraries Unlimited.

Kneale, R. (2009). *You don't look like a librarian! Shattering stereotypes and creating positive new images in the Internet age*. Medford, NJ: Information Today, Inc.

Law, D. (2009). Waiting for the (digital) barbarians. *Information Outlook, 13*(8), 15–18.

Special Libraries Association. (2003). *Competencies for information professionals of the 21st century*. Retrieved from http://www.sla.org/content/learn/members/competencies/index.cfm.

Special Libraries Association. (2009). *SLA alignment portal*. Retrieved from http://www.sla.org/content/SLA/alignment/portal/index.html.

SYSTEM VIEW

MAP LOCATION

H, 4

THREAD LOCATION

Page 36

SCAPE

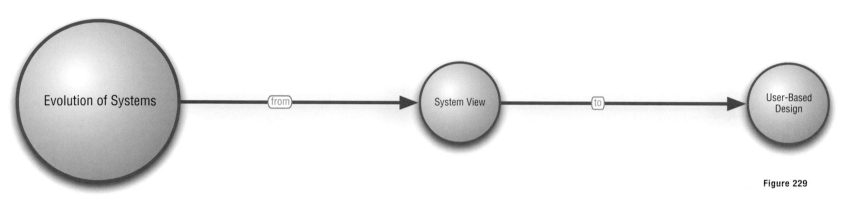

Figure 229

TCP-IP

MAP LOCATION

F, 5

THREAD LOCATIONS

Page 86

SCAPE

Figure 230

MAP LOCATION

A, B 4, 5

THREAD LOCATIONS

Pages 15, 31, 65, 83, 117, 137

SCAPE

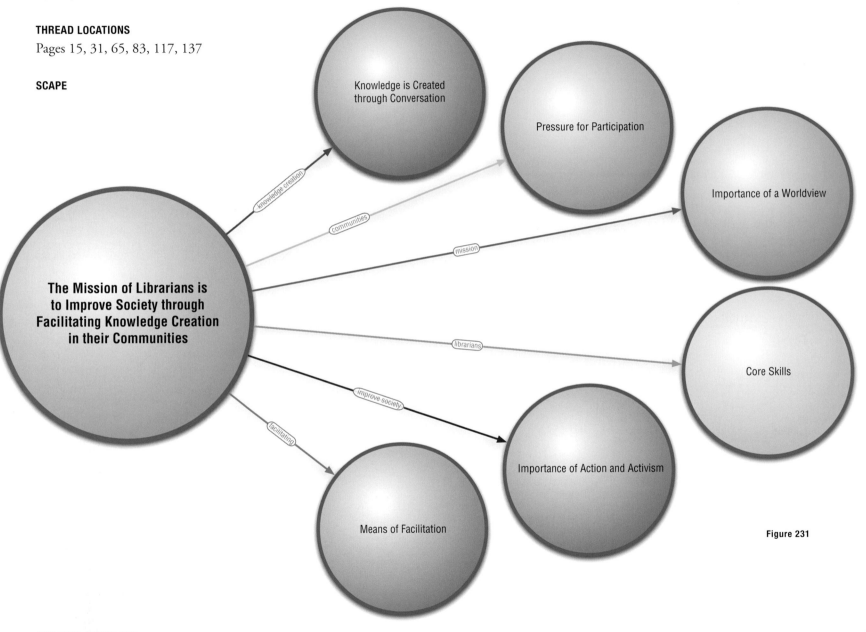

Figure 231

RELATED ARTIFACTS

"The Big Picture," Arizona State Library, Phoenix, AZ http://quartz.syr.edu/rdlankes/
blog/?p=716

TOPICAL CENTERS WITH CURRICULUM

MAP LOCATION

D, 4

THREAD LOCATION

Page 93

SCAPE

Figure 232

TRANSITION OF TRADITIONAL SKILLS

MAP LOCATION

D, 4, 5

THREAD LOCATION

Page 137

SCAPE

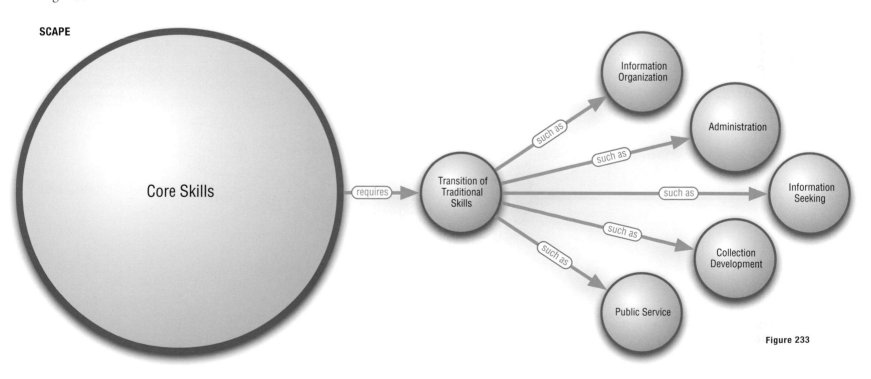

Figure 233

TRUE FACILITATION MEANS SHARED OWNERSHIP

MAP LOCATION

D, 1

THREAD LOCATION

Page 65

SCAPE

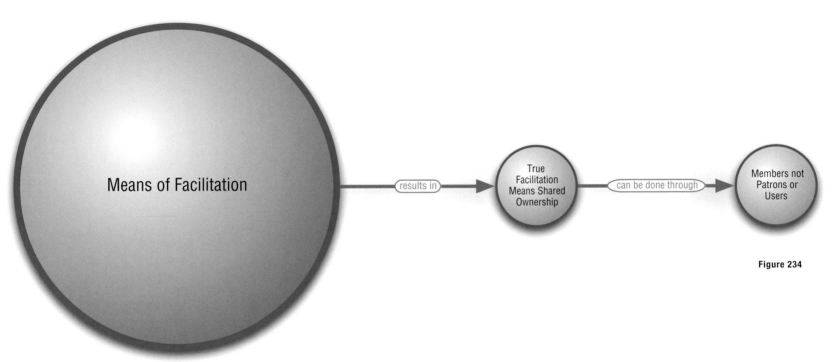

Figure 234

TRULY DISTRIBUTED DIGITAL LIBRARY

MAP LOCATION

E, 5

THREAD LOCATION

Page 114

SCAPE

Figure 235

RELATED ARTIFACTS

Sonnenwald, D. H. M., Wildemuth, B. M., Dempsey, B. L., Viles, C. R., Tibbo, H. R., & Smith, J. S. (1999). *Collaboration services in a participatory digital library: An emerging design.* In Aparec, T. et al. (eds.), *Digital libraries: Interdisciplinary concepts, challenges, and opportunities (COLIS 3)*, 141–152. Zagreb: Zavod.

USER

MAP LOCATION

E, 5

THREAD LOCATION

Page 90

SCAPE

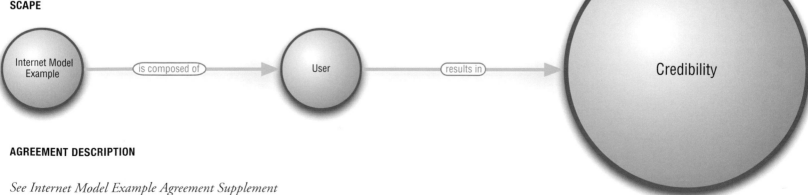

AGREEMENT DESCRIPTION

See Internet Model Example Agreement Supplement

Figure 236

USER SYSTEMS

MAP LOCATION

H, 4, 5

THREAD LOCATION

Page 38

SCAPE

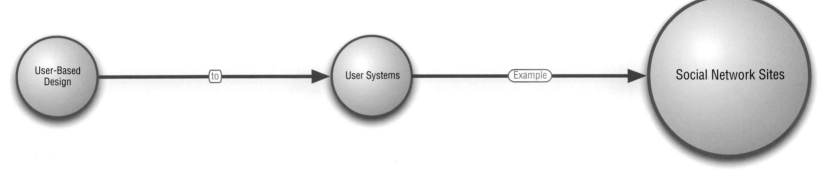

Figure 237

USER-BASED DESIGN

MAP LOCATION

H, 4

THREAD LOCATION

Page 37

SCAPE

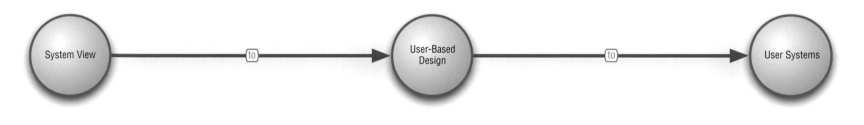

Figure 238

CONTRIBUTOR

Amy Edick

RELATED ARTIFACTS

Abels, E., White, M., & Hahn, K. (1998). A user-based design process for web sites. *Internet Research, 8*(1), 39.

> Annotation: This article went over the second leg of the experiments on user-based design. I think this article was important to include because it went over actual user-based input that was being used. It showed the stages and what it takes to include it.

Abels, E., White, M., & Kim, S. (2007). Developing subject-related web sites collaboratively: The virtual business information center. *Journal of Academic Librarianship, 33*(1), 27.

> Annotation: For some reason, I am always drawn to case studies. They seem to work no matter what topic you are using. I picked this study because it went through the process that is involved with user-based design.

Hippel, E, V. (1995, May). User learning, "sticky information," and user-based design. Retrieved from http://dspace.mit.edu/bitstream/handle/1721.1/2574/SWP-3815-32867610.pdf?sequence=1

> Annotation: This article goes over the working between the manufacturer and the user when creating the product needed. They make a good point that "user needs" change so much that it is hard to put out a product that is at the same level for everyone.

VITAL ROLES OF MENTORS

MAP LOCATION

E, 7, 8

THREAD LOCATION

Page 185

SCAPE

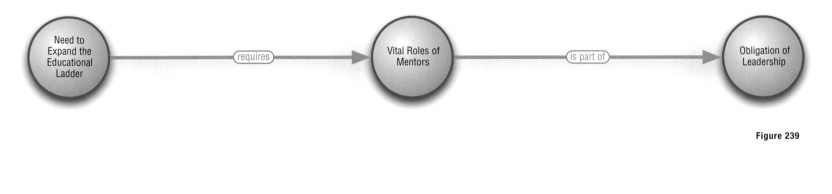

Figure 239

WAREHOUSING FUNCTIONS

MAP LOCATION

F, 8

THREAD LOCATION

Page 161

SCAPE

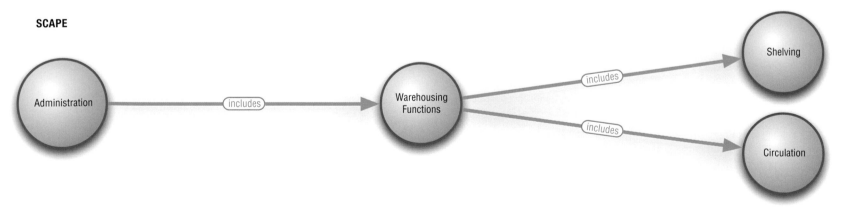

Figure 240

WEB 2.0

MAP LOCATION

F, 5

THREAD LOCATION

Page 89

SCAPE

Figure 241

WRITING CENTER

MAP LOCATION

F, 4

THREAD LOCATION

Page 99

SCAPE

Figure 242

ATLAS POSTSCRIPT

For more than a year, this manuscript has been a passion and, frankly, an obsession with me. I have written it in my office, late at night at home, on trains, on planes, and even on an iPhone next to a pool in the summer. I have slipped out of parties, events, and even church to scribble down some idea.

In many ways, it has been a process akin to sculpture. I rough in the basic shapes and forms, and then I go over and over it, tweaking, smoothing, and refining. I could spend easily another year in the process. The Agreements Supplement in particular cries out for more citations and more depth. But to continue to do so only continues a conversation with close colleagues and myself. It is time to invite the wider community in to continue the work and expand that conversation.

What lies ahead in that conversation I cannot say. Will it be contentious? Riotous? Resigned? Quiet? Apathetic? I don't know. I do know that if you wait for it to happen or if you wait for it to finish, it will never occur. If you remain on the sidelines, how can you expect others to jump into the fray? If you sit quietly with your criticism or comment, you abdicate the future. Let me say that again. By not choosing to engage in the conversation on the future of librarianship, you abdicate your power to shape it.

In our field, we have examples of those who chose to shape librarianship and strive for a better world. We can think of Dewey, of course, or of Cutter or Ranganathan. But I ask you also to think of Dinberg, von Dran, and Taylor.

When Donna Dinberg was diagnosed with terminal brain cancer, she did not quit, she did not hide. Instead, she worked until she was not able to, and then she told doctors to try any experiment they may have; if being a test subject to a possible cure for others was all she could do to improve the world in her final days, then she would do it.

Unlike Donna, Ray von Dran didn't have forewarning when pneumonia took his life, but he must have sensed something. Days before he died, he decided not to sell his dream car to a colleague but instead offered it to a staff member battling breast cancer because "she could use a pick me up."

Bob Taylor spent his last few days in Francis House. There was a memorial service a few months later for a man who in his career had been a sports reporter, an intelligence officer in the army, a librarian, a professor, and a dean. In his years, he can be easily credited for reinventing reference with his question negotiation work, LIS education by creating the first information school in the states, and beginning the era of user-based design with his work on value-added systems. Instead, those who talked spoke of a kind and thoughtful man. A man who, years earlier, on withdrawing from academia, devoted his life to care for his wife dying of Alzheimer's.

I retell these events to show you that Taylor, von Dran, and Dinberg are not just names but real people. They created a legacy not just through writings but actions and values that went beyond their professional lives. All of these people furthered the conversation of librarianship. They all faced struggles, they all faced resistance, and they all persevered.

Dewey, Cutter, Ranganathan, Dinberg, von Dran, and Taylor all created a legacy that we, by calling ourselves librarians, have become stewards to. This legacy is one to be respected and continued not simply enshrined and frozen. All of these giants, on whose shoulders we now teeter, never saw the field as finite, fixed, or passive. Unlike some fine sculpture or glorious piece of architecture, we preserve the legacy of these librarians by constantly tearing down convention for efficiency, structure for effectiveness, and past assumptions for future success.

I end the way I began the Atlas, with Israel Zangwill's quote[1]:

The Past: Our cradle, not our prison; there is danger as well as appeal in its glamour. The past is for inspiration, not imitation, for continuation, not repetition

Be proud of your heritage as a librarian. Ours is an old and noble profession that can count among our members radicals, missionaries, teachers, and more. They have started for you an amazing conversation full of richness and history. They have written this conversation into our values, our institutions, and our education. But they did not complete the work or finish the conversation. They held it open for you, for those you mentor, and for those who they mentor. The conversation that is librarianship is alive and waiting for your voice.

1. http://www.quotationspage.com/quote/4482.html.